DARFUR

THE ROAD TO PEACE

Darfur

The Road to Peace

DR DAVID HOILE

European-Sudanese
Public Affairs Council

First Published in March 2005
as *Darfur in Perspective*
Copyright © David Hoile 2005
The European-Sudanese Public Affairs Council
1 Northumberland Avenue
London WC2N 5BW

Second, revised edition published January 2006
Third, revised edition published July 2008

Telephone: 020 7872 5434
Telefax: 020 7753 2848
E-mail: director@espac.org
website: www.espac.org

ISBN 978-1-903545-41-6

Typeset by Amolibros, Milverton, Somerset
Printed and bound by T J International Ltd, Padstow, Cornwall, UK

CONTENTS

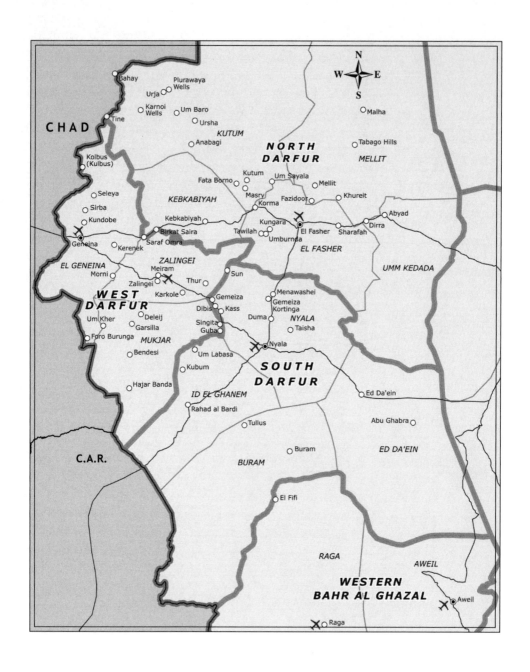

Map of Sudan showing Darfur

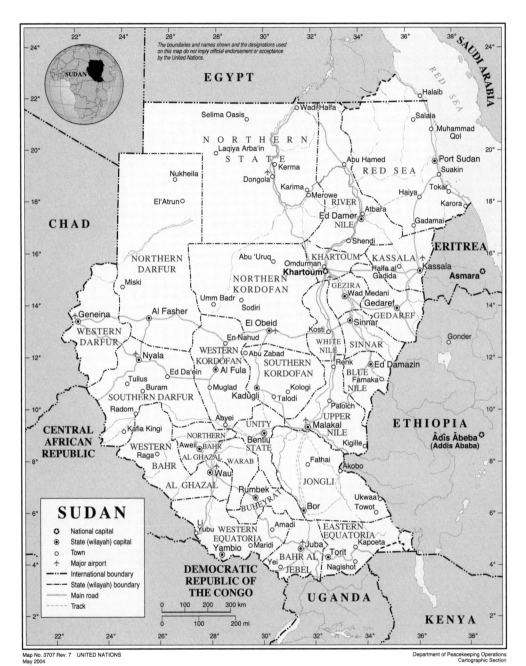

Map of Sudan

Map No. 3707 Rev. 7   UNITED NATIONS
May 2004

Department of Peacekeeping Operations
Cartographic Section

ABBREVIATIONS

AU	African Union
AMIS	African Union Mission in Sudan
BBC	British Broadcasting Corporation
CFC	Ceasefire Commission
CIJ	Coalition for International Justice
CNN	Cable Network News
CPA	Comprehensive Peace Agreement
CRED	Centre for Research on the Epidemiology of Disasters
DDDC	Darfur-Darfur Dialogue and Consultation
DOP	Declaration of Principles
DPA	Darfur Peace Agreement
DRDF	Darfur Reconstruction and Development Fund
ECHO	European Union Aid Office
EU	European Union
GAO	US Government Accountability Office
GOAL	Irish humanitarian organisation
GOS	Government of Sudan
HAC	Humanitarian Aid Commission
ICC	International Criminal Court
ICG	International Crisis Group
IDP	Internally Displaced Person
IRIN	UN Integrated Regional Information Networks
JAM	Joint Assessment Mission
JEM	Justice and Equality Movement
JIM	Joint Implementation Mechanism
MSF	Médecins sans Frontières
NATO	North Atlantic Treaty Organisation
NCP	National Congress Party
NIF	National Islamic Front

NMRD	National Movement for Reform and Development
NRF	National Redemption Front
OCHA	Office for the Coordination of Humanitarian Affairs
OLS	Operation Lifeline Sudan
PANA	Pan African News Agency
PC	Popular Congress
PDF	Popular Defence Force
SAF	Sudan Armed Forces
SLA	Sudan Liberation Army
SLA/MM	Sudan Liberation Army/Minni Minawi Faction
SLA/AS	Sudan Liberation Army/Abdel Shafi Faction
SLA/AW	Sudan Liberation Army/Abd al-Wahid Faction
SLM/A	Sudan Liberation Movement/Army
SMC	Sudan Media Center
SNMEM	Sudan National Movement for the Eradication of Marginalisation
SPLA	Sudan People's Liberation Army
SUNA	Sudan News Agency
TDRA	Transitional Darfur Regional Authority
UN	United Nations
UNAMID	UN-AU Mission in Darfur
UNICEF	United Nations Children's Fund
USAID	United States Agency for International Development
WFP	World Food Programme
WHO	World Health Organisation
WMD	Weapons of Mass Destruction

About the Author

Dr David Hoile is a public affairs consultant specialising in African affairs. He has studied Sudanese affairs for over ten years and is the author of *Images of Sudan: Case Studies in Propaganda and Misinformation* (2003) and *Farce Majeure: The Clinton Administration's Sudan Policy 1993-2000* (2000) and editor of *The Search for Peace in the Sudan: A Chronology of the Sudanese Peace Process 1989-2001* (2002). He is the author or editor of a number of other publications on African affairs, including *Moçambique: A Nation in Crisis* (1989) and *Moçambique, Resistance and Freedom: A Case for Reassessment* (1994). Dr Hoile is also a Research Professor at the Sudan University of Science and Technology and has been a Visiting Professor at the Institute of African-Asian Studies and the Department of Political Science at the University of Khartoum.

Introduction

Darfur: The Road to Peace is an extensively updated edition of *Darfur in Perspective*, a study of the conflict, first published in 2005. This new book seeks to examine both the search for a solution to the crisis and the obstacles to peace in Darfur. Those who are genuinely interested in peace in Darfur are fortunate in that both the solution and obstacles are well defined.

The war that has been fought in Darfur over the past four years between the Government of Sudan and a complex variety of rebel groups has been described by Alex de Waal, one of the few unchallenged experts on Sudan, in the following terms:

> Darfur is a typical north-east African civil war, consisting of multiple overlapping conflicts interspersed with large-scale offensives by the government army and its proxies and rebels. During 2001-2003, local disputes were exacerbated by the breakdown of local governance and combined with the ambitions of a frustrated provincial elite to fuel an insurgency, which escalated more quickly and bloodily than either side anticipated.[1]

The war has been a humanitarian disaster. The violence is said to have amounted to "a demographic catastrophe".[2] Hundreds of villages have been destroyed and many thousands of people have died as a direct or indirect result of the conflict. Many more have become internally displaced persons (IDPs) within Darfur, or refugees in Chad. The United Nations' *Darfur Humanitarian Profile*, published in July 2007, estimated that just over four million Darfurians had been affected by the conflict, of whom 2,152,163 were IDPs.[3]

There has also been a considerable international focus on the situation in Darfur. International involvement with the crisis has been both very positive and very negative. On the positive side, continuing conflict as a result of the political impasse notwithstanding, the aid work coordinated by the United

Nations has been outstanding. Darfur has become the world's largest humanitarian relief operation. The fighting peaked during several months in late 2003 into 2004, but not before it had precipitated a humanitarian disaster. As of January 2005, however, in very large measure due to the UN effort, the acute humanitarian crisis had started to ease. [4] The World Health Organisation confirmed that food and health access, water supply and sanitation services had made a significant difference in addressing the crisis.[5] In its 2004 year-end report, the Office of the United Nations Resident and Humanitarian Co-ordinator for the Sudan, reported that the 90-day humanitarian action plan, from June to August 2004, coordinated with the government, had been a success. It further reported that "by 31 December 2004 the humanitarian situation for most of the 2.2 million people affected...stabilized...The catastrophic mortality figures predicted by some quarters have not materialised".[6] The United Nations reported that a June 2005 mortality survey showed that "the crude mortality rate was 0.8 deaths per 10,000 people per day in all three states of Darfur." This was "below the critical threshold" of one death per 10,000 people per day. A year earlier, a similar survey showed crude mortality rates three times higher. As of September 2005 there were 184 fixed health centres in Darfur with an additional 36 mobile centres. The United Nations noted: "75% of accessible hospitals had been rehabilitated, providing free access to 70% of the IDPs and conflict affected population."[7]

The UN reported that the number of foreign and national aid workers in Darfur had increased from 200 in March 2004 to 8,500 by the end of 2004.[8] In September 2005 the number of humanitarian workers in Darfur had grown further to around 13,500 and that they were working for 81 NGOs and 13 UN agencies.[9] The tremendous achievements of the international humanitarian community in Darfur have subsequently been increasingly endangered by an escalation in rebel attacks on aid workers and humanitarian convoys. In 2005, the BBC noted that "after eight months of relative calm and improving security, the situation in Darfur is deteriorating once again. Banditry and attacks on aid convoys are increasing and the finger of blame is being firmly pointed at the SLA, Darfur's main rebel movement...The African Union said the rebels' provocative banditry and lack of cooperation was casting doubt over their commitment to negotiations."[10] By July 2007, as a result of often premeditated attacks on humanitarian personnel and property, the number of national and international aid workers had decreased to 12,070, working for 75 NGOs.[11] Rebels groups have also repeatedly attacked and murdered African Union peacekeepers.[12]

Nevertheless, mortality levels in Darfur have continued to drop. *The Los Angeles Times* reported in August 2007, for example, that UN figures showed that the mortality rate in Darfur is about 0.35 deaths daily per 10,000 people, a rate that is "near, or perhaps even below, the region's pre-conflict level. In sub-Saharan Africa, 0.44 deaths daily per 10,000 people is a common baseline." A Médecins sans Frontières doctor noted that "People in Darfur are now getting better healthcare than people in other parts of Sudan, such as the east and central regions", and better than in Khartoum.[13] This improvement was because of an unprecedented effort by the international community, UN agencies and non-governmental organisations. De Waal and Julie Flint, another long-time critic of the Khartoum government, have observed that "for the past two years, mortality rates among people reached by international aid have been lower than they were before the war. That's a tremendous achievement."[14] Flint has further observed noted that Darfur mortality levels are lower than in the Sudanese capital, and that "in southern Sudan, where conflict is stilled, children have higher death rates and lower school enrolment."[15]

Not all the international interest shown has been constructive. As one British commentator has observed "There is no civil war so bad that it cannot be made worse by the intervention of Western liberals."[16] One can quite clearly extend that truism to include the Bush administration. Darfur has been no exception. While it is clear that the world's humanitarian community is holding the ring in Darfur, keeping hundreds of thousands of people alive while the rebels dither about peace talks, on another level international involvement in the crisis has also served to prolong the conflict. The actions of the United States government, and several of Sudan's neighbours, for example, have artificially prolonged and extended the crisis. Propaganda and political opportunism are a feature of all wars. Pandering to powerful anti-Muslim and anti-Sudanese constituencies within the United States, the Bush administration declared that the Darfur crisis constituted genocide. Labelling Darfur as genocide was an unforgivable act of opportunism. There was also no doubt that Washington's deliberate use of the genocide term in Darfur was designed not just to placate domestic constituencies but also to help divert attention away from the growing Iraqi disaster. Not content with having cried wolf on weapons of mass destruction in Iraq, Washington has also prostituted claims of genocide.

With the exception of a handful of "Darfur advocacy" groups such as the Save Darfur Coalition, often with their own political and religious agenda, Washington has found itself alone in this claim. It is a matter of record that, in January 2005, the United Nations International Commission of Inquiry on Darfur reported back to the UN Secretary-General, stating that while there had been serious violations of human rights in the course of the war in Darfur, allegations of genocide were unfounded.[17] The Sudanese national commission of inquiry into human rights violations in Darfur also published its report in January 2005. Established by presidential decree and chaired by a former chief justice of Sudan, the commission visited Darfur on several occasions and spent several months taking evidence from hundreds of witnesses. The national commission also found that there was no evidence to support allegations of genocide in Darfur. The commission found that there had been grave violations of human rights and recommended the establishment of a judicial commission to investigate, indict and try those responsible for crimes in Darfur. It also recommended the setting up of compensation and administrative commissions to assist with reconciliation within Darfur.[18]

The part played by advocacy groups such as Save Darfur in prolonging the Darfur conflict is clear. Buoyed at least in part by the Bush administration's use of the genocide word, the anti-Sudan groupings within the United States have repeatedly pushed for a western-led United Nations military intervention in Sudan to destroy the nomadic "Janjaweed" militias in Darfur, seemingly blind to the disastrous international and regional consequences of yet another western military intervention in another oil-rich Muslim country and the inability of the world's military superpower to itself control a few thousand Shia militiamen three miles outside of the green zone in Baghdad.[19] Flint warns of "the dangers inherent in much of the uninformed comment on Darfur that emanates from the United States – driven, very often, by activists who have never been there and who perceive the war as a simple morality tale in which the forces of 'evil' can be defeated only by outside saviors."[20] Key Save Darfur activists have admitted that Save Darfur's framing of the conflict was from the start "severely simplified and almost ignorant of the rebel movement".[21] The founding executive-director of Save Darfur admitted that "the closer we could get to a bumper sticker, the better we'd be as an organization."[22] That is to say that the very complex Darfur crisis was reduced to a bumper sticker sound-bite within the United States.

A number of Save Darfur's statements have been shown to be false. It has claimed, for example, that 400,000 people had been killed in Darfur. The British advertising regulator ruled that this was untrue.[23] Calls made by Save Darfur for military intervention and "no-fly zones" in Darfur have also angered the American humanitarian community. Flint has noted, for example, that "Aid agencies are quietly but unanimously appalled by the prospect of a no-fly zone...A no-fly zone would be recklessly dangerous and would not address the real problems in Darfur. To endanger the region's humanitarian lifeline is not simply wrong-headed. It is inhumane."[24] The Zoe's Ark "kidnap" scandal involving a French charity's attempts to illegally remove alleged Darfurian "orphans" from Chad in October 2007 is one more example of the reckless self-righteousness of humanitarian interventionism. The children were in many instances neither orphans nor even Darfurian.[25] As *Newsweek* has noted, Darfur activists "may be doing more harm than good".[26]

De Waal has also noted the consequences of bumper-sticker politics, observing that in 2004 there was "much increased coverage of Darfur in the U.S. press and mounting activism among American advocacy groups. Although the pattern of the war was now changing...the underlying narrative in the U.S. [was that Darfur] was...genocide warranting American military intervention."[27] That is to say, having almost flippantly used the genocide word, the Bush administration was then caught up in the domestic consequences, renewed pressure to "do something". De Waal has outlined the resulting cynical nature of Washington's actions on Darfur:

> As the crisis unfolded in 2004-2005, the U.S. government had several different policies towards Darfur...Popular opinion demanded military intervention but the Pentagon had no intention of sending troops, aircraft or any other assets to Sudan. In the second quarter of 2005, the White House extracted a policy priority from these competing demands: AMIS should be handed over to the UN. The UN troops proposal began as a piece of political spin. It deflected the activists' ire from the White House to the UN and those Security

Council members not ready to support tough action against Khartoum.[28]

De Waal also observed that "There was an element of deception in the proposal. No UN mission would be able to deploy quickly...disarm the Janjawiid by force, or provide physical protection to more than a small minority of Darfurian civilians...Perhaps it is not too cynical to assume that President Bush's advisors calculated that once a UN force had been approved, any disappointments could be placed at the door of the UN...not the U.S." [29]

Having chosen for domestic reasons to go down a cynical path of spin, a UN deployment became an end in itself for the Bush administration. Washington devoted all of its efforts to forcing through a change from AU to UN forces, exerting tremendous pressure on the Sudanese government to accept a peace-keeping force which would have no peace to keep. At the same time it ignored the fact that the rebels were reluctant or unable to negotiate any peace agreement. Flint confirmed this American myopia, noting that since May 2006, "international diplomacy has been wholly focused on forcing Khartoum to accept a UN force of more than 20,000 men – even though it is doubtful whether such a force can, of itself, stop the fighting and protect civilians." [30] Flint returned to this issue, one year later: "The emphasis on getting UN peacekeepers into Darfur has bedevilled western policy for the past two years, driven largely by an interventionist lobby whose backing in the US Congress has intimidated the State Department and hindered any rational approach to Sudan."[31] In July 2007, UN peacekeepers in the form of a hybrid AU-UN mission, UNAMID, incorporating the African Union mission in Darfur, were authorised by the UN Security Council. The new force commander, General Martin Luther Agwai, has also warned of a deployment without a peace agreement: "Without a new peace deal, even with the force numbers we are bringing into Darfur, it will still be a big task because you cannot keep peace if there is no peace deal."[32] There is also the additional concern that Washington's calls for a UN force in Darfur plays directly into the hands of al-Qaeda. It will attract Islamic extremists from Algeria to Zanzibar.[33] In October 2007, al-Qaeda leader Osama bin-Laden once again called for *jihad* against any UN peacekeepers, and the Sudanese government for having agreed their deployment: "It is the duty of the people of Islam in the Sudan and its environs…to perform jihad against the Crusader invaders and wage armed rebellion to remove those who let them in."[34]

It is also ironic that the continuing calls for intervention come at the time when – in comparison with 2004 with several thousand deaths per month – a shooting war has given way to banditry, inter-tribal raiding and hit-and-run rebel attacks on aid convoys. *The Los Angeles Times* reported, for example, that UN figures showed that violence-related casualties in 2007 averaged 100 to 200 per month: civilian casualties were down 70% in the first half of 2007, compared with the same period last year.[35] And last year's casualty figures in turn were much less than the previous year's and vastly reduced in comparison with 2004. A western diplomat has noted: "The idea that thousands are still being killed by janjaweed is a myth."[36] De Waal and Flint have stated that the Sudanese air force "is rarely used" and that "there have been no large-scale offensives by the government in 2007."[37] The respected British journalist Jonathan Steele has noted that "Far more civilians are dying from Nato airstrikes in Afghanistan. Critics who demand that French or US planes shoot down Sudanese military aircraft should consider calling for a no-fly zone in Helmand province."[38] The pressure, nonetheless, for some sort of intervention has resulted in the African Union presence in Darfur being sidelined by UNAMID in a hybrid operation with all the potential for escalating violence that such an operation would bring with it. Violence could possibly escalate in two ways. The first way is that rebels would continue to attack peacekeepers, in this instance UN forces, and this would result in calls for western or NATO intervention; any such intervention in another Islamic country would in turn result in a *jihadist* focus on Sudan, with the potential of another Iraq, this time in the Sahel.

It is also worth noting that the anti-Sudanese constituencies within the United States, especially amongst conservative groupings, have also used the Darfur issue to indirectly attack China, whose economy depends in part on oil from Sudan. They have sought to extend the genocide debate to China, claiming that China was party to the Darfur conflict: there have been moves to campaign against the 2008 Beijing Olympics as the "genocide Olympics".

The role of the African Union in negotiating peace, peace-keeping and civilian protection within Darfur has been crucial. By August 2007, the African Union Mission in Sudan (AMIS), established by ceasefire protocols signed by all parties to the conflict in April 2004, had deployed 6,143 military personnel and 1,360 police officers in Darfur.[39] The AU mission, however, has been severely undermined by western governments and institutions in political calls for a UN force to replace it in Darfur. Both the United States and the European Union have also failed to follow through with funding pledges. Julie Flint has stated that the international community has failed Darfur on several occasions. One was the "organisation, management and forced pace of the AU-mediated Abuja peace talks. The US, the key player…committed too few resources too late." This has undoubtedly weakened the AU's ability to function as effectively as it might within Darfur. The July 2007 UN Security Council resolution establishing the 26,000-strong UNAMID force, incorporating and replacing AMIS, when there is to all intents and purposes no peace to keep, will see a new phase in the Darfur crisis. Professor Mahmood Mamdani, the Herbert Lehman Professor of Government at Columbia University in New York, and one of America's most distinguished Africanists, has noted:

> Significant changes are currently taking place on the ground in Darfur. The peacekeeping forces of the African Union (AU) are being replaced by a hybrid AU-UN force under overall UN control. The assumption is that the change will be for the better, but this is questionable. The balance between the military and political dimensions of peacekeeping is crucial. Once it had overcome its teething problems – and before it ran into major funding difficulties – the AU got this relationship right: it privileged the politics, where the UN has tended to privilege the military dimension, which is why the UN-controlled hybrid force runs the risk of becoming an occupation force.[40]

The commitment by all parties to a peaceful solution to the Darfur conflict is unclear. The new government of national unity in Sudan, established following the 2005 Comprehensive Peace Agreement, and bringing together Sudan's former north-south combatants, has repeatedly stated its commitment to peace talks.[41] Southern Sudan's new leadership in the shape of Sudanese First Vice-President (and President of an autonomous Government of Southern Sudan), SPLA leader Salva Kiir, committed itself to work for peace in Darfur.[42] In September 2005, Sudan's new foreign minister, veteran SPLA politician Dr Lam Akol, outlined a new plan to end the Darfur conflict.[43] The rebel position was marked by a seeming inability or disinclination on their part – despite having started the war ostensibly to address political grievances – to engage in a negotiated settlement of the conflict or to present a political programme. De Waal and Flint, have noted, for example, that because of rebel shortcomings "[b]y the end of [2004] there had not been a single day's discussion about a framework for a political settlement…In the AU's conference chambers, SLA delegates rage at the government, but don't articulate a political agenda."[44] Despite this the AU peace process saw significant movement with the signing of several humanitarian and ceasefire protocols including a declaration of principles – signed in July 2005 – outlining the framework for a political settlement of the conflict.

The Bush administration has continued to impede and undermine the Darfur peace process. In November 2005, the UN stated that the rebels were still blocking peace talks and the African Union threatened to impose sanctions on them because of their obstructionism.[45] The US prevented any such measure. Vice-President Kiir has urged the international community to press the Darfur rebels to seek a peaceful solution to the conflict.[46] The US was very heavy-handed in the African Union-mediated talks in Abuja which resulted in the signing of the May 2006 Darfur Peace Agreement (DPA) between the Government of Sudan and the Darfur SLA rebel movement led by Minni Minawi. This agreement was modelled on the Comprehensive Peace Agreement between the Government of Sudan and the rebel Sudan Peoples Liberation Army (SPLA), which ended the long-running civil war in southern Sudan. The DPA addressed issues relating to power- and wealth-sharing, security, land and humanitarian affairs said to be at the heart of the Darfur conflict. Flint, for example, described the US approach to the Darfur Peace Agreement as one of "sign or be damned". The US "had determined that peace could be forced…and had set a deadline that was going to be observed come hell or high water. Only one rebel leader signed…Four months later, the result of this high-handed impatience is, predictably, hell."[47] Two other rebel factions refused to support the agreement. Violence escalated. Washington's arrogance, incompetence and spin coupled with vocal and material support from American advocacy groups such as Save Darfur served to fuel rebel intransigence within the peace process. And all this while the very people on whose behalf the two rebel factions claimed to be fighting continued to live precarious lives in displaced peoples' camps the length and breadth of Darfur in the face of growing international donor fatigue.[48] The American and British governments warned that those parties that did not sign the DPA would be "outlaws" to the process and subject to sanctions. None followed.

Despite having signed the DPA, and continuing to press for a negotiated settlement of the conflict, it was the Sudanese government, however, and not the non-signatory rebel movements, that was subsequently the target of new sanctions by the United States. Apparent rebel indifference to the suffering of Darfurians has continued well into 2007 with continuing Western double standards. The October 2007 Darfur peace talks held in Libya provide another example of such hypocrisy. The Sudanese government declared a unilateral ceasefire and arrived for the internationally-mediated negotiations. Most rebel factions did not.[49] The British Prime Minister, Gordon Brown, then issued a statement noting "This is a critical and decisive moment for Darfur. Of course, if parties do not come to the ceasefire, there's a possibility that we will impose further sanctions on the government." The Sudanese government was understandably puzzled and angered. The Sudanese President Omar al-Bashir warned that the comments would encourage the rebels to ignore or derail the peace talks so as to secure further sanctions on Khartoum.[50]

Flint observed that "George Bush's megaphone diplomacy has resulted in a complete breakdown of communication with Khartoum".[51] This was echoed in September 2006 by Mark Malloch-Brown, on his retirement as UN deputy secretary-general: "The megaphone diplomacy coming out of Washington and London: 'you damn well are going to let the UN deploy and if you don't beware the consequences' isn't plausible."[52]

The Darfur crisis has also been made worse by other international actions. Following on from recommendations made by the UN Commission, the UN Security Council called upon the International Criminal Court (ICC) to investigate human rights abuses in Darfur – despite the fact that Sudan is not a signatory to the 2002 Rome treaty which established the court.[53] Attempts to assert that the ICC has jurisdiction in Darfur runs the clear danger of prolonging the crisis for several reasons. Flying in the face of traditional African reconciliation mechanisms and practical political reality, threats to arrest and detain those alleged to be involved in war crimes while a conflict is ongoing greatly reduce the incentives of all concerned to end a war. As one American commentator has noted: "Threatening leaders with life sentences in the Hague turns a situation that might conceivably be resolved by diplomacy into a fight to the death."[54] Similar attempts by the ICC to indict Ugandan rebel leaders have derailed a delicate peace process in that country. Additionally, moves within the United States and other countries to secure disinvestment from Sudan risks not just aggravating the solution to the Darfur crisis but damaging the pre-existing peace in southern Sudan. Given that both the southern rebels and those now fighting in Darfur stated that they were fighting for a greater share of Sudan's wealth, and given the fact that the biggest single generator of wealth is the Sudanese economy, attempts to weaken or destroy that economy by attacking any foreign investment in Sudan can only but undermine not just the existing peace in southern Sudan but will also damage any post-war settlement in Darfur itself. Where else is the money to rebuild and develop Darfur going to come from if not from the Sudanese economy?

The international media has also inadvertently served to prolong the Darfur conflict. Speaking in 2006, Jonathan Steele, a senior foreign reporter with *The Guardian* newspaper, noted eight fundamental mistakes made by the media in their coverage of Darfur: incorrectly reporting the war's origins; incorrectly transferring the template of Sudan's North-South war to Darfur; presenting the war as one between Arab and Africans; ignoring the economic roots of the conflict; ignoring the peace process and then overlooking the problems caused by the rebels – blaming the government for any lack of progress at the peace talks; ignoring the splits on the rebels' side and ignoring the humanitarian problems caused by the rebels. Steele definitely believed that undemanding Western media coverage of the Darfur conflict has artificially prolonged the crisis: "I believe that the media's role in making heroes out of the rebels and overlooking their misdeeds, as well as in constantly calling for sanctions on Khartoum or even military intervention, have had a malign effect. In my view it encouraged the rebels to be more intransigent in Abuja than they would otherwise have been. They felt confident that if they refused to sign but held out for more, they could have the media's support."[55] De Waal has confirmed that "the peace process has never been properly covered in the media."[56]

For all the column inches of media coverage of the war, there are still a number of essentially unanswered questions concerning the Darfur crisis. One of the first must be what triggered the systematic outbreak of violence in Darfur in February 2003? This question is at the heart of understanding the dynamics of the conflict. Given concerted international attempts at peace-making and offers of regional autonomy together with power- and wealth-sharing, a second question is: what sustains the conflict? A third question concerns whether any of the parties are dragging their feet in the peace process; and, if so, why? A fourth question is what is the real position with regard to humanitarian access to Darfur? A fifth question asks the extent to which flawed interpretations and questionable projections of the crisis – some of them the sort of propaganda invariably associated with war and particularly civil war – hinder both reconciliation and peace-building while at the same time skewing and adversely influencing international opinion. And, of course, following on from this question, is the credibility of claims of genocide and ethnic cleansing in Darfur.

Darfur in Outline

The Darfur region, divided into the states of North, South and West Darfur, is the western-most part of Sudan. Darfur's 160,000 square miles make up one fifth of Sudan. It is an expanse of desert in the north through to savannah in the south. Geographically, it is made up of a plateau some 2,000 to 3,000 feet above sea-level. The volcanic Jebel Marra mountain range runs north and south for a distance of some 100 miles, rising to between 5,000 and 6,000 feet. Darfur's six million or so inhabitants comprise one seventh of Sudan's population. They are made up of farmers growing sorghum, millet, groundnuts and other market vegetables and nomadic cattle and camel pastoralists.

Formerly an independent sultanate, and named after the Fur tribe ("Dar" means land – of the Fur), Darfur was incorporated into Sudan by the British government in 1917.[57] Some of its borders were not finalised until as late as 1938. Previously administered as one entity, Darfur was divided into three states in the early 1990s. Al-Fasher, historically the capital of Darfur, is now the capital of North Darfur state; Nyala is the capital of South Darfur state; and al-Geneina is the capital of West Darfur state. Each state has a regional assembly, and a governor appointed by central government. Darfur is strategically placed, bordering Libya to the north-west, Chad to the west, and the Central African Republic to the south-west. Culturally, Darfur is part of a belt from Mauritania to the Red Sea.

The largest ethnic group within Darfur are the Fur people, who consist mainly of settled subsistence farmers and traditional cultivators. Other non-Arab, "African", groups include the Zaghawa nomads, the Meidob, Massaleit, Dajo, Berti, Kanein, Mima, Bargo, Barno, Gimir, Tama, Mararit, Fellata, Jebel, Sambat and Tunjur. The mainly pastoralist Arab tribes in Darfur include Habania, Beni Hussein, Zeiyadiya, Beni Helba, Ateefat, Humur, Khuzam, Khawabeer, Beni Jarrar, Mahameed, Djawama, Rezeigat, and the Ma'aliyah.[58] Sudanese sociologists have suggested that the population in Darfur can also be divided into four groups: the *Baggara* (cattle nomads), the *Aballa* (camel nomads), the *Zurga* (a Darfur name for non-Arab peasants derived from the Arabic word for blue), and the inhabitants of the urban centres.[59] A more culturally-based classification distinguishes between four groups: the Arabs; the fully Arabised; the partly Arabised; and the non-Arabised. The "Arabs" are the native Arabic speakers: the Rezeigat, the Zeiyadiya, Beni Hussein, and the Djawama nomads who, as a result of intermarriage with the indigenous Darfurians, look much darker than other non-Sudanese Arabs. The "fully Arabised" group is made up of those Darfurians, such as the Berti, who have lost their native languages to Arabic. The third, "partly Arabised" group is made up of those communities such as the Fur, the Zaghawa, and the Meidob, who have kept their native languages, but also speak Arabic fluently. The last "non-Arabised" group consists of tribes that speak very little Arabic, for example, the Massaleit, some sections of the Zaghawa, the Berti, the Mima, the Tama, and the Kanein.[60] A linguistically based analysis would categorise as "African" those whose mother-languages belonging to the Nilo-Saharan language group.[61]

Darfur is an ecologically fragile area which had already seen growing – and often armed – conflict over natural resources between some 80 tribes and clans loosely divided between nomadic and sedentary communities. Sudanist academics such as Professors Richard Lobban and Sean O'Fahey have stated: "This conflict has emerged at the present in the context of persistent ecological crises of increased desertification and lack of production and limited grazing lands among the pastoralist and agricultural peoples."[62] O'Fahey has noted that "desertification accelerated by droughts led to pressure on water and grazing resources...Conflicts over wells that in earlier times had been settled with spears or mediation became much more intractable in an era awash with guns."[63] Desertification and drought had forced a number of tribal migrations from the 1970s onwards and by the late 1980s, as noted by Darfurian writer Ismail Abakr Ahmed, "the migrant groups increased in numbers, and in the absence of social harmony, tribal factions developed and culminated in violent conflicts."[64]

These inter-tribal and intra-tribal conflicts, some *between* nomadic communities and farmers, and some *within* nomadic and farming communities themselves, were a feature from the late 1950s onwards. The following are some of the armed tribal conflicts that have taken place within Darfur since independence: 1957, Meidob against Kababish caused by mutual raiding for camels and disputed territorial access; 1968, Rezeigat against Ma'aliyah, caused by disputed access and livestock theft; 1969, Zaghawa against northern Rezeigat, caused by disputed access to pasture and water and livestock theft; 1974, Zaghawa against Birgid, caused by disputed access to farming land and livestock theft; 1976, Beni Helba against northern Rezeigat, caused by disputed access to pasture and water and livestock theft; 1980, northern Rezeigat against Beni Helba, Birgid, Dajo, and Fur, caused by disputed access to pasture and water and livestock theft; 1980, Taisha against Salamat, caused by disputed access to pasture and water and livestock theft; 1982, Kababish and Khawabeer against Meidob, Berti and Zeiyadiya, caused by disputed access to pasture and water and livestock theft; 1984, Missairiya against Rezeigat, caused by disputed access to pasture and water and livestock theft; 1987, Gimir and Mararit against Fellata, caused by disputed access to pasture and water and livestock theft; 1989, the Fur of Kabkabiya against the Zaghawa, over disputed territorial access and livestock theft; 1989, the Fur against various Arab tribes, caused by disputed territorial access and political conflict; and 1989, Gimir against Zaghawa, caused by disputed territorial access and livestock theft.[65] Six of these 13 conflicts were fought between Arab nomadic communities: four of the conflicts were between parties who were both non-Arab. All of these were serious armed conflicts, sometimes involving thousands of tribesmen, with combatants increasingly well armed with automatic weapons and vehicles. As is also apparent from the tribes involved, the violence was both within and across ethnic divides. The Sudanese national commission documented 36 major inter- and intra-tribal conflicts from 1932-2001.[66]

John Ryle has noted: "Low-level fighting among communities in western Sudan (all of which are Muslim) has been endemic since the late 1980s, when a war broke out between the Arabs and the Fur, two of the ethnic groups involved in the present conflict."[67] Much of this violence also had cross-border implications, with affected communities, such as the Salamat, often straddling the Sudan-Chad frontier. From 1983-87, as some northern Darfur tribes moved south into the central farming belt because of the drought, the Zaghawa and Ma'aliyah came into armed conflict with Fur communities. This conflict and others involving the Fur led to thousands of deaths, tens of thousands of displaced Darfurians and the destruction of thousands of homes. It was settled by a government-mediated intertribal conference in 1989. The 1990s were marked by three distinct conflicts. In 1990 the southern Sudan People's Liberation Army unsuccessfully tried to start an insurgency, led by Fur activist Daud Bolad, amongst non-Arab communities; in 1996 there was a long-running conflict between the Rezeigat and the Zaghawa; and from 1997-99 there was fighting in western Darfur between the Massaleit and some Arab tribes. The SPLA-inspired insurgency was defeated within a matter of months and, generally speaking, inter-tribal conferences and conciliation, *ajaweed* and *mutamarat al sulh*, settled most of the other disputes.

Amnesty International's picture of Darfur pre-rebellion also overlaps with inter-ethnic tensions: "The lack of employment opportunities, the proliferation of small arms and the example of militia raiding and looting in Kordofan and the south, have encouraged banditry, acts of armed robbery and general insecurity."[68] The simple fact is that all these factors existed well before 2003. An insurgency amongst "African" tribes had been tried and had failed; tribal conflicts had come and gone; ecological factors had been there for some time; the region was awash with weapons. What was it that made the key difference in sparking and fanning the war in 2003? What was it that turned limited, low-intensity conflicts between the pastoral and arable farming groups in Darfur into a well-organised, well-armed and well-resourced insurrection? Why was it that for the first time ever warring tribes in Darfur had systematically attacked and killed soldiers and policemen – historically seen as arbiters within regional conflicts?

The answers possibly lie with the answer to a final question, perhaps the most elementary one – a question not asked by the international community and especially not by the media – which is the old Latin one of *Cui Prodest*, or whom does it benefit? Khartoum certainly has not benefited. Several years of painstaking diplomacy, together with the peace talks which culminated in the end of the civil war in the south, had brought Sudan to the verge of normalising its relations with the international community. To somehow believe that the Sudanese government set out to destroy all that work by recklessly embarking on "genocide" in Darfur just as it was poised to rejoin the community of nations would be naïve. This is a point raised by French academic, and noted Khartoum critic, Gérard Prunier: "[G]enocide began to be mentioned as an explanation [for events in Darfur] in early 2004 by more militant members of the international community…This hypothesis…failed to explain why Khartoum would have picked such an obviously wrong moment."[69] The Zaghawa and Fur communities have similarly not benefited, having borne the brunt of a ruthless insurgency and counter-insurgency and vicious intra-rebel and intra-tribal violence. The close involvement, both in the preparations for the insurgency, and then in the war itself, of veteran anti-government Islamist politicians such as Dr Hassan Turabi – an Islamist extremist sidelined in 1999 by the Khartoum government – and paramilitaries drawn from the his party, the Popular Congress, is evident. These forces have used Darfur as a battlefield on which to wage war against the Khartoum government – and ironically were, in large part, the same people who ruthlessly put down the attempted insurrection in 1990. Previously sidelined in Khartoum politics from 1999 onwards, the Darfur conflict has brought these radical Islamists back to centre stage, and, in so doing, the Popular Congress has changed the electoral dynamics of western Sudan

Chapter One

THE CAUSES OF THE DARFUR CRISIS

The conflict in Darfur has nothing to do with marginalisation or the inequitable distribution of wealth. Inherently it is a struggle between the two factions of the Sudanese Islamist movement, the (opposition) Popular Congress party and the ruling National Congress (party).

Sudanese Human Rights Activist Ghazi Suleiman[70]

the prism through which the war is commonly explained — ethnic animosity between Arabs and blacks — may be less applicable than other factors, including the environment.

Time Magazine[71]

In the decades to come, Darfur may be seen as one of the first true climate-change wars.

The Guardian[72]

The war in Darfur which began in February 2003 was markedly different from the conflicts which had previously been fought in the region. Two armed groups, the Justice and Equality Movement (*harakat al-adil wal-musawah*, JEM) and the Sudan Liberation Army (*jeish tahrir as-sudan*, SLA), launched attacks on policemen, government garrisons and civilians in the area.[73] While the first widely acknowledged attack was on Gulu, the capital of the Jebel Marra region of central Darfur, there had been attacks on government forces and civilians for several months prior to that. One of the first attacks was on an army post between Nyala and Tur in early 2002. The rebel groups appear to have been drawn from within "African" sedentary communities such as the Fur, Zaghawa and Massaleit. In October 2002, what would subsequently become the SLA (emerging from a loose group known as the Darfur Liberation Front) elected a leadership which allocated the three top positions along tribal lines. A Fur, Abd al-Wahid al-Nur, became chairman; Abdalla Abakkar, a Zaghawa and a former officer in Chadian president Idriss Déby's *Garde républicaine*, became chief-of-staff; and the deputy-chairmanship was allocated to a Massaleit, Mansour Arbab. When Abdalla Abakkar subsequently died in the fighting, another Zaghawa, Minni Arkou Minawi, replaced him, calling himself the secretary-general of the SLA. Mansour Arbab was also later replaced by Khamees Abdallah. The Justice and Equality Movement was publicly launched in 2001. Led by Islamist hard-liner Dr Khalil Ibrahim, a long-time associate of Dr Hassan Turabi, JEM is closely identified with the Zaghawa tribe.

A number of systematic and well-organised attacks, most notably on al-Fasher and Mellit, respectively the capital and the second largest city in North Darfur, followed on from the Gulu attack. The attack on al-Fasher was by hundreds of rebels, in dozens of vehicles, and there were significant military and civilian casualties. Prunier notes, for example, that the rebels murdered 200 army prisoners after they had surrendered.[74] The rebel forces are said to be "well-equipped".[75] The SLA was reported by Agence France-Presse to have "modern satellite communications".[76] UN media sources have also noted claims by tribal leaders that the rebels have better weapons than the Sudanese army.[77] The rebels have also been receiving military supplies by air.[78] The fighters, led by commanders with satellite telephones, are well-armed with rocket-propelled grenades, heavy machine-guns, mortars and automatic rifles, and transported in fleets of all-terrain vehicles – mainly Toyota "technicals" with mounted heavy machines guns, an infamous hallmark of the Somalian conflict. In the initial 18 months of conflict, the rebels killed over 685 policemen, wounded 500 others and attacked and destroyed over 80 police stations.[79] It is worth noting that most of the policemen killed or wounded were from "African" tribes.

In response to these attacks, government forces launched military offensives against the SLA. These resulted in the death of the SLA military commander, Abdalla Abakkar, and the recovery of most of the areas previously held by the rebels. The communities from which the rebels had recruited their fighters bore the brunt of much of the fighting. It is also clear that the Fur communities bore an additional burden. Julie Flint states that in the first year of the war, Darfur rebels "lived off the land – or more specifically, off the inhabitants". This was "a recipe for disaster" and Fur communities suffered "the abuses of undisciplined commanders". Flint also notes that "The lack of control generated by the all-consuming nature of the leadership dispute led to the emergence of rogue commanders answerable to none but themselves. The SLA leaders made little attempt to enforce discipline…Alcohol compounded the problem…There was rape too." [80]

In perhaps the most objective reading of the present crisis in Darfur, the UN media service has made this analysis: "The conflict pits farming communities against nomads who have aligned themselves with the militia groups – for whom the raids are a way of life – in stiff competition for land and resources. The militias, known as the Janjaweed, attack in large numbers on horseback and camels and are driving the farmers from their land, often pushing them towards town centres." [81]

The extent of popular support for the rebel actions has been unclear. In his 2005 study of the conflict, US scholar Victor Tanner found that "most of the Darfur people interviewed, rich and poor, Arab and African, victimized and not – and most of them supportive of the rebels' agenda for change – stated both their opposition to armed rebellion, and their belief that the current violence escalated in response to the insurgency." [82] Tanner and Tubiana have subsequently reported fluctuations in support since then but, by mid-2007, they observe that "Many Darfurians seem less sanguine about the prospects of future rebel victories, and some even blame them for some of the abuses and suffering that civilian populations continue to endure." [83]

The violence in Darfur has taken on several forms. The government has used its army and air force in its response to the rebellion. It has also drawn on local "popular defence forces", made up of national and local volunteers. And it has also recruited from amongst politically supportive local tribes to form additional irregular forces. It is also clear that a variety of other armed groups have been active in Darfur over the past two years, either as participants in the war or taking advantage of the turmoil the conflict has caused. The systematic murder by rebels of several hundred policemen and the destruction of over 80 police stations created a security vacuum, especially in rural areas. The rebels' targeting of tribal leaders and tribesmen from several "Arab" tribes, and the theft of thousands of head of livestock from these tribes, have resulted in an explosion of inter-communal violence with revenge attacks and livestock raids by equally well-armed nomadic tribes.[84] Darfur has also historically had a serious problem with armed banditry, the so-called "Janjaweed" phenomena, and heavily armed criminal gangs from both sides of the Chad-Sudan border have added to the chaos.

The war in Darfur spiked in late 2003 and early 2004. Government offensives ended any significant, large-scale rebel actions and culminated in a series of disjointed ceasefires. On 19 April 2004, however, the government and rebels signed a significant humanitarian ceasefire agreement mediated by the Chadian government as a first step towards a lasting peace. In November 2004 African Union mediation resulted in the government and rebel movements signing the Abuja protocols, extending the ceasefire and aid access agreements.[85] These were followed by the signing in July 2005 of a Declaration of Principles which outlined the basis of a possible political settlement, and the May 2006 Darfur Peace Agreement. The several thousand-strong African Union Mission in Sudan has provided both a forum for continuing peace talks and ceasefire supervision. Following pressure on the Sudanese government, the AU mission changed into a 26,000-strong AU-UN hybrid mission, the United Nations and African Union Mission in Darfur, UNAMID. It is essential that any peace agreements are honoured, monitored and followed through as the international community attempts both to address the humanitarian aid needs of those hundreds of thousands of civilians who have been displaced by the war and to facilitate a political solution to the conflict.

What Has Caused the Conflict?

It is essential for anyone seeking to bring the Darfur conflict to an end to examine closely the causes of the violence that has convulsed the region. To end the war, the precise reasons for why it started need to be examined. There are several contributory factors. The insurgents claim to be acting because of Darfur's marginalisation and underdevelopment. That Darfur is underdeveloped is self-evident. It is no more underdeveloped, however, than several other parts of Sudan. It is also clear that this historic underdevelopment – however it is measured – does not adequately explain the inter-communal violence in past decades. It is particularly difficult to accept that underdevelopment and marginalisation account for the level of focused and orchestrated violence aimed at the Government of Sudan since early 2003 – violence clearly planned for some considerable time beforehand.

It is difficult, for example, to ignore Khartoum's assertions with regard to development in Darfur since the present government came to power in 1989 in one of the poorest countries in the world. The government has stated that, before 1989, there were only 16 high schools in Darfur: there are presently some 250 schools; the number of primary schools had increased from 241 in 1986 to 786 in 2003. In 1989 there were 27,000 students in schools; in 2003 there were more than 440,000.[86] In 1989 there was not a single university in Darfur; there are now three. The number of hospitals in Darfur has increased under this government from three hospitals in 1988 to 23 hospitals by 2001; health centres had increased from 20 to 44 in the same period. Water pump production in greater Darfur has also increased from 1,200,000 cubic metres in 1989 to 3,100,000 cubic metres in 2003. During 2000-2003, the following water projects were implemented in greater Darfur: the installation of 110 deep ground wells, the rehabilitation of 133 ground wells, the building of 43 dykes and 30 dams, the drilling of 842 hand pumps and the rehabilitation of 839 hand pump wells. The total power generation in greater Darfur has risen under this government from 2,300 kilowatts in 1989 to 4,500 kilowatts by 2000. Before 1989 there was not a single airport in Darfur; there are now three, in al-Fasher, Nyala and al-Geneina, along with three aerodromes at al-Deain, Zallingi and Jama – this represents 40 per cent of airports outside of the national capital. There has been a three-fold increase in paved roads since 1989. And, politically, Darfur is very well represented at all levels of Sudanese society. As of early 2005 there were eight government ministers from Darfur and four Darfurian state governors.[87] Darfurians are also members of the supreme and constitutional courts. Darfurian representation in the National Assembly is second only to the southern states.[88]

The Sudanese government has also made the point that, far from showing interest in development issues for Darfur, rebels have repeatedly attacked key education and development projects and civilians involved in these projects. In April 2003, rebels murdered Engineer Ahmed Youssef Mahdi, the director of the Jebel Marra agricultural scheme. On 21 November 2003, for example, rebels murdered al-Tayeb Abdul Gadir al-Nour, a telephone engineer, while he was inspecting the fibreglass cable line linking Nyala and al-Geneina. On 27 November that year they murdered three water engineers working on rural water schemes. In March 2003 rebels attacked the school examination centre in Tina and stole the examination papers. This led to the abandoning of certain school examinations nationally, adversely affecting tens of thousands of school students and their families.[89]

Rebel attacks on development projects continued into 2004. In June 2004, for example, rebel attacks stopped work on an emergency water supply project for al-Fasher.[90] Their attacks on development and infrastructure projects have been criticised by several Darfurian community leaders. The chairman of trade unions in North Darfur, Alamir Altagani Ali Dinar, stated that it was "strange" that the rebels attacked the development projects in the state, while claiming lack of development as the cause of their movement. The general secretary of the Ministry of Social Welfare, Mohammed Nour Ahmed, said that the attacks delay development projects in Darfur.[91] By May 2005, in the state of North Darfur alone, all health facilities had been destroyed or affected by the war. Almost 40% of dispensaries and 80% of the wells in the state had also been destroyed or damaged.[92]

What is becoming increasingly obvious is that whatever legitimate issues may have arisen out of concerns about underdevelopment they have been hijacked by various opportunistic forces to serve different ends. The question that must be answered is what was it that turned limited, low-intensity conflicts between, and within, the pastoral and arable farming groups in Darfur into a well-organised, well-armed and well-resourced rebellion? Rebel claims that the war is simply the inevitable result of marginalisation have been contradicted by reputable, independent observers. A particularly credible observer is Ghazi Suleiman, Sudan's most prominent human rights activist. He has been described by Reuters as "a prominent non-partisan political figure"[93] and by the Knight-Ridder news service as a "well-known Sudanese human rights lawyer".[94] Suleiman has publicly stated: "The conflict in Darfur has nothing to do with marginalisation or the inequitable distribution of wealth. Inherently it is a struggle between the two factions of the Sudanese Islamist movement, the (opposition) Popular Congress party and the ruling National Congress (party)."[95]

De Waal has also made interesting points about the marginalisation issue. He has noted, for example, that the black Arabs of Darfur are "among the most disadvantaged of all Darfur's communities".[96] The Zaghawa community, on the other hand, has established itself commercially in Darfur and other parts of Sudan. De Waal has noted: "They cannot simply be described—as they often are—as 'nomads' or 'farmers': they are both, and more besides. For sheer business acumen, the Zaghawa surpassed all contenders in Darfur, making spare but impressive profits in an economy that seemed to have no surplus." In addition, the Zaghawa are the ruling *élite* in Chad – Chadian President Idriss Déby, and many of the ministers and army officers around him, are Zaghawa.[97] It is also the case that the rebels cannot in any case claim the full support even of their own communities. In April 2004, for example, SLA rebels kidnapped and murdered Abdel Rahman Mohammain, a prominent Zaghawa tribal leader, because of his opposition to them. The UN stated that this murder was "aimed at intimidating and deterring" local leaders in Darfur.[98]

Claims of Fur marginalisation are also very questionable. Prunier, for example, points out that, in January 1980, the Fur politician, Ahmed Diraige, became Governor of Darfur. The deputy governor was Mahmood Beshir Jama, a Zaghawa. The Speaker of Darfur's Parliament was another Fur.[99] Douglas Johnston has also shown that at the time of many of the pre-2003 conflicts between pastoralists – Arab and African, such as the Zaghawa, – and farmers, far from being marginalised it was the Fur who dominated government structures in Darfur: "With the upper levels of the regional government being occupied by Fur, the broader structural changes of regionalization from 1981 onwards led to a sharpening of partisan politics in the approach to pastoralist/ non-pastoralist confrontations."[100] Even Sharif Harir, a long-time critic of Khartoum and himself now closely identified with the Sudan Liberation Army, has noted that the appointment in 1981 of the Fur politician Ahmed Diraige as Governor of Darfur saw a Fur political ascendancy in the region. He also noted that Fur hegemony resulted in the crystallisation of two political alliances – with the Fur and elements of urban Darfurian elites on one hand, and the Zaghawa, nomadic Arab groups and the Islamist extremists on the other.[101] Harir even went so far as to state that "a deep hostility began to develop between the persecuted groups and the Fur-led government."

23

While citing marginalisation, it is clear that those sections of the Zaghawa, Fur and other tribes who are at the forefront of the rebellion in Darfur have themselves in large part dominated political and economic life in Darfur. Their motivations continue to be influenced by political ambition and, in the case of elements of the Zaghawa, by a continuing allegiance to Islamist politics and Dr Hassan Turabi.

The Islamist Roots of the Darfur Conflict

For all the claims of marginalisation, there is no doubt whatsoever that the conflict within the Sudanese Islamist movement following the government's sidelining of the Islamist *eminence grise* Dr Hassan Turabi in 1999 is central to the Darfur conflict. Once the mentor of the present government, Dr Turabi had long been seen by reformists within the Sudanese government/ruling élite as an obstacle both to the normalisation of relations with the United States and a peace agreement with southern rebels. The ruling National Congress party, *al-Mutamar al-Wattani*, split in 2000/2001 with hard-liners under Turabi, many of them from Darfur, forming the Popular Congress party, *al-Mutamar al-Sha'bi*, in opposition to any engagement with Washington and the West and peace in southern Sudan. (De Waal has observed: "It is almost unbearably ironic that just as southern Sudan is on the brink of peace, Darfur – and with it the entire north – is convulsed by another war. The linkage is not accidental."[102])

Sudarsan Raghavan, the Africa bureau chief for the Knight-Ridder news service, a veteran commentator on Darfur and critic of the government, has reported on the Islamist twist to the Darfur issue: "The violence in Sudan's western province of Darfur...is widely portrayed as an ethnic-cleansing campaign by Arab militias against black African villagers. *But it's also part of a long-running fight for political supremacy between Sudanese president Omar al Bashir and an Islamist who called Osama bin Laden a hero.* [Emphasis added] For 15 years, Hassan Turabi was Sudan's most powerful man, deftly manoeuvring its leaders from his perch as speaker of the parliament. He counted bin Laden among his close friends and once called the United States 'the incarnation of the devil'." Turabi has subsequently been very critical of Khartoum for "selling out" to Washington, including Sudan's considerable assistance in the war on terrorism and concessions Khartoum has made in the peace process.[103]

Raghavan asserts that "the government is deathly afraid of Turabi" and has noted: "many Sudanese believe…Turabi's supporters are the core of the rebel groups."[104] He also cites Ghazi Suleiman, whom he described as a "well-known Sudanese human rights lawyer", as saying of the war in Darfur: "It is a struggle to seize power in Khartoum, and the battlefield is in Darfur."[105] In a different interview, with Reuters, Ghazi Suleiman stated that "Turabi is the mastermind of the existing conflict in Darfur. If he is released and if the government tries to come to an agreement with him he will stop what is going on in Darfur in a week."[106] This line of analysis has also been confirmed by other anti-government commentators. Dr Tajudeen Abdul-Raheem, the general-secretary of the Pan African Movement and co-director of Justice Africa, a human rights organisation, has also said: "Darfur is a victim of the split within the National Islamic Front personified by…Dr Hassan al-Turabi and his former protégé, General Omar al-Bashir. Al-Turabi's support is very strong in Darfur…"[107]

The Justice and Equality Movement is increasingly recognised as being part and parcel of the Popular Congress. *Time* magazine has described JEM as "a fiercely Islamic organisation said to be led by Hassan al-Turabi" and that Turabi's ultimate goal is "the presidential palace in Khartoum and a stridently Islamic Sudan".[108] JEM leader Khalil Ibrahim is a long-time associate and protégé of Turabi's. He had been a leader of the Islamist student movement *al-ittijah al-islami* (the Islamic Orientation) and entered government following the 1989 coup which brought the Islamists to power in Sudan. He served as a state minister in Darfur in the early 1990s before serving as a state cabinet-level advisor in southern Sudan. Ibrahim was a senior member of the Islamist movement's secret military wing. The International Crisis Group has noted that "Khalil Ibrahim…is a veteran Islamist and former state minister who sided with the breakaway [Popular Congress] in 2002 and went into exile in the Netherlands."[109] He was closely involved in raising several brigades of the Popular Defence Force (PDF) and *mujahideen*, many of them personally recruited from Darfur tribes, to fight rebels in southern Sudan. He was known as the *emir* of the *mujahideen*.[110] Ibrahim recruited several hundred JEM fighters from the ranks of those Darfurian tribesmen he had led in the south, claiming that the Khartoum government had sold out to the southern rebels and Washington. Other pro-Turabi Islamists in JEM include Baha Idris Abu Garda, JEM vice-president and secretary-general, and Abubakar Hamid Nur Abdelrahman Firti, JEM's international relations chief. A key link between Turabi and JEM is Dr Ali al-Haj, a Turabi protégé, former government minister and party treasurer. Tanner and Tubiana note that Ali al-Haj is said to be JEM's key "money man".[111]

De Waal has mentioned that the student wing and regional Islamist cells followed Turabi into opposition following the split. Two other parts of the Islamist infrastructure that joined Turabi virtually *en masse* following the break were the financial cell and the military wing (which continued to exist separately of the Sudanese armed forces even after the 1989 coup which brought the present government to power, and which had previously administered the PDF and *jihad* fighters). Both had always been strictly controlled by Turabi. This military wing formed the core of JEM and the military structures which planned and initiated attacks in Darfur. In November 2003, the Popular Congress admitted that some party members were involved in the Darfur conflict.[112] In January 2004 Turabi admitted supporting the Darfur insurrection: "We support the cause, no doubt about it...we have relations with some of the leadership."[113] In the same month, Turabi admitted that 30 members of his Popular Congress party had been arrested in connection with activities in Darfur.[114]

The influential Egyptian newspaper *al-Ahram* was also explicit in its linking of JEM to extremist Islamism: "JEM is a militant Islamist organisation reputedly linked to the Popular National Congress Party (PNC) of the Sudanese Islamist ideologue and former speaker of the Sudanese parliament Hassan Al-Turabi."[115] *Al-Ahram* has also noted Turabi's involvement in Darfur: "Al-Turabi wields powerful influence among certain segments of Darfur society. Darfur, a traditional Islamist stronghold...The Sudanese government is especially concerned about the involvement of elements sympathetic to Al-Turabi in the Darfur conflict."[116]

The International Crisis Group has also noted the Darfur war's Islamist origins: "Darfur's crisis is also rooted in the disputes that have plagued Sudan's Islamist movement since it took power in 1989. Following a disagreement with Hassan el-Turabi, the architect and spiritual guide of the Islamist movement, a second split in the ruling Islamist movement had an equally destabilising impact on Darfur. In 2000, Turabi, then speaker of parliament, formed the Popular National Congress (later renamed the Popular Congress, PC) following a fierce power struggle with the ruling National Congress Party. To broaden its base, PC activists reached out to Sudan's majority but marginalised African population."[117] These roots have also been commented upon by human rights activists:

> The second rebel group is the Justice and Equality Movement (JEM), based mostly on the Zaghawa tribe. It is linked with the radical Popular Patriotic Congress party led by the veteran Islamist Hassan al-Turabi who has now fallen out with his former NIF disciples...The relationship between JEM and SLM remains one of the obscure points of the Darfur conflict, even if the two organizations claim to be collaborating militarily. The JEM is by far the richer of the two and the one with the greater international media exposure, even if its radical Islamist connections make it an unlikely candidate for fighting a radical Islamist government...The main financial support for the uprising comes...in the case of the JEM, from foreign funds under the control of Hassan al-Turabi. It is the importance of this last financial source that explains the fairly impressive and modern equipment of the rebel forces.[118]

De Waal has also written about the split between the Islamists and the Khartoum government: "It was a protracted struggle, over ideology, foreign policy, the constitution and ultimately power itself. Bashir won: in 1999 he dismissed Turabi from his post as speaker of the National Assembly, and later had him arrested. The Islamist coalition was split down the middle...The students and the regional Islamist party cells went into opposition with Turabi, forming the breakaway Popular Congress. Among other things, the dismissal of Turabi gave Bashir the cover he needed to approach the United States, and to engage in a more serious peace process with the SPLA – a process that led to the signing of the peace agreement in Kenya."[119]

The International Crisis Group has noted that "the alleged link between JEM (Justice and Equality Movement) and the [Popular Congress] is the most worrisome for [Khartoum], since it fears Turabi is using Darfur as a tool for returning to power in Khartoum at the expense of his former partners in the ruling National Congress Party (NCP)." [120] It has also further noted that "The belief that the Darfur rebellion has been hijacked by disaffected rival Islamists is a main reason behind the government's refusal to talk to the rebels, particularly JEM. The personal rivalry between Vice-President Taha and his ex-mentor Turabi for control of the Islamist movement and the country is being played out in Darfur, with civilians as the main victims." [121] Dr Richard Cornwell, the Sudan expert at the South African-based Institute of Security Studies, has said that many Sudanese believe that JEM was formed as result of the power struggle between President Bashir and Hassan Turabi: "The Turabi link is very important…there are some people who are of the opinion that Turabi's supporters in Khartoum and Darfur deliberately manufactured this crisis with a view of taking power." [122] Agence France-Presse has concluded that "disgraced Turabi loyalists of Muslim African origin…constitute the core of the JEM's current leadership…More than a liberation movement, the JEM is seen as an organisation used as a tool by members of the political opposition to destabilise Beshir's regime." [123] Tanner and Tubiana have noted that JEM has "clear roots in the Turabi branch of the NIF". [124]

The Government of Sudan was initially very reluctant to concede that Dr Turabi and the Popular Congress were intimately involved in the Darfur conflict. In May 2004, however, the then Sudanese Interior Minister, Major-General Abdul-Rahim Mohammed Hussein, admitted the connection: "The Popular Congress is involved in the incidences in Darfur and the JEM is just another face of the Popular Congress." [125] In September 2004, the Governor of West Darfur, Suleiman Abdullah Adam, stated that the Justice and Equality Movement was the military wing of the Popular Congress: "The JEM are the military wing of the Popular Congress and, as the military wing of the Popular Congress in Darfur, they try to escalate the situation." [126]

It is also becoming apparent that the Popular Congress has been using a dual – interconnected – strategy in its attempts to overthrow the Khartoum government. They have used orchestrated events in Darfur to weaken the government domestically and internationally – perhaps even to the extent of foreign military intervention. And they have also attempted, in combination, to mount a military uprising. In March 2004, military officers linked to the Popular Congress attempted a *coup d'état* in Khartoum. The BBC said: "Those detained are also being linked to the uprising in the Darfur region."[127] They also planned attacks on oil refineries and power stations.[128] In September 2004 the government also foiled another Popular Congress coup attempt.[129] Khalil Ibrahim admitted that JEM was involved in organising this attempted coup.[130] The Islamist plotters were accused of plotting to assassinate or kidnap government officials and take over strategic installations, including state radio and television.[131] The government captured a large arms cache "with which the conspirators planned to kidnap and kill 38 government officials and destroy strategic targets in Khartoum".[132] The trials of those involved in the coup attempts, including five retired members of the armed forces and a former cabinet minister, began in late 2004.[133] They were charged with possessing weapons, terrorism, undermining the constitutional system and plotting war. Twenty-one serving members of the armed forces were charged separately.[134] The Sudanese government began to move against Islamist extremists.[135]

It is clear that Turabi and Popular Congress deliberately chose Darfur to be the cockpit of their war against Khartoum. They also cold-bloodedly sought to project a racial element on the issue. Popular Congress activists originated and distributed a publication known as "The Black Book" alleging Khartoum's marginalisation and neglect of Darfur and claiming that Sudan's political elite was dominated by a northern Arab clique – seemingly the same clique once led by Turabi. *The Financial Times* confirmed that the "Black Book" had been written by Justice and Equality Movement activists. The newspaper also noted that "The appearance of the Black Book did coincide with a deep split in the regime, which has exacerbated tension in society."[136] Prunier specifically identified Khalil Ibrahim as the author of the book.[137] De Waal has also commented on the importance of the "Black Book" in subsequent events in Darfur: "The Islamist split quickly took on regional and ethnic dimensions. The west Africans and Darfurians who had come into the Islamist movement under Turabi's leadership left with him...In May 2000, Darfurian Islamists produced the "Black Book"...The Black Book was a key step in the polarization of the country along politically constructed 'racial' rather than religious lines, and it laid the basis for a coalition between Darfur's radicals, who formed the SLA, and its Islamists, who formed the other rebel organization, the Justice and Equality Movement."[138]

Charles Snyder, a former United States Acting Assistant Secretary of State for African Affairs, and the State Department's senior adviser on Sudan, has noted the visceral nature of the intra-Islamist struggle:

> The emergence of armed opposition in Darfur has profoundly shaken the government because it poses, in many respects, a greater threat than the activities of the SPLM in the south....Support for the JEM and SLM, however, comes from within the overwhelmingly Muslim population of Darfur; radical Muslim cleric Turabi, who was recently jailed by the current [government of Sudan], has links to the JEM. Moreover, over 50 percent of the Sudanese military is from Darfur, and that region is not far from Khartoum. A successful insurgency in Darfur would fuel potential insurgencies in other parts of the north. This, I believe, explains why the Government of Sudan has adopted such brutal tactics in Darfur. The GOS is determined to defeat the JEM and SLM at any cost...[139]

The linkage between Darfur's violence and the Popular Congress has an additional dimension. In February 2001, Turabi and the Popular Congress signed a joint memorandum with the SPLA, the southern rebel movement led by Dr John Garang, which called for the "the escalation of popular resistance" against Khartoum. A secret codicil to the Popular Congress/SPLA memorandum was an agreement by the SPLA to train Darfur rebels. The International Crisis Group, an organisation very critical of the Sudanese government, has noted that "numerous sources link the SPLA to the beginning of the SLA rebellion by providing arms, training, and strategy...It allegedly trained as many as 1,500 Darfurians near Raja, in western Bahr el-Ghazal, in March 2002."[140] These trainees subsequently formed the basis of the Sudan Liberation Army and Justice and Equality Movement. The SPLA clearly maintained their relationship with Dr Turabi and the Popular Congress, demanding that Turabi be invited to the January 2005 signing of the north-south peace agreement.[141] Prunier has had no hesitation in linking the Darfur insurgency to Turabi, the Popular Congress and the SPLA: "[t]he Turabi faction...had planned the insurrection since perhaps late 2000 or at least early 2001 and it had acted in cooperation with the SPLA."[142] It is also clear that

JEM has a national agenda. JEM fighters have been seen on the Sudanese border with Eritrea.[143]

In October 2004, the Sudanese government warned that a new armed movement with links to Dr Turabi had emerged in the central Kordofan region of Sudan. Called *Shahama*, this group was headed by Mussa Ali Mohammedin, another member of the Popular Congress. It was said to operate from bases in Bahr al-Ghazal.[144]

The intimate involvement of Islamist extremists such as Dr Turabi and his Popular Congress party in the Darfur insurgency has worrying implications for those eager to end the Darfur crisis. It is very difficult, for example, to end a conflict said to be about marginalisation and underdevelopment when at least one of major participants would appear to have a hidden agenda of overthrowing the Government of Sudan and replacing it with a more hard-line Islamist regime. Building schools and roads and drilling more water wells in Darfur, while doubtlessly useful, is not going to satisfy hard-line Islamist rebels in Darfur any more than reconstruction projects in Iraq have satisfied Islamist insurgents in that country.

The First Climate Change War?

There is no doubt that climate change and directly related environmental degradation have served to underpin the politics of conflict in Darfur. While the Darfur conflict has always been described as in some way a struggle over resources, the catalytic role played by climate change was first raised in an environmental magazine in August 2006 which sought to acknowledge "how the dispute began: Darfur may well be the first war influenced by climate change. In recent years, increasing drought cycles and the Sahara's southward expansion have created conflicts between nomadic and sedentary groups over shortages of water and land."[145] The UN Secretary-General, Ban Ki-Moon, has pointed to climate change as a major factor in causing the Darfur conflict:

> Almost invariably, we discuss Darfur in a convenient military and political shorthand – an ethnic conflict pitting Arab militias against black rebels and farmers. Look to its roots, though, and you discover

31

a more complex dynamic. Amid the diverse social and political causes, the Darfur conflict began as an ecological crisis, arising at least in part from climate change…It is no accident that the violence in Darfur erupted during the drought.[146]

Ban Ki-Moon's position was reflected in a report issued in June 2007 by the UN Environment Programme which stated that "Darfur…holds grim lessons for other countries at risk."[147]

This perspective was also examined in a key article in *The Atlantic Monthly* which observed that the Darfur crisis "has been profoundly misunderstood", and that while "the violence in Darfur is usually attributed to ethnic hatred…global warming may be primarily to blame". The article stated that some experts "see Darfur as a canary in the coal mine, a foretaste of climate-driven political chaos". The article cited Alex de Waal as saying that environmental degradation "creates very dry tinder. So if anyone wants to put a match to it, they can light it up." [148]

The Atlantic Monthly article went further in actually pointing to the origin of the catastrophic climate changes in the Sahel:

Why did Darfur's lands fail? For much of the 1980s and '90s, environmental degradation in Darfur and other parts of the Sahel (the semi-arid region just south of the Sahara) was blamed on the inhabitants. Dramatic declines in rainfall were attributed to mistreatment of the region's vegetation. Imprudent land use, it was argued, exposed more rock and sand, which absorb less sunlight than plants, instead reflecting it back toward space. This cooled the air near the surface, drawing clouds downward and reducing the chance of rain. But by the time of the Darfur conflict four years ago, scientists had identified another cause. Climate scientists fed historical sea-surface temperatures into a variety of computer models of atmospheric change. Given the particular pattern of ocean-temperature changes worldwide, the models strongly predicted a disruption in African monsoons. "This was not caused by people cutting trees or overgrazing," says Columbia University's Alessandra Giannini, who led one of the analyses. The roots of the drying of Darfur, she and her colleagues had found, lay in changes to the global climate.

As *The Atlantic Monthly* magazine makes clear, the United States along with the rest of the industrialised world may well have had a role in the Darfur crisis:

> Among the implications arising from the ecological origin of the Darfur crisis, the most significant may be moral. If the region's collapse was in some part caused by the emissions from our factories, power plants, and automobiles, we bear some responsibility for the dying…we, unconsciously and without malice, created the conditions that led to this crisis. [149]

This perspective has also been articulated by Julian Borger, the Washington correspondent of *The Guardian*, in a further study of the environmental underpinning of the Darfur crisis:

> Something fundamental has changed in this part of Africa, and it happened within a generation…What changed, the evidence suggests, was the climate….Back in the 1980s, the failure of the rains was widely blamed on the people who lived in the region. Their over-grazing, it had been thought, had led to soil erosion, replaced green cover with bare rock and sand, reflecting more heat into the atmosphere and diminishing the chance of rain. More recent computer modelling has suggested that rain patterns over Africa are influenced rather by ocean temperatures, and those in turn reflect global warming, and the rise of greenhouse gases in the atmosphere. In other words, droughts in Africa may be caused less by its hapless inhabitants and more by oversize cars and cheap flights in Europe and the US. [150]

Borger observes that those Arab communities that have been drawn into the conflict came "from the ranks of the desperate, ripped from their traditional way of life by a catastrophic change in the weather". He retells Alex de Waal's meeting with a nomadic leader, Sheikh Hilal Musa, in 1985 at the height of the drought as the Sahara desert was visibly advancing. De Waal noted: "Sheikh Hilal's moral geography had been disturbed; the cosmic order had given way to chaos." It is perhaps no coincidence that the one tribal leader most associated in the West with the "janjaweed" is that Sheikh's son, Musa Hilal.

An April 2007 *Time* magazine article touched on many of the same themes outlined above.

> What is often overlooked is that the roots of the conflict may have more to do with ecology than ethnicity. To live on the poor and arid soil of the Sahel – just south of the Sahara – is to be mired in an eternal fight for water, food and shelter. The few pockets of good land have been the focus of intermittent conflict for decades between nomads (who tend to be Arabs) and settled farmers (who are both Arab and African). That competition is intensifying. The Sahara is advancing steadily south, smothering soil with sand. Rainfall has been declining in the region for the past half-century, according to the National Center for Atmospheric Research. In Darfur there are too many people in a hot, poor, shrinking land, and it's not hard to start a fight in a place like that.[151]

Michael Klare, an expert on international security issues at Hampshire College, in the United States, and author of the book *Resource Wars*, has also seen the Darfur crisis as part of an emerging pattern of resource conflict in Africa:

> I don't think you can separate climate change from population growth, rising consumption patterns and globalization... It's really one phenomenon... In a place like Africa, where the infrastructure and the government are weak, all these pressures are multiplying...and it's creating conflict and schisms, which often arise along ethnic and religious lines, because that's how communities are organized. But they're really fighting over land or water or timber or diamonds.[152]

The *Time* report also cited Philip E Clapp, president of the Washington-based National Environmental Trust, who warned that Darfur may be "an advance warning" of climate-related apocalypses to come: "Darfur is small by comparison with what is projected. It may be our last warning before the consequences of climate change become so enormous that they are beyond the capacity of industrialized nations to deal with."[153]

That the conflict in Darfur is clearly linked to the environment has also been recognised by European politicians. In February 2007, for example, then British Defence Secretary John Reid publicly pointed towards global warming as a driving force behind the Darfur crisis: "[Environmental] changes make the emergence of violent conflict more rather than less likely...The blunt truth is that the lack of water and agricultural land is a significant contributory factor to the tragic conflict we see unfolding in Darfur."[154] On 17 April 2007, his colleague British Foreign Secretary Margaret Beckett hosted the first-ever debate on climate change and armed conflict at the UN Security Council. Beckett asked: "What makes wars start?" Her answer was blunt: "Fights over water. Changing patterns of rainfall. Fights over food production, land use. There are few greater potential threats to our economies too... but also to peace and security itself."[155]

There is also an increasing realisation on the part of Western defence and security analysts of the increasing part played by climate change in conflict in Africa. A 2004 US defence report warned that climate change is a greater threat to the world than terrorism.[156] A further report by 11 American admirals and generals, released in April 2007, echoed these concerns, warning that climate change "presents significant national security challenges to the United States". The report stated: "Projected climate change will seriously exacerbate already marginal living standards in many Asian, African, and Middle Eastern nations, causing widespread political instability and the likelihood of failed states."[157] It warned that climate change will act as a "threat multiplier" fuelling instability around the world by worsening water shortages, food insecurity, disease, and flooding that lead to forced migration.

Time magazine left its readers with a clear warning about the environment and Africa:

> The devastation of Darfur highlights the potentially catastrophic effects of climate change on societies across Africa. The U.N.

estimates that the lives of as many as 90 million Africans – most of them in and around the Sahara – could be "at risk" on account of global warming. Many of Africa's armed conflicts can be explained as tinderboxes of climate change lit by the spark of ancient rivalry.[158]

Dr Emeka E Obioha, one of the world's leading experts on climate change and resultant clashes over resources, places the Darfur conflict into its environmental context:

In North East Nigeria there are many conflicts, which are environmentally induced. These are conflicts over grazing land, over cattle, over water points and over cultivable land. While there are conflicts over grazing land and over cattle amongst pastoral people, there are also conflicts over cultivable land amongst peasant farmers within the same ethnic group and also between ethnic groups. Such conflicts amongst pastoralists are common and widespread in Nigeria. This is similar to what happens in the Karamajong of Uganda and the Pokot of Kenya who have been fighting over grazing land and over cattle for more than three decades.[159]

The UN's Integrated Regional Information Networks (IRIN) reported the killing of 70 people in northern Kenya's Marsabit district in July 2005 as demonstrating "a frequent pattern of conflict between communities living in arid areas over scarce resources and inter-communal animosity exacerbated by political rivalry". Hundreds of armed raiders, believed to have been members of the Borana ethnic group, attacked villages inhabited by the Gabra community in the Turbi area of Marsabit, near the Kenya-Ethiopia border. Some 70 people were killed, including 22 children. Some 6,000 people fled their homes following that raid. IRIN reported: "In similar incidents, dozens of people were killed and thousands displaced around the Kenya-Somalia border between January and March 2005 in clashes between two ethnic Somali clans, the Murule and the Garre." About 23,000 people were displaced in the clashes. The fighting was said to have been sparked by competition for resources among rival clans. An arbitration committee identified causes of the conflict as disputes over pasture and water that had been allowed to fester without resolution and disagreements over locations and criminal acts such as murder and rape. IRIN also reported clashes between the Garre and Marehan clans: "The Garre feel marginalised in their own territory and are trying to drive the Marehan out of Boru-Hache, while the Marehan want to drive the Garre out of Gedo." IRIN reported that the Kenyans were forced to close the country's border with Somalia after Marehan militia crossed the frontier in two separate incidents during which they killed one person and stole 39 head of cattle.

The United Nations also reported that a similar conflict between the Borana and the Gabra communities in Marsabit should also be seen in the same light – "rivalry over resources, accentuated by local politics". Mohammed Sheikh Adan, a humanitarian team leader, also attributed intermittent clashes between the Gabra and the Rendile or the Turkana and the Rendile in other parts of Marsabit "to disputes over water and pasture and cattle rustling".[160] In May 2006, there was further fighting over pasture between ethnic groups on the Kenyan-Ugandan border.[161] This violence has continued into 2007, with the deaths of well over one hundred civilians and the displacement of tens of thousands of others.[162]

Despite all these concerns it has, however, been far easier, and of more political value, for the Bush administration to avoid any possible responsibility for the environmental degradation documented in Darfur – and attributable to western energy consumption and pollution – and rather to claim events in Darfur are genocide than to look towards any blame on its own part for the crisis.

External Involvement in the Darfur Conflict

Whatever the factors were within Darfur that helped to spark off the conflict, the resultant crisis has been deliberately fuelled by external actors. The Darfur rebels were reported by Agence France-Presse to have "weapons, vehicles and modern satellite communications".[163] The insurgents have also been receiving military supplies by air.[164] The rebels are operating in groups of up to 1,000 men in four-wheel drive vehicles.[165] All of these would inevitably require support from outside of Darfur itself. It is a matter of record that the Darfur insurgents have had considerable external assistance. The SLA and JEM has been receiving arms and support from Eritrea.[166] Eritrea has militarily, logistically and politically assisted the Darfur gunmen in its continuing attempts to destabilise Sudan. Khartoum has lodged official complaints about this involvement with the United Nations and African Union.[167] The Sudanese government has also pointed to the agreement signed in the Eritrean capital between Darfur insurgents and elements of the Beja Congress, an armed anti-government group based in Eritrea.[168] Eritrean military involvement with the Darfur rebels has also been confirmed by the International Crisis Group.[169]

The United Nations reported in January 2006 that "Eritrea hosts large offices for both JEM and SLA" and that "the Government of Eritrea has provided, and probably continues to provide, arms, logistical support, military training and political support to both JEM and the Sudan Liberation Army (SLA). Training of JEM and SLA has reportedly occurred at a number of camps on the Eritrea-Sudan border." It was also noted that the training of Darfur rebels "occurred…in 2003 and 2004".[170] In a subsequent report in October 2007, the UN noted that arms were still being provided through Eritrea to rebels.[171]

The Justice and Equality Movement is said to be receiving assistance from Chad, Islamist groups and al-Qaeda.[172] Roland Marchal has confirmed Chadian military assistance to JEM and the SLA. He has also reported that the grouping brought together by JEM to coordinate those factions that chose not to sign the 2006 Darfur Peace Agreement, the National Redemption Front, was established in Eritrea and assisted by Chad.[173] Chadian involvement in JEM is deep. It is also worth noting that there have been serious questions about whether or not Justice and Equality Movement fighters are actually Sudanese. A senior Chadian government official has claimed, for example, that up to 85% of JEM was Chadian – something which the International Crisis Group has said is "a widely shared belief among Darfurians as well".[174] Many of JEM's leaders, including its first military commander, have served as officers in the Chadian army. Questions about both the nationality of JEM fighters and the level of support provided to them by Chadian officials were illustrated by a UN report about an August 2006 JEM attack, involving over 40 armed rebel vehicles, on an AMIS protection force escorting a convoy of 27 fuel tankers, 60 kilometres outside of al-Fasher. Several AMIS soldiers were killed and wounded, and 18 tankers were stolen by the assailants. The rebel vehicles carried JEM and NRF identification and the UN reported that "the assailants reportedly spoke in French and Arabic, with Chadian accents." The stolen vehicles and rebel vehicles crossed over into Chad, where a Chadian army colonel assumed command of the convoy.[175]

The ICG has also noted that Libya has important links to both the SLA and JEM. SLA chief, Minni Minawi, and JEM leader Khalil Ibrahim were reported to be "close to President Khaddafi and his intelligence apparatus". Khaddafi's involvement in Darfur and Sudan dates back to the 1970s, with Libya using Darfur as a staging post for intervention in Chad.[176] The Libyans have held several rounds of Darfur consultations and attempts at reconciliation since October 2004.[177] In 2006, the UN reported that it had received "information from a number of sources that military equipment and supplies for both SLA and JEM have transited through the Libyan Arab Jamahiriya". The UN ascertained, for example, that Darfur rebels had received 35 Land Cruiser vehicles from Libyan security officers in July 2005 and then 60 more in November 2005.[178]

The Sudanese government has had grounds to doubt the credibility of their counterparts in the North-South Naivasha peace process, and subsequent partners in government, the late Dr John Garang and the Sudan People's Liberation Army. While engaged in peace talks with Khartoum, the SPLA had both trained and helped arm the Darfur rebels. As observed above, the International Crisis Group has noted SPLA involvement in training Darfur rebels. The ICG has also commented on the SPLA involvement with the Darfur rebels: "While the exact ties between the SPLA and the Darfur rebels have not been documented, there appear to be at least important tactical links. The SPLA – which has always recognised that the more rebellion could be extended to the rest of Sudan the better positioned it would be – encouraged the Darfur insurgents as a means to increase pressure on the government to conclude a more favourable peace deal at Naivasha."[179] The internationally-funded Small Arms Survey has also observed that "The SPLA provided the Darfur rebels with early support in the form of weapons and training."[180] De Waal and Flint note that SPLA influence saw the change of name of the Darfur Liberation Front to the Sudan Liberation Army/Movement. On 16 March 2003, the SLA released its "Political Declaration". As de Waal and Flint note, this manifesto "bears a striking resemblance to the SPLA's vision of a united 'New Sudan'".[181] De Waal and Flint also record that "the SPLA argued that the Darfurians should not join the Naivasha process. First, they should fight – advised by a senior SPLA commander who was sent to Darfur to coordinate with them."[182] The UN has reported that rebels have confirmed that there were as many as ten "SPLA-sponsored" flights into Darfur carrying weapons to the insurgents.[183] Flint has recorded that 22 SPLA officers were sent into Darfur in February 2003 to help with the training of rebel recruits. She states that they also acted as military advisers and may have participated in some attacks.[184] Despite mounting evidence to the contrary, SPLA spokesmen were still claiming as recently as September 2004 that the SPLA "has nothing to do with the present rebellion in Darfur".[185]

There have also been reports of some degree of American involvement in sustaining the insurgency. Writing in August 2004, veteran Canadian foreign correspondent Eric Margolis noted: "[The] CIA has reportedly supplied arms and money to Darfur's rebels...Washington is using Darfur's rebels, as it did in southern Sudan's thirty-year old insurgency, to destabilize the Khartoum regime, whose policies have been deemed insufficiently pro-American and too Islamic. More important to the increasingly energy-hungry US, Sudan has oil, as well as that other precious commodity, water."[186] The Sudanese government has alleged that the American government trained and armed Darfur rebels. President al-Bashir, speaking in September 2004, stated "I must again point out that the United States is supporting the rebels in Darfur to the hilt." He stated that the American government "took the rebels to Eritrea, and set up training camps for them, spent money on them, [and] armed them."[187] Allegations of western support for the rebels have continued into 2007. In February 2007, for example, President al-Bashir alleged that the Darfur rebels that had not signed the Darfur Peace Agreement had been encouraged by the West: "The elements that reject the agreement move with freedom in Western capitals and receive financial and military support."[188]

Disturbingly, some level of American assistance to the Sudan Liberation Army has been documented.[189] The close involvement in Darfur of the United States Agency for International Development (USAID), led by long-time anti-Sudan activist Roger Winter, provides the continuity for reports of such support. There is no doubt, for example, that USAID has been at the heart of the "talking up" of possible deaths from the ongoing conflict, and has played a central role in the declaration of "genocide" in Darfur by the United States.[190]

The United Nations has also reported that the Sudanese government had provided details of Israeli weapons captured from rebels that had been manufactured by Israel Weapons Industries. They included Tavor and Galil assault weapons.[191]

Some rebel leaders have stated that they began their war to secure more resources for Darfur and with one eye on the negotiating process that ended the north-south civil war. The international community, through its close involvement in the negotiations in Kenya, may have also inadvertently played a role in inciting armed insurrection in Darfur in 2003. In their paper "The Hidden Costs of Power-Sharing: Reproducing Insurgent Violence in Africa", for example, Tull and Mehler argue that "the West's preferred instrument of conflict resolution – power sharing agreements – turns the rhetoric of conflict prevention on its head in that it inadvertently encourages would-be leaders elsewhere to embark upon the insurgency path." The institutionalisation of this practice provides political pay-offs for violence.[192]

The involvement of foreign governments, such as Eritrea, and foreign terrorist networks, in encouraging the destabilisation of Darfur, and their support for, and arming of, insurgents is very serious. Any attempts to stop the war by seeking to address any marginalisation or underdevelopment – if that was ever the motivation for the violence – will cut no ice with these forces.

Chapter Two

THE DARFUR PEACE PROCESS

There has been a breakdown in negotiations because of unacceptable rebel demands. The talks have been suspended: it's a failure.

Chadian Government Peace Mediator, December 2003 [193]

The SLA started this war, and now they and Justice and Equality Movement are doing everything possible to keep it going.

American State Department Official, October 2004 [194]

The rebels came with preconditions from the start of this meeting, only to scupper any talks.

Peace Talks Mediator, January 2005 [195]

The need to find a peaceful solution to the horrendous war in Darfur is painfully self-evident. The peace process that has unfolded over the past four years has, however, been a difficult one. The Government of Sudan has repeatedly declared its commitment to a peaceful solution to the crisis.[196] It unilaterally declared a ceasefire at the start of internationally-mediated peace talks in Libya in October 2007.[197] On the eve of signing the historic January 2005 Comprehensive Peace Agreement ending Sudan's long-running north-south conflict, President Bashir reiterated his commitment to attaining a settlement of the war in Darfur.[198] This was echoed by the head of the government's negotiating team, the then agriculture minister Dr Majzoub al-Khalifa, who stated that the government would carry on negotiating until there was a final peace deal.[199] The new government of national unity in Sudan, formed in September 2005 and bringing together Sudan's former north-south combatants, restated its commitment to peace talks[200] The government announced in January 2005 that Vice-President Ali Osman Mohamed Taha, the man who negotiated an end to the long-running war in the south, would be focusing on the Darfur crisis.[201] Vice-President Taha has stated that the conflict should be easier to resolve than the north-south war.[202] The government has also involved northern opposition parties, including the National Democratic Alliance, in the search for peace.[203] The war was not of Khartoum's making and it is abundantly clear that the Sudanese government has the most to lose in any continued conflict.

Sudan has welcomed the close involvement of the international community, the African Union, Libya and Chad as mediators, and also agreed to and urged the deployment of thousands of African Union peace-keeping forces.[204] The African Union has committed itself to attaining peace in Darfur. In January 2005, the chairman of the African Union, Nigerian president Olusegun Obasanjo, stated: "I want to give you one assurance on behalf of Nigeria and the AU. We will not rest until there is peace and perfect peace in Darfur and in the whole of Sudan." [205] The African Union mission in Sudan has subsequently been augmented by the AU-UN hybrid force, UNAMID.

As early as 2002, the government sought to address any nascent problems within Darfur. Following the declaration of the Darfur Liberation Front (which subsequently became the Sudan Liberation Army) the government convened a conference of the Fur tribe from 16-22 August 2002 to address local problems in the Nairtati area; it convened a conference of 60 tribes from 11-13 September 2002 with regard to issues within the Jebel Marra area; in October and December 2002, the government sent delegations of Fur tribal leaders to address issues with rebels in the Jebel Marra; in November and December 2002, the government had meetings with members of the armed opposition in al-Fasher; in February 2003, it convened a general meeting of Darfur tribes in al-Fasher, a meeting attended by over one thousand Darfurian leaders[206]; in February and March 2003, the government sent three delegations of the Fur, Zaghawa and Arab tribes to meet with rebel leaders in the Jebel Marra, Dar Zaghawa and Jibal Kargu to address their grievances. A government delegation made up of the federal Minister of Education and the governor of Nile State, leading Darfurian politicians, together with 31 other Darfurian leaders from various tribes, spent a month in talks with the rebels in Darfur. No agreement was reached.

Large-scale rebel attacks throughout Darfur followed in the wake of these attempts to negotiate any grievances opposition groups may have had. Government attempts to end the violence continued nevertheless. Sudanese Vice-President Ali Osman Taha had meetings with veteran Darfurian opposition leader Ahmed Ibrahim Diraige with a view to an immediate ceasefire.[207] Vice-President Taha and Mr Diraige agreed that the proper way to settle the conflict is through "dialogue".[208] The then Sudanese interior minister's January 2004 commitment to peace talks was typical: "Whenever (the rebels) are ready to talk, we are ready to talk to them. We have no conditions at all."[209] It is also clear that the government appears to have had no reservations about negotiating with any rebel organisations, including those movements that have been formed more recently. This had included peace talks from 2004 onwards with a third force, a JEM breakaway calling itself the National Movement for Reform and Development.[210]

In 2003, the Chadian government, parts of which are drawn from the Zaghawa tribe, offered to mediate between the government and rebels. The Sudanese government welcomed and has continued to welcome ongoing Chadian mediation in the conflict.[211] The government of Chad was instrumental in negotiating ceasefires in western Sudan in September 2003 and earlier. It has been a challenging task. On 3 September 2003, however, as the result of indirect talks hosted by President Déby, the Sudanese government and rebels signed a six-week ceasefire in Abeche, Chad. On 17 September, the government and the SLA signed an agreement allowing "free and unimpeded" humanitarian access within Darfur. The government and rebels agreed to a tripartite ceasefire monitoring commission made up of five members from both sides and five Chadian military officials. In subsequent Chadian-brokered peace talks, the rebels proved to be intransigent. Chadian Government mediators declared in December 2003, for example, that the rebels had stalled peace talks: "There has been a breakdown in negotiations because of unacceptable rebel demands. The talks have been suspended: it's a failure."[212] Chad's president called rebel demands "unacceptable".[213] In what was seen as a deliberate attempt to derail the peace talks, the SLA demanded military control of the region during a transitional period, 13% of all Sudan's oil earnings and SLA autonomy in administering Darfur.[214] It was claimed that Islamic fundamentalist opponents of the Sudanese government had been instrumental in sabotaging these negotiations.[215] The government named senior Popular Congress members Hassan Ibrahim, Suleiman Jamous, Abubakr Hamid and Ahmed Keir Jebreel as having been responsible.[216] JEM had hitherto displayed a stop-start attitude to joining mediated peace talks.[217]

In March 2004, the Government of Sudan reaffirmed its commitment to a just and peaceful solution to the conflict in Darfur through consensus: "Through political dialogue a final agreement can be reached in the region."[218] Sudan's then deputy Foreign Minister, al-Tigani Salih Fidhail, said his government was willing to take part in a conference Chad has reportedly offered to host between Khartoum and the Darfur rebels: "We are ready to negotiate peace with any party but we reject any preconditions."[219]

The April 2004 Humanitarian Ceasefire Agreement on the Darfur Conflict

On 8 April 2004, in Ndjamena, the Government of Sudan and both rebel movements signed a *Humanitarian Ceasefire Agreement on the Darfur Conflict and a Protocol on the Establishment of Humanitarian Assistance in Darfur*.[220] Ahmad Alammi, the spokesman of the Chadian mediation team, noted: "The humanitarian ceasefire was a priority, but at the same time it includes political clauses."[221] Under the Ceasefire Agreement, the parties agreed, amongst other things, to: cease hostilities and proclaim a ceasefire for a period of 45 days automatically renewable, unless opposed by one of the parties; establish a Joint Commission and a Ceasefire Commission, with the participation of the international community, including the African Union; free all prisoners of war and all other persons detained because of the armed conflict in Darfur; facilitate the delivery of humanitarian assistance and the creation of conditions conducive to the delivery of emergency relief to the displaced persons and other civilians victims of war, in accordance with the Protocol on the Establishment of Humanitarian Assistance in Darfur, referred to above. The parties also agreed to: combine their efforts in order to establish a global and definite peace in Darfur; meet at a later stage within the framework of a conference of all the representatives of Darfur to agree on a global and definite settlement of the problems of their region, especially concerning its socio-economic development; contribute to create an environment conducive to negotiation and stop hostile media campaigns.

Sudan welcomed the decision by the African Union to send monitoring teams to follow up implementation of the ceasefire agreement between the government and the armed groups in Darfur.[222] The AU's commissioner for peace and security, Said Djinnit, said: "Nigeria, Ghana, Senegal and Namibia have agreed to send military officers to be deployed as observers in Darfur. They will be on the ground as soon as possible."[223]

Almost immediately, SLA spokesmen stated that they would not honour the ceasefire and would not attend peace talks aimed at establishing the envisaged joint ceasefire monitoring commission. On 17 April 2004, however, Reuters reported that they had changed their minds and would go after all: "Rebels from western Sudan said on Friday they would go to peace talks and had not threatened to withdraw from a ceasefire, adding that previous reports to the contrary were incorrect...Earlier on Friday SLM/A spokesman Musa Hamid al-Doa said the Justice and Equality Movement (JEM) would not go to the peace talks and would not abide by a ceasefire in effect since Sunday...But Al-Doa later said he had been given misleading information and another spokesman retracted his comments." Mohammed Mursal, a spokesman for the SLA secretary-general, stated: "No officially sanctioned statements were made by the Sudan Liberation Movement/Army (SLM/A) to imply that we would not abide by the ceasefire or not go to Addis Ababa or Chad." Reuters reported that "Analysts say there is infighting in the SLM/A's leadership with a power struggle between prominent figures in the armed and political wings." Mursal said there would be an internal investigation to establish what had led to the confusion.[224]

The International Crisis Group documented some of the rebel splits during the April 2004 peace talks: "The presence in N'djamena of exiled political activist Sharif Harir as a coordinator for the SLA team was a precursor of some of these internal tensions. He apparently sidelined SLA chairman Abdel Wahid...A similar split occurred in JEM. Hassan Khames Juru, a self-proclaimed political coordinator, announced the dismissal of the JEM president, Khalil Ibrahim, his brother Jibril, the general secretary, Mohamed Bechir Ahmed, and the coordinator, Abubakar Hamid Nour, who had led JEM negotiators at the ceasefire talks. JEM's military spokesman, Colonel Abdalla Abdel Karim, quickly denounced the statement and said Juru represented only himself."[225] The International Crisis Group also noted the results of these splits: "Confusion reigned among the rebels at the political talks in late April [2004], with the two groups eventually repudiating the deal their delegations accepted. The mixed signals are indicative of serious infighting between the military and political wings…The SLA sought to settle some of these differences in prolonged consultations between its chairman, Abdel Wahid Mohamed Nour, and its military coordinator, Minni Minawi. JEM, reflecting the strong position of its political leader, Khalil Ibrahim, took a different approach, firing dissident commanders and political cadres deemed disloyal."[226] In April 2004, for example, Khalil Ibrahim dismissed the movement's second-in-command, Jibril Abdel Karim Bare.

The two rebel groups rejected government proposals for round-table conferences on Darfur – despite having agreed on 19 April 2004 to attend a peace and development conference in Khartoum for all Darfur leaders, including the rebels, to be chaired by Idriss Déby, the Chadian president. A 130-strong preparatory committee were planning for some 1,700 delegates. The JEM leader stated: "We will not participate in this conference nor do we recognise it."

In late April 2004 the rebels declared once again they would not participate in the ceasefire talks in Addis Ababa or the political negotiations in Ndjamena. Reuters reported that Darfur rebels were unlikely to attend peace talks to end the fighting in Darfur. The SLA had said "it would not attend the political talks due to reconvene on April 24 in Chad, adding it wanted Eritrea to mediate instead of [Chadian] President Idriss Debby [sic]." Reuters noted that "Sudan has poor relations with Eritrea." Reuters also quoted JEM leader Khalil Ibrahim: "I don't think we are going to Chad. The Chadian President should not chair any meeting nor any of his executives."[227] Even the hitherto rebel-friendly United States warned the rebels against boycotting the talks aimed at creating a commission to monitor the Darfur ceasefire. A State Department spokesperson stated: "The United States expects the parties…to actively engage in the planning and implementation of the ceasefire monitoring team. Failure of any party to fully participate in this crucial part of the ceasefire agreement is a clear statement of bad faith and will affect our relationship with them."[228]

To work out logistical details for the ceasefire monitoring commission, the AU sent a reconnaissance mission to Darfur and Chad, from 7 to 13 May 2004.

It was made up of representatives from the UN, EU, US and France. On 22 May, the SLA rejected AU proposals to meet with the government in Addis Ababa and finalise the formation of a ceasefire commission, claiming that Ethiopia was too closely aligned to the Sudanese government.[229]

The eventual establishment of the African Union Mission in Sudan (AMIS) as part of the ceasefire protocol was of critical importance to efforts to end the crisis. AMIS was headed by the Special Representative of the Chairperson of the Commission of the African Union (SRRC), initially Ambassador Baba Gana Kingibe. There were also two deputy special representatives, one based in Khartoum and one in al-Fasher. The Deputy SRRC in al-Fasher normally chaired the Ceasefire Commission (CFC). AMIS was made up of a Joint Commission and the Ceasefire Commission. AMIS was authorised by a meeting on 25 May 2004 of the African Union's Peace and Security Council. This meeting sanctioned the deployment of an AU observer mission and a protection force to support the work of the ceasefire commission.

On 28 May 2004, the government and rebels signed an *Agreement on the Modalities for the Establishment of the CFC and the Deployment of Observers in Darfur*, creating a joint ceasefire commission along with arrangements for international observers. The Ceasefire Commission was to be chaired by the AU, the international community (represented by the European Union) as the deputy chairman, Chadian mediators, the Government of Sudan, JEM and SLA. The CFC reports to the Joint Commission, which is made up of two senior members each from the Parties, the Chadian government, the AU, USA and EU. The operational arm of the CFC is the AU Monitoring Mission, made up of observers from the Parties, Chad, AU member states and other members of the international community.[230] On 4 June 2004, the African Union and other international observers finalised an agreement with the government setting out the terms of the ceasefire observer mission agreed in the April ceasefire protocol. The agreement set out the relationship between Khartoum and the ceasefire committee in Darfur and which gives the observers free entry into Sudan and free movement inside the country. In total, an initial group of 120 observers from the AU, the European Union, the United States, the Sudanese government, the two rebel groups in Darfur and the mediation team from neighbouring Chad was to be deployed in the region.[231] On 9 June 2004, the African Union established a headquarters in al-Fasher from which to monitor the ceasefire, and from which to deploy these military observers.[232] The CFC became fully operational on 19 June.

An AU meeting held on 20 October 2004 decided to strengthen AMIS with a renewable one-year period with the following mandate: to monitor and observe compliance with the humanitarian ceasefire agreement; to assist in confidence building between the Parties; and to contribute to a secure environment for the delivery of humanitarian relief and the return of IDPs and refugees. An AMIS strength of 6,171 military personnel and some 1,560 civilian police personnel was agreed. AMIS units were drawn from Nigerian, Rwandan, Senegalese, Gambian, Chadian, Kenyan and South African soldiers.

In early July 2004, both the SLA and JEM stated that they would not attend further peace talks in Chad. An SLA leader said: "We do not want Chad to mediate for the political issues because they were not fair in the humanitarian talks."[233] The president of the African Union, Alpha Oumar Konare, announced that the first round of AU-mediated political negotiations between the warring parties to try to end the crisis were to begin in mid-July in Addis Ababa: "The problem with Darfur is political, its solution is political, hence the necessity for the parties to quickly begin political negotiations...on July 15 in Addis Ababa. We hope that all the parties are properly represented".[234] The Justice and Equality Movement declared, however, that it would not be joining political negotiations in the Addis Ababa aimed at ending the crisis: "These negotiations are coming too quickly." It is worth noting that the United Nations placed on record a renewal of attacks on humanitarian convoys in Darfur by gunmen from this date onwards.[235] The rebels' commitment in any instance to talks in July was questionable. Al-Jazeera reported: "AU officials who struggled for three days to convene a rebel-government meeting said their task had never looked very promising because Darfur's top rebel leaders had chosen instead to attend a Sudanese opposition conference held in Eritrea."[236]

Rebel attacks on humanitarian aid personnel continued. In the first week of July 2004, the SLA attacked 26 aid workers working for Save the Children UK, delivering emergency assistance in northern Darfur. They also stole six vehicles. On 13 July, the British government urged Sudanese rebels to return the stolen vehicles.[237] Rebels also attacked a relief convoy near Orishi in North Darfur, murdering nine civilians and several policemen. They also attacked another aid convoy north of al-Fasher, killing four truck drivers. Rebels also abducted Abass Daw Albeit, the traditional leader of all the tribes of eastern Darfur.[238]

In early August the African Union announced that the Sudanese government had agreed to an increase in peacekeeping forces and monitors in Darfur from 300 to 2,000 soldiers.[239]

The second round of African Union-sponsored inter-Sudanese peace talks was held in Abuja, Nigeria, from 23 August to 17 September 2004. The government declared: "Our concern is to find a quick peaceful solution to all the unresolved questions."[240] The Nigerian President, Olusegun Obasanjo, hailed the adoption by both sides of a broad agenda of humanitarian, security and political issues as a "first step in the right direction". The negotiations were almost immediately deadlocked when the Darfur rebel groups backtracked on the previously agreed agenda. Abd al-Wahid, leader of the Sudan Liberation Army, stated: "We in the movement reject this agenda completely." The rebels' move was described by mediators as a "blow to the African Union". The leader of the Sudanese government delegation, Dr Majzoub al-Khalifa, reiterated that "We adopted this agenda in front of President Obasanjo and AU and UN representatives this morning, and we are good to our word. We are very keen to continue these negotiations." The Sudanese government also accused the rebels of several breaches of the existing ceasefire agreement, including an attack in which four Sudanese humanitarian workers and two journalists were kidnapped. The government spokesman Ibrahim Mohammed Ibrahim stated: "Despite all that, we will continue to participate in these negotiations with the same spirit. Hopefully there will be an agreement between us and the rebel groups."[241] The agenda, made up of the following items – humanitarian issues, security issues, political issues and socio-economic issues – was eventually agreed. On day three of the talks, the Sudanese government agreed to accept a larger African Union peacekeeping force in Darfur if the troops were used to contain and demobilise rebel forces. The African Union had suggested the supervised cantonment of rebel and government forces as a step towards a peaceful solution to the crisis.[242] Rebel leaders subsequently refused to discuss the issue of cantonment. The JEM spokesman stated: "We insist that this point be taken off the agenda."[243]

Rebel intransigence was being increasingly noted. *The New York Times'* Scott Anderson observed in late 2004: "In recent months, the SLA has repeatedly stalled peace talks being brokered by the African Union by setting unrealistic preconditions or quibbling over such details as where the talks should be held; for its part the Justice and Equality Movement faction had, until recently, boycotted the talks altogether." Anderson cited an American diplomat: "The first notion anyone's got to disabuse themselves of is that there are any good guys in this. There aren't. The S.L.A. started this war, and now they and Justice and Equality Movement are doing everything possible to keep it going."[244] In August 2004, American journalist Sam Dealey pointed to possible reasons for apparent rebel indifference to peace talks: "The international community may wish to restrain from setting early deadlines for intervention. Such deadlines only encourage rebel intransigence in pursuing peace deals, as last month's unsuccessful talks in Ethiopia proved. With outside action threatened, there is little incentive for the rebels to negotiate a lasting cease-fire."[245] This was a general point also raised by the Sudanese foreign minister during his September 2004 address to the United Nations general assembly.[246]

The talks nevertheless ended with the agreeing of a *Protocol on the Improvement of the Humanitarian Situation in Darfur* which addressed the issue of free movement and access for humanitarian workers and assistance as well as the protection of civilians. Sudan agreed to the deployment of more than 3,000 AU peacekeeping troops in Darfur.[247] The parties also agreed the establishment of a Joint Humanitarian Facilitation and Monitoring Unit – based in al-Fasher – to ensure a more effective monitoring of the commitments they had entered into. It was also agreed to request the UN High Commission for Human Rights to expand the number of its human rights monitors in Darfur.

In the lead-up to the next rounds of talks the rebels intensified their attacks in Darfur, attacks which severely impeded the delivery of emergency aid to Darfur. In October 2004, the UN confirmed rebel responsibility for attacks in Darfur, quoting the Special Representative of the UN Secretary-General to Sudan: "Mr Pronk said rebel groups – the Sudan Liberation Army (SLA) and the Justice and Equality Movement (JEM) – were responsible for much of the recent violence, which is restricting humanitarian access to many areas within Darfur, a vast and desolate region in western Sudan."[248]

The third round of African Union-mediated Darfur peace talks was held in Abuja from 21 October to 9 November 2004. Despite the urgent and immediate ongoing humanitarian crisis, the rebels refused to discuss humanitarian issues. A JEM leader said: "The government is insisting on discussing the humanitarian issue. It only wants to waste time and avoid the real issue on the ground."[249] The rebels also stalled the peace talks because of the African Union's seating plans, stating they did not wish to sit near the government negotiators. Abubakr Hamid, the coordinator of the joint JEM/SLA team, declared: "We are not going to participate…because they are trying to force us to sit with government delegates."[250] He added: "We'd rather the African Union appoints two separate teams to negotiate with the two groups."[251] When the rebels returned to the negotiations, having agreed to sit with the government, they then continued to refuse to sign a humanitarian aid agreement essential for the provision of relief to those affected by the war. A European diplomat said: "We've told the rebels that for them to be seen as blocking the signature of the humanitarian protocol is not very good…The rebels should not take the international community for granted. They think they have all the international sympathies, but if they are seen as the ones who are stalling they will have to pay a price."[252] The second round of AU-sponsored talks had focused on the humanitarian crisis but the rebels refused to sign new humanitarian arrangements. JEM's Haroun Abdulhameed said that the rebels would focus only on power-sharing: "We are not going to harp on humanitarian issues. There is no need for that…The government in insisting on discussing the humanitarian issue only wants to waste time…" The Sudan Liberation Army spokesman stated: "We must tackle the political issue above everything if we are to make any progress…"[253]

After considerable time invested in mediation, this round of talks resulted in the signing of a *Protocol on the Enhancement of the Security Situation in Darfur* and the signing of the *Protocol on the Improvement of the Humanitarian Situation in Darfur*, as discussed and agreed at the previous round of talks on 9 November 2004. The government and rebels agreed to renew a cessation of hostilities and, for the first time, the government agreed to renounce "hostile" military flights over Darfur, except in cases of self-defence.[254] The two sides had also initiated discussion on a draft Declaration of Principles which would constitute the basis for a just, comprehensive and durable settlement of the conflict.[255]

In early November 2004, in an official report, the UN Envoy to Sudan pointed to deliberate attempts by the rebel movement to provoke government responses: "Some commanders provoke their adversaries by stealing, hijacking and killing."[256] In November, the Sudanese government attacked the United Nations for not highlighting rebel involvement in attacks and human rights abuses, while focusing undue attention on the government. The humanitarian affairs minister, Ibrahim Hamid, said the international community must pressure rebel groups, and not the government alone, to end the Darfur conflict: "The silence of the United Nations and its reluctance to denounce the rebels and exercise pressure on them has encouraged the rebels to go on with their violations and spur insecurity. We believe...the international community should exercise pressure on the rebels instead of seeking to condemn the government over minor issues."[257]

Despite having signed the Abuja ceasefire protocols on 9 November 2004, less than two weeks later the SLA mounted several systematic attacks on police and civilians in Darfur. The African Union noted that "in late November, the Sudan Liberation Movement/Army (SLM/A) carried out attacks on various places, including Tawila, in North Darfur, Adwah village, in South Darfur, the town of Um-Asal and at Draida. These attacks constitute serious and unacceptable violations of the...N'djamena Agreement and the Abuja Protocols."[258] The rebels coordinated attacks on, amongst other targets, Tawila in North Darfur and Kalma in South Darfur. On 22 November 2004, some 80-100 rebels attacked the police station on the edge of the Kalma IDP camp in South Darfur. This resulted in the death of four policemen, and the wounding of several others. The WFP confirmed the attack and stated that "ominously, the attack appeared to have been launched from inside Kalma camp".[259] The UN Envoy to Sudan said that he condemned "in the strongest terms the killing of policemen and civilians around Kalma camp".[260] In a separate attack, coordinated to start at the same time as the assault on Kalma, several hundred SLA rebels, travelling in land-cruisers and lorries, attacked Tawila, killing a doctor, 22 policemen and several civilians, and by their actions, forcing the evacuation of aid workers from the surrounding refugee camps.[261]

As *The New York Times* noted, these attacks, and the ones that preceded them, ended the stability, a "respite" that had been achieved in Darfur – especially with regard to the provision of humanitarian assistance to war-affected communities: "But what respite had been achieved over the last several months has steadily unravelled in recent days." The government noted that the Tawila and Kalma attacks had brought the number of rebel violations since the signing of the Abuja ceasefire protocol to 19: 12 in South Darfur, six in North Darfur and one in West Darfur: "Now the international community has seen for itself. We consider this a very serious escalation and a very alarming index of the rebel attitude."[262] That the attacks had disrupted a period of relative peace was also confirmed by the African Union's own ceasefire monitoring commission. In its October 2004 report, for example, the ceasefire commission noted that there was a "relative calm".[263] The British aid agency Oxfam confirmed that there had been "improving humanitarian access" but that the attacks had reversed any gains that had been made: "Humanitarian access is worse than it was 6 months ago."[264]

These attacks, and particularly the one on Tawila, were very important for several reasons. It illustrated once and for all the indifference the Darfur rebels displayed to the internationally mediated peace and ceasefire protocols it had signed only a few days previously. They were designed to provoke a government reaction in the lead-up to several important international meetings on Sudan – at the expense of suffering to hundreds of thousands of the very people the rebels were claiming to be protecting. This was confirmed by British television news coverage some days after the attack: "What happened here was an act of war. But it was an act of war provoked by the rebels to make the government look bad ahead of this week's peace talks." [265] The attacks also showed that the indifference of the rebel movements to the devastating humanitarian consequences of its actions. The attack on Tawila shut down WFP operations in North Darfur: "All WFP staff and many NGOs were withdrawn from the field." The rebel action resulted in 300,000 IDPs being "cut off from WFP food aid".[266] It was also significant because it was one of the first occasions when the international community chose to unambiguously challenge the Darfur rebels.

The New York Times described the attack and some of the consequences:

> At dawn on Monday, according to the United Nations, the rebel Sudan Liberation Army, or SLA, attacked a strategic town just west of [al-Fasher], called Tawilah, killing nearly 30 police officers and taking control of the town...Insurgents from a second group, called Justice and Equality Movement, seized another Darfur town, called

Gareida, before pulling back. In a refugee camp in South Darfur, rebels struck at a police post in the middle of the night. Rebels battled government troops in Kuma, just north of [al-Fasher], on the edge of rebel-held territory last weekend. The human consequences of the rash of violent actions are getting grimmer. Practically all roads out of El-Fashir, the North Darfur state capital, are off limits to aid workers, for security reasons…Mobile clinics that once roamed to rebel-held villages north and south of here are now staying off the road.[267]

International criticism of these attacks was universal, immediate and unambiguous. The UN Envoy to Sudan Jan Pronk stated that the SLA was solely responsible for breaching the ceasefire and restarting the fighting in north Darfur: "This was a unilateral violation of the agreement by SLA, not by the government."[268] He declared that: "I do really think that the international community should hold them (SLA) accountable for not complying with international agreements and their own promises."[269] The rebel attacks were also condemned by the American government. The State Department said: "The latest incidents of violence were instigated by the Sudan Liberation Movement/Army, and they have resulted in the suspension of humanitarian activities in the areas of fighting."[270] Chris Mullins, Minister of State at the Foreign and Commonwealth Office, noted that: "The recent difficulties have been caused by a series of violations predominately initiated by the rebels." He cited the finding by the UN Envoy to Sudan that "the rebels have been the principal cause in the last two months of incidents that have caused the breakdown of the ceasefire…"[271] His views were echoed by the British international development minister, Hilary Benn: "Recent rebel attacks on Tawila and on humanitarian convoys in Darfur, along with the murder of two Save the Children UK staff, are particularly horrific."[272]

In early December 2004, the SLA admitted to kidnappings, attacks on civilians and obstructing aid workers. The organisation promised there would be no more incidents.[273] On 5 December 2004, the Sudanese government released documents which it said showed that the rebels had killed 89 people in more than 300 armed robberies since the April 2004 ceasefire. A Sudanese interior minister stated that the number of armed robberies in Darfur in eight months following the ceasefire was higher than in the previous 15 months. The documents indicated that from 1 January 2003 to April 2004 there were 251 armed robberies in which 80 people had been murdered. From April until the end of November there were 320 armed robberies during which 89 people were killed.[274]

Keeping the Aid Corridors Open

In its December 2004 briefing, the Sudanese government recorded that rebels had attacked over 200 trucks: "The policy, we understand, is aimed at strangling the main towns in Darfur. The rebels seem to not be keen on committing themselves to the accords they signed. Although we are committed to the letter to the agreements and protocols ... the state could not be expected to tolerate this nonsense."[275] This point was also restated later in December: "[The rebels] block roads, impede commercial activities, rob people and commit all sorts of crimes. No responsible government can fold its hands when things like these are happening."[276] This underpins the quandary facing the government. While committing itself to a ceasefire, government forces cannot stand by and let humanitarian and other traffic be attacked on its main roads. Such attacks do indeed strangle the logistics needed to feed the hundreds of thousands of displaced people in camps throughout Darfur. Not to do so would result in deaths and more misery amongst displaced communities. When Khartoum does militarily respond, with or without airpower, it is then accused of violating the ceasefire.

This dilemma was reported upon by the United Nations Secretary-General in his report of January 2005.[277] The Secretary-General stated, for example, that the fighting which broke out on 7 December 2004 was a result of "government road-clearing operations, which the Government defined as operations aimed at clearing the roads of banditry". The Secretary-General noted that the government had briefed the United Nations on their intentions and that Khartoum had "specifically stated that it was not intending to attack or occupy SLM/A-held areas during these operations". The government went on to identify several key aid corridors. The Secretary-General also noted that in its attempts to keep aid corridors open the government had previously offered to place any necessary police forces under African Union command.

The UN noted that this offer had been declined at the 24 November 2004 meeting of the Joint Implementation Mechanism.[278] The Secretary-General also noted government concerns about SLA attacks on roads. In addition to obstructing the flow of aid to war-affected communities in Darfur, these attacks "have brought constricting pressure to bear on supply lines, leading to rising commodity prices and insecurity of strategic goods to the population of state capitals". The Secretary-General himself also noted "SLM/A vehicle and fuel hijacking operations aimed at vital tactical commodities". He also reported on a "new trend" in the pattern of attacks on, and harassment of, international aid workers: "While previous incidents have only been aimed at looting supplies and goods, December has seen acts of murder and vicious assaults on staff, forcing some agencies to leave Darfur."[279]

The government position was a clear one. It called for the complete deployment of all the AU forces envisaged for Darfur: "If the African troops can't defend the roads and civilians, the government must do that. We can't leave the rebels to cut the roads that reach (the 5 million civilians in Darfur)."[280]

In January 2005, the UN noted that the government "reminded the Joint Implementation Mechanism that…the Government's offer to provide police who would operate under AU command and assist it in protecting the roads had been declined by AU at the 24 November 2004 meeting of the Mechanism on the grounds that to do so would compromise its impartiality. AU clarified later that although it had some reservations initially, it had not totally rejected the offer and consideration was being given to the possibility of working with Sudanese police in protecting roads in Darfur."[281]

In early December 2004, nonetheless, Sudan's Minister for Humanitarian Affairs, Mohamed Yusif Abdallah, reaffirmed Khartoum's desire for a negotiated settlement to the crisis, stating that a settlement for Darfur could be part of a broader constitutional reform that also affected other regions: "The southern peace agreement will have a positive impact on Darfur…I hope the situation becomes like the south where the rebels commit themselves seriously to a ceasefire."[282] The first week of December, however, saw continuing rebel attacks which forced the withdrawal of more aid workers from Darfur. Attacks, for example, on Saraf Ayat in north Darfur, had resulted in Médecins Sans Frontières evacuating its staff and the displacement of 2,000 civilians. Some 4,500 people were affected by this attack and others.[283]

In December 2004, the SLA, and its obstruction of the peace process, came under close scrutiny by *The New York Times*. The newspaper reported that: "The SLA has been accused of stalling at the last round of African Union-mediated peace talks in Abuja. Despite promises, it has yet to disclose the location of its fighters, on security grounds. Privately, some aid workers and diplomats accuse the SLA of sowing the seeds of further conflict by acts of provocation." *The New York Times* gave an example of such provocation: "For instance, the rebel group has blocked the seasonal migration routes of a large and powerful nomadic Arab tribe just south of [Thabit]. To date, the leaders of the tribe have remained neutral in the Darfur conflict, but blocking the movement of their animals and thus threatening their livelihood and their way of life could be disastrous." The newspaper quoted a Western diplomat as saying that the rebels were "broadening the conflict base. The SLA knows what they are doing."[284]

Under pressure from the international community, the rebels came back to the peace table. The fourth round of African Union-mediated Darfur peace talks was held in Abuja from 11 to 21 December 2004. Reuters reported that the government indicated its wish to reach a peace deal in the African Union talks which had recommenced in Abuja. Dr Majzoub al-Khalifa, head of Sudan's delegation, said there was "a lot of common ground for agreement". He said: "We are very much hoping to come to a final peace agreement in this round", adding that the government would do its best to reach an agreement "before the end of this year so that peace in Sudan will be finalised by January in all parts of Sudan". JEM leader Khalil Ibrahim dismissed the meeting, declaring "[t]his is not a serious round of talks" and that JEM had lost faith in African Union sponsorship of Darfur peace efforts.[285] News agencies reported in mid-December that the rebels had pulled out of the Abuja peace talks.[286] This also coincided with new rebel attacks aimed at disrupting peace process. The African Union confirmed as much.[287] The African Union's chief mediator, Sam Ibok, said that all the international representatives at the talks had advised against the walk-out because "there was no justification for such a suspension." The Sudanese government commented that: "Only negotiation and talks will solve the problem of Darfur. Withdrawal from the talks means more trouble for Darfur."[288]

The rebels returned to the AU-mediated talks and progress appeared to have been made during these negotiations. The government agreed to withdraw its forces from positions it had moved into following the rebels' November offensive in Tawila and elsewhere.[289] And while the rebels rejected new proposals for peace,[290] they promised no more attacks and violations of the ceasefire agreements.[291] The SLA and JEM committed themselves "to cease all attacks against humanitarian and commercial activities and to restrain their forces from attacks on government infrastructure, including police posts".[292]

The rebels broke their word within days with two serious attacks. On 27 December, rebel forces attacked the town of Ghubaysh. The United Nations said that "notably" this was "the second attack by the SLA since 19 December when the Government of Sudan agreed to an immediate cessation of hostilities."[293] In late December Reuters reported that JEM had refused any continuing African Union mediation in the Darfur conflict, citing a rebel spokesman: "JEM is rejecting the African Union. We are not going to Abuja again under the auspices of the African Union."[294] This was a particular blow to the peace process as the future rounds of peace talks were to focus on the political solution to the Darfur conflict. The government had already announced a range of proposals focusing on a federal solution to the problem.[295]

The Sudanese government showed its frustration at the unwillingness of the Darfur rebels to seriously commit to the peace talks: "At the last round in Abuja where the vital political issues was to be discussed, [the] government came ready with six ministers. That shows we were here for business. But the rebels had a different agenda. They delegated very junior officers who could not agree on anything. It is no wonder that [they] keep frustrating the talks via incessant walkouts."[296]

In early January 2005, the rebels announced that they would be leaving the ceasefire commission in Darfur. Reuters reported that the UN had said "a rebel threat to withdraw from a cease-fire monitoring commission in Sudan's troubled Darfur region would spell disaster for the faltering peace process". A UN spokesperson warned: "Obviously, if the SLA make this threat a matter of fact…that would be a disastrous thing to happen because we do not believe that any of the parties have any interest in destroying the little fragile gains they have (made)."[297] Reuters reported that officials at the January 2005 ceasefire talks "blamed the rebels for the meeting's failure". A peace mediator stated: "The rebels came with preconditions from the start of this meeting, only to scupper any talks."[298] The rebels subsequently suspended their participation in the ceasefire committee and rebel attacks continued.[299]

It also emerged that while promising no new attacks – having clearly been stung by the international community's criticism following the Tawila and Kalma attacks – the SLA had used front groups for some of its new attacks. In December 2004, a group styling itself the "Sudanese National Movement for the Eradication of Marginalisation" (SNMEM) commenced attacks on civilians and policemen. It attacked an oil field at Sharif in Darfur and then a town in western Kordofan, an area neighbouring Darfur, killing 15 people.[300] Reuters reported in early January 2005 that "[the] government and some observers have said the group is a front for...the Sudan Liberation Army".[301] The government stated: "There is evidence showing the involvement of the Sudan Liberation Movement in the attack."[302] Reuters cited an international observer as saying: "It seems the SNMEM is the SLM with a different name. They feel that if they use another name, they can act without being bound by the agreements they have signed with the government."

On 13 January 2005, the Sudanese government urged the complete deployment of the African Union peacekeeping force in Darfur. The foreign minister, Dr Mustapha Osman Ismail, stated that less than half of the 3,320 troops committed by the African Union had arrived: "We are still waiting for the African troops."[303] This echoed his previous call on 1 December 2004 for the African Union to fulfil its commitment to Darfur.[304]

The United Nations has repeatedly noted the government's commitment to a peaceful solution to the Darfur conflict. In his February 2005 comments to the United Nations Security Council meeting on Sudan, the UN Special Envoy to Sudan, Jan Pronk, stated: "The good news is that the government has shown a willingness to negotiate, toughly, but seriously, on the basis of principles concerning the sharing of power and wealth that have resulted in the Naivasha peace agreement. The Government has recently confirmed its commitment to such talks. President Bashir and Vice-President Taha have made it quite clear: the objective is peace through negotiations, in Darfur and elsewhere in Sudan."[305]

By contrast, the UN Secretary-General's February 2005 assessment of the preceding six-month period with regard to the rebel movements was bleak: "Over this period, the rebel movements have become less cooperative in talks.

Their attacks on police have increased and often seemed intended to invite retaliation."[306] In a further complication, tensions between SLA military commanders and the exiled political leadership resurfaced in early 2005. The military leadership were reported to have distanced themselves from the SLA chairman Abd al-Walid Mohamed al-Nur and the Secretary-General Minni Minawi.[307]

In March 2005 the UN reported that the SLA had been involved in "a number of attacks against civilians", including attacks on Haraza and Wazazen villages in South Darfur. JEM was also reported to have attacked the village of Rahad El Fate.[308] The UN Secretary-General also commented upon "the rash of attacks during March on international personnel operating in Darfur".[309]

There were clashes between the Government and rebel movements throughout April 2005. The UN's report for April noted that "[i]n most cases, Government forces were on the defensive as the rebel movements conducted small-scale attacks against Government convoys or small units of army or police personnel. Of the two [rebel] movements, it appeared that SLA was more often the instigator of the clashes…Not only were the rebel movements more active militarily against Government forces, but both SLA and JEM attacked villages and other civilian targets."[310]

The United Nations reported that:

> The Sudanese Liberation Army and the Justice and Equality Movement (JEM) carried out a number of attacks on police and militia in April and continue to take commercial, private and non-governmental organization vehicles at gunpoint on a scale that suggests that these acts are approved by their leadership. There are reliable reports that the vehicles are taken with the aim of converting them into battlefield platforms. Abductions, theft of livestock, restrictions on freedom of movement and general intimidation of civilians and humanitarian workers, including United Nations personnel, by rebel movements, were reported throughout April.[311]

In late May 2005, an 80-strong rebel force attacked the village of Amo, near Kutum in North Darfur. They wounded several civilians, killed 50 camels and stole several thousand more.[312]

The UN noted that "banditry continued to plague Darfur in May". The Secretary-General also reported that "those criminal acts are increasingly being committed by rebel and militia fighters, in addition to common criminals acting without a political agenda. Banditry threatens all commercial and humanitarian traffic in Darfur." As a result of these activities, on 26 May, the Government informed the African Union that it intended to clear bandits from the Tawila-Kebkabiya road in North Darfur if the attacks did not stop.[313] It should also be noted that the UN or AMIS have often chosen not to identify rebel forces with acts of banditry they have committed.

In May Libya hosted a six-way African heads-of-state summit on Darfur; it was also attended by the Arab League. The rebel movements refused to attend.[314] In early June 2005, Reuters reported that "[t]he African Union says Khartoum has stopped military flights over Darfur and shown restraint in clashes with rebels in the past few months. Government troops have also withdrawn from areas they occupied during a December offensive and handed over to the AU." The UN Special Envoy to Sudan observed that: "It's over now…there's no reason anymore to fight, [the rebels] don't have any reason anymore not to negotiate."[315]

The July 2005 Declaration of Principles

The fifth round of AU-led Darfur peace talks opened in Abuja on 10 June 2005, and ended in early July. The UN reported that there were considerable difficulties with regard to important procedural matters, including the roles to be played by Chad and Eritrea. The rebels restated their objections to Chadian mediation in the peace process, claiming that Chad was seeking to prolong the war. The Chadian foreign minister, Nagoum Yamassoum, challenged rebel assertions: "The rebels create problems with Chad – what interest do we have in creating problems that prolong the conflict or the presence of refugees which costs money, adds security risk, damages the environment?" The Chadian foreign minister went on to state: "[the rebels] say they don't want us because we say the truth which is that the rebel political leaders do not want peace. The people who live in Amsterdam, London, Paris…who are in these five-star palaces, who have not even seen Darfur since 5-6 months, and for whom the Darfur, the war, has given some authority, they are received by heads of state

– they do not really want that to stop." He also observed of the leaders "[t]hey are contesting with each other – who are the real leaders? No one knows who they are and that's been the difficulty with the conflict here since the beginning. There is no real leadership of these rebels."[316]

The UN Secretary-General also noted: "There were also sharp differences within and between the two movements. In the case of JEM, breakaway groups called into question the legitimacy of its representatives in Abuja."[317] These talks nevertheless concluded with the signing of a *Declaration of Principles for the Resolution of the Sudanese Conflict in Darfur* which the African Union envisaged as paving the way for substantive discussion on the key issues of power and wealth sharing. The Declaration of Principles addressed issues such as power- and wealth-sharing, unity, religion, land use and ownership and security arrangements. The next round of peace talks was scheduled to be held in late August. On 18 July, JEM and the SLA signed an agreement in Libya which sought to unify the rebels' positions on key issues.[318] The August peace talks were called off by the rebels, something criticised by the Sudanese government.[319]

Ambassador Kingibe, the head of the African Union Mission in Sudan, speaking in mid-July 2005, noted that "over the past few months the security situation on the ground in Darfur has generally calmed down in the sense that fixed combats between the parties…has more or less vanished. What we had in the run-up to the resumption of the Abuja peace talks in June, from May to the first half of June, was fighting between the rebel elements…that too has now died down."[320] Asked about the peace negotiations, Ambassador Kingibe observed: "I must say the progress has been slow. When negotiations resumed on 10 June, the first item on the agenda was the adoption of the DoP – declaration of principles…[negotiations] dragged on and on for almost a month. New demands were raised by, I must say, the rebel movements. The government…were prepared to sign the draft as it was. But the rebels raised all sort of issues…"[321]

The following week, however, the SLA attacked a humanitarian convoy guarded by a government detachment in South Darfur. The rebels also attacked several villages.[322] The AU confirmed the rebel attack.[323] The Sudanese military responded by attacking rebel positions. Nevertheless, in an interview in early August 2005, the UN Special Envoy Jan Pronk confirmed that "the security situation has changed. There is no longer war between the government and the SLM/A. There is a ceasefire that is not breached to a great extent." He said that there were about 100 violence-related deaths per month attributable "to a great extent [to] banditry, looting, crime, which goes hand-in-hand with a no-peace-no-war situation".[324]

The UN's July 2005 report noted that "violence in Darfur has diminished greatly since the period from early 2003 to mid-2004, which was prior to Security Council decisions and the deployment of AMIS. There can be little doubt that the situation in Darfur is less dangerous for civilians than it was a year ago. Attacks on civilians have declined significantly over the past 12 months, and humanitarian relief workers have access to far more people in need than they had at the time the joint communiqué was signed, in July 2004. These developments should be welcomed by the international community."[325]

This was all to change in the last week of July. On 23 July 2005, the SLA attacked two convoys that were being escorted by government forces on the Nyala-al Fasher road. The government responded by action against SLA forces in the same area. The United Nations also noted in the Secretary-General's report on 11 August that there had been "a considerable rise in abductions, harassment, extortion and looting by both the Justice and Equality Movement (JEM) and the Sudan Liberation Movement/Army (SLM/A) victimizing civilians and jeopardizing humanitarian activities".[326] The Secretary-General spoke of a "descent into lawlessness by the armed movements".[327]

Rebel banditry continued throughout August and into September, with UNICEF's Darfur representative Keith McKenzie noting on 31 August: "There has been a tremendous rise in banditry. Not a single day goes by without two, three or four attacks on aid convoys. You never know when you are going to be hit or where. They seem to be targeting the humanitarian community and workers."[328] An AU spokesman noted: "There is a lot of banditry…The area is lawless and they (gunmen) are attacking everyone." An aid official also observed that "[t]he situation got worse from around April, May, June…They (gunmen) are taking vehicles. We have lost trucks and aid commodities."[329]

On 1 September, SLA gunmen attacked a seven-vehicle aid convoy on the road from Kongo Harasa to al-Geneina in western Darfur. All of the humanitarian workers, drawn from International Aid Services and Tearfund, were severely beaten. The vehicles and their contents were then stolen by the rebels.[330]

On 2 September 2005, the African Union publicly criticised the Darfur rebels:

> The Special Representative condemns not only the provocative banditry of the SLA/M, but also their continuing refusal to cooperate with the AMIS intermediaries. He notes that from past experience, such incidents, coming so close to the resumption of the Abuja talks, not only destabilizes the quiescent security situation on the ground, but also impacts negatively on the Talks. The continuing non cooperation of the SLA/M casts doubt on the commitment of the Movement to a smooth resumption of the Abuja talks…"[331] A few days later, the AU Special Representative in Sudan, Ambassador Kingibe, described the Darfur rebels as "thieves".[332] Associated Press noted that "[t]he United Nations and Sudanese government have condemned the recent increase in rebel-related banditry and attacks in Darfur.[333]

The United Nations' September 2005 report on Darfur noted that the SLA "maintained an aggressive stance, establishing new checkpoints and attacking vehicles, in particular in South Darfur".[334] The UN corroborated AMIS reports that the SLA had attacked nomadic herders near the village of Malam in South Darfur, abducting seven people and stealing over 3,000 camels. The UN noted that the SLA was refusing to assist AMIS with its enquiries.[335]

On 9 September 2005, the Joint Commission monitoring the ceasefire condemned rebel involvement in repeated attacks on civilians, aid workers and AMIS peacekeepers.[336] The United Nations warned that Darfur risked sliding into a perpetual state of lawlessness because of banditry, and continuous attacks by armed groups on aid workers, Arab nomads and villages. The UN noted that there had been at least ten serious attacks on humanitarian workers since mid-August.[337] *The Guardian* reported in September that "[a]n upsurge in attacks by Darfur's main rebel force, including the capture of a key government-held town, is undermining the latest internationally sponsored talks on bringing peace to Sudan's western regions, according to senior UN officials…The rise in violence by the Sudan Liberation Army (SLA), the largest of the two rebel groups, comes after months of relative calm since African Union monitors fanned out across Darfur and the UN security council imposed a no-fly zone and sanctions on the Sudanese government."[338] The BBC noted that "after eight months of relative calm and improving security, the situation in Darfur is deteriorating once again. Banditry and attacks on aid convoys are increasing and the finger of blame is being firmly pointed at the SLA, Darfur's main rebel movement…The African Union said the rebels' provocative banditry and lack of cooperation was casting doubt over their commitment to negotiations."[339]

It was against this backdrop that the sixth round of inter-Sudanese Peace Talks on the Conflict in Darfur was held in Abuja from 15 September – 20 October 2005. The UN noted that "the talks opened with an air of uncertainty regarding the cohesion of the SLM/A delegation and the degree to which the faction of SLM/A Secretary-General Mini Arkoy Minawi was participating." The UN subsequently noted that "negotiations had not begun by the end of September. Internal division within the SLM had paralysed the talks for one week." [340] The UN Secretary-General publicly urged the leaders of the rebel movements "to definitively choose the road of peace and negotiations rather than that of combat, and to demonstrate a serious interest in substantive peace talks rather than in internal, and selfish, debates". [341] A few days into these negotiations, on 20 September 2005, the Sudan Liberation Army launched several attacks on government positions in South Darfur, seizing the town of Sheiria.[342] The government accused the rebels of attempting to undermine the Darfur peace process.[343]

On 15 October 2005, the Darfur ceasefire commission called on the Darfur rebels to withdraw without delay from the areas of Labado, Ashma, Gareida and Marla in South Darfur. These areas had previously been controlled by the government and had then been handed over to the African Union. Rebel forces had then taken these areas over. The commission condemned these actions as well as rebel violations of the ceasefire and their attacks on AU forces and relief workers. The commission also called on the rebels to provide their locations to AMIS in keeping with previous commitments they had made. The AU also noted that: "There is a division in the rank of the Sudan Liberation

Movement as to who should represent the movement in the talks…As long as the problem is not solved we cannot make much progress."[344]

The sixth round of peace talks ended in an impasse. The end-of-talks communiqué stated that there had been agreement on the issues of human rights and fundamental rights and criteria and guidelines for power sharing.[345] At the same time a spokesman for the United Nations described September 2005 as the worst by way of insecurity for aid workers: "The month…was probably the worst month in terms of the number of direct attacks…we haven't stopped humanitarian operations but we have had to adjust them. For example, we have deployed extra helicopters so that humanitarian workers aren't spending time on the roads because the roads are where they're most vulnerable."[346]

In October 2005, the International Crisis Group concluded: "The SLA, the dominant rebel force on the ground, is increasingly an obstacle to peace. International divisions, particularly among its political leadership, attacks against humanitarian convoys, and armed clashes with JEM have undermined the peace talks and raised questions about its legitimacy. JEM, while less important militarily and suspect among many Darfurians for its national and Islamist agenda, has similar problems."[347] A Reuters article in late October 2005 reported on the growing impatience within Darfur at rebel intransigence regarding peace negotiations: "People in the camps were impatient for the rebels to engage in earnest at the AU talks in the Nigerian capital and swiftly move towards the dividends that a deal can bring."[348]

The seventh round of peace talks began on 29 November 2005. They stalled for two months. In February 2006, Abd al-Wahid announced the end of the effort to coordinate a negotiating position with the SLA/MM and JEM. The AU mediators agreed separate bilateral talks between the government and Abd al-Wahid's faction. De Waal states that during these talks the government:

> Almost clinched a deal with Abdel Wahid, whose chief negotiator, a Darfurian professor of ancient languages called Abdel Rahman Musa, actually initialled an agreement. But Abdel Wahid hadn't prepared his SLM colleagues for such a dramatic step. There were no proper structures for consultation and decision-making – there wasn't even any record-keeping – and Abdel Wahid had simply

instructed Abdel Rahman Musa to go ahead. Nineteen SLM delegates denounced Abdel Wahid's move and withdrew their support. The dissenters called themselves SLM-Unity and this group is now the main fighting force in north Darfur opposing the government. [349]

The following month, nineteen SLA-Abd al-Wahid field commanders formed what became known as G-19. Mainly Zaghawa, these commanders criticised both Minni Minawi and Abd al-Wahid, before leaving the SLA-Wahid because they thought he was about to sign a deal with Khartoum. This group has also called itself SLA-Unity and SLA-Mainstream, and by October 2006 had come to be led by Adam Bakhit Abdelrahman, a Zaghawa commander who had challenged Minni for the SLA leadership at the Haskanita conference.

The Darfur Peace Agreement

On 25 April 2006, the AU mediation team presented the parties with a compromise document that would become the Darfur Peace Agreement and gave all parties a five-day deadline to accept or reject it. De Waal explains the rush: "The fatal problem with the mediation was...that it was rushed to a premature conclusion in the first days of May. The reason for this was that the UN Security Council demanded that the mediation meet a wholly artificial deadline of 30 April to conclude the talks. The mediation rushed to complete a text a week before this deadline, knowing that it could not possibly be properly negotiated in the days remaining." [350]

On 30 April, despite a number of reservations, the Government of Sudan agreed to sign the agreement. The Darfur rebel movements dragged their feet. The US Deputy Secretary of State, Robert Zoellick and the British International Development Secretary, Hilary Benn, arrived in Abuja to apply pressure to all parties. The AU extended the deadline twice to accommodate the rebel movements. The then incumbent chair of the AU, President Sasso Nguesso of Congo Brazzaville, and Nigerian President Olusegun Obasanjo pressed the Sudanese government for additional concessions – which were given – and urged the rebels to sign. SLA leader Minni Minawi signed but Abd al-Wahid and JEM refused. Abd al-Wahid's chief negotiator, Abdel Rahman Musa, representing a group (largely non-Fur, and including members of the Birgid, Daju, Berti and Tunur tribes) within the SLA, signed the agreement. Musa stated that he was forming his own Front for Liberation and Renaissance, which would take half of Abd al-Wahid's camp with him, including 15 commanders, and they supported the peace agreement. He said of Abd al-Wahid that "I don't think he is seeking peace." He said because his group was new, it might not have status to formally sign the peace agreement, but that the African Union and the international community "will acknowledge our will for peace and then we will find a way to negotiate with the government".[351] On 15 May, the AU Peace and Security Council gave SLA/AW and JEM until 31 May to sign. A group of non-Zaghawa commanders declared their support for the DPA and left JEM to form the JEM-Peace Wing.

More than two dozen heads of state and other leaders from Africa, Europe and the Middle East gathered at the talks in Abuja. The international community, especially the United States, presented the DPA as a take it or leave it option – with severe ramifications for those who chose not to sign. The US Deputy Secretary of State Robert Zoellick stated publicly that those rebel forces who continue to engage in violence were "likely to be treated by the international community as outlaws and renegades and they will have to pay the appropriate price". [352] Zoellick noted that the Justice and Equality Movement was "dismissive of the need for peace". JEM's spoiling role in the peace talks was clear. *The New York Times* reported that JEM had "sought the most radical changes to the peace agreement, most of which were not accepted".[353] Zoellick warned the non-signatories: "For the parties that left the table, they run the risk that all of us made very clear about what happens to them in the future if they choose a path of violence." [354] Zoellick was very specific in his comments to Abd al-Wahid: "I conclude that you are not serious about an agreement. Going forward, we are parting ways for good. If you think there is an alternative, you are dead wrong. And I mean, dead wrong. I will not accept bad faith...You will not see me again until there is accountability for actions at the UN Security Council." Zoellick publicly warned Abd al-Wahid and JEM: "Those who don't sign are outlaws to the process."[355] The British government was reported to have told the rebels that they "must realise that no deal will meet their full requirements – but this agreement is a fair and just one. It offers them participation in government and a political platform from which they can influence Darfur's future." London also warned: "The international community will not understand if they fail to take this opportunity to bring peace to Darfur and security to its people. We have already made clear that those who impede the peace process will face sanctions. The rebel movements need to understand that this is their opportunity for a just settlement and such an opportunity is unlikely to recur."[356]

The Darfur Peace Agreement, signed on 5 May 2006, was the result of more than two years of intensive negotiations. It consists of three protocols, on power-sharing, wealth-sharing and security arrangements as well as a framework for Darfur-Darfur dialogue and reconciliation. With regard to the permanent status of Darfur, the agreement provides for a referendum on whether to retain Darfur's three states or create a Darfur region – this to be held within 12 months of the general elections in Sudan (by July 2010). A Transitional Darfur Regional Authority (TDRA) was created with responsibility for coordinating the implementation and follow-up of the DPA and facilitating better cooperation between the three state governments.

With regard to participation in government, pending elections, the rebel movements are to nominate people to the following posts, making a special effort to nominate women: one Special Assistant to the President (also chair of the TDRA), and one presidential advisor; one federal cabinet minister and two federal state ministers (in addition to three cabinet minister and three state minister posts which will continue to be filled by Darfurians); 12 seats in the National Assembly and chairmanship of one of the National Assembly's parliamentary committees; one ministerial position in the Khartoum State government; a governorship of one of Darfur's states and deputy governorship of each of the other two, plus two ministers and one advisor in each of the states and a senior member of each state ministry; 21 of the 73 seats in each state assembly, including the deputy speaker of each assembly; six local commissioners and six executive directors in Darfur; membership of the Council of States is to be non-partisan and to follow consultation with Darfurians. Fifty per cent of places in Darfurian universities and 15 per cent of places in Khartoum's universities are reserved for Darfurians. Historical land rights (*hawakeer*) are recognised, subject to rulings by state-level Land Commissions.

The DPA would also establish both a Darfur Reconstruction and Development Fund (DRDF) with seed funding of US$300 million in 2006 and a further US$200 million per annum in 2007 and 2008 and a Joint Assessment Mission (JAM) to determine priorities. With regard to protection and compensation, a Darfur Rehabilitation and Resettlement Commission (DRRC) is established to coordinate humanitarian provision and access and the safe and voluntary return of IDPs and refugees. A Property Claims Committees will resolve disputes. A Compensation Commission is established with an initial budget of US$30 million.

The DPA set out a specific timeline and organisational structures for (1) disarming the pro-government militias within five months, (2) incorporating members of the rebel groups into the Sudanese military forces or assisting their integration into civilian life, and (3) returning principal responsibility for law enforcement in Darfur to a reformed civilian police force. The agreement stated that pro-government militia will be confined to their camps and must relinquish all heavy weapons before any rebel forces are asked to withdraw and demobilise. The agreement prohibits armed forces from displaced persons camps and other civilian areas, including humanitarian supply routes. The DPA also granted expanded powers to the African Union-run Ceasefire Commission, including to identify those responsible for ceasefire violations and to recommend measures against them by the AU Peace and Security Council. These security arrangements were to be monitored by African Union peacekeeping forces. A comprehensive ceasefire was to come into force within 72 hours of signing; a Joint Humanitarian Facilitation and Monitoring Unit (including representatives of AMIS, the UN, the international community and the parties) is to monitor and report. Four thousand former combatants from the rebel movements were to be incorporated into the Sudanese Armed Forces; education and training are to be provided for a further 3,000.

The Darfur-Darfur Dialogue and Consultation mechanism (DDDC) is to serve as a means for mobilising support for, and implementing, the DPA. Sixty per cent of delegates will be tribal and community representatives, the remaining 40 per cent from political parties, civil society, religious organisations and the diaspora; observers are to be sent by international community and others. It was specified that the DDDC process was to be chaired by an "African of independence and integrity" and assisted by a team of elders from Darfur, and shall have between 800 and 1,000 delegates, to include sheikhs and tribal leaders, refugees, internally displaced persons, women, rebel groups, militias, civil society, and other local parties. The DPA stated that this process was to be organized by a Preparatory Committee appointed by the African Union and to include members of the rebel groups and the Government of Sudan, as well as tribal leaders and representatives of civil society and international organizations including the African Union, United Nations, and Arab League. It empowered the DDDC to make recommendations to the relevant local and national authorities, and to establish a permanent Peace and Reconciliation Council to continue its work.

Much of this process has been placed on hold. The stalling of the DPA has been attributed to the international community by key participants such as Alex de Waal. De Waal has described how Abd al-Wahid reacted to international pressure as the AU deadline approached: "If they give me 24 hours or 24 days or 24 years I will not sign . . . the AU will not determine the future of my people. If the whole world has come – and this is exactly what happened – and tells me to sign, I will not sign." Fourteen days later, Abd al-Wahid once again rejected international pressure to sign, warning: "Remember these words: all of you, the international community will create big chaos in Darfur, endless fighting, endless suffering, endless chaos." De Waal noted that "Deadlines, pressure and inflexible insistence on the letter of agreement simply don't work in Sudan. The US line was that there could be no renegotiation of the DPA: not one word could be changed."[357]

The comments in this respect of de Waal, a member of the AU mediation team, are very informative: "The breakdown did not happen because the peace agreement was faulty, but because the political process was brought to an abrupt and premature end when Minawi signed." De Waal stated that "The disaster of the DPA was that the book was closed on 5 May and those who failed to sign were shut out of any further formal negotiation. All the high-powered mediators left Abuja." De Waal observed that "the outstanding differences between him [Wahid] and Khartoum were small" and that Wahid declared the DPA's security arrangements "acceptable" and the wealth-sharing provisions "95% acceptable" and that "Wahid did agree with Khartoum on a comprehensive ceasefire, including withdrawal of forces to designated zones of control, demilitarisation of displaced camps and humanitarian supply routes, restriction of the Janjaweed leading to ultimate disarmament, and much more robust mechanisms for monitoring and reporting violations...But that counted for naught when he was given the 'take it or leave it' option on the whole package."[358]

Another international mediator, Laurie Nathan, one of de Waal's colleagues in the AU mediation team, has also been critical of the "deadline diplomacy" practiced by the international community: "The manipulation and threats of the international partners undermined the AU's authority in the eyes of the parties, compromised Minawi, and created suspicion of the DPA in Darfur." Nathan states that this approach was "too simplistic and rigid for the purpose. The conflict...required a multi-faceted plan." The tight deadlines made it difficult for the mediators to communicate with groups not represented at the negotiating table and the "haste induced by the deadline diplomacy precluded effective mediation". In short, Nathan noted that: "Instead of mediation, the deadline diplomacy led to a mediator-produced agreement covering cardinal issues on which the parties still bitterly disagreed; to an unreasonably brief period for the parties to consider and approve the document; and to a fierce burst of pressure in the dying moments of the negotiation process. Each of these elements was antithetical to the parties' ownership of the DPA. In the final analysis, the mediators, rather than the parties, owned the DPA."[359]

In June 2006, the National Redemption Front, (*jebhat al-khalas al-watani*, NRF), was formed by JEM in Asmara as an umbrella for groups opposed to the signing of the DPA. Flint notes that "Dr. Khalil took the gamble of escalating the war. With the backing of Chad and Eritrea, and the support of many of the SLA Splinters that are critical of the peace agreement, he launched the National Redemption Front and a new military offensive."[360] The NRF was supported by Eritrea, Chad and Libya. JEM and G-19 agreed to coordinate military activities. Some SLA non-signatories informally associated themselves with the NRF. NRF-associated forces launched a number of attacks in the months following the DPA, against both government and Minni Minawi SLA forces. The JEM Zaghawa domination of the NRF has become increasingly evident. At least partly in response to JEM's control over the NRF, G-19 and the Fur SLA groupings led by Abd al-Wahid and Abdel Shafi agreed to coordinate their activities. Abd al-Wahid stated:

> There is no organization called the NRF. Behind this name there is in reality only JEM – and we are convinced JEM is part of the Islamist

movement. We refuse any attempt, today as tomorrow, at a rapprochement between JEM and us, politically as militarily. There is no meeting point and no hope there will be one. We are different in everything. We will never become close.[361]

A further pro-DPA grouping emerged out of SLA-Wahid in September 2006. This was led by SLA field commander Abdel-Gasim Imam al-Haj. Abdel-Gasim subsequently signed a Libyan-brokered peace agreement with the government. He was appointed the governor of West Darfur state.

The international community also misjudged issues with regard to the Darfur Ceasefire Commission. This has been set up following the April 2004 N'djamena ceasefire. The commission had not been very effective but the question was what to do with the groups that were now not signatories to the DPA? De Waal records that: "The AU team discussed the problem in the days after 5 May and decided that the non-signatories must stay on – to succeed, a ceasefire commission had to include all those who were firing – but should not be party to the complex arrangements for monitoring the withdrawal of government troops to barracks, enforcing the ban on hostile military flights, or disarming the Janjawiid. There would therefore have to be a two-tier ceasefire commission." De Waal notes however that "The government and Minawi both assert that Kingibe never explained this to them, let alone got their consent, and as soon as the JEM representatives walked into the ceasefire commission meeting on 23 June, Minawi's delegates walked out. The commission was paralysed."

De Waal states that Abd al-Wahid's erratic behaviour "killed the [peace] process" which in turn led to a further split in the SLA:

The last straw for Abdel Wahid's lieutenants, including Ahmed Abdel Shafi, who had been with him from the very beginning, came in Nairobi on 3 June. Having changed his mind twice in as many days, Abdel Wahid finally agreed to the latest attempt to get his mainstream SLM into the peace accord, and said he would fly to southern Sudan the next day to meet with Salva Kiir, who had taken up the mantle of mediation. Kiir arrived at the town of Yei in mid-morning to discover that Abdel Wahid was still in Nairobi demanding a personal guarantee of his security. Kiir called Nairobi and, after waking Abdel Wahid up, gave the assurance. Abdel Wahid sent emissaries to finalise the logistics, only to call them back when they were halfway across town. They turned their taxi round, returned to Abdel Wahid's flat and discovered that their leader had gone into hiding for unspecified "security reasons". On 25 July, Abdel Shafi announced that 30 SLM commanders had "ousted" Abdel Wahid and that he would serve as interim chairman until a conference could be held. In reality, it was another split: the SLM has fragmented into as many as a dozen different groups.

The Abdel Shafi faction came to be known as SLA-Classic or SLA-AS. The following month this group declared that they had ousted Abd al-Wahid from his post as SLA chairman. Fighting between the groups ensued.

International activity on Darfur continued. On 31 August 2006, the UN Security Council approved a resolution to send a new UN force of 17,300 to the region. The Sudanese government expressed strong opposition to the resolution. The Sudanese president depicted it as a colonial plan, stating that "we do not want Sudan to turn into another Iraq." The AU, whose peacekeeping force mandate expired on 30 September 2006, stated they would leave. The next day, however, the US government stated that the AU force might remain in the region past the deadline, citing this possibility as a "viable, live option". On 2 October, the AU announced that it would extend its presence in the region until 31 December 2006. Two hundred UN troops were sent to reinforce the AU force.

On 13 October 2006, US President George W Bush imposed further sanctions against those deemed complicit in the Darfur atrocities under the so-called Darfur Peace and Accountability Act of 2006. The measures were said to strengthen existing sanctions by prohibiting US citizens from engaging in oil-related transactions with Sudan (although US companies had been prohibited from doing any business with Sudan since 1997), freezing the assets of complicit parties and denying them entry to the US. On 1 November, the US announced that it would formulate an international plan which they hoped the Sudanese government would find more palatable.

On 9 November, senior Sudanese presidential advisor Dr Nafie Ali Nafie told reporters that his government was prepared to start unconditional talks with the National Redemption Front but noted he saw little use for a new peace agreement. The NRF did not respond. In late 2006, Darfur Arabs started their own rebel group, The Popular Forces Troops.

President Sasso Nguesso, chairman of the African Union, observed that the peace process continued: "The train of peace has left, and we hope that those other wagons will follow us. We hope before the next station, they will want to join us and we will slow down for them to catch up."[362] On 9 November 2006 the AU announced the launch of the long-awaited Darfur-Darfur Dialogue and Consultation mechanism. On 13 November 2006 the AU invited JEM and the non-signatory SLM factions back to the ceasefire commission. On 17 November, there were reports of a potential deal to place a "compromise peacekeeping force" in Darfur.

On 8 February 2007, the Libyan government sought to address the tensions which had developed between Sudan and Chad regarding Chadian support for Darfur rebels. The Tripoli Agreement established an African Ministerial Level Committee chaired by Libya and made up of the Foreign Ministers of Chad, Sudan, CAR, Libya, Congo Brazzaville, Burkina Faso and the Chairman of the Executive Council of the Community of the Sahel-Saharan States (CEN-SAD) to assist in bringing the two countries together. Supported by the African Union and the European Union, the agreement also called for the establishment of a joint border surveillance force consisting of Libyan, Eritrean, Chadian and Sudanese monitors. Following up on this process, on 3 May 2007, Sudan and Chad signed an agreement in Riyadh aimed at reducing tensions on their common border. Both governments agreed that support for the Darfur Peace Agreement would reduce tension on their border. The Riyadh communiqué echoed the Tripoli agreement. On 5 May, the Sudanese president issued a presidential decree establishing a high level committee to oversee the implementation of the Riyadh Agreement. The UN Secretary-General said the "agreement is a positive step towards normalising the relations between Chad and Sudan".

In April 2007, appearing before the US senate foreign relations committee, the US Presidential special envoy to Sudan, Andrew Natsios, affirmed a continuing American commitment to the DPA:

As the central basis for negotiations, the U.S. supports the Darfur

Peace Agreement (DPA) signed by the GOS and the faction of the Sudan Liberation Movement headed by Minni Minawi (SLM/MM) on May 5, 2006. Despite some limitations, the DPA is a good agreement that outlines ways to address the root causes of the conflict, creates space for the delivery of humanitarian aid, and gives international forces a robust mandate to protect civilians and humanitarian workers. In further negotiations among non-signatories and the GOS, we support adding amendments, annexes, or clarifications to the DPA. What we do not support is starting from scratch and spending another year negotiating a new agreement that will likely be worse for the rebel movements and the people of Darfur. We have made this point to all parties involved.[363]

Natsios also discussed some of the difficulties now faced in negotiating a peaceful resolution to the Darfur conflict:

The number of rebel groups now operating in Darfur also complicates a negotiated settlement...We now confront a confusing array of rebel factions, the number of which fluctuates up to as many as fifteen at any given time. Rebel leaders frequently appear more focused on their own ambitions than on the well-being of people in Darfur...In January I met with rebel leaders to gain their perspective and to deliver a strong message from the U.S. government that they need to unify politically and support humanitarian operations. I stressed that while the people of the United States are appalled by the atrocities committed against the people of Darfur, the rebels should not translate that into support for their political movements, many of which are personally based and the goals of which are obscure. I have urged them to renounce the violent overthrow of the government of Sudan, which some have been publicly advocating, and which is an impediment to peace negotiations.[364]

On 18 April President Bush gave a speech at the US Holocaust Memorial Museum criticising the Sudanese government and threatening the use of sanctions if the situation did not improve. On 24 April 2007, in accordance with the DPA, the Transition Darfur Regional Authority was established. The AU welcomed its creation as "a central part of the powersharing arrangements of the DPA and its launching marks a major milestone in its implementation".[365] In late April 2007, Libyan leader Muammar Khaddafi accused Darfur rebels of seeking to internationalise the conflict and warned the international community to stay out of the crisis: "There are rebel groups in Darfur which are trying to involve the world in this issue. It is not in the interests of the international community to intervene in an affair in which one of the parties does not want a solution."[366]

From 28-29 April 2007, Libya hosted a high-level meeting on the Darfur peace process. All the key regional and international actors participated, including Sudan, Chad, Egypt, Eritrea and Libya, as well as the five permanent members of the UN Security Council. The Tripoli Consensus, which was adopted at the meeting, reaffirmed the importance of a comprehensive and sustainable political solution to the Darfur crisis and stressed the need for all national, regional and international peace initiatives to converge under AU-UN leadership. On 8 June, the joint AU-UN road map for the Darfur political process was finalised. It consists of three phases: convergence of initiatives and consultations; pre-negotiations; and negotiations. The AU and UN have stated that they expected all parties to declare their serious commitment to achieving a political solution to the crisis.

In a joint UN and AU communiqué issued on 8 May, Rodolphe Adada of the Republic of Congo was appointed as the Joint AU-UN Special Representative for Darfur. Adada, the Congolese foreign minister in his own country – and party to the Ministerial Committee set up in the course of the Tripoli Agreement, was tasked with overall responsibility for the peacekeeping mission in Darfur and with oversight of the implementation of the Darfur Peace Agreement.

In mid-May, the Sudanese government acknowledged that the signing of the Darfur Peace Agreement with one rebel faction had led to an imperfect agreement. Presidential Advisor Mustafa Osman Ismail admitted that this had resulted in the factions that did not sign seeking to weaken the faction that did sign. Dr Ismail emphasised that the government was committed to the Abuja Agreement and had no preconditions for talks with the non-signatory rebel factions. He further reiterated Sudan's commitment to the Tripoli agreement.[367]

In July 2007, the UN and AU special envoys convened a Darfur peace meeting in Tripoli, Libya. Held from 15-16 July, this meeting sought to gain consensus on a unified approach to a UN-AU mediation effort. This marked the end of the initial convergence phase and opened up the beginning of the pre-negotiation phase of the road map. From 3-6 August 2007, the UN and AU convened a follow-up meeting with a range of Darfur leaders in Arusha, Tanzania. There was movement towards establishing a common platform for the final negotiations on power-sharing, wealth-sharing, security arrangements, land and humanitarian issues, as well as the criteria for, and level of, participation in the final negotiations, and the inclusion of IDPs, refugees, tribal leaders, women and other civil society groups. All the main non-signatory factions were present at the meeting with the exception of Abd al-Wahid's SLA group. They included, JEM, NMRD, Sudan Federal Democratic Alliance, SLA-Unity and SLA-Abdel Shafi.

On 29 August 2007, in an escalation of the conflict, rebel forces attacked a police station in Wad Banda in west Kordofan. They killed 41 policemen. The AU denounced the raid: "AMIS would like to register, in the strongest terms, its condemnation of this deliberate attack, and of all acts of violence in Sudan, especially at this time when the African Union, the United Nations and the entire international community have converged all efforts towards upcoming peace negotiations."[368] Writing in September 2007, de Waal reported that that month had seen the first significant armed hostilities between the Sudan government and rebel forces since October 2006. He noted that "The fighting was initiated by the rebels. It was provocative, even reckless, and there has since been internal disagreement among rebel commanders over the wisdom of launching these raids, which began in a historically Arab part of Darfur and then crossed the boundary into Kordofan."[369]

On 14 September 2007, the Sudanese government stated that it was prepared to call a ceasefire ahead of peace talks with rebels in Libya. President al-Bashir said: "We stated that we are prepared for a ceasefire for the start of negotiations in order to create a positive climate conducive to a positive end to the negotiations. We hope that the negotiations in Tripoli will be the last and that they will produce a definitive peace."[370]

On 29 September 2007, however, rebels attacked an AMIS base in Haskanita in southern Darfur. They killed at least ten peacekeepers; dozens more were reported missing.[371] The UN Secretary-General called it a "shocking and brutal" act. The UN Mission in Sudan (UNIMIS) described the attack as "unprovoked and barbaric".[372] De Waal stated

> The assault was one of very few instances in history in which there has been a clearly-planned and premeditated attack on international peacekeepers. Most instances in which peacekeepers are killed occur in the context of coercive operations... or are the outcome of error and miscalculation by either peacekeepers or belligerent parties, or both, in the heat of the moment. The murderous attack at Haskanita puts the attackers in the same select category as the Rwandese soldiers who slaughtered 13 Belgian peacekeepers in cold blood in Kigali in April 1994, in one of the first acts of the Rwanda genocide. That observation speaks for itself.[373]

De Waal went on to note that "the principal culprits have been clearly identified as members of the Darfur armed movements...enough is known to be able to point the finger with certainty at the rebels. This is an immense moral comedown. Darfur's moral and political landscape is changed in the aftermath of this crime. It will have repercussions on the prospects for peace and for peacekeeping. The leadership of the armed movements faces a huge challenge in restoring its credibility." [374]

In keeping with its road map to peace, the international community scheduled what were hoped to be pivotal peace talks in Libya in late October 2007. The Sudanese government sent a high-level delegation, hoping to bring the war to an end. The AU Commission chief, Alpha Oumar Konare, reiterated the Khartoum government's hope that the Libyan talks would be a success: "We hope that all our other Sudanese brothers have the same inclination...It's time for peace, it's the moment for peace and we cannot lose time."[375] Most of the rebel movements chose to snub the talks. [376] *The Christian Science Monitor* reported that "the rebels are at risk of becoming the key stumbling block to peace."[377]

Additional Government Measures within the Peace Process

In addition to engagement within the peace process, the government has also been party to a number of other measures aimed at stabilising Darfur. On 7 April 2004, the Sudanese government announced the formation of a Ministerial Committee "to end security and relief problems in Darfur region". The Committee was tasked with the following: to control and disarm militias and non-regular forces that target the civilian population or hinder the delivery of relief; to open all relief corridors and to secure unimpeded access to the area for humanitarian assistance; to provide basic needs for affected population in the area; and to create a conducive atmosphere for the stabilisation and normalisation of the situation in Darfur. The Committee visited the affected areas on 8 April 2004, accompanied by diplomatic representatives of the USA, EU, and France, as well as representatives of UN agencies. The government informed the African Union that the representatives of the international organisations had confirmed an improvement in the humanitarian situation.

On 10 April 2004, the Sudanese government announced an immediate investigation to prosecute those responsible for the violence in the Darfur region. In May 2004, President Omar Bashir announced the setting up of a national commission to probe allegations of human rights violations in Darfur. The committee was chaired by former Chief Justice Dafallah al-Haj Yousif and made up of retired police general Hassan Ahmed Sidik, former army general al-Sir Mohammed Ahmed, a former commander of the Western Command, Dr Fatma Abdul-Mahmoud, National Assembly member, Hamadto Mukhtar, Chairman of the National Assembly's Human Rights Committee, Nazir Mohammed Sarour Mohammed Ramli, a representative of the Darfur administration) and Fuad Eid, a former administrator. It was tasked with investigating claims relating to killings, torture, the burning of villages and the seizure of property.[378] The Commission reported back in January 2005 and made a number of recommendations including judicial investigation of the human rights abuses and the establishment of a compensation commission and administrative commission to address any underlying social causes of the insurrection.

A central recommendation of the Commission was the establishment of a national judicial commission to investigate abuses of human rights in Darfur.

Local authorities established similar committees. The UN noted that, by May 2005, the national commission had indicted 70 persons and armed parties for involvement in crimes in Darfur. The charges ranged from murder and rape to looting and arson.[379]

Gender-based sexual violence has been a feature of the Darfur crisis. In July 2004 it was also announced that the Minister of Justice had established three committees to investigate allegations of rape in Darfur.[380] In August the justice ministry established a special committee made up of female judges, police and justice ministry officials to investigate rape cases. In March 2005, the government and UN raised awareness of the rape issue in a joint mission to the province. The mission clarified that rape victims were entitled to medical treatment whether or not they had completed forms required by local courts that document a victim's injuries and serve as medical evidence of the injuries and/or rape.[381] In August 2005, the government announced further measures to eliminate violence against women in Darfur. These measures included awareness-raising activities, police training, the establishment of police liaison officers in six community centres, human rights training, support for legal aid to assist rape victims and the establishment of a joint committee of the Government of National Unity and UN agencies to revise criminal procedure laws in order to secure compliance with international standards. The UN has noted that many of the measures reflect key recommendations contained in a July 2005 report, *Access to Justice for Victims of Sexual Violence*, prepared by the United Nations Mission in the Sudan.

The government had helped facilitate numerous visits from human rights organisations and experts. From 21 April-2 May 2004, for example, a UN High Commission on Human Rights investigative team visited Darfur. Amnesty International delegations visited Darfur in January 2003 and in September 2004. A delegation from the African Human Rights Commission visited Darfur in July 2004. The Special Rapporteur on violence against women, Professor Yakin Ertürk, visited Darfur from 25 September to 2 October 2004. All these visits were at the height of the war. Numerous other human rights delegations have also visited subsequently.

The Government of Sudan has agreed to and fully cooperated with the deployment of United Nations human rights officers in Darfur. The first OHCHR officers arrived in Darfur in August 2004, and are now fully integrated into the United Nations Mission in the Sudan. In July 2005, the UN noted that government "cooperation with human rights officers has been good, with regular meetings held with the police, prosecutors and the judiciary. Extensive human rights training for local police and the judiciary has been provided by the United Nations Development Programme, supported by the OHCHR and the International Rescue Committee."[382]

In May 2004, the government announced a number of measures aimed at facilitating the arrival of humanitarian aid in Darfur and enabling war-affected civilians in Darfur to return to their home areas and to prepare for the coming agricultural season. These measures were said to be "aimed at reducing the impacts of war and facilitating the work of Sudan's partners in the humanitarian aid field". To this end the government relaxed entry visas for aid workers entering Sudan.[383] Visas had hitherto been granted within a framework that was already heavily bureaucratic. This had often resulted in delays in granting access to Darfur.

In June 2004, the Sudanese President appointed the then Interior Minister, Major-General Abdul-Rahim Mohammed Hussein, as his Special Representative for Darfur, to oversee the implementation of government measures.[384] On 18 June, the President announced seven decrees: a declaration mobilising all sectors of government to restore law and order in Darfur; the establishment of special courts to prosecute criminals; the deployment of police forces to protect villages to enable civilians to return home; all ministries, particularly Agriculture and Finance, to assist with making available seeds for the coming planting season; all relevant ministries were instructed to implement the contingency plan for the development and provision of basic services in Darfur; calls for all governmental and non-governmental organisations to provide humanitarian assistance to internally-displaced people; and the promotion of a national conference to promote a national dialogue. These were followed up by further measures. On 6 July 2004, the Sudanese President's Special Representative in Darfur, Major-General Hussein, issued 15 decrees aimed at addressing and alleviating the crisis in Darfur. These addressed security issues, the easing of aid and relief access to Darfur, human rights monitoring and the presence and work of African Union observers.[385]

On 3 July 2004, the then Sudanese foreign minister Dr Mustafa Osman Ismail and the UN Secretary-General signed a joint communiqué establishing a Joint Implementation Mechanism (JIM), to oversee the carrying out of a mutually agreed plan of action. In addition to the government and United Nations, participation in JIM includes several partner countries and members of the League of Arab States, as well as Nigeria representing the African Union in its capacity as current AU chairman. It has since met on a number of occasions. A joint verification mission visited Darfur in late July and ascertained that the government was holding to a policy of voluntary returns and that humanitarian access had improved.[386] It was realised that commitments to disarm all militias within 30 days was unrealistic, as noted by the Secretary-General on 30 August 2004: "Making an area the size of Darfur, with the amount of armed men and violent recent history, safe and secure for all civilians takes more than 30 days."[387] The government committed itself to three steps: ending all offensive military operations; identifying parts of Darfur that could be made safe within 30 days; and identifying those militias over whom it had control and instructing them to lay down their weapons. Areas in each state were identified, and as agreed through JIM, the government commenced the large-scale deployment of some 6,000 policemen to maintain security and protect displaced persons' camps in Darfur. They would be tasked with assisting with the delivery of relief supplies and the provision of medical supplies.[388] An additional 2,000 policemen were deployed in mid-August.[389] By the end of 2004, some 12,000 policemen had been moved from other areas of Sudan into Darfur. The United Nations noted that "the enlarged police force appears to be of a well disciplined quality."

In his 30 August 2004 report, the Secretary-General noted that "the disarming of members of the [Popular Defence Forces]…has started. The second joint verification mission observed a demobilization ceremony of about 300 PDF soldiers in West Darfur…In South Darfur, the joint verification mission on 27 August inspected 157 arms in Kass that had been given up by members of the PDF the previous day, and was told about similar efforts in other locations in South Darfur."[390]

In keeping with the United Nations plan of action, the government convened a conference of local leaders from Darfur. This was held in Khartoum from 11-12 August 2004. The conference reviewed draft legislation on "the native administration of the three Darfur states". The United Nations Secretary-General noted that "the participants adequately covered the three Darfur states, and all major tribes and the interests of both pastoralists and nomads were well represented. Most of the traditional local leaders were present, including leaders who were known to have political views at variance with those of the Government." The Administration Law for the Three Darfur States was passed by presidential decree on 19 August 2004 and the United Nations states that it "contains criteria for the selection of local administrators and provisions relating to administrative, security, judicial, executive and other issues. The law provides for a general framework…to help address the conflict in Darfur in a transparent and sustainable manner." [391]

In building the case for peace in Darfur, the government has sought to encourage a process of inter-tribal reconciliation – a process which has previously helped to end similar conflict. As but one example, Khartoum convened a meeting in Nyala, South Darfur, for the leaders of six tribes caught up in the conflict. The tribes agreed to a ceasefire and to waive claims for compensation and blood money. [392] These sorts of tribal reconciliation meetings have continued. In April 2006, for example, the UN reported that "The Government of the Sudan has initiated tribal reconciliation processes for particular incidents and for geographical areas." UN officials, meeting with representatives of the tribal reconciliation committee in North Darfur, were told that "tribal reconciliation processes will be essential to any sustained peace in Darfur." [393] The work of these committees has continued into 2007.

Problems Facing the Peace Process

There are clearly a number of serious problems facing the Darfur peace process. These relate to the rebel movements, the international community, and the peace process itself – problems which explain in part the inability or unwillingness of the rebel movements to negotiate within the peace process and the slide into banditry by rebel gunmen.

A Pattern of Rebel Provocation

In addition to the uncertainty of a rebel commitment to the peace process, it is a matter of record that the rebels have on a number of occasions been party to behaviour that can only be described as deliberately provocative to both the government and Arab tribes within Darfur. De Waal and Flint have recorded SLA attempts to provoke the biggest Arab tribe in Darfur into involvement in the conflict. In July 2004, for example, the SLA deliberately began attacks into the south-east of Darfur, within areas belonging to the Rezeigat, Darfur's most powerful tribe – a tribe which had not been caught up in the war. The SLA attacked Rezeigat villages, killed civilians and stole livestock, attacks which in the words of de Waal and Flint threatened to "plunge the hitherto calm Rizeigat land into bloody conflict".[394] The Rezeigat militia defended themselves and pursued SLA forces back to their bases. Rezeigat tribal leaders ordered their men not to attack any further and to return to their own tribal areas. The SLA continued to provoke the Rezeigat until they eventually responded to threats by retaliation.[395]

The United Nations has documented several instances of rebel provocation within the peace process. The SLA had attacked a nomadic community in early 2005, killing ten members of the Miseriyya tribe and stealing livestock in South Darfur. This attack had been reported to the African Union who were unable to respond effectively. On 7 April 2005, a Miseriyya tribal militia retaliated with an attack on the village of Khor Abeche. This attack resulted in the displacement of several thousand people.[396] This pattern of activity has continued.

And, as mentioned above, both UN and AMIS documented the SLA attack on nomadic herders near the village of Malam in South Darfur in August 2005, abducting seven people and stealing over 3,000 camels. The SLA refused to assist AMIS it its attempt to resolve the incident.[397] The African Union severely criticized the SLA for its attitude. The African Union noted with regard to the Malam incident "the restraint shown by the Arab nomads and their commitment to follow the path of mediation".[398] Regrettably, having waited in vain for AMIS intervention, the nomad communities in question chose to take the law into their own hands and attempted to recover the abducted members of their tribe as well as the stolen livestock. Forty people died in the clash. A source within the nomadic community stated: "Following a week-long truce, the AU was unable to convince the SLA to return the camels. A few evenings after the truce ended, a large group of nomads attacked an SLA stronghold in the Jebel Marra mountain area."[399] *The Guardian* had also noted that the Malam incident had "sparked a chain of clashes" and confirmed that tribal leaders had appealed to the AU for assistance. When that was not forthcoming the nomads tried to forcibly recover their livestock. When asked by *The Guardian* if government forces had been involved in the recovery, the governor of North Darfur denied any government presence: "There was not a single soldier with them. The camel owners waited 13 days for the AU and the international community to respond."[400]

The International Crisis Group also noted deliberate provocation regarding Malam on the part of the rebels, stating that "An outbreak of fighting in early and mid-September…can be traced back to the SLA division. The looting at the beginning of that month of several thousand cattle from Arab nomads near Malam was committed by SLA soldiers connected with Minni Minawi. The camels were taken to Jebel Marra, leading to retaliatory attacks by Arab tribes. In mid-September, the SLA attacked at least three towns in South Darfur, briefly capturing Sheiria."[401] The ICG further noted that a rebel leader had stated "that the camels were purposely brought by Minni's faction to Jebel Marra in order to give the impression that the Fur were behind the attack."[402] That is to say, Zaghawa SLA rebels deliberately provoked nomads into attacking a Fur community in order to recover their livestock.

Intra-Movement Conflict

It is now widely recognised that the Sudan Liberation Army, disorganised from the outset, has been caught up in ethnic, political and personality conflicts which have led to its splintering into several factions. To an extent this was predictable. De Waal and Flint, for example, observed: "The SLA emerged into the political arena as a marriage of convenience rather than of conviction – a coming together of tribally organized armed groups on the basis of what united them, with very little discussion of what divided them."[403]

One of the most apparent divisions within the SLA factions has been a tribal one, between Fur fighters represented by Abd al-Wahid, and others, and Zaghawa combatants led by Minni Minawi. De Waal and Flint noted that the war which unfolded within the Jebel Marra in 2003 soon led to "mistrust between Fur civilians and Zaghawa fighters", with the Fur seeing the Zaghawa as a "threat".[404] The Fur-Zaghawa relationship continued to sour to the extent that when Fur SLA groups under Abd al-Wahid were surrounded by government forces to the south of the Jebel Marra in early 2004, Minawi refused to send any help. He was also said to have diverted deliveries of urgently-needed weapons from Abd al-Wahid's Fur forces to his own in North Darfur. These tensions were later further exacerbated when, forced out of North Darfur by government offensives, hundreds of Zaghawa SLA fighters loyal to Minawi relocated to the Jebel Marra and other areas of South Darfur. Vicious inter-tribal intra-SLA fighting between Fur and Zaghawa rebels allied respectively to Abd al-Wahid and Minawi, subsequently ensued in the Jebel Marra area. Minawi's Zaghawa continue to control parts of the Jebel Marra with a largely Fur population, and inter-tribal tensions continue. The International Crisis Group reported in October 2004 that "there are reports of serious abuses of the civilian population in the areas east of Jebel Marra controlled by, or exposed to, the operations of [the Minawi] faction".[405]

There is a clear pattern of inter-tribal violence by factions of the SLA. In November 2005, the United Nations reported that the SLA had abducted members of the Fellata tribe and demanded that ransom be paid for their return. The Fellata attacked the SLA and freed their kinsmen. This led to further fighting. On 6-7 November, 1,500 armed tribesmen attacked the villages of Dar es Salaam, Jamali, Funfo, Tabeldyad, Um Djantara and Um Putrumf in the Gareida area, burning most of them. In a separate incident, members of the largely Zaghawa JEM organisation attacked villages near Serguela: 62 JEM fighters were reported to have been killed. Ten thousand, largely Massalit, civilians fled to Gareida as a result of this fighting.[406]

Leadership within the SLA had gradually polarised between Abd al-Wahid and Minni Minawi, and their respective tribal constituencies. Minawi and his largely Zaghawa fighters started to push for control of the SLA. De Waal and Flint, for example, cite a Zaghawa SLA commander who stated: "The fighters on the ground in Darfur are Zaghawa. They control all of North Darfur and half of South Darfur. Most SLA commanders are Zaghawa."[407] Abd al-Wahid opposed any changes in the leadership arrangements for the movement. The SLA became an essentially Zaghawa dominated organisation. The tribal divisions subsequently started to come into sharp focus.

Another deep division opened up within the SLA between the movement's SLA's external and internal components. Both Minawi and Abd al-Wahid left Darfur in 2004. Once outside Darfur, both began to lose touch with SLA commanders in the field. De Waal and Flint noted that "[a]n 'internal-external' divide was added to the ethnic split."[408] Abd al-Wahid split his time between Eritrea, Kenya and Europe – de Waal and Flint state that Fur leaders began to refer to him as a "hotel guerrilla".[409] An additional division that was to emerge within the SLA was that of age. A generation of young gunmen had emerged as SLA commanders. As early as 2004, a SLA leader noted that "[t]he SLA problem is a leadership problem. They are young and inexperienced and leave no openings for intellectuals or men of experience. They have no political system. They are not democratic."[410] The International Crisis Group confirmed this development: "As the divisions grew between the leaders in exile, a gulf predictably grew between them and the field commanders. This has led to new leaders in the field, a gradual breakdown in military command and control, including a sharp rise in banditry, and the loss of legitimacy for the external leadership in the eyes of the international community as well as some elements of the SLA."[411]

Minawi returned to Darfur in May 2005. Abd al-Wahid remained outside of Darfur until late October 2005. Flint records that when Abd al-Wahid visited SLA-controlled areas of the Jebel Marra in October, after an absence of 18 months, he said he was "deeply shocked" by what he found: commanders who had had been "accused of killing many, many people", abuses of power leading to the imprisoning of civilians without charge or trial, often as the result of a personal grudge; poor control over combatants and "thousands of underage soldiers".[412] Minawi pushed for a SLA conference to be held in Darfur – to include the field commanders – knowing that the Fur were poorly represented in the SLA military leadership. He subsequently convened what was said to have been an SLA reconciliation meeting and conference near the village of Haskanita, in a part of rebel-held eastern Darfur, in late October 2005.[413] Abd al-Wahid and his faction boycotted the meeting.[414] The conference was dominated by Minawi and another Zaghawa, Juma Haggar, the SLA's military commander-in-chief, and was widely seen as having widened the split within the rebel movement.[415] The UN stated that it did not attend the meeting because it was "not an all-inclusive conference".[416] Minawi was challenged unsuccessfully for the chairmanship by Adam Bakhit Abdelrahman, who had fought alongside Déby in Chad in the late 1980s and had later trained in Iraq.

Two SLAs emerged out of the Haskanita conference; a Fur SLA led by Abd al-Wahid, and based in Jebel Marra; and a Zaghawa SLA in northern, eastern and southern Darfur led by Minawi.

In the light of these deep divisions perhaps the first question that must be asked is whether or not the rebel movements themselves actually want to end the war they started? This question is central to the issue of what motivated the conflict in the first place. It is clear that what they claim to have been fighting for is on offer. As the International Crisis Group has quite rightly noted:

> Darfur's problems are negotiable – under the right circumstances – and could fit relatively smoothly into the governance structures being negotiated between the government and the SPLA at Naivasha. In particular, the state autonomy models for the northern states of the Nuba Mountains and Southern Blue Nile could offer the basis for a resolution in Darfur. They provide for a high degree of autonomy for sub-national states and greatly increased provincial control over decisions affecting local administrations, including on education and legal systems, and could offer a template with which to begin discussions on a political settlement for Darfur.[417]

Autonomy has already been put on the table by the Sudanese government.[418] The question is whether or not one or more of the rebel movements have been pursuing a different agenda other than that of "overcoming" marginalisation through some level of power and wealth sharing. This is of particular concern with regard to the Justice and Equality Movement. Is their war less one against marginalisation and more of an Islamist war by proxy in Darfur with the objective of re-instating Turabi or the Popular Congress in power? If this is the case then they will presumably continue to seek ways of weakening or destabilising the Khartoum government by keeping the conflict going, hoping that there might be some sort of Western military intervention which the ultra-Islamist Popular Congress would then be able to exploit domestically.

There are also question marks over whether any of the SLA factions have a genuine commitment to the peace process, even when it was a single movement. The SLA's transparent attempt to launch attacks in December 2004, in violation of international ceasefire agreements, by using front groups such as the "Sudanese National Movement for the Eradication of Marginalisation" did not augur well. The SLA factions have not only continued to violate ceasefires but have also engaged in deliberately provocative attacks on government forces and Arab tribes and civilians, often in the lead-up to, or during, rounds of peace talks. It demonstrates a cynical intention on the part of the SLA to continue violence while paying vestigial lip-service to a peace process. That all the major rebel factions have procrastinated within, and delayed, the peace process is a matter of record. In addition to being obstructionist during the rounds of peace talks, they have also sought to destabilise the peace process itself by first objecting to the Chad government's attempts at mediation, and then by refusing to continue with African Union mediation. Even assuming that the rebel movements want peace, and they genuinely seek a political solution to the Darfur crisis, defining their political demands has been problematic. For one thing, as the ICG has noted, although the rebel movements are arguing for democracy "their own democratic credentials remain open to question".[419]

Leaving JEM's political agenda to one side, that of the Sudan Liberation Army, even when it was one movement, was far from coherent. *Time* Magazine noted that "The SLA's ultimate goals remain murky. Over the years, its leaders have advocated everything from secession to greater representation in local government to the capitulation of the central government." The anti-Khartoum International Crisis Group has also observed: "They haven't to this day clarified their political objectives or presented them in a coherent way."[420] The implication of this incoherence has been spelled out in October 2004 by *The New York Times*: "The rebels' political goals have never been clear, beyond vague demands for the sharing of wealth and power in Sudan. That could be a potential stumbling block in [peace] talks."[421] Two months later, in the wake of the Tawila attack, *The New York Times* returned to the issue: "[J]ust what does [the SLA] want politically and how does it intend to reach its objective through its gunmen?...Nearly two years after the insurgency began, its political demands remain vague – beyond claims for a greater share of Sudan's economic and political spoils."[422]

In the absence of any coherent political agenda on the part of the Sudan Liberation Army factions looms the spectre of Somalian-type warlordism. In

November 2004, the UN Special Envoy to Sudan spoke of this possibility.[423] Pronk said that rebel leaders must control their forces or "we may soon find Darfur is ruled by warlords".[424] The SLA's track record in this respect has been appalling leading to direct African Union criticism of the behaviour of its members: "[W]e don't think it is right or normal for any movement that is trying to be a political movement to be involved in banditry." [425]

There is also considerable concern about the rebel movements' control over their own forces. Perhaps the most benign reading of the November 2004 attacks on towns such as Tawila is that it revealed apparent rebel difficulties with regard to control of their fighters in Darfur. The UN described the rebel attack as an example of "a crisis of leadership" within the SLA. Knight-Ridder's Sudarsan Raghavan described the situation as "an obstacle to achieving peace in Darfur". Raghavan confirmed that "rebel forces now appear to be launching many of the disputed attacks. Black African rebels have stolen camels from Arab tribes, kidnapped civilians and attacked police stations."[426] The African Union also stated that "It appears...that there are some problems with the chain of command of some of the movements, especially the SLA."[427] The SLA representative to the African Union, Abdou Abdallah Ismail, denied any such problem, and insisted that the SLA "has full control over its commanders". Ismail was clearly aware of international criticism: "I want to send a message to the international community. My guys are not going to act like bandits. We're a movement. How can we act like thieves and protect people?" [428]

The New York Times also addressed concerns about rebel command and control:

> The problems are exacerbated by what appear to be contradictory bluster and promises from the rebel camp. It remains unclear whether the attack on Tawilah, for instance, was ordered from on high, or whether it was the result of a flimsy chain of command...Their message has not been consistent. Rebel leaders late this week scrambled to publicize their commitment to a cease-fire, even after at least one of their spokesmen earlier in the week declared the truce to be over...The latest spate of hostage-taking and attacks on government targets has brought unusually harsh criticism of the

SLA...Whether rebel leaders are stepping up attacks for the sake of trying to gain leverage at coming peace talks in Abuja, or whether the attacks simply signal a breakdown in their command-and-control structure also remains unknown.[429]

In the event, *The New York Times* reported the more benign view of Tawila, "Whatever the case, it is clear, say aid workers, United Nations officials and senior Sudanese government officials, that the Sudan Liberation Army remains a poorly organized insurgency, one whose rank-and-file fighters may be unaware of the promises made by their political leaders." [430]

There has also been an obvious question mark with regard to the SLA factions' ability to engage constructively or coherently in the AU-led peace negotiations. It is very obvious, for example, that the fighting between SLA factions quickly manifested itself in the peace negotiations. The ICG noted, for example: "[t]he rivalry between the two factions has crippled the SLA's negotiating efforts, undermining its ability to offer a credible and united front. For example Minni and Abdel Wahid routinely submit separate lists of delegates to the AU for accreditation. The divisions were most evident in the June/July 2005 round."[431] These divisions were also evident during the October 2005 negotiations, and the round of talks which culminated in the Darfur Peace Agreement. The BBC noted:

Peace talks in Nigeria – which should have addressed fundamental issues of power and wealth sharing – have instead been dominated by wrangling over who should represent the SLA. No substantive discussions took place at the sixth round of negotiations which ended in Abuja on the 20 October. For three weeks the SLA argued among themselves over the make up of their delegation. Abdul Wahid had changed the SLA's list of negotiators from the previous round to exclude Minnawi and his faction. The official SLA delegation now just consisted of Abdul Wahid's supporters – even his personal bodyguard was included.[432]

De Waal and Flint cite an observer at the peace talks: "We should be talking about two or three separate SLAs. The only thing keeping Abdel Wahid and

Minni talking to each other is that the Americans insist that they have one delegation."[433] This is exactly what was to unfold. Additionally, factional in-fighting and actual inclination to negotiate aside, there are doubts over the SLA's ability to engage constructively in any peace or political process. De Waal and Flint note that:

> The SLA and JEM negotiating teams were catapulted into major negotiations with almost no experience or preparation. Lacking political structures or strategy, the SLA compensated for lack of quality with quantity and sent ever-larger numbers to the talks....Most of its delegates were poorly prepared at best, but still insisted on being party to every discussion...Abdel Wahid rarely turned up or sent clear instructions...Without a negotiating strategy...the talks did not get beyond acrimonious preliminaries. By the end of the year, there had not been a single day's discussion about a framework for a political settlement...Armed men are given legitimacy as decision-makers for people who have not elected them...In the AU's conference chambers, SLA delegates rage at the government, but don't articulate a political agenda.[434]

That is to say that the rebel movements would appear to have launched a bloody insurrection, killing thousands of people within Darfur, and provoking a ruthless counter-insurgency campaign affecting many thousands more without any clear agenda beyond mouthing a number of superficial slogans, most of them questionable in themselves.

Reuters has noted also that "Internal differences, conflicting goals and a lack of coordination among Sudanese rebel groups are obstructing international efforts to reach a peace agreement with the government over Darfur, diplomats and aid workers say."[435] Reuters quoted an African Union official as saying: "The factionalism of the (rebel) leadership almost derailed talks in N'Djamena and set back the talks in Addis Ababa." They have also paralysed much of the Abuja negotiations. Reuters also pointed to the problem of "a pattern of often contradictory rebel statements from spokesmen who change frequently". Abd al-Wahid tried to explain differences of opinion away by stating that "There are mistakes sometimes from some officials who say things that are not our policy." Reuters observed that "[al-Nur] said he was the overall leader of the group and took the final decision in political matters. But another SLM leader, Minni Arcua Minnawi, had previously told reporters he was the leader of the group." An aid worker who deals with the SLA leadership on a regular basis noted: "It is often unclear who speaks for the group or what section of the group they speak for. It is also unclear who speaks for the group at all and who doesn't."[436] This dramatically affected the peace talks.

The Justice and Equality Movement has its own limitations. Tanner and Tubiana note that a central feature of JEM "is its extremely narrow tribal base...the Kobe branch of the Zaghawa, from Tina on the Sudan-Chad border". The Kobe numbers in Darfur are limited. They also state that JEM "remains essentially Kobe" and that the movement has "even had trouble building consensus among the Kobe". JEM, for example, is opposed by the present Kobe sultan.[437] Tanner and Tubiana have observed that "Khalil is increasingly seen as a Zaghawa, rather than Darfurian, leader."[438] While the Justice and Equality Movement, in that it is essentially Zaghawa both in leadership and membership, has not been troubled by ethnic divisions, it has experienced several political splits. JEM's leadership has always been externally-based which has led divisions within the organisation. In 2004, JEM's chief-of-staff, Gabril Abdul Kareem Badri, a former officer in the Chadian *Garde républicain*, with which he had served in the Central African Republic and Democratic Republic of Congo, formed a breakaway group, the National Movement for Reform and Development (*al-haraka al-watania lil-islah wat-tanmia*, NMRD). NMRD broke away from JEM because of a disagreement over the influence of the Popular Congress and Dr Turabi over the rebel movement.[439] Nourene Manawi Bartcham, a veteran of Chadian and Sudanese politics, served as its political leader until September 2005, when he rejoined JEM. It was reported that subsequent clashes between JEM and breakaway rebel fighters had left 20 dead and dozens injured.[440] Other factions have also left the organisation. In early 2005, the former JEM third-in-command, Mohamed Saleh Hamid, "Harba", broke away to form the Field Revolutionary Command. These splits were described by the African Union official as "a dilemma" which would get worse: "This is particularly a concern with JEM...With JEM we have had splinter groups claiming to talk for the whole group...it's difficult to know who talks for the group."[441]

The continuing emergence of further armed groups, in Darfur and in other parts of Sudan, has undoubtedly complicated attempts to end the conflict. A number of new groups, of varying credibility, have appeared on the scene.[442] Reuters has reported, for example, that the African Union presently "recognizes the SLA and the other main rebel group, the Justice and Equality Movement (JEM), and the National Movement for Reform and Development, which split from JEM and agreed to respect a cease-fire after talks with Khartoum". Reuters quoted Major-General Festus Okonkwo, the Nigerian commander of AU forces in Darfur, on the issue of new groups: "If we recognize too many groups, then more groups will take up arms. So the AU will not recognize any more groups."[443]

There are now up to twenty rebel factions. They include the SLA/Abd al-Wahid, SLA/Minni Minawi, SLA/Abdel Shafi, Justice and Equality Movement, the Justice and Equality Movement/Siddiq Abdul Kareem faction, NRF, G-19, NMRD, FRC, the Sudan Federal Democratic Alliance, Khamees Abdallah's United Front for Liberation and Development and the Sudan National Liberation Movement.

The Darfur rebels have clashed with traditional leaders, even to the extent of murdering senior tribal figures. There has also been a generational clash. Most of the field commanders are young and there is tension between them and older political activists. There is additional tension between field commanders and those rebel leaders, political and military, who have spent or are spending most of their time outside of Darfur in various foreign capitals. Flint has noted: "As 2007 began, the two men who had dominated the SLA since it first took up arms – Minni Minawi and Abdel Wahid Mohamed al Nur – appeared increasingly irrelevant. Their place was taken by a new group of field commanders who wanted unity, reform of the SLA, and peace."[444] With regard to Abd al-Wahid, Flint also observed

> He squandered every ounce of political capital that he had until, in the months after he refused to sign the Darfur Peace Agreement in Abuja, even his closest and most loyal comrades turned against him. His basic flaw is his personality: he is disorganized, indecisive…it is common for him to make a decision one day and reverse it the next. He has on occasion countermanded critical decisions within the

hour…Slowly but surely, Abdel Wahid lost the support of the movement."[445]

Inter-Movement Conflict

It is also clear that there are deep political differences and tensions between JEM and the SLA. As early as May 2004, the International Crisis Group quoted a leading SLA member as saying: "Continued coordination is unclear, because they [JEM] have some ambiguous political backing."[446] In October 2004, Reuters reported: "The rebel movements negotiating with Sudan's Islamist government to try to end the 20-month-old conflict in Darfur have been unable to come up with a common political framework, presenting separate documents to mediators instead."[447] *The New York Times* has noted of the SLA that "splits are inevitable with its cousin rebel factions".[448] The issue of the separation of religion and state has been cited as a major area of divergence between the two groups. Reuters noted that "the leadership of the two rebel groups have very different backgrounds. JEM's leaders are widely believed to have retained prior links with Sudan's opposition leader and Islamic ideologist Hassan al-Turabi, an advocate of Sharia law."[449]

The April 2005 African Union report on Darfur noted that "the SLM/A has been experiencing leadership problems during the past months. The relationship between its Chairman, Abdelwahid Mohamed Nour, and its Secretary-General, Minni Arcou Minawi, has deteriorated considerably. Since then, each one of these two leaders has proceeded to work with his own group of followers, which makes decision-making within the Movement difficult."[450]

The United Nations and the African Union have documented several of the violent clashes between the SLA and JEM. In June 2005, for example, the AU stated that it was deeply concerned at "the deteriorating security situation" in South Darfur:

Exclusive responsibility for this lies squarely on the Sudan Liberation Movement and the Justice and Equality Movement whose military elements have engaged in clashes for control of territory. The genesis of the current offensive and counter offensive goes back to March 2005 when JEM was forced out of Muhajeriya by the SLA.

Consequently, the JEM occupied Graida despite requests by AMIS forces for them to relocate some 6 Km outside Graida. On the 3rd June, 2005, the SLA attacked the JEM positions in Graida with heavy bombardment and the firing of mortar bombs which killed 11 persons, wounded 17, and burnt several houses. They constitute a serious breach of the Ndjamena Humanitarian Ceasefire Agreement.[451]

Cantonment of Combatant Forces

One of the long-running obstacles to effective peacekeeping within Darfur has been the rebel reluctance to adhere to cantonment plans as laid down in ceasefire agreements. An AU-monitored separation of combatant forces in Darfur is an essential component of bringing the conflict to an end. All parties to the crisis have signed protocols agreeing to cooperate in this process. The UN has emphasised the importance of this cantonment: "Such a plan would contribute to improving the situation on the ground by stabilizing the ceasefire and creating better conditions for the African Union monitors to carry out their work. It will also create a climate more conducive to negotiating a peaceful resolution to the conflict in Darfur."[452]

In the 25 November 2004 meeting of the Joint Commission, the parties were requested to comply, within one month, with their commitment to provide information on the locations of their respective forces.[453] The Government of Sudan provided the stipulated cantonment details. In January 2005, the UN noted that the government "reminded the Joint Implementation Mechanism that it had taken steps to comply with its obligations in good faith, providing AU with maps indicating the area under its control, as stipulated in the Abuja Security Protocol. SLM/A, on the other hand, had not yet done so."[454]

In February 2005, in his review of the previous six months, the UN Secretary-General reported that "over this period, the rebel movement have become less cooperative in talks. Their attacks on police have increased and often seemed intended to invite retaliation. These attacks and provocations have at times indirectly impaired humanitarian access. Some rebels groups have directly impeded humanitarian work by looting cars and trucks and putting pressure on, or even abducting, national staff of humanitarian organizations. Many of these actions have severely reduced the delivery of assistance."[455]

In his March 2005 report, the United Nations Secretary-General noted that the seventh high-level meeting of the Joint Commission in N'djamena on 16-17 February 2005, attended by, *inter alia*, the Presidents of Chad, Gabon, Congo-Brazzaville and the Sudan, decided to dispatch a team to Darfur to "verify the positions occupied by the forces on the ground, with a view to working out a separation plan of forces. A clear delineation of the territory controlled by the various forces on the ground is a crucial element of any viable ceasefire agreement and a vital precursor to the disengagement of forces."[456] The African Union reported that the Joint Commission "demanded that the SLM/A and the JEM communicate without delay to the CFC the positions occupied by their forces. The Movements have still not submitted their locations."[457] The African Union further noted that this non-compliance with commitments was "clearly unacceptable, as the notification of positions is a basic requirement under the Abuja Protocol on the Enhancement of the Security Situation in Darfur".[458] This was echoed by the UN Secretary-General.[459]

The United Nations reported that in April 2005 both SLA and JEM were "repositioning their forces to new locations that are off limits under the terms of either the ceasefire or other ad hoc agreements. Most recently, JEM reoccupied the town of Gereida in Southern Darfur on 29 May, despite the agreement reached in February among the Government, the rebel movements and AMIS that all combatants would vacate Gereida and three other towns."[460]

In May 2005, the UN special envoy to Sudan noted with regard to attempts by an AMIS team to ascertain the position of combatant forces: "While the government has shown its concern with the task of the team, the other parties have not yet shown the required response. The locations of positions and separation of the feuding forces are provided for in all agreements of the joint ceasefire observation commission and in the UN Security Council Resolution 1591."[461]

In October 2005, the African Union called upon "the rebel movements to submit to the verification of their locations and urges especially SLM/A to refrain from further violation of the N'djamena Agreement and the Abuja Protocols by attacking GoS positions and military convoys, as well as hindering

AMIS patrols and the free flow of commercial and humanitarian traffic on the roads."[462]

Rebel Attacks on African Union Peacekeepers

An increasingly serious problem within the peace process in Darfur has been repeated rebel attacks on African Union peacekeepers – attacks which have included the murder of dozens of AMIS personnel and injury to many others.

The UN Secretary-General reported that African Union peacekeepers had come under fire on no fewer than seven occasions in February 2005: "No excuse or explanation offered by the SLM/A leadership can possibly justify their forces firing on aircraft or vehicles that are clearly marked as belonging to the United Nations, the African Union or relief agencies and organizations. I condemn these acts."[463]

An April 2005 an African Union report noted: "A new phenomenon on the security scene is the deliberate targeting and firing at AMIS personnel and equipment, lately by unidentified gunmen. Recently, there have been a series of unprovoked attacks on AMIS vehicles and aircrafts. So far, a total of five separate attacks on AMIS vehicles and PAE fuel tankers, with AMIS escort, have been recorded. While the immediate motives for these gunmen are unknown, it is obvious that the Mission is now operating in a less benign environment. On 29 March, unknown gunmen fired at an AMIS vehicle carrying two military officers and one Sudanese civilian guide…in Sector 2 (Nyala). The AMIS Team leader was shot at the neck and the other two suffered light shrapnel wounds…The Team is of the opinion that the perpetrators were SLM/A fighters."[464]

The UN also noted that the rebel movements became "increasingly obstructionist" towards African Union peace-keepers in the course of May 2005. On 10 May, for example, the SLA detained 18 members of an AMIS team.[465]

In his July 2005 report on Darfur, the UN Secretary-General noted that the rebel movements were "actively seeking to hinder [peace] monitoring activities. In addition, AMIS is not infrequently confronted by local SLM/A commanders who deny their patrols access to an increasing number of rebel-held areas. These AMIS patrols have reported that the SLM/A commanders have attempted to justify their refusal to grant access on the grounds that AMIS was conducting espionage against SLM/A, without attempting to substantiate the allegation."[466]

The UN Secretary-General reported that on two occasions in February 2005, clearly marked UN WFP helicopters came under heavy machine-gun fire passing by Siyah en route to Malha Wells in North Darfur. The SLA admitted that they had fired on the second occasion and the Secretary-General stated that "one may assume its responsibility for the first incident as well." On 8 October 2005, SLA gunmen killed three Nigerian AU peacekeepers and two civilian drivers in an ambush: two other Nigerian soldiers were captured and subsequently executed. The African Union stated that it unreservedly condemned the killings "and holds the SLA responsible for this wicked and atrocious act".[467] Associated Press noted that "the violence occurred in generally SLA-controlled territory with a history of previous rebel interference and attacks against African Union teams, according to a statement released by the African Union Mission in Sudan."[468] A further 36 AMIS personnel were kidnapped by another Darfur rebel faction on 9 October. The government condemned the murder and abduction of AMIS members: "Serious measures should be taken by the African Union to halt this targeting of AMIS personnel, of the civilians and of relief workers in Darfur by the rebels." [469]

In April 2006, the UN stated that its panel of experts on the Darfur conflict "gathered a significant body of information on acts of harassment or attack against AMIS personnel that pose a serious impediment to the work and mission of AMIS." The UN noted that "AMIS personnel have been threatened by NMRD and SLA combatants. SLA has on a number of occasions...forcibly entered AU camps and abused the facilities and personnel" and that Darfur rebels had been responsible for the death and wounding of AMIS personnel.[470]

Rebel attacks on AMIS personnel have continued into 2007. Two AMIS soldiers were murdered by rebels in Gareida on 5 March 2007. AMIS reported that later that month there was "a clearly targeted" attack by rebels on an AMIS helicopter carrying the AMIS deputy force commander, Brig. General Ephreim Rurangwa. This was followed by the killing of five AMIS peacekeepers in Umbaro on 1 April. AMIS noted that "these attacks have been launched against the backdrop of an increasing spate of harassments, hijackings, threats and blackmail that have been made against the Mission and its top leadership by some of those it is supposed to work with and assist."[471] This pattern culminated in the September 2007 murder by rebels of ten peacekeepers in an attack on an AU base in Haskanita, southern Darfur.

Foreign Involvement in Darfur

There is another difficulty which has posed a problem in the search for peace in Darfur – the existence of foreign governments and constituencies who, for their own political interest, would wish to see continuing conflict in Darfur and the continued destabilisation of Sudan in Darfur and elsewhere. Eritrea is an obvious candidate in this respect. The United Nations has clearly documented military, financial and political assistance to the Darfur rebels emanating from Eritrea, Chad and Libya. The International Crisis Group has also commented upon the sometimes less than helpful role played by international observers at the peace talks themselves, citing one observer as saying "The process had too many players. It was too hard to keep the international actors united. They were a fractured, agenda-ridden group. It was a political catfight. The observers never settled their own differences."[472] There were also accounts of how the Darfur rebels were being encouraged by United States officials to procrastinate during peace talks in late 2004.[473]

The former UN Special Envoy to Sudan, Jan Pronk, has clearly pointed to the fact that some foreign governments have encouraged the Darfur rebels – and, if these same foreign interests now want peace in Darfur, will now have to put pressure on them to negotiate a peaceful settlement: "Some people have been told: 'If you fight, you get some outside support.' But the same countries who made such risky statements will have to tell these people in the field: 'If you fight, you won't get any support any more from us; you have to participate in the political dialogue.'"[474]

The simple fact which must be borne in mind by those who wish to see peace in Darfur is that the rebel movements may believe that it is not in their best interests to have peace. Continued war means a continuing humanitarian crisis which in turn means continuing pressure on Khartoum, with rebel hopes that this might translate into some form of foreign military intervention which the SLA or JEM would then be able to exploit domestically.[475] This would at least in part explain the reluctance of rebel factions either to engage in any meaningful negotiations or then to abide by any commitments they may have signed.

Chapter Three

HUMANITARIAN AID ACCESS IN DARFUR

It is strange to see that there is still the notion in the world that nothing is happening and we're completely blocked from accessing Darfur. We are reaching some 800,000 people at the moment with some sort of assistance and food.

Jan Egeland, UN Under-Secretary-General for Humanitarian Affairs, July 2004[476]

Most of the underserved areas remain rebel-held, many of which have not been accessible to UN agencies because of a series of security incidents and a delay in obtaining SLA agreement and understanding of humanitarian rules and principles laid out in agreements.

United Nations Report, December 2004[477]

There has been considerable sensationalism with regard to humanitarian aid access to Darfur. Attempts have been made to claim that the government has been systematically denying humanitarian access to Darfur and its war-affected communities. The reality is that ensuring humanitarian access to the war-affected communities while a political solution is sought is the single most important task facing both the Sudanese government and the international community. At the same time it is clear that a continuing humanitarian crisis, especially one in which aid workers cannot gain access to war-affected communities, is in the best interests of the rebel movements. It is now equally obvious that the rebel movements have not only been seeking to deny humanitarian access to government-controlled areas by attacks on aid workers – attacks which in turn result in aid agencies suspending activities in parts of

Darfur – and by attacks on humanitarian aid convoys: they have also denying the international community access to rebel-controlled areas, thereby severely affecting the very people they claim to protect. All of this in an attempt to further ratchet up international pressure on the Sudanese government.

Any study of the Darfur crisis must examine the aid issue in some depth. Humanitarian access to displaced communities in Darfur is essential in addressing the crisis. The international community must be aware of the extent to which emergency relief and food aid in such circumstances can and has been manipulated.

The initial bureaucratic difficulties were clear and overcome.[478] The Government of Sudan would appear to have acted responsibly with regard to humanitarian access to Darfur. The facts speak for themselves. In September 2003, the Government of Sudan and the SLA signed an agreement allowing "free and unimpeded" humanitarian access within Darfur.[479] In less than 12 months the Sudanese government had agreed and facilitated an increase in aid workers present in Darfur, from two foreigners and a few dozen nationals in September 2003, to just under 6,000 aid workers – over 700 of them expatriates – by August 2004.[480] By the end of 2004, there were 9,100 aid workers in Darfur.[481] By September 2005, the UN was able to confirm that the number of humanitarian workers in Darfur had grown further to around 13,500 and that they were working for 81 NGOs and 13 UN agencies.[482]

The signing of the April 2004 ceasefire made it safer and thus much consequently easier for aid agencies to operate in Darfur. The UN 2004 end-of-year humanitarian action report stated that "much credit has to be given to the [government] Humanitarian Affairs Ministry whose officials worked tirelessly to enforce the provision of the Joint Communiqué of 3 July [guaranteeing access]."[483]

On 6 July 2004, the government issued 15 decrees which included measures to enhance security in Darfur; the establishment of police stations in displaced people camps; to facilitate the ceasefire commission and African Union monitoring force; to streamline the granting of visas for aid workers in Darfur; the exemption of all humanitarian aid imports from any restrictions, customs tariffs or personal fees; the repeal of measures regarding specifications on the humanitarian aid imports into Darfur; to facilitate freedom of movement for those working in the humanitarian aid organizations in Darfur; to facilitate the flow of humanitarian aid to displaced people in Darfur; to exempt humanitarian aid from the health and medical regulations in Darfur; the exemption of agricultural inputs, fodders, and seeds in Darfur from any restrictions, customs tariffs or personal fees; exemption from import restrictions of humanitarian aid imports into Darfur; to activate the measures regarding the governments of the Darfur states to guarantee the flow of humanitarian aid and humanitarian aid imports into Darfur and to encourage the return of the displaced to their villages; and to facilitate the work of the fact-finding commission in regard to the allegations of human rights violations committed by armed groups in Darfur.

As of October 2004, there were 155 locations assisting with internally displaced people in the three Darfur states, and the World Food Programme was present in 136 of these centres.[484] Speaking in June 2004, the outgoing UN Humanitarian Coordinator for Sudan, Kevin Kennedy, confirmed that visas were generally being granted within 48 hours – as promised by the Government of Sudan – and that "people are experiencing very few visa difficulties".[485] That there have been propagandistic attempts to claim that the government was deliberately blocking access to Darfur by aid workers is apparent. The United Nations Under-Secretary-General for Humanitarian Affairs, Jan Egeland, speaking in July 2004, commented on some of these claims. He said: "It is strange to see that there is still the notion in the world that nothing is happening and we're completely blocked from accessing Darfur. We are reaching some 800,000 people at the moment with some sort of assistance and food."[486] By September 2004, the World Food Programme was feeding some 940,000 conflict-affected people in Darfur.[487] The presence of over 13,000 aid workers in Darfur provides clear evidence of the Khartoum government's commitment to the provision of food and medical relief to Darfur's war-affected communities.

The international community must be aware of the extent to which humanitarian issues can be manipulated for political effect.[488] For rebels a humanitarian crisis is a no-lose situation. A humanitarian crisis always reflects badly on the government in the country affected. And a humanitarian crisis is something which can be created and deepened. One of the goals of most insurgencies is to internationalise the conflict to which they are a party. One of the easiest means of doing so is to provoke a humanitarian crisis. This is precisely what the Darfur rebels succeeded in doing. Merely starting the war in Darfur initiated a humanitarian crisis in western Sudan. The escalation of the conflict and the government's response to it led to a deepening crisis and considerable displacement of populations – a feature of most wars. The rebels, however, have deliberately sought to heighten the humanitarian crisis they created by starting the war by additionally seeking to escalate food insecurity knowing full well that this would be the focus of immediate international attention. As early as July 2003, for example, the UN news service reported on rebel attempts to disrupt food security in the affected areas: "SLA rebels regularly attacked and looted villages taking food and sometimes killing people…The attacks present a real threat to people's food security and livelihoods, by preventing them from planting and accessing markets to buy food."[489]

The provision of humanitarian relief such as food aid and medical supplies has historically also been a bonus to rebel movements. Firstly, international access impinges upon the national sovereignty of the country concerned, a net propaganda victory for anti-government forces as it brings with it international attention. Secondly, international agencies provide food and emergency supplies which help to sustain communities within rebel-controlled areas and can often be diverted by rebel forces. It was widely acknowledged, for example, that vast amounts of food aid were diverted during the war in southern Sudan. In July 1998, in one instance, the Roman Catholic Bishop of the starvation-affected diocese of Rumbek, Monsignor Caesar Mazzolari, stated that the SPLA were diverting 65 percent of the food aid going into rebel-held areas of southern Sudan. Agence France-Presse also reported that: "Much of the relief food going to more than a million famine victims in rebel-held areas of southern Sudan is ending up in the hands of the Sudan People's Liberation Army (SPLA), relief workers said."[490] It is also clear that rebel forces in Darfur are also directly misappropriating food aid and equipment stolen from relief agencies. This is a point made by humanitarian aid expert, Professor Sarah Kenyon Lischer. Interviewed in January 2005, she noted that: "Recently, the World Food Program has had over a dozen of its trucks hijacked. And the aid that was on those trucks has been stolen. The trucks reportedly have been repainted and used for military purposes by the rebels. And so that's just a very obvious way that aid can be used for war."[491] That this had happened was confirmed by the United Nations: "The United Nations said it was also concerned about reports that Darfur-based rebel forces have stolen 13 commercial all terrain trucks leased to WFP and loaded with food in the last two weeks. These thefts are in addition to multiple losses of commercial and aid agency vehicles to armed groups in recent months, [the UN said]. More alarming are reports that the rebel group that stole them may now be using some of these trucks for military purposes, it said."[492] The UN Sudan Envoy Jan Pronk stated: "Such misuses of humanitarian assets should cease immediately. All trucks and other equipment taken by armed groups from humanitarian organizations should be returned without delay so that relief operations are not hindered further." [493]

From the earliest days of the insurgency, the rebels have sought to escalate humanitarian access difficulties by deliberately targeting aid workers. They murdered nine World Food Programme truck drivers, and wounded 14 others, in an attack on a relief convoy in October 2003.[494] All this followed a set pattern by rebels in other parts of Sudan, tactics which have previously succeeded in creating a humanitarian crisis in southern Sudan. The veteran American journalist Robert Kaplan noted, for example: "On June 1, 1986, twelve Kenyan truck drivers bringing food into the south from the Ugandan border town of Nimule were ambushed...The drivers were bound by ropes to their steering wheels, and then grenades were lobbed at the trucks. This put a virtual halt to the World Food Program's overland relief operation. Only 600 of the 90,000 tons had been delivered."[495]

In November 2003 the Government accused rebels in Darfur of killing two of its relief workers and abducting three others in an attack on an aid convoy. Humanitarian Aid Commissioner Sulaf Eddin Salih said his government is worried about the "continued" rebel attacks which he said "threaten the humanitarian operations and result in losing human lives and worsening the humanitarian situation". He appealed to the international community to intervene to halt and denounce the "repeated" armed operations on the humanitarian assistance convoys.[496]

Put quite simply, insecurity severely curtails humanitarian aid access. In the words of a UN humanitarian relief spokesman: "You can't give aid when there are bullets flying."[497] In January 2004, for example, UN media sources reported that "about 85 percent of the 900,000 war-affected people in

Darfur…are inaccessible to humanitarian aid…mainly because of insecurity."[498] In December 2003, the UN quoted the government as saying "The problem is in areas controlled by the SLM. Our experience has made us hesitant to send relief to areas under the SLM because of kidnapping and attacks on trucks."[499] In October 2003, in the wake of the above-mentioned attacks, the United States government asked the Sudanese government for help with security and access.[500] One month later, rebel gunmen killed two other relief workers and abducted three others.[501] Rebels have also kidnapped other relief workers. In a further example of interference with humanitarian work, JEM gunmen admitted abducting five aid workers working for the Swiss humanitarian group Medair.[502]

On 11 February 2004, JEM declared its intention to close down every road within Darfur. It would have been aware of the devastating consequences this would have on the ability of the government and aid agencies (national and international) to provide emergency assistance to those communities suffering in Darfur. This was at precisely the same time, in February 2004, as the United Nations high commissioner for refugees warned of a humanitarian catastrophe in Darfur. Médecins Sans Frontières (MSF or Doctors without Borders) had also warned that there was not enough food or water in the desert region.[503]

In February 2004, the Sudanese Minister of State for Humanitarian Affairs, Mohammed Youssef Moussa, commented on an attack on Save the Children: "It is true that (the rebels) have started causing damage and today, in particular, they planted a land mine near the town of Ambro that went off, wounding a lorry driver and his assistant. The lorry was carrying medical supplies and belonged to Save the Children Fund-UK. So if this is what they are talking about, then they are…abandoning all humanitarian principles."[504]

In early January 2004 the Sudanese government said its troops were trying to secure deliveries of humanitarian aid to people caught up in the Darfur conflict. The ministry of humanitarian affairs said a government delegation had completed a nine-day tour of West and South Darfur states during which it had examined the obstacles hindering the delivery of assistance to parts of the region. The ministry stated that the obstacles included insecurity and instability. The delegation said the government armed forces "are working to tighten their grip on the situation" which would ease the delivery of relief supplies to some areas. The delegation instructed the offices of the

Humanitarian Aid Commission (HAC) in Darfur to speed up distribution of relief supplies.[505]

On 10 February 2004, the United Nations said that aid access had improved within Darfur. The UN spokesman for the humanitarian coordinator for Sudan, Ben Parker, stated: "There are signs and indications that we will be able to reach more places in the coming weeks and the government is assuring us that the access situation will improve." The government had told aid agencies that it had opened 10 new corridors in Darfur for relief convoys to move through.[506] Egeland described the agreement with the Sudanese government to provide improved aid access to Darfur as a breakthrough.[507] As part of the UN-government agreement, on 18 February 2004, the UN announced that a 13-person UN logistical team arrived in Darfur to assess humanitarian needs in the area. The team would assess aid requirements in the cities of Nyala, al-Geneina and al-Fasher as UN agencies work to deliver and pre-position food, water and medical supplies for around 250,000 displaced people.[508]

Rebel attacks on relief convoys continued. A senior UN official in Sudan stated in February 2004 that rebels have made it too dangerous to take aid into parts of Darfur. Aid convoys were still being attacked by armed groups. The spokesman also cited the danger of landmines."[509] In March 2004, the Sudanese government held rebels responsible for blocking deliveries of humanitarian aid in Darfur. Deputy Foreign Minister al-Tigani Salih Fidhail said: "The armed groups constitute the main obstacle to the delivery of relief in Darfur." He called on the international community to hold the rebels "fully responsible".[510]

A high-level UN humanitarian assessment mission, under the leadership of World Food Programme Executive Director James Morris, visited Darfur in late April 2004. Rebel attacks on aid workers continued. At the same time the SLA attacked a humanitarian convoy and abducted and murdered a traditional leader of the Zaghawa, Abdel Rahman Mohammain, whose communities would have received this assistance.[511] The International Crisis Group noted continuing rebel obstruction in May 2004: "The SLA issued several statements in the first half of May to the effect that it will refuse to allow into areas it controls any humanitarian relief that originates in government-controlled areas – where most UN and international NGOs are based."[512]

In early June 2004, Associated Press reported the abduction by rebels of 16 aid workers. Those kidnapped worked for the International Rescue Committee, Save the Children UK, the UN Office for the Coordination of Humanitarian Affairs (OCHA), United Nation's World Food Programme, UNICEF, the Norwegian Refugee Council, ECHO, the Humanitarian Aid Office of the European Commission, and Sudan's Humanitarian Aid Commission. They were stopped while they were conducting assessments to prepare the way for delivery of relief assistance for displaced people in the vicinity of Al Hilief in North Darfur despite driving vehicles clearly bearing the UN insignia.[513] They were eventually released by the rebels. The UN Emergency Relief Coordinator, Jan Egeland, condemned the detention and delayed release of the 16 aid workers as "totally unacceptable" and "contradicts solemn promises" made by the SLA. Egeland said: "Too much time has already been lost in this race against the clock to save more than a million lives threatened by indiscriminate violence, starvation and disease." The UN stated that "[t]he incident not only threatened the safety and security of humanitarian workers, but has interrupted and delayed aid to desperately needy civilians in Darfur."[514]

On 8 June 2004, Agence France-Presse reported that rebels had seized nine trucks loaded with relief items, medicines and tents on the road between Nyala and al-Fasher. The rebels abducted four of the drivers and beat a fifth one.[515] Later that month, rebels attacked a humanitarian relief convoy in Darfur, stealing 57 tons of UN food aid. The Sudanese minister of humanitarian affairs said: "These types of rebel action are the most serious threat to the humanitarian and security situation."[516]

In the first week of July, the SLA attacked 26 aid workers, working for Save the Children UK, delivering emergency assistance in northern Darfur. They also stole six vehicles and a large amount of cash. On 13 July 2004, the British government publicly urged Sudanese rebels to return the stolen vehicles.[517] It was reported on 12 July 2004 that rebels had attacked several towns in north Darfur. These had included Al Liayet, Al Towaisha and Um Keddada. Several civilians had been killed, and a judge and bank manager had been kidnapped. The government of North Darfur stated that there had been over 50 rebel violations of the Ndjamena ceasefire agreement.[518] At about the same time rebel militias were also accused of kidnapping 32 children during attacks on several villages.[519]

There were a number of systematic rebel attacks on aid workers in August 2004. The African Union confirmed that, on 22 August, SLA forces had abducted humanitarian affairs workers on their way to a meeting in the Abgaragil area, and that on 23 August rebels had abducted medical aid workers engaged in an inoculation campaign in Kutum.[520] At the end of August 2004, Darfur rebels abducted six aid workers in north Darfur. Three were from the World Food Programme and three from the Sudanese Red Crescent. WFP condemned the targeting of humanitarian workers. WFP Senior Deputy Executive Director Jean-Jacques Graisse said that WFP was "delighted that our people, as well as those working for the Sudanese Red Crescent, have been freed unharmed. This is not, however, the first time that humanitarian workers have been targeted in Darfur. At a time when all agencies are battling the rainy season, poor infrastructure and an unpredictable security environment to deliver desperately needed humanitarian assistance, this kind of incident can only further worsen the plight of the needy in Darfur. We call upon all armed groups in the region to stop targeting those involved in humanitarian work and allow them to do their duty without fear of intimidation. Any continuation or escalation of incidents such as the one just resolved is likely to have far-reaching consequences for the relief operation."[521] On 31 August 2004, JEM insurgents detained 22 Sudanese health workers near Nyala in south Darfur.[522] In late August, the United Nations humanitarian coordinator for Sudan, Manuel Aranda da Silva, stated that he was encouraged by Sudan's actions to improve the humanitarian situation in Darfur.[523]

In October 2004, the Sudanese government's chief negotiator at Abuja, Dr Majzoub al-Khalifa, warned that the rebels were seeking to worsen affairs in Darfur: "They need to stimulate all these governments and all these organizations on their side by making the situation worse on the ground."[524] October also saw rebel threats to kill aid workers.[525] Two other Save the Children workers, one British and one Sudanese, were killed in October by a landmine laid by SLA rebels.[526] The United Nations special envoy to Sudan, Jan Pronk, unambiguously confirmed rebel involvement in these deaths: "It was the rebels who are responsible for attacking relief workers and convoys, they are responsible for...landmines which killed two relief workers."[527]

That same month, the United Nations reported that "UN spokesman Fred Eckhard said in New York that the operations of humanitarian agencies in

North Darfur State have become limited because some roads remain closed to them. Other areas have become dangerous for transporting aid supplies. Last Saturday, forces from the rebel Sudan Liberation Army (SLA) hijacked seven commercial trucks on a road about 120 kilometres east of the state capital El Fasher."[528] A spokeswoman for the UN Advance Mission in Sudan (UNAMIS) stated that "[t]he repeated ceasefire violations of the past month have had a very serious impact on the UN's ability to deliver humanitarian assistance to affected populations."[529]

In mid-November 2004, the United Nations said that nearly 200,000 needy people, especially in the mountainous Jebel Marra area in central Darfur and the northern part of North Darfur, had been cut off from relief aid because of escalating violence. The German press agency reported: "The U.N. said tension in the region had risen as rebel groups, in particular the Sudan Liberation Army (SLA), had increased their operations in an apparent attempt to claim more territory." The UN Humanitarian Coordinator for Sudan, Manuel Aranda da Silva, said an estimated 150,000 people have been driven from their homes due to the escalating violence during the past month. The UN also reported several attacks on buses and aid convoys around Darfur. Travellers had been abducted and even killed and vehicles looted by the attackers.[530] By the end of November, *The New York Times* was reporting that the rebels had been "sharply ratcheting up attacks" which in turn was preventing relief work.[531]

In November 2004 the rebels were accused of attacking a joint WHO/Ministry of Health medical team. One doctor was killed and four other health workers were injured. The team was also robbed.[532] In the same month both the Dublin-based GOAL aid agency and the Spanish branch of Médecins Sans Frontières were forced to withdraw their staff from the Jebel Marra area in central Darfur after "repeated" rebel acts of aggression targeting the humanitarian personnel and the relief supplies intended for people in need.[533] Both MSF and GOAL complained that rebels had attacked their vehicles.[534] On 27 November 2004, *The New York Times* revealed the degree of rebel obstruction of aid delivery and aid workers: "On the ground, many aid workers, too fearful of giving their names for fear of jeopardizing their work, say that rebel officials have made unreasonable demands on aid groups operating in their territory, at one point insisting on a certain number of expatriates to accompany Sudanese staff, whom rebels distrust as potential government spies. Aid workers have also been detained in rebel territory in recent months."[535]

Amnesty International noted a similar pattern of rebel activity: "over the past two months, a number of World Food Programme commercial trucks have been attacked in South Darfur."[536] It also noted that: "After Sudan Liberation Army forces reportedly hijacked seven commercial trucks east of al-Fasher on 23 October, the road between al-Fasher and Um Kedada in North Darfur was closed and has only just been re-opened. Because of heavy fighting in the area, the road between al-Fasher and Kutum remains a no-go zone."

In early December 2004, *The Christian Science Monitor* confirmed the results of rebel action: "[R]ecently they've stepped up attacks and have even looted international aid convoys. The violence adds to the instability – and to aid groups' growing inability to help the displaced millions."[537] Two Save the Children aid workers, members of a mobile medical clinic, were murdered by rebels on 12 December 2004. They were deliberately shot dead in an attack on an aid convoy. The director of Save the Children's international operations said: "We deplore this brutal killing of humanitarian workers in Darfur." The charity said its vehicles were clearly marked as belonging to Save the Children.[538] The African Union and United Nations confirmed the SLA's responsibility for the deaths of the aid workers. In addition to the murdered aid workers, one other worker was injured and three are missing. African Union officer Nigerian Major-General Festus Okonkwo stated: "SLA was involved in the attack as two Land Rovers belonging to Save the Children (UK) were recovered from [the] SLA camp in Jurof."[539] Rebel involvement in the murders was established by the UN.[540] In mid-December the United Nations suspended aid operations in South Darfur in December in the wake of these murders.[541] *The Guardian* reported that an aid worker was shot on the same road in the summer but survived.

The then UN Envoy to Sudan, Jan Pronk, said of the rebel attacks and interference with aid deliveries: "They have to stop. Otherwise they are blocking access to the very people they say they are protecting."[542] In December 2004, the Sudanese government made the obvious point that "[w]here the rebels create insecurity, it is not the government denying access."[543] The United Nations *Darfur Humanitarian Profile* released in December 2004 stated, for example, that: "Despite prevailing insecurity in the three Darfur States, 79%

of Darfur conflict affected population is currently accessible to UN humanitarian workers. *Most of the underserved areas remain rebel-held, many of which have not been accessible to UN agencies because of a series of security incidents and a delay in obtaining SLA agreement and understanding of humanitarian rules and principles laid out in agreements.*"[544] [Emphasis added] The rebels are endangering the lives of hundreds of thousands of civilians already malnourished and badly affected by the conflict in Darfur.

On 15 December 2004, the United Nations reported further rebel attacks on food aid convoys: "WFP reports that food distribution has been seriously disrupted by ongoing insecurity. On 18 December 2004, the SLA detained a total of 13 trucks. Five of them were released on the same day but the rest were kept until 21 Dec…the disruption affected food distribution in Marla and Sania Fundu. Food assistance has also been halted in Labado, Al Juruf, Muhujarija, Khor Abechi, Manawashi, Mershing, Rokero and Gildo Labado."[545]

On 22 December 2004, *The New York Times* also reported that: "The chaotic situation in Darfur has hampered the work of agencies trying to reach the estimated 2.3 million people who rely on aid to survive. Aid organizations in the region say rebels have been attacking convoys carrying aid and goods along the road between Nyala and El Fasher, where two Save the Children UK workers were killed recently."[546]

Ongoing rebel attacks, particularly that on the market town of Ghubaysh on 27 December, had disastrous effects on the delivery of food aid to affected communities. The United Nations noted:

> The World Food Programme (WFP) has suspended food convoys to the Darfur States following a large scale attack yesterday by rebel forces on the market town of Ghubaysh…WFP has halted three convoys of seventy trucks carrying more than 1,300 MT of WFP food aid destined for El Fasher and Nyala…this recent insecurity has cut off assistance to some 260,000 people who will miss their December rations in the South Darfur as well as eastern parts of West Darfur…Notably, it is the second attack by the SLA since 19 December when the Government of Sudan agreed to an immediate cessation of hostilities. This latest insecurity has serious consequences for the UN and NGOs operations in Darfur, as it

effectively blocks overland access from central Sudan to the Darfur region. This has a particular impact on WFP's provision of life-saving food aid, as it must rely heavily on road deliveries to support its Darfur humanitarian operation. The United Nations is also concerned about reports that Darfur-based rebel movement forces have stolen in the last two weeks thirteen commercial all terrain trucks leased to WFP, loaded with urgently required WFP food commodities for the affected people of Darfur dedicated to the transportation of food aid to Darfur... The latest thefts are in addition to multiple losses of commercial and aid agency vehicles to armed groups in recent months. More alarming are reports that the rebel groups that stole them may now [be] using some of these trucks for military purposes.[547]

A World Food Programme spokeswoman said: "The attacks followed a week of insecurity in Darfur and this has caused difficulties, in terms of providing assistance. It will delay urgently required food for 260,000 people in South Darfur and the eastern parts of West Darfur."[548] AMIS noted that the rebel attack on Ghubaysh was "the second carried out by the rebels since 19 December, when the Sudanese government agreed to an immediate cessation of hostilities". The UN Envoy to Sudan concluded: "The problems of Darfur cannot be solved through military means. The parties to the conflict have to live up to their commitments, including their responsibility to ensure the safety and wellbeing of their own people and their unhindered access to humanitarian assistance."[549]

The rebels' murder of aid workers has served to intensify the humanitarian crisis in Darfur with the ultimate rebel aim of forcing some sort of military intervention. It has gone hand-in-hand with the SLA's deliberate breaking of ceasefire agreements with attacks in northern Darfur. This precipitated the current humanitarian crisis in Darfur. Associated Press reported that: "The United Nations has condemned a rebel attack in Darfur province, saying it violates a cease-fire agreement and jeopardises the lives of tens of thousands of people who will not receive aid because of the fighting."[550] The international community has roundly condemned these rebel actions.[551] These systematic rebel attacks have placed hundreds of thousands of war-affected communities in danger of starvation. The Director of Save the Children UK, Mike Aaronson, stated that: "We are devastated that we are unable to continue to offer health care, nutritional support, child protection and education to the approximately 250,000 children and family members served by our current programs. However, we just cannot continue to expose our staff to the unacceptable risks they face as they go about their humanitarian duties in Darfur."[552]

Erwin Van Der Borght, deputy director of Amnesty International's Africa programme, has also noted the effect of rebel attacks: "Attacks knowingly and intentionally directed against personnel involved in humanitarian assistance in armed conflict may constitute war crimes. Insecurity within Darfur hinders movement to whole districts, so that food, medicine and other non-food items can not be brought in. This increases enormously the sufferings of an already vulnerable population." Amnesty International noted that "After such attacks, the district or road is likely to be declared a no-go area for international humanitarian staff for several days" and pointed out that it stopped aid reaching "thousands" of displaced people.[553]

On 31 December 2004, *The Daily Telegraph* reported that SLA attacks in December had "forced the United Nations to suspend supply convoys into Darfur": "The SLA attacks seemed to be designed to isolate Darfur. The rebels struck police stations in the town of Ghibaish and al-Majrour in the neighbouring province of West Kordofan, killing 99 people. The ensuing battle closed Darfur's main communication artery."[554]

In his January 2005 report on Darfur, the United Nations Secretary-General reported on what he termed a "new trend" in the pattern of attacks on, and harassment of, international aid workers: "While previous incidents have only been aimed at looting supplies and goods, December has seen acts of murder and vicious assaults on staff, forcing some agencies to leave Darfur."[555] The Secretary-General's February 2005 assessment of the preceding six month period with regard to the rebel movements was also bleak: "Their attacks on police have increased and often seemed intended to invite retaliation. These attacks and provocation have at times indirectly impaired humanitarian access. Some rebel groups have directly impeded humanitarian work by looting cars and trucks and putting pressure on, or even abducting national staff of humanitarian organizations. Many of these actions have severely reduced delivery of assistance."[556]

In his January 2005 report the Secretary-General noted that Save the Children UK had decided to cease its operations in Darfur and to withdraw its 350 staff members due to the murder of four of its staff by Darfur rebels.[557] In January, the United Nations further noted:

The level of humanitarian access has continued to decline in SLM/A- and JEM-controlled areas due to the frequent lack of cooperation by field commanders and a lack of communication between them and their leadership. While work does continue in some of these areas, much more assistance is required and cannot be provided while SLM/A and JEM commanders continue to restrict movements and place unnecessary and impossible conditions on humanitarian agencies.[558]

In January 2005 the UN Secretary-General noted that "rebel-held areas in north and south Darfur remain the least accessible for humanitarian agencies."[559]

In February 2005, the UN Secretary-General reported that: "Rebel groups have also detained and harassed humanitarian workers and confiscated humanitarian assets, such as vehicles and water drills. Allegations of political and proselytizing activity directed at NGOs, largely unfounded, are counterproductive and risk undermining the critical efforts of those brave and resourceful organizations that work together with the Sudanese to address the humanitarian crisis in Darfur."[560] He also stated that, on two occasions in February 2005, clearly marked UN WFP helicopters came under heavy machine-gun fire passing by Siyah en route to Malha Wells in North Darfur. The SLA admitted that they had fired on the second occasion and the Secretary-General stated that "one may assume its responsibility for the first incident as well." He further noted that African Union peacekeepers had come under fire on no fewer than seven occasions in February: "No excuse or explanation offered by the SLM/A leadership can possibly justify their forces firing on aircraft or vehicles that are clearly marked as belonging to the United Nations, the African Union or relief agencies and organizations. I condemn these acts."[561]

In his March 2005 report, the UN Secretary-General stated that "Relief workers continue to face dangerous challenges. On 21 February, seven staff members of an international NGO were detained overnight by the National Movement for Reform and Development (NMRD) rebels in Arosharo, near the Jebel Moon area..."[562] In his April 2005 report, the UN noted that access to SLA-held Dar Zaghawa in North Darfur was held up for three weeks. The Secretary-General also noted that

> incidents targeting humanitarian supplies and personnel on major roads have rendered the movement of supplies erratic and inconsistent, affecting assistance to beneficiaries. A peak in the number of attacks on commercial trucks used by WFP was reported in March, especially on the two major road routes into Darfur. A sizeable proportion of these security incidents have been carried out by SLA elements; the balance are attributable to bandits or militias...The Government of the Sudan also took steps to move in convoy from Ed Da'ein to Nyala a backlog of 250 trucks that had built up because of the insecurity.[563]

The African Union noted in April 2005 that "the armed Movements have been involved in a number of attacks against commercial convoys land humanitarian organizations, as well as continued acts of harassment of relief workers." The Chairperson of the Commission of the African Union urged the rebels "to put an end to these actions, which run contrary to the letter and spirit of the Agreements they had signed. Failure by the Movements to take immediate and remedial action can only but cast a doubt on their willingness or ability to end the conflict in Darfur and the suffering of the civilian population."[564]

The UN reported that in May 2005 the rebel movements became "increasingly obstructionist...towards relief workers...SLA, in particular, was involved in a number of incidents that delayed or diverted the passage of humanitarian supplies or personnel."[565]

The United Nations reported that in May the "SLA ambushed several convoys and vehicles belonging to or engaged by humanitarian organizations along the Kabkabiya-El Fashir road...During the reporting period, continued insecurity and banditry on the Ed Daein-Nyala road (Southern Darfur) seriously hampered access for humanitarian relief operations. Trucks belonging to the World Food Programme (WFP) were looted regularly by armed bandits on this road during the beginning of May, and two drivers were murdered on 8 May. In addition...five non-governmental organization staff members were abducted and held for three hours by suspected SLA elements in Sanamanaga in Southern Darfur."[566]

In his July 2005 report on Darfur, the UN Secretary-General noted that the rebel movements were "actively seeking to hinder relief...activities."[567] The UN reported that SLA and JEM rebels attacked humanitarian convoys in the month of June.[568]

The Secretary-General's August 2005 report stated that rebel activities were "jeopardizing humanitarian activities". He noted that: "The abduction of national staff of non-governmental organizations reached alarming proportions at the beginning of July, with 10 members of non-governmental organizations being held by SLA. Six people have been released, but four individuals abducted in Western Darfur are still being detained. The armed movements also abducted teams from the Ministry of Health carrying out polio vaccinations in Northern and Southern Darfur. Though they subsequently released the drivers, they have not returned the cars. As a result, this vaccination campaign was not able to reach people living in some areas where SLA is active."[569]

Rebel attacks on humanitarian workers and vehicles escalated in September and October 2005. In mid-October, the UN spokesperson in Khartoum noted that "the issue of looting and banditry is taking quite serious proportions. We have been monitoring this phenomenon since it started and I can tell you that I remember days when we could have one incident of banditry in one week in the whole of Darfur. Now we have lost count, and when I look at our reporting, I can't tell you how many because there are so many."[570]

Reporting in May 2006, Human Rights Watch stated that "Rebel attacks against humanitarian convoys have been a persistent problem for well over a year." It reported that "According to several humanitarian sources, the rebels have regularly looted humanitarian convoys, particularly vehicles. Human Rights Watch has received numerous reports of incidents in North and South Darfur in which vehicles, particularly rental cars and trucks used by humanitarian organizations, were stolen by SLA forces." Human Rights Watch also noted that a May 2005 UN Security Council report on Darfur stated that the frequency with which SLA and JEM fighters hijacked commercial, private and NGO vehicles suggested that the attacks had the approval of rebel leaders.[571] Human Rights Watch noted that rebel groups were conducting attacks on humanitarian convoys and aid workers that have diverted food assistance and hindered access to the population in need, and that "this interference appears to be increasing". In April 2006, for example, the UN special envoy, Jan Pronk, threatened to suspend UN aid to 450,000 people in northern Darfur "unless rebel attacks against United Nations and other relief operations...stop immediately."[572] The UN has concluded that the rebels were taking humanitarian vehicles with the aim of converting them into battlefield platforms.[573]

In addition to regularly attacking aid convoys, Darfur rebels have also sought to interfere with humanitarian air missions. In November 2005, for example, the NMRD threatened to shoot down UN helicopters on humanitarian missions in areas of West Darfur, including Seleah and Jebel Moon. Unable to visit by road for security reasons, aid workers were therefore unable to visit Seleah, near the border with Chad, for several months. The UN Humanitarian Air Service (UNHAS) also had to suspend flights to other areas north of al-Geneina, West Darfur (including Sirba and Kulbus) following similar, credible threats.[574]

In October 2006, the UN reported that

> Often the most important factor for decreased access [to the affected populations] is the intolerably high incidence of increasingly violent hijackings of humanitarian vehicles with a debilitating effect on the organizations' transport means. Between July and September, 21 humanitarian vehicles have been hijacked and 31 convoys ambushed and looted, during which six humanitarian workers and two AU Military Observers were killed...Various factions of the rebel movements have often resorted to the hijacking of humanitarian vehicles, to be used in combat.[575]

These hijackings had meant that aid organisations have had to withdraw from affected areas of Darfur. As but one example, due to the hijacking at gunpoint of five of their vehicles in August 2006, humanitarian groups had to withdraw from Tawila in North Darfur.[576] This trend continued into 2007. The April 2007 *Darfur Humanitarian Profile* once again noted that

A greatly debilitating factor for humanitarian outreach remains the intolerably high incidence of increasingly violent hijackings of humanitarian vehicles. Between January and March, 21 humanitarian vehicles have been hijacked and five attempts thwarted, during which 18 humanitarian staff members were temporarily abducted. In the same period, 15 convoys were ambushed and/or looted, and one Ministry of Health nurse wounded by gunshot.[577]

The report also noted that since May 2006, 97 aid vehicles had been hijacked and 79 convoys ambushed. Various factions of the rebel movements as well as Chadian rebels have often been involved in the hijacking.[578]

In August 2007, rebel commanders, meeting in Tanzania, pledged to stop attacks on aid organisations and AU peacekeepers, and to allow free access by humanitarian groups to Darfur's affected communities.[579] Rebel attacks on aid workers and vehicle continued nevertheless, to the extent that Oxfam, a British aid organisation with a very large presence serving hundreds of thousands of civilians in Darfur, warned that it might have to cease operations in the region. The Sudanese government urged aid organisations to consider the option of military escorts for their convoys. A government spokesman stated that "In so many cases, we offered to protect the convoys of the U.N. agencies and international agencies operating in Darfur and this offer has been turned down so many times, because they see that if they accept it this will affect their neutrality…But, whenever we are asked to render this service we are ready." The spokesman also noted that aid agencies were reluctant to publicly identify the rebels as having carried out the attacks: "we always prefer that any organizations who are attacked to indicate who attacked them, because people might think that, if an NGO did not mention where and when and who attacked it, it might be understood that the government is involved in one way or another, which is not true."[580]

Into early 2007 it became apparent that Sudanese government bureaucracy was impeding the unfettered activities of humanitarian organisations, to the extent that one NGO discontinued all its activities in Darfur. On 28 March, a new Joint Communiqué was signed between the UN and the Government of Sudan. This established a Tripartite Joint Technical Committee and a High Level Committee made up of representatives of the Government, UN and

NGOs to monitor the implementation of the Communiqué, especially the envisaged "fast track procedures".[581]

Rebel Militarisation of IDP camps

The rebel movements have also extended their activities into IDP camps within government-administered areas in Darfur. They have launched attacks from within camps on policemen protecting IDPs, have encouraged unrest amongst IDPs and have discouraged IDPs from returning back to the places of origin. Rebel agitators have also discouraged attempts by humanitarian organisations to obtain accurate figures for people within IDP camps. In January 2005, for example, the African Union placed on record that the rebels were active within IDP camps, activities which endangered civilians and aid workers: "[I]t is worth mentioning reports of an increase in the recruitment and control of IDPs by SLM/A and JEM, which is undermining the safety of those populations and that of humanitarian and human rights workers."[582] The UN Secretary-General also noted that the SLA had abducted and threatened humanitarian personnel at the Zam Zam IDP camp near al-Fasher in North Darfur.

In August 2005, the UN stated with regard to unrest within IDP camps in West Darfur that:

> Insecurity in camps for internally displaced persons in Western Darfur is a major concern. On 8 July, the registration process was violently disrupted in seven out of eight such camps around Geneina and 10 humanitarian workers were wounded. Violent incidents again took place on 16 July during a food distribution in Mornei camp, where exchanges of gunfire between armed elements and Government police killed 2 and injured 15 to 20 people. Most humanitarian staff were forced to evacuate the camp. On both occasions, there was strong evidence of incitement by sheikhs within the camp, whose manipulation of the ration-card system is threatened by the registration process. As a result, the delivery of humanitarian relief activities has been seriously affected.[583]

Rebels have continued to use the IDP camps as a base for attacks on policemen. In August 2007, as one more example, gunmen attacked a police post at the al-Salam camp in southern Darfur. A UN humanitarian aid official stated that "We are concerned by the increasing number of attacks...and the presence of armed men in IDP camps."[584]

It is equally clear that it is in the rebel movements' interest for the numbers of IDPs in camps to continue to be artificially inflated. In October 2005, the UN reported that the registration in the al-Geneina camps, town and surrounding villages had been resolved with the assistance of the government. The UN noted that the problem had been one in which "corrupt internally displaced person leaders had misappropriated humanitarian assistance for many months".[585] It also noted that a number of camps, including Kalma camp in North Darfur, still needed to undergo a re-registration process.

The IDP camps, administered by the UN and international NGOs, not the government, have continued to become politicised, militarised and dominated by rebel movements. In September 2006, for example, the UN reported that "the militarization of some internally displaced person camps continued unabated." It noted that members of two SLA factions had harassed civilians within camps in northern and southern Sudan.[586] In January 2007, the Darfur Humanitarian Profile confirmed "an increased presence of armed groups within camps...The protection of IDPs in camps has been further undermined by a reduced number of AU patrols around the IDP gatherings and decreased [Government of Sudan] police presence inside the camps."[587] In October 2007, *The Guardian* reported the presence of small arms, heavy-machine guns and RPG-7 rocket launchers inside the huge Kalma camp in South Darfur state. The newspaper also reported that Fur activists had set up a military organisation in the camp and that there had been clashes between Fur and Zaghawa residents resulting in the death of 17 people. The UN reported that attempts by the army and police and AMIS to enter the camp to restore order had been abandoned after resistance and that the camps were considered too dangerous for aid agencies and outsiders.[588]

Chapter Four

THE "JANJAWEED" AND DARFUR

Comprehensive, forcible disarmament is hazardous at best, impossible at worst. Before effective disarmament (or more realistically, regulation of armaments) can take place, a workable definition of the Janjawiid is needed.

The Justice Africa human rights organisation [589]

In Darfur, Janjaweed is a word that means everything and nothing.

The Reuters Sudan Correspondent [590]

One of the biggest problems facing any analysis of the Darfur conflict, and subsequently any attempt to resolve it, is the extent to which the international community, responding to a combination of poor analysis, shallow media reporting or, in some instances, straightforward propaganda projections of one sort or another, has reduced the crisis to one or two images and demands. The "Janjaweed" phenomena is one such image and with it comes a demand, that the government of Sudan immediately stop all "Janjaweed" activity and disarm these people.

The simple fact is that no-one has arrived at an objective definition of the term "Janjaweed". Darfur analyst Ali Haggar, writing in Alex de Waal's *War in Darfur and the Search for Peace*, has stated that "There is no agreement on the origin or definition of the word 'Janjawiid.'"[591] It has seemingly been used as a blanket term to describe any armed nomadic tribesman in Darfur today, and particularly anyone involved in attacks on "African" communities in the region. The United Nations International Commission of Inquiry on Darfur adopted a typically questionable definition of "Janjaweed". It noted that there were two "precisions" in a definition of "Janjaweed", that attackers were Arab and armed with modern weapons. The Commission further noted that outside of these "precisions" it is "probably impossible to define the 'Janjaweed'". The Commission also stated that "where victims describe their attackers as Janjaweed, these persons might be from a tribal Arab militia, from the PDF or from some other entity..."[592] It is clear that the Commission, by its own admission, followed a muddled and subjective rather than an objective definition of what constituted "Janjaweed".

The difficulties in coming to a definition of "Janjaweed" have been addressed by other UN observers. The UN media service has described the "Janjaweed" as being made up of "Sudanese and Chadian horse and camel-riding Arab nomads, opportunists and 'criminals'".[593] The team leader for the UN Office for the Coordination of Humanitarian Affairs in North Darfur, Niels Scott, commented in November 2004: "The Janjaweed takes many different forms. It could be a local tribal issue, or it could be plain banditry. Or it could be plain banditry. It could be profiteering...This Janjaweed business – I shy away a bit from it. Janjaweed – as an historical concept – has been around for years. What we are seeing now is...criminality." Asked if the lawlessness was being directed from Khartoum, Niels Scott said: "There's no direction."[594] His views have been echoed by other relief workers. The field coordinator for the Irish aid agency GOAL in North Darfur, Terri Morris, has noted that: "There is a lot of banditry in the whole of Darfur, also in rebel-controlled areas and if you ask people who are responsible they say 'janjaweed', which means in the rebel areas that the 'janjaweed' are in fact rebel fighters."[595] Her predecessor, Fionna Gannon, similarly noted: "They (the Arab nomads) say that they are the most despised people in the world because of the way the western media portrayed the conflict. Not every Arab nomad on a camel with a Kalashnikov is a janjaweed, far from it. I don't believe that the Janjaweed are under government control."[596]

There can be no simple reading of the issue.[597] The difficulty in adequately defining the term has been seen as a problem by Human Rights Watch. In its publication *Empty Promises? Continuing Abuses in Darfur, Sudan*, it observed:

[I]t is increasingly clear that the term 'Janjaweed,' while used by victims to describe any armed attacker, is in fact a misnomer, and that there are at least two types of forces encompassed by the description: 1) the government-backed militias used as proxy forces in the government's military campaign; and 2) opportunistic armed elements taking advantage of the total collapse of law and order to settle scores, loot and raid cattle and livestock.[598]

UN Special Envoy Jan Pronk has also noted the problem with regard to definitions of what makes up the Janjaweed. He has said that the government "have a different understanding of [who make up] the Janjawid from the international community". Pronk also observed that "the IDPs call everybody Janjawid". Pronk admitted that "[t]he government has indeed taken some steps to…disarm the officially mobilized persons in the Popular Defense Force. They, through talks, also tried to control – with some success – militias which have stayed closely related to Arab tribes, in a reconciliation process. They do not control the real Janjawid, who they call outlaws, who they cannot stop, they say." He also pointed out one of the major impediments on any government action on the janjaweed. He admitted that the international community "do not want the [Sudanese] military to become active…to take action." Pronk had added that the government have said "if we can't use the military – our police are not strong enough." [599]

Pronk has also observed that the international community "also need to talk, at a certain moment, with Arab tribes, who do have control over their militia, including the Janjawid, in order to address some of the concerns of these Arab tribes, because they also have concerns, which are being used as a legitimization, by these groups, to take up arms."[600]

Darfur is an ecologically fragile area and had already been subject to growing – and often armed – conflict over access to water and pastures. The war has greatly exacerbated previously existing tensions. In perhaps the most objective reading of the crisis in Darfur, the UN media service observed: "The conflict pits farming communities against nomads who have aligned themselves with the militia groups – for whom the raids are a way of life – in stiff competition for land and resources. The militias, known as the Janjaweed, attack in large numbers on horseback and camels and are driving the farmers from their land, often pushing them towards town centres."[601] There is also no doubt that these militias, and criminal gangs, have exploited the security gap which opened up in Darfur following the murder by rebels of over 685 policemen and the destruction of dozens of police stations in a region the size of France or California in which law enforcement infrastructure was already badly stretched. The International Crisis Group has noted that "the term 'Janjaweed' has been used for decades to describe bandits who prey on the rural populations through cattle rustling and highway robbery. These criminals were generally rejected by their communities because of their contempt for tribal codes and communal values."[602] The ICG also reported that a senior Chadian official had stated that "Chadian Arabs can establish themselves in Darfur and use the Janjaweed as a cover for their anti-Déby activities."[603]

The scale of the violence in Darfur, even before the outbreak of rebellion in 2003, had led to Khartoum introducing special measures, including the declaration of a state of emergency and the establishment by presidential decree of eight special criminal courts to deal with offences such as murder, tribal clashes, armed robbery, arson and the smuggling of weapons.[604]

The UN media service has reported "that there was nothing new about tribal clashes between nomads of Arabic extraction and village farmers belonging to local African tribes in Darfur, but these days they have become much more deadly because the raiders were better armed." A foreign diplomat noted: "The Janjawid have kept their traditional values and ways of living. They do the same as they used to: they steal to get. Only this time, their weapons are more sophisticated."[605]

It has also become apparent that the Darfur issue has been caught up in the sort of propaganda and misinformation that has characterised previous coverage of Sudan. Several commentators appear to have opted for a partisan or lazy analysis of events in Darfur, seemingly unable to resist projecting the image of government-supported "Arab" – "Janjaweed" – militias attacking "African" villagers (and in doing so often merely echoing questionable rebel claims). The allegations that the government of Sudan is using militias to launch genocidal attacks on African communities falls at one of the first hurdles. As Haggar notes, "Shortly after the SLA attacked al Fashir in April 2003, the Sudan Armed Forces began a major recruitment drive for the Popular Defence Forces. Both Arab and non-Arab tribes were targeted."[606] This has also been confirmed by Julie Flint who has observed that "In the first months, General Ismat al

Zain, head of western command, armed Arabs and non-Arabs alike."[607] It is somewhat unbelievable that those committing genocide would have actively sought to militarily train and arm those it was intending to exterminate.

The Sudanese authorities have repeatedly and consistently denied that they are sponsoring "Janjaweed" gunmen in Darfur. Sudanese leaders from the President and ministers downwards have described "Janjaweed" gunmen as "outlaws".[608] The then Sudanese foreign minister, Dr Mustapha Osman Ismail, has noted: "The problem is the word Janjaweed has become a coverall for so many things. There are militias that are outside the rule of law, and this is one of the things we are going to crack down on."[609] Simplistic readings of events in Darfur claim that Khartoum is in control of all those groups labelled as "Janjaweed" – this despite increasing evidence that these forces are out of control.[610]

The Sudanese national commission of inquiry into human rights abuses during the Darfur crisis also highlighted the difficulties surrounding the definition of "Janjaweed": "There was all-round agreement that the meaning and connotation of the term 'the Janjaweed' is obscure and that opinions differ as to how it should be understood and interpreted. That disagreement now constitutes the primary focus of all the decisions and resolutions promulgated by foreign entities with respect to the Sudan."[611] There have also been several accounts of how nomadic communities have suffered through the unjustified and inaccurate use of the "Janjaweed" label. A UN media report noted that "[due] to the increasingly polarised political atmosphere, many of Darfur's residents equate Arab nomads with the notorious 'Janjawid'." An aid worker observed that: "People confuse the nomads with the Janjawid. They are considered the same – the same entity – but they're not." Arab nomads stressed that "there was no relation between the nomadic defence groups and the Janjawid, as the latter were mere bandits who attacked farmers and nomads, alike." A member of the Aregat – a clan belonging to the "Arab" Rezeigat tribe – stated that: "The Aregat have been attacked by the Janjawid many times. They are thieves. They don't differentiate between the tribes. When they see the opportunity to steal, they will." [612]

Assertions that the government controls the "Janjaweed" – and that it can turn their activities off and on like a tap – have distorted the reality of events. Human rights groups, for example, have confirmed Janjaweed attacks on policemen and police stations. Julie Flint, for example, in a report for Human Rights Watch, has also reported on a Janjaweed attack on the police station at Terbeba. She does not mention what happened to the policemen inside, but states the police station was burned down.[613] Amnesty International has noted the fact that policemen are often targeted for attack by Janjaweed gangs.[614]

The UN Commission of Inquiry on Darfur noted examples of Janjaweed attacks on police, reporting, for example, that victims of attacks stated that "the police were indeed targeted during the attacks on the villages" and that they "mainly blamed the Janjaweed for these actions".[615] The Commission reported that there have been instances where Janjaweed gunmen have attacked and killed policemen defending villagers from Janjaweed attack. It recorded, for example, that Janjaweed raiders killed 17 policemen in an attack on Kailek, in South Darfur.[616] Sudan's national commission of inquiry confirmed that numerous policemen had been killed in attacks by "Janjaweed" gunmen.[617] The US government also reported in September 2005 that "Janjaweed" gunmen attacked al-Geneina "to confront Government of Sudan (GOS) police and take hostages, in retaliation for a September 19 incident in which GOS police killed one jingaweit and apprehended another during an attempted truck robbery outside Geneina. GOS police and jingaweit clashed in the Geneina city market". The Janjaweed gunmen freed their gang member from police custody.[618]

One clear example, amongst many, of a "Janjaweed" attack and a government response, was that involving an attack by between 800 and 1,000 heavily armed members of a nomadic group that attacked the Shattayia area in North Darfur on 10 February 2004. This attack was against a Fur community and was in revenge for the killing of two members of the nomadic Salamat tribe and one member of the Beni Halba tribe by members of the Fur tribe. Government forces responded to this inter-tribal attack and engaged the nomadic attackers. Eleven policemen and six members of the Popular Defence Force were killed in the engagement. A large number of "Janjaweed" raiders were killed in the action. In another engagement, on 4 February 2004, Sudanese armed forces, including air force units, responded to an attack by nomadic tribes on Zaghawa and Massaleit communities east and north of Nyala. Seven hundred and fifty head of livestock were recovered by government forces from these "Janjaweed" raiders.[619] "Janjaweed" gangs are also reported to have attacked Arab tribes.[620]

The UN Commission provided a clear example of the scale and violence of some *ad hoc* inter-tribal revenge attacks pre-dating the 2003 rebellion. It documented the case known as *Jagre al-Hadi al Makbul and others*, which involved the Rezeigat and the Ma'aliyah tribes, both Arab, and related to events in April and May 2002. One member of the Rezeigat tribe was killed by two members of the Ma'aliyah tribe. On 18 May 2002, 40 days after the incident, 700-800 Rezeigat tribesmen, dressed in military uniforms and heavily armed, attacked a Ma'aliyah community, killing 54, wounding another 24, burning the settlement and looting cattle and household property. The Commission noted that government forces were not involved.[621] There have been countless instances of the sort of violence described above since early 2003 and in the wake of the dislocation of law and order. Inter-tribal revenge and opportunistic raids have led to a spiral of similar attacks and counter-attacks well outside of the control of the government.

A May 2004 United Nations media report stated that diplomats and Chadian government officials "question how much control Khartoum has over these nomadic horsemen".[622] That the militiamen that have come to be known as "Janjaweed" are out of control is clear. Many of these gunmen have on several occasions attacked civilians in Chad.[623] That Sudan would have had very little to gain from attacks on Chad is equally obvious. Chad is a mediator in the Darfur conflict. Chadian President Déby has in fact been accused of being sympathetic towards Khartoum, having, for example, previously committed several hundred Chadian soldiers to joint operations with the Sudanese army.[624] Ahmad Allami, President Idriss Déby's official spokesman, stated: "Now, there is the feeling that Sudan does not have control over the militia and needs assistance."[625] Chad's acting Defence Minister, Emmanuel Nadingar, announced that, on 5 May 2004, the Chadian army clashed with a raiding party of Janjaweed 25 kilometres inside Chadian territory and killed 60 of them. One Chadian soldier was killed and seven others were wounded in the battle. The UN report stated that "One captured Janjaweed fighter who was presented to the press in Chad this week confirmed fears that the militia were operating on their own initiative without necessarily following orders from Khartoum." The gunman stated: "Nobody sent us to Chad."[626] The idea that the Khartoum authorities would have directed militiamen under its control to attack Chadian civilians and President Déby's forces would make no sense – and clearly demonstrates the anarchy associated with those groups labelled as "Janjaweed".

The Khartoum authorities have taken several steps to end abuses in Darfur. In June 2004, the Sudanese President ordered security forces to disarm all groups, including rebels and pro-government militia, in the conflict-ridden region of Darfur: "What happened in Darfur is bloody and severe for all Sudanese people, not only the Darfurians."[627] The Sudanese President announced a few days later that both Sudan and Chad had agreed to cooperate in the disarming of militias on both sides of their border: "We have completed an agreement with Chad to collect arms in Darfur and the Chadian lands neighbouring Darfur at the same time…To disarm the groups in one area without the other would not help in resolving the problem."[628] Khartoum's commitment to crack down on armed groups and gunmen in Darfur has been repeated on several occasions, including during the visit to Sudan by American Secretary of State Colin Powell.[629]

The Reuters correspondent in Sudan, Nima el-Baghir, has outlined the difficulties in defining the term "Janjaweed": "In Darfur, Janjaweed is a word that means everything and nothing. It is a composite word deriving literally from *jinn* – which in Arabic means devils or spirits, carrying G-3 rifles on a *jowad* (horse)."[630] Her conclusion has also been echoed by other journalists. *The Los Angeles Times*, for example, has noted that "[t]he word 'janjaweed' means different things to different people. The term, traditionally used to refer to bandits and criminals, is a combination of Arabic words that convey the idea of evil gunmen on horseback." Haggar reports that "Those versed in the culture of Arab tribes in Darfur state that the word 'Janjawiid' has been in use for a long time, perhaps since the 1960s, when it was used as a pejorative term to describe poor vagrants from Arab tribes." [631]

In her article Ms el-Baghir interviewed an Arab tribal leader and asked him if he would call himself a Janjaweed leader.

> He responds furiously: 'What is this word "militia"? What are "Janjaweed"? These words mean nothing.' For years, he says, his people have defended themselves without government help. 'Would you entrust those you are responsible for, your women and children, to a government which is so far away?' He pauses as the voices of his men chorus around him in agreement. 'When they came to us

and said we will give you weapons to fight against the rebels, we said: keep your weapons. Let us use our own.' Abdullah falls quiet, while some of the men with him proudly show me their guns. One says, 'The government rifles were old but ours are from abroad and they are better. We bought them from Zagawa traders.'

In a different interview, Musa Hilal, a Darfurian tribal leader accused of being a Janjaweed leader, also addressed the use of the term. "Janjaweed means nothing, but it is a word used to encompass all evil, a convenient way for Americans to understand who are the good guys and who are the bad. When the rebellion began last year, the government approached us and armed us. My sons were armed by the government and joined the Border Intelligence. Some tribesmen joined the Popular Defense Force."[632] He has also pointed to the vagueness of the term: "The rebels spread the word Janjaweed as if it were an organisation. As a political group there is no specific concept called Janjaweed...It means nothing, but has been used to mean everything." Hilal explained his tribe's involvement in the fighting as an inter-tribal conflict. He stated that his clan had suffered from "acts of banditry", including the murder of young men and livestock theft, carried out by the neighbouring Zaghawa tribe. The Zaghawa and Fur then entered into an alliance against Arab tribes. Human Rights Groups and the UN have confirmed that there was tit-for-tat violence in the lead up to the rebellion.[633] There is no doubt that Hilal is the leader of paramilitary forces raised by the government in response to the rebellion, forces separate from those groups of criminal opportunists that have increased their activities since the destruction of the police force in 2003. That some of these organised paramilitaries have been involved in questionable activities is clear. Their activities must be divorced from the other essentially criminal activities which have gone on in Darfur since before the rebellion and which have escalated since. One can only hope that the government is able to control the sorts of forces seemingly commanded by people like Hilal. He has stated his view with regard to disarmament: "As far as we as a tribe are concerned, whenever we feel the situation is completely secure and the ceasefire is being respected, we will hand in our weapons. The reality is that this is a country where everyone has weapons."[634]

One Janjaweed leader, interviewed by the London *Sunday Times*, denied any alignment with the government: "We are not with the rebels, we are not with the government…we look for our due…We fight all governments in Sudan. We get nothing from the government." When asked about possible international intervention by the UN, the USA or Britain, the Janjaweed stated: "We will fight them. We hate them and we will attack the foreigners. We refuse to be like Iraq – surrendered, confused and occupied. We will fight them more than the mujaheddin in Afghanistan." [635] *The Sunday Times* also outlined some of the difficulties facing the government: "Disarming these warring factions may be impossible. If Khartoum dispatches more troops to Darfur, it will be in violation of its ceasefire with the two main rebel groups. Disarmament would in any case enrage the Janjaweed and the African and Arab tribal militias, who may turn their guns on aid workers and Sudanese soldiers alike, detonating any chance of relief efforts." [636]

A largely sensationalist, and on occasion disingenuous, media has lumped together as "Janjaweed" regular army forces, popular defence forces, police units, tribal militias, vigilantes and armed robbers through to any armed "Arab" tribesman. It is a bit like claiming that the British government controls not only all army and army reserve units and police and police reserve units in Northern Ireland but is also controls and is also responsible for all anti-republican or anti-Catholic loyalist organisations, paramilitaries, gunmen and criminal rackets in the province. The simple fact is that virtually all of Darfur's 80 tribes and groups will have members who are armed, some with members on both sides of the conflict. Some tribal militias will not disarm unless rival tribes also do so. A western diplomat in Khartoum has noted: "There are many gangs or groups that (the Sudanese government) doesn't control or who may be partly under their control or controlled by the local authorities. So this is not a clear-cut picture. That makes you understand how difficult (disarmament) is logistically." [637] According to the United Nations Under-Secretary-General for Humanitarian Affairs, Jan Egeland "There are many armed groups and many armed criminal gangs in Darfur." He referred to the Janjaweed as "a monster that nobody seems to be able to control". [638] In early November 2004, the UN Envoy to Sudan also observed: "The government does not control its own forces fully. It co-opted paramilitary forces and now cannot count on their obedience…The border lines between the military, the paramilitary and the police are being blurred." [639] Pronk returned to this theme in his February

2005 comments before the United Nations Security Council: "The militias are strong and well organized. And there seems to be a sort of an invisible hand behind their actions. There are forces in the back in Sudan, not inside the Government, yet powerful, that have the capacity to spread terror on the ground..."[640]

The human rights group Justice Africa has addressed the need for a sustainable definition of "Janjaweed":

> Who are the Janjawiid? A clear definition of the Janjawiid is a requirement for their disarmament. The term 'Janjawiid' has been used to denote Arab militias since the late 1980s, but not always to refer to the same entities. Noting the term 'Arab' is ambiguous and fluid in Darfur, we can note the following different armed Arab groups in the region: Armed pastoralists. Every community in Darfur is armed. For pastoralist groups, disarmament is out of the question as long as there is no effective law enforcement...The Rizeigat (Abbala) Janjawiid...The Beni Halba Fursan...Other Baggara militia, such as the Janjawiid drawn from the Terjam group that lives in the environs of Nyala. Chadian Arabs, including the Salamat group, which lives on both sides of the Chad-Sudan border. Their numbers are unknown but are rumoured to be substantial...The Rizeigat (Baggara) Murahalin...Emergent militias among groups that have not thus far been involved in the conflict...The Popular Defence Forces...[641]

In addition to the groups mentioned above by de Waal, and separate from the national army and police force, the popular defence force, *Difaa al Sha'abi*, and popular police force, *Shorta al Sha'abi*, there are several other armed pro-government groups. These include the 'Peace Forces', *Quwat al Salaam*, the nomad protection forces, the Um Bakha irregular forces and the Um Kwak forces. The Chadian Arab factor has not been adequately studied by the international community. Haggar's study has noted that "all the major conflicts in Darfur over the last twenty years have been associated with the presence of armed Chadian groups and that armed Chadians constitute a significant proportion of the Janjawiid." He observes, for example, that Chadian tribal leader "Acheikh Ibn Omer and the [Conseil Démocratique Révolutionaire] began the 1987-1989 Arab-Fur war." Haggar has also stated that the Arab-Masalit wars involved a large number of Chadian Arabs, and that the wars since 2001 "have also involved armed groups of Chadian origin on a large scale." [642] Quite how the international community expects the Sudanese government is meant to exercise control of any number of Chadian groups is puzzling.

Those who attribute every single act of violence or criminality to the "Janjaweed" and claim that all these acts are on the instructions of the Sudanese government are either naïve or are seeking to deliberately mislead the international community. In either instance they ill serve the people of Darfur. It is essential to cut away the propaganda that is already clouding the Darfur issue. That Khartoum must address the criminality and armed banditry that has undermined law and order in Darfur is obvious. At the same time, however, lazy commentators and human rights organisations cannot have it both ways in criticising the Sudanese government for inaction and then attacking Khartoum for responding firmly to terrorism and lawlessness.

Claims That All Militias in Darfur can be Disarmed in 30 Days

Unrealistic expectations, often based upon naïve claims, have not assisted with a resolution of the problem. One issue has been the problem of disarming the many armed groups and individuals in Darfur. In July 2004, for example, the UN Security Council adopted Resolution 1556 threatening action against Sudan if it did not disarm gunmen in Darfur within 30 days. [643] Charles Snyder, a former United States acting assistant Secretary of State for African Affairs and the US State Department's senior representative on Sudan, stated at the time, however, that there were no "30-day, 90-day quick fixes" to the problem. He also admitted: "This is going to take, in my view, 18 months to two years to conclude the first phase" of making the region safe for people to return to their homes. [644] De Waal has also warned of international naivety with regard to "disarming" the Janjaweed:

> On July 30, the UN Security Council gave Khartoum 30 days to disarm the Janjawid. But how? There are many different militia groups, ranging from entire nomadic clans that have armed

themselves to protect their herds, to brigades of trained fighters headed by Musa Hilal and some of his Chadian Arab comrades in arms. The Janjawid paramilitaries are the direct responsibility of Khartoum and can be demobilized, but the armed nomads will be more difficult. In a region where every community has armed itself, confiscating all arms is frankly impossible: what can be done is community-based regulated of arms, gradually marginalizing criminal elements through a process of political reconstruction. [645]

The international community appears to have realised the problems inherent in the 30-day "fix-all" demands. As much was noted by the UN Secretary-General in a report on 30 August 2004: "Making an area the size of Darfur, with the amount of armed men and violent recent history, safe and secure for all civilians takes more than 30 days." [646] The government committed itself to three steps: ending all offensive military operations; identifying parts of Darfur that could be made safe within 30 days; and identifying those militias over whom it had control and instructing them to lay down their weapons. The UN reported that the government had, nonetheless, started a process of disarming those militias that were under its command. [647] Janjaweed members have been both arrested and convicted.[648] Four hundred had been arrested by July.[649]

Justice Africa, the human rights organisation, has outlined realistic measures that can be undertaken with regard to disarmament:

> The most realistic option is twofold. On the one hand, [the government] can control the paramilitary forces it has established under the command of Musa Hilal and other commanders. Secondly, it can initiate a process of arms regulation, whereby communities are permitted to hold arms for legitimate self-defence, in accordance with norms and procedures agreed by all groups, and they themselves become partners in disarming the illegitimately armed groups. This kind of disarmament will be gradual, founded on community-based security provision, and will take place concurrently with political negotiations, reconciliation and reconstruction.[650]

It is obvious that every effort must be made to remove both weapons and the motivation or need to carry weapons, from the Darfur situation. Increasingly shrill demands for an immediate disarmament of armed forces within Darfur in the face of the reality outlined by the United Nations, Charles Snyder and de Waal serve no purpose other than enflaming an already fraught situation.

Washington's Janjaweed Problem

Washington's demands for the immediate disarming of militias in Darfur have been made despite (and some would say because of) the fact that there is no working definition of what constitutes the "Janjaweed". Several questions arise regarding the Bush Administration's stance. Is Washington's intelligence regarding, and analysis of events and circumstances in, Darfur really as poor as it seems? Is the Bush Administration making demands of Khartoum that it knows to be unrealistic in order to have a pretext for Western intervention in yet another oil-rich Muslim nation? In addition to making unrealistic demands of Sudan's government over the Darfur militia issue, Washington has also opened itself up to charges of rank hypocrisy.[651] A simple comparison with circumstances within Iraq highlights this hypocrisy. While making demands of the Sudanese government regarding disarming militia, US forces have been unable to disarm the plethora of pro-and-anti government and religious militias within Iraq, some of them present, armed and active in the Iraqi capital itself despite the fact that the armed Arab militias in Iraq are to a large degree well-defined and known forces.[652]

They have engaged American forces, and killed and wounded American servicemen, on numerous occasions. The Americans maintain 180,000 military personnel in Iraq, supported by unprecedented air and naval power, all part of the world's biggest and most sophisticated military machine. Despite this immense force they are clearly unable to disarm Iraqi militias made up of several thousand gunmen. *The New York Times* has noted that "Iraq's various ethnic and sectarian militias continue to exist…There are a growing number of small, homegrown, paramilitary-style brigades being formed by local tribes, religious leaders, and political parties. Some battle Iraq's largely Sunni insurgency alongside official Interior and Defence ministry troops, others operate without official assistance or sanction. The larger, more established militias…are tied to Iraq's leading political parties, organized along sectarian lines, and enforce order in their respective regions."[653]

Matt Sherman, an American government adviser to the Iraqi government from 2004-2006, notes that "armed militias have roamed [Iraq]…as they see fit". Writing in *The New York Times*, Sherman further noted that "having spent two years in Baghdad as the American policy adviser to Iraq's Interior Ministry" he had "a sense of just how strong these militias really are and just how destabilizing they can be." Sherman stated that there were nine major militias operating in Iraq – one which had "slowly gained virtual control of the Interior Ministry". Sherman concluded: "Unfortunately, the militias are part of the social fabric in Iraq. They cannot be simply eliminated or disarmed."[654]

One of the Iraqi militias in question is the "Mahdi" militia led by Iraqi Shia leader Moqtada al-Sadr. Unlike militias in Darfur, over a thousand kilometres from the Sudanese capital, the "Mahdi army" and other militias are present in Baghdad itself, some four or five kilometres away from the "Green Zone", the command centre of the United States occupation forces in Iraq. *Newsweek* magazine has highlighted this contradiction:

> At one time…there was a murder warrant out for the arrest of Moqtada al-Sadr, on the charge of killing an ayatollah in 2003. U.S. Army Gen. Richardo Sanchez later publicly vowed that coalition troops in Iraq would 'kill or capture' Sadr, and not rest until they had destroyed his militia…Today his militia is back, and bigger than ever: He is now estimated to have 15,000 armed followers, three times as many as when he fought U.S. forces in 2004..[655]

Newsweek has noted that despite Sadr's militia's clear involvement in violence "The American military no longer talks about killing or capturing Sadr: in fact, they're careful to not even point a finger of blame at him." Two of Sadr's followers control ministries in the new government, health and transportation. Sadr is allowed by the Americans to tour Middle Eastern capitals. Sadr's militia is described by *Time* magazine as "the most potent of the armed militias that have carved Baghdad into fiefdoms". *Time* notes that "Even though he has attacked U.S. troops countless times, no one will touch him." *Time* also pointed out that Iraqi military forces "are powerless in the face of the Mahdi army". *Time* notes that "The U.S. would prefer that the Iraqi security forces disarm the militias, but it hasn't happened. A senior military official in Baghdad says the U.S. is deliberately avoiding confrontations with the militias."[656]

Sadr's militias have fought pitched battles with US forces on several occasions. His forces have killed American servicemen. Have the Americans disarmed his militia? No. The height of the American response has been calls by the US Ambassador for Sadr to moderate his rhetoric. The "Janjaweed" are a problem for Washington for two reasons. Having helped to create the "Janjaweed" propaganda theme, if Washington genuinely wishes a solution to the Darfur crisis it must play a considerably more constructive role – something which would involve it helping to dismantle its own propaganda. Washington's demands for disarmament of the "Janjaweed", given its own chronic failings in Iraq, have additionally opened it up to charges of hypocrisy. The patently unrealistic demands made by both the Security Council and the Bush Administration for immediate disarmament of militias in Darfur discredit both the UN and Washington. It shows the absurdity of "quick-fix" solutions in such complex conflict situations – and highlights the hypocrisy of the Bush Administration. Washington's demands for yet another "quick-fix", the introduction of NATO/UN military forces in Darfur, are equally flawed. Simply put, Washington's hypocrisy on Darfur goes a long way to validating the Sudanese government's reluctance to entertain such an intervention.

Chapter Five

ALLEGATIONS OF GENOCIDE IN DARFUR

I don't think that we should be using the word "genocide" to describe this conflict. Not at all. This can be a semantic discussion, but nevertheless, there is no systematic target — targeting one ethnic group or another one. It doesn't mean either that the situation in Sudan isn't extremely serious by itself.

Dr Mercedes Taty, Médecins sans Frontières deputy emergency director[657]

Our teams have not seen evidence of the deliberate intention to kill people of a specific group.

Médecins sans Frontières — France President
Dr Jean-Hervé Bradol [658]

In September 2004, the American Secretary of State, Colin Powell, declared that events in Darfur constituted "genocide". This was despite having stated two months previously that the Darfur crisis did not "meet the tests of the definition of genocide".[659]

Claims of genocide are amongst the most heinous allegations that can be made. De Waal sums it up succinctly: "The term 'genocide' consigns its architects to the realm of pure evil, beyond humanity and politics."[660] Mahmood Mamdani has also observed: "It seems that genocide has become a label to be stuck on your worst enemy, a perverse version of the Nobel Prize, part of a rhetorical arsenal that helps you vilify your adversaries while ensuring impunity for your allies."[661] It must be noted, however, that over the past decade or so a number of similarly grave but ultimately deeply questionable claims have been made about Sudan. These have included allegations that Sudan possessed and manufactured weapons of mass destruction. On 20 August 1998, for example, the Clinton Administration launched cruise missile attacks on the al-Shifa pharmaceutical factory in Khartoum alleging that the plant was making chemical weapons as part of Osama bin Laden's infrastructure of international terrorism. Every one of the American claims proved to have been false. The London *Observer* newspaper spoke of "a catalogue of US misinformation, glaring omissions and intelligence errors about the function of the plant".[662] These claims are now accepted internationally to have been unfounded.

One of the other widely-publicised sensationalist claims about Sudan has been allegations of government-sponsored "slavery" and "slave trade" in Sudan. As "proof" for this, a great number of newspaper articles "reported" instances of "slave redemption" in which alleged "slaves" were said to have been "bought" back from "slave traders". These sorts of claims began to be exposed as questionable where not simply false as early as 1999.[663] In February 2002, in an unprecedented international focus, and as the result of some excellent investigative journalism, *The Irish Times*, London's *Independent on Sunday*, *The Washington Post* and *International Herald Tribune* chose to publish articles definitively exposing the deep fraud and corruption at the heart of claims of "slave redemption" in Sudan.[664] *The Irish Times* reported: "According to aid workers, missionaries, and even the rebel movement that facilitates it, slave redemption in Sudan is often an elaborate scam."[665] Washington's claims about genocide can be seen in the same light.

Powell's September flip-flop, in the lead-up to the US elections, was widely seen as both an attempt to divert media attention away from the disastrous events in Iraq and to pander to the large and well-established anti-Sudan and anti-Muslim constituencies within the United States.[666] It appears that the Bush administration had decided that it was to its electoral advantage for the sensationalism and inaccuracy that has obscured events in Darfur to continue. It was a simple enough equation. The 2004 US election was seen at the time by the Bush White House as possibly being a very close run affair.[667] The war in Iraq was a key electoral issue, and that war continued to go badly.[668] The day before Powell's Darfur comments had seen the American military death toll in Iraq since 2003 reach over one thousand.[669] Declaring Darfur to be a genocide was useful to Republican party strategists for very simple reasons. It appeased several domestic constituencies and the more US television coverage and column inches devoted to Darfur at the time, the less media time focused on the worsening situation in Iraq.

That the declaration also served a second political purpose, relieving domestic political pressure, is also clear. The Bush administration had come under considerable pressure from a range of constituencies to declare Darfur a genocide. These calls had come from pre-existing anti-Sudan structures. Key Save Darfur activists Rebecca Hamilton and Chad Hazlett have noted that anti-Sudan activism previously focused on southern Sudan had "created not only a pool of experienced and well-connected advocates, but also a contingent of Congressional 'champions' for Sudan. These committed legislators...provided a ready source of allies for Darfur activists."[670] The first American politician to allege genocide in Darfur, Representative Frank Wolf, came from this contingent. He alleged genocide in Darfur in the US Congress on 2 April 2004.[671] This was followed by other long-time opponents of the Khartoum government, Senators Mike DeWine, John McCain, and Jon Corzine. On 24 June 2004, Representative Donald Payne and Senator Sam Brownback introduced concurrent resolutions in the House and Senate, declaring that genocide was occurring in Darfur. In June 2004, 52 senators pressured Colin Powell to take punitive action on Darfur. Powell subsequently visited Darfur, arriving in Sudan on 30 June. He stated that the Darfur crisis did not constitute genocide. His position came under immediate and sustained attack from Congress and pressure groups. In July 2004, the US Congress passed the concurrent, nonbinding resolution labelling the violence in Darfur as genocide.[672] Further Congressional and media pressure ensured. Of the 83 editorials and op-eds on Darfur appearing in *The New York Times*, *The Washington Post*, *The Wall Street Journal* and *The Washington Times* from March to September 2004, almost half alleged "genocide" or potential "genocide", many of them invoking the spectre of Rwanda.[673] On 9 September 2004, in an appearance before the US Senate Foreign Relations Committee, Powell reversed his previous position and stated that "genocide has been committed in Darfur...and that genocide may still be occurring."[674] The same day, President Bush issued a statement stating that as a result of State Department investigations, Washington had concluded that genocide had taken place in Darfur. President Bush called on the UN "to undertake a full investigation of the genocide and other crimes in Darfur".[675] President Bush restated this assertion when he addressed the UN General Assembly on 21 September. In a subsequent presidential debate he again restated the genocide allegations. [676]

While ultimately coming down to sheer political opportunism, Powell's use of the genocide word has undoubtedly further tarnished the image of the American government, not least of which because at the time of making the genocide declaration he also stated that the United States would not act upon this finding. Bizarrely, having made a public declaration of genocide before the Senate, Powell then stated that "[n]o new action is dictated by this determination...So let us not be too preoccupied with [it]".[677] Bush subsequently reconfirmed that the US would take no further action: "We shouldn't be committing troops."[678] This lack of concern can be seen as confirmation in itself that the declaration of genocide was made more as the result of internal political pressure and politics and less on the reality of events.

There is no doubt that Save Darfur activists saw a direct link between their work and the genocide declaration. Hamilton and Hazlett have spoken of "the first accomplishment of Darfur advocacy: the genocide determination".[679] In their words, "For the burgeoning Darfur movement, getting the U.S. government to use the 'G-word,' as activists referred to it, was an unimaginable coup".[680]

The extent to which the Bush administration's approach to the Save Darfur movement was a cynical one did not escape activists. Hamilton and Hazlett have observed: "To date, the movement's efforts to pressure the U.S. government may have, somewhat perversely, forced the Administration to place a higher priority on 'managing' activists than finding a workable solution for Darfur."[681] This analysis is echoed by de Waal who has described the US use of the genocide label as "the outcome of intra-beltway political calculus".[682] De Waal also observed that it was the result of "a very specific set of political processes in Washington D.C. in which interest groups were contending for control over U.S. policy towards Sudan. In this context, the call to set up a State Department inquiry into whether or not there was genocide in Darfur was a tactical manoeuvre designed to placate the anti-Khartoum activists circling around Congress".[683] Even anti-Sudan activists such as Eric Reeves have termed Bush's position on genocide "hopelessly opportunistic".[684]

De Waal has outlined some of the American domestic pressure pushing for Darfur to be labelled as genocide:

> The impetus for the genocide ruling did not come from Washington's neocons, but rather from liberal human rights activists and members of the religious right. The origins of this coalition lie both in genuine outrage at the conditions of life in Sudan, but also in the politics of support for the SPLA...which intersected with influence trading in Congress [bringing] together the Black Caucus, the Israeli lobby, the religious right (for whom Sudan is a crusade) and the human rights groups...Several of these groups were frustrated that the State Department, under the Republicans, had switched from a policy of regime change in Khartoum to a pursuit of a negotiated peace for Southern Sudan.[685]

That the Bush administration in essence caved into domestic political pressure was confirmed by Senator John Danforth, President Bush's special envoy to Sudan and subsequently US ambassador to the United Nations. In a July 2005 BBC interview he stated that the use of the genocide label "was something that was said for internal consumption within the United States". When asked whether he meant the Christian Right, Danforth agreed.[686] *The Financial Times* has also noted that Powell was under intense domestic pressure, notably from Christian lobby groups, to reach the genocide definition.[687] In any instance, it is also clear that the Bush administration's declaration of genocide in Darfur was against the advice of its own legal experts. George Taft, a counsel within the State Department's Office of the Legal Adviser stated in August 2005, sometime after Powell's statement, that events in Darfur did not constitute genocide and that he had opposed the use of that term.[688]

The administration's cynicism in using the term had unexpected results, however, as outlined by Hamilton and Hazlett: "Use of the 'G-word' may have been an early attempt by the Administration to assuage activists – but if so, the strategy had the opposite effect. Calling it genocide elevated Darfur above other atrocities with high death tolls, seemingly highlighting it as the crisis most deserving of attention. The legitimacy the term gave to Darfur advocacy emboldened a fresh and growing pool of activists, convinced that the 'worst crime imaginable' demanded an uncompromising response."[689] The administration was hoist by its own petard.

Assuming for one moment that the Bush administration had not been as crassly cynical as it seems, there are two further possible explanations for its use of the genocide label. The first is that this declaration was simply based on poor intelligence. This is of course equally disturbing but not totally unimaginable. It is a matter of record that this declaration of genocide came from an administration and intelligence community that has come to be characterised by systemic intelligence failures.[690] It would appear, for example, that Washington's intelligence on Iraq, both pre-and-post invasion was abysmal – even though it was presumably, from an American intelligence perspective, the most watched and studied country in the world. What would the intelligence community necessarily know about a region on the edge of the Sahel? Confidence in American intelligence and analysis was not enhanced by former Defense Secretary Donald Rumsfeld's admission that: "Reports that say something hasn't happened are always interesting to me because as we know, there are known knowns; there are things we know we know. We also know there are known unknowns; that is to say we know there are some things we do not know. But there are also unknown unknowns – the ones we don't know we don't know."[691]

The second explanation, one which has gained momentum within sections of the American left and internationally, is that the Bush administration declared genocide in Darfur in order to lay the ground for a military intervention in yet another oil-rich Muslim country just as WMD had been used as a pretext for the US invasion of oil-rich Iraq.

Whichever explanation holds, the American record for crying wolf, in the wake of the Iraqi weapons of mass destruction fiasco, has not improved.[692] Only 18-months earlier, the same Colin Powell had been wheeled out by the Bush administration to state that Iraq possessed weapons of mass destruction, forcefully alleging, amongst other things, the existence of a nuclear weapons programme, mobile bio-weapons laboratories, 500 tons of chemical agent, tons of VX nerve gas, thousands of litres of anthrax and biological weapon-armed rockets and warheads. Powell stated that "every statement I make today is backed up by sources, solid sources. These are not assertions. What we are giving you are facts and conclusions based on solid evidence." [693] It perhaps goes without saying that the American media accepted Powell's claims with enthusiasm. The reality is now all too clear. There were no WMD. The Bush administration had lied. [694] Powell has subsequently had the good grace to admit his disastrous mistake, stating that he felt "terrible" at having been misinformed.[695] Powell's chief-of-staff described Powell's claims as "a hoax on the American people, the international community, and the United Nations Security Council."[696]

It is now evident that Powell made similarly misinformed allegations about genocide in Darfur. Brendan O'Neill, the British political commentator and prominent blogger, clearly saw an ulterior motive in Powell's Darfur declaration:

> Powell's labelling of the Darfur conflict as genocide was a cynical stunt – and even many of those of an anti-war persuasion who saw through his rubbish about Saddam having WMD, as spouted at the UN in February 2003, fell for it hook, line and sinker. Washington's decision officially to define Darfur as a genocide was motivated more by the fallout from Iraq than by events in Sudan. As Gulf War II proved both a practical and political disaster – leaving Iraq in a mess and causing endless embarrassment for the American and British governments – Washington launched what we might call an intervention-lite into the affairs of Sudan, hoping that posturing over a conflict that could be presented in black-and-white terms (and where there were no WMDs to worry about) would help them win back some of their fast-collapsing international moral authority.[697]

That this move was a cynical one appeared to have been borne out almost immediately by Washington's statement that no action on its part would follow. It is interesting to note, in the light of Powell having been used to front the Iraqi WMD claims, that French academic, and noted Khartoum critic, Gérard Prunier, stated that he was "assured that Secretary of State Colin Powell had practically been ordered to use the term 'genocide' during his high profile 9 September 2004 testimony to the Senate Committee on Foreign Relations but that he [had] also been advised to add in the same breath that this did not oblige the United States to undertake any sort of drastic action...Thus President Bush tried to be all things to all men on the Sudan/Darfur question...Predictably the interest level of US diplomacy on the Sudan question dropped sharply as soon as President Bush was re-elected."[698] This begs the question of whether Powell was more than aware of the weakness in his claim. One wonders if he will have the courage to admit that his claim of genocide in Darfur was as fraudulent as his WMD allegation.

The first question, therefore, that must be asked is whether or not the Bush administration would play political games with allegations of genocide. It was a question posed by genocide activist Gerald Caplan:

> What would have been the point of making this declaration unless significant action was being planned...Had the historic declaration of genocide been nothing more than an opportunistic political ploy by the Bush administration to assuage some domestic pressure groups? Could even the Bush neo-cons be so cynical as to play politics with genocide? If not, how could this wholly unanticipated development be explained? How could the esteemed Colin Powell participate in this destructive exercise, which had done so much to debase the currency of the Genocide Convention?" [699]

This crucial question, which lies at the heart of Washington's genocide declaration, is perhaps best answered by Arianna Huffington, the syndicated US columnist: "Almost every day brings fresh evidence that Bush and his crew believe they can get away with just about anything – no matter how shocking, offensive, corrupt, underhanded or in-your-face the transgression."[700] And, it should be noted, Huffington was summing up the Bush administration *before* the Iraqi invasion and subsequent WMD fiasco. Her view is shared by David Corn, the Washington editor of *The Nation*. Writing in his *New York Times* list bestseller, *The Lies of George W. Bush. Mastering the Politics of Deception*, Corn quite baldly stated: "George W. Bush is a liar. He has lied large and small, directly and by omission. He has mugged the truth – not merely in honest error, but deliberately, consistently, and repeatedly."[701]

It is also worth noting that even the fig-leaf used by Powell to justify his

Darfur genocide claim has subsequently been discredited. *The Washington Post* reported that as the basis for his claim, "Powell cited a report released by the State Department...that found a 'consistent and widespread pattern of atrocities committed against non-Arab villagers'."[702] The report, *Documenting Atrocities in Darfur*, was written by an 'Atrocities Documentation Team' made up of State Department and USAID officials and members of the Coalition for International Justice. It was said to have been based on 1,136 interviews with refugees in Chad, in which 61 percent were to have witnessed the killing of a family member. USAID Administrator Andrew Natsios stated: "The Atrocities Documentation Project was a critical part of the evidence that led the [United States Government] to conclude that a genocide had taken place."[703] Bush has also cited this report as justification. If this was indeed the justification, then Washington's theoretical case for claiming genocide was a very weak one. Firstly, it should be noted that the report itself did not use the word "genocide". Secondly, the prestigious World Health Organisation-affiliated Centre for Research on the Epidemiology of Disasters (CRED) pointed to a flaw at the heart of the project: "These interviews...were not designed in any way to function as a mortality survey not was there an overall systematic sampling methodology used that could make it representative of the roughly 200,000 refugees that fled to eastern Chad, much less of the entire 2.4 million people affected in Darfur."[704] The definitive 2006 American government study of mortality in Darfur, carried out by international experts, *Darfur Crisis: Death Estimates Demonstrate Severity of Crisis, but Their Accuracy and Credibility Could Be Enhanced*, echoed CRED's criticism, stating that "many experts felt that Atrocities Documentation Team's survey was not a reliable or appropriate source of data to estimate violent deaths for a cumulative death estimate on Darfur, based on public documentation on the survey, as well as supplemental information on the survey's design, implementation, and sampling...obtained from representatives at the Coalition for International Justice."[705]

Having opportunistically declared Darfur to be "genocide", the Bush administration has continued to demonstrate contradictory positions regarding this term aware as it must be that the declaration was unfounded. In the words of anti-Sudan activist Eric Reeves, "The Bush administration...has attempted to 'walk back' the g-word."[706] In April 2005, Robert Zoellick, the then US Deputy Secretary of State, was the first senior American official to travel to

Khartoum following Powell's genocide declaration in September 2004. It was clear that he was uncomfortable with the term. When asked if the US believed genocide was being committed in Darfur, he stated: "I don't want to get into a debate over terminology." Zoellick did however speak of "crimes against humanity", in line with the findings of the United Nations commission of inquiry.[707] In October 2005, the US ambassador to the UN blocked a briefing on Darfur by the UN secretary-general's special adviser on genocide.[708] In early February 2006, the US Assistant Secretary of State for African Affairs, Jendayi Fraser, would not respond to questions as to whether events in Darfur still constituted "genocide". Fraser stated that the situation was "very different than it was…It is a very serious situation and it's a series of small attacks and incidents. It is not the government directing the militia attacking civilians."[709] Yet, two weeks later, the US Secretary of State, Condoleezza Rice, speaking before the US Congress, stated that "genocide" continued in Darfur.[710]

And then, one year later, in February 2007, at a meeting at Georgetown University, Andrew Natsios, President Bush's special envoy to Sudan, stated that "The term genocide is counter to the facts of what is really occurring in Darfur."[711] Interestingly enough, a week or two after Natsios, the US point-man on Darfur, a man with decades of experience of Sudanese affairs, declared claims of genocide to be counter to what was happening in Darfur, the US Department of State's annual human rights report claimed that "genocide continued to ravage the Darfur region of Sudan."[712] At a subsequent hearing before a US Senate Foreign Relations Committee hearing on 11 April 2007, in a heated exchange with Senator Robert Menendez, Natsios repeatedly refused to characterise the ongoing violence in Darfur as genocide. Natsios was asked "Do you consider the ongoing situation in Darfur a genocide, yes or no?" He responded: "There is very little violence in Darfur right now." When pressed, he replied: "There is very little fighting between rebels and the government and very few civilian casualties going on in Darfur right now." A press release by Senator Menendez confirmed that "Natsios…refused to give Menendez a straightforward answer as to whether the conflict in Darfur can still be deemed a genocide."[713] Later in 2007, President Bush returned to the genocide theme. Speaking in a UN Security Council meeting on Africa, he declared that "when we find genocide it's time to do something about it. Time is of the essence." Bush gave what appeared to be his somewhat open-ended definition of genocide: "If you've been raped...if you're mercilessly killed by roaming bands, you know it's genocide."[714]

Outside of the Washington Beltway, the Bush administration's claim of genocide has been regarded with scepticism. In late September 2004 Secretary of State Colin Powell admitted that the Bush Administration was alone in having alleged that genocide was happening in Darfur: "I must say, I am disappointed that not more nations have made this clear statement of what's happening there."[715] The international community has shunned the American declaration. United Nations Secretary-General Kofi Annan, for one, contradicted American claims: "I cannot call the killing a genocide even though there have been massive violations of international humanitarian law."[716] The African Union's position was clearly outlined by its Peace and Security Council in July 2004: "Even though the crisis in Darfur is grave, with unacceptable levels of death, human suffering and destruction of homes and infrastructure, the situation cannot be defined as a genocide."[717] The then AU Chairman, Nigerian President Olusegun Obasanjo, also stated in early December 2004 that events in Darfur did not constitute genocide: "Now, what I know of Sudan it does not fit in all respects to that definition. The government of Sudan can be condemned, but it's not as ... genocide." Obasanjo stated that "the real issue of Darfur is governance. It is a political problem which has mushroomed into a military (one) when the rebels took up arms."[718] Speaking at a press conference at the United Nations Headquarters in New York on 23 September 2004, President Obasanjo had previously stated: "Before you can say that this is genocide or ethnic cleansing, we will have to have a definite decision and plan and program of a government to wipe out a particular group of people, then we will be talking about genocide, ethnic cleansing. What we know is not that. What we know is that there was an uprising, rebellion, and the government armed another group of people to stop that rebellion. That's what we know. That does not amount to genocide from our own reckoning. It amounts to of course conflict. It amounts to violence." It should also be noted that the African Union had hundreds of observers on the ground throughout Darfur, whose first-hand observations would have shaped President Obasanjo's conclusions.

Similarly, the European Union's fact-finding mission concluded that, although there was widespread violence, there was no evidence of genocide. A spokesman for the mission stated: "We are in not in the situation of genocide there. But it is clear there is widespread, silent and slow, killing going on, and village burning on a fairly large scale."[719] The Arab League took the position that events in Darfur were neither genocide nor ethnic cleansing and accused the Bush administration of seeking to exploit the crisis for electoral gain. Even Israel, a state founded in large part by survivors of a genuine holocaust, has perhaps indirectly demurred from Washington's claim in publicly turning away Darfurian refugees.[720]

Given the level of international concern about allegations of genocide in Darfur, and partly in response to President Bush's call for such a measure, the United Nations Security Council established the International Commission of Inquiry on Darfur pursuant to Security Council resolution 1564 (2004), adopted on 18 September 2004. A five-member body, chaired by Italian jurist Antonio Cassese, was appointed by the Secretary-General in October 2004. The Commission was tasked "to investigate reports of violations of international humanitarian law and human rights by all parties" and "to determine also whether or not acts of genocide have occurred". It was requested to report back to the Secretary-General by January 2005. The Commission reported that while there had been serious violations of human rights in Darfur, genocide had not occurred.[721]

Of particular significance, perhaps, has been the fact that Washington's genocide claims have been pointedly criticised by well-respected humanitarian groups such as Médecins Sans Frontières.[722] In 2004, MSF pointedly criticised the unfounded use of words such as genocide: "By screaming 'the crime of all crimes', mixing military with humanitarianism…to justify intervention, words do have concrete implications and often serve political interests." The organisation also noted of the allegations of genocide in Darfur: "Resorting to this terminology says much about the racist representation of African conflicts in the West (the conflict in Darfur reduced to an inevitable antagonism between Blacks and Arabs). It also demonstrates, as if it were necessary, that words are used by States, not for what they mean but for the political objectives that they might serve." MSF cautioned that to continue with its job would entail "distancing ourselves from propaganda and resisting this era of confusion".[723] MSF-France President Dr Jean-Hervé Bradol subsequently described American claims of genocide in Darfur as "obvious political opportunism".[724] Dr Bradol had previously stated that the use of the term genocide was inappropriate: "Our teams have not seen evidence of the deliberate intention to kill people of a specific group. We have received reports of massacres, but not of attempts to specifically eliminate all the members of a group."[725] Dr Mercedes Taty, MSF's deputy emergency director, who worked with 12 expatriate doctors and 300 Sudanese nationals in field hospitals throughout Darfur at the height of the emergency, has also warned: "I don't think that we should be using the word 'genocide' to describe this conflict. Not at all. This can be a semantic discussion, but nevertheless, there is no systematic target – targeting one ethnic group or another one. It doesn't mean either that the situation in Sudan isn't extremely serious by itself."[726]

Médecins Sans Frontières is an exceptionally credible observer with regard to allegations of genocide for three reasons. Firstly, MSF was amongst the first humanitarian groups to establish a presence in Darfur as the conflict unfolded. MSF is very heavily involved in the provision of medical and emergency services in all three of the states that make up Darfur, deploying 2,000 staff. [727] It has been actively assisting hundreds of thousands of people displaced by fighting throughout the region. Médecins Sans Frontières is also present and engaged in Chad. MSF, therefore, has a unique institutional awareness of events in Darfur. Secondly, MSF's reputation is quite simply beyond reproach. Médecins Sans Frontières was the recipient of the Nobel Peace Prize in 1999. It has also received numerous other awards recognising its outstanding humanitarian work throughout the world.[728] And, thirdly, MSF's record with regard to genocide is also unambiguous. Dr Bradol, cited above, headed MSF's programs in Rwanda in 1994, and spent several weeks assisting the surgical team that struggled to remain in Kigali during the genocide. Dr Bradol and MSF called for armed intervention in Rwanda stating "doctors can't stop genocide". Dr Bradol has stated that "Genocide is that exceptional situation in which, contrary to the rule prohibiting participation in hostilities, the humanitarian movement declares support for military intervention. Unfortunately, an international military intervention against the genocide never came to pass and the Rwandan Patriotic Front did not win its military victory until after the vast majority of victims were killed." Given the clear position with regard to genuine genocide taken by Dr Bradol and MSF, their unambiguous position in pointedly criticising allegations of genocide in Darfur is all the more powerful.

Dr Bradol has also criticised the way in which the truth was twisted in order to claim genocide in Darfur: "The need to revive the notion of race to support the premise of genocide in Darfur is not the only point of weakness in the genocide argument. Public statements of the intent to destroy a human group have been no more obvious than the existence of distinct races. No traces of this intent can be found in statements by the Sudanese dictatorship or in the country's laws. In short, the alleged intent to destroy a human group is not obvious, and the definition of the group of victims is based on a category that was rightly invalidated many years ago."[729] Interestingly, MSF's comments about allegations of genocide were echoed by other medical organisations. Interviewed in April 2005, Dr Gino Strada, a war surgeon and founder of Emergency, a humanitarian NGO that had worked through the Rwandan genocide, and in Darfur, stated that "I will say there is no genocide at all in Darfur. There is a big humanitarian disaster, and the problem is to act toward that humanitarian disaster." Dr Strada further noted that "All this business of genocide in Sudan...I think has come up as an idea to sort of pave the ground for a possible military intervention. And next door there is the...Democratic Republic of Congo, where four million people have died because of the conflict, and no one has ever thought about mentioning genocide...A country comes to the light of the media when there are some political agendas from very powerful nations behind them."[730]

There has also been criticism of the Bush administration's questionable declaration of genocide from American elder statesmen such as the former president, Jimmy Carter. Speaking during a visit to Darfur, Carter, whose charitable foundation, the Carter Center, worked to establish the International Criminal Court, said that Washington's use of the term "genocide" was both legally inaccurate and "unhelpful". He went on to say that: "There is a legal definition of genocide and Darfur does not meet that legal standard. The atrocities were horrible but I don't think it qualifies to be called genocide. If you read the law textbooks...you'll see very clearly that it's not genocide and to call it genocide falsely just to exaggerate a horrible situation I don't think it helps."[731] Carter also noted that: "Rwanda was definitely a genocide; what Hitler did to the Jews was; but I don't think it's the case in Darfur. I think

Darfur is a crime against humanity, but done on a micro scale. A dozen janjaweed attacking here and there. I don't think the commitment was to exterminate a whole group of people."[732]

The first American academic study of the Bush administration's declaration of genocide in Darfur has also questioned the true motivation for such a finding, especially when compared to the inaction of the Clinton administration during the Rwandan genocide, noting that "especially perplexing is that while the Clinton administration sought to deny what (they and) the international community knew about genocide in Rwanda, the Bush White House sought to brand the situation in Darfur as genocide despite significant uncertainty as to whether this was, in fact, the case. Bush continues to do so despite a UN inquiry in January of 2005 that concluded that genocide had *not* taken place."[733] The study notes:

> That the UN came to a different conclusion than the United States regarding genocide in Darfur is relevant to the present concern for at least two reasons. First, as a circumstantial matter, it is curious, to say the least that the United States would find it expedient to label the Darfur atrocities 'genocide,' request a UN investigation only to have its claim challenged and then continue to use the rhetoric of genocide despite the UN's contradictory findings…The second reason…has to do with the simple fact that Darfur is not Rwanda. While Darfur as been characterized as 'Rwanda in slow motion', the atrocities in Rwanda are qualitatively and quantitatively different from those in Rwanda 10 years earlier. Eight hundred thousand deaths in 100 days are scarcely comparable to an estimated 70,000 in 10 months. Thus, when the United States continued to use the rhetoric of genocide despite the UN's contrary findings…led to charges by several leaders – mainly in the Islamic and Arab worlds – that the United States was employing the rhetoric of genocide as a pretext to invade another oil-rich and predominately Arab and Muslim state.[734]

The study also concludes that "the word 'genocide' undoubtedly has entailments that…other atrocities do not: it is more inflammatory, more reproachful, and entails at least a moral (if not legal) obligation to stop such acts...and it is why the Bush administration's characterization of the Darfur crisis as genocide created a groundswell of controversy in world capitals in 2004...It may indeed be a truism to say that the United States and those elites who represent it will only use the rhetoric of genocide if they stand to gain something from doing so."[735]

Interestingly, Professor Francis Fukuyama, once the intellectual centre of the neo-conservative movement within the United States, has also noted the difference between Darfur and instances of unambiguous genocide: "If the conflict in Darfur is genocide, it is also quite different from German treatment of the Jews or the Hutu slaughter of Tutsis in Rwanda."[736]

Mahmood Mamdani has also pointed to the double-standards in any instance of the American position on genocide. Mamdani has succinctly pointed out the contradictions in Washington's Darfur genocide declaration:

> The similarities between Iraq and Darfur are remarkable. The estimate of the number of civilians killed over the past three years is roughly similar. The killers are mostly paramilitaries, closely linked to the official military, which is said to be their main source of arms. The victims too are by and large identified as members of groups, rather than targeted as individuals. But the violence in the two places is named differently. In Iraq, it is said to be a cycle of insurgency and counter-insurgency; in Darfur, it is called genocide. Why the difference? Who does the naming? Who is being named? What difference does it make?[737]

Speaking about the "politics around genocide", Mamdani has asked when is the killing of civilians a genocide? He stated that "genocide is being instrumentalized by the biggest power on the earth today, which is the United States." Deaths "which implicate its adversaries are being named as genocide and those which implicate its friends or its proxies are not being named as genocide".[738] Mamdani has compared the American response to Darfur to its non-response to Congo, the dimensions of which "give it a mega-Darfur quality: the numbers killed are estimated in the millions rather than the hundreds of thousands; the bulk of the killing, particularly in Kivu, is done by paramilitaries trained, organised and armed by neighbouring governments; and the victims on both sides – Hema and Lendu – are framed in collective rather than individual terms, to the point that one influential version defines both as racial identities and the conflict between the two as a replay of the Rwandan genocide." Mamdani then points out that the neighbouring governments, Rwanda and Uganda, are allies of the United States: "Could the reason be that in the case of Congo, Hema and Lendu militias – many of them no more than child soldiers – were trained by America's allies in the region, Rwanda and Uganda? Is that why the violence in Darfur – but not the violence in Kivu – is named as a genocide?"[739]

The opportunistic underpinnings of the use of the genocide term in Darfur has also been highlighted by Professor Richard Lobban of Rhode Island College, a veteran scholar of Sudan, a past chairman of the Sudan Studies Association in the United States and a long-time critic of the Khartoum government. Writing in Macmillan's *Encyclopaedia on Race and Racism*, Lobban stated with regard to the genocide claim that "Notably three non-African and non-Arab nations were the most interested in applying this term. Perhaps for reasons of domestic pressures, or as diversionary efforts were England, the United States and Israel."[740] Professor Hisham Aidi, a Columbia University professor, has elaborated on Lobban's comment about Israeli interest in the genocide term, stating that pro-Israeli scholars have focused on Darfur as a means of shifting the international spotlight away from Palestine.[741]

The Save Darfur movement's use of Elie Wiesel to support its assertions of genocide in Darfur has also been opportunistic.[742] Wiesel has previously been criticised for flip-flopping on genocide issues, and picking and choosing which "genocide" he wishes to acknowledge and when he chooses to do so. In 1982, for example, Wiesel was scheduled to be the honorary chairman of a conference on genocide in Israel. When Armenia was scheduled for discussion, Wiesel pulled out of the event, and urged noted Israeli Holocaust historian Yehuda Bauer to also boycott the conference. Norman Finkelstein has pointed out:

> Elie Wiesel and Rabbi Arthur Hertzberg as well as the AJC and Yad Vashem withdrew from an international conference on genocide in Tel Aviv because the academic sponsors, against Israeli government

urging, included sessions on the Armenian case. Wiesel also sought, unilaterally, to abort the conference and, according to Yehuda Bauer, personally lobbied others not to attend. Acting at Israel's behest, the US Holocaust Council practically eliminated mention of the Armenians in the Washington Holocaust Memorial Museum, and Jewish lobbyists in Congress blocked a day of remembrance for the Armenian genocide.[743]

Professor Noam Chomsky has also pointed to this instance as an example of Wiesel "serving Israeli state interests".[744] It should also be noted that Wiesel has subsequently put his name to a declaration by Nobel Prize winners that the Armenian genocide did actually take place.[745]

Bloggers have also been active in highlighting the inconsistencies in Washington's genocide finding. Writing on the "Dissidentvoice" blog, Glen Ford notes: "Possibly a quarter million people have lost their lives in Darfur, western Sudan, in ethnic conflict. The US government screams its head off in denunciation of genocide, in this case. In the Democratic Republic of Congo (DRC), as many as five million have died since 1994 in overlapping convulsions of ethnic and state-sponsored massacre. Not a word of reproach from Washington. A human death toll that approaches the Nazis' annihilation of Jews in World War Two – an ongoing holocaust – unfolds without a whiff of complaint from the superpower."[746] Conor Foley, a British academic, humanitarian aid worker and blogger, has also repeatedly challenged the misuse of the genocide label in Darfur, stating that given the current political climate in Sudan, it "is bit like crying 'fire' in a crowded theatre".[747] The American blogger, David Peterson, spoke for many when he asked the question: "Imagine invoking the 'G'-word – politically and morally and legally combined, the single most invidious word in the lexicon…– in as deliberately ostentatious a fashion as the Bush Administration just has, and then adding by way of footnote: No new action is dictated by our use of the 'G'-word."[748]

Reputable British newspapers have also voiced concern at the claims made by Colin Powell. The London *Observer* newspaper reported that international aid workers in Sudan were claiming that American warnings that Darfur is heading for an apocalyptic genocidal catastrophe, as voiced by the United States Agency for International Development, had been widely exaggerated by

Administration officials in Washington. An aid worker interviewed by *The Observer* newspaper also touched on the apparent lack of concern shown by Powell: "It suited various governments to talk it all up, but they don't seem to have thought about the consequences. I have no idea what Colin Powell's game is, but to call it genocide and then effectively say, 'Oh, shucks, but we are not going to do anything about that genocide' undermines the very word 'genocide'."[749] It was claimed that a desire for regime change in Khartoum had coloured their reports. *The Observer* pointed out that American genocide claims had been "comprehensively challenged by eyewitness reports from aid workers and by a new food survey of the region. The nutritional survey of Sudan's Darfur region, by the UN World Food Programme, says that although there are still high levels of malnutrition among under-fives in some areas, the crisis is being brought under control." Many aid workers and officials interviewed by *The Observer* were puzzled that Darfur had become the focus of such hyperbolic warnings when there were crises of similar magnitude in both northern Uganda and eastern Congo.[750]

The Observer noted that "Concern about USAID's role as an honest broker in Darfur has been mounting for months, with diplomats as well as aid workers puzzled over its pronouncements and one European diplomat accusing it of 'plucking figures from the air'." The newspaper also pointed out that two of USAID's most senior officials, director Andrew Natsios, a former vice-president of the Christian charity World Vision, and Roger Winter, a former director of the US Committee for Refugees, have long been hostile to the Sudanese government.[751] Winter had already attempted, in the course of the civil war in southern Sudan, to use "genocide" propaganda. While he was director of the US Committee for Refugees, the organisation published *Quantifying Genocide in the southern Sudan 1983-1993*.[752] As Sudan historian Douglas H Johnson has noted: "At the release of this report the U.S. Committee for Refugees pre-empted criticism by suggesting that anyone questioning that figure was denying the scale of human devastation. Herein lies the value of the exercise: it is designed to attract attention."[753] Johnson then quotes statistical expert David Henige: "Numbers wielded for the immediate benefit of others – whether statistics collected on crowd sizes or numbers of homeless estimated – need have no relation to reality, since it is only the impression that matters."[754] Considerable caution, therefore, needs to be exercised before accepting any of the statistical claims made by American-commissioned reports of war-related deaths in Darfur.[755] In any instance, USAID claims projecting hundreds of thousands of deaths were contradicted by the United Nations 2004 end-of-year report which stated that "The catastrophic mortality figures predicted by some quarters have not materialised".[756] Interestingly, while content to use statistical extrapolations and projections in its ongoing propaganda campaign against Sudan on Darfur, Washington has been noticeably shy of accepting any similar statistical extrapolations with regard to its war in Iraq.[757]

Washington's shallow use of the term genocide has had several negative effects. Juan Méndez, the Special Adviser to the UN Secretary-General on the Prevention of Genocide, has stated that the discussion of whether or not the Darfur situation constituted genocide had been "sterile and paralysing".[758] *The Financial Times* has reported that "Amnesty and Human Rights Watch say that debating the definition of the atrocities has detracted from a key issue: action by the international community to help end the violence and ensure those responsible are brought to justice."[759]

Perhaps the most telling contradiction of claims of genocide in Darfur also applied to similar – and equally propagandistic – claims of genocide in southern Sudan. The simple fact is that victims of genocide do not move towards those engaged in their slaughter. Jews within Germany in the 1930s and 1940s were seeking to flee Germany not move towards Berlin or other urban centres. Jews elsewhere in Europe were not moving towards Germany. Similarly, during the Rwandan genocide, Tutsis were not heading towards Kigali or other Hutu government-controlled centres; they were fleeing into the countries neighbouring Rwanda. During the 50-year civil war in southern Sudan, however, at least half of the southern population voluntarily trekked northwards – often in difficult circumstances – to seek refuge in northern Sudan, and particularly Khartoum. They could more easily have gone to live in Uganda, Kenya, Ethiopia or the Congo, often amongst their own extended tribal kin. Many thousands more chose to live within government-controlled cities and towns in southern Sudan. Similarly, most of those displaced in Darfur have chosen not to flee to Chad, to live amongst their extended kin, but have chosen instead to move to government-controlled urban areas such as al-Fasher, Nyala and al-Geneina. Most people do not flee toward "genocidal" assaults.

This was a point touched on by *Guardian* journalist Jonathan Steele: "Grim though it has been, this was not genocide or classic ethnic cleansing. Many of the displaced moved to camps a few kilometers from their homes. Professionals and intellectuals were not targeted, as in Rwanda. Darfur was, and is, the outgrowth of a struggle between farmers and nomads rather than a Balkan-style fight for the same piece of land. Finding a solution is not helped by turning the violence into a battle of good versus evil or launching another Arab-bashing crusade."[760] Marc Lavergne, of the French National Centre for Scientific Research in Paris, has made the similar observation that the violence has not been aimed at Darfurian identity: "Darfurians who live in Khartoum are not targeted."[761]

Short of saying that the vast majority of Darfurians are suffering from collective "false consciousness", it is impossible for groups such as the Save Darfur coalition to explain away this simple fact.

In her groundbreaking 1999 study of media accountability, *Compassion Fatigue: How the Media Sell, Disease, Famine, War and Death*, Professor Susan Moeller made several points which are borne out by recent media coverage of the Darfur crisis, points relevant to current attempts to label events there as "genocide". Unlike many journalists, Moeller has asked the key question "How does genocide differ, for example, from ethnic, tribal or civil war?" and warned that "In common parlance and in the media the term genocide has lost its specific meaning and become almost commonplace. It has become synonymous with massacre and gross oppression or repression."[762] Charles Lane, writing in *Newsweek*, has also observed: "The world is full of places where one ethnic group is feuding with another...In every case, the fighting is characterized by atrocities, and the victims cry genocide."[763]

This is also a point touched on by David White, the Africa editor of *The Financial Times*:

> The word genocide is too freely used. Deliberate attacks on civilians, including indiscriminate bombing and executions, can certainly be categorised as war crimes or crimes against humanity. Despite official denials, there is overwhelming testimony that attacks by Arab militia riders have been undertaken in joint operations with government forces. But this is not genocide in the sense of a deliberate plan to

kill a whole population group, as happened in Rwanda. A more plausible version is that, by exploiting traditional tensions in the region, the authorities unleashed forces beyond their control and had difficulty coming to terms with the consequences. Clashes between farmers and nomadic herders go back for generations in Darfur. Conflict over land, access to water and the raiding of cattle have got worse in the past 20 years as a result of drought, desertification and the availability of modern weapons. At its origin it is a conflict about resources, not racial hatred. The standard labelling of 'Arabs' as opposed to 'black Africans' is misleading inasmuch as both groups are black and both are Muslim. The distinctions are more tribal and cultural.[764]

The issue was also addressed in *The World Today*, the journal of the Royal Institute of International Affairs. Peter Quayle, an expert working with the International Criminal Tribunal for the Former Yugoslavia, said that it would be wrong to label events in Darfur as genocide: "The conflict is a complex social, political and military struggle for wealth and power. Although it coincides with racial differences, the ongoing destruction is a coincidental not motivating purpose." Referring to the 1954 Genocide Convention, Quayle notes:

The Convention's two invidious questions ought to be asked. Are non-Arab Darfurians a people that the Convention protects as a group in whole or in part? And is this group, if protected, attacked as such? The group appears not to be a protected group partly because it relies on a regional definition. In answer to the second unhappy question – are these people being attacked only because they are members of a protected group? No, Darfurians are targeted because of the possibility they shelter and sustain rebels. Outside the conflict zone they are unharmed.[765]

Michael Clough is another human rights and Africa expert who quite clearly stated that the genocide label is inaccurate: "Genocide is not being committed in Darfur...But to call what's happening there 'genocide' when it's not is unlikely to help the people of Darfur."[766] Clough was director of the Africa program at the Council on Foreign Relations from 1987 to 1996. He is the author of *Free at Last? United States Policy toward Africa and the End of the Cold War*. As Human Rights Watch's interim advocacy director for Africa from September 2004 to July 2005, during which time he helped to publicise the organisation's findings in Darfur, Clough followed the unfolding Darfur crisis very closely.

Clough stated that "lawyers and researchers within Human Rights Watch…concluded that the events in Darfur did not rise to the level of genocide, a legal designation in international law, because there was no proof of 'intent to destroy, in whole or in part, a national, ethnic, racial or religious group, as such' That didn't stop activists — inspired in part by Samantha Power's book, 'A Problem from Hell: America and the Age of Genocide' — from invoking the emotive power of the word 'genocide' to mobilize the international community." [767]

Convenient sound-bites about the tenth anniversary of the Rwandan genocide do not make the events in Darfur genocidal. Michael Clough has rebutted attempts by activists to liken events in Darfur to the Rwandan tragedy. They had "buttressed their case by drawing attention to the fact that the atrocities in Darfur were coming to light as the world was holding ceremonies commemorating the 10th anniversary of the genocide in Rwanda". Clough noted, however, that

> the pattern of human rights abuses in Darfur is very different from what happened in Rwanda. As Alison Des Forges, a senior advisor to the Africa division of Human Rights Watch, and others have documented, the slaughter in Rwanda was carefully planned and ruthlessly carried out in a matter of weeks; the clear intent was to eliminate the Tutsi population of Rwanda. In all, 800,000 people were butchered. In Darfur, the Sudanese government has targeted African villagers. But it is not clear that the government's intent is to wipe out these Africans. The assaults followed successful rebel attacks on some government military facilities. In unleashing janjaweed and targeting the rebels' base of support, the government used the same counterinsurgency tactics it employed in a decades-

old war against southerners...The Sudanese government is certainly not the first to combat an insurgency by attacking sympathetic villages and displacing civilians.[768]

Clough has also noted that before the current crisis previous inter-tribal "clashes were chiefly the result of environmental pressures and competition for land, not deep-seated ethnic or racial animosities. And, until 2003, Darfur was relatively peaceful. By contrast, the genocide in Rwanda was presaged by a history of attempts by Hutus and Tutsis to slaughter each other."[769]

The way in which Washington's "genocide" label has been used has been illustrated by the statements of SLA leader Abd al-Wahid. In November 2005, in the months leading up to the signing of the Darfur Peace Agreement, he declared himself to be fighting "to stop the genocide".[770] After the DPA was signed, he declared genocide again and asked "how can we negotiate with someone who is committing genocide against our people?"[771] What Abd al-Wahid neglects to mention is that in between his protests about "genocide" in Darfur, he came very close to signing the DPA itself. The AU mediators in Abuja paint a picture of a man who was holding out for some more million dollars and an extra ministerial post in each of Darfur's three state governments.[772]

Given that genocide is not being carried out in Darfur, something which is very obvious to many observers in the West, and especially within the developing world – and that the political opportunism of such claims is equally clear – the Khartoum government is able to use Washington's claims to strengthen its position within the Third World. This was a point noted by *The Washington Post*'s Emily Wax: "Sudan's government has used the genocide label to market itself in the Middle East as another victim of America's anti-Arab and anti-Islamic policies."[773]

It should also be noted that in their propagandistic frenzy, anti-Sudan activists have also reduced the issue of genocide to the level of a video game. Called "Darfur is Dying", and designed and launched by the MTV music channel and Darfur activists, the free game is said to "raise awareness" of events in Darfur. Players would adopt the role of a Darfurian teenager running away from a Janjaweed gunman.[774]

If not genocide, the question must be asked then what is it? De Waal and

Flint have an answer. Noting that any outside western observer would expect to find a "a sort of slow-motion Rwanda in the desert" in Darfur they stated: "What will you find on arrival? A reality that's complicated and messy. A Darfur that has more in common with Chad, southern Sudan and – dare we say it? – Somalia."[775]

Allegations that the Darfur Conflict is Racial

One of the other sensationalist themes encountered with respect to the conflict in Darfur is that it is a racial one in which light-skinned "Arab" tribes have been engaged in the "ethnic cleansing" of black "African" tribes.[776] These sorts of claims are particularly inflammatory and very questionable. Mamdani has noted that "The implication that these are two different races, one indigenous and the other not is dangerous."[777] The simple fact is that there is very little, if any, racial difference between the many tribes of Darfur, "Arab" or "African". Both communities are black. Prunier has noted: "In terms of skin colour everybody is black."[778] The London *Observer* newspaper has reported, for example, that "[c]enturies of intermarriage has rendered the two groups physically indistinguishable".[779] The UN media service noted: "In Darfur, where the vast majority of people are Muslim and Arabic-speaking, the distinction between 'Arab' and 'African' is more cultural than racial."[780] This reality has also been confirmed by de Waal and other anti-government activists. Ryle has noted that Arabs and non-Arabs "are generally physically indistinguishable".[781] *The New York Times* has exemplified contradictory reporting on this issue, with articles on one hand by their columnist Nicholas Kristof alleging, for example, that "black Africans have been driven from their homes by lighter-skinned Arabs in the Janjaweed"[782] while also publishing subsequent news articles such as "In Sudan, No Clear Difference Between Arab and African".[783] Kristof has subsequently found it necessary to explain away the fact that Sudanese President al-Bashir's family "appears to come from an African tribe". Kristof then chose to disingenuously point to political rather than racial roots for his claims of genocide in Darfur.[784] Even "African" Darfurian anti-government figures such as Dr Eltigani Ateem Seisi contradict the dangerously lazy shorthand of Kristof in *The New York Times*. Speaking at a conference in Brussels he stated with reference to "Arabs" and "Africans" in Darfur that "we all look alike" and that one "can't tell from the features if he is Arab or African". He added that he, an "African", had a lighter skin than many "Arabs".[785]

De Waal has also pointedly challenged the "Arab" versus "African" stereotype, stating that "Characterizing the Darfur war as 'Arabs' versus 'Africans' obscures the reality. Darfur's Arabs are black, indigenous, African Muslims – just like Darfur's non-Arabs."[786] He has also said:

> We will see that the story is not as simple as the conventional rendering in the news, which depicts a conflict between 'Arabs' and 'Africans.' The Zaghawa...are certainly indigenous, black and African: they share distant origins with the Berbers of Morocco and other ancient Saharan peoples. But the name of the 'Bedeyat', the Zaghawa's close kin, should alert us to their true origins: pluralize in the more traditional manner and we have 'Bedeyiin' or Bedouins. Similarly, the Zaghawa's adversaries in this war, the Darfurian Arabs, are 'Arabs' in the ancient sense of 'Bedouin,' meaning desert nomad...Darfurian Arabs, too, are indigenous, black, and African. In fact there are no discernible racial or religious differences between the two: all have lived there for centuries.[787]

A Policy of Ethnic Cleansing in Darfur?

There has obviously been a vast displacement of civilians within Darfur, especially amongst those communities from which the rebels have recruited and presumably sought other support. A sensationalist media and human rights industry has claimed that the government has pursued a policy of ethnic cleansing in Darfur.[788] The Sudanese junior foreign minister Najeeb Alkhair Abdelwahab has stated with regard to claims of ethnic cleansing in Darfur that: "The situation in Darfur is neither one of ethnic cleansing nor genocide. It is primarily a clash over resources."[789] Médecins Sans Frontières has noted that "there is no systematic target – targeting one ethnic group or another one". Jan Egeland has also stated that the term "ethnic cleansing" did not fit events in Darfur: "I think we have more reports actually of a kind of scorched earth [policy] – and that nobody has taken over....It's complex, because some have said that it doesn't fit the legal definition of ethnic cleansing. The same tribes are represented both among those who are cleansed and those who are cleansing."[790] Egeland's views have been echoed by key human rights experts. Asma Jehangir, the UN rapporteur on extra-judicial summary and arbitrary executions, for example, has said: "I wouldn't categorise it as ethnic cleansing at the moment because that is not the impression that I am getting. It could be an unintended purpose."[791]

Dr Charles King, the Chairman of the Faculty, School of Foreign Service, Georgetown University, has also highlighted in any instance difficulties with the "ethnic" label:

> The 1990s seemed to be the age of ethnic conflict. Around the world, the end of superpower competition heralded a sudden upsurge in age-old animosities. Federations collapsed and genocidal wars broke out, each one over basic differences of religion, language, and history. This is one common reading of the last two decades, but it is in large measure inaccurate. In the first place, the very label "ethnic conflict" is largely a product of perception and representation, not an analytical tag that describes a unique kind of social violence. No violent conflict ever involves all, or even most, members of one ethnic group suddenly rising up and deciding to kill all the members of another group. This is the cartoon version of ethnic war, but it is seriously out of step with reality...Mobilized ethnic groups certainly can and do have an effect on politics, but the opposite can also be true: politics can help create mobilized ethnicity in the first place. In other words, "ethnic conflict" is not a meaningful category of analysis unless we untangle what we, and the belligerents themselves, really mean by that label.[792]

French academic Gérard Prunier is clear in his views about claims of "ethnic cleansing" in Darfur:

> The notion of 'ethnic cleansing', implying that the GoS had been trying to displace African tribes in order to give their land to 'Arabs', is not backed by any evidence other than the shouts hurled at the

victims by the perpetrators themselves. Although they (the perpetrators) might have hoped for such an outcome of the massacres, it is doubtful that a policy of that kind had been clearly thought out in Khartoum. This does not exclude the possibility that some in the GoS might have wished for that outcome, but the few instances of 'Arabs' settling on the land abandoned by African peasants do not seem very convincing. The 'Arabs' are mostly nomads who do not seem much interested in becoming agriculturalists. [793]

Allegations of ethnic cleansing have also been clearly contradicted by Sudanese government actions. Far from wishing to see the displacement of "African" Darfurian communities, the government has self-evidently been very eager to see these communities returned to their homes. In the Plan of Action signed on 5 August 2005, the Government committed itself to signing an agreement with the International Organization for Migration (IOM) to oversee and assist in the voluntary return of internally displaced persons. The UN Secretary-General has noted with regard to this agreement that "since the Management and Coordination Mechanism was established, progress has been made in reaching definitions of appropriateness and voluntariness and establishing standard operating procedures, and these definitions have been practically implemented".[794] This agreement was signed by the government, IOM and the United Nations on 21 August. In November 2004, Khartoum reported to the UN that 270,000 displaced people had been returned to their places of origin. The Sudanese humanitarian affairs minister stated: "More than 270,000 people have voluntarily returned to their homes. This is a very good sign and indicator that the situation in Darfur is improving."[795] Jan Pronk, the then UN Special Envoy to Sudan, was said to be concerned because neither the UN High Commissioner for Refugees nor the UN Organisation for Migration had been consulted prior to the repatriation.

While there may well be some concern as to whether all the returns were voluntary, Khartoum's eagerness to return refugees to their place of origin is manifest. The United Nations has noted government pressure on displaced people to return home, and has undertaken profiling exercises which "will inform appropriate and timely planning of interventions when conditions for return are in place".[796] Attempts to compare Darfur to Kosovo or any other example of ethnic cleansing fail to explain why it is that – unlike in Kosovo and other parts of the former Yugoslavia, for example, where there were clear attempts by governments to permanently exclude people from their homeland – in Darfur the government is being criticised for trying to return people to where they came from.[797]

Allegations of a concerted, planned genocide or ethnic cleansing in Darfur also jar with the fact that in addition to several thousand AMIS peacekeepers and policemen, Khartoum has also allowed 13,500 aid workers, many of whom are foreigners, into the region. It has also allowed hundreds of foreign reporters into Darfur. These have included journalists from virtually every Western nation, and have included reporters from the BBC, Reuters, *The Times*, *The New York Times*, *The Washington Post*, *The Chicago Tribune*, *The Financial Times*, *The Christian Science Monitor*, *The Daily Telegraph*, *The Sunday Telegraph*, *The Independent*, *The Guardian*, Sky, CNN, *Time*, Knight-Ridder news service and *The Economist*. Several of these journalists have spent several weeks, and some several months, in Darfur. Most governments involved in a programme of genocide go out of their way to prevent any outsiders, especially journalists, from roaming around the area in question.

De Waal has pointed to several of the negative consequences of Washington's cynical use of the genocide label. It has distanced Washington from the rest of the international community – something which he believes has been exploited by the Sudanese government:

> The fact that the US media and government have mischaracterized the Darfur war as 'Arabs' killing 'Africans' has allowed Khartoum to portray it as (another) American conspiracy against Arabs. The US determination that genocide has been committed...has appeared to put Washington out on its own in its opposition to Khartoum. From the perspective of Khartoum (and indeed many other capitals in Africa and the Middle East), the genocide determination appears to be the cynical use of a new tool to legitimize US interventionism and demonize Arabs...At the very minimum, this new-found Arab solidarity will buy time for the Sudan government. At the maximum, the way in which the US has declared 'genocide' will disqualify it from contributing to any solutions in Sudan. [798]

Additionally, de Waal has pointed out that "the genocide finding is being internalized into the politics of the region…The Islamists in the Justice and Equality Movement have a strategy for regime change, using the atrocities in Darfur to delegitimize the Khartoum government internationally, thereby to bring it down. The SLA…has yet to develop a full political programme, and is instead largely reacting to events…It seeks intervention as a best option."[799]

De Waal's concerns have been echoed by *The Washington Post*'s East Africa bureau chief, Emily Wax, who has stated that "The 'genocide' label made [the Darfur conflict] worse". She noted that "Many of the world's governments have drawn the line at labelling Darfur as genocide. Some call the conflict a case of ethnic cleansing, and others have described it as a government going too far in trying to put down a rebellion." She has observed that the American government's labelling of the conflict as a "genocide" "only seems to have strengthened Sudan's rebels; they believe they don't need to negotiate with the government and think they will have U.S. support when they commit attacks. Peace talks have broken down seven times, partly because the rebel groups have walked out of negotiations."[800] The UN's special adviser on the Prevention of Genocide warned that the "genocide" debate had adversely affected the resolution of the conflict.[801]

The extent to which the genocide label has been devalued was also demonstrated by the fact that in June 2005 JEM accused the Chad government of committing genocide in Darfur.[802]

Prunier has asked perhaps the most pertinent question about allegations that the Sudanese government has sought to carry out genocide in Darfur: "genocide began to be mentioned as an explanation [for events in Darfur] in early 2004 by more militant members of the international community…This hypothesis…failed to explain why Khartoum would have picked such an obviously wrong moment."[803]

Prunier also examined what did happen in Darfur. He concluded that: "Darfur is a bad case of poorly conceived counter-insurgency carried out with completely inadequate means."[804] Commenting on de Waal's description of events in Darfur as "counter-insurgency on the cheap", Prunier asks whether "refined" or "efficient" forms of counter-insurgency exist. He added:

The predicament at the time of writing of the Israeli army in Palestine and even more of the US army in Iraq are cases in point. Even if the dominant army tries to restrain its forces and kill only when necessary, and to keep repeating public relations slogans to the point of dulling peoples' receptivity, the results tend to be poor...'Careful' or 'focalised' repression techniques aimed at separating an insurgency from its causes are largely a techno-military dream.[805]

Brendan O'Neill has perhaps best summed up the dangers of the opportunistic use of terms such as genocide:

The liberal use of the word "genocide" to describe civil wars, brutal clashes and Stalinist repression is deeply problematic for two reasons. Firstly, it distorts history...It belittles the greatest horror of human history by suggesting that similar things happen all the time in various war-zones or under tinpot dictatorships. No, they do not. Something like Germany's industrialised slaughter of half of Europe's Jews has never been repeated since...Secondly, over-use of the G-word obscures a true understanding of wars that take place today. Instead of struggling to understand why there is a war in Darfur, what is sustaining it and how it might be resolved, we simply denounce one side of the conflict as "evil" and deserving of punishment... Stop using the Holocaust in this way. It relativises history and simplifies the present. It is time we took a more grown-up and less hysterical approach to international affairs.[806]

Michael Clough has also pointed out how self-defeating such claims are: "Over the long run, peace in Darfur will require Africans and Arabs to live together. Calling their conflict 'genocidal' won't make that easier."[807]

Chapter Six

THE DARFUR MORTALITY SURVEYS

The advocacy powers of Prof Reeves and [Coalition for International Justice] are clearly stronger than their statistical ones...Using badly constructed numbers for sensational attention does not help the cause...unsubstantiated figures and exaggerations are easily discredited and do the beleaguered Darfur population a great disservice.

The Centre for Research on the Epidemiology of Disasters [808]

The United Nations says overall mortality rates in Sudan's...western Darfur region have dropped for a third consecutive year.

Voice of America, 21 October 2006. [809]

A particularly fertile propaganda battlefield has presented itself over how many people have died as a direct or indirect consequence of the conflict in Darfur. Alex de Waal has observed that "The estimation of mortality ought to be a purely scientific affair, free from moral coloring. But it never is...In Darfur, the figures have become more politicized than any in recent history." [810] Far from being an academic discussion, questionable figures have been central to many of the claims of genocide in Darfur. Claims about the deaths in Darfur have ranged from under 10,000 up to 500,000. [811] Whatever the variation in estimates may be, the simple fact is that thousands of civilians have died in Darfur over the past four years, and hundreds of thousands more have been displaced within the region. The danger, however, is that exaggerated and sensationalist claims about Darfur, if they do prompt misjudged military intervention in Sudan, would only lead to an ever-greater tragedy engulfing not just Darfur but the whole Sahel region. One clear example of this tendency has been the Save Darfur Coalition's multi-million dollar international advertising campaign within the United States and in Europe which claimed in a series of full-page newspaper advertisements and television commercials that 400,000 civilians had been killed, and used this claim to urge western military intervention.[812] It is also clear that the Bush Administration hyped the mortality figures, claiming in June 2004, for example, that between 300,000 and 1 million people might die in 2004.[813]

Given the controversy about mortality in Darfur it is essential that reputable and independent figures are examined. There have been several surveys of mortality in Darfur, and as is now clear they have been of varying reliability. It is worth noting that the war in Darfur, and with it the massive displacement of civilians and resultant food insecurity, was at its peak from late 2003 until early 2004. The first ceasefire agreement in April 2004 reflected this reality. Since then, while there have been numerous spikes in violence, the humanitarian situation broadly stabilized with the presence of over ten thousand aid workers and the deployment of several thousand African Union peacekeepers. While imperfect, the AU presence undoubtedly helped to stabilise the situation. A UN-commissioned World Health Organization mortality survey during critical months in 2004 estimated 10,000 deaths per month.[814] This death toll dropped off dramatically as the large-scale fighting came to an end and the UN aid effort had kicked in. The UN reported that by the end of 2004 the situation had stabilised and that the "catastrophic mortality figures predicted by some quarters have not materialised".[815] An unprecedented international humanitarian effort was on the ground in Darfur caring for the food and medical needs of the hundreds of thousands of civilians who had been displaced. It was widely reported in January 2005 that 70,000 people may have died from all causes to that date.[816] In a 14 January 2005 interview with *Spiegel International*, the Associate Director for Human Rights Watch, Carroll Bogert, stated that "In Darfur we're talking about the deaths of over 70,000."

In March 2005, the UN emergency relief coordinator, Jan Egeland, responding to questions from the press about Darfur mortality, gave his own, off-the-cuff, updated figure. It is clear that he extrapolated from a 2004 UN WHO mortality survey and multiplied that survey's figure of 10,000 deaths per month by 18 months, coming up with a new figure of 180,000 deaths.[817] Egeland's figure was very questionable. This estimate was not based on any new data collection or analysis other than multiplying the earlier 2004 WHO figure, and – as can be seen from other UN accounts – deaths in Darfur had not remained at a constant monthly figure of 10,000. The WHO figures were also subsequently found to be higher than they should have been, and any extrapolation based on them necessarily flawed. This was documented in the same month as Egeland's *ad hoc* claims. In mid-March 2005, for example, Professor Debarati Guha-Sapir, director of the World Health Organization-affiliated Centre for Research on the Epidemiology of Disasters at the Catholic University of Louvain (CRED)[818], noted that the Complex Emergencies Database (CEDAT), which monitors conflict mortality from surveys, reviewed more than 30 survey results from UN agencies and non-governmental organizations:

> These show that death and malnutrition rates in most parts of Darfur improved over the latter half of 2004 despite insecurity and political stalemate. Death rates for the displaced have halved since June 2004. All this is thanks to an efficient and effective donor response supporting an increasingly professional community of private and voluntary organizations and to the U.N. World Food Programme, the U.N. World Health Organisation and the U.N. Children's Fund, Unicef.[819]

Several wildly inaccurate mortality claims followed, based largely on the 2004 WHO report and the Chad-based "Atrocities Documentation Team" briefing. These were advanced by groups such as the self-styled Coalition for International Justice (CIJ) and activists such as Eric Reeves. They were challenged by scientific studies. In April 2005, for example, the US State Department issued a new report which estimated "excess", war-related, deaths in Darfur as between 63,000 and 146,000.[820] The US State Department also noted that "The fact that many prognosticators overemphasize the degree to which violent deaths contribute to large-scale mortality in a region as big and diffuse as Darfur continues to result in grossly overestimated projections of overall deaths."[821] In early May 2005, Professor Guha-Sapir commented upon the "unseemly fight" that "has broken out in the US over how many have died in Darfur". She was referring to the criticism of the State Department estimates by Eric Reeves and the Coalition for International Justice who claimed that 400,000 people have died. Professor Guha-Sapir noted:

> The advocacy powers of Prof Reeves and CIJ are clearly stronger than their statistical ones. Deaths of 300,000-400,000 are now quoted by the UK House of Commons, the UN Office for the Co-ordination of Humanitarian Affairs and a series of respectable newspapers…making those who plod systematically through evidence and come up with less sensational figures look like uncharitable scrooges…Using badly constructed numbers for sensational attention does not help the cause…unsubstantiated figures and exaggerations are easily discredited and do the beleaguered Darfur population a great disservice. [822]

In late May 2005, CRED published *Darfur: Counting the Deaths. Mortality Estimates from Multiple Survey Data*, a mortality survey based on the application of mortality estimates from UN population figures for each region in Darfur. This study estimated that between 63,000 – 146,000 people had died between March 2003 and January 2005 in Darfur and eastern Chad. Their deaths could be attributed to violence, disease and malnutrition because of the conflict during this period.[823] The report examined previous mortality surveys and found that some had been misused. Referring to materials cited by CIJ and Reeves, the Centre noted that:

> These interviews…were not designed in any way to function as a mortality survey nor was there an overall systematic sampling methodology used that could make it representative of the roughly 200,000 refugees that fled to eastern Chad, much less of the entire 2.4 million people affected of Darfur…The inappropriate misuse of these interviews…as a proxy for the aggregate Darfur population for the entire conflict (despite the availability of other more reliable data) has been a major basis of overestimation of deaths (common in most estimates).[824]

The Centre has also pointed out that an earlier 2004 "WHO mortality survey and the WHO mortality projections have often been confused and misguidedly used interchangeably." Incorrect assumptions have "led to double counting of violent deaths in many subsequent projections".[825] De Waal found CRED's work to be credible: "The most reliable study is the one conducted by the Centre for Research on the Epidemiology of Disasters." He also noted "The least reliable estimates were those provided by John Hagen and Eric Reeves. In fact, de Waal's only criticism of the CRED study is that "the authors were careful to make pessimistic assumptions at every stage." De Waal notes that "this is unusual—normally they would have made medium or marginally optimistic assumptions about mortality. The reason for the pessimism was that the figures for mortality in Darfur had become politicized, with many advocates speaking about extremely high death rates that were not, in fact, supported by systematic evidence. CRED's researchers did not want to be accused of minimizing the crisis. Personally, I would have preferred to have seen CRED stick to median assumptions, and therefore come with a slightly lower figure for estimated excess deaths." [826]

CRED's study was supported by other sources. The United Nations in Sudan, present throughout Darfur, stated in June 2005, for example, that "mortality in Darfur has significantly declined".[827] The World Health Organisation noted in July 2005 that "Mortality overall has declined substantially since the first WHO survey in all three states." The WHO stated that there had been a "three-fold drop in mortality" and that mortality indicators were "below the international crisis threshold".[828] In August 2005, Jan Pronk, the UN Sudan envoy, stated that there were about 100 people being killed in Darfur per month in the course of the conflict and even this, he stated, was "to a great extent" due to "banditry, looting, crime, which goes to hand-in-hand with a no-peace-no-war situation".[829] On 13 November 2005, Pronk noted further: "The mortality and malnutrition rates are even below those before the outbreak of the war in Darfur..." On 22 September 2006, he also confirmed that: "In 2005 the malnutrition and mortality figures decreased drastically. Aid has saved the life of tens of thousands of people." In April 2006, Pronk noted that on average 100 people a month were dying as a result of the conflict in Darfur.[830]

The December 2005 CRED published its second study, *Darfur: Counting the Deaths (2). What are the Trends?* This found that mortality in Darfur had declined and that even its own estimates of excess deaths were "likely to be over-estimations". CRED also stated that the baseline figure was actually lower that the Sub-Saharan average.[831]

The World Health Organisation has been very active in tracking morbidity and mortality trends in Darfur. In its report, the *Darfur Morbidity and Mortality Bi-Annual Report 22 May 2004 – 30 December 2005*, the World Health Organization provided details of the WHO outreach in the region.[832] The report stated that in week 21 of 2004 only 10 percent of Darfur's Internally Displaced Persons were under EWARS surveillance. By week 52 of 2004, 1,139, 825 were under surveillance; one million in week 1 of 2005; 1, 930,000 in week 41 of 2005 and it remained between 1.5 – 1.8 million per week afterwards. The average population under surveillance in 2005 was 1,435, 935, covering an average of 73.3 % of the IDP population (1,960,000) and 54.8% of the total affected population in Greater Darfur. The May-December 2005 *Darfur Morbidity and Mortality Bi-Annual Report* stated that acute respiratory tract infection was the primary cause of morbidity in Darfur for that period, resulting in 123 deaths in Darfur in 2005. The report stated that there were 59,819 injury cases in 2005, resulting in 134 deaths of persons over 5 years of age, and 7 children under five. The report also stated that 123 people died from severe malnutrition in 2005. UNICEF noted a decrease in severe malnutrition from 3.9% in 2004 to 1.4% in the IDP population in October 2005. EWARS data indicated a further reduction to less than 1% in the fourth quarter of 2005.

The World Health Organization's *Weekly Morbidity and Mortality Bulletin* is a crucial resource for monitoring deaths and mortality trends in Darfur. In December 2006, for example, the WHO had approximately 1,723,000 civilians under surveillance as part of its Early Warning and Alert Response Surveillance (EWARS) system. Between 3-9 December 2006, the WHO reported 29 deaths in all age groups as the result of 42,207 cases of health events.[833] While the World Health Organization EWARS system obviously does not monitor the entire war-affected population in Darfur, it does cover a vast amount of the population at risk. And, regarding those parts of Darfur which aid workers find it hard to cover, Julie Flint reports that in "many of the areas controlled by the rebels...life is returning to normal".[834]

This has continued through to present day. At the end of 2006, UNICEF reported that mortality rates in Darfur had "dropped for the third year running", and that malnutrition rates had dropped below the emergency threshold and "remained significantly below the 2004 malnutrition rates".[835] Professor Debarati Guha-Sapir's 18 December 2006 letter to *The Financial Times* clearly states that the Centre for Research on the Epidemiology of Disasters revised estimate of deaths in Darfur between 2003 and 2005 was 125,000. Professor Guha-Sapir also states that about one in five was due to violence. She further states that "During 2006, mortality in Darfur decreased below emergency levels." This was further confirmed by UNICEF which at the end of 2006 reported that mortality rates in Darfur had "dropped for the third year running", and that malnutrition rates had dropped below the emergency threshold and "remained significantly below the 2004 malnutrition rates". The WHO emergency threshold is one death per day per 10,000 of the population.

De Waal points to three "pretty reliable rules of thumb" concerning mortality during humanitarian crises:

> Number one, if an informed source gives a range of estimates for actual or predicted deaths, say '50,000 to 200,000 dead in the next year,' the press and the humanitarian advocates will seize on the high end figure and neglect the low end or the middle range. Even when post-crisis studies bring the numbers down, the headline figure somehow remains imprinted on the historical record...Number two, the high end figures rarely if ever materialize and the low end ones turn out to be more accurate...Number three, a crisis of mass displacement follows a regular and predictable mortality curve. There is a sharp peak, followed by a decline that slowly levels off, bringing death rates down to normal levels and often slightly below normal...The reason for the 'slightly below' normal is a combination of (a) good health facilities provided by relief agencies and (b) lower fertility rates during the crisis, which means fewer young children, and as children under five represent about two thirds of the mortality in a Sudanese population, ipso facto this reduces the crude death rate. A relief intervention can blunt the peak of mortality, accelerate the decline, and prevent further bumps as the crisis stretches on, but cannot change the basic pattern. Thus it is common to have a

protracted humanitarian crisis in which mortality rates in displaced populations are lower than pre-crisis levels. In Darfur, the peak followed the big offensives of 2003-04. [836]

Commenting on mortality since the end of 2005, de Waal noted that "The data for the displaced populations indicate a pattern, familiar from protracted emergencies, of crude death rates at normal levels, albeit with occasional bumps...Since the end of the major offensives in 2004, reports of violent deaths are compiled by the UN on a regular basis, though not published. There are peaks and lulls but the reports—which cover all significant incidents—indicate between 6,000 and 7,000 fatalities over the last two and a half years." [837] Regarding violence-related mortality, De Waal noted that "Violent deaths peaked between September 2003 and June 2004. According to the most thorough study (CRED), an estimated 35,000 people were killed by violence in this period through to January 2005. Over the last 24 months, the data contained in UN reports indicate that violent deaths have averaged 100-200 individuals per month, with occasional spikes of twice that number." [838]

De Waal has noted that "all surveys agree that mortality peaked in June 2004" and that "The WFP and UNICEF claim that the Darfur-wide crude mortality (CMR) rate fell as low as 0.35 deaths per 10,000 per day, which is much lower than the 1/10,000/day emergency threshold and similar to what would be considered normal for such a population in peacetime." He has also recorded that "Crude and under-5 mortality rates, the most important indicators of a population's health, peaked in early 2004, fell sharply through the end of year and have remained constantly below the emergency threshold since 2005."[839]

WFP and UNICEF's *Emergency Food Security and Nutrition Assessment in Darfur 2006* shows that food security in Darfur has been stable over the last year: "The number of people requiring assistance is not expected to vary significantly even after taking into account the prospects of the forthcoming harvest, due to the limited number of the food insecure households who have planted a significant acreage of cereals this season".[840] Commenting on that report, de Waal observed: "In addition, Global Acute Malnutrition (GAM) and Severe Acute Malnutrition (SAM) prevalence rates in Darfur fell sharply from 2004 to 2005 from 21.8 to 11.5 (GAM) and from 3.3 to 1.4 (SAM)...Since then, the prevalence rates appear to have stabilized." [841]

Writing in March 2007, both Dr Jean-Hervé Bradol, president of Médecins Sans Frontières, and Fabrice Weissman, Médecins Sans Frontières research director, supported CRED's mortality findings, citing the reported 131,060 conflict-related deaths in the September 2003-June 2005 period, of which one-quarter were killed in the war; the others from hunger and disease. Bradol and Weissman noted that "Although living conditions in the camps remain precarious, mortality and malnutrition rates are well below emergency thresholds (and in many camps, well below pre-war levels)". They also pointed out that while "still at unacceptable levels", violence against civilians has fallen in comparison with 2004: "Since the second half of 2006, the United Nations mission in Sudan has recorded an average of 200 civilian deaths per month, peaking above 400 in September-November." They reported that the "renewed outbreak of violence" was linked to fighting between the government and rebel groups that were not party to the DPA, and between rival armed groups.[842]

The simple fact is that WHO's mortality and morbidity bulletins, together with the statistics provided by other non-governmental organisations such as UNICEF actually on the ground in Darfur, do not in any way bear out the sort of figures being claimed by anti-Sudan "advocacy" groups and anti-Sudan activists such as Eric Reeves – figures subsequently recycled by Save Darfur and "Globe for Darfur" in their advertisements.

It is in this light that the claims of anti-Sudan activists such Eric Reeves should be assessed.[843] Reeves is the person most identified with claims that more than 400,000 people have been killed in Darfur. It is apparent that he took the 2004 WHO mortality survey as his baseline and multiplied each subsequent month by 10,000 regardless of the real situation on the ground. His inconsistencies are self-evident. He claimed, for example, that as of January 2005, 400,000 people had died in the Darfur conflict.[844] It is worth noting that this 400,000 figure itself jumped from claims he had made that deaths were "already approaching 100,000" in late June 2004.[845] That is to say, for example, that Reeves claimed that between July and December 2004 alone, over a third of a million civilians, 50,000 per month, died in Darfur – apparently without being documented either by the aid agencies or the many foreign journalists, diplomats and soldiers in Darfur, and at a time when the UN stated things were improving. Reeves' 400,000 figure continues to be cited in *The New York Times* and *The Washington Post*.

It comes as no surprise therefore that reputable groups such as CRED, and the American government, have criticised Eric Reeves for the propagandistic way in which he has approached quantifying the suffering of the people in Darfur. In December 2006, the United States government's accountability office (GAO) published *Darfur Crisis: Death Estimates Demonstrate Severity of Crisis, but Their Accuracy and Credibility Could Be Enhanced*, a comprehensive report examining Darfur mortality surveys.[846] This study was based on evaluations made by the world's top ten experts in the field. The report stated that most experts rated Reeves' "level of objectivity...as low. The experts thought that the estimates were more characteristic of advocacy or journalistic material than of objective analysis."

When asked whether Reeves' mortality estimate was based on methodologically sound source data, the ten experts responded negatively, seven saying "generally no" and three saying "definitely no". When asked whether they felt that Reeves had made "appropriate or inappropriate extrapolations from the source data to the affected population", all twelve experts stated that Reeves had used inappropriate extrapolations, with seven experts going further to state that Reeves had used "very inappropriate" extrapolations. When asked whether in their view the experts considered the assumptions made Reeves in his claims to be reasonable or unreasonable, eleven stated that he had made unreasonable assumptions: seven experts declared his assumptions to be "very unreasonable". The remaining expert stated that Reeves had made "as many reasonable as unreasonable assumptions".

When asked whether Reeves had sufficiently or insufficiently described appropriate limitations, including sources of possible over or under estimation, eleven experts stated that Reeves had insufficiently addressed this issue: seven thought that this was handled "very insufficiently". When asked to rate Reeves' level of objectivity as reflected in his mortality claims, all twelve of the experts described his objectivity as either "low" or "very low". When asked to describe their level of confidence in Reeves' estimates all twelve of the experts described it as low: eight experts stated that they had a "very low" level of confidence in Reeves.

The Definitive Survey of the Surveys

The official United States government report mentioned above, *Darfur Crisis:*

Death Estimates Demonstrate Severity of Crisis, but Their Accuracy and Credibility Could Be Enhanced, provided an objective assessment of at least some of the sensationalist claims about Darfur. This was a report to the US Congress.[847] The GAO stated that it commissioned this study because "While few would dispute that many thousands of Darfur civilians have died, less consensus exists about the total number of deaths attributable to the crisis. Estimates by the Department of State and other parties report death tolls up to about 400,000 for varying populations and periods of time between February 2003 and August 2005." The report was based on "the views of experts convened by GAO and the National Academy of Sciences, interviews with estimate authors, and a review of relevant literature". De Waal, who was invited to join the panel but was unable to do so as he was present at the Abuja peace talks, has stated that he supported the GAO conclusions and that his own assessment did "not differ from the consensus of the experts". [848]

To evaluate the Darfur death estimates, the GAO report reviewed and analysed public information on the estimates and interviewed the estimate authors regarding their studies' data, methods, and objectives. The GAO provided this information and summaries of the interviews to a group of 12 experts in epidemiology, demography and statistics, and convened an experts' conference in April 2006 in collaboration with the National Academy of Sciences.[849] The GAO also consulted "with officials from USAID, State, and the Centers for Disease Control and Prevention (CDC) in the U.S. Department of Health and Human Services".

The GAO report studied six estimates that were publicly available in March 2006. They were produced by (1) the World Health Organization (WHO); (2) the United States Department of State; (3) the World Health Organization-affiliated Centre for Research on the Epidemiology of Disasters (CRED) in Brussels, Belgium[850]; (4) Dr Jan Coebergh, a Dutch medical doctor who had worked in Darfur; (5) the Coalition of International Justice (written by John Hagan, Wynnona Rymond-Richmond, and Patricia Parker[851]); (6) Eric Reeves.

The World Health Organization estimated between 35,000 – 70,000 excess[852] deaths in Darfur between March – September 2004; the State Department estimated between 63,000 and 146,000 excess deaths between March 2003 and January 2005; CRED estimated a high-end 141,800 excess deaths between September 2003 and June 2005; Coebergh estimated 253,573 excess deaths; the

Coalition of International Justice estimate by Hagan *et al* was a total of 396,563 deaths. Reeves estimated "over 370,000 excess deaths".

The report noted that "Estimating deaths in a humanitarian crisis such as that in Darfur involves numerous challenges. For example, in Darfur, difficulties in collecting mortality data, such as lack of access to particular geographical regions, impacted the data's quality and led to data gaps. Because of such data gaps, some Darfur death estimates relied on potentially risky assumptions and limited contextual information. Further, limitations in estimates of Darfur's population before and during the crisis may have led to over- or under-estimates of the death toll. Finally, varying use of baseline mortality rates—the rate of deaths that would have occurred without the crisis—may have led to overly high or low death estimates."

Having reviewed the estimates, the GAO report stated that "Most of the experts had the highest overall confidence in estimates by the Centre for Research on the Epidemiology of Disasters (CRED)", followed by the State Department's estimate and then that of the World Health Organization. The GAO report stated that "most of the experts expressed the least confidence in three estimates that reported the highest number of deaths" – that is to say the three estimates ranging from 253,573 to 396,563 deaths. The experts "cited several shortcomings in these estimates, such as a reliance on unrealistic assumptions regarding fixed levels of mortality for all populations and time periods included in the estimate".

With regard to the CRED estimates, the report stated: "Overall, the experts rated CRED's estimates most highly in terms of data, methods, objectivity, and reporting of limitations." It further noted that: "Most experts said that the data CRED used for its two estimates (drawing from a total of about 30 mortality surveys in Darfur and Chad) were generally sound. CRED reported checking the reliability and validity of the surveys included in its estimates, which experts found to be a strength."

With regard to CRED's methods, including its extrapolations and assumptions, the report noted that "some experts found CRED's method of using disparate data sources to estimate total deaths to be innovative and logical. Additionally, more than half of the experts rated CRED's assumptions and extrapolations as somewhat appropriate or reasonable. For example, several experts found the Sudan baseline mortality rate that CRED used more accurate than the baseline mortality rates derived from a larger region of sub-Saharan Africa used in some of the other estimates."

With regard to objectivity the report stated that "experts viewed CRED's death estimates as having the highest level of objectivity. Two authors of other estimates also concluded that the CRED estimates were likely to be more reliable and more scientific than other Darfur death estimates, including their own". With regard to "sufficiency of reporting", the report stated that "experts noted that, among the estimates they evaluated, CRED most sufficiently reported the limitations and potential sources of over-or underestimation in its estimates."

With regard to the three highest estimates, the study stated: "Almost all experts expressed a low level of confidence in the estimates by Coebergh, Hagan, and Reeves." The report stated that "the majority of the experts viewed the estimates by Coebergh, Hagan, and Reeves as too high". Eight out of ten experts thought that Coebergh's estimates of 253,573 excess deaths and 306,130 excess deaths were "too high": all the experts concluded that the Coalition's estimate of 396,563 total deaths was "too high". Similarly, all the experts concluded that Reeves' estimate of "over 370,000 excess deaths" was "too high". The GAO noted: "The experts cited several methodological shortcomings in the Coebergh, Hagan, and Reeves estimates, including the use of problematic data and application of unrealistic assumptions about the levels of mortality over time and affected populations." In respect of source data

> Many experts found shortcomings in each of the three Estimates'
> use of certain survey data. A number of experts noted problems in
> the design, sampling, and data collection in the Atrocities
> Documentation Team's survey of Chad refugees on which all three
> estimates based, at least in part, their numbers of violent deaths.
> Experts also pointed out that, because the survey's intended purpose
> was to document levels and types of victimization, the estimates by
> Dr. Coebergh, Dr. Hagan, and Dr. Reeves should not have
> extrapolated the survey findings to a broader population or time
> period in order to estimate total deaths. In addition, many experts
> observed that the estimates by Coebergh and Hagan inappropriately
> used findings from the 2004 WHO survey to calculate only non-

violent deaths without taking into account the fact that some deaths reported by the WHO were due to violence or injury.

With regard to the methods used, including extrapolations and assumptions, the report stated that

most experts found that the Coebergh, Hagan, and Reeves estimates used unrealistic extrapolations and assumptions to fill information gaps and estimate total deaths. For example, many experts thought that each of the three estimates relied on too few data points extrapolated to an excessive degree. As a result of this type of extrapolation, the experts observed, a sensitivity analysis changing one or two assumptions could swing the total number of deaths from 100,000 to half a million, making the estimates unreliable. Moreover, several experts believed that some of the authors had inappropriately assumed constant rates of mortality for different population groups in Darfur at different periods in the conflict. Two of the estimates (Coebergh's and Hagan's) also used 'fixed' estimates of the affected population over time, a method that some experts thought was inappropriate because the affected population grew over the course of the conflict. Additionally, the three estimates involve assumptions that some experts viewed as questionable, such as using unsupported numbers to estimate the number of deaths among populations inaccessible to aid or assuming all missing persons were likely to be dead."

Additionally, with regard to sufficiency of reporting shown in the three higher estimates, the report noted that "most of the experts found that the three estimates did not sufficiently describe limitations that may have resulted in under-or overestimation of total deaths."

It is worth noting that the GAO study asked the authors of the various death estimates what they were seeking to achieve: "The authors of the CRED estimates said that their aim in conducting their estimate was to develop a method that, rather than extrapolating mortality from a single survey to the entire region and conflict period, took into account variations over time and space." Interestingly, Dr Coebergh stated that his estimate was intended as "a political statement". It is a matter of record that much the same can be said for the work of Eric Reeves. The essentially political nature of the three highest claims was touched on in the GAO study. With regard to the level of objectivity reflected in the three highest estimates, the GAO stated that "Most experts rated the level of objectivity of the three estimates as low, particularly those by Drs. Coebergh and Reeves."

With regard to the objectivity of the Department of State estimate, the study stated that "nine of the 12 experts rated the State estimate's level of objectivity as high. Several experts generally believed that the estimate represented a 'good faith effort' to use available evidence in an unbiased way." Regarding the structure of the U.S. government estimate, the reported noted: "In assessing State's estimate, the experts identified methodological strengths related to each of the four elements but also noted some shortcomings. Strengths included its use of multiple types of information, including contextual data from other sources besides surveys, such as reporting of attacks." Regarding source data the report stated: "Many experts cited as one strength the estimate's use of different types of data, including mortality survey data and contextual information, to triangulate findings and estimate mortality, and one expert deemed this approach a 'pioneering attempt' in the field of death estimates in humanitarian crises… However, just over half of the experts thought that the data used were methodologically sound…Some experts said that several of the mortality surveys used in State's estimate may have had methodological limitations in areas such as survey design, implementation, or accessibility to insecure regions, resulting in unrealistically low mortality rates."

Regarding the World Health Organization survey, the report stated: "Several experts found strengths in the data and level of objectivity of the WHO's estimate, which it presented in a short briefing in October 2004." With regard to source data, the report noted: "The WHO estimate of IDP deaths in Darfur for 7 months in 2004 relied primarily on findings from the organization's 2004 mortality survey. Several experts noted that this survey followed standard methods and was generally reliable." Half the experts thought that "the WHO estimate's level of objectivity was equal to CRED's and State's."

Limitations in Population Data and Baseline Mortality Rates Affect Reliability of Death Estimates

The GAO study also noted several key factors affecting accurate mortality estimates:

> Limitations in the population data before and during a crisis such as Darfur's can also impact researchers' ability to produce reliable death estimates. No definitive estimate of Darfur's pre-crisis population exists, and estimates of the current population vary considerably, from around 4 to 7 million. The difficulty of estimating the region's population is compounded by the fact that migration was widespread in Darfur before the crisis, making it difficult to get accurate counts. Because the death estimates essentially extrapolate the mortality rates from the surveys to the entire population affected by the crisis, an estimate of the affected population that is too high or too low will lead to an over-or underestimate of the death toll.

The report correctly pointed out that the use of varying baseline mortality rates can significantly affect the accuracy of the mortality estimates:

> Varying approaches to the selection of a baseline for normal mortality can raise or lower death estimates, possibly making the totals overly high or low... For example, CRED's use of a baseline mortality rate of 0.3 subtracted about 16,000 deaths from the total estimate of 134,000, resulting in 118,000 'excess' deaths. If CRED had used a baseline of 0.5, it would likely have subtracted about 26,000 deaths, obtaining a somewhat lower estimate of deaths from the crisis... The experts we convened proposed various baseline mortality rates, ranging from 0.3 to 0.75 deaths per 10,000 affected persons per day... About half of the experts said that deaths that would have occurred regardless of the crisis should be subtracted from the death toll attributed to the crisis.

The simple fact is that the work done by the Centre for Research on the

Epidemiology of Disasters and borne out by the World Health Organisation's mortality and morbidity bulletins, together with statistics provided by other non-governmental organisations such as UNICEF actually on the ground in Darfur, do not in any way bear out the sorts of figures being claimed by anti-Sudan "advocacy" groups such as the Save Darfur Coalition or by anti-Sudan activists such as Eric Reeves. The opinion of international experts such as those brought together for the American government's *Darfur Crisis: Death Estimates Demonstrate Severity of Crisis, but Their Accuracy and Credibility Could Be Enhanced* report clearly documented the slapdash way in which "advocates" had sought to twist Darfur mortality figures.

Chapter Seven

DARFUR, HUMAN RIGHTS AND HYPOCRISY

[T]he simplistic characterization – used, for example, by Human Rights Watch – of 'Arabs' killing 'Africans' doesn't fit.

Human Rights Activist Alex de Waal [853]

All wars, and particularly civil wars, lead to human rights violations. Civilians are inevitably caught up in war and are invariably its primary victims. The conflict in Darfur has been no exception. The Government of Sudan has admitted that there have been serious abuses of human rights in the course of the Darfur conflict.[854] The government is also cooperating with a number of UN protection-oriented agencies, with British funding, in human rights training programmes for Sudanese armed forces and police. The government has also opened Darfur to human rights investigators. Numerous human rights delegations and specialists have visited the region. These include the a United Nations High Commission for Human Rights mission from 24-30 April 2004; the United Nations special rapporteur on extrajudicial, summary or arbitrary executions, Asma Jehangir, who visited for several days in June 2004; the African Human Rights Commission visited Darfur in July 2004; the United Nations High Commissioner for Human Rights, Louise Arbour, and the Secretary-General's special adviser on the prevention of genocide, Juan Méndez, 20-24 September 2004, and again in 2005; the UN special rapporteur on violence against women, Professor Yakin Ertürk, visited Darfur from 25 September to 2 October 2004; Amnesty International visited Darfur in September 2004; the five-member United Nations commission of enquiry into allegations of genocide in November 2004; and so on. All have noted that there were no restrictions placed on their visits. Numerous other visits have followed.

And, as is so often the case in war, the conflict has been caught up in the propaganda and misinformation that comes with it and that has certainly characterised previous coverage of Sudan. The Sudanese government, for example, has claimed that: "Those with their own agendas are trying to give a very sad view of what is happening. The propaganda in the west is trying to exaggerate what is taking place in Darfur."[855] It is, of course, essential that human rights are protected, and that those who violate human rights are reported on and that action against human rights violators is taken. It is also commendable that there are dedicated organisations that focus exclusively on human rights issues. Sadly, all too often, many of the western human rights organisations follow political agendas set by a western élite that through prejudice or pressure group politics badly serve the developing world. It must also be noted that the United Nations High Commissioner for Human Rights, Ms Arbour, undermined her credibility and that of the United Nations, when in her October 2004 report on Darfur she stated that she had "received no credible reports of rebel attacks on civilians as such".[856]

De Waal's point, made above, about the human rights industry's use of simplistic characterisation is right. Much of the human rights reporting on the Darfur crisis, and especially that by Human Rights Watch, has been simplistic. It has also been inaccurate, unbalanced and in some cases biased. This is something which has not helped with analysing and thereby seeking to remedy, what is a complex situation. Human rights commentators, for example, have not been able to differentiate between the activities of government paramilitary forces, those of armed nomadic tribes or those of the heavily-armed criminal gangs that roam Darfur. As a result they have made unrealistic – and indeed impossible – demands on the Sudanese government. Their continual criticism of the government for not doing things that are in many instances beyond their control, which adversely colour western international opinion about Khartoum, merely serves to discredit the western human rights community in the eyes of the governments and people of much of the developing world. The human rights industry certainly appears to have opted for partisan or lazy analysis of events in Darfur, seemingly unable to resist projecting the image of government-supported "Arab" – "Janjaweed" – militias attacking "African", Fur or Zaghawa, villagers (and in doing so often merely echoing questionable rebel claims).

The United Nations International Commission of Inquiry on Darfur, tasked "to investigate reports of violations of international humanitarian law and human rights by all parties" and "to determine also whether or not acts of genocide have occurred", provided a classic example of the unacceptable shortcuts taken by the human rights industry. The most obvious flaw was with regard to the standard of evidence the Commission said it required:

> In view of the limitations inherent in its powers, the Commission decided that it could not comply with the standards normally adopted by criminal courts (proof of facts beyond a reasonable doubt), or with that used by international prosecutors and judges for the purpose of confirming indictments (that there must be a prima facie case). It concluded that the most appropriate standard was that requiring a reliable body of material consistent with other verified circumstances, which tends to show that a person may reasonably be suspected of being involved in the commission of a crime.[857]

That is to say it chose to make findings based on material from which it might said that a person – or entity – may reasonably be suspected of having been involved in the commission of a crime. That this is an unsatisfactory standard is clear, especially given the serious nature of the alleged crimes. It was a standard, however, that the Commission did not extend to others. The Commission demanded that the Government and affected citizens of Darfur produce "concrete information or evidence" to support their claims.[858]

A large number of claims and allegations have been made regarding events in Darfur despite the scarcity of reliable information. United Nations media sources, for example, have noted "a lack of accurate information on the conflict"[859] and Reuters has also stated that "it is hard to independently verify claims by government or rebels in Darfur."[860] Human rights reports have consistently reported – and attributed – human rights abuses within Darfur in circumstances in which independent confirmation of such assertions is impossible. *The New York Times*, while echoing many of these allegations of human rights abuses, was candid enough to admit that "it is impossible to travel in Darfur to verify these claims".[861] Claims of Khartoum's control over the "Janjaweed" persist despite increasing evidence that they are out of control.[862] The absence of verifiable information regarding events in Darfur was a point raised by Louise Arbour, the UN High Commissioner for Human Rights. Reporting to the UN on her return from Darfur, Arbour noted: "There is a great need on the part of the international community to improve its capacity to collect, coordinate and analyse information and reports of human rights violations. This is critical to ensure that we have available empirically-founded concrete data if we are to counter the rumours and manipulation of information that is rife in Darfur. Such a capacity will be invaluable to the international community, allowing it to assess trends and further tailor its response to the crisis. It will be invaluable, too, for the Government of Sudan which clearly feels aggrieved by what it perceives to be an exaggeration by the international community as to the extent of the crisis."[863]

Contradictions in claims by human rights organisations about events in Darfur have also led to question marks about some of the serious allegations that have been made. While Human Rights Watch, for example, eagerly chose to label the conflict as "ethnic cleansing"[864] and has skirted close to using the "genocide" label, Amnesty International researchers have said that observers should be "cautious" about describing clashes as ethnic cleansing.[865] Such labels have also been challenged by the United Nations and senior aid workers on the ground within Darfur.[866] Nonetheless, the claims of "ethnic cleansing" have echoed around the world. Other, far less objective, groups claiming to be human rights organisations have embraced very questionable claims about Darfur. The Jacob Blaustein Institute for the Advancement of Human Rights, a project of the American Jewish Committee, for example, has claimed both "genocide" and a mortality figure of 400,000 people in Darfur.[867]

Human Rights Watch: Questionable Sources, Questionable Reports

There is little doubt that groups such as Human Rights Watch and Amnesty International have once again relied upon questionable sources with regard to Darfur. It has also been clear that in some cases their analysts are partisan and their previous methodology with regard to Sudan has been flawed. Human Rights Watch's counsel and Sudan researcher Jemera Rone has, for example, previously eulogised a Sudanese rebel commander as "thoughtful...curious and intellectual" and with a "respect for the rights of all". This was in the face of the rebel commander's direct and indirect responsibility for massive human rights violations including the murder, rape or torture of hundreds if not thousands of civilians, many of whom were women and children. The rebel eulogised by Rone was also directly responsible for the abduction of thousands of under-age children for use as child soldiers and their transportation to Ethiopia. Nearly 3,000 of these children subsequently died from malnutrition or disease: many more died as child soldiers. Rone's eulogy was an astonishing statement for someone supposedly concerned with human rights to have made and provides a clear insight into the sort of anti-government bias that has coloured key "human rights" reports on Sudan.[868] Many of Human Rights Watch's claims about Darfur, and much of its analysis, must be seen in this light.

Perhaps unsurprisingly, therefore, Human Rights Watch's reports have been marked by their lack of focus on rebel abuses in Darfur. In its April 2004 report, *Darfur in Flames: Atrocities in Western Sudan*, for example, Human Rights Watch devotes ten lines within the 49-page publication to rebel violations of human rights claiming to have had "limited access to information about abuses by JEM and SLA". All it reports, for example, is that in November 2003, JEM "apparently" killed 20 civilians in West Darfur and that in late 2003 the SLA "apparently" killed a prisoner in a police station. HRW also states that both rebel movements are using child soldiers.[869] What little did appear in this report was stated to have come from "interviews" in Chad. HRW researchers appear not to have been in touch, even by telephone, with United Nations officials in Darfur. The UN information network, part of the Office for the Coordination of Humanitarian Affairs – and active in Sudan, publicly documented in July 2003, for example, that "SLA rebels regularly attacked and looted villages, taking food and sometimes killing people…The attacks present a real threat to people's food security and livelihoods, by preventing them from planting and accessing markets to buy food."[870] Neither do they appear to have even read BBC news items reporting that the rebels had murdered nine World Food Programme truck drivers, and wounded 14 others, in an attack on a relief convoy in October 2003.[871] In the wake of this attack, the United States government asked the Sudanese government for help with security and access.[872] The following are just a few of the many publicly-reported instances of rebel human rights abuses – just on aid workers alone –

which never made in into Human Rights Watch's April 2004 report. In November 2003 the Government accused rebels in Darfur of killing two of its relief workers and abducting three others in an attack on an aid convoy.[873] One month later, rebel gunmen killed two other relief workers and abducted three others.[874] Rebels also kidnapped other relief workers with JEM gunmen admitted abducting five aid workers working for the Swiss humanitarian group Medair.[875] On 11 February 2004, the Equality and Justice Movement declared its intention to close down every road within Darfur. Rebel attacks on relief convoys continued. A senior UN official in Sudan stated in February 2004 that rebels have made it too dangerous to take aid into parts of Darfur. Aid convoys were still being attacked by armed groups. The spokesman also cited the danger of landmines."[876] The Sudanese government repeatedly held the rebels responsible for blocking deliveries of humanitarian aid in Darfur.[877]

Human Rights Watch's August 2004 human rights "report", *Empty Promises? Continuing Abuses in Darfur,* was even more unbalanced. Its 37 pages contained one sentence alleging a rebel human rights abuse – the "temporary" abduction of aid workers – who were then returned "unharmed". This was sourced to the United Nations. The organisation's excuse was that it had not been able to get visas for government-controlled areas of Sudan, and therefore was not able to report on rebel abuses. The disingenuousness of this line is breathtaking. Human Rights Watch has constantly relied upon second-hand or previously published news items for the bulk of its "reporting" on human rights in Sudan. Indeed the only rebel human rights abuse they cited in *Empty Promises? Continuing Abuses in Darfur* was sourced to the United Nations. As can be seen from the very small sample outlined above, there are numerous well-documented human rights abuses – including many sourced by the United Nations – which Human Rights Watch could easily have included in its reports. That they chose not to do so is telling evidence of the organisation's clear bias and hence unreliability with regard to human rights reporting and analysis.

It was also perhaps unsurprising that Human Rights Watch chose to use British journalist Julie Flint as a researcher. Flint, although presenting herself as an "independent journalist" when speaking before the American Senate's foreign relations committee, is a long-time anti-Sudan activist.[878] Flint's testimony was predictably light with regard to rebel abuses. She did, however, admit that rebel attacks on government targets "took heavy civilian casualties".

She mentioned that rebels had abducted humanitarian aid workers but did not cite any of the numerous instances of their murder. She stuck to the official position that, despite having been provided with a "list of ceasefire violations and attacks on villages" by the government and other groups in Darfur, they were unable to investigate them because they had not visited government-held areas. This has not, however, prevented HRW from reporting as fact other alleged, government abuses within government-held areas. Flint drew heavily upon her guided tour, by rebels, through a rebel-controlled area of Darfur. Flint and Human Rights Watch did admit that "It is...difficult to ascertain what exactly is happening in a place the size of Darfur." It is all the more difficult to ascertain what is happening if one ignores numerous well-documented accounts by journalists, United Nations workers and other non-governmental sources.

Interestingly, it is also worth noting that, although Human Rights Watch's main Sudan researcher Jemera Rone went on record to criticise the credibility of Eric Reeves, Flint has no such reservations. She accepts Reeves' claim of 400,000 deaths in Darfur, describing them as "a serious analysis of mortality" in Darfur.[879] This despite the fact that at the time Human Rights Watch worked with the World Health Organisation figure of 70,000.[880] Unusually for a supposed human rights researcher, Flint has also acted as an apologist for rebel war crimes, stating that rebel human rights abuses, including the murder of aid workers, were the responsibility of "rogue rebel commanders".[881] In short, Flint provides a telling example of the sort of partisan anti-government activist who so often double-up as "independent", supposedly objective, human rights workers.

Not only has Human Rights Watch been economical with certain facts, it has totally misrepresented others. Its Sudan report for 2003, for example, stated that Sudan "had backed out of peace talks sponsored by Chad".[882] It is somewhat difficult to reconcile Human Rights Watch's claim with that of the official Chadian Government peace mediator who went on record in December 2003 to state: "There has been a breakdown in negotiations because of unacceptable rebel demands. The talks have been suspended: it's a failure."[883] This is only one of many mistakes and omissions on the part of Human Rights Watch – but is certainly one of its most significant in the slant it put on a crucial aspect of the Darfur crisis. The same 2003 section claimed that Khartoum was "trying to use southern militias, previously used against the SPLA, to fight in Darfur." This is another particularly off-the-wall claim, unsupported by any evidence whatsoever.

Amnesty International and Darfur

Amnesty International's reporting on Darfur has been similarly flawed. In its February 2004 report, *Darfur: "Too Many People Killed for No Reason"*, Amnesty International stated that it "had received very little information regarding killing of civilians by the armed opposition the SLA and the JEM". Amnesty qualified its position by stating that "in some cases, the armed political groups appear to have put the lives of civilians at risk".[884] This despite having mentioned in the same report that the United Nations had reported regular rebel attacks upon, and looting of, villages and the killing of civilians. Amnesty International would appear to share the Human Rights Watch methodology of turning a blind eye to independent, publicly-documented accounts of rebel human rights abuses.

All of Amnesty International's publications on Darfur have been unbalanced and misleading. In Amnesty's "Sudan Crisis – Background", it accepts, at face value, the usual rationale for the initiation of violence in Darfur, that the rebels began the war as a result of "marginalisation and underdevelopment of the region".[885] In its April 2004 report, *Deliberate and Indiscriminate Attacks against Civilians in Darfur*, Amnesty does not once mention rebel human rights abuses.[886] In its lengthy 2004 report, *Arming the Perpetrators of Grave Abuses in Darfur*, Amnesty devotes three sentences to the rebels. While calling for an end to any supply of weapons, and vehicles, to the government, it is silent with regard to supply of weapons – by Eritrea and others for example – to the rebels.[887] And, in its December 2004 *Open Letter to All Members of the Security Council*, Amnesty does not mention the rebels once.[888] Any semblance to objectivity and quality research that Amnesty International may once have tried to claim with regard to its work on Sudan was in any instance starkly contradicted by allowing discredited out-and-out propagandists and apologists for rebel human rights abuses such as Eric Reeves to write on Sudan in their publications.[889]

It is also worth noting that previous Amnesty International reports on Sudan in general have been flawed by deeply questionable methodology. Key reports have been largely reliant on newspaper reporting – often utilising second- and third-hand newspaper accounts by partisan journalists. In these reports Amnesty International's lack of professionalism was also been manifested by its turning a blind eye to independent, reputable, first-hand accounts of rebel use of child soldiers and the daily bombardment of towns. It chose instead to publish claims made by rebel commanders.[890]

Amnesty International has been accused of double standards with regard to its position on Darfur. Writing in October 2004, journalist Paul de Rooij pointed to hypocrisy on the part of the human rights organisation:

> Consider AI's statement issued regarding the situation in Darfur: "The United Nations Security Council should stop the transfer of arms being used to commit mass human rights violations in Darfur [AI] urged today while releasing a report based on satellite images showing large-scale destruction of villages in Darfur over the past year." The situation may be awful in Darfur, and the measure suggested may be warranted. However, the curious aspect of this statement is that AI has never called on the UN or any other body to impose an arms embargo on Israel, although there are ample grounds for such a recommendation. An American academic inquired about this double standard, and she received the following answer from Donatella Rovera, AI's principal researcher on Israel-Palestine: "The situations in Sudan and in Israel-Occupied Territories are quite different and different norms of international law apply, which do not make it possible to call for an arms embargos on either the Israeli or the Palestinian side. The West Bank and Gaza Strip are under Israeli military occupation (not the case for the Darfour region in Sudan). Hence, certain provisions of international humanitarian law, known as the laws of war (notably the 1907 Hague Convention and the Fourth Geneva Convention) apply in the Occupied Palestinian Territories (and not in the Darfour region)." AI is couching its double standards in dubious legalese, but consider what Prof. Francis Boyle (Professor of International Law at Univ. of Illinois Champaign) has to say about Rovera's statement: "This is total

197

gibberish. When I was on the Board of Directors of Amnesty International USA near the end of my second term in 1990-92, we received the authority to call for an arms embargo against major human rights violators, which Israel clearly qualified for at the time and still does – even under United States domestic law. Of course no one at AI was going to do so because pro-Israel supporters were major funders of Amnesty International USA, which in turn was a major funder of Amnesty International in London. He who pays the piper calls the tune – especially at AIUSA Headquarters in New York and at AI Headquarters in London.[891]

As so often has been the case in their reporting of Sudan, the reliability of the assertions of groups like Human Rights Watch and Amnesty International should not be taken at face value.

The Hypocrisy of the Human Rights Industry on Darfur

In addition to often overt bias, and factual inaccuracies, on the part of human rights groups, there has also been considerable hypocrisy with regard to Darfur. While claiming that the Arab "Janjaweed" raiders are sponsored by the government, Human Rights Watch and Amnesty International ignore the fact that the government has regularly taken very firm action against "Arab" tribesmen who have attacked "African" communities. In April 2003, for example, Sudanese courts sentenced 24 Arab armed bandits to death for their involvement in the murder of 35 African villagers in attacks on pastoralist villages. Judge Mukhtar Ibrahim Adam described the attacks as "barbaric and savage conduct" reminiscent of "the dark ages".[892] In the same month, 44 tribesmen were killed, and 22 injured, in a tribal clash between Arab and Massaleit tribes in West Darfur. Police units contained the violence.[893] In a further example of the government's firm stance, in October 2003, 14 other Arab tribesmen were also sentenced to death for the murder of non-Arab villagers during attacks and arson within villages in south Darfur state.[894] There is also abundant evidence of the sorts of lawlessness that has plagued Darfur, including considerable "Arab" on "Arab" violence. In one incident alone in May 2002 50 Arab tribesmen were killed in such clashes between the Arab tribes.[895] (Would this qualify as "Janjaweed" on "Janjaweed" violence?) A special criminal court sentenced 86 Arab tribesmen to death for involvement in the murder of other Arab tribesmen.

The stance of the human rights industry on criminal violence in Darfur has been contradictory. Amnesty International, for example, has previously criticised government inaction in responding to the violence and banditry in the region. In February 2003 Amnesty International stated that "government responses to armed clashes have been ineffective".[896] Amnesty has then condemned the government for taking measures to restore order, such as arresting tribesmen suspected of involvement in violence.[897] The scale of the violence had led to Khartoum introducing special measures. Yet these have also been criticised by Amnesty International. They, for example, have condemned the special criminal courts created by presidential decree to deal with offences such as murder, armed robbery, arson and the smuggling of weapons., and the firm sentences these courts have subsequently handed down.[898] And at the same time these measures are being taken against the very Arab tribesmen that it is alleged the government is supporting militarily.

The fact is that scores of Sudanese soldiers and policemen have been killed in tribal clashes and while trying to apprehend those suspected, including "Janjaweed", of criminal acts. (Even Amnesty International admits to as much in its more objective moments.[899]) Many more Sudanese policemen have also been murdered by rebels, often while carrying out their job of protecting internally displaced peoples.

An Incomplete Picture

Another way in which the human rights industry has distorted perceptions of events in Darfur is through often incomplete or inaccurate analysis of events in Darfur and Sudan. The overriding goal for anyone concerned about human rights should be to end the conflict that is leading to human rights abuses. Merely focusing upon the symptoms and not the cause is an inadequate response. In this respect, however, the human rights groups have been very disappointing. Amnesty International, for example, takes rebel claims about their motivation at face value, asserting without reservation that the Darfur rebels "took up arms in February 2003 to protest at what they perceive as the lack of government protection of the settled population against attacks by nomads and the underdevelopment and marginalisation of Darfur". Human Rights Watch unquestioningly echoes the stated rebel position when it claims "Both rebel groups were formally created in early 2003 in response to the perceived political marginalization and chronic underdevelopment of Darfur".[900] Amnesty International would appear to be unaware, and certainly have not noted in their publications, the view of Sudan's premier human rights activist, Ghazi Suleiman, about the Islamist dimension to the conflict. In so doing, the simplistic analysis of groups such as Amnesty International and Human Rights Watch merely serves to advance rebel propaganda and misinform those observers who may rely upon those organisations for accurate information on this issue.

Rebel Human Rights Abuses

One of the reasons for the international community's distorted picture of the Darfur crisis – with the resultant flawed analysis and demands that have ensued – is the under-reporting of the activities of the rebel movements. Having by and large ignored large-scale rebel human rights abuses in the course of 2003, human rights groups are now belatedly starting to document their activities. Even the SLA has had to admit to human rights abuses, accepting in early December 2004, for example, that it had been involved in attacks on civilians, kidnappings and obstructing aid workers.[901]

Almost eighteen months after they first began, Human Rights Watch is now conceding that rebel attacks on towns in early 2003 resulted in considerable loss of civilian life. Even Julie Flint had to admit, in June 2004, that "heavy civilian casualties" were caused during these attacks. She admitted that the April 2003 attack on al-Fasher "resulted in the deaths of numerous civilians".[902] Prunier states that the rebels murdered 200 army prisoners after they had surrendered.[903] In its November 2004 report, in a section entitled "Attacks on Civilians", Human Rights admitted that "the rebel movements have been responsible for direct attacks on civilian objects in violation of international humanitarian law, and for causing deaths and injuries to civilians."

Rebel human rights abuses have followed a pattern. They have included systematic attacks on nomadic communities and the destruction of numerous

Arab villages. They have included the murder, wounding, and abduction of civilians and the rape of women. These attacks on civilians have continued despite the rebels having signed several internationally-mediated ceasefire agreements, including the November 2004 Abuja protocol. In early December 2004, for example, the governor of North Darfur, Osman Yusuf Kibir, accused rebels of attacking villages and raping women.[904] In January 2005, the government reported that rebels had destroyed eight villages and killed many civilians in attacks in South Darfur.[905] Rebels have also carried out hundreds of armed robberies throughout Darfur, and in so doing killing many civilians. They have also been involved in the theft of thousands of head of livestock – the very lifeblood of many of Darfur's tribal communities. The Sudan Liberation Army have also murdered several aid workers, foreign and Sudanese, and abducted scores of others. They have also attacked and looted dozens of relief convoys carrying food aid to Darfur's displaced communities. The rebels have also recruited and armed child soldiers.

In addition to attacks on rival forces and communities, the Darfur rebels were also accused by human rights organisations of endangering civilians by stationing their forces in their midst.[906] This criminal behaviour has continued throughout the conflict. Writing in September 2007, *The Times* Africa correspondent, Rob Crilly, stated that that he had "met a former rebel commander in El Fasher. He had quit the movement two years earlier after becoming frustrated at the leadership's preference for using civilian villages as bases. 'They seemed to want to use civilian suffering caused by government and Janjaweed attacks in their PR campaign,' he told me in the offices of the human rights organisation where he now works."[907]

Both before and after the signing of the Darfur Peace Agreement in May 2006, much of the human rights abuses within Darfur were the result of fighting within various rebel factions, and attacks by rebel factions on the sections of the African population seen to be supporting rival factions. This led to rebel attacks on Fur, Zaghawa and other tribes. These abuses and others were reported by the UN. A March 2007 UN report stated that "Rebel abuses of human rights and humanitarian law…continue. Civilians have been targeted in armed rebel attacks, and acts of rape and torture by rebel forces have also been documented. There have been reports of attacks on aid convoys by rebel forces, putting the populations in those areas in a particularly precarious situation. Many of the violations committed by rebels relate to the fragmentation of rebel groups and intra-rebel fighting."[908]

Despite significantly under-reporting rebel human rights abuses, newspapers and human rights organisations have provided some glimpses into the scale of earlier rebel human rights violations.

A Snapshot of Rebel Human Rights Abuses: Malam, South Darfur.

In its November 2004 report, Human Rights Watch provides the outside world with a snapshot of rebel human rights abuses. It reported, for example, on rebel attacks in and around one specific area – Malam, located on the eastern side of the Jebel Marra, approximately one hundred kilometres north of Nyala, in South Darfur. Human Rights Watch has cited numerous examples of the murder of civilians, the rape of women and abduction of young children by Sudan Liberation Army rebels in and around this town, a location inhabited both by Fur and people from the Beni Mansour tribe. SLA rebels have been attacking civilians in this area – one of many in Darfur – since they began the war. Human Rights Watch, for example, noted that it had received a list of sixty Beni Mansour women and girls who were said to have been raped or assaulted by rebels in attacks between 10 February and 7 July 2004 – but stated that it was not able to "verify" these claims.[909] In one attack in the area, on 21 April 2004, the rebels killed ten civilians. Six more civilians were murdered in an attack in nearby Um Dashur in early June 2004. Human Rights Watch also reported that in mid-June 2004 rebel gunmen were said to have raped several Beni Mansour women near Malam. Rebels attacked Malam again in October 2004, killing three civilians, including a 12-year-old girl, and injuring several more. Human Rights Watch stated that their apparent intention had been to loot. It also reported that it had received a list of thirty-nine people, including two children, said to have been abducted in the Malam area between 2 August 2003 and 10 July 2004, adding that their whereabouts remained unknown. In January 2005, the United Nations reported that between 24 and 36 civilians had died and 26 others were wounded in fresh rebel attacks on villages in and around Malam.[910] Rebel human rights abuses in and around Malam provide the international community with documented – albeit imperfectly – examples of rebel abuses in one small specific area of Darfur. From all accounts it is a pattern of abuses that has been repeated throughout Darfur – the vast majority of which have gone unrecorded by human rights organisations or other outside observers.

It is a matter of record that systematic rebel attacks on civilians in the vicinity of Malam continued into 2005.

The Economist has provided us with an equally brief snapshot of rebel abuses, in West Darfur. It reported that rebels burned down 12 villages in the area of Ishbara, located some 120 miles north of Al-Geneina, in West Darfur. They had "killed anyone who crossed their path." Those civilians who survived now live in the Wadi Bardi refugee camp. Another five villages were said to have been abandoned by petrified villagers. These civilians were from the African Gimir tribe, traditional rivals of the Zaghawa tribe. *The Economist* reported that SLA rebel leaders had stated that because the Gimir were rivals to the Zaghawa they must therefore be pro-government, and that was why they were attacked.[911] In reality, it comes down to inter-tribal – and in this case intra-African – rivalry. *The Daily Telegraph*, reporting on the same attacks, pointed out that rebel "brutality at least equals that of" the Janjaweed, and that the rebels "have received none of the international condemnation heaped upon the Janjaweed".[912] *The Independent* has also reported on claims that the rebels were "driving Arabs from their villages."[913] It provided a glimpse of the ten thousand Arab villagers packed into the Mossei refugee camp, near Nyala in South Darfur, reporting on their claims to have "been attacked, driven from their homes, and abandoned to face pending epidemics of cholera, malaria and hepatitis. They say their persecutors are African tribes in league with the Sudan Liberation Army, with their own campaigns of driving out another community."[914]

Even in their minimalist references to rebel abuses Human Rights Watch and *The Economist* provides a disturbing picture.

Rebel Armed Robberies and Attacks on Road Transport

Rebel involvement in armed robberies of civilians and civilian premises is clear. These have included any number of civilian premises, including banks and other businesses. An example of a typical attack was that on Yassin, in South Darfur, in January 2004. In this attack rebels looted offices, commercial premises and the *zakat* (charity) office. In early December 2004, the Sudanese government released documents indicating that the rebels had been involved in 571 armed robberies since early 2003 in the course of which they had killed 169 people.[915] Rebels were said to have attacked over 200 trucks. [916] Human Rights Watch also reported rebel attacks on trucks and the theft of "commercial goods from trucks and vehicles in Darfur". It also noted that: "These attacks on civilian property are a violation of international humanitarian law."[917] In November 2004, African Union ceasefire monitors confirmed that the SLA had attacked convoys of Nigerian pilgrims on four separate occasions in Darfur. In one attack on three civilian trucks, the rebels killed seven people. Eight others were injured.[918] These systematic attacks prompted an unprecedented intervention by Amnesty International in early November 2004 which directly criticised rebel attacks on civilians and humanitarian convoys. It noted that in one case "Eighteen passengers from nomad groups were taken off a bus between Niyertiti and Thur in South Darfur state by soldiers of the Sudan Liberation Army...Amnesty International has grave concerns about their fate. Thirteen of them are said to have been killed."[919]

These attacks have continued and intensified up to the present day.

Rebel Theft of Livestock

The rebels have been engaged in systematic theft of livestock throughout Darfur. Human Rights Watch has underlined the seriousness of these thefts: "Given the importance of livestock as the primary family asset, looting of cattle and camels can render the owners destitute. This is particularly true for nomads who depend almost entirely on livestock for their income."[920] Human Rights Watch has stated that it has received reports of SLA "attacks on convoys of camels that were being taken across traditional trade routes in North Darfur". These attacks had involved significant numbers of livestock. Human Rights Watch has provided the outside world with a few examples of these attacks. One nomadic leader in South Darfur had reported the theft from the Ma'aliyah tribe of more than 2,500 camels. In another documented attack, in May 2004, SLA gunmen in Land cruisers attacked a camel drive north of Atrum, in North Darfur. They stole 1,100 camels and abducted 38 civilians – whose whereabouts remain unknown. Rebels were said to have stolen more than 4,000 camels in the course of 2003 in attacks on the nomadic Aulad Zeid tribe in North Darfur. These attacks had involved the use of automatic rifles, rocket-propelled grenades and machine-guns. The rebels had arrived in Land cruisers and trucks. Human Rights Watch mentioned that "many of the herders were killed defending their animals".[921] Human Rights Watch has called on rebel groups to "Cease all attacks on civilians and civilian property including livestock." The three incidents Human Rights Watch reported are probably the tip of the iceberg with regard to the scale of livestock theft. Given the visceral seriousness with which blood vendettas and livestock theft are taken, there is no doubt that attacks such as these have led to considerable inter-tribal tit-for-tat raids and violence to recover livestock and avenge murdered tribesmen. Nomadic tribes would have raided the communities and villages from which the SLA men would have been drawn, as well as the villages in which they were harbouring. While, in passing, documenting what may well have been the cause of a number of reprisal attacks by nomadic tribes on tribes seen as complicit in livestock theft, this has not in any way been reflected in Human Rights Watch accounts of attacks on "African" villages. Human Rights Watch attributes all such attacks as government inspired. This is one more example of a critical failure in analysis by human rights organisations.

It is a matter of record that large-scale livestock theft by the rebel movements has continued up to and including 2007.

Rebel Attacks on Humanitarian Aid Workers and Relief Convoys

Rebel attacks on humanitarian aid convoys have been particularly serious. These attacks have been throughout the course of the humanitarian crisis in Darfur, and have gravely endangered the delicately-balanced emergency feeding programme keeping hundreds of thousands of civilians – many of them from the communities the rebels were claiming to protect – alive in Darfur. Human Rights Watch has called on rebel groups to "Cease all attacks on civilians and civilian property including…humanitarian aid convoys." The pattern of rebel human rights abuses in attacks on aid convoys and workers is a clear one. The following are a random selection. They murdered nine truck drivers, and wounded 14 others, in an attack on a relief convoy in October 2003.[922] The following months, rebel gunmen killed two relief workers and abducted three others.[923] Later in November JEM gunmen admitted abducting five aid workers.[924] In early June 2004, Associated Press reported the abduction by rebels of 16 aid workers. On 8 June 2004, Agence France-Presse reported that rebels had seized nine trucks loaded with relief items, medicines and tents on the road between Nyala and al-Fasher. The rebels abducted four of the drivers.[925] Later that month, rebels attacked aid vehicles and stole 57 tons of UN food aid.[926] In the first week of July, the SLA attacked 26 aid workers, stealing six vehicles and a large amount of cash. There were a number of systematic rebel attacks on aid workers in August 2004. The African Union confirmed that, on 22 August, SLA forces had abducted humanitarian affairs workers in the Abgaragil area, and that on 23 August rebels had abducted medical aid workers in Kutum.[927] At the end of August 2004, Darfur rebels abducted six aid workers in North Darfur. WFP condemned the targeting of humanitarian workers.[928] On 31 August 2004, rebel gunmen detained 22 Sudanese health workers near Nyala in south Darfur. A SLA landmine killed two Save the Children Fund workers, one British and one Sudanese, in October 2004.[929] The United Nations special envoy to Sudan Jan Pronk unambiguously confirmed rebel involvement in these deaths: "It was the rebels who are responsible for attacking relief workers and convoys, they are responsible for…landmines which killed two relief workers."[930]

United Nations reported that in late October "forces from the rebel Sudan Liberation Army (SLA) hijacked seven commercial trucks on a road…east of …El Fasher."[931] In mid-November 2004, the United Nations reported several attacks on buses and aid convoys around Darfur. Travellers had been abducted and killed and vehicles looted by the attackers.[932] By the end of November, *The New York Times* was reporting that the rebels had been "sharply ratcheting up attacks" on civilian traffic which in turn was preventing relief work.[933] In November 2004 rebels attacked a joint WHO/Ministry of Health medical team. One doctor was killed and four other health workers were injured. The team was also robbed.[934] In November GOAL and the Spanish branch of Médecins Sans Frontières withdrew from the Jebel Marra area in central Darfur after "repeated" rebel attacks on aid personnel, vehicles and relief supplies.[935] Amnesty International noted the pattern of rebel activity: "over the past two months, a number of World Food Program commercial trucks have been attacked in South Darfur."[936] On 12 December 2004, rebels murdered two more Save the Children aid workers, members of a mobile medical clinic travelling in clearly-marked vehicles.[937] Rebel responsibility for their deaths was confirmed by both the African Union and United Nations.[938] In addition to the murdered aid workers, one other worker was injured and three are still missing. Rebel involvement in the murders was established by the UN.[939] Rebel attacks on aid convoys continued into December. At the end of December 2004, the United Nations stated that rebel forces had stolen 13 commercial all-terrain trucks leased to WFP and loaded with food: "These thefts are in addition to multiple losses of commercial and aid agency vehicles to armed groups in recent months."[940]

As touched upon in earlier chapters, rebel attacks on aid workers have continued and intensified up to and including 2007.

Rebel Use of Child Soldiers

Human Rights Watch has clearly documented that both the Sudan Liberation Army and the Justice and Equality Movement use child soldiers. It has correctly pointed out that "it is unlawful…to deploy children as combatants, whether or not they were forcibly recruited or joined on their own accord."[941] The Rome Statute of the International Criminal Court classifies the use of child soldiers as a war crime. *The Independent* newspaper has reported the presence of hundreds of child soldiers, some as young as ten, with the rebels.[942] Human Rights researchers in North Darfur in July and August 2004 observed and photographed SLA child soldiers, some as young as twelve.[943] Unsurprisingly perhaps, Human Rights Watch sought to contextualise this blatant war crime, virtually presenting the SLA as juvenile social workers. In a different report, however, a child eyewitness, Mubarak, abducted from Kutum in southern Darfur, presented a different picture. A former SLA child soldier, he stated that following an attack on his school, rebels had abducted "several dozen frightened boys…and marched them off into the countryside. The heavily armed men asked the boys if any of them wanted to go. Eight of them raised their hands and…the rebels told them they could run away. Mubarak said he still remembered the loud bangs when the men shot two of the escaping boys. The remaining boys became rebels. 'I had to join them,' Mubarak said. 'I was afraid I would be killed, too.'"[944] The African Union has also confirmed that the Sudan Liberation Army is arming and using child soldiers.[945] The SLA is obviously aware that it is illegal to use child soldiers. Journalists who reported seeing fighters who "seem to be no more than schoolboys" who, when asked their age, reply with "the stock answer": "I have just become 18, sir. I am not a child soldier."[946]

Reuters was also able to report on the rebel use of child soldiers. A February 2005 article mentioned the presence of children as young as twelve within rebel ranks.[947]

Air Power and Rebel Use of Civilian "Human Shields"

One of the issues frequently raised with regard to human rights issues has been the government's use of air power in its war against insurgents in Darfur with the focus upon any resultant civilian casualties or displacement. That governments reserve the right to use air power in war is obvious. Air power has been used in every recent conflict – not least of which during the Iraq war and subsequent occupation. That civilians are often killed, injured or displaced during even the most clinical bombing attacks against insurgents has also been amply demonstrated in Iraq. The use of air power in Darfur has been no different.

That the rebel movements have wittingly or unwittingly drawn air attacks upon the civilian population in Darfur is a matter of record. The government's position has been predictable. In November 2004, Reuters reported government claims that "rebels…have drawn army fire and aerial bombardment on to Darfur villages by using them as cover and as bases for military operations." A senior government security chief said that rebels would often have camps next to villages, which were near water sources, and on many occasions attacked the army from within the villages."[948] Predictable or not, the government's claims appear to have been at least partly borne out when SLA rebels subsequently admitted as much when they revealed that the Sudanese air force had killed 25 fighters in a raid on a village in north Darfur. The village was 25 miles south of al-Fasher.[949] A British television news item also reported on the rebel presence within villages, in this instance Thabit: "This village is full of rebel soldiers from the Sudan Liberation Army. Eight were wounded in the bombing of Thabit. What happened here was an act of war. But it was an act of war provoked by the rebels to make the government look bad ahead of this week's peace talks." [950] Amnesty International's Benedicte Goderiaux has also pointed out rebel complicity: "Of course it's the government's duty to distinguish the SLA from civilians, but the SLA doesn't help in making that distinction."[951] In a report to the United Nations human rights commission, UN officials noted that: "There are some claims that [the rebels] operate from or near civilian areas and rely on towns and villages composed of certain ethnicities for support and supplies. This has endangered civilians in many areas and appears to feed into certain groups being considered as hostile to the Government."[952]

It has also been claimed, and subsequently confirmed, that rebels have been using displaced persons camps from which to stage attacks on relief convoys and government officials, actions which clearly endanger civilians by provoking a possible military response by government forces. In October 2004, for example, the government stated that an attack on a relief convoy 20 kilometres southwest of al-Fasher had been staged from the Tawila displaced camp.[953] Security forces had also discovered an arms cache near the Zam Zam displaced camp near al-Fasher. In late November 2004, the UN World Food Programme reported that, on 21 November 2004, rebels attacked a police station on the edge of the Kalma IDP camp. This resulted in the death of several policemen. The WFP confirmed that "ominously, the attack appeared to have been launched from inside Kalma camp".[954] The Sudanese government reported further examples of rebel use of refugee camps, claiming in December 2004 that rebels were using a presence in at least one refugee camp to target and attack policemen.[955] The rebels have also sought to cause unrest within IDP camps, opposing re-registration of IDPs as well as opposing their return to their villages. These attacks by rebels from IDP camps have continued up to and including 2007.

Unbalanced, misleading and incomplete reporting, coupled with equally misleading or simply inaccurate analysis, by human rights groups confuses and misinforms international perceptions of the conflict. The human rights industry has sadly been party to all these failings in its reporting on Sudan. While all too often taken at face value in a handful of Western capitals, such flawed reporting gravely undermines the credibility of organisations such as Human Rights Watch and Amnesty International in the rest of the word.

Chapter Eight

Darfur and the International Criminal Court

There's one big problem with [the ICC and Darfur]: Most of the perpetrators in Darfur can't be tried before the ICC because Sudan hasn't ratified the court's founding statute. The panel's failure to admit this limitation is staggering.

Stéphanie Giry, international lawyer [956]

We don't want the International Criminal Court. We want peace... Will the court really bring peace, or fuel the war again?

Ugandan war victims, northern Uganda [957]

On 31 March 2005, following on from the recommendation of the UN Commission of Inquiry into Darfur, and despite the fact that Sudan is a non-state party, the United Nations Security Council passed Resolution 1593 (2005) referring the prosecution of those allegedly responsible for atrocities committed in Darfur to the International Criminal Court (ICC).[958] On 7 April 2005, the ICC prosecutor opened a sealed list of 51 individuals named by the United Nations International Commission of Inquiry as being suspected of international crimes in Darfur. The list was said to advisory and not mandatory for the prosecutor to follow. It is believed that in addition to several rebel commanders, a number of Sudanese government ministers also featured on the list. The issue of the ICC and Darfur has been caught up in controversy, not least of which the question as to whether or not the ICC has jurisdiction, and the charge that the ICC is not impartial and that ICC investigations can prolong rather than stop conflict. We have also seen the arrogance of the ICC

Chief Prosecutor Luis Moreno-Ocampo who stated in September 2007 that there would be no end to the conflict without the prosecution of individuals named by the ICC.[959]

Moreno-Ocampo informed the UN General Assembly in October 2006 that the court had started pre-trial investigations, including more than fifty missions to fifteen countries and the screening of close to 500 potential witnesses. The ICC had also visited Khartoum on three occasions to assess national proceedings. He noted that the ICC was unable to open an office in Darfur and its office in Chad had been temporarily closed in 2006 due to violence. On 27 February 2007, Moreno-Ocampo announced that he would ask the pre-trial chamber of the ICC to issue summons against two Sudanese nationals, Ahmed Muhammad Haroun, a former Minister of State for the Interior of the Government of Sudan, and currently Minister of State for Humanitarian Affairs, and Ali Muhammad Ali Abdel-Rahman, also known as Ali Kushayb, an alleged militia leader. The application stated that the Office of the Prosecutor had concluded that there are reasonable grounds to believe that these two persons bear criminal responsibility for crimes against humanity and war crimes committed in Darfur in 2003 and 2004.

The Sudanese government has repeatedly stated it will not cooperate with the court. President Omar al-Bashir has on several occasions unambiguously declared that Sudan will not hand over any Sudanese national to a foreign court. There have also been very large demonstrations within Sudan against any idea of such a legal action.[960] The President has also refused to relieve Ahmed Muhammad Haroun of his duties as a government minister, stating that Haroun "will not resign or be fired and will not be interrogated...The former secretary of state for interior was only performing his duty to defend the citizens and their property from the aggressors at the time of the events (in 2003-2004)." The then Sudanese Foreign Minister Lam Akol also stated that the ICC "has no right to put any Sudanese citizen on trial" for alleged war crimes in Darfur.[961]

On 2 May 2007, the ICC issued warrants of arrest for alleged crimes against humanity and war crimes for Haroun and Ali Kushayb.[962] Sudan's Justice Minister Mohamed Ali Al-Mardi stated: "We do not recognize the International Criminal Court ... and we will not hand over any Sudanese even from the rebel groups who take up weapons against the government."[963]

The International Criminal Court

The International Criminal Court was established in 2002 as a permanent tribunal to prosecute individuals for genocide, crimes against humanity, war crimes, and the crime of aggression, although it is unable currently to exercise jurisdiction over the crime of aggression. The court can only prosecute crimes committed on or after 1 July 2002, the date its founding treaty, the Rome Statute of the International Criminal Court, entered into force. The International Criminal Court was established by a multilateral treaty which states that it can only exercise territorial jurisdiction or personal jurisdiction in relation to states that are parties to the Rome Statute. The court "inherits" the jurisdiction of state parties to the Rome Statute, which gives the court jurisdiction over crimes committed in the territory of a state party and over crimes committed by nationals of a state party. The ICC does not have universal jurisdiction of its own. The court might also come to deal with a case by way of a United Nations Security Council referral. Article 13(b) of the court's statute envisages a situation where the Security Council, acting under its Chapter VII authority, refers a situation to the ICC for investigation and possible prosecution.

The Court is designed to complement existing national judicial systems: it can only exercise its jurisdiction when national courts are unwilling or unable to investigate or prosecute such crimes. Primary responsibility to exercise jurisdiction over suspected criminals is therefore left to individual states. As of October 2007, 105 states are members of the Court, and a further 41 countries have signed but not ratified the Rome Statute. However, a number of states, including the United States, Russia, China and India are critical of the Court and have not joined. The ICC's claim to be an international institution is clearly undermined by the fact that pivotal states, representing almost half the world's population are outside of its jurisdiction. Sudan is a non-state party. It has not ratified the Rome statute.

There has been considerable criticism of the ICC. The American scholar John Rosenthal has noted one of its central dangers:

> The failings of the Rome Statute are glaring. Its provisions flout the elementary principles of international law that have formed the express basis of the international system since the founding of the

U.N. after World War II. Most gravely, they undermine the principle that has formed the very cornerstone of the U.N. system: namely, what the U.N. Charter in its article 1.2 calls the "principle of self-determination".[964]

What is the US position on the ICC?

The US has opposed the establishment of the International Criminal Court from the start. Washington has stated that the ICC's apparent jurisdiction over nationals of non-party states and the resultant binding nature of the Rome Statute on non-party states is the "single most fundamental flaw in the Rome Treaty".[965] The then American Ambassador-at-Large for War Crimes Issues, David Scheffer, told the US Senate Foreign Relations Committee that "the treaty purports to establish an arrangement whereby US armed forces operating overseas could be conceivably prosecuted by the international court even if the US has not agreed to be bound by the treaty...This is contrary to the most fundamental principles of treaty law."[966]

The American government has also noted that "Under the Rome Statute, the ICC claims the authority to second guess the actions taken and the results reached by sovereign states with respect to the investigation and prosecution of crimes."[967] The danger of politicised prosecutions was also pointed to by the United States: "We are also concerned that there are insufficient checks and balances on the authority of the ICC prosecutor and judges. The Rome Statute creates a self-initiating prosecutor, answerable to no state or institution other than the Court itself. Without such an external check on the prosecutor, there is insufficient protection against politicized prosecutions or other abuses."[968]

The United States has moved beyond merely objecting to the premise of the International Criminal Court. It has actively penalised states that support the ICC. The Council on Foreign Relations noted that "U.S. legislation continues to penalize countries that are signatories to the Rome Statute...Since 2002, the United States has sought bilateral immunity agreements (BIAs)— which protect U.S. soldiers from the ICC—with as many countries as possible. Under the 2004 Nethercutt Amendment, those that have signed on to the ICC but refused to sign BIAs are penalized with cuts in foreign assistance. As of

August 2006, some one hundred BIAs had been signed, and fifty-three countries had publicly refused signing."[969]

With regard to Darfur and the ICC, the Bush administration's actions have clearly illustrated the political nature of the process. Having long claimed that it did not support the ICC because it was unsound and that politically motivated prosecutions would ensue – against the United States for one – Washington had long shunned anything to do with it. Washington's subsequent decision not to veto a UN Security Council resolution purporting to give the ICC jurisdiction in Darfur, enabling the very action against a non-party state that it had longed warned about, was itself clearly motivated by political pressures, domestically and internationally.

Recently released cables have shown how the US disdained the ICC. In early January 2005, upon learning that the UN commission of inquiry was to recommend ICC referral, UN Ambassador John Danforth cabled Secretary of State Condoleezza Rice for instructions: should the US seek to block the ICC referral altogether, or secure a US exemption (wording in the resolution that would grant immunity to any Americans that might be caught up in the investigation). Danforth recommended the later course, saying that that it was the easier option. The Bush administration went for the first option, and for the next three months Washington attempted to block a resolution giving jurisdiction to the ICC, because in the words of a cable from Foggy Bottom "we do not want to be confronted with a decision on whether to veto a court resolution in the Security Council." Rice directed the US mission to the UN to "position ourselves to table our text before any other member formally proposes language seeking accountability through the ICC." During these three months, the United States proposed creating an alternate "accountability venue" that would be an African Union-United Nations hybrid court instead of the ICC. When European Union members of the Security Council resisted the AU-UN hybrid option, the administration sought to circumvent them: "The proposal might gain momentum...if the Africans supported it," reads one cable. Pierre-Richard Prosper, the US Ambassador-at-Large for War Crimes Issues, travelled to Africa to press AU member states to agree to the American proposal for a hybrid, AU-UN court. The US failed to convince African countries. Under political pressure, from within the United States and internationally, the United States abstained from Resolution 1593, which sought to give the ICC jurisdiction, with American exemptions, to investigate crimes in Darfur.[970]

The Sudanese position on the ICC and Darfur

The Sudanese government does not recognise any ICC jurisdiction over its sovereignty or nationals. It has not ratified the Rome treaty and is a non-state party. The simple fact is that in claiming jurisdiction over Darfur, the ICC is moving beyond its legal powers. The South African think-tank, the Institute for Security Studies, has noted that the Darfur case "is a monumental moment for the court as it steps beyond its classical treaty-based constraints to exercise jurisdiction over a non-party state, Sudan."[971] This has also been recognised by international legal experts. Commenting on the recommendations made by the UN Commission of Inquiry on Darfur to refer the situation in Darfur to the ICC, Stéphanie Giry, an international lawyer formerly with the UN Office of Legal Affairs, has noted that

> There's one big problem with it: Most of the perpetrators in Darfur can't be tried before the ICC because Sudan hasn't ratified the court's founding statute. The panel's failure to admit this limitation is staggering. It is so staggering, in fact, that coming from a group of respected experts, it may not be an oversight at all. More likely, it's a daring strategy to expand the court's ambit over one of the world's worst humanitarian crises. Unfortunately, it's also a losing strategy.[972]

The fact that Sudan has not signed the statute is an insurmountable impediment to any ICC action. Rosenthal has also pointed to the fact that "The Rome Statute is a treaty. It is a self-evident principle of the law of treaties – one explicitly confirmed by article 34 of the 1969 Vienna Convention – that treaties create no obligations per se for states that are not parties to them." [973] South African legal experts have also pointed out the difficulties of the ICC position: "Sudan is not a state party to the ICC and, as such, owes no treaty obligations to the court. This is an inevitable problem with the referral of situations involving non-party states to the ICC, as the referral extends the court's jurisdiction beyond the parameters of the Rome Treaty, but does not concomitantly extend the court's power to enforce that jurisdiction."[974]

The International Criminal Court in Action

In recommending that the Security Council refer the situation in Darfur to the ICC, the UN Commission of Inquiry on Darfur argued that there would be several benefits from such a referral: the prosecution of the crimes would be conducive to peace and security in Darfur; the ICC, as the "only truly international institution of criminal justice" would ensure justice is done because the ICC sits in The Hague, far from the alleged perpetrators' spheres of influence; the cumulative authority of the ICC and the Security Council would be required to compel those leaders responsible for atrocities to acquiesce to investigation and potential prosecution; the court is the "best suited organ for ensuring a veritably fair trial of those indicted by the Court Prosecutor" owing to its international composition and established rules of procedure; it was claimed that the work of the ICC would not necessarily involve a significant financial burden for the international community; and, finally, it was also claimed as a benefit that the ICC could be activated immediately, without any delay.[975] Of all of these, only the last assertion might go without challenge.

Before examining these claims, it must be noted the credibility of the Security Council in referring matters to the ICC is itself deeply questionable given the fact that three of three five permanent members of the Security Council are not even ICC members. With regard to the UN Commission of Inquiry's assertions, the statement that the ICC's prosecution of crimes would be conducive to peace and security in Darfur is dangerously unrealistic. Academic studies of peace note that:

> When a conflict is ongoing, the immediate concern will be to bring an end to the bloodshed. Although the pursuit of justice can potentially contribute to long-lasting peace through the imposition of the rule of law...punishment has the potential to reinforce hostility and impede efforts to encourage rival parties to agree. For

those most at risk in the conflict, it is more than likely that it will be peace and not justice that is of greatest concern.[976]

This has been echoed by the Council on Foreign Relations regarding similar international courts: "Critics say the tribunal exacerbates current conflicts."[977]

The ICC and Uganda is a key case in point, and one with clear implications for Darfur. A savage civil war between the Ugandan government and a largely Acholi-based rebel movement calling itself the Lord's Resistance Army (LRA), has raged in northern Uganda for several decades. Tens of thousands of civilians have died and millions more have been displaced into government-controlled IDP camps. The prospect of a peaceful solution to the war came sharply into focus from November 2004 onwards when the Ugandan President Yoweri Museveni announced a unilateral ceasefire in parts of northern Uganda. The initial ceasefire period was extended and a major breakthrough seemed imminent.

President Museveni had, however, in December 2003 previously called upon the ICC to investigate the "situation concerning the Lord's Resistance Army", the first state referral that the ICC had received since its inception. On 29 January 2004, the ICC Chief Prosecutor participated in a joint press conference in London with President Museveni to announce the referral. On 29 July 2004 the ICC announced that it would undertake a full investigation of the situation in northern Uganda. A delegation of senior northern Ugandan leaders travelled to The Hague in February 2005 and on April 14-16, 2005 to urge the ICC not to issue arrest warrants while peace negotiations were ongoing.[978] In October 2005, nevertheless, the ICC issued indictments and arrest warrants for several Ugandan LRA rebel leaders. The peace process suffered a major reversal as LRA leaders returned to the bush.

Religious and community leaders in war-affected northern Uganda criticised the issuing of ICC arrest warrants for Ugandan rebel leaders. The day after the UN announced the ICC indictments, Uganda's Roman Catholic Church warned that the threat of legal action could put the peace process in the north at risk. Catholic Archbishop John Baptist Odama stated "The peace process has been put in jeopardy...we do feel that the presence of the court here and its activities are in danger of jeopardising efforts to rebuild the rebels' confidence in peace talks. How can we tell the LRA soldiers to come out of the bush and receive amnesty when at the same time the threat of arrest by the

ICC hangs over their heads?" [979] Monsignor Matthew Odongo, the vicar-general of the Roman Catholic diocese of the northern district of Gulu, said: "This is like throwing a stone in water that had settled. Any move that adds to the suffering of the people will not be good." Odongo, speaking on behalf of the Acholi Religious Leaders Peace Initiative, an inter-faith peace group said he was also concerned about the timing of the announcement, coming as it did just as the LRA had announced its commitments to peace talks.[980]

Peter Onega, the head of the Uganda Amnesty Commission, a statutory body set up by the government to encourage the peace process, said the decision by the international court had left their work in "total confusion". Onega warned that the indictments would provide rebel hardliners with the tools to consolidate the rebel ranks: "They will be at liberty to tell these people that 'this is just the beginning, don't think we are the only ones wanted by the ICC – your turn is coming' and very few will come out [of the bush] if such a message was driven home". Onega expressed the fear that the ICC indictments could only encourage more atrocities because the LRA leadership could act as "desperately as a wounded buffalo". He also warned of the negative effect on reconciliation:

> The ICC should have known all the consequences before they issued the warrants. They should have also considered another issue in all this – reconciliation. Does the taking of only five people for prosecution at The Hague bring about reconciliation among the divided Acholi [northern ethnic group] people? The warrants are not any good for national unity if you have people who will go to testify against others.[981]

The Guardian reported in January 2007 on the local opposition in northern Uganda to the ICC: "hostility to the ICC in Gulu is so widespread that Norbert Mao, the chief elected representative for about 300,000 people in the district around the town and a member of the opposition Democratic party, has warned the court's investigators that their lives are at risk." He stated: "What would be the point in taking these LRA leaders to a prison in Stockholm? Would that be a definition of justice for us? I think this is the ICC grandstanding as it's its first case."[982]

The Council on Foreign Relations has also noted: "Ugandans are increasingly dissatisfied with the ICC, which they say fails to respect their desire for traditional reconciliation and is undermining efforts for genuine peace in their country."[983] Reuters, reporting in April 2007, stated "Since peace talks started, a wave of popular opposition to the ICC amongst northern Ugandans – the main victims of Kony's cult-like rebel group – has dismayed rights groups. Northerners say only a lifting of the indictments will bring lasting peace."[984] Senior UN officials such as Jan Egeland, the under secretary-general for humanitarian affairs, for example, have been confronted by northern Ugandan leaders on the issue. The leader of a camp of 25,000 displaced persons – victims of the conflict – told him to his face "We don't want the International Criminal Court. We want peace...Will the court really bring peace, or fuel the war again?"[985] Even the Ugandan government, faced with the prospect of continuing conflict, has indicated that it wishes to approach the ICC to drop indictments against the LRA leadership if a peace deal is signed. In September 2007, the Ugandan Defence Minister, Ruth Nankabirwa, stated Uganda had contacted the ICC "to request them to relax or to withdraw the warrants of arrest to enable Uganda to handle the culprits."[986]

In respect of Uganda, Arsanjani and Reisman question "What contribution to the settlement of the dispute accrues from transferring the problem, at this juncture, to the International Criminal Court, a body that was neither intended not equipped to resolve, through judicial means, a longstanding political problem of a government."[987] They have also asserted that Uganda's referral of the situation to the ICC amounts to "washing its own hands of an insoluble internal problem" and sets a bad example as it is "a move that could encourage [other] governments to externalize to the Court the domestic problems they are unable or unwilling – because they do not wish to invest the necessary resources – to manage or resolve."[988]

Richard Dowden, director of the Royal African Society, has argued that the intrusion of "international law" into African conflicts such as Uganda and the DRC, can cause problems for local peace deals, as in Africa peace deals have usually included losers in government and tying them into a peaceful settlement rather than punishing combatants for the conflict. Dowden has stated that concerns that the ICC's western-inspired, universalist idea of justice might come into conflict with local forms of law, jeopardising the process of reconciliation "may turn out to have been justified".[989] He has warned that a global justice system "must have its ideas of justice informed by cultures other than our own. The ICC cannot hand out justice in Sudan as if it were Surrey...If the ICC cannot bring peace and reconciliation to the victims of war, what is the point of its justice?" As Dowden has stated "If the ICC is going to step into Africa's complex wars, it must understand the local contexts and think through the effects of its actions. Local input and outcomes based on peace and reconciliation must be as close to the heart of the ICC's mission as justice." [990] Dowden further states that it is Western, not African, imperatives that push for international courts: "Who is it for? I suspect it is for us, watching these wars on television...The court may be a salve for our consciences for doing nothing about the wars in the first place."[991] Even keen supporters of "international law" such as South African Judge Richard Goldstone appear to confirm that such a process can impede peace: "if you have a system of international justice you've got to follow through on it. If in some cases that's going to make peace negotiations difficult, that may be the price that has to be paid."[992] That is, of course, easy for Goldstone to say from the safety and comfort of his judges chambers and residence.

The impact on peace within Sudan of the Darfur indictments is clear. They will have a very negative effect on the Darfur peace process, serving to radicalise both sides to the conflict. They bolster the fragmented rebel movements, who may think all they have to do is sit tight, continue the conflict and wait for regime-change by indictment. On the other government side, as pointed out by Christopher Caldwell of *The Weekly Standard*, "Threatening leaders with life sentences in the Hague turns a situation that might conceivably be resolved by diplomacy into a fight to the death."[993]

Rather than speeding up resolution of the Darfur conflict, therefore, the ICC involvement will have the opposite effect. In the short term it is often cited as a reason why the Sudanese government will not entertain the idea of UN military forces in Darfur. International observers have noted, for example, that "the media has often talked about the threat of the ICC hanging over the dominant National Congress Party as a possible reason for its intransigence on the question of a UN deployment in Darfur, for fear that such a deployment would assist the ICC in its task of gathering evidence of war crimes."[994] Such concerns would have been fuelled by statements by senior American officials, cited by the Council on Foreign Relations: "Ambassador David Scheffer, who led the U.S. delegation in UN talks to establish the ICC, says the investigation won't be able to have a presence in Darfur until there are UN peacekeepers on the ground. Analysts say this is one of the main reasons behind the Sudanese government's opposition to a UN-only force."[995]

There is also foreign speculation that the ICC referral will not just prolong the Darfur conflict but will also unravel the existing north-south Comprehensive Peace Agreement by seeking to remove the principal northern Sudanese architects of that peace:

> Moreover, the principle of "Command Responsibility" which has been incorporated into the international criminal courts including the Rome Statute of the ICC makes it possible for the courts to punish superiors and commanders for crimes committed by their subordinates. What the first two summonses by the ICC prosecutor allege is that an intimate link exists between the Sudanese state authorities and the perpetrators of crimes against humanity. Should the rot go deeper to the highest echelons of the NCP, what can we expect to happen to that document of international legitimacy – the Comprehensive Peace Agreement?[996]

The ICC indictments have also caused concern for the safety of UN personnel within Sudan. UN radio reported that "The UN mission in Sudan has expressed fears for the security of its staff after the International Criminal Court accused two Sudanese officials of war crimes in Darfur." The acting UN special envoy to Sudan confirmed that the mission had warned its staff: "There could be reactions from people. Yes, the ICC is seen as part of the UN system. But we have no mandate on what the ICC does." [997]

The second claim made by the UN, that the ICC, as the "only truly international institution of criminal justice", would ensure justice is done because the ICC sits in The Hague, far from the alleged perpetrators' spheres of influence. This claim is at best a half-truth. While it may be an international mechanism, it is naïve to claim that the ICC is immune from political influence by governments and activists. The ICC is seen as an extension of the UN Security Council – itself perceived throughout much of the world as a body ultimately dominated by the US. One clear example of this was that the Government of Sudan received an offer from the Bush administration that it would halt ICC proceedings in return for Khartoum's consent to deploy UN troops in Darfur. The Minister of State at the Sudanese Ministry of Foreign Affairs, Ali Karti, stated: "This shows this court has been formed for political purposes and not to serve justice."[998]

The assertion that the cumulative authority of the ICC and the Security Council is necessary to compel those leaders allegedly responsible for atrocities to acquiesce to investigation and potential prosecution is questionable. It is just simply not the case. The authority and credibility of the ICC and Security Council is weakened in any instance from the very start by the United States not being liable for any prosecution. It is precisely the fact that the Security Council is involved that will contaminate it. The reality is that the ICC will only be able to focus on alleged cases within the developing world. The West will to all intents and purposes be immune from prosecution. A South African analysis has succinctly observed "we cannot ignore the global context of intervention, which is presently dominated by the apparent failure of international action in Iraq. How is the international community to play honest broker when images of the Middle East and the UN's particular inability to prevent violations of international law in Israel and Palestine feed local paranoia in Sudan?"[999]

The truth is that the ICC is as independent as the UN Security Council (and some claim, by default, the United States) will allow it to be. Rosenthal has punctured the myth of the ICC's independence: "It is a self-evident principle that the independence and hence impartiality of a court is only as sure as the independence of its financing....None of us would put faith in the impartiality of a local or national court if it depended upon the largesse of private individuals or corporations, who, by definition, might have an interest in the outcome of particular proceedings."[1000] The ICC is financed out of the general UN budget. Additionally, article 116 of the Rome Statute also provides for voluntary contributions "from Governments, international organizations, individuals, corporations and other entities." Rosenthal observes "Thus, the ICC's very statute openly invites contributions from a whole range of 'entities,' any of whom could have an interest in the outcome of proceedings and some of whom, notably "Governments" might even have been parties to the hostilities in which the alleged crimes over which the court claims jurisdiction are supposed to have occurred." Rosenthal also points out that the ICC is clearly itself aware of how this might be read. In September 2002, the ICC's Assembly of State Parties passed a "remarkable resolution" which asked all such "entities" making such contributions to declare that their contributions "are not intended to affect the independence of the Court." Rosenthal notes that "much in the spirit of the statute itself, verbal assurances were here offered as the equivalent of substantive protections." He concludes: "The ICC is not merely a matter of good intentions gone awry in the face of stubborn political realities…The ICC…has been made to be abused." [1001]

The Council on Foreign Relations has also noted that:

> Human rights organisations have criticised the ICC for a lack of transparency in how cases are chosen. So far all have come from Africa. Four situations have been publicly referred to the Prosecutor of the ICC: Three state parties (Uganda, Democratic Republic of the Congo and Central African Republic) have referred situations occurring on their territories, and the UN Security Council has referred the situation of Darfur, Sudan. While prosecutor Moreno-Ocampo has defended his choices as the "gravest admissible situations" within his jurisdiction, potential ICC action over US actions in Iraq was dismissed in 2006. [1002]

A further and clearly related criticism has been that the ICC has excluded weapons of mass destruction and terrorism from its jurisdiction. The government of India, for example, has expressed concern that "the Statute of the ICC lays down, by clear implication, that the use of weapons of mass destruction is not a war crime. This is an extraordinary message to send to the international community." [1003] It is clear that this limitation of jurisdiction is very much in favour of the permanent members of the Security Council and those other western countries who possess immense arsenals of such weapons.

It has also been pointed out that for all the claims of the ICC needing the authority of the Security Council to compel those leaders responsible for atrocities to acquiesce to investigation and potential prosecution, this is naïve. As Louise Parrott notes, "Having no police force of its own, the ICC must rely on international cooperation in order to effect the arrests. Giving the ongoing nature of the conflict, this is likely to require security forces, which increases the control of states." [1004] Certain nation states may well, for their own particular reasons, acquiesce in requests to militarily assist in ICC investigations or the enforcement of arrest warrants against its own nationals. This may adversely affect some national perceptions of the impartiality of the ICC. An example of this would be if the ICC used Ugandan government forces to execute its mission. And Parrott also points out that "while it may be more desirable…to rely on United Nations peacekeeping forces for enhanced security in undertaking investigations and efficiency in carrying out arrests, the use of UN forces also presents various problems. Not only could the neutrality of the forces be compromised if they were perceived as part of the operation that was building a case against a party to the conflict." [1005] Should Sudan not cooperate with the ICC, the court could report this "non-compliance" to the UN Security Council, which in turn considers appropriate action. One is then back to the independence or otherwise of the Security Council.

Fourthly, in calling for Darfur to be referred to the ICC, the UN claimed that the court is the "best suited organ for ensuring a veritably fair trial of those indicted by the Court Prosecutor" owing to its international composition and established rules of procedure. The legitimacy of the ICC will depend on its ability to maintain an appearance of impartiality. As Allison Danner points out: "[i]f the Prosecutor becomes identified with any political agenda other than seeking justice, the role of the Court in providing an impartial, independent forum for individuals accused of the most serious crimes will be severely compromised."[1006] Louise Parrot has noted that this is a problem that has already arisen with regard to Uganda in that "only LRA rebels have been targeted, making the Court open to claims that its purpose is to selectively rid Uganda of the rebels rather than to impartiality prosecute the crimes committed." [1007] She went on to observe that the Ugandan government hoped "that joining the ICC would help it prosecute the rebels…These recent developments raise numerous issues, not least of which is the desirability of the ICC becoming involved in ongoing conflicts, particularly where the referring government is one of the parties. As a result, questions arise about the impartiality of the Prosecutor, the feasibility of enforcement and ultimately the prospects of peace."[1008]

Human Rights Watch has also confirmed that the ICC's impartiality has come into question almost immediately regarding its involvement in Uganda: "The ICC badly needs to regain the confidence and trust of the people whose interests it is pursuing. It must correct the image it has acquired of an institution subject to manipulation by the Ugandan government for political expediency. It must restore the image of a credible international institution." Human Rights Watch felt it necessary to urge the ICC to "quickly act to demonstrate the court's impartiality", noting that "Civil society remains concerned that the ICC is being manipulated by President Museveni, whose statements have not dispelled that impression."[1009] These questions have also been voiced by Ugandan political leaders such as Norbert Mao: "When the ICC first came they said they would investigate both sides. In the eyes of many people the ICC is serving the interests of the Ugandan government, not justice."[1010] *The Guardian* has also noted: "While the LRA's crimes have been widely exposed, the actions of the Ugandan army have not been subjected to the same scrutiny. It has been involved in wholesale forced removals, often brutally carried out, of hundreds of thousands of people from their homes to deny the rebels support. People in the area also accuse government soldiers of rape and killings." [1011]

Impartiality aside, there have also been questions about whether or not the ICC is able to offer a fair trial. These questions arose from the very start in the ICC's first case. In November 2006, the ICC began its case against an alleged former militia leader, Thomas Lubanga Dyilo from the Democratic Republic of Congo. The court has been accused of unfair treatment. Resources allocated to the defence are inadequate; his evidence and witness statements have been slow to arrive and many documents are impossible to read because they have been so heavily redacted by the ICC. The International Bar Association has supported concerns raised by Dyilo's legal defence team.[1012] The Council on Foreign Relations has also noted that "some in Africa are questioning the court's ability to provide justice".[1013]

And as for the claim that the institution of criminal proceedings before the ICC, at the request of the Security Council, would not necessarily involve a significant financial burden for the international community, this is another surprisingly naïve assertion. In the first year or so of its investigations, ICC personnel conducted more than fifty well-funded missions to fifteen countries.

Rosenthal has summed up the dangers of the ICC:

> If we consider the ICC's erosion of the classical U.N. principles, the contempt for due process written into its statute, and – last but by no means least – its mode of financing, what will become abundantly obvious is the risk it presents of being an interventionary court subordinated to the geostrategic aims of its richest and most powerful member states, whether singular or in league. In short, the ICC's practice threatens to be nothing other than the continuation of war by quasi- or pseudo-judicial means.

In conclusion, with regard to the ICC and Darfur one might end with the comments of the Justice and Peace Commission in Gulu, northern Uganda: "[t]o start war crimes investigations for the sake of justice at a time when the war is not yet over, risks having, in the end, neither justice not peace delivered."[1014] And, in the case of Sudan, two peace processes may unravel.

Chapter Nine

THE MEDIA, SENSATIONALISM AND IRRESPONSIBILITY

> *For all that it deals with events and realities...news has a prodigious capacity for myth-making. Like a huckster on the high street it hawks its wares regardless of their quality.*
>
> *Former BBC Correspondent Martin Bell* [1015]

> *American media coverage of complex emergencies will likely continue to be limited, random and unreliable.*
>
> *Andrew Natsios, USAID Director* [1016]

The veteran British journalist Nick Davies' 2007 book, *Flat Earth News: An Award-winning Reporter Exposes Falsehood, Distortion and Propaganda in the Global Media*, was billed as an insider's view on a "profession corrupted to the core" where journalists are content to peddle myths "from the millennium bug to the WMD in Iraq" – dressed up as genuine stories. While he did not focus on coverage of Sudan, his criticism of the media could not be more apt with regard to media coverage of the Darfur crisis.

It should not have been unexpected. It is a simple matter of fact that a significant amount of the international press coverage of Sudan over the past two decades has been questionable. Disinformation and propaganda has been an ever-present feature of most, if not all, wars over the past 50 years or so. Sudan in general and Darfur in particular have been no exception. The international news media have been a target for those who wish to manipulate the way in which conflicts are presented. This is for obvious reasons.

International "reporting" is in many instances the only image many outside observers will have of the country itself. International press coverage is also sometimes the only material many commentators and even legislators will have in mind when addressing issues either directly or indirectly related to Sudan. Journalists have in many instances managed to get away with some appalling reporting on Sudan. There has been a mixture of simply bad journalism and misinformation.

Speaking in December 2004, Chris Mullins, the then Minister of State at the British Foreign and Commonwealth Office, noted the dysfunctional nature of much of the media coverage of the Darfur conflict. After viewing a British television news item on Darfur, he stated that the news item was "the first one to acknowledge there are actually two sides in this dispute"[1017] – that is to say 18 months after the war had begun. It is a sad reality that Mullins' comments can be applied virtually across the board with regard to media coverage of the Darfur crisis.

It is worth placing the reporting on Darfur into context. Over the past decade or so the international news media have carried a number of deeply questionable claims about Sudan. These have included allegations that Sudan possessed and manufactured weapons of mass destruction. These were, of course, particularly grave allegations to have been made. Foreign media outlets "reported", for example, that Khartoum had used weapons of mass destruction in the course of the then civil war in southern Sudan. The allegations were also shown to have been baseless. In one instance anti-government rebels claimed in July 1999 that Sudanese armed forces had used chemical weapons in attacks on their forces in southern Sudan.[1018] These claims were repeated by several British newspapers as well as the BBC. They were also carried in other international media.[1019] The United Nations investigated the claims and arranged for detailed tests which "indicated no evidence of exposure to chemicals".[1020] The claims were false.

One of the other widely-publicised sensationalist claims about Sudan has been allegations of government-sponsored "slavery" and "slave trade" in Sudan. As "proof" for this, a great number of newspaper articles "reported" instances of "slave redemption" in which alleged "slaves" were said to have been "bought" back from "slave traders". These claims were widely and sensationally reported in the international media from 1996 onwards but gradually came to exposed as questionable where not simply false, as early as 1999.[1021] In February 2002, in an unprecedented international focus, and as the result of some excellent investigative journalism, newspapers such as *The Irish Times*, London's *Independent on Sunday*, *The Washington Post* and *The International Herald Tribune*, exposed the deep fraud and corruption at the heart of claims of "slave redemption" in Sudan.[1022]

Interestingly, allegations of chemical weapons use have surfaced within the Darfur conflict. In September 2004, the conservative German daily newspaper *Die Welt* published allegations that the Sudanese and Syrian governments were using chemical weapons in Darfur.[1023] The article had a specific racial tone as the article claimed that the weapons were to be tested on "the black African population". The newspaper claimed western intelligence services as its source. Similar allegations surfaced at the same time in Norwegian state media. The story was soon discounted, by, amongst others, the American government and German intelligence, but not before it had been picked up and republished by major news agencies and by the media world-wide.[1024] German intelligence sources blamed the fabrication on Sudanese exile groups.[1025] The British government subsequently stated that it had "seen no credible evidence" to support the allegation.[1026] The Norwegian variant on the story was sourced back to the Sudan Liberation Army through Norwegian People's Aid, an anti-Khartoum organisation with a history of fabricating propaganda stories – including earlier disproved "chemical weapons" claims in southern Sudan.[1027]

"Genocide" in Darfur

The latest sensationalist claim has been "genocide" in Darfur. The US media in particular has carried a number of reports alleging "genocide" and "ethnic cleansing" in Darfur. This has been despite the fact that such claims have been challenged by seasoned aid groups such as Médecins Sans Frontières, and only really advanced by a politically opportunistic Bush Administration.

With few exceptions, the international media's coverage of the Darfur conflict has been self-evidently lacklustre. The very dynamics of the conflict has not even been adequately analysed or reported. Most coverage has taken at face value rebel claims that they are fighting against underdevelopment and marginalisation in Darfur. As we have seen this has been challenged by fiercely anti-government critics such as Ghazi Suleiman. Neither Dr Turabi's name, nor the Islamist involvement, featured much in media coverage of the conflict, particularly earlier coverage.

Susan Moeller's clinical description of how the media handles crises is instructive – a description that fits the way in which the Darfur crisis has been presented:

> Almost every night, [the crisis] will become a front-page, top-of-the-news story. Print and television reporters, photographers and camerapeople flood the area. At this point, the story is grossly simplified: clear victims, villains and heroes are created; language such as "harrowing," "hellish," "unprecedented," "single worst crisis in the world," [crisis] of the century' is employed; huge numbers are tossed off frequently and casually, with few references to sources…[The crisis] dominates coverage of international news, and for a while even domestic events. It becomes the focus of presidential and congressional debate and action. It becomes a cultural and moral bellwether for the nation…By this stage, the story has become a runaway engine…The success of that morality play story line rests on the fact that it is easy to understand and appreciate…The set piece is ideal material for television and superficial print coverage.[1028]

This is precisely the course followed by the US media on Darfur. In her chapter in de Waal's *War in Darfur and the Search for Peace*, Deborah Murphy produced the first detailed analysis of US media coverage of Darfur in 2004. Murphy reviewed 83 editorials and op-eds on Darfur appearing in *The New York Times*, *The Washington Post*, *The Wall Street Journal* and *The Washington Times* from March to September 2004. She stated that the narrative contained in these articles "assigned polarized Arab and African identities to the perpetrators and victims, usually labelled it a genocide, and assumed the government controlled the violence". Almost half of the articles reviewed described the violence as genocide or potential genocide; fourteen of the twenty-four articles which appeared between March and early June did so. Twenty-eight of the articles, and more specifically eleven of the sixteen appearing between March and April 2004, referenced the Rwandan genocide, describing the Darfur crisis commonly as "the new Rwanda", "another Rwanda", "the worst humanitarian crisis since Rwanda" and so on. She further noted that this general narrative "probably accounts for a great deal of the success had by human rights advocates in attracting attention to Darfur...and proved to be a powerful formula for demonstrating the need for intervention". Murphy states that while comparing Darfur to Rwanda, "few efforts were made to illuminate the similarities and differences between the conflicts." [1029] Murphy also noted that "little attention was paid to the role of the rebels". For example, only 23 of the 83 articles reviewed stated that the violence was a response to armed insurrection. Only eleven articles mentioned the long-running conflict between nomads and farmers over scarce land and water resources as a factor in the crisis. [1030]

Perhaps the study of the American media most relevant to the American media's unquestioning acceptance of the Bush administration's Darfur genocide claims is Herbert Gans' *Deciding What's News*, a detailed examination of how news stories are selected by key media outlets. Gans states that most media stories are based on statements by prominent elected and government officials such as the President, cabinet members and congressmen. He also notes that because reporters get most of their stories from these "official" sources, they are subservient to their sources. Gans states that reporters "must concentrate on stories that please their sources, since angering them may endanger their closeness or rapport, thus ending the reporter's usefulness on the beat". [1031]

Gans' study was amply demonstrated by the then *New York Times* star reporter Judith Miller and her reporting on Iraq. Miller became infamous for unreservedly accepting false Bush administration claims about Iraq: "My job isn't to assess the government's information and be an independent intelligence analyst myself. My job is to tell readers of The New York Times what the government thought about Iraq's arsenal." [1032] This is, in effect, exactly what virtually all the American media have done with regard to Washington's claims about Darfur and genocide: no assessment, no analysis, merely repetition.

An unquestioning reliance on official US government claims, and an apparent disinclination on the part of western media to do their homework, is also central to criticism of western media coverage of Darfur made by *The*

Guardian's senior foreign correspondent, Jonathan Steele: "Good journalism is not about getting powerful TV footage or dramatic interviews. Good journalism involves sifting through a variety of sources, talking to experts, reading well-researched academic and other historical accounts, and closely following websites run by the United Nations and those of the numerous aid agencies who work in Darfur or have recent access to it." [1033] Far too many journalists have opted instead for the Miller approach to journalism. Nicholas Kristof, Miller's colleague at *The New York Times*, is her equivalent on Darfur.

In her study of disaster reporting Moeller cites one disaster reporter as noting that there is "a common period in disaster reporting – exaggerating the immediate and long-term impact. We will *always* gravitate towards the largest kill count...We will *always* speculate...the cosmic consequence."[1034] Darfur provides a case study of this sensationalism. Media claims of genocide in Darfur have gone hand in hand with wildly exaggerated mortality figures. Darfur mortality figures have been addressed elsewhere in this book. The Darfur war was at its peak from late 2003 until 2004. The death toll which may have been several thousand per month dropped dramatically. The UN reported that by the end of 2004 the situation had stabilised and that the "catastrophic mortality figures predicted by some quarters have not materialised".[1035] An unprecedented international humanitarian effort was on the ground in Darfur caring from the food and medical needs of the hundreds of thousands of civilians who had been displaced. It is useful, therefore, to record a snap-shot of international media reporting on the mortality figures at the junction when mortality levels plummeted (and have continued to drop ever since). The Knight Ridder news service reported on 9 January 2005 that "the war in Darfur has taken an estimated 70,000 lives." On 11 January 2005, Associated Press stated that "about 70,000 people have died through disease, hunger and attacks in Darfur." On 12 January 2005, Reuters stated that "70,000 are estimated to have died in Darfur." On the same day the BBC reported that "about 70,000 people" had died. The Voice of America reported on 14 January 2005 that "two years of fighting between rebels and government-backed militias have claimed an estimated 70,000 lives". On 16 January 2005, Agence France-Presse wrote that the conflict "has claimed the lives of 70,000 people". As has been outlined elsewhere in this book, from late 2004 onwards war-related deaths dropped to between one and two hundred per month, with occasional spikes. American newspapers do not appear to have let facts get in the way of a good story. A little over one year later *The New York Times* was reporting that as many as 450,000 people had died in Darfur.[1036] Some months later *The Washington Post* claimed 450,000 civilian deaths in Darfur.[1037] The venerable *National Geographic News* even pushed the figure up to 500,000.[1038] Even reputable British newspapers have been caught up in sensationalism and hyperbole. A September 2006 editorial on Darfur in *The Times* of London was run under the title "The next Rwanda?" The editorial claimed that "at least 200,000 villagers – and possibly double that, according to credible US estimates – have been killed."[1039]

That there has been superficial and exaggerated press coverage of the Darfur crisis is clear. That many news reports have accepted rebel propaganda is unsurprising. Much of this reporting has been done by journalists who were taken on guided tours by the rebels in Darfur.[1040] Only one of these journalists subsequently contacted the government of Sudan stating that he wished to visit government areas to give the government's position. That the reporting by these journalists in large part reflected claims made by the rebels is self-evident. This despite the fact that, as also noted by Reuters, "it is hard to independently verify claims by government or rebels in Darfur."[1041] It is also clear that some of these journalists are long-time anti-Sudan activists (such as Julie Flint) who have previously made several questionable claims about events in Sudan.[1042] And, in addition, there are also those journalists who wish to present one side as exclusively good and the other as exclusively bad. An example of this was the Scottish *Sunday Herald*'s August 2004 article "And With Darfur's Rebels", which actually used the phrase "guys in white hats" with regard to the SLA.[1043]

Professor Mahmood Mamdani has been particularly critical of the shortcomings of media coverage of Darfur, from both a macro and micro perspective. The media's general approach has been simplistic:

> Journalism gives us a simple moral world, where a group of perpetrators face a group of victims, but where neither history nor motivation is thinkable because both are outside history and context. Even when newspapers highlight violence as a social phenomenon, they fail to understand the forces that shape the agency of the perpetrator. Instead, they look for a clear and uncomplicated moral

that describes the victim as untainted and the perpetrator as simply evil. Where yesterday's victims are today's perpetrators, where victims have turned perpetrators, this attempt to find an African replay of the Holocaust not only does not work but also has perverse consequences.[1044]

He also noted that rather than providing any coherent analysis, media coverage has obsessed on sensationalist details:

Newspaper writing on Darfur has sketched a pornography of violence. It seems fascinated by and fixated on the gory details, describing the worst of the atrocities in gruesome detail and chronicling the rise in the number of them. The implication is that the motivation of the perpetrators lies in biology ('race') and, if not that, certainly in 'culture'. This voyeuristic approach accompanies a moralistic discourse whose effect is both to obscure the politics of the violence and position the reader as a virtuous, not just a concerned observer.[1045]

Eight Media mistakes on Darfur

In a keynote speech at the Royal United Services Institute for Defence and Security Studies in London, in July 2006, *The Guardian*'s Jonathan Steele bluntly criticised western media coverage of Darfur: "The media, in my view, have consistently failed to cover Darfur properly. Reporters have made repeated mistakes, and not been honest with their readers. Commentators have ignored or slanted key aspects of the conflict. Even though much of their work has been well-intentioned, aiming to alert the world to the tragedies of Darfur in the hope of getting them stopped, I believe their work has had the opposite effect. Bad journalism has helped to prolong the war."[1046]

Steele outlined eight mistakes the media had made in their coverage of Darfur.

Mistake number one was not to get the war's origins right...The fact that hostilities began with a rebel attack on the Sudanese air force base at El Fasher in February 2003 and the deaths of dozens of soldiers was usually not mentioned...Mistake number two was to transfer the template of Sudan's North-South war to Darfur. So we heard a good deal about how the Islamic fundamentalist regime in Khartoum was trying to impose Islam and sharia on Darfur just as it had done for years on the Nilotic peoples of south Sudan. It took months before most of the media discovered that almost everyone in Darfur is Muslim. Mistake number three, a variant of mistake number two, was to portray the war as one between Arab and Africans. OK, the war wasn't about religion. It was about race...This simplistic Arab versus African template ignored the complexity of Darfur's tribal structure and the long history of tension between the various tribes and ethnicities. It also ignored the long history of tribal reconciliation mechanisms which had managed over decades to keep the peace in Darfur or restore it when it was occasionally broken. Mistake number four was to ignore the economic roots of the conflict... If the media did not understand or bother to report the context of the war in Darfur, they were equally bad at failing to report the options for peace... Mistake number five by the media was to ignore [the] peace process. Instead the bulk of the op-ed pieces and comments was to demand Western intervention and sanctions on Khartoum as though there was no peace track on offer...The trouble was that at various points the rebels walked out or refused to return after a break. Once they took on board that peace talks were happening, media mistake number six was to overlook the problems caused by the rebels. All the blame for the lack of progress at the peace talks was put on the government. Media mistake number seven was to ignore the splits on the rebels' side. It was not until two of the three rebel movements refused to sign the Abuja deal in May that many reporters woke up to the fact that the rebels were not united...Media mistake number eight was to ignore the humanitarian problems caused by the rebels. In their eagerness to portray the struggle in simple terms as good guys versus bad guys, attacks by the rebels on aid convoys were not covered. Attacks by the rebels on villages which also displaced thousands of Darfurians also went unreported.

Alex de Waal has also confirmed that "the peace process has never been properly covered in the media."[1047] Steele went on to ask "Does all this matter to anyone except a handful of students of the press?" His clear answer was yes. Steele strongly believed that undemanding western media coverage of the Darfur conflict has artificially prolonged the crisis and the suffering:

> I believe that the media's role in making heroes out of the rebels and overlooking their misdeeds, as well as in constantly calling for sanctions on Khartoum or even military intervention, have had a malign effect. In my view it encouraged the rebels to be more intransigent in Abuja than they would otherwise have been. They felt confident that if they refused to sign but held out for more, they could have the media's support. As it is, two of the three groups refused to sign the deal, and it was little short of a miracle that Minni Minawi, the leader of the largest military faction, eventually did sign it.[1048]

Much of the media would once again appear to have gone for the sensationalist story in Sudan – at the expense of professionalism. Andrew Buckoke, a British foreign correspondent who has written for *The Guardian*, *The Economist*, *The Observer*, *The Financial Times* and *The Times*, has provided an insight into the mindset – even on non-controversial issues – which should be borne in mind when reading claims of "genocide" and "ethnic cleansing" in Darfur. He cited the example of the sensationalistic coverage of the floods in Sudan in August 1988. Torrential rain on the headwaters of both the White Nile and Blue Niles had resulted in intense press prediction and speculation that Khartoum "would disappear under a gigantic whirlpool".[1049] Buckoke was sent to cover this impending disaster and found there was none to report on: "The Nile never did burst its banks, nor was any significant damage due to the downpour evident in central Khartoum."[1050] This, however, did not stop "the story still being taken very seriously in the outside world, and I was rebuked by a telex demanding more drama and detail". Despite being a non-event, "the floods were the biggest story out of black Africa".[1051] Buckoke questions the international coverage: "How did the coverage...get so distorted and imbalanced, as they so often do when Africa is involved?"[1052] He also notes that "the whole story was out of control. Journalists, aid agency workers, the government and donors had been caught from the beginning in a self-sustaining spiral of exaggeration."[1053]

It can be argued that Andrew Buckoke's use of the term "self-sustaining spiral of exaggeration" applies equally to sensationalistic claims of "genocide" in Darfur. What has happened there is bad enough. Given the expected story-line set by editors it would be a brave journalist indeed who returned from a week of milling around in the sands of Chad or along the border with Sudan or even a week or so in Khartoum's hotels without filing the some sort of story of "ethnic" cleaning or genocide. This does not, of course, in any way excuse the unprofessional way in which Sudan continues to be covered by many journalists. Given the track record of questionable claims about Sudan, one would have expected professional journalists to have taken a much more cautious approach to events in Darfur.

Prunier has been critical of media coverage of the Darfur crisis, noting that "the first US article on [Darfur] focused immediately on the 'Black versus Arab' side of the problem, an aspect which, even if justified, was going to obscure rather than clarify the essential elements in the following months because of its misleadingly 'evident' explanatory power."[1054] He further observes that following the anniversary of the Rwanda violence, and attempts to link Darfur to Rwanda:

> Newspapers went wild and the *New York Times* started to write about "genocide". The "angle" had been found: Darfur was a genocide and the Arabs were killing the Blacks. The journalists did not seem unduly concerned by the fact that the Arabs were often black, or that the "genocide" was strangely timed given Khartoum's diplomat goals in Naivasha…What is conventionally known as "world opinion" now cared about Darfur, even if the actual mechanics of what was happening remaining obscure. But the moral outrage which was felt tended to overshadow, if not hide completely, the political nature of the problem. Some specialized articles started to disentangle the various lines of causality but soon got lost amid the loud humanitarian demands for action.[1055]

Prunier also specifically examined the media's embracing of the genocide label: "The reason seems to be the overriding role of the media coupled with the mass consumption need for brands and labels. Things are not seen in their reality but in their capacity to create brand images, to warrant a 'big story', to mobilize TV time high in rhetoric. 'Genocide' is big because it carries the Nazi label, which sells well. 'Ethnic cleansing' is next best (though far behind) because it goes with Bosnia, which was the last big-story European massacre. But simple killing is boring, especially in Africa."[1056]

There are numerous instances of poor journalism on Darfur. The following are a few examples.

The New York Times: Questionable Journalism

In the course of 2004, *The New York Times* published a number of articles alleging that genocide is taking place in Darfur. The newspaper has also published articles alleging that there has been systematic "ethnic cleansing".[1057] Mark Lacy, for example, has claimed that the "Janjaweed" have been purging "villages of their darker-skinned black African inhabitants".[1058] Nicholas Kristof, a former editor of *The New York Times* turned columnist, has repeatedly claimed genocide in Darfur, asserting that the "Arabs" have been targeting "blacks", citing claims that "The Arabs want to get rid of anyone with black skin...there are no blacks left."[1059] In another article Kristof alleges that "black Africans have been driven from their homes by lighter-skinned Arabs in the Janjaweed".[1060] These sorts of claims are particularly inflammatory and very questionable. (The racial dimension of their claims would also be called into question by subsequent articles by *The New York Times* with titles such as such as "In Sudan, No Clear Difference between Arab and African".[1061]) The discrepancy between simple factual Darfurian realities and the "reporting" and claims of people such as Kristof and Lacy exposes either poor reporting (of very sensitive issues) or reporting that has been purposefully skewed. Either is simply unacceptable. It is perhaps worth noting that Kristof's reporting on other issues has been repeatedly criticised for its shortcomings. His previous coverage of Africa in general had been described as cynical and distorted and "bizarre" by African academics.[1062] It should also be noted that Kristof is no stranger to blunders, managing to get his newspaper sued over claims made in the wake of the post-September 11 anthrax scare when he erroneously pointed the finger at an American scientist as being responsible.[1063]

Even *The New York Times*, while blithely claiming genocide, has admitted at the same time that "it is impossible to travel in Darfur to verify these claims".[1064] Despite these circumstances, Lacy, Kristof and others have rushed in to make the most serious claims imaginable. And, as we have seen above, claims of "genocide" in Darfur have also been categorically contradicted by seasoned humanitarian groups with hands-on experience of events within Darfur such as Médecins Sans Frontières. Dr Mercedes Taty, MSF's deputy emergency director, was one of those aid workers who have gone on record to refute allegations of genocide and ethnic cleansing. Amazingly enough, Nicholas Kristof has actually quoted from Dr Taty in one of his articles claiming genocide in Darfur. He apparently did not ask the most obvious question, or if he did he chose to ignore the answer. He obviously thought that his one- or two-day visits to the Chad border, running after third- and fourth-hand stories provided him with a better picture than someone such as Dr Taty, and MSF, whose thousands of workers have worked at the heart of the crisis.

Kristof's apparent disinclination to even discuss MSF's reservations is a strange one journalistically. As Moeller has noted: "The central heroes of [crisis] are the western aid workers." She quotes a commentator as saying that "the age of the 'French doctors'" has come.[1065] Moeller also notes: "In contrast to the victims, the relief workers are extensively quoted. As the on-scene mediators in the [crisis] world, their comments are used both as the 'deus ex machina' of the stories and as providers of verbal 'color.' Their words give the political and social context and much of the anecdotal fillip."[1066] In the words of Michael Maren, a journalist and former aid worker cited by Moeller, journalism can become "impervious to facts that do not fit the popular story line".[1067]

Going hand in hand with his questionable assertion of genocide in Darfur have been his claims about mortality figures. In March 2004, Kristof estimated the death toll at a thousand a week. Two months later, on 29 May, he revised the estimates dramatically upwards, citing statements by USAID that between 100,000 and 500,000 might die that year. On 23 February 2005, in an apparent moment of clarity, Kristof admitted that "the numbers are fuzzy." He cited a low of 70,000 deaths, which he dismissed as "a UN estimate", to "independent estimates" in excess of 220,000. He also stated that "the number is rising by about ten thousand a month." On 3 May, Kristof cited the latest estimate of deaths from the Coalition for International Justice as "nearly 400,000, and rising by 500 a day". As Mamdani points out, "In three months, Kristof's estimates had gone up from 10,000 to 15,000 a month." On 27 November 2005, Kristof warned that "the death toll could then rise to 100,000 a month." Mamdani provides a measured critique of Kristof's numbers game, noting that:

> Anyone keeping a tally of the death toll in Darfur as reported in the Kristof columns would find the rise, fall and rise again very bewildering. First he projected the number of dead at 320,000 for 2004 (16 June 2004) but then gave a scaled down estimate of between 70,000 and 220,000 (23 February 2005). The number began once more to climb to "nearly 400,000" (3 May 2005), only to come down yet again to 300,000 (23 April 2006). Each time figures were given with equal confidence but with no attempt to explain their basis. Did the numbers reflect an actual decline in the scale of killing in Darfur or was Kristof simply making an adjustment to the changing mood internationally?[1068]

Mamdani has been critical of the simplistic and misleading way in which Kristof's writing on Darfur has sought to frame the issue:

> The journalist in the US most closely identified with consciousness-raising on Darfur is the New York Times op-ed columnist Nicholas Kristof, often identified as a lone crusader on the issue. To peruse Kristof's Darfur columns over the past three years is to see the reduction of a complex political context to a morality tale unfolding in a world populated by villains and victims who never trade places and so can always and easily be told apart. It is a world where atrocities mount geometrically, the perpetrators so evil and the victims so helpless that the only possibility of relief is a rescue mission from the outside, preferably in the form of a military intervention.[1069]

Mamdani points out that Kristof has been careful not to let facts interfere with his morality tale: "In the Kristof columns, there is one area of deafening silence, to do with the fact that what is happening in Darfur is a civil war. Hardly a word is said about the insurgency, about the civilian deaths insurgents mete out, about acts that the commission characterised as 'war crimes'."[1070] It should also be noted that – in common with many Save Darfur advocates – while pushing for Western military intervention in Darfur, Kristof opposed Western military intervention in Iraq, and at the same time as urging Western, preferably non-American, soldiers into Darfur he is calling for American forces to "cut and walk" from Iraq. In so doing he notes that the Western military presence in Iraq is perceived as a grab for Iraqi oil, and is "legitimising extremists…and aggravating civil war". He has also warned of the Western intervention spilling out further into the Middle East.[1071] He cannot apparently see that this is precisely what would happen in Darfur should the outside military intervention that he has been calling for ever take place.

For all its sensationalism and inaccuracies, Kristof's reporting succeeded in adversely influencing thinking within the United States. *Foreign Affairs* magazine, for example, noted that "[t]he genocide debate took off in March 2004, after New York Times columnist Nicholas Kristof published a number of articles making the charge." These were said to have "stimulated…calls for action from an unlikely combination of players – Jewish-American, African-American, liberal, and religious-conservative constituencies."[1072] The lessons of previous mistakes have clearly not been learnt. Professor Susan Moeller has stated that "conventional wisdom" has it, as Senator Paul Simon wrote in 1994, that "The media brought the disaster of Somalia into our living rooms. The American people and our government were moved to action."[1073] It is, of course, now widely accepted that the American "Blackhawk down" intervention in Somalia had disastrous consequences – for the Somali people, for American military prestige and for American foreign policy.

Despite the deep fault lines running through his superficial Darfur reporting, Kristof received the 2006 Pulitzer Prize. It was awarded to Kristof "for his graphic, deeply reported columns that, at personal risk, focused attention on genocide in Darfur and that gave voice to the voiceless in other parts of the world".[1074] This was perhaps as skewed an award as the infamous 1932 Pulitzer Prize given to his fellow *New York Times* journalist Walter

Duranty for his glowing accounts of life in Stalin's Russia. It is now clear that Duranty's Pulitzer should never have been granted. A report subsequently commissioned by *The New York Times* in 2003 into Duranty's work has said that the reporting had a "serious lack of balance," was "distorted," and was "a disservice to American readers of the New York Times…and the peoples of the Russian and Soviet empires."[1075] Much the same can be said about Kristof's Darfur work. Although different in many ways, both Pulitzers were awarded essentially because the reports upon which they were based reflected a perceived consensus of the day. One can only hope that *The New York Times* will not take as long as 70 years to review Kristof's Pulitzer.

The Washington Post: A Recruiting Sergeant for al-Qaeda?

The Washington Post's editorial stance on Darfur has been both remarkably shallow and sensationalist – never a good combination. In a series of editorials in the course of 2004, the newspaper repeatedly described events in Darfur as genocide.[1076] Its 7 June 2004 editorial, "300,000 Deaths Foretold", for example, merely echoed, and in some instances updated, much of the misinformation that has previously so clouded perceptions of Sudan. In some instances it was simply untruthful. The editorial sought to draw parallels between events in Darfur and the recently concluded civil war in southern Sudan. It additionally attempted to compare the situation in Darfur with Rwanda or even Cambodia. These attempts – which are little more than crude opportunism – were all the more shameful given that they come from a newspaper of record.

The editorial claimed genocide and ethnic cleansing in Darfur. In attempting to make its case, *The Washington Post* has made assertions that are at best very questionable where not simply untruthful. It claimed that "almost no foreign aid workers operated in the region" – this despite the fact that there were over a thousand present at that time. A prime example of *The Washington Post*'s crassness was its claim that "Sudan's government is delighted with the war's 'slaughter'". The editorial staff had not even asked of themselves the most elementary of questions: who benefits from the Darfur situation? Khartoum has not. The Zaghawa and Fur communities have not. The only people to benefit from Darfur are those Islamist extremists who succeeded in drawing Khartoum into a war in the region, and those within the anti-Sudan lobby who have not hesitated to continue with their long-standing propaganda war against Sudan.

The Washington Post was also caught out in more lies. Much of the debate about Darfur now evolves around the need to provide war-affected communities in Darfur and refugees in Chad with humanitarian assistance. In trying to argue that Khartoum wants 300,000 of its own civilians to starve, *The Washington Post* claimed that in "its long war against the country's southern rebels" the government has used "starvation" as a weapon stating that Khartoum's response to humanitarian access was "always late and inadequate". This could not be a more blatant lie. Humanitarian relief to the war-affected parts of southern Sudan is provided by Operation Lifeline Sudan (OLS). OLS began in 1989 under the auspices of the United Nations, and with the full approval and cooperation of Sudanese government. OLS was unprecedented in as much as it was the first time that a government had agreed to the delivery of assistance by outside agencies to rebel-controlled parts of its own country, something confirmed by *The Journal of Humanitarian Assistance*: "It was the first time a government agreed on a violation of its own national sovereignty by accepting that humanitarian organizations aid rebel-held areas. Further, the negotiators decided that non-government areas would be supplied from Lokichoggio, Kenya, consequently establishing the first legitimate cross-border operation for the delivery of humanitarian assistance."[1077]

As *The Guardian* also observed: "Governments involved in civil wars usually refuse to authorise cross-border feeding."[1078] Far from using "starvation" against southern Sudan, independent observers confirmed that the number of Khartoum-approved OLS feeding sites in southern Sudan served by air grew within five years from ten in 1992 to over 200 sites by the end of 1997 – a twenty-fold increase.[1079] Each and every one of these sites had been agreed upon by the Sudanese government. Khartoum could have refused to increase the number from the initial ten. There was also a similar increase in the number of approved non-governmental organisations operating within southern Sudan. There had only been six or seven NGOs working in the southern sector in 1992.[1080] OLS brings together over 40 non-governmental organisations, including the UN World Food Programme and UNICEF. It is additionally worth noting that these increases in food delivery sites were also agreed by the Khartoum authorities despite it being widely known that the southern rebels were diverting very sizeable amounts of this aid for its own uses.[1081] Far from starving civilians, there were unanimous United Nations resolutions acknowledging "with appreciation" Khartoum's cooperation with agreements and arrangements facilitating "relief operations".[1082]

In projecting its claims of genocide in Darfur, *The Washington Post*'s figures for those who have died as a consequence of the crisis have grown exponentially. In February 2004, Amnesty International cited the United Nations figure of 3,000 deaths.[1083] By August 2004, *The Washington Post* was citing 80,000 deaths.[1084] In October 2004, the death toll is variable with figures ranging from 50,000 to 70,000 to 300,000 – a figure provided by established anti-Sudan activist Eric Reeves, described disingenuously by the newspaper as "an independent Sudan watcher".[1085] By November 2004, the figure is unquestioningly said to be 300,000.[1086] *The Washington Post*'s choice of Reeves, one of the most jaundiced and inaccurate commentators on Sudan and the description of his figure of 300 – 400,000 as the "best" estimate available, is revealing.

To make its case *The Washington Post* has also had to ignore the fact that the rebel movements have been at the heart of so much of the violence, and disruption of essential food aid deliveries, over the past several months. Indeed, when it is forced to mention repeated rebel attacks in November and December 2004, the editorial line is that the murder of policemen and aid workers, and attacks on aid convoys, are little more than a rebel cry for help.[1087]

The Washington Post's editorial position has also neglected to note any Islamist involvement in the Darfur crisis, accepting rebel claims about "marginalisation" being the reason for the conflict. Interestingly, *The Washington Post* editorialists called on European countries to militarily intervene in Darfur, stating that "the United States is overcommitted militarily in Iraq and elsewhere". The United States is overcommitted for the simple reason that it is mired in increasingly unsuccessful military interventions in two other Muslim countries, Iraq and Afghanistan. These interventions have served to galvanise anti-American forces, armed and unarmed, across the political spectrum within those countries and internationally, as well as attracting vast numbers of al-Qaeda fighters. Western military intervention in Sudan, another Muslim country, would have a similar effect. Simply put, *The Washington Post*'s editorial stance has put propaganda before both people in need and national security.

In yet another double-standard, *The Washington Post* repeatedly cites 450,000 deaths in Darfur, based on clearly questionable claims – and equally questionable methodology – while at the same time downplaying civilian deaths in Iraq. In its weekly round-up of Iraq casualties, it has consistently cited very low estimates of civilian deaths. In its 21 April 2007 figures, for example, it cited a "minimum count" of 62,144 and a "maximum count" of 68,141 Iraqi civilian fatalities. This is despite the fact that it has reported on very much higher death counts. In October 2004, for example, it noted that American health and emergency studies experts had estimated that 100, 000 civilians had died as a result of the American invasion. The survey was designed by the Center for International Emergency, Disaster and Refugee Studies at the Johns Hopkins Bloomberg School of Public Health in Baltimore and Columbia University in New York.[1088] Two years later, the newspaper reported that "a team of American and Iraqi epidemiologists estimates that 655,000 more people have died in Iraq since coalition forces arrived in March 2003 than would have died if the invasion had not occurred." The estimate is more than 20 times the estimate of 30,000 civilian deaths that President Bush gave in a speech in December 2005. It is more than 10 times the estimate of civilian deaths made by the British-based Iraq Body Count research group. The survey was overseen by epidemiologists at Johns Hopkins University's Bloomberg School of Public Health.[1089] Both the 2004 and 2006 findings were published by the British medical journal *The Lancet*. In September 2007, a British research organisation raised the estimated number of Iraqi civilian deaths to one million.[1090] One can only but assume that these findings have been ignored by *The Washington Post* because the editorial opinion was that the methodology of the findings was questionable. With regard to Darfur, however, in the face of clear and, frankly, unanswerable criticism about their methodology, the newspaper accepts partisan claims of 450,000 civilian deaths in Darfur.[1091]

A last indication of *The Washington Post's* apparent determination to frame the Darfur issue in keeping with its in-house line was provided by de Waal in August 2007. De Waal and Flint had written an op-ed piece for the newspaper which they wished to have headlined "Darfur: Simple, It Isn't". *The Washington Post* headlined it "In Darfur, From Genocide to Anarchy" instead.[1092]

The London Sunday Times Magazine: A Study in Inept Journalism:

On 11 July 2004, the London *Sunday Times* magazine carried an article written by AA Gill, on the situation in Darfur. Written by someone better known as a restaurant critic, the article was described as the "first of our series of stirring reports from around the world" and featured a picture of Gill swathed in a head-scarf on the magazine cover. Entitled "Welcome to Hell", the article demonstrated almost every facet of the poor journalism that has characterised media coverage of the Darfur crisis. His first piece of foreign reporting, Gill rushed at the Darfur issue with all the enthusiasm of a cub reporter – and made all the mistakes one would have expected from one.

Gill chose the easy option on Darfur, echoing sensationalist claims, stating for example that "there are rumours of war, of genocide, of ethnic cleansing" before moving on to assert that there is "ethnic cleansing and genocide", and then concluding that the Sudanese government is a "blatantly racist, genocidal regime". Gill's inept journalism, based on a short visit to the Chadian side of the border, was illustrated by his attempt to produce evidence for the "genocide". As proof of genocide and ethnic cleansing Gill pointed to the fact that in the refugee camps he visited "all the refugees are black: there are no Arabs here." Here Gill made his first mistake. As we have seen, both "African" and "Arab" in Darfur are black. Any number of anti-government sources have shown Gill's claims to be dangerously lazy racial shorthand. Perhaps Gill was expecting "Arabs" to be Omar Sharif lookalikes. The discrepancy between simple Darfurian realities and the "reporting" and claims of people such as Gill exposes either poor reporting or reporting that has been purposefully skewed. Either is simply unacceptable: in Gill's case it was all too obvious that it is merely poor journalism.

AA Gill chose to make serious claims of genocide in Darfur – this despite the unambiguous observations of groups such as Médecins Sans Frontières. This was even more surprising as what little "front-line" colour there was in Gill's report came out of visits to MSF camps and facilities on the border. While visiting their camps, Gill seemingly neglected to ask MSF for their view of claims of genocide. Gill would have also come across these views had he done even a basic internet search. He opted, however, for easier, more sensationalist and less demanding story-lines.

Gill was equally strident in his claims that humanitarian access to Darfur is being blocked by the Khartoum authorities, claiming: "invariably the promised visas for observers and NGOs never materialise...There are 500 applications from humanitarian agencies alone gathering dust." This claim would come as a surprise to aid workers in Darfur. Jan Egeland, the United Nations Under-Secretary-General for Humanitarian Affairs (and a fierce critic of the government), stated in early July – a week before Gill's article – that he was surprised to see claims that aid was not reaching Darfur: "It is strange to see that there is still the notion in the world that nothing is happening and we're completely blocked from accessing Darfur. We are reaching some 800,000 people at the moment with some sort of assistance and food."[1093] Gill may also have been interested that three weeks before his *Sunday Times* magazine article, Kevin Kennedy, the outgoing acting UN Humanitarian Coordinator for Sudan, stated that visas were generally being granted within 48 hours and that "people are experiencing very few visa difficulties".[1094] Gill's claims were also somewhat dented by the United Nations announcement one week prior to his article that two million children in Darfur had been immunised against measles.[1095] This was carried out by 2,000 health teams made up of WHO, UNICEF and other humanitarian workers – all of whom would presumably have needed visas of some sort.

AA Gill's gullibility appeared to know no bounds. He rounded off his lacklustre piece on Darfur by repeating a few more stale and discredited claims about Sudan. He states, for example, that Khartoum has "attempted to develop chemical and nuclear weapons". This will come as news to the International Atomic Energy Agency and the Organisation for the Prohibition of Chemical Weapons. The Clinton Administration's farcical 1998 cruise missile attack on the al-Shifa aspirin factory in Khartoum and its subsequent inability to substantiate its claims (and Gill's) about Sudan and chemical weapons was painful and public.[1096]

The Independent on Sudan: Lies and Hypocrisy

The Independent, a British newspaper, has over the years established itself as a newspaper which showed a genuine interest in Africa and African issues. Sadly, its coverage of the Darfur crisis has also demonstrated every shortcoming associated with Western media coverage of the continent: inaccurate reporting, sensationalism, prejudice and hypocrisy. In a mirror image of *The Washington Post*, *The Independent*'s editorial line has claimed that events in Darfur were genocide and has called for military intervention. The newspaper enthusiastically proclaimed Colin Powell's 9 September 2004 claim of genocide in Darfur with a banner-page headline, "Genocide", the following day.[1097] Given that *The Independent* has hitherto been very cautious about believing anything claimed by Colin Powell it is very surprising that it unreservedly accepted at face value Powell's claim of genocide in Darfur, let alone to have given his assertion such prominence in the paper.[1098] (Ironically, *The Independent* was the first paper to subsequently report that Powell's claim was made to please the religious Right within the United States.)[1099]

This leads to the first surprise about this newspaper's embracing of claims of genocide. Not many months previously, *The Independent* had been at the forefront of opposition to any American military intervention anywhere, and was particularly prominent in the opposition to the American-led war in Iraq. It published several editorials and numerous comment pieces and news items critical of the war. It warned about American claims leading up to the Iraq war.[1100] It reported on the horrific nature of the American-led war in Iraq.[1101] It reported on the gradual disintegration of the American reasons for invading Iraq in the first place.[1102] And it has reported on the consequences of the American invasion of Iraq.[1103] *The Independent* has also asserted that President Bush and Colin Powell led Britain into an illegal war in Iraq.[1104] Yet, the newspaper's editorialists appear to be blind to the fact that in their unquestioning acceptance of clearly questionable American claims about another Muslim country – and in their calls for military intervention – they have reduced *The Independent* to nothing more than a mindless cheerleader for action that could be every bit as badly thought-out and disastrous as Iraq.

It is worth noting that *The Independent* was very critical of Prime Minister Tony Blair for supporting the Bush Administration's invasion of Iraq. It has claimed he was suckered into doing so by untrue American claims about the country.[1105] It is ironic that with regard to American claims about Darfur, unlike Blair – who has been far more cautious and better informed about the issue on this occasion – it is *The Independent* that appears to have been suckered by Washington.

In any instance, the case made by *The Independent* to support its claim of genocide and call for military intervention is flimsy. The editorial which accompanied its "Genocide" front-page banner headline, for example, claimed that "By any civilised standards, the slaughter of 50,000 people constitutes genocide" and pressed for military intervention.[1106] Given that the figure cited was a controversial statistical extrapolation, and included those who may have died from malnutrition and disease, the use of the term "slaughter" was immediately questionable, as was the inference that any war in which 50,000 may have died automatically qualifies as "genocide". The intellectual and linguistic sloppiness of *The Independent*'s editorial team is manifest. This has not stopped it making repeated claims of genocide in Darfur.

Johann Hari, a regular columnist with *The Independent*, has led the newspaper's attempts to describe events in Darfur as genocide. In so doing he has made repeated references to, amongst other things, the film "Schindler's List" and the Rwandan holocaust.[1107] Indeed, in his enthusiasm, he has trivialised concern for the Nazi Holocaust: "If we don't intervene in Darfur, you can toss your tear-stained copies of 'Schindler's List' on to a bonfire."[1108] Amazingly enough, however, in his article of 23 April 2004 claiming genocide, he quotes from one Mercedes Tatay [sic], whom he describes as "a Darfur-based physician with the aid group Medecins Sans Frontieres", as giving "a glimpse into the state of a country where journalists are being denied access". This is, of course, Mercedes Taty, the deputy emergency director of Médecins Sans Frontières, someone who had indeed been based in Darfur, and who had been interviewed on 16 April by MSNBC. Hari cites Taty's comments about the destroyed villages in Darfur, but conveniently ignores the fact that she unambiguously said events in Darfur did not constitute genocide – and that there was no systematic targeting of one ethnic group or another: Taty also said the crisis could not be described as ethnic cleansing. Hari's article was one more example of appalling, two-faced journalism on Darfur. In his enthusiasm to claim genocide in Darfur, however, Hari actually compares Darfur to the Holocaust, Nazi death camps and IBM.[1109] Unsurprisingly, given this sort of word-blindness, Hari's Darfur articles regurgitate all the standard propaganda lines on the issue. He writes about "racist Sudanese militias" engaging in "attacks against black people", and their disruption of "basic food and medicine supplies".[1110] He has claimed that "the Arab majority is continuing to rape and slaughter the black minority".[1111] And just as the United Nations tells us that things are getting better, the situation has stabilised, war-affected communities are being fed, Hari, once again claiming genocide, informs his readers that "the situation…is getting worse".[1112]

In early October 2005, Hari produced his most skewed article. Entitled "The first genocide of the twenty-first century is drawing to an end", this article claimed that "the holocaust in western Sudan is nearly over…because there are no black people left to cleanse or kill." He asserted that the Sudanese government had killed 400,000 black Darfurians.[1113]

Hari's grotesque distortion of the reality of events in Darfur complemented the newspaper's general Darfur coverage. Despite having published a glowing account of Médecins Sans Frontières in July 2004, *The Independent*'s editorialists conveniently overlooked MSF's views on claims of genocide in Darfur.[1114] It has also published blatant untruths. In January 2005, for example, it alleged that the charity Save the Children "was expelled from the country last year".[1115] The reality was that Save the Children had voluntarily left Darfur following the murder by rebels of four of their staff. This had even been reported on by *The Independent*'s own correspondents.[1116] *The Independent*'s editorialising about the murder of aid workers also demonstrated its slant. The newspaper had ignored the fact that the Darfur rebels had murdered a number of aid workers – including the four Save the Children personnel, had abducted dozens of others and had repeatedly attacked aid convoys over several months in 2004. It chose to editorialise when another aid worker was killed in cross-fire during an engagement between government forces and rebels. Its editorial then accused the government of the "deliberate targeting of aid workers" and inferred that the government had killed the four Save the Children workers, thereby forcing the organisation out of Darfur.[1117]

It is still puzzling that *The Independent* finds itself in the lonely position of enthusiastically articulating American claims about genocide in Darfur – claims which even the American government appears not to take too seriously – in the face of precisely the sort of concerns it raised about previous American assertions about Iraq: widespread international unease about the American claims, the horror of the military intervention that would be needed and the unpredictable outcome and legality of any such intervention. The question it has not posed or answered is that, given the chaos that we now see in Iraq, whether the people of Darfur would be any better off with a similar intervention in their homeland. Would Darfur – and Sudan and possibly some of her neighbours – merely become the latest extension of Afghanistan or Somalia, a failed state with no international humanitarian presence?

BBC Panorama, "The New Killing Fields", 14 November 2004

British foreign minister Mullins has also been critical of BBC coverage of the Darfur crisis: "I continually hear reports of the situation in Darfur, often on the BBC, as if only one party – the Government of Sudan – were involved…we do ourselves no service in improving our understanding of what is happening there if we continually pretend that it is all due to the Government of Sudan. That is not the case."[1118] "The New Killing Fields", a BBC Panorama programme, presented by American reporter Hilary Andersson and screened on 14 November 2004, provided clear evidence of this poor reporting. The programme deviated significantly from the journalistic standards normally associated with the flagship Panorama series and violated the BBC's own *Producers' Guidelines*. These guidelines declare that "[a]ccurate, robust, independent, and impartial, journalism is the DNA of the BBC" and called for people to be able to rely on the BBC for "unbiased and impartial reporting and analysis to help them make sense of events; and where a debate can take place in which relevant and significant voices are heard".

It goes without question that any journalistic investigation of allegations of genocide must be thoroughly professional and objective. Anything less is simply unacceptable. The BBC's "The New Killing Fields", fell considerably short in both respects. The thrust of the programme was clear. It argued a case for genocide in Darfur – the title of the programme made that clear from the start – but in making its case it presented an incomplete and questionable picture of events to support its assertions.

Ms Andersson's report essentially cut and pasted footage in an attempt to put her case for genocide in Darfur. This undermined the report's chronological integrity from the very beginning of the programme. It is a simple fact that the bulk of the actions that framed the tragedy of Darfur happened up to April 2004. The April ceasefire and the deployment of thousands of policemen in Darfur essentially stabilised the situation in Darfur. Ms Anderson reported from Darfur during this earlier period and did not then assert that genocide had taken place. It is hard to see how not having seen or reported "genocide" then, that a subsequent visit to Darfur during a period of comparative stability during which the UN and other aid agencies were able to reach most if not all of those Darfurian communities in need of humanitarian assistance, Ms Andersson was then able to insinuate that genocide has/is taking place in Darfur. Ms Andersson's attempt to update her coverage of Darfur from earlier in 2004 did not produce anything remotely supportive of her assertions of genocide in Darfur. By way of evidence Ms Andersson produced interviews and a Sudan Liberation Army rebel videotape which – even if taken at face value – point to the sorts of appalling human rights abuses that are tragically a hall-mark of many African and European civil wars. However much Ms Andersson and Panorama may have sought to package the suffering of those she interviewed; it was simply not evidence of "genocide".

While there were several examples of questionable and lacklustre journalism in the BBC programme, two issues stood out. The first point is that there was a clear failure to reflect "all significant strands of opinion" as stipulated in the BBC's *Producers' Guidelines*. The guidelines state: "Openness and independence of mind is at the heart of practising accuracy and impartiality. *We will strive to be fair and open minded by reflecting all significant strands of opinion, and by exploring the range and conflict of views. Testing a wide range of views with the evidence is essential if we are to give our audiences the greatest possible opportunity to decide for themselves on the issues of the day.*" [Emphasis added] With regard to "accuracy" and "achieving accuracy", the Guidelines state that "The BBC must be accurate. Research for all programmes must be thorough. We must be prepared to check, cross-check and seek advice, to ensure this. *Wherever possible we should gather information first-hand by being there ourselves or, where that is not possible, by talking to those who were.* [emphasis added] Accuracy can be difficult to achieve. It is important to distinguish between first and second-hand sources."

With regard to "impartiality in general", the BBC's *Producers' Guidelines* clearly states that: *"No significant strand of thought should go unreflected or under represented on the BBC."* [Emphasis added] The Panorama programme clearly did not reflect "all significant strands of opinion" on allegations of genocide in Darfur. Ms Andersson also did not talk to "those who were [there]". Her programme pointedly ignored the views of the most respected, independent, vocal and accessible authority on the issue of genocide in general and allegations of genocide in Darfur in particular – the views of Médecins Sans Frontières, the biggest humanitarian aid agency present in Darfur.

There were therefore several question-marks over this BBC programme. Was Ms Andersson or the BBC aware of Médecins Sans Frontières' stance with regard to allegations of genocide in Darfur? Why were the clearly relevant views of Médecins Sans Frontières ignored in her report? Why did Ms Andersson not interview Médecins Sans Frontières about allegations of genocide in Darfur? Did she really believe that MSF's view on the issue of genocide was irrelevant or not significant? If she was not aware of MSF's position would that not indicate inadequate background research on this grave issue? It is all the more surprising that Ms Andersson did not approach Médecins Sans Frontières given that she filmed MSF facilities in Darfur. Why did Panorama chose to use MSF as a prop and not a commentator? Could this have been because Ms Anderson knew they may well have contradicted the core of her report?

Similarly, it is strange that while interviewing African Union officials in Darfur, she pointedly chose not to ask their position with regard to allegations of genocide in Darfur. Like Médecins Sans Frontières, the African Union has a presence in Darfur, albeit subsequent to that of MSF, and, as we have seen above, its position that there is no genocide in Darfur is a clear one. Given that Ms Andersson self-servingly interviewed African Union officials about allegations of human rights abuses, why did she not interview the African Union about allegations of genocide in Darfur? Was she aware of the African Union's stance with regard to allegations of genocide in Darfur? If she was not aware of the African Union's position, would that not indicate inadequate background research on this serious issue?

Secondly, the BBC's *Producers' Guidelines* note the importance of using "accurate language", stating that "it is not sufficient that we get our facts right. We must use language fairly. That means avoiding exaggeration. We must not use language inadvertently so as to suggest value judgements, commitment or lack of objectivity." The title "The New Killing Fields" was simply unacceptable. They are words that directly refer to the genocide in Kampuchea in the 1970s – and were the title of a well-known film about the Kampuchean genocide. The absence of a question mark in the title was even more insidious. The use of this title implied precisely the sort of value judgement and lack of objectivity warned against in the *Producers' Guidelines*.

The *Producers' Guidelines* additionally refer to "hurtful or inaccurate stereotypes" and under a section headed "misleading images" states that "Programmes must not allow offensive assumptions or generalisations in scripted material, and interviewees who express them need to be challenged wherever possible." The BBC programme resorted to inaccurate stereotyping regarding Darfur, repeatedly referring either to "black Africans" or "Arabs". Ms Andersson referred, for example, to "black African rebels", "black Africans", "black African civilians", "African families", "black African population", "black African civilian areas" etc. She also referred to "Arab militias", "Arab-looking" and "the Arabs". In so doing Ms Anderson wittingly or unwittingly perpetuated the patently inaccurate stereotype that the conflict in Darfur has been a racial one in which light-skinned "Arab" tribes have been engaged in the "genocide" of black "African" tribes. These sorts of claims are self-evidently inflammatory and very questionable. Ms Andersson may have spent only a short time in Darfur but it cannot have escaped her notice that "Arab" and "African" communities in Darfur are both black – a reality repeatedly confirmed by prominent critics of the Khartoum government. Why was it that in the hour-long Panorama programme, Ms Andersson did not even address the fundamental issue of identities outlined above? While there could conceivably be a case for referring to "African" and "Arab" in the cultural context cited above, Ms Andersson's repeated use of the term "black" within the Darfur context, however, in which both "Arab" and "African" are equally black-skinned is either deliberately self-serving and sensationalist or simply lazy journalism. Neither should have a place in BBC journalism.

A subsequent BBC Panorama programme, entitled "Never Again", and presented by Fergal Keane, echoed many of the sloppy claims made by Hilary Andersson. The title of the programme demonstrated the slant the programme was to take. Keane interviewed exclusively anti-Sudanese sources and – following Andersson's lead – chose not to talk to anyone or any group such as Médecins Sans Frontières in a position to contradict what was clearly a pre-determined conclusion. Even when one of his key interviewees, former US senator and US ambassador to the UN John Danforth, revealed that the US government had only used the genocide label to appease the Christian right within the United States, Keane persisted with the innuendo of "never again".[1119]

It is worth noting that Gérard Prunier is critical of claims of "ethnic cleansing" in Darfur: "The notion of 'ethnic cleansing', implying that the [Government of Sudan] had been trying to displace African tribes in order to give their land to 'Arabs', is not backed by any evidence other than the shouts hurled at the victims by the perpetrators themselves. Although they (the perpetrators) might have hoped for such an outcome of the massacres, it is doubtful that a policy of that kind had been clearly thought out in Khartoum." [1120] He noted that "[t]he term 'ethnic cleansing' was first used in connection with Darfur in a BBC commentary on 13 November 2003 and it was soon expanded into the accusation of genocide."[1121]

An American Media Critique of Itself

A September 2004 article in *The Village Voice*, a liberal New York newspaper, provided one of the most insightful critiques of American news coverage of Darfur. It is worth quoting it at length:

> For news outlets covering the conflict in Sudan, the killings, rapes, and razing of villages boils down to one factor – race. *The Washington Post* and *The New York Times* have repeatedly characterized attacks by the Arab riders of the government-backed Janjaweed as a war against "black Africans." The Associated Press has referred to the turmoil in the Darfur region as fighting between Arabs and "ethnic Africans." Clinging to race as an explain-all theory might make for more readable stories, but it has a central flaw. Many of the Sudanese "Arabs" are as dark as the "ethnic Africans" they are at war with...."If you look at most of the media coverage, you get the impression that Sudan is made up of white people, who are mostly Arabs, attacking black people who aren't Arab," says Bill Fletcher, president of TransAfrica Forum. "Some of the Africans in question are Arab, some are not. But they are almost all black – at least the way we understand it. Being Arab is a matter of culture and language. Arabs

look all kinds of ways, but you'd never get that impression."...The narrative of Darfur involves issues of religion, climate, and competition for land...Nuanced and accurate, this kind of explanation has little chance of making it into the morning papers...In much of its coverage [*The New York Times*] has been sucked in by the siren song of race. An August 20 piece cited "the war in western Sudan, pitting the Arab-led government against black Africans in Darfur."[1122]

In the *Online Journal*'s independent critique of Eric Reeves' activity on Sudan – he "may be the major source of disinformation (he calls it 'analysis') about Darfur" – the gullibility of the American media is also criticised: "How curious that the American media latches on to Mr Reeves' one-sided falsehoods by way of presented out-of-context half-truths while at the same time ignoring the dispatches of other journalists, including those who have provided eyewitness accounts...Reeves' pieces altogether comprise of several dozens of pages which have the same basic thrust, yet he utterly ignores the realities of the two-decades-plus Civil War in Sudan and even the more recent background of violence... for Reeves, and by extension, the newspapers that publish him, morality is clearly a one-way morality. In other words, a hypocritical immorality." The *Online Journal* concludes: "In sum, what the American media has poured down an unsuspecting public's throat is a hellish brew of selective half-truths, sophistry, and *ad hominem* pseudo-arguments."[1123] That any newspaper worth that name would publish material by Reeves is surprising. There can be no greater indictment on the ethics and standards of American journalism. Reeves, however, has provided students of the media-propaganda dynamic with a snap-shot of gullibility and culpability. In an attack on "shamefully irresponsible journalism" – that is to say those newspapers and wire services that have not accepted his claims of 400,000 dead in Darfur – Reeves provides us with a list of those "news organizations, editorial boards and journalists" that have. They include "the editorial boards of the Washington Post and Boston Globe; Bloomberg News; the Canadian Broadcasting Corporation; and experienced Sudan journalists such as Julie Flint."[1124] The *Online Journal* states that *The Washington Post* has, indeed, been "a major conduit for Mr Reeves' misinformation".[1125]

In her study of media reporting and compassion fatigue Professor Moeller has also pointed to other media shortcomings which can also be applied to reporting of the Darfur crisis:

> The media should commit to covering international affairs as they cover domestic crime. If they report on the arrest of a suspect, they have an ethical responsibility to follow up and report on the outcome of that arrest. Was there a plea bargain or a trial? Was the defendant found innocent or guilty? Too often the media cover an international crisis as they would a dramatic incident like an arrest, but then the story is dropped, and the public never learns whether the victim survived or whether the suspect arrested was really the person responsible. The media also too infrequently revisit stories six months or even six years later.[1126]

That the media rarely follows up on its stories was confirmed by former NBC News president Bill Small: "It is rarely done but whenever it is, one finds insights in the follow-up, and, often, the discovery that the original story was either wrong or lacked vital ingredients that the follow-up discovers."[1127] It is worth noting that in the small number of cases when there has been follow-up on sensationalist stories on Sudan – on "slave redemption" and weapons of mass destruction stories, for example – much of the original story, as outlined above, was wrong or deeply questionable.

Andrew Natsios, before becoming USAID director, had pointed to the shortcomings of American reporting of emergencies: "American media coverage of complex emergencies will likely continue to be limited, random and unreliable...Media coverage of most emergencies has been so inaccurate or so superficial that it has in some cases encouraged counterproductive responses."[1128] Natsios also noted that "[t]he American electronic media influences public and therefore congressional opinion."[1129]

Coverage of Darfur has led to considerable debate amongst journalists, including several exchanges in the *Press Gazette*, British journalism's in-house magazine, with articles questioning the close relationship between the media and non-governmental organisations in Darfur. One keynote piece asked whether some "kind of deliberate misinformation about the Sudan was being engineered by some…NGOs that had become players in the civil war in the south or had been involved in media manipulation through friendly journalists?"[1130] One journalist expressed his concern "that a number of aid and humanitarian organisations continue to hid their own political agenda and a larger number of journalists and media organisations resort to lazy racial stereotyping…Many humanitarian crises caused by civil wars are in inaccessible places and appear too complicated…but it is exactly the duty and function of journalism to highlight the crisis and explain its background."[1131]

Mediocre and sensationalist media coverage of the Darfur crisis has, and will have, a number of deplorable consequences. Firstly, given that the some of the media – journalists such as Kristof – have, for whatever reason, labelled events in Darfur as genocide when there have already been several credible denials that that is the case, there is a clear danger of interest in the issue waning as a result. This is a point made by Moeller: "There is another problem stemming from the labelling of crises by images and metaphors. Once an audience is familiar with a label, it becomes easy to dismiss the event itself by rejecting the label. And that rejection can become a form of compassion fatigue."[1132] Secondly, any role the US media may have had in forcing the US Administration into a declaration of genocide in Darfur – in circumstances in which that description was at best deeply questionable and at worst undeserved – will, in the light of clearer examinations of the issue, have the effect of presenting the United States as once again crying wolf. In the wake of the "weapons of mass destruction" fiasco over Iraq, this "weapons of mass distraction" controversy will ill serve the reputation of the United States. And on a related issue, the mis-labelling of events in Darfur as genocide will – as was the case with American policy after Somalia – make the United States reluctant to recognise genuine instances of genocide in the future. Thirdly, shallow media coverage of Darfur claiming genocide and calling for foreign military intervention would not only have resulted in an Iraqi-style quagmire but would also have had a disastrous knock-on effect on the delicate north-south peace deal in Sudan.[1133] The irresponsibility of shallow, and in some cases self-serving, media coverage of Darfur could not be clearer.

Moeller's warnings about the importance of responsible reporting, and their relevance to Darfur, are equally clear: "Reporting the news is both a political and a moral act. An element of shame is involved in not reporting responsibly and reporting equitably. If the media don't bear witness truthfully and thoughtfully, the good/bad stereotypes endure and the lack of concern persists."[1134]

Darfur Advocacy Groups and the Media

In addition to the reporter-government relationship described by Gans which has skewed reporting of Darfur, there have been additional pressures on American media outlets from the increasingly assertive Save Darfur movement.

The "BeAWitness.org" campaign is a project of the Genocide Intervention Network and the American Progress Action Fund. Recognising that "the vast majority of Americans continue to rely on broadcast and cable television as their primary source of information", this is an online campaign designed to pressure major media outlets to describe events in Darfur as "genocide". The campaign estimates that "three-quarters of Americans state that they get their information from broadcast or cable television. No other source of information—not newspapers, magazines, or the Internet—comes close to the power of television to inform the public." "BeAWitness.org" follows the standard Darfur advocacy group line taken by the Genocide Intervention Network, asserting that up to 400,000 people have died in Darfur and states that coverage of the "genocide" on American television is the easiest way to provoke international intervention in Darfur. It also claims that "every day hundreds of people are dying in Darfur".

The campaign has taken two significant forms. The first is a concerted attempt to get CNN, Fox News, NBC/MSNBC, ABC, CBS and other TV channels to use the term "genocide" in coverage of events in Darfur. To this end, the campaign provides activists with both a model email and emailing mechanism to reach the big five channels. The model email states:

> I am writing concerning your network's coverage of the genocide in Darfur. Genocide is the ultimate crime against humanity. And a government-backed genocide is unfolding in the Darfur region of the Sudan. As the horror in Darfur continues, our major television news networks are largely missing in action. During June 2005, CNN, FOX News, NBC/MSNBC, ABC, and CBS ran 50 times as many

stories about Michael Jackson and 12 times as many stories about Tom Cruise as they did about the genocide in Darfur...Increased television coverage of the genocide in Darfur has the power to spur the action required to stop a devastating crime against humanity. Increased coverage will raise public awareness and put pressure on our government to help accelerate the deployment of the African Union forces to the region, to apply coordinated international pressure on the Sudanese government, to insure that the guilty are held accountable, and to build a lasting settlement for peace. In short, increased television coverage of the genocide in Darfur has the power to help save thousands of lives...What recent coverage shows...is that...precious time is being devoted to matters of far less consequence than the massive loss of life in Darfur. And so I am calling on your network to be a witness to genocide. Give the Darfur genocide the coverage it so clearly deserves.

The second form the campaign has taken is to seek to force the big five channels to air pro-military intervention Darfur advertisements. Entitled "Tell NBC, CBS and ABC to Air Our Ad – Genocide IS News", it also provided activists with a ready email mechanism to contact "NBC, CBS, ABC, NBC-4, CBS-9, ABC-7, Gannett (the parent corporation of CBS-9) and Allbritton Communications Company (the parent corporation of ABC-7)" and ask "them why they have refused to air our ad and to reconsider this decision". The model email stated:

As a member of the BeAWitness.org community, I am writing today to ask you to reconsider the decision not to air the BeAWitness TV ad purchased by the American Progress Action Fund and the Genocide Intervention Fund. Every day hundreds of people are dying in Darfur and while the solution to this tragedy is complex, one thing is certain: Genocide IS News. If you continue to refuse to air the BeAWitness ad, I would appreciate an explanation for this rejection. Additionally, I would hope that your news division makes more of an effort to cover the genocide in Darfur in the coming weeks and months.[1135]

Writing about the Advertising Standards Authority's August 2007 adjudication that whole-page Save Darfur newspaper adverts claiming that 400,000 people had been killed in Darfur were untrue, Brendan O'Neill has made a point about the British media which is also applicable to the US media. He criticised the British media's reluctance to report on what he saw as a crucial judgement: "why has there been a deafening silence on the ASA's adjudication, and why has it been left to a grey, censorious body to raise awkward questions about the Coalition's sensationalist claims?" O'Neill concludes that this is "Perhaps because many in the British media have uncritically, and continually, repeated the Save Darfur Coalition's claim that the Khartoum government is pursuing a genocide against Darfuris which has left 400,000 innocent people dead. And thus the ASA judgement is as embarrassing for them as it is for the Coalition." To have reported on the adjudication would have meant that "the media would have to own up to the fact that they themselves relied on 'sensational' figures, which are judged by experts to be 'deficient' and 'unreasonable' and are now described by the ASA as being in the realm of opinion rather than fact."[1136]

Chapter Ten

DARFUR ADVOCACY: LOBBYING FOR DISASTER

Having an honest and serious foreign policy debate is not an easy thing in contemporary American political culture. Television sound bites, bumper-sticker clichés passing for ideas, single-issue interest groups and highly partisan politics all work against a thoughtful evaluation of realistic U.S. options.

Dimitri K. Simes, President of the Nixon Centre [1137]

I believe it is among nations as with individuals, that the party taking advantage of the distresses of another will lose infinitely more in the opinion of mankind and in subsequent events than he will gain by the stroke of the moment.

George Washington, Observations on July 28, 1791 [1138]

The Darfur issue has been taken up by a number of advocacy groups, especially within the United States. While these groups are motivated by a number of factors, most if not all call for western-led military intervention in Darfur; some call for regime change in Sudan. These groups represent a number of anti-Sudanese, anti-Muslim and anti-Chinese constituencies. Salih Booker, the Executive Director of the Washington-based Africa Action, and a veteran Africa activist and advocate, has agreed that a political industry that has a vested interest in sensationalising Darfur is at work.[1139] For some the Darfur issue is an ideological one, an extension of a propaganda war against Islam or the Chinese government. For others it is merely a lucrative fund-raising opportunity. A number of books about Darfur have also been published –

books which have generally reflected the claims of American advocacy groups. The activities of these groups and individuals have in general served to confuse and complicate an understanding of the Darfur crisis. There is little doubt that all these groupings are engaging in advocacy. What is less than clear is whose interests they are advocating. They do not represent the average American. Only ten per cent of Americans considered Darfur a top foreign policy priority, according to an NBC News poll in October 2006.[1140]

From a common-sense point of view it is in no-one's interest for there to be western military intervention in Darfur, least of all the Darfurians. What can be clearly stated is that the activities of the Darfur advocacy groups, in demonising yet another Muslim country, draw attention away from the failed United States-led military fiascos in Iraq and Afghanistan and the deteriorating impasse in the Palestinian territories. In calling for western military intervention (and ultimate occupation) of yet another oil-rich Muslim country, they possibly also reflect the oil- and resources-driven foreign policy agenda of the sorts of neo-conservative think-tanks that led the United States and Britain into the Iraqi debacle. At the very least they represent the musings of a naïve foreign policy outlook which has yet to learn from the law of unintended consequences.

Far from helping the people of Darfur towards peace, the Darfur advocacy groups have themselves become a significant obstacle to the peace process. They have artificially prolonged the suffering of the Darfur people. This is for several reasons. The Darfur advocacy groups have consistently presented an acutely mono-dimensional picture of events in Darfur – a picture that has been further skewed by often deliberate exaggerations of facts and figures. In so doing they have consciously sought to focus all the international pressure regarding Darfur upon the government of Sudan. This ignores the simple fact that it is the rebel movements in Darfur that are dragging their feet in the search for peace. The government and one major Darfur rebel group signed the internationally brokered 2006 Darfur Peace Agreement. Two other rebel groupings consciously chose to remain outside of the agreement and have repeatedly attacked rival rebel factions, African communities identified with those rebel factions, government forces and humanitarian workers. Such naivety on the part of the advocacy groups prolongs war in Darfur. There is also a second way in which the advocacy groups have extended the Darfur crisis. Alex de Waal has clearly stated that outsiders have "often encouraged"

Darfur rebels "to believe that their salvation would come through an international military intervention"[1141]. This has artificially hardened rebel positions in round after round of peace talks.

Alan J. Kuperman, an assistant professor of public affairs at the University of Texas, and the editor of *Gambling on Humanitarian Intervention: Moral Hazard, Rebellion and Civil War*, has also criticised attempts by advocacy groups to present the Darfur rebels as freedom fighters, noting that "America, born in revolution, has a soft spot for rebels who claim to be freedom fighters." He argues, however, "We must withhold support for the cynical provocations of militants who bear little resemblance to our founders."[1142] He also notes that "Darfur's rebels...took up arms... to gain tribal domination" and that "the rebels have long wasted resources fighting each other rather than protecting their people".[1143]

Not content with merely prolonging the Darfur conflict, the advocacy groups – in their repeated calls for unilateral western military intervention in Sudan – are pushing for a dramatic escalation in the crisis, something that would inevitably lead to an Iraqi-type conflagration not just in Darfur but throughout the Sahel.

Human Rights Watch's former advocacy director for Africa, Michael Clough, has also criticised the use of the genocide label by Darfur advocacy groups: "The debate about what to do in Darfur — and the use of anti-genocide rhetoric to arouse public concern — has only deepened my misgivings about the way the United States responds to African crises."[1144] There was "a grave risk in raising the specter of genocide to galvanize a global response to the human rights abuses in Darfur — the international community may be less inclined to react to serious abuses that don't rise to the level of genocide". Clough also pointed out the possible long-term dangers of crying wolf about "genocide" in Darfur. Such behaviour "could even make it harder to mobilize the public to respond to similar crises in the future".[1145]

The most prominent of the Darfur advocacy groups, and deliberately or naively at the heart of prolonging the conflict in Darfur, has been the Save Darfur Coalition.[1146]

The Save Darfur Coalition

At the centre of the anti-Khartoum "Darfur" campaign has been the self-styled Save Darfur Coalition. The coalition was established in July 2004, at a meeting of 40 non-governmental organisations hosted by the American Jewish World Service and the United States Holocaust Memorial Museum. The coalition describes itself as "an alliance of over 170 faith-based, advocacy and humanitarian organizations". *The Jerusalem Post*, however, has challenged this description: "Little known…is that the coalition, which has presented itself as 'an alliance of over 130 diverse faith-based, humanitarian, and human rights organization' was actually begun exclusively as an initiative of the American Jewish community. And even now…that coalition is heavily weighted with a politically and religiously diverse collection of local and national Jewish groups." *The Jerusalem Post* noted that "The coalition's roots go back to the spring of 2004…An emergency meeting was coordinated by the American Jewish World Service, an organization that serves as a kind of Jewish Peace Corps as well as an advocacy group for a variety of humanitarian and human rights issues. At the meeting, which was attended by numerous American Jewish organizations and a few other religious groups, it was decided that a coalition would be formed based on a statement of shared principles." [1147]

The executive committee of the Save Darfur Coalition includes representatives from the United States Holocaust Memorial Museum, American Jewish World Service, Jewish Council for Public Affairs, National Association of Evangelicals, National Coalition of Churches of Christ in the USA, Union for Reform Judaism and the United States Conference of Catholic Bishops. [1148]

The Coalition defines its "mission" as raising "public awareness about the ongoing genocide in Darfur and to mobilize a unified response to the atrocities that threaten the lives of two million people in the Darfur region." This is done through "media outreach, public education, targeted coalition building and grassroots mobilization to pressure policymakers and other decision-makers in the United States and abroad to help the people of Darfur." [1149]

Save Darfur activists Hamilton and Hazlett have admitted, however, that Save Darfur's framing of the conflict was from the start "severely simplified and almost ignorant of the rebel movement". [1150] This was confirmed by the former executive-director of Save Darfur, David Rubenstein, who stated that "after many difficult hours of mulling [over] policy alternatives, we realized that the closer we could get to a bumper sticker, the better we'd be as an organization."[1151] That is to say that an issue as incredibly complex as the Darfur crisis was reduced to the level of a bumper sticker in order to better market it to an American audience.

The respected American writer on humanitarian affairs, David Rieff, has criticised this "simplistic, mostly-without-nuance view of the conflict in Darfur".[1152] Rieff asks why Save Darfur has "offered an incomplete picture of what's happening?...Even naming an organization Save Darfur is an oversimplification, in that it implies that there is an innocent victim...and a group from whom they need to be saved", something which has become increasingly unclear.[1153] Brendan O'Neill states that: "The Save Darfur brigade has effectively transformed Darfur into a morality tale...And as with all morality tales, facts are less important than feelings, and the truth comes a poor second to creating a childishly simplistic framework of 'good' and 'evil'."[1154]

Mamdani has also commented on the dangers that this gross simplification of the movement's message brought with it: "The Save Darfur campaign's characterisation of the violence as 'Arab' against 'African' obscured both the fact that the violence was not one-sided and the contest over the meaning of 'Arab' and 'African'...The depoliticisation, naturalisation and, ultimately, demonisation of the notion 'Arab', as against 'African', has been the deadliest effect, whether intended or not, of the Save Darfur campaign."[1155]

In a mirror image of the ill-informed and misjudged steps which led to the fiasco in Iraq, the Save Darfur Coalition states very clearly that it wishes to see a multinational western-led military intervention in Sudan: "As the strongest of member states, we believe that the United States, under the President's leadership, must lead the international effort to raise and deploy that UN peacekeeping force."[1156] It has also called for the establishment and enforcement of "a no-fly zone over Darfur, Sudan", and has spent millions of dollars in an international media campaign including full-page ads to this effect in major newspapers in the United States, Britain and Europe. The most serious criticisms of Save Darfur – from the humanitarian community itself – have arisen out of these reckless demands for military intervention in Darfur and its inaccurate claims about the situation on the ground. It is a matter of record that a growing divide has opened up between Save Darfur and the humanitarian groups and personnel working on the ground in Darfur and across the border in Chad over this issue.

Rieff has reported that a number of aid groups in Darfur (most notably, Médecins sans Frontières, which has one of the largest and most effective programmes in the region) have "been privately complaining about Save Darfur's activities in the U.S.". He stated that the complaints were prompted by "a series of ads run by Save Darfur calling for more aggressive action in Darfur, including the imposition of a 'no-fly' zone over western Sudan, the effect of this…would be to put the on-the-ground aid effort at risk." Rieff cited an Action Against Hunger statement that such a move would "have disastrous consequences that risk triggering a further escalation of violence while jeopardising the provision of vital humanitarian assistance to millions of people".[1157] Mamdani has also pointed to the irresponsibility of the Save Darfur ads:

> A full-page advertisement has appeared several times a week in the *New York Times* calling for intervention in Darfur now. It wants the intervening forces to be placed under 'a chain of command allowing necessary and timely military action without approval from distant political or civilian personnel'. That intervention in Darfur should not be subject to 'political or civilian' considerations and that the intervening forces should have the right to shoot – to kill – without permission from distant places: these are said to be 'humanitarian' demands.[1158]

The ads in question were a matter of considerable concern to the humanitarian community. In March 2007, Sam Worthington, the head of InterAction, the grouping bringing together all the US aid organisations involved in Sudan, sent the following communication to David Rubenstein, the then director of Save Darfur:

> As the President of InterAction, the largest coalition of US humanitarian organizations who are helping keep close to 2 million people in Darfur alive, I want to privately convey to you our

strongest objection to the wording used in your current Save Darfur media and e-mail campaign. As someone who like you is a strong advocate for human rights and the protection of populations who do not have a voice I am deeply concerned by the inability of Save Darfur to be informed by realities on the ground and to understand the consequences of your proposed actions. If we are unable to bridge this reality gap at some point InterAction will need to go public and state to the press that: 1) Save Darfur does not represent any of the humanitarian organizations on the ground in Darfur; 2) Save Darfur is misstating the facts; and 3) Save Darfur's proposed endorsement of a Plan B that includes the items listed in your ads would set into motion a series of events that could easily result in the deaths of hundreds of thousands of individuals. I have no desire to make any of this public but actions by Save Darfur are increasingly making our silence untenable. Every week members of our staffs are killed and with thousands of staff in Darfur we are fully aware what is going on as we help shelter, care for, and feed the victims of this disaster. I will be in touch with the 14 InterAction members that are associated with Save Darfur and will share with them these concerns. Coming from a family of activists I have welcomed the way your coalition has galvanized this important issue but advocacy that is disconnected from NGOs operating on the ground and their knowledge of that reality is simply not responsible.

More criticism was to follow. Steve Fake and Kevin Funk, two American social justice activists, writing in *Foreign Policy in Focus*, observed:

The Save Darfur Coalition has often legitimated concerns that it is patently unaware of or even supportive of Washington's plans for the region, and ignorant of fundamental issues of the conflict. More prominently, the Coalition has at times been guilty of sidetracking Darfurian and Muslim activists, describing the conflict in harshly oversimplified ethnic terms…the movement as a whole has demonstrated considerable myopia in both its actions and rhetoric.

Fake and Funk further criticised Save Darfur for having "failed to realize that a Western-backed [intervention] force would not be equivalent to 'the armed wing of Amnesty International.'" [1159]

A subsequent British Advertising Standards Authority adjudication regarding Save Darfur's "misstating the facts" also deeply embarrassed the movement.[1160] An op-ed piece in *The New York Times* noted that the ruling was "more than just a minor public relations victory for Khartoum: it exposes a glaring problem in Save Darfur's strategy…[Save Darfur] has hampered aid-delivery groups, discredited American policy makers and diplomats and harmed efforts to respond to future humanitarian crises."[1161] *The New York Times* observed that "Save Darfur's inflated estimate…only frustrates peace efforts…Inaccurate data can also lead to prescriptive blunders…Ultimately, the inflated claims fuel a death race in which aid and action are based not on facts but on which advocacy group yells the loudest." The article concluded that "Two-hundred thousand dead in Darfur is egregious enough. No matter how noble their intentions, there's no need for activists to kill more Darfuris than the conflict itself already has."[1162] Referring to the advertising watchdog adjudication, O'Neill notes that "The ASA story shows the deep divide between Western campaigning on Darfur and the reality on the ground; between sensational Western claims about a twenty-first century genocide and the fact that, while things no doubt remain terribly grim in Darfur, the situation there has improved since the intense conflict period of 2003-2005. Western agitation for action in Darfur…is divorced from real events in Darfur or Sudan."[1163]

The Save Darfur Coalition has engaged in a number of other anti-Sudanese activities. On 22 January 2006, for example, it launched the "Million Voices for Darfur" campaign with the aim of collecting one million signed postcards to send to President Bush urging the United States government to support military intervention in Darfur. This particular campaign ended on 29 June 2006 with Senate Majority Leader Bill Frist and Senator Hillary Clinton said to have signed the 1,000,000th and 1,000,001st postcards. The Coalition also organised a "Save Darfur: Rally to Stop Genocide" event on the National Mall in Washington, DC on 30 April 2006. Reuters reported that "several thousand" people had attended the rally.[1164] The Coalition claimed that 50,000 people attended. Among the speakers were actor George Clooney, Nobel Prize winner Elie Wiesel, Senator Barack Obama, Rwandan hotel manager Paul

Rusesabagina, Olympic Gold medallist Joey Cheek, US House of Representatives Democratic party Leader Nancy Pelosi, Brian Steidle and Reverend Al Sharpton. The Coalition claimed that "There was extensive television coverage, with more than 800 stories broadcast in the U.S. and Canada. Articles about the rally were published in newspapers that reached a world-wide readership of an estimated 31 million people." The rally also served as the conclusion of Steidle's 21,000-mile, 22-city photo "Tour for Darfur: Eyewitness to Genocide" exhibit. In their haste to set their own particular agenda for the rally, however, the Save Darfur Coalition forgot to include any voice from Darfur. *The Washington Post* reported that: "Organizers rushed this week to invite two Darfurians to address the rally after Sudanese immigrants objected that the original list of speakers included eight Western Christians, seven Jews, four politicians and assorted celebrities – but no Muslims and no one from Darfur."[1165]

Reporting on the clear involvement of the American Jewish community in this rally, *The Jerusalem Post* stated that a "collection of local Jewish bodies, including the Jewish Community Center in Manhattan, United Jewish Communities, UJA-Federation of New York and the Jewish Council for Public Affairs, sponsored the largest and most expensive ad for the rally, a full-page in The New York Times on April 15…the Jewish Community Relations Council, a national organization with local branches that coordinate communal activity all over America, has put on a massive effort to bus people to Washington on Sunday. Dozens of buses will be coming from Philadelphia and Cleveland. Yeshiva University alone, in upper Manhattan, has chartered eight buses." *The Jerusalem Post* also commented upon the "absence of major African-American groups like the NAACP or the larger Africa lobby groups like Africa Action. When asked to comment, representatives of both groups insisted they were publicizing the rally but had not become part of the coalition or signed the Unity Statement declaring Save Darfur's objectives."[1166] The newspaper also reported that the organisers of the rally "consistently played down" the "Jewish origins and character of the rally". David Rubenstein, the director of the Save Darfur Coalition, was quoted as saying that given that the groups who started the coalition were Jewish, "it's not surprising that they had the numbers of more Jewish organizations in their rolodexes."[1167]

There was a second rally, entitled "Save Darfur Now: Voices to End

Genocide", in New York City's Central Park, on 17 September 2006. This rally also urged military intervention in Darfur. In addition to activities within the United States, the Coalition has also organised a number of "Global Day for Darfur" events. The Coalition claimed that on the 2007 "Global Day", "From Austria to Mauritius to Jordan, Nigeria to Mongolia to Bahrain, Pittsburgh to Bamako to Budapest, and at over 400 locations in as many as 40 countries, people of conscience gathered at rallies, marches, 'die-ins,' conferences, vigils and other events to demonstrate their solidarity with those suffering in Darfur".

These events have also come in for withering criticism. Anne Bartlett, the Director of the London-based Darfur Centre for Human Rights and Development, has pointed to Save Darfur's "series of expensive, symbolic stunts: [they] do little…They are usually costly and do more for the people taking the action than for the intended recipients."[1168] This is a view shared by *The Boston Globe*: "What effect have all the fashion shows, wristband sales, and celebrity drop-ins – did someone mention George Clooney? – have on the millions of displaced persons in Darfur? None whatsoever."[1169] O'Neill has also echoed one of Bartlett's points: "'Save Darfur' activism – from Hollywood celebs calling for Western military action to the growth of campaigning commentary on the conflict – has not really been about Darfur. Rather, it has been about creating a new moralistic and simplistic generational mission for campaigners and journalists in America and Europe."[1170]

In common with other Darfur advocacy groups, the Coalition has exaggerated war-related mortality in Darfur, claiming, for example, in its ads that "at least 400,000 people have been killed" in Darfur. The Coalition has also used the genocide word inaccurately. What the Coalition is unable to address is the fact that impeccable sources such as such as Médecins Sans Frontières have publicly stated that there is no genocide in Darfur; this despite the fact that the Coalition cites Médecins Sans Frontières in its so-called "Unity Statement" as an "independent" organisation.[1171] Save Darfur was sensationalist from its inception. The founding "Unity Statement" of the Save Darfur movement was itself seriously flawed. Produced in 2004, this statement anchored the movement's *raison d'être* on the claims that between 350,000 and one million people could die "in the coming months" in 2004.[1172] That claim and subsequent allegations that 400,000 people had been killed have since been discredited in a landmark judgement by the British Advertising Standards Authority which stated that such assertions were inaccurate and misleading.

Save Darfur's reliance on deeply flawed sources for its claims is self-evident. In its unsuccessful defence of having alleged 400,000 deaths in Darfur, the organisation cited the work of John Hagan, a professor of sociology and law at Northwestern University in the United States. It is clear that Hagan's peers have been very critical of his claims about Darfur mortality. The US government's Government Accounting Office study asked the 12 experts it had convened with the National Academy of Sciences in April 2006 a number of questions about the claims made by Hagan and others. When the experts were asked about their level of confidence in Hagan's estimates, 11 out of 12 experts stated they had either low or very low confidence in Hagan, of which 8 stated that had very low confidence in his estimates. When asked, in their view, whether Hagan's work was based on methodologically sound source data, 9 out of the 11 experts stated that Hagan's mortality estimates were not based on methodologically sound source data. The experts concluded that Hagan's "estimates were more characteristic of advocacy or journalistic material than of objective analysis".[1173]

The online Wikipedia encyclopaedia has summarised several of the general criticisms of the Save Darfur Coalition:

> In non-Western media the 'Save Darfur' movement has received some criticism...the campaign is criticized for presenting a one-sided picture of a ceaseless campaign of ethnic cleansing by the janjaweed against defenseless villagers, without presenting details on the region's rebels, who have committed some abuses of their own. In Iranian media the campaign has been compared by some outlets to the British 'liberal imperialism' of the late 18th and 19th centuries. Some groups on the radical left have accused the movement of anti-Arab bias. From the perspective of various left-wing groups, the movement is a U.S.-government supported propaganda campaign targeting the Sudanese government for its opposition to the U.S.-led occupation in Iraq, support for the Palestinian cause, and strengthened economic ties to China. Other leftwing groups have

decried the 'Save Darfur Coalition' for its original make up, and the fact that its earliest rallies had no Sudanese or Muslim speakers. They also oppose many of the groups that originally formed the coalition, describing them as 'Christian fundamentalists, Zionists, and pro-Iraq war neo-conservatives.' They are also against the calls for intervention in Sudan on the grounds that such an intervention will only serve the rich in the U.S. and Europe, and will in fact make the situation for ordinary Sudanese people worse. Yoshie Furuhashi, a Monthly Review editor, has criticized the 'Save Darfur' campaign for U.S. intervention as 'imperialism' in humanitarian guise, combined with a strong tinge of anti-Arab prejudice. There have also been accusations of strong Jewish and Christian fundamentalist agendas behind the campaign.

The Save Darfur Coalition has been openly criticised for helping to worsen and prolong the violence in Darfur. Kuperman has been one such critic. He has stated that the Save Darfur advocacy groups, in pressing for western military intervention, contributed to some rebel movements shunning the 2006 peace agreement:

> this rejection of peace by factions claiming to seek it is actually revelatory. It helps explain...how the Save Darfur movement unintentionally poured fuel on the fire...their persistent calls for intervention have actually worsened the violence...Because of the Save Darfur movement...the rebels believe that the longer they provoke genocidal retaliation, the more the West will pressure Sudan to hand them control of the region...The key to rescuing Darfur is to reverse these perverse incentives". [1174]

This observation has been echoed by Brendan O'Neill:

> The narcissistic campaigning of the Save Darfur Coalition and others has helped to prolong and even intensify violent clashes in the region. The good-and-evil presentation of the conflict has warped its dynamics. State Department officials claim that, during the height

of the conflict, some Darfuri rebels "let the village burnings go on, let the killing go on, because the more international pressure that's brought to bear on Khartoum, the stronger their position grows". Furthermore, the intense international and celebrity pressure on Khartoum has had the effect of inflaming and encouraging other rebels, based in eastern Sudan, to renew their war against the Khartoum government. In Africa, Western do-gooding can prove deadly indeed. Save Darfur activism is one kind of porn that really has given rise to violence in the real world.[1175]

The editor of *Monthly Review*, Yoshie Furuhashi, has also drawn a clear link between the Save Darfur Coalition "Save Darfur" rally on 30 April 2006 and the intransigence of Darfur rebels in the Abuja peace talks:

> The timing of the rally was perfect, designed to coincide – and scuttle – the Abuja peace negotiations between the rebels and Khartoum brokered by the African Union, whose deadline is midnight today. And sure enough, the rebels rejected the peace deal. Really, why should the rebels accept any peace deal, when Washington, given an excuse by the pro-war rally organized by an odd alliance of evangelicals and establishment Jews is pushing for NATO interventions just at this moment? The rebels would naturally think: "Why don't we wait till Washington sends us NATO or UN or US troops to weaken the government's hands, so we can get a better deal?"[1176]

There have also been repeated questions about Save Darfur's financial affairs. The Save Darfur movement had quickly emerged as a commercial venture. To this end it sells a wide range of items, green "Save Darfur" wristbands and ribbons, bumper stickers, lawn signs, banners that state "A call to your conscience: save Darfur" for display in "community centres, houses of worship, schools and other institutions". Even Eric Reeves has noted that: "They seemed more interested in merchandizing, and establishing their claim as the default organization – than in making any of the necessary policy decisions"[1177] The movement has also solicited and raised very large funds from its outreach. There has also subsequently been considerable unease as to where this money has gone. Anne Bartlett, for example, has explicitly questioned the money-making side of Save Darfur: "With the level of fundraising running into hundreds of millions of dollars, how much of that money has seen the light of day in Darfur? How many people have been helped by the wearing of green wristbands or fundraising dinners? How many kids have been educated with this money? How many families have been able to eat? The answer is not many." Bartlett has also observed that "Darfur has become a social club where everyone but the Darfurians are invited".[1178] Mamdani has also sought to follow the money trail, asking UN humanitarian officials in Sudan "What assistance does the Save Darfur Coalition give?" The answer was "Nothing". Mamdani goes on to state that "And I would like to know. The Save Darfur Coalition raises an enormous amount of money in this country. Where does that money go? Does it go to other organizations which are operative in Sudan, or does it go simply to fund the advertising campaign?"[1179]

Mamdani has also asked whether or not the public was being misled: "people...give money not to fuel a commercial campaign, but expecting that this money will go to do something about the pain and suffering of those who are the victims in Darfur, so how much of that money is going to actually – how much of it translates into food or medicine or shelter? And how much of it is being recycled?"[1180] These questions were finally answered in a *Washington Post* article in June 2007: "None of the money collected by Save Darfur goes to help the victims and their families."[1181] It was revealed that the funds go towards sustaining a staff of thirty and Save Darfur's annual budget of $15 million. The combination of very questionable ads, which enraged the US humanitarian community, and questions about where Save Darfur funds were going – in large part to fund the questionable ads – led to the removal of David Rubenstein as director in June 2007.

Prominent US officials such as Andrew Natsios, President Bush's special envoy to Sudan, have questioned the continuing relevance of Save Darfur. Speaking in September 2007, Natsios said that the group may have more useful in the past. He further observed that "Some of the advocacy groups want to inflict pain for pain's sake" against the government in Sudan.[1182]

Referring to the debate about Save Darfur's failings, de Waal noted that "the principle 'do no harm' was adopted to guide humanitarian engagement. The same 'do no harm' principle applies to advocacy too, and I think that what is happening in Sudan today will soon turn into soul-searching by activist organizations. How could they have inadvertently done harm (or failed to do good)?"[1183] De Waal said that the Save Darfur campaign had to answer several questions:

> Could the focus on Darfur mean that the challenges of consolidating the North-South peace have been neglected?...Could the Darfur campaign have driven the Bush administration to adopt hardline rhetoric that made Khartoum less cooperative, while at the same time encouraging the rebels to believe that they could win a military intervention if they held out long enough? Could it in fact have impeded the search for a compromise between government and rebels? Has the stress on genocide...misrepresented the situation? Has this meant that they have missed more appropriate actions. [1184]

A October 2007 *Newsweek* feature has echoed de Waal's concerns, noting that Darfur activists "may be doing more harm than good".[1185]

Helping or endangering Israel?

The close involvement of the American Jewish community in the Save Darfur movement is clear. It is no longer the elephant in the room and has been widely acknowledged, and debated, within the community itself, with questions as to whether such a close involvement was a good thing. One Jewish activist noted that Jewish involvement on Darfur is "promoted" as being "ecumenical":

> But the ecumenical language of the Coalition is somewhat of a facade. The Save Darfur Coalition is heavily (overly?) Jewish, and was created by the United States Holocaust Memorial Museum and the American Jewish World Service. It appears that intensive Jewish leadership and organizational support is viewed with cynicism from other possible allies for the Darfurians, including crucial African-

American organizations...Could it be that our commitment to Darfur is somehow viewed with suspicion when the Jews are calling for yet another intervention against Islamic aggression?[1186]

Many commentators, several of them clearly anti-Zionist and anti-Israeli, have questioned Jewish involvement and alleged that it serves Israeli interests.[1187] A *Counterpunch* article noted, for example, that: "several US-based zionist groups have taken up the Darfur issue for...cynical ends. Pushing the Darfur issue is viewed among some of these groups as a means of deflecting attention from Israel, suggesting that the situation in Darfur is worse and therefore 'why single out Israel'...The situation in Darfur was also exploited after the Israeli war of aggression against Lebanon in 2006; as soon as the war ended, the media focus shifted immediately and preponderantly to cover the Darfur situation in order to deflect attention from a criminal war by US/Israel."[1188] There is no doubt that the Sudanese government sees a clear relationship between Save Darfur and Israeli and Jewish interests. In July 2007, for example, Sudan's defence minister, Abdul-Rahim Mohammed Hussein, has very specifically accused 24 Jewish organisations of "fuelling the conflict in Darfur".[1189] These are groups that have been caught up in the Save Darfur bandwagon. As Ruth Messinger, the executive-director of the American Jewish World Service stated, understandably, that genocide "has particular meaning to Jews who have sworn never again".[1190] As has been argued elsewhere in this study, however, there are at the very least many doubts about whether or not genocide has occurred in Darfur. Quite a strong case can be made that it has not and that the issue itself has been deliberately distorted by an opportunistic White House and pre-existent anti-Sudan industry. The simple fact is that given the awesome implications of the term genocide – and the memory of the Holocaust – any ambiguity as to whether or not it is accurate in Darfur is very dangerous not just for the international community as a whole, but for the Jewish community in particular. It should also be noted that Israel itself has not bought into the genocide in Darfur issue – and has expelled Darfur refugees, something a state born out of the Holocaust would presumably not have done had they been seen as genuine victims of genocide.[1191]

It is dangerous for several reasons. The first relates to the misuse of the genocide term. Crying wolf on genocide can only but denigrate the memory of the reality of the Holocaust in Europe during the Second World War, encourage Holocaust deniers and badly damage the reputation of those organisations that make such claims. Given that many previous serious allegations made about Sudan (including claims made by previous American administrations) have proven to be deeply questionable where not simply false, the danger of reputable Jewish organisations echoing claims made by the Bush Administration of genocide in Darfur is clear. The reputations of American Jewish leaders, and the organisations they represent, can only but suffer as a result. If, in the coming months or years, it emerges that American claims about Darfur were opportunistic and false it further weakens American claims to international leadership. There are further physical dangers. Ironically, in undermining Khartoum, claims of genocide have strengthened the position of ultra-Islamists in Sudan, notably the key Darfur rebel movement involved in the Darfur conflict, the Justice and Equality Movement. JEM is widely seen as an ultra-Islamist movement closely identified with Islamist ideologue Dr Hassan Turabi. Political action on Darfur and the material assistance provided by Jewish groups on Darfur directly benefits a *jihadist* movement. At the very least it encourages JEM, and other Darfur rebels, to avoid or prevaricate on peace talks and in so doing artificially prolonging the conflict – in the hope of further weakening the increasingly pro-Western government in Khartoum, a country that has been a staunch ally in the American war on terror.

There is a further, linked, danger, one that relates to Israel. Many Jewish – and several pro-Israeli – groups have joined the Save Darfur call for western military intervention and "no-fly zones" in Darfur. The law of unintended consequences is one which should be required study by all advocates. Many pro-Israeli activists were at the forefront of calls for the invasion of Iraq. Four years on only a fool would suggest that that invasion has made Israel any safer. It is clear that the Middle East is a far more dangerous place as a result. The simple fact is that the sort of western military intervention called for by Jewish constituencies could very easily lead to another Iraq-type catastrophe in the Sudan – and in this case in a country bordering directly with Egypt. An Iraq in the Sahel would inevitably destabilise and engulf Egypt, Israel's only peace partner in the Middle East.

The American Jewish community is right to draw attention to events in Darfur. It was wrong, however, for it to have unquestioningly echoed repeatedly discredited Bush Administration claims of genocide in western Sudan. At the very least it will damage the credibility of the American Jewish community in speaking out on genuine instances of genocide elsewhere in the years to come. At worst, it may indirectly further jeopardise the security of Israel.

The Genocide Intervention Network (GI-Net)

The "Genocide Intervention Network" (originally the Genocide Intervention Fund) was established in 2004 by students at Swarthmore College in the United States, "to give concerned Americans the opportunity to help protect civilians from genocide". GI-Net states that it seeks private contributions in support of peacekeepers in Darfur, "the site of the twenty-first century's first genocide". The "Genocide Intervention Network" claims to have US $500,000 from individual private donations for civilian protection in Darfur stating that "more than half of every donation we receive goes directly to civilian protection in Darfur".

GI-Net is also at the centre of a Sudan "divestment" campaign. It claims that the state of California was the first in the United States "to adopt the Genocide Intervention Network's targeted divestment model". It organises a toll-free hotline providing its supporters with "an easy way to contact their elected officials. Without being put on hold or having to look up the number, callers have the option of being connected directly with their members of Congress, governor or the president. Before being connected to the relevant office, callers hear an up-to-date briefing about the specific actions elected officials must take to stop genocide." Since the launch in February 2007, the hotline has generated hundreds of calls as part of campaigns targeting a particular state or district. GI-Net has also produced a "congressional scorecard on Darfur", which it claims has been used by more than 27,000 people to date and which "grades each member of Congress on his or her record on ending the Darfur genocide". The "Darfur scorecard empowers citizens with the tools and knowledge to more effectively pressure their elected officials".

As an indication of the exaggeration that has accompanied all its activities, GI-Net claims that "more than 450,000 people have been killed" in Darfur.

A Student Anti-Genocide Coalition

STAND, "A Student Anti-Genocide Coalition", formerly known as "Students Taking Action Now: Darfur", is the student wing of the "Genocide Intervention Network". It describes itself as "an umbrella organization of over 600 high school and college chapters dedicated to putting an end to genocide, specifically the ongoing genocide in Darfur, Sudan". It further claims that it was formed out of "the rapidly growing student movement to protect Darfur and works to unify this anti-genocide movement under one message by providing students with informational, educational and organizing resources, empowering them through an extensive network of impassioned student activists and advocating for a change in the world's mentality towards genocide". STAND claims to have become "a student movement that encompasses over 600 college, university, and high school chapters across the United States and around the world". In 2007, STAND activists protested at Chinese economic ties with Sudan by forming a human chain spanning 12 blocks in New York City, and calling on the state of New York to "break the chain" and divest from Sudan. Interestingly, in the "learn about Darfur" section on their website, STAND states that the Darfur rebel groups launched an uprising against the Khartoum government because they were "frustrated by poverty".[1192] Quite how destroying the Sudanese economy will help alleviate poverty in Sudan and Darfur is not explained.

STAND states that it works with several partner organisations, including the United States Holocaust Memorial Museum's Committee on Conscience, Hillel: The Foundation for Jewish Campus Life, the Save Darfur Coalition, American Jewish World Service and the Sudan Divestment Task Force.[1193] Along with the Save Darfur Coalition, STAND also calls for western-led military intervention in Sudan.

In common with its parent organisation, GI-Net, STAND has also grossly exaggerated mortality in Darfur, claiming that the Darfur crisis "has claimed 400,000 lives" and that "more than one hundred people continue to die each day".

The Aegis Trust

The Aegis Trust states that it was established in 2000 by James Smith and

Stephen Smith. Its creation was said to have "emerged from the experience of the UK Holocaust Centre, established by the Smith family in 1995". While the Aegis Trust states that it "works with a wide range of partners, including governmental, non-governmental, educational and academic institutions around the world" it is clear that Aegis is the British extension of the Save Darfur Coalition. It is extremely well funded. Aegis echoes many of the Coalition's demands, including calls for unilateral western military intervention in Sudan. Aegis Trust director James Smith, for example, has stated that the "UN must be ready to intervene without Sudan's consent".[1194] That is to say, invade Sudan.

In common with its Save Darfur Coalition partner the Aegis Trust has also exaggerated events in Darfur. Aegis claims, for example, "genocide" in Darfur and that "civilians in Darfur continue to perish at a rate of 10,000 per month". On one page on its website Aegis stated that "combined mortality from violence, malnutrition and disease from the beginning of the conflict in February 2003 until now could be more than 300,000 people."[1195] On another page, Aegis claimed that "in March 2005 it was estimated that as many as 350,000 Africans have been killed."[1196] On yet another page, Aegis states that 400,000 people have been killed.[1197] Together with Save Darfur Aegis placed the "Globe for Darfur" newspaper ads which were the subject of a British advertising standards watchdog's admonishment for inaccuracy.

Following the American model, Aegis has also set up a Sudan divestment division, "Sudan Divestment UK". Sudan Divestment UK admits that it works "in partnership with the Aegis Trust, an NGO which campaigns against genocide". Sudan Divestment UK also "admits that it works with "the US-based, Sudan Divestment Task Force". This organisation also gives a skewed picture of events in Darfur. Sudan Divestment UK claims, for example, that "the conflict in the Darfur region of Sudan is the first genocide of the 21st century" and that "between 250,000 and 400,000 are dead".[1198] It is ironic that although James Smith identifies a lack of investment in Darfur as a catalyst for rebellion in Darfur, Smith is an enthusiastic advocate of divestment from Sudan with all the implications for the aspirations of all Sudanese, Darfurians included.[1199]

Darfour Urgence

The Save Darfur Coalition's counterpart in France is *Darfour Urgence*, which was established in 2005. It is perhaps unsurprising that this "advocacy" group also claims that 400,000 civilians have been killed in Darfur.[1200] Referring to calls by *Darfour Urgence* for international military intervention in Darfur – a policy supported by five candidates in the 2007 French presidential elections – Dr Jean-Hervé Bradol, the president of Médecins Sans Frontières, and Fabrice Weissman, MSF research director, publicly described the calls as "a risky and dangerous initiative".[1201] Bradol and Weissman declared themselves to be "disturbed that our presidential candidates have blindly signed on to the recommendations put forth by the Urgence Dafour Committee, and thus promised the people of Darfur that their salvation will come from a foreign military intervention, whose chances of deployment and success are slim." They were also critical of *Darfour Urgence* for jeopardising humanitarian assistance to civilians in Darfur:

> The only way to reduce violence in Darfur is to resume negotiations among the government, rebel groups and paramilitary militias. Joint action on the part of the international community addressing civilian needs for aid and protection is thus critical. Unfortunately, and at the risk of undermining one of the most effective aid operations of the last twenty years, a group with the standing to summon the major presidential candidates has chosen to participate in bellicose rhetoric rather than encourage European governments to commit firmly to a policy of mediation. [1202]

Darfour Urgence's repeated misinformation about Darfur and calls for military intervention has drawn further criticism. On 29 March 2007, Robert Ménard, the secretary-general of Reporters sans Frontières, and Stephen Smith, a journalist, wrote an article in *Le Monde* which was entitled, in English translation, "Darfur: Make Peace not War!" This article was a blistering critique of *Darfour Urgence*, arguing that the organisation's suggested course of action in Darfur was half-baked and a naïve, Manichean simplification of a complex situation. The writers also made the point that the information reaching the west about Darfur was limited – given that it was coming from journalists and activists who been based in or had visited the IDP camps; it was, they suggested, similar to making an assessment of the whole of France after visiting just its hospitals. They were also critical of those in the west who demand that UN forces drawn from the developing world should intervene in Darfur. If they felt so strongly, they should go themselves: "What right [do] these journalists have to ask United Nations forces from the third world to die in their place?" The article also challenged the mortality claims made by *Darfour Urgence* in support of its calls for military intervention in Darfur. Ménard and Smith state that rather than 400,000 or 200,000 deaths in Darfur, the death toll is 40,000 killed and 90,000 indirect deaths as a result of the conflict.[1203]

The dangers of *Darfour Urgence*'s distortion of reality manifested themselves in late 2007. *Arche de Zoé*, Zoe's Ark, was established in 2004 by Eric Breteau, a French fireman. In 2007, spurred on by the claims made by *Darfour Urgence*, Zoe's Ark turned its attention to the Darfur issue and started a campaign to "rescue" war-orphans from Darfur. The claims made by Zoe's Ark in the course of its lucrative fund-raising were staggeringly false: "550,000 people murdered, four million civilian victims... A child dies every five minutes in Darfur. In a year's time, 800,000 will have died."[1204] Reporting on the affair, *The Observer* newspaper noted "They are deeply questionable figures, some massively inflated, that fly in the face of the best estimates." [1205] In the event, Zoe's Ark proceeded to do something even more questionable. In October 2007, it tried to illegally remove over one hundred children from Chad, many of whom were neither orphans or from Darfur. Six of the charity's workers were arrested by the Chadian authorities and were charged with child trafficking offences. Chadian President Idriss Déby strongly criticised Zoe's Ark: "Here's the truth about this Europe that portrays itself as helping, this Europe which seeks to give lessons to Africa. It's dreadful. I am revolted. I cannot accept it."[1206] The governor of Abeche in Chad, the home to many of the families involved, summed up the anger in Chad surrounding the Zoe's Ark incident: "We feel like white people come here under false pretences, as do-gooders...In Africa, there are not many orphans, because children who lose their parents are taken care of by the extended family. I spoke to one of the girls in the orphanage. She was kidnapped. Her mother is dead, but her father was working in the fields when the abductors came. It hurts us when people come here with their ideas and, just because they are bringing food, they must impose their values." [1207]

The Observer noted that "The damage caused by Zoe's Ark and its apparently over-zealous and misguided humanitarianism is considerable." [1208] British academic Chris Bickerton further noted that "Many have seen Zoe's Ark as a sorry example of where humanitarian intervention has ended up." He also pointed to the fact that leading humanitarians such as Rony Brauman, the co-founder of Médecins Sans Frontières, chose not to blame the fanaticism shown by Zoe's Ark: "Instead, Brauman targets his ire at the political establishment. French foreign minister Bernard Kouchner is to blame, apparently, having irresponsibly labelled events in Darfur a genocide and recommended some kind of humanitarian intervention. Blame has also been laid at the door of Bernard Henri-Lévy, a French public intellectual who has also been active in drumming up support for intervention." [1209] Bickerton has further noted that

> The charge is that individuals such as Kouchner and Henri-Lévy have too often been willing to compromise on the facts in order to prompt Western governments into action. Darfur was therefore erroneously labelled a genocide, and casualty figures were grossly inflated by groups such as the Save Darfur Coalition in the US and Urgence Darfour in France. As a result, groups have sprung up – outside of the more regulated world of mainstream NGOS – and have taken such campaigns at their word...This has been the philosophy of Zoe's Ark: do-it-yourself humanitarianism. [1210]

In summarising the Zoe's Ark fiasco, Bickerton concluded that "The notion that legal right should give way to Western moral indignation has been challenged and exposed as an arrogant assumption. This should be a lesson not just for the naive and self-righteous aid workers of Zoe's Ark, but for all those wedded to the tenets of humanitarian intervention." [1211]

Globe for Darfur

Globe for Darfur states that it is a coalition made up of a number of organisations, including the Save Darfur Coalition, STAND, Aegis, Aegis

Students, the American Jewish Committee, the American Jewish World Service, *Darfour Urgence*, the World Evangelical Alliance, the European Union of Jewish Students, Human Rights Watch and the International Crisis Group. While Globe for Darfur states that it "was originally conceived by a group of NGOs working on Darfur and concerned about the slow response of the international community to the crisis", "Globe for Darfur" functions essentially as the international division of the Save Darfur Coalition. It is administered on behalf of the Save Darfur Coalition by the Aegis Trust.

Globe for Darfur has been used by the Save Darfur Coalition to project its claims and objectives internationally. To this end, Globe for Darfur has held a range of activities across the world. On 17 September 2006, the Globe for Darfur coalition held its first "Global Day for Darfur", with over 60 events in 42 cities. On 10 December 2006, Globe for Darfur organised activities around the world to call for military intervention in Darfur. On 29 April 2007, Globe for Darfur claimed that it organised events and activities in "more than 200 cities worldwide".

Like the Save Darfur Coalition, Globe for Darfur has made several very questionable claims about the Darfur crisis. For example it has produced seriously flawed claims that "Several hundred thousand people have been killed or seriously injured" in Darfur. In advertisements placed by Globe for Darfur it has also claimed that 400,000 people had been killed. The advertisements in question were placed in the British media by Save Darfur and Aegis using the Globe for Darfur name.

In advertisements widely published in British newspapers, Globe for Darfur misled British readers.[1212] Firstly, the advertisements started by stating: "In 2003, Sudanese President Omar al-Bashir moved to crush opposition by unleashing vicious armed militias to slaughter entire villages of his own citizens." This distorted simple facts about the Darfur conflict, leaving the reader with the impression that the "opposition" in question was parliamentary or was made up of civil society groups engaged in peaceful activity. As is clear, the facts are very different.

As has been previously outlined, the war in Darfur was initiated by the rebels themselves in early February 2003 with attacks on civilians, policemen and government garrisons in Darfur, including systematic attacks on al-Fasher and Mellit, respectively the capital and the second largest city in North Darfur.

The attack on al-Fasher was by hundreds of rebels, and there were significant military and civilian casualties. The rebels also murdered 200 army prisoners after they had surrendered. The rebels were very well equipped. It is also a matter of record that the Darfur rebels killed over 685 policemen, wounded 500 others and attacked and destroyed over 80 police stations in the course of theirs attack on government forces in 2003, something which destroyed law and order within an already lightly policed region. In response to these attacks, government forces launched offensives against rebel groups in Darfur. The second clearly misleading area of concern in the Globe for Darfur advertisement was the claim that 400,000 civilians have been killed in Darfur.

Evangelising Darfur?

The involvement of groups such as the Kansas-based evangelical group, Sudan Sunrise, on the Darfur issue is also indicative of the true nature of Darfur "advocacy" groups. The Sudan Sunrise website stated that it sought to convert the people of Darfur from Islam to Christianity, stating that the organisation was engaged in "one on one, lifestyle evangelism to Darfurian Muslims living in refugee camps in eastern Chad". It appealed for money to "bring the kingdom of God to an area of Sudan where the light of Jesus rarely shines". The references to evangelising Darfur on the website were quickly changed when it drew adverse attention.[1213]

Brian Steidle on Darfur: Opportunistic or Just Gullible?

Brian Steidle, a former US Marine, who worked with an African Union monitoring team in Darfur for five months from late 2004 into 2005, has become a centre-piece of Save Darfur Coalition activities. Photographs that he took during his work with African Union have been exhibited and presented as evidence to support sensationalist claims of "genocide" in Darfur across the United States.[1214] Far from illustrating genocide, however, his pictures are images of an intermittent low-intensity bush war in which civilians, as in any war, have been caught up in the violence. Would Steidle be able to claim that any number of pictures of dead and injured Iraqi civilians including children – caught up in American attacks on urban areas and villages during which many were burned alive, attacks involving helicopter gunships – was evidence of "genocide" in Iraq? The answer is, of course, no.

His written account, *The Devil Came on Horseback. Bearing Witness to the Genocide in Darfur*, founders on equally shallow claims.[1215] The book is a prime example of the sloppy, self-serving hyperbole that has been taken at face value and warmly embraced by the anti-Sudan industry within the Washington Beltway and by anti-Sudan and anti-Muslim constituencies world-wide. The book reveals that he was very much out of his depth in Darfur. It would appear that had obviously had very little if any hands-on experience of war during his service with the American military: he was certainly very uneasy when his personal safety was in any way threatened. Steidle's is a clearly skewed perspective from the very start. He admits, for example, "I was close to the JEM and SLA." [1216] He claims that an "appropriate term for [JEM and SLA] would be 'freedom fighters.' They would never even consider using their fellow civilians and tribe members as shields." [1217] This despite considerable evidence that rebel combatants have done just that. *The Times* reporter, Rob Crilly, for example, has written about a former rebel commander admitting that the rebel leadership had a "preference for using civilian villages as bases". He cited the rebel: "They seemed to want to use civilian suffering caused by government and Janjaweed attacks in their PR campaign".[1218] Steidle's naivety shows through in other respects. JEM, the Justice and Equality Movement, one of the two main rebel movements in Darfur, and "freedom fighters" to Steidle, is a very hard-line Islamist organisation, whose concept of freedom would be very different to Steidle's.

Given that Steidle has presented himself – and has been presented by the Save Darfur Coalition and others – as an expert on genocide, it is interesting that Steidle states that he formed his opinion that there is "genocide" occurring in Darfur, from looking at a third-party's photographs of an attack on a village in Darfur in which civilians had been killed, while Steidle was in the Nuba mountains – months before he had even stepped foot in Darfur. He notes that "the entire village was in ashes…what is going on here is…most definitively 'genocide'. There is no question about that." [1219] Steidle's intellectual dishonesty and selective memory are all too clear, however. Identical attacks by SLA rebels in which civilian villages are burnt to ashes, and in which old men, women and children are slaughtered, including children who were burnt to death, and which his AU teams investigated, are conveniently glossed over. He writes, for example, that in January 2005 his AU team was called on to investigate reports of rebel attacks on four civilian villages near Malam, approximately one hundred kilometres north of Nyala, in South Darfur. In his attempt to gloss over the involvement of his SLA friends in war crimes, Steidle admits he "hurried through the investigation" and states that "there were only two dead bodies, most likely SLA fighters". What he does not tell the reader is that the African Union documented that dozens of civilians, including many women and children were horrifically killed and injured in these rebel attacks – first-hand information to which Steidle would presumably had have access. In January 2005, reporting on the very incidents which Steidle "investigated", the African Union and United Nations confirmed that between 24 and 36 civilians had died and 26 others were wounded in these rebel attacks on villages in and around Malam, which had been burned to ashes.[1220] The reason for Steidle's dishonesty is clear. His litmus test for genocide is the killing of civilians, rape, the burning down of villages and the subsequent displacement of civilians. By this yardstick, his SLA friends would be equally guilty of genocide, something which would discredit his deeply-flawed, morality tale.[1221]

It is also worth noting that before "investigating" these attacks around Malam Steidle also claimed that "This was the first incident we had heard of rebel forces attacking civilian villages."[1222] In its report for 2004, however, Human Rights Watch cited numerous examples of the murder of civilians, the rape of women and abduction of young children by Sudan Liberation Army rebels in and around this very area in the course of 2004. Human Rights Watch, for example, noted that it had received a list of sixty women and girls who were said to have been raped or assaulted by rebels in attacks between 10 February and 7 July 2004.[1223] In one attack in the Malam area, on 21 April 2004, the rebels killed ten civilians. Human Rights Watch also reported that in mid-June 2004 rebel gunmen were said to have raped several women near Malam. Human Rights Watch stated that rebels attacked Malam again in October 2004, killing three civilians, including a 12-year-old girl, and injuring several more. Human Rights Watch stated that their apparent intention had been to loot. It also reported that it had received a list of thirty-nine people, including two children, said to have been abducted in the Malam area between 2 August 2003 and 10 July 2004, adding that their whereabouts remained unknown. Thousands of villagers had been displaced by these attacks. Despite being in the area, Steidle appears to have been unaware of any of these incidents.

Steidle is also clearly unconcerned about mastering any of the complexities of the dynamics in Darfur. He consistently lumps together all Darfur Arabs, armed or not, as "Janjaweed". Speaking of the Popular Defence Force (PDF), the Sudanese equivalent of the American National Guard or the British Territorial Army, he admits that he "considered all of them Janjaweed, though there was a slight distinction between the PDF, a more formal force, and other Arab nomad militias, which were less formally organized."[1224] (This is tantamount to describing the insurgency in Iraq as a united, cohesive whole.) It is enough for Steidle for someone to tend camels for someone to be a "Janjaweed". To him, all Arabs in Darfur are "Janjaweed", just as a previous generation of Americans would have used the pejorative term "Gook" for all Vietnamese, armed or otherwise, during their wars in Indochina. He is hard pressed to explain away the obvious disconnect he sees in actions carried out by Arab tribes, often in response to livestock theft, actions carried out by government forces and actions carried out by "Janjaweed" elements: when an incident does not fit his stereotype he dismisses it as having "possibly" been committed by "an out-of-control Janjaweed force".[1225] He makes no attempt to reconcile his description of the "Janjaweed" as "the government's loyal attack dog" with reports he received of fighting between the Janjaweed and government forces. While he has subsequently claimed to "have seen clear evidence that the atrocities committed in Darfur are the direct result of the Sudanese government's military collaboration with the militias"[1226], in his book he admits ignorance about the command and control this would have entailed: "we didn't know much about how the Janjaweed were given their orders to move."[1227]

Steidle either dishonestly or naively describes several instances of inter-tribal raiding to recover rustled livestock as somehow equating to genocide. Far from in any way producing evidence for "genocide" in Darfur, however, his book inadvertently illustrates the resources-driven nature of so much of the localised fighting that has taken place in Darfur. He records that much of the work with the AU was investigating instances where Arab tribesmen had complained to the AU about the murder or kidnapping of civilians and the theft of thousands of camels. In example after example he documents attacks by tribesmen from one village on the tribesmen of another village in order to recover stolen livestock. Far from a "genocidal" motivation, it is all too clear that the attacks are focused on recovering animals. Four of Steidle's own examples will perhaps suffice.

In November 2004, Steidle's AU team went to the villages of Tiesha, Mirrel and Nitega to talk to tribal leaders: "We were following up on something that threatened to escalate into a major crisis." Steidle relates that "Reportedly, rebels had stolen 350 camels from the Janjaweed and this is what caused the Janjaweed, willing to die for their camels, to plan an attack on the SLA stronghold of Muhajeriya. Over a few days, they had already burned 14 or 15 villages." He cites an Arab tribesmen, a "Janjaweed" naturally, who stated that "Rebels stole 350 of our camels and 600 cattle. My men went to take them back when rebels in 20 vehicles ambushed us near Labado. They shot the camels we were riding on and killed 15 people!" Steidle noted that "the men were now walking back to their settlement on foot, clearly furious and probably paranoid."[1228] In Mirrel village, Steidle meets the sheikh of Nitega, whom he describes as the "tribal and military leader of the Janjaweed in all of South Darfur". Steidle relates that the sheikh is clearly annoyed. He had just returned from meetings in Khartoum and stated that "The government offers us no recognition. They are coming down hard on us." The sheikh confirmed the livestock theft and subsequent ambush of his tribesmen. Steidle states that the tribesmen "had been burning villages as they tracked their stolen camels".[1229]

Also in November 2004, Steidle's AU team investigated a "Janjaweed" attack on the village of Um Louta. Thirty-four people were said to have been killed in the incident. Steidle interviewed the sheikh of the people said to have been responsible for the attack. He related that the region had always been fairly secure and peaceful but rebels had stolen some of his own livestock. He and his men had tracked down the animals. They were then attacked by gunmen at a water hole outside Um Louta. A prolonged gun battle ensued with the rebels using mortars and heavy machine-guns. Some of the sheikh's men were killed and wounded. They were only able to evacuate their wounded the following day and they were attacked again. In the course of the fighting the village of Um Louta was destroyed. Asked if the "Janjaweed" were involved, the sheikh denied this and said that he did not wish to be associated with them.

In mid-December 2004, Steidle relates that his AU team visited Adwah village to investigate an Arab complaint of stolen cattle. The tribal leader (as always, described by Steidle as a "Janjaweed") reported to the AU that the previous week the SLA had kidnapped and killed several tribesmen and that they had stolen camels and other livestock. The tribal leader also "brought up an incident that reportedly took place either in 2003 or 2004...rebels purportedly stole 1,050 camels and abducted 75 people in an ambush while the nomads were travelling to Libya. The militia leader was furious that the AU had not yet done anything about the situation." He then informed the AU that his tribesmen had tracked the camels from Adwah to Jurof, Hamada and Khor Abeche and he threatened to attack those villages unless they got their camels back, stating: "No one can stop us. You can't stop us."

In another instance, in January 2005, he re-states that Arab tribesmen (yet again dubbed "Janjaweed") had complained to the AU the previous year about the theft of 1,050 camels and the kidnapping of 75 people. The Arab tribesmen had contacted the AU again to report more recent theft of camels. Steidle writes that the Arab leader "repeated his threat: if the rebels didn't return their people and their camels, he would attack Hamada Forest, Khor Abeche, and Muharjeriya. He was prepared to move today but had heard the AU was coming, so he decided to give us one more chance." Steidle then relates how Hamada was subsequently attacked and a large number of people were killed in the fighting.[1230] Steidle also records that there had been an attack on a village called Sanam Al Nanger. He writes that there had been a dispute between tribes over a water-hole on 2 November 2004. A week later, Arab tribesmen attacked and were said to have stolen 300 cattle. The villagers tried to recover their livestock and there was more fighting. On 12 November, there was another attack on the village and more fighting ensued: six people were said to have been killed and many wounded. The local tribal leader stated that he had complained to the police, but had heard nothing: "If we do not receive a response in the next two days, we intend to retaliate."[1231] This fighting between tribal communities – essentially to recover stolen livestock – is somehow magnified by Steidle to qualify as "genocide".

Steidle inadvertently explains away the visceral nature of attempts to recover livestock, admitting the value of camels within Darfur society: "I knew how seriously they took [livestock] theft. There were only a few banks in rural

Sudan, and obviously no opportunities to invest in the stock market. Instead, you bought a cow, and when that cow reproduced, you doubled your money. Camels were even more valuable."

Steidle did actually get see some genuine fighting, namely government forces fighting with SLA insurgents in and around the village of Labado. This was clearly a set-piece engagement involving thousands of government soldiers and militiamen operating with helicopter gunship support. Steidle was able to confirm that there was fighting between the government and SLA, and that Sudanese soldiers had been wounded. He also describes the fighting as evidence that an "all-out war" was in progress and then a few paragraphs later states that the same fighting was "systematic genocide".[1232] For Steidle it appears that any act, whether it is recovering stolen livestock or fighting in a village between soldiers and rebels, constitutes genocide.

Steidle's inclination towards exaggeration and hyperbole continues to unfold in his book. In the course of one of his team's investigations in South Darfur he came across what he says was an al-Qaeda training camp, something that was in reality obviously a Sudanese military training facility. He then also sees an Arab militiaman with a Dragunov sniper rifle and states that seeing this was "as significant as discovering an active al-Qaeda training camp. Someone was seriously investing in these Arab nomads – and the destruction of Darfur's black population."[1233] Perhaps Steidle is unaware that the Dragunov rifle is over forty years old – it first saw service in the Soviet army in 1963. There are literally hundreds of thousands of such rifles in the Third World, and particularly within countries such as Sudan that had historically been equipped with Soviet bloc weapons.

In October 2004, Steidle is told by the SLA that chemical weapons have been used in an attack on a village. As evidence, the SLA handed him an RPG rocket propelled grenade round. Steidle reports that "It had a screw cap on top and looked to me like it could contain a chemical or biological agent, possibly CS gas, commonly called tear gas. I had no idea that the GOS had the capability to use chemical or biological weapons or that it would use them on civilian villages. It just kept on getting worse." The SLA claimed that there had been "gas clouds". [1234] As he makes clear, however, it was obvious that the AU viewed Steidle's naïve claims as not worth progressing.

Steidle's naivety is manifested in other ways. He was quite clearly the recipient of what can only be described as disinformation from "Dan", one of his American embassy "contacts". "Dan" provides Steidle with what he describes as an official-looking document with an English translation. An all too obvious and clumsy forgery, this hand-written document – in the name of "the Light and Frightful Forces of Musteriha" – speaks of alerting all Arab leaders in the whole region of Darfur to implement "the aims of the Arab Coalition in Darfur" in order to "change the demography in Darfur and make it void of any African tribes and face the rebels and destroy them with poisonous weapons". The document called those to whom it was addressed to raise "the Arab Coalition flag". Somewhat conveniently, it recorded that "ninety vehicles have been received equipped with Iranian weapons and munitions and materials for the manufacture of rockets and twenty personnel from the forces who are graduates in preparation [or field] of traditional poisonous [chemical] weapons…" The document also states that "sums of money have been allocated to be transferred to abroad in some Arab countries to destroy the American interest".[1235]

Steidle embraces this "document" with glee: "I couldn't believe what I was holding in my hand. Here was clear evidence of order to commit genocide against the black African tribes of Darfur – from the government – 'to change the demography,' as the directive so clinically put it." He does, however, have the good grace to admit that he was "amazed" that the government had "held a meeting to hand down its strategy for carrying out widespread ethnic cleansing".[1236]

Steidle's book is also useful in the sense that while claiming that the SLA and JEM are freedom fighters, and that they are fighting to protect their communities, in describing the work of his AU team, he inadvertently documents numerous examples of rebel attacks on humanitarian workers in Darfur. He relates an SLA attack in October 2004 on two trucks carrying NGO supplies, including medicines. Interestingly, in describing this attack, Steidle acts an apologist for this behaviour: "The SLA had been known to steal goods to sustain operations."[1237] In another incident, on 1 November, Steidle's team investigated and confirmed an attack by rebels on trucks carrying medical supplies for MSF.[1238] Steidle also documented the attack by SLA rebels on a Save the Children humanitarian convoy north of Nyala. The SLA had murdered two aid workers and stolen four Save the Children vehicles. An AU team recovered the vehicles the following day. Once again Steidle acts as an apologist, this time for murder, by claiming that the SLA commander responsible for this attack was drunk at the time. He was assured by the SLA that the commander had been "executed".[1239] Steidle's team was also able to physically confirm that the SLA had hijacked eleven World Food Program trucks.[1240]

It is worth noting that in a subsequent film documentary based on his book, also called 'The Devil Came on Horseback', released in 2007, Steidle repeats many of his assertions, adding for good measure that the African Union were party to the "genocide". A film reviewer relates, for example, that Steidle "discovered...a united effort by the African Union to completely expel its own people" from Darfur. The film states that Steidle was encouraged by his sister to "share his evidence... that the African Union was in on the genocide". The reviewer acknowledges that "this is not a movie about the complexities of why the genocide, or Darfur conflict (whatever term you want to use), is happening and why the U.S. government isn't taking effective action to stop it. In fact, Steidle (our guide and narrator) is content to call the militant Janjaweed just plain 'evil' and nothing more."[1241]

It is also worth noting that Steidle and his claims have also been treated with scepticism by independent sources. Keith Harmon Snow, an American investigative journalist, human rights researcher and Africa expert, has been blunt in his criticism of Steidle: "The suggestion that Steidle is an objective and impartial observer is ridiculous." Snow has also suggested that: "The Darfur 'mission' of U.S. Marine Brian Steidle offers another perfect example of how information and involvement about the Darfur conflict is turned completely on its head, such that truth becomes lie and lie becomes truth...[Steidle is] a ubiquitous fixture in the U.S. propaganda campaign for Darfur."[1242]

Steidle has also been described by his own colleagues as opportunistic and self-serving. He admits that at least one of his fellow workers in Sudan "thought I was trying to exploit the suffering of the people in Darfur for my own financial gain". He also admitted that he heard that NGOs, the UN and the AU were upset by his behaviour and claims. Steidle also concedes that the American government has discredited his claims.[1243] His claims about Darfur certainly gave him Warhol's "15 minutes of fame": he has lucratively dined out on his

Darfur claims for more than two years and projected his all too naïve claims about Darfur in hundreds of speaking events and interviews.

Steidle's own words provide observers with the scope he has had to present his deeply questionable and self-serving claims about Darfur. It is little wonder that American grass-roots perceptions of Darfur remain as dangerously skewed as they are at present:

> Since Brian's return from Darfur, he has spoken at over 100 public awareness events in communities and at universities across the country, including Harvard, Princeton, Stanford and UCLA. The Save Darfur Coalition sponsored a special speaking tour in Spring 2006 which took Brian 22,000 miles across our nation for over 50 events. Brian has met with U.S. Secretary of State Condoleezza Rice, U.S. Deputy Secretary of State Robert Zoellick, U.S. Ambassador and Alternate Representative to the UN on Special Policy Issues Holliday, and U.S. Ambassador to the UN on War Crimes Prosper. He has spoken before the UN Human Rights Commission, the British House of Commons, the Congressional Black Caucus and the Senate Republican Steering Committee, and he has officially testified before the Human Rights and Africa Subcommittee of the Congressional Foreign Relations Committee. He remains an advisor to numerous NGOs regarding their policies on Darfur.[1244]

Perhaps the kindest explanation for Steidle's claims is that he is naïve and was overwhelmed by events in his first shooting war. He claims to have come across – and survived – al-Qaeda in Darfur, the use of chemical weapons, evidence of Iranian chemical weapon munitions, evidence of an international Arab conspiracy to attack the United States, and, of course, genocide in his five months stay in Darfur. Steidle's naivety once again manifests itself in his avid support for international divestment from the Sudanese economy.[1245]

Steidle admits that his attitude was that of an "idealistic college protestor". Those who know Darfur well will know the danger of such naivety in attempts to describe or resolve Darfur's all too complex problems.

"Not on our Watch": Prendergast and Cheadle

Another of the gratuitously self-serving books to emerge on the Darfur crisis was *Not on Our Watch. The Mission to End Genocide in Darfur and Beyond* by John Prendergast and Don Cheadle.[1246] Prendergast works for the International Crisis Group, and is a former Clinton Administration Africa director. He is also on the executive committee of the Save Darfur Coalition. Cheadle is an American actor who starred in Hotel Rwanda. The book seeks to be the touchstone for Darfur "advocacy" and provides both of the authors a platform for self-congratulation. It is a comic-book approach to a deeply complex crisis.

The somewhat semi-detached way in which Prendergast sees himself is also revealed in the book. He actually compares himself to "The Mighty Thor, Captain America, Batman, Daredevil, and the Silver Surfer...all guys who hated injustice and put their lives on the line for it...I wanted to be like them somehow."[1247] This would also in large part explain why, despite "a number of good arguments" against using the term, Prendergast has chosen to cry genocide in Darfur. For Prendergast the genocide label is self-evidently self-serving. Without "genocide" in Darfur he cannot assume his "Captain America" or "Batman" superhero role.

As a result, the central platform of Prendergast's book is, of course, that genocide is taking place in Darfur. Bearing this in mind it is perhaps unsurprising that the most relevant section of *Not on Our Watch*, the debate about whether there is a genocide in Darfur, is relegated to a footnote. In this footnote Prendergast admits:

> Whether the crimes against humanity committed in Darfur should be regarded as genocide has been the subject of some debate. A United Nations Commission of Inquiry and several reputable research and advocacy organisations – including the International Crisis Group, Human Rights Watch, and Amnesty International – do not use this description. They have a number of good arguments, perhaps best summed up by Gareth Evans, the President and CEO of the International Crisis Group and member of the UN Advisory Panel on Genocide Prevention, who argues that, here, as in a number of other cases, use of the term genocide can be unproductive, non-

productive, and even counter-productive. Unproductive, because there are always lawyers' arguments about whether the legal definition in the UN Commission on the Prevention and Punishment of the Crime of Genocide has been satisfied, and this can be a real distraction from the immediate imperative of protecting the victims of what everyone agrees are crimes against humanity. (The Convention definition requires that certain acts be "committed with intent to destroy, in whole or in part, a national, ethnical, racial, or religious group," and it is extremely hard to establish that element of specific intent to destroy non-Arabs in Darfur.) Non-productive, because, as the U.S. response to Darfur illustrates, even when the term is invoked there is no legal obligation under the genocide convention for countries that use the term to actually do anything. And counter-productive when expectations are raised that a particular situation is genocide, but then lawyers' arguments prevail that some necessary element is missing, as was the case with the UN commission in Darfur: in these circumstances the perpetrators of what are unquestionably mass atrocities or crimes against humanity achieve an utterly unearned propaganda victory. All of this demonstrates that right-thinking people can disagree about the use of the term genocide.[1248]

Despite having clearly admitted that the grounds for labelling the Darfur crisis as genocide are very debatable, Prendergast nonetheless willingly goes down the sensationalistic propaganda route regarding Darfur, given that this is the received wisdom amongst his activist friends, and states that "for us the crisis in Darfur is one that constitutes genocide".[1249]

It is also surprising that Prendergast continues to tout himself as an Africa expert let alone someone qualified to comment on Sudan and Darfur. It is even more surprising that anyone takes him seriously. His track record on all these issues is abysmal. Prendergast served as director of African affairs at the National Security Council during the Clinton Administration and then as special advisor to the American assistant secretary of state for African affairs, Susan Rice. Prendergast's current comments relating to Darfur should be assessed in the light of his record on Sudan and Africa during his time within the Clinton Administration. Prendergast was intimately associated with all of the Clinton Administration's disastrous Africa policies – policies which caused and built upon deadly conflict almost wherever they touched the continent.[1250] It was an African-American Democratic Congresswoman, Cynthia McKinney, a member of the House of Representatives Committee on International Relations and Committee on National Security, who summed up the Clinton Administration's Africa policy during Prendergast's watch in a 1999 letter to President Clinton:

> I feel compelled to report to you that crimes against humanity are being committed…throughout Africa, seemingly with the help and support of your administration. I would suggest to you that U.S. policy in the Democratic Republic of Congo has failed and it is another example of our policy failures across the continent. One only has to point to diplomatic duality in Ethiopia and Eritrea, indecisiveness and ambivalence in Angola, indifference in Democratic Republic of Congo, the destruction of democracy in Sierra Leone, and inflexibility elsewhere on the continent. The result is an Africa policy in disarray, a continent on fire, and U.S. complicity in crimes against humanity….your Africa policy has not only NOT helped to usher in the so-called "African Renaissance," but has contributed to the continued pain and suffering of the African peoples.[1251]

Representative McKinney was one amongst many such critics. The American periodical, *The New Republic*, also observed: "The Clinton administration's Africa policy will probably go down as the strangest of the postcolonial age; it may also go down as the most grotesque…Indeed, confronted with several stark moral challenges, the Clinton administration has abandoned Africa every time: it fled from Somalia, it watched American stepchild Liberia descend into chaos, it blocked intervention in Rwanda…Clinton's soaring rhetoric has posed a problem that his predecessors did not face – the problem of rank hypocrisy…the Clintonites have developed a policy of coercive dishonesty." *The New Republic* pointed out that Africa specialists on Capitol Hill have described the Clinton Administration's dishonesty on Africa as "positively Orwellian".[1252] John Prendergast was at the heart of this flawed analysis, policy failure and dishonesty.[1253]

There is no clearer example of this flawed analysis, policy failure and dishonesty than the Clinton Administration's Sudan policy, policy drafted by Prendergast, including the refusal of Sudan's 1996 offer to extradite Osama bin Laden to the United States.[1254] De Waal has also highlighted Prendergast's poor track record on Africa, pointing out that he had been

> a senior official on African policy in an administration that fired cruise missiles that destroyed a pharmaceutical factory in Khartoum and which endorsed regime change by rebels in both Sudan and Zaire. In the latter case, that regime change happened and ushered in the humanitarian disaster that is the Democratic Republic of Congo today. Do you ever ask yourself what you might have done differently to avert that disaster? [1255]

On Darfur, de Waal has also observed that Prendergast showed a "wanton ignorance about the peace process in Abuja". [1256]

The dangers of taking Prendergast seriously in any of his views, especially when they are on the incredibly complex situation in Darfur are, therefore, self-evident. Having blundered into igniting what has been described as World War Three – the horrific multi-national war within the Democratic Republic of Congo, which has resulted in four million deaths, Prendergast and his calls for western military intervention in Darfur could just as easily plunge the whole Sahel into another Iraqi-type conflagration.

Prendergast's crass arrogance is clearly revealed in *Not on Our Watch*. When he hears that Minni Minawi, the prominent SLA rebel leader, has signed the Darfur Peace Agreement in May 2006, Prendergast dismisses Minawi out of hand: "He's on the other side now. He's becoming a government lackey."[1257] The white, middle-class activist Prendergast thinks that he knows more about how things should happen in Darfur than the leader of one of Darfur's largest rebel groupings, a man who had actually fought a war in Darfur for several years.

As for Cheadle (clearly Robin to Prendergast's Batman superhero persona), given that he is a Hollywood actor, perhaps the best advice he can take is that offered by Clint Eastwood's iconic character Inspector Harry Callahan in 'Magnum Force', "a man's got to know his limitations". He should perhaps focus more on his acting career. It is ironic that Cheadle cites his role in the film Hotel Rwanda – playing the part of hotel manager Paul Rusesabagina – which was set against the backdrop of the Rwandan genocide, as to why he is active on Darfur. The Rwandan president Paul Kagame has subsequently criticised the Oscar-nominated film as inaccurate. He specifically disputed the film's portrayal of Rusesabagina as in any way a hero: "Someone is trying to rewrite the history of Rwanda and we cannot accept it."[1258] Very much the same can be said of Cheadle's involvement in the Darfur issue.

George Clooney: Batman in Darfur?

Unlike Prendergast, George Clooney comes with the advantage of once having actually starred in the role of a comic-book hero, Batman. Clooney has become one of the most visible Hollywood figures calling for the western military invasion of Sudan.[1259] Clooney has been quoted as stating that if NATO or the United Nations did not invade Darfur "I'm not quite sure what they are there for." He apparently realises that American soldiers will not be sent to invade Sudan. He wants someone else's soldiers to do it: "we're going to have to build our alliances and find someone who is willing to do it."[1260]

On the subject of celebrities and Darfur, it is worth repeating Alex de Waal's view on their value: "In Darfur in 1986 I coined the term 'disaster tourists' to refer to the senior aid officials, dignitaries and celebrities who made fleeting visits to famine zones. I found the media circus surrounding those visits rather distasteful, and sometimes the careful posing of stick-thin children, grossly distressed but apathetically silent, frankly obscene. During the 1992 Somali famine my colleague Rakiya Omaar used the phrase "disaster pornography" to describe some of this imagery." De Waal went on to note that "One way of looking at the celebrity issue is a balance sheet. The plus side is more aid resources and political pressure...The minus is an oversimplified and sometimes degrading portrayal of the situation and a stress on outside silver bullets.[1261]

Clooney has stated that "You have to be incredibly well-informed. So, if you're going to go out and talk about poverty or AIDS in Africa or Darfur, you better know your shit. And you better know it better than any of the jackasses that are going to try to somehow make what you're trying to do (look) bad."[1262] Yet he has ignored, or is obvious ignorant of, a plethora of analyses of the Darfur crisis contradicting his flawed stance on Darfur, many from opponents of the Khartoum government. Clooney prefers to say of the Darfur crisis that "it's not a political issue."[1263] (Compare that response to a summary provided by Laurie Nathan, a South African academic and African Union mediator during the Darfur peace talks: "Given the nature of the conflict in Darfur, what was required was a multifaceted plan with objectives, strategies, taskings, and resource allocations not only in relation to the parties in Abuja, but also in relation to Sudan's neighboring states, the people of Darfur, AU and UN headquarters, key AU member states, and the power blocs that comprise the Sudanese state."[1264]) The simple fact is that Clooney has been wrong on Darfur time and time again. Referring specifically to Clooney, de Waal has stated, for example, to with regard to his calls for international intervention, that: "In my view, the focus on bringing UN peacekeepers to Darfur has been a damaging distraction from the central issue of peace...George Clooney's statement to the UN Security Council on September 15 last year [was]...hyperbole. Clooney predicted that millions would die in the absence of peacekeepers and gave a specific date: October 1. It didn't happen... Clooney's prediction of complete collapse of the aid operation and two million dead was a wild exaggeration and simplification."[1265]

It is interesting to note that Clooney's real motivation in his Darfur activities has been challenged by human rights activists such as Nina Shea. Shea, the director of Freedom House's Center for Religious Freedom, has dismissed Clooney's Darfur advocacy as "antics", and as "partisan". She has accused Clooney of "exploiting Darfur" to engage in "Bush bashing". She has further described Clooney as having a "simplistic conception of foreign affairs and diplomacy".

Shea described Clooney's envisaged "solution", a "multi-national" Darfur intervention force, as "preposterous". She also notes that "Clooney's voice was nowhere to be found" during alleged human rights abuses during the war in southern Sudan. Shea asks the question: "Could it be that, since most of those deaths occurred during the Clinton administration, and President Bush took the lead in successfully ending it, Clooney sees no political gain in bringing it up?" Shea has also warned: "He risks betraying the beleaguered people of Darfur and setting a tragic precedent in the process. It is a foolish display by Clooney, but an abundance of wisdom has never been the fault of this self-righteous Hollywood crusader."[1266]

The contradictions of Clooney's position on Darfur are clear. *The Sunday Times* reported that "His one regret is that the Democratic party he has always supported failed to confront the Bush administration in the run-up to the war in Iraq." Clooney says that "The Democrats were scared on Iraq and the truth is they backed themselves into a corner." Clooney was fiercely criticised by the American conservative establishment for not supporting the war in Iraq. "He was scornfully portrayed by Bush supporters as a Hollywood airhead who was not only ignorant of the issues involved but was also somehow jeopardising American security by daring to disagree with the president." [1267]

Speaking of his opposition to the Iraq war, Clooney stated: "All I had done…was say, 'Well, I think we have some questions to ask before we send 150,000 kids to get shot at.'" *The Sunday Times* noted that "he plainly relishes his new status as Hollywood's leading liberal: "Yes, I'm a liberal and I'm sick of it being a bad word…Vietnam was wrong and strip-bombing Cambodia was probably stupid. We've been on the right side of all these issues."

Brendan O'Neill has criticised Clooney's double-standards: "It is striking the extent to which the opponents of the Iraq war are doing exactly the same with Darfur as they attacked Bush for doing with Iraq and more recently Iran; reducing it to a simple black-and-white issue and calling for a moral crusade to make it all better. Bush was lambasted by Clooney, numerous other celebs and media commentators for believing that there was such a thing as good and evil, and that America was good and Saddam was evil…Yet now Clooney declares of Darfur: 'There is only right and wrong.'".[1268]

What is surprising is that while Clooney appears to be commendably sceptical of current American foreign policy entanglements, observing "The truth is, you still have to ask questions. We do have Syria, Iran and North Korea. We've got a lot of other issues and we don't want to have to go into these with an (ideological) agenda, and then fake whatever information we need to back up our agenda again," he has himself failed to ask even the most rudimentary of questions and is pushing for western military intervention in yet another developing Islamic country on the basis of yet more questionable claims by the Bush administration. [1269] He wants tens of thousands of someone else's kids to get shot at. Quite how this sits with his liberal status is unclear.

On the issue of celebrities such as Clooney, de Waal poses the question: "Why do we think it is appropriate for celebrities to have such a high profile in our (western) dealings with African crises? Why do we (Americans and Europeans) think that singers and actors have something useful to say?" His answer is that

> the narrative structure of media coverage of African disaster… follows a folk tale pattern. We have an innocent and helpless victim, a villain (sometimes the weather, sometimes an embodiment of human evil, sometimes even a callous bureaucrat), and a hero— who is a foreign savior bringing a magical solution. We like to believe that a combination of our goodwill, technology and funds will solve their problems. Complicated histories are reduced to simplistic moral stereotypes. We identify with the western celebrity as the personification of our concern. It's often a travesty. If celebrity engagement with Africa becomes the occasion for a more intelligent engagement with the problem at hand, it is a fabulous opportunity. If it makes Africa into a giant screen onto which we (westerners) can project our salvation fairy tales, it's part of the problem. In the American imagination, Darfur is stuck as a simplistic morality tale. It needs to graduate…[1270]

Eric Reeves: The Return of the Ugly American

One of the long-standing anti-Sudan activists who have particularly focused on Darfur has been Eric Reeves, an English teacher at Smith College in Massachusetts. He has been active for some time in a campaign against Sudan. In the course of this campaign Reeves has written dozens of articles making serious allegations about events within Sudan. On examination many of these claims have fallen apart at the seams. Several measured criticisms of Reeves' approach, methodology, and especially the sources he has relied upon for his claims, have been published and republished.[1271] Reeves continues to make, or repeat, serious claims about the situation in Sudan – most recently on Darfur

– without any means of verifying them. He has, for example, made numerous allegations of genocide and ethnic cleansing in Darfur.[1272]

In a deliberate attempt to equate events in Darfur with the horrific case of Rwanda, Reeves has even used the term *genocidaires* in referring to the Sudanese government.[1273] He has claimed that as of January 2005, 400,000 people had died in the Darfur "genocide" – this being almost three times the number of people who are credibly estimated to have died through violence or disease.[1274] In early 2007, he then upped this figure to 500,000.[1275] Reeves' January 2005 figure of 400,000 deaths jumped from his late June 2004 claim that deaths were "already approaching 100,000".[1276] That is to say Reeves claimed that between July and December 2004 over a third of a million civilians died in Darfur – apparently without being documented either by the aid agencies or the many foreign journalists and diplomats in Darfur, at a time when the UN stated conditions were improving and when every reputable news agency was reporting an estimated 70,000 deaths from all causes. Amazingly he made these sorts of assertions while at the same time acknowledging that such claims are based on "second-hand accounts" and "fragmentary" accounts. He has also acknowledged that verification of such claims has been impossible: "There have been virtually no first-hand accounts by journalists, and the observations by humanitarian organizations are necessarily scattered."[1277]

In common with several people who have claimed genocide in Darfur, Reeves has turned a blind eye to any of the reservations made by groups such as Médecins Sans Frontières about such claims. This is particularly disingenuous given that Reeves has repeatedly cited MSF as a credible source on Darfur.[1278] Indeed, he states that it was through Médecins Sans Frontières that he first heard about Sudan.[1279] He cites a "life-changing" conversation with the executive director of MSF as the reason he become involved with Sudan.[1280] Reeves' selectivity with regard to which MSF material he wishes to use, especially if it contradicts his case, is deeply questionable. Despite having previously noted that Médecins Sans Frontières "has performed superbly in the field", Reeves has abruptly turned on MSF, accusing the organisation of being "disingenuous" and that it had made "ignorant and presumptuous statements about the issue of genocide" in Darfur. He dismissed comments by Dr Jean-Hervé Bradol as a "particular disgrace"[1281], presumably because they contradicted his claims.

Given this level of intellectual gerrymandering it is little wonder, therefore, that Reeves has even been criticised, especially on the genocide issue, by other established long-time anti-Sudan activists. In July 2004, for example, Jemera Rone, the Human Rights Watch Sudan specialist – whose work on Sudan has previously been described by Reeves as "assiduously researched", "distinguished", "unsurpassed" and "trenchant"[1282] – publicly asked whether "people like Eric Reeves are abusing the legal term [genocide] to try and rouse people to act?"[1283]

Reeves' credibility on Darfur is questionable across the board. In a 17 December 2004 commentary, for example, Reeves acted as an apologist for the cold-blooded murder by SLA gunmen of two Save the Children (UK) aid workers, in an attack on their clearly marked vehicle, in Darfur on 13 December 2004.[1284] The United Nations special envoy Jan Pronk unambiguously confirmed rebel involvement in these deaths. Reeves, however, claims there were "somewhat conflicting accounts" of the crime. He claims that the "perpetrator was drunk" while admitting this may not be true. He claims that there was "a heated debate…about what to do with the aid workers". Reeves then claims: "The person responsible for shooting the two aid workers…was himself summarily shot and killed by his fellow combatants." All these assertions are untrue. Reeves attempted to downplay the murders by claiming that "the insurgents have shown inadequate discipline, even as they confront appalling provocation." Quite what "appalling provocation" by aid workers helping to keep civilians in Darfur alive justifies cold-blooded murder is not made clear by Reeves. He also queried whether the SLA had been responsible for the October 2004 murder of two other Save the Children aid workers in a land-mine attack. The United Nations confirmed SLA responsibility.[1285] Reeves' attempt to downplay the December 2004 murders as an "action…by a single drunken soldier" is sickening. This rebel attack on aid workers was part of a clear and systematic pattern and follows recent rebel threats against aid workers.[1286] In his January 2005 report on Darfur – and referring to rebel actions – the United Nations Secretary-General reported on what he termed a "new trend" in the pattern of attacks on, and harassment of, international aid workers: "While previous incidents have only been aimed at looting supplies and goods, December has seen acts of murder and vicious assaults on staff, forcing some agencies to leave Darfur."[1287] Reeves has also claimed that there are "no credible reports of rebel attacks on civilians as such". This further attempt to whitewash the atrocious human rights record of the Darfur rebels was breathtaking in its dishonesty.

Far from demonstrating the objectivity, discernment and research skills one would have expected from a Smith College teacher, he has shown crass selectivity. It comes, however, as no surprise. He has previously embraced similarly serious claims about Sudan. In 2000, for example, Reeves accepted at face value outlandish newspaper claims that China was deploying 700,000 soldiers to Sudan to protect Chinese interests in the Sudanese oil project.[1288] Reeves called it an "explosive report" stating "it is highly doubtful that the report comes from thin air, or that important sources are not behind it."[1289] When asked about this allegation, however, the British government stated that "We have no evidence of the presence of any Chinese soldiers in Sudan, let alone the figure of 700,000 alleged in one press report."[1290] Even the Clinton Administration, as hostile as it was to the Sudanese authorities, dismissed the claims, stating that even "the figure of tens of thousands of troops is just not credible based on information available to us".[1291] He has also relied upon dubious sources for some of his other claims about Sudan. These sources have included South African Islamophobes such as Derek Hammond.[1292] Hammond's website has overtly championed the "Christian" fight against "the evil of Islam", referring to the "anti-Christian religion of Islam".[1293] Amazingly enough, given this sort of track record, Reeves has been allowed to write on Sudan in Amnesty International publications.[1294]

In an independent critique of media coverage of Darfur, *Online Journal* has openly criticised Reeves' claims about Darfur, stating that he "may be the major source of disinformation (he calls it 'analysis') about Darfur which is then spread throughout the U.S.A...How curious that the American media latches on to Mr Reeves' one-sided falsehoods by way of presented out-of-context half-truths while at the same time ignoring the dispatches of other journalists, including those who have provided eyewitness accounts."[1295]

War Propaganda

Leaving aside the activities of groups such as the Save Darfur Coalition, which in their own way amounts to war propaganda, the war in Darfur has also seen the sorts of propaganda that is associated with any armed conflict. Propaganda has been a feature of previous conflicts in Sudan, propaganda which has already served to distort perceptions of the Darfur crisis and Sudan.[1296] The Sudanese government has stated that: "Those with their own agendas are trying to give a very sad view of what is happening. The propaganda in the West is trying to exaggerate what is taking place in Darfur."[1297] That the Darfur issue has been enmeshed at least in part in propaganda images and claims is clear. It would be naïve not to factor such a dimension into any study of the crisis. There have been allegations of genocide, ethnic cleansing and the use of chemical weapons in Darfur. Claims, for example, of the use of chemical weapons in the region have unravelled. A prominent conservative German newspaper, *Die Welt*, alleged that the Syrian and Sudanese governments had used chemical weapons against civilians in Darfur.[1298] This claim, although exposed as misinformation, was widely repeated and serves as a further illustration of the propaganda war surrounding Darfur.[1299] It is worth noting that Brian Steidle sought to raise similarly flawed rebel claims of chemical weapon use at roughly the same time. Similarly sensationalistic claims, while serving any number of short-term political goals, complicate and distort an already complex issue.

Much of the propaganda which has come out of the Darfur conflict has emanated from the rebels. Rebel claims across the board have proved to be questionable. As we have seen, rebel claims to be fighting against marginalisation have been contradicted by reputable sources such as Ghazi Suleiman. In November 2004, for example, the SLA initially denied any involvement in the November attacks in north Darfur, claiming that Khartoum's claims were "totally erroneous".[1300] The international community was in a position to verify the rebels' complicity and the UN, USA, Britain and others roundly condemned the attacks, stating they had once again clearly violated the cease-fire agreement.[1301] Even day-to-day assertions such as the SLA's January 2004 claim to have shot down three Apache helicopter gunships have shown their unreliability.[1302] That Khartoum had a fleet of Apache attack helicopters would have come as news to the American government who have strictly controlled purchases of the Apache helicopter: Apaches have not yet even been fully deployed by the British army. The *Die Welt* "chemical weapons" propaganda story outlined above was sourced back to the SLA.[1303] Flint has also documented rebel disinformation. In 2007, she reported that following a helicopter gunship attack on a village in North Darfur, she was contacted by "a faction of the rebel Sudan Liberation Army…[who] put out a statement alleging that the attack had killed 26 civilians, including four pregnant women". She was contacted shortly after by a rebel humanitarian coordinator who stated that the real death toll was three.[1304]

Interventionism, Naiveté and Double Standards

Perhaps the most disturbing aspect about the Save Darfur advocates is their naiveté. Samantha Power is a case in point. A journalist and Harvard University academic, she is the author of *A Problem from Hell: America and the Age of Genocide*, often taken as a text by interventionists within the United States. Power has taken centre stage with the Save Darfur movement in claiming genocide in Darfur and calling for military intervention. Her credibility – outside of the Washington Beltway at least – is very questionable. A critique of her book – and thereby also her stance – has revealed the weakness of her intellectual stance:

> In order to make her case that the U.S. is derelict in its duty to stop genocide Ms. Power presents a warped and decontextualized version of events…omitting key facts and distorting others. Events are reduced to simple tales of bad leaders who do bad things and need to be stopped or countered by the U.S. and its allies…the reader is left with a wildly flawed but typically American view of the designated enemy as 'irrational' or 'evil,' with war as a positive thing or at least the lesser evil. Most disturbing is Power's refusal to deal honestly with the crimes of the United States and hold her government to an equal level of accountability as the various enemy states she decries…[her book] is an attempt to obscure the real problem from hell: Western intervention.[1305]

Power's apparent ability to wish untold misery on Third World civilians is manifest. When asked, for example, if the intervention in Sudan that she sought might risk *jihad*, Power stated "I think so."[1306] That is to say Power is clear that the action she calls for might reduce Darfur – and Sudan – to the horrific state of Iraq or Afghanistan, but it must proceed regardless, all in the name of flawed academic theory. Nowhere is her naiveté more telling than in her testimony before the US House of Representatives that a 10,000 strong intervention force would suffice in Darfur [1307] when contrasted with the statement by UN High Commissioner for Refugees Antonio Guterres that even a force of 100,000 peacekeepers could not secure peace in the Darfur region: "Even if you have 100,000 policemen in Darfur, they will not be able to cover the whole territory... Without peace, there is no miracle. No security force will be able to guarantee security in the whole of Darfur. Darfur is very big".[1308] A case of an ivory tower bumping up against Darfurian realities could not be clearer. The journalist Paul de Rooij's comments about the academics who call for war are also relevant: "The neocon chickenhawks are best known for urging the US military to go to war while they remained safely ensconced in their think tanks. The leftists or Liberals who have jumped on the humanitarian war bandwagon engage in very much the same hypocrisy. When anyone today prescribes 'intervention', they are really only urging the military of their state to attack other countries, while they themselves are sitting pretty. Someone else will die for the positions they propound."[1309]

Brendan O'Neill has summed up criticisms of the Darfur advocacy movement: "Many campaigners and writers in the West have cynically and opportunistically turned Darfur into 'Our Mission'. They have done this through propaganda and deed. Propagandistically, they insist that the conflict is a simple case of African savages trying to wipe out African victims, and they have exaggerated the current scale of the suffering to suit the purposes of their own Heroes vs New Nazis morality tale. Increasingly, commentary on Darfur is not intended to clarify what is happening there but rather to indulge and flatter readers' sense of self-serving anger. Indeed, campaigners and writers have demanded Western military action to end a conflict that has actually been in decline since 2005 (although there have been renewed outbursts in recent months); and now they have got what they wanted, in the shape of the 26,000-strong UN force. Every bit as cynically as the Bush administration's intervention in Iraq, these activists have sought to turn someone else's country and conflict into outlets for their own moral self-gratification."[1310]

The American public should step back from the precipice to which the various Darfur advocacy groups have led them. They would do well to heed the advice of Ambassador Joseph Wilson, the man central to the unravelling of the Bush administration disinformation about Iraqi weapons of mass destruction and Africa. Speaking of the pressure from the Bush White House to invade Iraq, Wilson warned his fellow Americans: "Democracy asks us, requires us, to be engaged with issues, to become involved and not to accede to the loudest voices without questioning them."[1311] It would also serve the American public well to question at least some of the motivation of groups such as the Save Darfur Coalition.

Chapter Eleven

THE INTERVENTION DEBATE

[western military intervention in Sudan is] a fantasy that draws on the neocon vision that got us into Iraq

Stephen Morrison, Center for Strategic and International Studies[1312]

The idea of foreign troops fighting their way into Darfur and disarming the Janjaweed militia by force is sheer fantasy.

Alex de Waal, [1313]

Madness in great ones must not unwatch'd go.

Hamlet, Act III, Scene 1

The most benign reading of President Bush's predicament regarding Darfur would see him as a victim of his own propaganda. Having labelled events in Darfur as genocide for its own domestic reasons, the Bush administration then found itself under more and more domestic pressure to "do something" from an "anti-genocide" lobby within the United States that has taken on a life of its own. That something has become "intervention". Less benign interpretations would see President George Bush's drive for intervention in Darfur as yet another attempt to destabilise another Muslim country with massive oil reserves. While the sort of Iraq-style intervention demanded by anti-Sudanese constituencies, and echoed by the Bush administration, has not come about, as a result of American pressure, the Sudanese government has nevertheless agreed to accept the augmentation of the already present African Union, AMIS, peace-keeping force with UN forces. The resultant hybrid AU-UN force has been designated the African Union-United Nations Hybrid

311

Operation in Darfur (UNAMID) by the UN Security Council by its resolution 1769 of 31 July 2007.

The Bush administration's lobbying for an international Western-led intervention is a matter of record. In early February 2006, Washington called for a straight UN military intervention in Darfur to replace the African Union peacekeeping force that had been in place since 2004.[1314] On 19 February, Bush specifically urged a NATO-led UN military intervention in Darfur, in western Sudan. He called for "NATO stewardship, planning, facilitating, organizing" together with "double the number of peacekeepers that are there now". A Pentagon official confirmed that NATO would play a significant lead in any such intervention.[1315] Several days later Bush personally telephoned NATO's Secretary-General Jaap de Hoop Scheffer to discuss the issue. US Senator Joseph Biden demanded: "NATO must deploy troops."[1316] Bush also pressed the former French President Jacques Chirac on NATO intervention[1317] During its presidency of the UN Security Council in early 2006, the United States avidly supported UN military intervention in Darfur. The US Ambassador to the UN, John Bolton, admitted that the US was alone in doing so: "Right now, we're probably farther out front in advocating that than any of the council members and so be it."[1318] In April 2006, Washington again raised the issue of NATO intervention. *The Washington Post* reported that "The move would include some U.S. troops and mark a significant expansion of U.S. and allied involvement in the conflict."[1319] Responding to US pressure, the then UN Secretary-General, Kofi Annan, also called for intervention and asked for US troops to form part of any Darfur UN force.[1320]

Some contradictions should be noted in passing. The Bush administration's calls for a UN intervention in Darfur jar with its marked reluctance for UN forces to be deployed in similar circumstances such as Lebanon and Timor.[1321] Similarly, while calling for a UN military force in Darfur, Kofi Annan said that a similar force would not be appropriate in Chad and the Central African Republic until all parties agree to a ceasefire and start talks aimed at a political solution.[1322]

In examining calls for military intervention in Darfur, several issues must be addressed. First, and foremost, is the justification put forward for any such action. Secondly, without necessarily being too cynical, establishing the real motivations for intervention. Thirdly, the feasibility of an intervention. And, fourthly, the probable consequences of any such action within Darfur itself, Sudan, the Sahel region and internationally.

Justifying Intervention

The first issue is dealt with quite easily. As is clearly demonstrated by the claims and activities of groups such as the Save Darfur coalition, any such military action would be to stop "genocide" in Darfur, coupled to claims that up to 500,000 civilians had been killed in Darfur. The *casus belli* – that genocide was underway in Darfur – has turned out to be false, and has fatally weakened any moral justification for military intervention of the sort advocated by the Bush administration. Many intolerable things have happened in Darfur, but genocide is not amongst them. It has also been shown that the mortality claims being made by Save Darfur have proved to be false, and that the upper end estimate is that perhaps between 140,000 and 200,000 people may have died from all causes in Darfur.

These attempts to justify Western military intervention have, in any case, been widely challenged as inconsistent. Commentators have pointed out that perhaps as many as five million civilians have been killed or died as the result of ethnic violence in the Democratic Republic of Congo since the late 1990s.[1323] A conservative estimate, by the International Rescue Committee, published in *The Lancet* in early 2006, stated that 3.9 million people had died, a death toll which equates to 38,000 per month.[1324] Others have cited monthly mortality rates of 77,000 deaths.[1325] The UN has estimated a monthly death rate of one thousand people.[1326] John O'Shea, chief executive of Irish relief agency GOAL, has stated that the DRC was "the worst humanitarian tragedy since the Holocaust. The greatest example on the planet of man's inhumanity to man."[1327] Jan Egeland, the UN humanitarian affairs chief, stated in November 2003, that the war in northern Uganda was "the biggest forgotten, neglected humanitarian emergency in the world today."[1328] He subsequently declared that the DRC is "experiencing perhaps the worst humanitarian crisis in the world for several years."[1329] In March 2005, AlertNet, the Reuters Foundation's humanitarian webservice, published the results of a poll of humanitarian professionals as to which humanitarian emergencies deserved the most attention. The Sudan (south and west) came third behind the DRC and

Congo.[1330] Iraq can also clearly be added to the list above Sudan. *The Lancet* subsequently published a mortality study, for example, which stated that there may have been as many as 655,000 excess deaths since the US invasion of Iraq in March 2003.[1331] This figure has been extrapolated and updated by academics who have arrived at a figure of a million excess deaths among Iraqis.[1332] In November 2007, top UN officials declared Somalia to be the world's worst humanitarian crisis, stating that the country had higher malnutrition rates, more bloodshed and fewer aid workers than Darfur.[1333] If suffering from a humanitarian crisis is justification for military intervention, Darfur comes somewhat down the list. The simple fact is that the Darfur crisis, with a monthly death figure of 100-200 people, pales into relative insignificance when compared to the situation in the DRC, where a thousand civilians die per day, or Somalia.

There has also been a growing realisation, even within neo-conservative groupings in the United States, that several claims about Darfur are questionable. This is the view, for example, of Christopher Caldwell, a senior editor at *The Weekly Standard*. He warns that "Darfur is a problem the west should touch only with a very long stick...Americans may have enough patience to unravel the misadventure in Iraq, but they are not calling for an encore." Caldwell argues that Bush's description of Darfur as "genocide" was a mistake:

> The pictures being evoked in western minds are oversimplifications. Darfur is not just sadists on one hand and victims on the other. It is a war. We have only the vaguest picture of what kind of war it is. Is it a race war, pitting the Arabs of Khartoum against the blacks of Darfur? Is it a civil war over money and natural resources? (The rebels, too, have looted aid convoys and clashed with African Union peacekeepers.) Is Khartoum running a classic, Guatemalan-style, dry-up-the-fishpond counter-insurgency?

Motivations for Intervention

The real motivation for military intervention in Darfur is more difficult to assess. There are without doubt ideologically based constituencies within the United States, and to a much lesser extent elsewhere, for whom regime change in Sudan has been a long-standing objective. For these groups the 2005 comprehensive peace agreement ending Sudan's long-running north-south civil war was an unwelcome diversion from their goal of attacking, weakening and overthrowing the Sudanese government, the world's first modern Islamic republic. Darfur has provided these anti-Sudanese groups – and the anti-Sudan industry that has grown up around them – with a very convenient weapon with which to pursue their goals. For these groups, an international military intervention, preferably by NATO forces, would inevitably be opposed by the Sudanese government, which in turn would be removed from office – as happened in Iraq. Even if this were possible, the consequences of such a course of action are clear, as pointed out by Stephen Morrison, the Africa specialist at the prestigious Center for Strategic and International Studies in Washington-DC, who noted "[western military intervention in Sudan is] a fantasy that draws on the neocon vision that got us into Iraq". He also conveniently points to the ideological stable motivating these calls for military action.

It is a matter of record, however, that the very same people who headed the Project for the New American Century (PNAC), which provided the intellectual primer for the invasion of Iraq, have advocated similar action against Sudan.[1334] In September 2004, PNAC chairman, William Kristol, called for American troops to intervene in Darfur. He stated that if there is to be regime change in Sudan, "The United States will eventually act on Darfur…Washington must be a leader in the effort…the coalition of the willing that goes into Sudan is going to have to be largely organized, sustained and financed by the United States, most likely without a U.N. mandate."[1335] Another of the key (former) neo-conservative thinkers, Francis Fukuyama, has also advocated the sort of intervention that resulted in the Iraqi disaster, demanding that "Washington…make it clear that if Sudan refuses to accept a United Nations force, we will press NATO to act even without the consent of the Sudanese government – including a no-flight zone…And we would bring further sanctions to bear."[1336]

It is a matter of fact that the Bush administration had planned to invade Sudan well before having the pretext of a humanitarian intervention in Darfur. General Wesley Clark, the Supreme Allied Commander of NATO during the Kosovo war, and unsuccessful candidate for the Democratic Party's presidential nomination in 2004, revealed the existence of plans for military action during an interview in early 2007. Clark stated that during a visit to the Pentagon in October 2001, a US army general showed him a memorandum he had just received from the Secretary of Defense's office, explaining that "This is a memo that describes how we're going to take out seven countries in five years, starting with Iraq, and then Syria, Lebanon, Libya, Somalia, Sudan and, finishing off, Iran." Clark asked if the document was classified. The officer said "Yes, sir".[1337] The extent to which those plans are still on the table and being molded around the Darfur crisis is unclear.

There are also those constituencies for whom any action which would damage, destabilise or demonise an Islamic country, and particularly one with an Islamist party in power, is welcome. Neo-conservative groupings have long advocated "strategic chaos" as a strategy, encouraging political confusion, disorder, and fluidity within targeted parts of the developing world in the belief that a new and better dispensation would emerge: the Iraqi fiasco has been a result. The continuing chaos in the Palestinian territories is another case in point. Moving beyond the Palestinian situation, it is also a matter of record that Israel has pursued a similar policy of encouraging instability both within and around the Arab world, and in so doing for example supporting both Kurdish and southern Sudanese insurgents. It would be naïve not to believe that forces within Israel continue with this policy. For these groups and activists any continuing destabilisation – up and including regime change – serves any number of strategic and tactical purposes. Take, for example, the comments made by prominent American anti-Muslim activist Daniel Pipes about the bombing of the Askariya shrine in Samarra in Iraq February 2006: "[this] was not an American or a coalition tragedy. Iraq's plight is neither a coalition responsibility nor a particular danger to the West. Fixing Iraq is neither the coalition's responsibility, nor its burden. When Sunni terrorists target Shi'ites and vice versa, non-Muslims are less likely to be hurt. *Civil war in Iraq, in short, would be a humanitarian tragedy, but not a strategic one.*"[1338] (Emphasis added.) Continuing conflict in Darfur or renewed civil war within Sudan would not be strategically unwelcome to activists such as Pipes or the sorts of constituencies his views represent.

The Financial Times, in seeking to explain the Bush Administration's intelligence failure regarding Iraq, noted that: "For too long, they have allowed their information to be driven by both ideology and Israeli intelligence sources."

Warning about current American policy, the newspaper cautions, "The same danger looms today over US policy – or rather, non policy – towards Iran. If that goes wrong, and leads to the same inexorable spiral of sanctions and military action, it could prove far more costly than the war in Iraq."[1339] Exactly the same can be said about American policy towards Sudan on Darfur.

There have been other schools of thought which have sought to contextualise the Bush Administration's push for western military intervention in Darfur. The Bush Administration's policy of demonising Sudan with regard to Darfur has been seen as cynically self-serving in several ways, apart from appeasing domestic political constituencies. There is an increasing realisation that the American government is very interested in the large reserves of oil (and other strategic resources) that are said to be present in Darfur and Sudan. This particular line of argument would claim that the American government has deliberately highlighted the Darfur crisis, encouraging some of the rebel groups to continue the war and describing events as genocide in an attempt to prepare the ground for an international intervention that would result in a Kosovo-isation of Darfur or even a western occupation of Sudan. Sudan would then be dismembered into several smaller states in order to make the acquisition of oil concessions easier. American oil companies and interests would then be allowed in to Darfur and Sudan to exploit the oil wealth in the same way as US oil companies have done so in Iraq, and in so doing displacing Chinese involvement in the Sudanese oil industry. It is a matter of record that the Sudanese authorities believe this to be a factor. President al-Bashir has commented that "There are some invisible hands that continue to manipulate the question of Darfur for tearing up the unity of Sudan in preparation for controlling and looting its resources."[1340] President Bashir's concerns are shared by other developing world leaders such as the Libyan leader, Moamar Khaddafi, who has said that the Darfur issue is a western ruse to grab Sudan's oil.[1341]

The Pentagon has made Africa's strategic importance to the United States very clear: "Africa is...of strategic value to the U.S. as a supplier of energy; by 2015 it will supply 25 to 40 percent of our oil." US General Charles F. Wald has admitted the extent of Washington's dependency on African oil: "We import more oil from Africa than the Middle East – probably a shock to a lot of people – and that share will grow."[1342] Veteran American Africa researcher, Keith Harmon Snow, has been blunt in his explanation of American interest in

Darfur: "People need to know they are being lied to [in regard to Darfur]...Sudan and the Darfur region have a lot of oil, and it has two-thirds of the world's supply of high-quality gum Arabic. Corporations such as Coke, Pepsi, and Pfizer rely on cheap supplies of gum Arabic.[1343] The mass media and Hollywood are fooling the public about what's really happening in Sudan."[1344]

That the Bush administration is obsessed with energy issues is clear. Many observers have stated that the 2003 invasion of Iraq was merely an attempt to establish American control over one of the Middle East's biggest oil reserves. Even key politicians in countries allied to the United States have linked the invasion to oil. The senior British Labour party politician and former environment minister, Michael Meacher, has stated that the reason for the American invasion of Iraq was "was principally, totally and comprehensively to do with oil". Meacher said: "The reason they attacked Iraq is nothing to do with weapons of mass destruction, it was nothing to do with democracy in Iraq, it was nothing to do with the human rights abuses of Saddam Hussein."[1345] That the Americans have been willing to project military force to secure oil reserves is self-evident. That this has been disastrous for Iraq – the region, and internationally – is also self-evident. The American neo-conservative magazine, *The Weekly Standard*, has noted that American foreign policy is perceived as being focused on energy supplies and not much else: "Much of the Muslim world believes the US attacked Afghanistan for its natural gas reserves, not because of 9/11."[1346] Even before the war began, *The Washington Post* noted that "a U.S.-led ouster of Iraqi President Saddam Hussein could open a bonanza for American oil companies long banished from Iraq, scuttling oil deals between Baghdad and Russia, France and other countries, and reshuffling world petroleum markets, according to industry officials and leaders of the Iraqi opposition."[1347]

Referring to international military intervention in Yugoslavia, and that the US had artificially prolonged the conflict there, *Monthly Review* editor Yoshie Furuhashi has stated that "It's the same dynamics in Sudan . . . except the prize this time is more valuable than territories: 'Sudan has proven reserves of some 563 million barrels of oil, with the potential for far more in regions of the country made inaccessible by conflict (Esther Pan, 'China, Africa, and Oil,' Council on Foreign Relations, 12 January 2006). Putting an end to the Darfur conflict now would consolidate Beijing's dominant position in Sudan's oil industry…Who wants peace in Darfur? Certainly not Washington . . . at least till it gets its share of black gold."[1348]

There is no doubt that there are untapped oil reserves in Darfur itself – in addition to the huge proven reserves in other parts of Sudan. An Alert Net article, which reported on the presence of oil in Darfur, has asked the obvious question: "Whether oil will give a motive for warring parties to speed up moves towards peace or make the conflict even harder to solve." Mike Aaronson, director general of British NGO Save the Children, has commented that "The issue of oil in Darfur isn't very different from the issue of oil anywhere else. It's potentially a tremendous blessing, and potentially a tremendous handicap. It's not without reason that people talk about the oil curse. The reality is that many countries that have the greatest mineral wealth are also the ones with the conflicts."[1349]

The feasibility of intervention

Calls for military intervention in Darfur must be evaluated in the light of the feasibility of such action. Dr Jean-Hervé Bradol, the President of Médecins Sans Frontières, is sceptical in general of any such action: "[S]upport for the genocide argument implies the belief that the permanent members of the Security Council have the resolve and power to put an end to the most serious crimes all over the planet…the naivety of this position is astounding."[1350]

The former UN Special Envoy to Sudan, Jan Pronk, has been very critical of the US calls for intervention. It was reported that he had criticised Western diplomacy with regard to Sudan as "lacking intelligence". Pronk condemned Washington's call for NATO-led UN intervention as a misbegotten idea that would infuriate all Muslims because of the association with events in Afghanistan and Iraq. He stated that "Western diplomacy is indeed extremely foolish at this moment."[1351]

Even if the action was limited to Darfur itself, and did not expand outside of the region, it is not practical. Alex de Waal has been particularly blunt about this: "Those who are clamouring for troops to fight their way into Darfur are suffering from a salvation delusion. It's a simple reality that UN troops can't stop an ongoing war, and their record at protecting civilians is far from perfect."[1352] De Waal also warns of the consequences of such an intervention:

> The knock-down argument against humanitarian invasion is that it won't work. The idea of foreign troops fighting their way into Darfur and disarming the Janjaweed militia by force is sheer fantasy. Practicality dictates that a peacekeeping force in Darfur cannot enforce its will on any resisting armed groups without entering into a protracted and unwinnable counter-insurgency in which casualties are inevitable. The only way peacekeeping works is with consent: the agreement of the Sudan government and the support of the majority of the Darfurian populace, including the leaders of the multitudinous armed groups in the region. Without this, UN troops will not only fail but will make the plight of Darfurians even worse.[1353]

The Weekly Standard's Christopher Caldwell has been similarly cautious about the practicality of the numbers of troops necessary for such an action:

> The number of troops necessary to pacify Darfur is often placed at 20,000, with only 5,000 elite western troops necessary to do the "heavy lifting"...These numbers may be wild underestimates...However humanitarian their motivations, though, military operations turn political the moment they are launched, with consequences that are wildly unpredictable.[1354]

The United Nations has itself acknowledged that even a force of 100,000 peacekeepers could not secure peace in Darfur.[1355]

Julie Flint has also pointed out the impracticality of military intervention in Darfur itself, both in forces and commitment needed:

> Those who advocate a Chapter VII solution should ask themselves just how many troops will be needed to return two and a quarter million people – internally displaced persons and refugees – to their homes in the absence of agreement and in the face of opposition from Janjaweed forces who began hiding their weapons after the

first cease-fire agreement the government signed almost two years ago. To protect the people of Darfur and get them home will require far, far more troops than anyone is currently prepared to offer or fund. Even if powerful countries put their money where their mouth is – and there is little sign of that at present – it is highly improbable that any force, whether UN, NATO, or AU, or a combination of all three, will be able to do anything but keep a peace that is agreed between the parties. [1356]

It is clear that the Sudanese government vigorously opposes any such intervention. Sudan has repeatedly stated its opposition to any UN military intervention in Darfur, noting in February 2006, for example, that "Government consent is an essential precondition for taking any such a move by the world organization."[1357] The Government of National Unity restated its opposition later that month.[1358] Sudan's President has also noted: "We have witnessed what happened in Iraq and Afghanistan and learned lessons that shouldn't be repeated on the African continent." He restated Sudan's commitment to the AU mission: "We will spare no effort to create the conducive atmosphere for the African Union mission to carry out its task until we reach a negotiated comprehensive settlement in Darfur in the very near future."[1359] It is clear that even Sudanese opposition groups are hostile to UN intervention in Darfur. While making clear that they were opposed to Khartoum's Darfur policies, anti-government National Democratic Alliance (NDA) parliamentarians also rejected the presence of UN forces in Darfur.[1360]

The sheer scale of military intervention that would be necessary should Khartoum oppose such an action is colossal. In June 2004, in a report to the UN Security Council, the then UN secretary-general Kofi Annan set out the scale of challenge in Sudan were the UN to intervene. Annan pointed out that Sudan is 35 times larger than Sierra Leone, which had been the focus of one of the largest UN peacekeeping operations in the world, involving 17,000 troops and costing several billion dollars. The BBC reported: "Mr Annan did not make the calculation, but the implication was clear. If it took 17,000 troops to pacify Sierra Leone – where there was also a signed peace agreement – might it therefore take 35 times that number, or some 600,000, to do the same thing in Sudan?"[1361]

MSF's Bradol and Weissman have also clearly warned about the danger of any military action resulting in a state of war with the Sudanese government:

> According to African Union and United Nations military experts, it would take a lot more than the 20,000 blue helmets called for under Security Council Resolution 1706 to reestablish order and prevent new killings—assuming, of course, that the parties to the conflict accept this deployment. That is not the case, however, as the Sudanese government is opposed. Ignoring its refusal would mean invading western Sudan or, in other words, declaring war on the Sudanese government, without any assurance that such an action would enhance civilian safety. [1362]

They also note that:

> An international intervention in Darfur presents tougher problems than in Kosovo, East Timor and Sierra Leone. Those were small areas, held by well-identified armed groups, and the overwhelming majority of the people living there agreed to foreign intervention. An invasion of western Sudan could end in a bloodbath that would include civilians, like Operation Restore Hope in Somalia (1992) and Operation Iraqi Freedom. [1363]

Calls for intervention have also focused on demands for a "no-fly zone" over Darfur. General Henri Bentegeat, the head of the European Union's top military body coordinating the defence policy of the bloc's 27 members, dismissed American-backed proposals for such a "no-fly zone". The Bush Administration had proposed the idea in April 2007 and Britain urged the UN Security Council to impose a no-fly zone on Sudan as part of sanctions including broadening an arms ban.[1364] Bentegeat stated that such a plan was unfeasible: "A no-fly zone is technically impossible. Darfur is around the same size as France. You would need at least 60 combat aircraft [in order] to enforce it correctly. And there would be the question of distinguishing between helicopters." Bentegeat warned of possibly lethal confusion between Sudanese,

U.N. and other aircraft.[1365] This is a point that has also been taken up by humanitarian aid agencies and non-governmental organisations. De Waal, for example, states that "a no-fly zone is inefficient, nearly pointless, and almost sure to be counterproductive—and there are other options worth trying…air attacks have never been the most important element in the government's war…They kill a lot more livestock than they do human beings. There are no reliable figures for fatalities from air attacks this year, but it is likely that they number in the dozens."[1366] Flint has noted that "Aid agencies are quietly but unanimously appalled by the prospect of a no-fly zone." Aid organisations were concerned that their flights would inevitably be grounded in a region dependent on aid delivered by air. She went on to observe: "Today, stopping military flights wouldn't make much of a difference to the Darfuri people…The humanitarian's first obligation is to do no harm. Talk of coercive military action must end. A no-fly zone would be recklessly dangerous and would not address the real problems in Darfur. To endanger the region's humanitarian lifeline is not simply wrong-headed. It is inhumane."[1367] There is also a clear double-standard at play with regard to calls for no-fly zones. Enforcing a no-fly zone is extremely expensive and have been made at the same time as it has become self-evident that the AU peacekeeping mission in Darfur has been chronically under funded.

It is clear, however, that the American body politic is still in grip of powerful anti-Sudan and pro-intervention constituencies. This was reflected in the positions taken by Democratic Party presidential candidates during debates in 2007. Senator Joe Biden, for example, urged direct US military intervention, stating that 2,500 American soldiers would be enough to "stop the genocide". He also called for a no-fly zone. While not supporting the idea of US troops on the ground, Senator Hilary Clinton endorsed a no-fly zone. Senators Chris Dodd and Barack Obama have also backed such a call.

The suitability of the United Nations

In the absence of its preferred options of a US or NATO intervention in Darfur, the Bush administration has pushed for a UN intervention. The very suitability of the United Nations, however, to carry out any intervention or peacekeeping function is itself in question. It is puzzling, for example, that Washington is currently pushing the UN into an intervention in Darfur given the Bush administration's studied disdain – and that of its neo-conservative supporters – for the organisation. Francis Fukuyama, for example, has noted that:

> The conservative critique of the United Nations is all too cogent…the United Nations lacks both democratic legitimacy and effectiveness in dealing with serious security issues. The solution is not to strengthen a single global body, but rather to promote what has been emerging in any event, a 'multi-multilateral word' of overlapping and occasionally competing international institutions that are organized on regional or functional lines.[1368]

To start with there is the simple fact that the United Nations, and particularly the Security Council, is not perceived to be a politically neutral force. It is seen in Sudan, on the Arab street – and throughout much of the developing world – as being an instrument of American foreign policy. The recent war in Lebanon, and the UN Security Council's delay in calling for a ceasefire in order to give Israeli forces more time to engage with Hezbollah, is a case in point. The BBC reported that UN Secretary-General Kofi Annan criticised the UN's failure to act sooner to end fighting in Lebanon. He said the widely perceived delay in drafting a resolution had "badly shaken" global faith in the UN.[1369] This is a point also made by Alvaro de Soto, the former UN special representative for the Middle East Peace Process. He resigned his post in May 2007 in protest at the way in which the UN Secretariat had become an uncritical instrument for American and Israeli policies in the Middle East.[1370] That the UN was no longer seen as neutral in conflict zones was also admitted by Mark Malloch-Brown, the former UN deputy secretary-general under Kofi Annan.[1371] The former UN Special Envoy to Sudan, Jan Pronk, has also admitted that the US government circumvented the UN Security Council in the debate about the invasion of Iraq.[1372]

The UN's ability to carry out any military or peacekeeping mission in Darfur is itself also in question. The Department of Peacekeeping Operations may simply not up to the job required of it. Lee Feinstein of the New York-based Council on Foreign Relations has stated that "They are simply not equipped to do it. That's not to disparage them. That is the result of the deliberate choices of the [UN] membership." Reuters has also reported that "recently, U.N. and U.S. investigators last year began looking into possible corruption in the purchase of millions of dollars of goods for peacekeeping missions".[1373]

In March 2006, *The Economist* noted that the UN's international peacekeeping capacity was already severely compromised. A study by New York University's Center of International Co-operation has also warned that a new mission in Darfur could take the UN's peacekeeping efforts "past the point of overstretch".[1374] This has been admitted by the UN's head of peacekeeping, Jean-Marie Guéhenno. Speaking in late 2006, he observed: "When I think of the scope of what we are doing, with 18 different situations, I think we are badly overstretched."[1375] It has also been estimated that a UN Darfur peacekeeping force would cost up to $1.7 billion per year at a time that the UN is experiencing funding difficulties.[1376] It is also a matter of fact that the UN's deployment of peacekeepers within southern Sudan – to assist with the implementation of the CPA – fell behind schedule. In 2005, for example, it took nine months to get just two-fifths of the peacekeeping force deployed in the south. Delays have continued. These concerns were echoed by Bruce Jones, the co-director of the Center on International Cooperation and the series editor of the *Annual Review of Global Peace Operations 2006*:

> Such missions also put a strain on the greatly stretched headquarters staff. Whereas NATO, now running three peace operations worldwide, has about 1,000 military planners, the U.N. has 18 missions and 157 planners. It is not surprising that internal U.N. investigations have found evidence of serious corruption affecting peacekeeping finances. Where there is overstretch, there is limited oversight – and effective oversight is crucial. More seriously, the will and resources of U.N. member-states are being tested. In 2005, the mission to Sudan took nine months to get just two-fifths of its authorized strength on the ground. When the U.N. Secretariat requested an extra 3,000 troops for Congo later that year, the proposal was rejected.[1377]

The UN has had to investigate hundreds of allegations that its peacekeepers have been involved in sexual abuse and sexual exploitation in the course of missions ranging from Bosnia and Kosovo through to Cambodia, East Timor and West Africa. Over two hundred incidents alone were reported in the Democratic Republic of the Congo.[1378] UN forces already deployed on peacekeeping duties in southern Sudan have become embroiled in sex scandals involving the rape and abuse of children.[1379] There have been almost no prosecutions as a result of these sex crimes. There have also been a number of allegations of UN involvement in the killing of civilians in the course of peacekeeping operations, most recently in the DRC and Haiti.[1380]

There are a number of possible consequences of international military intervention in Darfur. If the intervention takes place without a peace in place – a peace to keep – any military "peacekeeping" action will inevitably be drawn into conflict, a conflict which will not be limited to Darfur or even Sudan as a whole. To think otherwise is to repeat the American delusion that their invasion forces in Iraq would be welcomed by cheering crowds. It is an unavoidable fact that even a debate about intervention is ultimately counterproductive from the point of view of peace – all it does is strengthen the resolve of rebels to wait it out until an international military force engages their enemies.

It is also unclear in what way any UN intervention force would differ from the present African Union mission in Darfur in terms of the circumstances it would encounter. Those outsiders who think that a UN military presence would provide the knights in shining armour needed for Darfur, or that they would necessarily be effective in that role are deeply unrealistic. The track record of UN intervention and peacekeeping in Africa is not a good one.

In his study of international intervention in Sierra Leone in the late 1990s, for example, Damien Lewis provides a clear insight into the short-comings of the United Nations peacekeeping operation in that country. The United Nations Mission in Sierra Leone (UNAMSIL), then the biggest UN peacekeeping mission to date, was described by Lewis as a "multinational peacekeeping force that had been made to look hopelessly foolish and incompetent by the rebel forces…More than a thousand UN troops had been taken hostage en masse and had scores of their vehicles stolen, while the rebels had wrought havoc across the country."[1381] Amongst other things, hostages taken by rebel forces reported that UN elements were providing rebel forces with ammunition, food and alcohol – ammunition that was then used by the rebels to attack other UN peacekeepers in Sierra Leone.[1382] Lewis concluded that:

> In a sense, the UN itself is not even to blame for its abysmal record on peacekeeping in Africa. The UN has no standing army of its own...When the UN sent 13,000 peacekeeping troops to Sierra Leone it had to beg its member states to provide them from within their own armed forces...The UN Mission in Sierra Leone ended up with 13,000 troops from nine different countries speaking several different languages...Equipped with different and incompatible radio communications systems, the various UN contingents were often unable even to communicate with each other. They were hardly the best-quality, most highly motivated soldiers in the first place. But parachuted into Sierra Leone's civil war with an inadequate mandate (they had to have really, really good reasons to shoot any of the rebels), incompatible comms equipment and a defunct command-and-control structure, is it any wonder the UN mission imploded?...The UN invariably ends up being provided with the world's least competent soldiers to carry out the world's most difficult peace missions, a guaranteed recipe for failure.[1383]

The UN military commander in Sierra Leone, Indian army general Vijay Muar Jetley, was himself unequivocal about the UN's failings. Interviewed by ABC in August 2000, General Jetley noted: "It is time to take stock of the manner in which we conduct peacekeeping operations. Firstly, the mental preparedness to do this is lacking with most countries who contribute to UN forces. There's a misconception that peacekeeping means being very well turned out, wearing a nice blue helmet or cap and being in a white vehicle with a blue flag fluttering around and marching up and down, and that's peacekeeping. It is not."[1384] The British journalist Hugo Young noted of UNAMSIL in *The Guardian* in May 2000:

> The force in Sierra Leone is the largest UN peacekeeping army in the world. Yet it is pathetically failing. It has become hostage to the armed gangs of the rebel forces who are destabilising the regime it

should be defending…If this massive UN presence is incapable of sustaining peace against a disorderly and largely untrained rabble, one must ask what future there can ever be for the entire principle of humanitarian peacekeeping intervention by the UN.

The short-sightedness of committing peacekeepers in Darfur ahead of any settlement is clear. Damien Lewis has warned of the dangers of sending in peacekeeping forces when there was no peace to keep:

[I]n the complex mix of civil wars and rebel factions and guerrilla insurgencies, old-style peacekeeping doesn't always fit the bill. In Sierra Leone, for example, there simply was no peace to keep. This is what the UN failed to realise when it sent 13,000 peacekeeping troops to that country – and it learned its lessons there the hard way. At the time, UNAMSIL was the largest United Nations peacekeeping effort in the world – yet its role in Sierra Leone was to prove an embarrassing debacle…In short, in Sierra Leone the UN lost the peace.[1385]

The lessons for Darfur are stark. If the UN fails, if it merely haemorrhages equipment and resources to rebels or armed criminals as has happened on a regular basis to the AMIS mission, if it suffers fatalities or if it sees its personnel taken hostage, the already mistaken venture of putting UN forces into Darfur will then probably be compounded by demands – by the same people who demanded UN intervention into a situation where they could only but fail – for more "robust" action, intervention by NATO or American or British or European forces. This would merely serve to add fuel to the fire – with all the ingredients for another Iraqi or Afghanistan-type disaster. One of which all the analysts will say later they "miscalculated" or for which they were "unprepared".

A Declaration of War?

An uninvited military intervention in Darfur would in effect amount to the invasion of a sovereign country, and would be treated as a hostile military action by the Sudanese government. The Sudanese president, Omar al-Bashir, has repeatedly voiced Sudan's opposition to such an intervention.[1386] Even the threat of intervention has resulted in considerable anger within Sudan. In August 2004, for example, the BBC reported that the Sudanese army had called the July 2004 UN resolution on the conflict in Darfur (which demanded the disarmament of "Janjaweed" militias within 30 days) "a declaration of war" and threatened to fight any foreign intervention. A military spokesman, General Mohamed Beshir Suleiman, stated: "The Security Council resolution about the Darfur issue is a declaration of war on the Sudan and its people. The Sudanese army is now prepared to confront the enemies of the Sudan on land, sea and air. The door of the jihad is still open and...it will be opened in Darfur."[1387] There is little doubt that the Sudanese military would react very negatively to any actual uninvited international military incursion in Darfur.

That the Sudanese population would be in large part hostile to any such action is also clear. Bush's calls for western intervention led to a number of large demonstrations within Sudan against any such UN involvement in Darfur.[1388] Veteran British journalist Simon Jenkins has noted that "A Western military presence would give the Janjawid exactly the pretext it wants to present itself as Africa's new Mujahidin. 'We will attack any foreigners,' one of its leaders is reported as saying. 'We refuse to be like Iraq – surrendered, confused and occupied.'"[1389] The extent of resistance to any foreign intervention was made clear to senior UN officials in July 2006. Mowadh Jalaladin, a leader of the Berti tribe, warned that UN forces would mean "foreign occupation and intervention" and would remind the Sudanese of their colonial past. He warned that if the UN intervened in Darfur "We are declaring *jihad* against it. It means death. It means defending Sudan and Islam." The significance of these comments is that the Berti tribe are one of Darfur's "African" tribes, the very people those intervening would be claiming to be intervening on behalf of.[1390]

Even southern Sudanese opponents of the government have warned about any Western military intervention. Bona Malwal, a veteran politician and southern Sudanese leader, has cautioned:

If a foreign military intervention takes place in Darfur, it will not be confined to Darfur. Darfur is part of Sudan. All the Sudanese should oppose any foreign military intervention in their internal affairs. Such foreign military interventions by powerful states coming from so far away to impose their own solutions on our problems have serious repercussion that are far reaching, not only for the people of Sudan as a whole, but for the continent of Africa as well.[1391]

In late February 2006, the then UN Special Envoy to Sudan, Jan Pronk, warned that sending a NATO-led UN military force into Darfur would be "a recipe for disaster". He further noted that such an intervention "would really start a Jihad (holy war) against it". Pronk also said that "There is fear in Khartoum that the transition will be a conspiracy which will bring Sudan into the same situation as Iraq." [1392] Any uninvited international military action in Darfur would inevitably precipitate a crisis with the government of Sudan and within Sudan itself.

Weakening the Humanitarian Activities of the United Nations

The UN's entertainment of military intervention has already undermined the vital political and even humanitarian role, especially within the north-south peace process, that it has been playing in Sudan. The vital role played by the UN in coordinating and carrying out humanitarian activities in Darfur is clear. The former UN Special Envoy to Sudan Jan Pronk outlined the negative effect that Washington's call for a NATO-led UN military intervention in Darfur had already had upon the United Nations presence in Sudan: "The climate in Khartoum against the UN is heating up very strongly. There are threats, warnings. They speak of recolonization, invasion, imperialism, (a) conspiracy against the Arab-Islamic world." [1393] A month later he warned:

The political climate in Sudan towards the UN is deteriorating. In the press statements have been published citing civil society organizations calling for "resistance against foreign intervention", "raising the flag of Jihad", warning both the international community and Sudanese authorities not to "help the colonization to come to Darfur", referring to the West as "the devil", calling for martyrdom and a readiness to sacrifice and "to repulse any attack", announcing a "graveyard for the invaders". In most statements reference is made to the examples of Afghanistan and Iraq.[1394]

Pronk went on to further note:

> Opinion leaders and the public do not make a distinction between the UN and the US or NATO. Those who are aware of the difference express their fear that the UN will pave the way for the US and NATO or say that the UN is an instrument in the hands of the US...The attacks on the United Nations cannot be attributed to the Government only. The Government is under pressure from powerful groups.

He notes also that the government is aware that "matters might get out of control".[1395] Put bluntly, uninvited UN military action in Darfur will in all probability lead to attacks by any number of extremists – foreign and domestic – on the UN as an institution, irrespective of the particular functions or activities of the agencies or missions present. The most disturbing aspect of how extremists have previously conflated the two was the devastating bombing of the UN headquarters in Baghdad, an action which saw the UN withdraw from Iraq. Pronk has also pointed out the hostile climate in Sudan was making it difficult for the UN to carry out its agreed work: "It's also a feeling which is true for many people in the streets of Khartoum, and in that very difficult situation we at the moment are working."[1396]

The sad reality is that any military action by the UN, albeit the military division, will inevitably drag the civil activities of the UN into the firing line. Médecins Sans Frontières has warned of precisely this circumstance:

> Whatever their legitimacy, armed interventions intended to assist and protect civilian populations put aid workers' safety at risk from the moment they are deployed under the humanitarian banner. If a protection operation is to be serious, it necessarily involves the use of force against the enemy and, thus, potential non-combatant victims. How can a humanitarian organization provide aid to victims if it is equated with the "humanitarian" protection force in the

fighting? This is the danger that threatens aid organizations in Sudan today. By brandishing the threat of armed intervention in Darfur, the Security Council and certain Western nations are including humanitarian actors in their camp. In so doing, they are designating those actors as enemies in the eyes of Khartoum's authorities. And the authorities see threats of intervention as a genuine "declaration of war".[1397]

Médecins Sans Frontières officials, Dr Bradol and Fabrice Weissman, have confirmed the consequences on humanitarian work in Darfur: "Such an intervention would also inevitably result in the collapse of aid programs—as in Kosovo, Sierra Leone, East Timor, Afghanistan and Iraq—during the offensive." [1398]

Weakening the Comprehensive Peace Agreement

Any intervention would inevitably adversely affect the crucial role the UN has been playing within the 2005 Comprehensive Peace Agreement (CPA) which ended Sudan's fifty-year-old off and on north-south civil war. The United Nations has its hands full in securing the CPA, let alone engaging in military adventurism in Darfur. In mid-March 2006, the United Nations admitted that the deployment of 10,000 peacekeepers in southern Sudan was running behind schedule.[1399] In April 2006, for example, the International Crisis Group warned that stronger international engagement is needed to prevent the unravelling of the CPA.[1400] Anything which discredits the UN and its involvement in the CPA undermines peace not only in Sudan but also regionally.

The Consequences of Intervention

It is said that every American president tries to formulate one foreign policy doctrine. James Monroe's was defence of the Americas, Harry S. Truman's was containment of the Soviet bloc, Ronald Reagan's was confronting, and rolling back, the Soviet empire. George W. Bush's doctrine has been a policy of pre-emptive war to defeat terrorism and spread democracy. It has failed.

The simple fact is that American foreign policy under Bush has been an unmitigated disaster. Patrick Buchanan, a prominent American conservative leader and former presidential candidate, has said that, within the areas Zbigniew Brzezinski once called the "arc of crisis", "U.S. foreign policy appears to be disintegrating."[1401] A July 2006 *Time* magazine cover somewhat optimistically read, "The End of Cowboy Diplomacy". In 2005, the *Arab Human Development Report*, produced by Arab intellectuals under the auspices of the UN Development Programme, whose work had previously been lauded by Bush, bluntly stated that the Bush administration was "causing chaos in the Arab World".[1402] The probable consequences of any uninvited US-sponsored military action in Darfur or Sudan are starkly predictable. One just has to look at events in Iraq and Afghanistan – events which followed naïve and ill-thought out unilateral western "humanitarian" actions. President Bush has noted of American strategy in Iraq: "Every war plan looks good on paper until you meet the enemy."[1403] This is a tragic understatement of the fiasco that has unfolded in Iraq due to American incompetence. This incompetence stems from intelligence and policy failure on the part of the Bush administration and the Blair government. The law of unintended consequences also features strongly. Professor John Harper, in his key study entitled "Anatomy of a Habit: America's Unnecessary Wars", notes "The final feature of America's unnecessary wars, including those that have ended in victory, is that they exhibit a kind of law of unintended consequences. More often than not, they have failed to advance the interests of the individuals and political parties who have pursued them." Harper cited Machiavelli's warning that "anyone can start a war when he wants to, but not finish it".[1404]

Given that the main push behind the commitment of a NATO-led UN Darfur intervention comes from Washington, it follows that much of the intelligence and planning will be provided by the United States government. It is now clear how flawed the American involvement in Iraq has been, starting with the allegations – based on "intelligence" – used as an excuse for intervention. In December 2005, President Bush conceded that the US waged war on Iraq based on false intelligence.[1405] *The Financial Times* of London sought to explain Washington's intelligence failure regarding Iraq: "For too long, they have allowed their information to be driven by both ideology and Israeli intelligence sources. The same danger looms today over US policy – or rather, non policy – towards Iran. If that goes wrong, and leads to the same inexorable spiral of sanctions and military action, it could prove far more costly than the war in Iraq."[1406] The same forces are pushing for military action in Sudan.

Secretary of State Condoleezza Rice has admitted to continuing American intelligence failures, including, for example, the 2006 electoral victory by Hamas in Palestine: "I don't know anyone who wasn't caught off guard by Hamas' strong showing…I've asked why nobody saw it coming and I hope that we will take a hard look, because it does say something about perhaps not having had a good enough pulse on the Palestinian population." Rice also noted that: "There is a huge transition going on in the Middle East, as a whole and in its parts. The outcomes that we're seeing in any number of places, I will be the first to say, have a sense of unpredictability about them."[1407] *Newsweek* noted with regard to the Hamas victory that Washington had been "Caught by Surprise. Again."[1408]

The likelihood of American intelligence being any more accurate on the forces at play in Darfur is very low.

What has been the result of international intervention in Iraq? In short, Iraq has been torn apart by the forces unleashed as a result of western occupation. In March 2006, Iyad Allawi, the former interim prime minister of Iraq, chosen by Washington to lead Iraq after the overthrow of Saddam Hussein, stated that Iraq was in the middle of a civil war.[1409] Allawi noted: "If this is not civil war, then God knows what civil war is." President Bush chose to contradict Allawi.[1410] Earlier in March, US envoy Zalmay Khalilzad observed that the American invasion of Iraq had "opened the Pandora's box" and that the conflict could lead to a regional war and the rise of extremists who "would make Taliban Afghanistan look like child's play".[1411]

The Daily Telegraph of London has stated the Iraq war was "huge and intractable" and "how inevitable it already seems in retrospect". It further noted that "Since 2003, the insurgency has become increasingly dominated by jihadists from across the Middle East. These are people…who apparently couldn't believe their luck when the invasion began."[1412] The *Economist* has been particularly downbeat for some time about American success in Iraq, noting in March 2006 that "[t]hree years after American invaded, Iraq is as violent as ever". It has observed that: "Iraq is not in the throes of a single insurgency, but three distinct although often overlapping conflicts", conflicts involving political power, nationalism, tribalism, religious extremism, resources and Iraqi and international *jihadists*.[1413] Forced international military intervention in Darfur would see precisely these sorts of conflicts replicated.

In March 2006, Condoleezza Rice admitted that the United States had made thousands of tactical errors in Iraq.[1414] This stance was described by a senior American state department official as "More delusion as a solution in the absence of a solution."[1415] American economist Joseph Stiglitz has estimated the cost of the Iraq war was US$ 2 trillion.

The policy failure that led in large part to the Iraqi fiasco has been the subject of considerable attention. The London *Independent* newspaper has described the Iraq fiasco as "an ideological war. From its creation by the loonies of the American right…to the hell-disaster that Iraq now represents, the real war had to be turned into a myth; nightmares into dreams; destruction into hope; terrible truths into profound mendacity. Even today the occupation forces tell awesome lies." [1416] It is also clear that the much-heralded US "reconstruction" projects in Iraq have been failures. An American government report has stated that six out of eight projects hailed as successes by the Bush administration have failed amidst allegations of spiralling corruption.[1417]

Every one of the American foreign policy blunders towards Iraq can be applied to Washington's approach to Sudan and Darfur and its calls for western intervention. There is no doubt that any adventurism in Darfur would result in even more political alienation amongst the Islamic world, at least in part because of the flimsy US justification for such a move. There is also no doubt that the sort of military intervention in Darfur as advocated by Washington would result in military failure and political chaos.

Western, NATO-led military intervention in Afghanistan has been similarly disastrous. The US Institute of Peace stated in 2006 that Afghanistan was more dangerous for American troops than Iraq.[1418] *Newsweek* has also described the present situation in Afghanistan as "dangerously weakened".[1419] An eminent British military historian and journalist, Sir Max Hastings, has stated that NATO's intervention in Afghanistan has been a disaster, and that "the west is far out of its depth". He also observed that the American and British governments had consistently "bungled and lied" in both Iraq and Afghanistan.[1420] The commander of the NATO force in Afghanistan has warned that the country is "close to anarchy".[1421] NATO's involvement in Afghanistan has caused considerable tension within the organisation. *Time* magazine has reported that Europe's military role in Afghanistan is "poorly planned": *Time* has concluded with regard to NATO involvement in Afghanistan that "what started as a clever political sidestep to allow the Europeans to make up with Washington without going to Iraq now seems a lot less clever. It may end up doing more harm than good." [1422]

The Bush administration's response to Iran's quest for a nuclear capability, in the light of the Iraqi fiasco, has led to considerable skepticism on the part of observers, with articles such as "Been there, botched that" appearing in newspapers such as *The Boston Globe*.[1423] Even conservative supporters of Bush such as Andrew Sullivan have said that "there is something unreal about the bellicose statements coming from some sources in the Bush administration towards Iran." Sullivan has noted of any American military assault on Iran that "the gain would be fleeting" and "the costs could be enormous".[1424]

An Iraq in Africa?

As with Afghanistan and Iraq, any Western military intervention in Darfur would serve as a rallying point for Islamist extremists, both within and outside of Darfur and Sudan. Darfur in any instance is fertile ground for militant Islamic groups such as al-Qaeda and JEM. *Al-Ahram*, for example, has described Darfur as a "traditional Islamist stronghold".[1425] It was from the Fur and *Baggara* that Muhammad Ahmed, the "Mahdi", drew the fundamentalist shock troops that crushed Egyptian rule in Sudan and held the British Empire at bay for ten years up till 1898, as noted by Margolis:

> One of the Islamic World's first anti-colonial movements, known in the west as the Dervishes, burst from the wastes of Darfur in the 1880s. Led by the fiery 'Mahdi', the Dervishes drove the British imperialists from the Sudan, and event immortalized in the splendid Victorian novel, 'Four Feathers.' The Dervishes took Khartoum, slaying Britain's proconsul, Sir Charles 'Chinese' Gordon.[1426]

There can be very little doubt that any American-heralded NATO-led UN military intervention in Darfur would also have a similar effect to that seen in Iraq of motivating and galvanising radical Islamic *jihadists* from across the Middle East and North Africa. This is a point that has been made by Dr Paul Moorcroft, a British Africa expert and former Ministry of Defence media specialist:

> UN troops have been accepted in the largely non-Muslim south; they would be treated very differently in the fervently Islamic west. At the beginning of March [2006] nearly a million militant Sudanese pledged to fight a jihad if western troops intervened. Every crazy from A to Z, Algeria to Zanzibar, would flock in as mujaheddin, further enflaming the already al-Qaeda-prone Sahel, and destabilising the whole fragile Horn of Africa.[1427]

Moorcraft's warning is similar to those stated by British ministers and international analysts. In 2004, British foreign minister Chris Mullins rejected the "suggestion that some people are urging upon us, that somehow there's some western force that could come riding over the hills and everything will be alright again, but it's not like that." He warned:

> The odds are that if any western force did intervene it would become bogged down and that some new cause for all the Jihadists in the world would emerge and we'd find ourselves very quickly being shot at by all sides. Plus we would probably destabilise the whole of Sudan which is the size of Western Europe and the last thing we want is a failed state the size of Western Europe on our hands in Africa.[1428]

Dominique Moisi, the deputy director of the French Institute of International Relations in Paris, has also warned: "If we do it through NATO we'll give further encouragement to all those who are condemning the white man and are fuelling the clash of civilizations, they will use it against us." [1429] London-based experts on Islamist groups have also warned of the dangers of uninvited intervention. Kamil al-Tawil, of *al-Hayat* newspaper, has observed:

"If Darfur becomes a U.N. mandate in spite of the Sudanese government's opposition, people will flock there. I fear it will become another Iraq."[1430]

The Sudanese authorities have also pointed to the dangers of Darfur attracting foreign militants. In late February 2006, the Sudanese government warned that should UN military forces be deployed in Darfur it would be difficult to protect them. The Sudanese justice minister, Mohamed Ali al-Mardhi, had stated that sending "international forces to Darfur would pave the way for infiltration of elements in Sudan across the borders with neighboring countries a matter which will complicate the protection and safety of the international forces."[1431]

Al-Qaeda and Darfur

Before his retirement, General Tony Zinni was the chief of the US military's Central Command, overseeing operations in the Middle East and South Asia and confronting at first-hand the most challenging foreign policy questions facing the United States. In his book *The Battle for Peace: A Frontline Vision of America's Power and Purpose*, Zinni lists what he thinks America's strategic goals ought to be, including, amongst other things, keeping regions and countries stable, making unstable countries stable, and working alongside regional partners to address instability: "The real threats do not come from military forces or violent attacks; they do not come from a nation-state or hostile non-state entity. They do not derive from an ideology…The real new threats come from Instability. Instability and the chaos it generates can spark large and dangerous changes anywhere in the land."[1432]

There is no doubt that al-Qaeda is deeply interested in Darfur for precisely those reasons. This is based on several calculations. One is the location of Darfur. American counter-terrorism expert Richard Miniter, in his book, *Shadow War: The Untold Story of How Bush is Winning the War on Terror,* has reported that the al-Qaeda network has for some time been establishing itself in the Sahel area, an area which includes the Maghreb, Nigeria, Niger, Mali through to Chad and Sudan.[1433] Dozens of al-Qaeda terrorists were killed in Chad in 2004.[1434] In March 2004, Chadian soldiers, trained by American forces under the US Pan Sahel Initiative, were involved in operations against Algerian terrorist groups in Chad: the Pentagon initially declined any US involvement but later admitted that U.S. support included a Navy P-3 Orion aircraft operating from Algeria together with 100 American servicemen; other operational support included communications, intelligence and reconnaissance. The US military delivered food, medical supplies and other assistance to Chad, said to be in support of "government troops there who had battled suspected terrorists linked to al-Qaida". Miniter states that al-Qaeda involvement in Darfur "dovetails with other reports from North Africa. The desert wastes have become al-Qaeda's latest battleground."[1435] In July 2007, the US military warned that al-Qaeda was growing in North Africa after a "merger" of several groups under its umbrella.[1436] There is no doubt that al-Qaeda is already seeking to turn parts of the Sahel – and in this case Darfur – into the next Iraq or Afghanistan.[1437] There are many all-too-familiar ingredients. Darfur's physical inaccessibility, its Islamist heritage, its proximity to several failed or semi-failed states, porous borders, and its inaccessibility to western intelligence services make it a very attractive location to hide in and from which to attack.

On 23 April 2006, al-Jazeera television broadcast an al-Qaeda audiotape. In this tape, Osama bin-Laden called upon al-Qaeda fighters to begin travelling to Darfur to prepare for a "long-term war against the crusader thieves in Western Sudan". He claimed that the United States was manipulating the Darfur crisis to "send crusader troops to occupy the region and steal its oil under the guise of preserving security there". Bin-Laden also called upon the mujahideen to prepare well for their presence in Darfur because "it has been said that a man with knowledge can conquer land while land can conquer the ignorant." He also criticised the Sudanese government for having abandoned sharia law and said that al-Qaeda's "differences with it are great". The UNIMIS commander in Sudan treated bin-Laden's threat with "whole seriousness". The London *Daily Telegraph* has also warned of the al-Qaeda threat in Sudan: "Intelligence reports warn that the number of al-Qa'eda terrorist agents in Sudan is already increasing."[1438] With headlines such as "Bin Laden calls for war against UN peacekeepers", "Bin Laden calls for jihad in Darfur" and "In Tape, Bin Laden Urges Fighters to Sudan", in the western media, it cannot be said that western governments have not been made aware of al-Qaeda's intentions regarding Darfur.[1439]

In September 2007, al-Qaeda leader Ayman al-Zawahri renewed al-Qaeda's call for *jihad* in Darfur. He urged Muslims to fight the AU-UN hybrid force which he said was invading Sudan: "The free mujahideen sons of Sudan must organise jihad against the forces invading Darfur." Al-Zawahri criticised Sudanese President al-Bashir for having abandoned his Muslim brothers to appease the United States.[1440] These calls were echoed by Osama bin-Laden in October 2007: bin-Laden called for *jihad* against any UN peacekeepers and the Sudanese.[1441]

Former UN envoy Jan Pronk warned of an al-Qaeda presence in Sudan, stating that there is "a lot of talk about Al Qaeda in Khartoum". Citing multiple sources, Pronk reported that there is "intelligence information that there are [Al Qaeda] people in Khartoum who have not been there before". He added that Bush's calls for a NATO-led UN military intervention in Darfur had led to the climate against the UN in Khartoum "heating up" with a number of warnings of action against the UN. Pronk warned that it would be "foolish not to take such warnings [of Al Qaeda attacks against a UN force] seriously".[1442]

It is also a matter of record that al-Qaeda is hostile to the government of Sudan. Sudan expelled bin Laden from Sudan in 1996, and has actively cooperated in the war on terrorism. In June 2005, al-Qaeda leader Ayman al-Zawahri launched an unprecedented attack on the Khartoum government for their cooperation with the United States. Al-Zawahri singled out Saudi Arabia, Egypt and Sudan in his attack: referring to Khartoum, he warned that "somebody will have to pay a very high price for it".[1443]

Senior US military officers have predicted that al-Qaeda forces are moving to the "vast ungoverned spaces" of the Horn of Africa.[1444] American concern about the terrorist threat posed by Islamist extremists within the Sahel is self-evident. The US military has established a separate African Command and currently has at least six major ongoing military programs spanning the African continent, including the Africa Crises Response Initiative (ACRI), and its various sections such as the Joint Command Exchange Training Program (JCET); the Pan-Sahel Initiative, which stretches across Mali, Mauritania, Niger, Chad and Sudan; and the "Golden Spear" program, which involves Kenya, Uganda, Rwanda, Tanzania, Ethiopia and Djibouti. In June 2003, President Bush announced the commitment of $100 million for an East Africa Counterterrorism Initiative (EACTI) to provide counterterrorism equipment, training, and assistance to six countries in the region: Djibouti, Eritrea, Ethiopia, Tanzania, Uganda, and Kenya. The Pentagon has also created another program called the Trans Sahara Counterterrorism Initiative (TSCTI). Part of the US Central Command's mandate for its presence in Djibouti is "to intercept al Qaeda operatives fleeing Afghanistan for East Africa."

Tom Vraalsen, the UN secretary-general's special envoy for humanitarian affairs for Sudan, has pointed out some of the regional implications of the Darfur conflict: "A continuation of the problems in Darfur could have serious political repercussions in the sense that it could destabilize the area along the Chad-Sudan border and it could have repercussions also regionally if it continues. It has to be brought to an end."[1445] Dr Ali Ali-Dinar, a Darfurian critic of the government, has made the simple point that "Peace in Darfur is necessary for stabilising the surrounding regions which include southern Sudan, Chad, and Central African Republic and to prevent the conflict spreading. The future of the region is at stake."[1446] This is also precisely why ultra Islamist groups such as al-Qaeda would be interested in a continuing cycle of violence in Darfur.

And, in Dr Turabi's close involvement with JEM, there is already a clear al-Qaeda link. Knight-Ridder Africa editor Sudarsan Raghavan described Turabi as "preaching a strict brand of Islam that made Sudan a haven for extremists such as bin Laden, whom Turabi once called a hero".[1447] That bin Laden and Turabi are close is undisputed. Richard Clarke, the Clinton Administration's anti-terrorism supremo, described Turabi as a "soul mate" of Osama bin Laden who shared his "vision of a worldwide struggle to establish a pure Caliphate".[1448] Bin Laden is also reportedly married to Turabi's niece.[1449] Many of those members of the military wing of the Popular Congress now involved with JEM trained with al-Qaeda members in the 1990s. Miniter states that al-Qaeda instructors, including specialists in guerrilla and urban warfare and logistics, have been involved in training Justice and Equality insurgents in Darfur. *Al-Ahram* has already noted connections: "JEM also is suspected of having links with several militant Islamist groups in Africa and around the world."[1450] It is also worth noting that amongst the rebels there is a self-styled "Tora Bora" militia – named after the Afghan mountain range in which Osama bin Laden, al-Qaeda and the Taliban fought one of their major battles, and from which bin Laden escaped American capture.[1451]

In another analogy with Afghanistan, blind western support for the Darfur rebels, and especially JEM – for whatever short-term political reasons – runs the risk of repeating the mistake of building up Islamist fundamentalist forces which then themselves pose national and regional threats to western interests. Providing Afghan and Arab fundamentalists, amongst them a young Osama bin-Laden, with hundreds of millions of dollars worth of military and logistical support in the 1980s has been seen as a tactical error which led to the birth of the modern international terrorist movement we see today.

The possible al-Qaeda-Darfur connection is of concern to the United Nations. The Irish newspaper *The Sunday Tribune* reported in December that "[t]he threat of al-Qaeda opening another front against western aid organisations and personnel in Darfur is real, according to UN officials in Sudan". A senior UN official noted that Darfur rebels had already made a specific threat to aid workers. According to *The Sunday Tribune*: "It fitted the pattern of violence against western aid organisations and personnel in Afghanistan and Iraq."[1452] The fundamentalist involvement has been poorly reported, but some details have emerged. In July 2004, for example, a Saudi national said to have been "preaching holy war" within a refugee camp in Chad was arrested. There had been violent scenes at the camp in which two refugees had been shot dead by local security forces. Arms caches had also been seized in the camp.[1453]

It is worth noting that the pattern of terrorism in Darfur has echoed al-Qaeda and Islamist tactics in Iraq, especially with regard to attacks on policemen and police stations.[1454] Over 685 policemen have been murdered, and hundreds more wounded, in terrorist attacks on policemen in Darfur. These attacks continued. The United Nations Secretary-General noted in his October 2004 report to the Security Council, for example, that Darfur rebels had attacked a police station in Medo, in North Darfur, on 12 September 2004 and that "further SLA attacks on police posts were reported on 14, 15, 17, 18, 19 and 22 September. Further SLA attacks on police in Ghubayash village, Western Kordofan, in the last week of September indicates that these violations may not remain confined to Darfur."[1455] The Secretary-General's November report noted the "SLA reportedly attacked police posts nine times in October, killing at least nine policemen."[1456] European Union military observers mission have confirmed rebel attacks on policemen in Darfur: "The SLA has been attacking continuously police stations."[1457] These are just a few examples of UN reports of attacks on policemen in Darfur. The African Union has also confirmed that "innocent policemen" have been the "major victims" of the rebels.[1458] Knight-Ridder has also confirmed rebel attacks on police stations.[1459] Human Rights Watch has reported: "Rebels have attacked many police stations and posts in Darfur."[1460] These attacks are of deep concern for at least two reasons. Firstly, as agreed with the United Nations, and outlined in the joint government-UN action plan, the deployment of police forces within Darfur was to protect displaced people and displaced peoples' camps from attack by criminal elements, Janjaweed or otherwise. Attacks on police stations, therefore, fuel civilian insecurity in the region. Secondly, Darfur rebel attacks on policemen have not only mirrored attacks in Iraq, but have also been part of a pattern of similar attacks on police stations within the Sahel.

Almost identical sorts of attacks to those in Iraq and Darfur have occurred as far apart as northern Nigeria and Liberia.[1461] This pattern of attacks also begs a simple question. Why is the murder of hundreds of poorly armed policemen in Iraq deemed by the United States to be terrorism – with all the consequences of that definition – while the murder of hundreds of poorly-armed policemen in Darfur appears not to be terrorism? Disturbingly, it would seem that the United States is actually helping to fund some of the activities of the very gunmen involved in killing the policemen – gunmen who if not themselves Islamist extremists are nevertheless closely allied with the Justice and Equality Movement. [1462]

The potential for regional Islamist activity, even before any possible NATO and UN military intervention in Darfur, is clear. *The Guardian* noted:

> Somalia could become the next "war on terror" battleground as the US zeroes in on al-Qaida and Islamist groups reportedly trying to exploit a power vacuum in the world's most anarchic state. Western defence officials have warned that al-Qaida was trying to re-establish a presence in Somalia, eastern Ethiopia and Sudan.[1463]

Reuters has warned that "Somalia's worst outbreak of fighting in years has raised fears that the troubled Horn of Africa state may become a proxy battleground for Islamic militants and the United States." [1464] The Islamist insurgency in Somalia is growing in strength.[1465] The Horn of Africa and east Africa is in the throes of a terrible drought affecting millions of people which will further destabilise the region.[1466] In April 2007, Islamist militants, said to be numbered in the hundreds, killed 12 police officers in northern Nigeria in the latest in a series of such attacks. These militants were said to have crossed into Nigeria from Chad. Twenty-five militants were subsequently said have been killed in clashes with Nigerian security forces.[1467] In the same month, Islamist militants identifying themselves as "Al-Qaeda in the Magreb" exploded car bombs in Algeria and Morocco. This new group is based on the Algerian terrorist groups known as the "Salafist Group for Preaching and Combat".[1468]

It is also the case that geographically Darfur borders on Egypt, which is a long-standing al-Qaeda target. It goes without saying that anything that destabilises Darfur and Sudan also destabilises Egypt.

There would also be any number of additional consequences of a US-created Iraqi-type fiasco in the Sahel. Such a conflict would impact on North Africa, the soft underbelly of Europe, resulting in hundreds of thousands of refugees and migrants. African migrants, from countries such as Mali, Gambia, Nigeria and elsewhere in West Africa, regularly use routes through Mauritania and by boat in the Mediterranean sea towards southern Italy or into Ceuta and Melilla, two Spanish territories on the northern coast of Africa. Even as things stand, European immigration specialists have stated that "We are just seeing the start of something much, much bigger." Officials from the Red Crescent, the Muslim counterpart of the Red Cross, have also noted that "We are victims of an immigration that we cannot control."[1469] The political and security impact in Europe of hundreds of thousands of Muslim migrants from northern Africa can only be imagined.

The International Impact of Intervention

The impact any western military intervention would have in mobilising militant Islamic activists both as an international issue and in terms of terrorist action against western forces both in Sudan and outside cannot be understated.

A case study for such cause and effect is the western intervention in Iraq. It is a matter of record that American intelligence agencies have stated that the

American invasion and occupation of Iraq has helped spawn a new generation of Islamic radicalism and that the overall terrorist threat has grown since the 11 September 2001 attacks on the United States. The 2006 US *National Intelligence Estimate*, the first formal assessment of global terrorism by United States intelligence agencies since the Iraq war began, and representing a consensus view of the 16 separate intelligence agencies inside the US government, stated that Islamic radicalism has spread across the globe and that "the Iraq war has made the overall terrorism problem worse". In September 2006, the US House of Representatives Intelligence Committee also warned of the growing *jihad* movement stating that "Al Qaeda leaders wait patiently for the right opportunity to attack." In early 2005, the National Intelligence Council concluded that Iraq had become the primary training ground for the next generation of terrorists. The CIA director, General Michael Hayden, warned in April 2006, that "New jihadist networks and cells, sometimes united by little more than their anti-Western agendas, are increasingly likely to emerge." In 2006, the U.S. Council on Global Terrorism, an independent research group of terrorism experts, concluded that "there is every sign that radicalization in the Muslim world is spreading rather than shrinking."[1470] *Jane's Intelligence Review* has called Iraq "a new Afghanistan" and noted that "The war in Iraq has helped the global Salafist jihad from the outset."[1471] Michael Scheuer, the head of the CIA's Bin-Laden section from 1996-99, and author of *Imperial Hubris*, described the invasion of Iraq as a "Christmas gift" to bin Laden and al-Qaeda.[1472] In January 2007, President Bush himself admitted that his actions had made international terrorist attacks on America more likely.[1473]

This warning has been echoed by the British intelligence services. *The Sunday Times* has reported that British intelligence chiefs have warned the British government "that the war in Iraq has made Britain the target of a terror campaign by al-Qaeda that will last 'for many years to come'". The memorandum from the Joint Intelligence Committee warned that the war in Iraq has provided "additional motivation for attacks" against Britain; that it is "increasing Al-Qaeda's potential" and "energising" terrorist networks engaged in *jihad*. It also reported that Iraq is being used as a "training ground and base" for terrorists to return to carry out attacks in Britain and elsewhere.[1474] British Muslim leaders have also warned their government that its foreign policy provided "ammunition to extremists" and put British lives "at increased risk".[1475] In April 2006, *The Sunday Times* also pointed to the existence of a network of Iranian "suicide bombers" prepared to strike at American and British targets should Washington or London attack Iran.[1476]

There can be no doubt whatsoever that uninvited western military intervention in Sudan would reinvigorate anti-western forces and radicalise even more people within the Muslim and developing world.

Economic sanctions

International intervention has also taken the form of attempts to pressurise Sudan by way of economic sanctions. Such intervention must also be carefully thought out if it is not have unintended consequences. The divestment campaign within the United States, which seeks to end all foreign investment in Sudan, is an example of the danger of naïve attempts at popular action. Simon Caldwell has warned about economic sanctions: "The one action with the best chance of changing the mind of Khartoum – destroying or blockading its oil industry – would greatly impoverish the 35m Sudanese who are not Darfuri."[1477] More specifically, Sudan has just emerged from a fifty-year north-south civil war, which was fought at least in large part for a more equitable distribution of wealth and power within Sudan. This has also been the stated objective of the rebel movements who started the war in Darfur in 2003, and is an issue that has been the subject of considerable attention at the Abuja peace talks. It is difficult to see how western activists think that they are contributing to peace by starving the Sudanese people and economy of the very thing – wealth – that at least two civil wars have been fought over. The reconstruction of those areas devastated by war, in southern and western Sudan, will take immense resources. Reliance on international funds for reconstruction is questionable. The necessary funds will have to come from the Sudanese economy and revenues accruing to the government. Attempts to destroy, damage or obstruct the Sudanese economy, therefore, can only but negatively impact on the post-peace process in Darfur and elsewhere.

Conclusion

It is clear that the Sudanese government needs assistance in ending the conflict in Darfur. The massive UN humanitarian programme has saved countless lives and alleviated the suffering of millions of Darfurians. AU forces succeeded in stabilising and protecting large parts of Darfur. Constructive international intervention, guided by reality and not ideology, has had very positive results in Darfur. The chronic under-funding of the AU and the resultant imposition upon a noticeably reluctant Khartoum government of a UN-AU hybrid peacekeeping force in Darfur when there is no peace to keep are worrying developments.

The case against intervention in general, and particularly in Darfur, has been made by the distinguished British journalist, Simon Jenkins: "Any fool can call for 'action to end the fighting' anywhere on earth, without giving a thought to what this involves. It usually involves other people dying to no good purpose."[1478] Peter Hallward, the author of *Absolutely Postcolonial*, has been direct: "Fresh from an illegal and deceitful war of aggression, Anglo-US forces now have only one moral responsibility: to stay at home."[1479] Julie Flint has also warned of the dangers of UN intervention and the calls made by groups such as Human Rights Watch and the International Crisis Group for an intervention under Chapter VII of the UN Charter:

> This is not the solution…If any military force is to have a chance of success in Darfur, peacemaking is needed before peace-keeping – not just between the parties represented at the inter-Sudanese peace talks in Abuja, whose ability to deliver on any agreement reached is far from certain, but among a much broader cross-section of Darfur society. Without such talks, increased militarization of Darfur, strongly opposed by both the Sudanese government and neighboring Libya, will lead only to greater violence and loss of life.[1480]

Continuing calls within the United States for direct American military intervention and no-fly zones over Darfur demonstrate that Washington has not learnt the lessons of its disastrous involvement in Iraq and Afghanistan, that allegedly humanitarian interventions can go very wrong.

Chapter Twelve

THE DARFUR ROAD-MAP

The political solution to Darfur ultimately lies in the federal process within Naivasha – that is the decentralisation of power.

US State Department official Charles Snyder [1481]

The positions of all sides on the issues are the same. They share a lot in the area of power sharing. They all agree on a united Sudan. They all agree on [the] need to devolve more power downwards.

Sudanese government official [1482]

Douglas H. Johnson, perhaps the best historian of Sudan's recent conflicts, has provided a particularly apt analogy for events in Darfur. He has written that Sudan's civil war reminded him "of his own great-grandmother's tales of survival in the border states during the American Civil War, where the great motivating principles of that horrific conflict were scarcely evident in the behaviour of its local protagonists. My home-state of Missouri (to which my great-grandmother fled in the mistaken hope of finding greater security) was then the battleground of the most vicious internal guerrilla war in American history, where all the cruelties of civil conduct were magnified."[1483] Johnson cites the American historian Michael Fellman's characterisation of the war in Missouri as "the war of ten thousand nasty incidents [where] justice was impossible" and in which "restraint and forbearance had not been the guiding qualities".[1484] And in its mishmash of different forces – federal, Confederate, government, regular, state, county and irregular, diverse militia – together with *ad hoc* armed bands of raiders and criminal and semi-criminal gangs that produced the likes of the James and Younger brothers, all within a framework of national conflict, local grievances and vendettas, the Missouri border wars provide some sort of an insight into the Darfur crisis. Even then it is an insight which does not take into consideration the extra complications of considerable external involvement within the Darfur conflict. And, for all the bitterness and violence at the time, peace and reconciliation did come, and unity and political consensus were re-established.

The reality of the Darfur crisis is all too apparent. There has been a vicious civil war in Darfur between two rebel movements, now splintered into a dozen or more factions, and the Sudanese government. It has truly been a "war of ten thousand nasty incidents". Tens of thousands of people have died and hundreds of thousands of civilians have been displaced in the conflict. It has been a human disaster.

The international community's response to the crisis in Darfur, especially by way of media coverage, has been varied and in some instances short-sighted. A key question that has not been asked very often is a simple one. Where does the international community want to be five years from now with regard to Darfur in particular and Sudan in general? There are two related questions. How do we get from A to B and what are the obstacles? In the rush to judgement on Darfur – premature, misguided and misinformed in some cases – we are losing sight of these key questions.

Any attempt to shape a road-map must start with two words of caution. Firstly, to address the Darfur crisis it is essential that events there are evaluated as objectively as possible. To do so, observers must cut away the propaganda, media sensationalism and pressure group politics – especially within the United States – that has already distorted perceptions of the Darfur crisis and Sudan. That Darfur has been enmeshed in propaganda is clear. This study has touched upon some examples. There have been allegations of genocide, ethnic cleansing and the use of chemical weapons in Darfur. Propaganda such as this, while serving any number of short-term political goals for those party to it, complicates an already complex issue. Any solution to the Darfur crisis has to break through this propaganda wall and move on. Such propaganda merely serves to encourage rebel groups in obstructing peace talks in the unfounded hope of some form of outside military intervention. And, secondly, as outlined by Richard Dowden, "Darfur may be a remote province but its politics link directly into the government in Khartoum. What happens here may lead to a fragmentation of the whole country. A settlement on terms too favourable to the rebels could spark revolts among other marginalised peoples."[1485] The international community must tread carefully. The destabilisation of Sudan is something that must be ended as soon as possible.

The Objectives of a Road Map

What are the objectives that would be set for a Darfur road-map? Again they are clear. When asked what the solution to Darfur was, Ghanaian Major-General Henry Anyidoho, the joint deputy special representative for UNAMID, the AU-UN hybrid force, said that it was threefold: "First, a complete ceasefire. Second, talks involving a cross-section of Darfurians. They must agree. And third, the government has a big role to play. This is not a failed state; there is a sitting government."[1486] Going hand in hand with this must be the protection of humanitarian aid work and the re-establishment of the rule of law in Darfur and, where possible, identification and prosecution of those people guilty of crimes and war crimes. Darfur's infrastructure must be rebuilt and developed and those communities that have been displaced must be returned to their homes. It is also essential for Sudan to complete its long-standing goal of normalising its international relations. Compensation for losses and inter-tribal reconciliation will be an integral part of any settlement.

Ceasefire and Peace Talks

We are fortunate in that a peace framework exists. Internationally-brokered peace talks have taken place in Chad, Ethiopia, Nigeria and Libya. An African Union-mediated ceasefire agreement between the Government and rebels was signed in early April 2004.[1487] In Abuja in November 2004 the Government and rebel movements extended ceasefire and aid access agreements.[1488] At face value negotiating a political solution to the Darfur crisis should not be difficult.[1489] The signing of the July 2005 Declaration of Principles established the framework for a negotiated settlement including power and wealth sharing. The two rebel movements that began the war claimed to have done so because of the marginalisation and underdevelopment of Darfur. JEM spokesmen, for example, have stated: "The regions should elect their own government and hold it to account. The regions should have their own constitutions. We're not seeking to separate from our country."[1490] In 2003, the then SLA secretary-general Minni Minawi encapsulated his movement's demands: "The SLM/A shall struggle to achieve a decentralised form of governance based on the right of Sudan's different regions to govern themselves autonomously through a federal or confederal system."[1491] As early as 2004, the government publicly committed itself to a federal system of government in Darfur which would "ensure" that Darfur states would "have their own constitutions...elected governors [and] elected legislative assemblies" as well as "suitable" Darfurian "participation in the central institutions" and "wealth sharing".[1492] This was also echoed by Dr Mustapha Osman Ismail, the then Sudanese foreign minister: "The people from Darfur state should have the right to have a parliament, to have a governor, to have a government to be elected by the people of Darfur."[1493] President Bashir has also stated that Darfur will be ruled by local, tribal law, and not by central legislation.[1494] Taken at face value, these issues are adequately addressed by the Naivasha formula, which has defined devolved regional government in southern Sudan, a formula at the heart of the January 2005 Comprehensive Peace Agreement settling the long-running north-south civil war.[1495] Senior Sudanese government ministers have stated that the Naivasha arrangements could be a model for Darfur.[1496] The key US State Department official on Sudan, Charles Snyder, has also noted: "The political solution to Darfur ultimately lies in the federal process within Naivasha that is the decentralisation of power."[1497]And, should Darfur be endowed with as yet undiscovered and unexploited oil reserves, they should be subject to a wealth-sharing arrangement similar to the southern formula. All these issues, and more, were built upon, expanded and entrenched in the 2006 Darfur Peace Agreement. De Waal has himself noted how close the DPA came to being signed by a majority of the Darfurian rebel movements.[1498]

It is important to note that the 2005 north-south peace agreement was itself the end result of a process of reform, liberalisation and engagement in Sudan that can be traced back to the 1999 ouster of hard-line Islamist leader Dr Hassan Turabi. In April and in mid-May 2000, towards the end of the obstructive Clinton Administration, Khartoum restated its readiness to enter into "an immediate and comprehensive ceasefire" and to restart negotiations for the achievement of a lasting peace. Throughout 2001, the Sudanese government repeatedly called for a peaceful resolution of the southern conflict and called upon the SPLA to do the same.[1499] With the Bush Administration's support, the ensuing peace process resulted in the 2002 Machakos protocols and 2004 Naivasha agreement which were turned into the 2005 comprehensive peace settlement.

It is essential that Sudan remains committed to the course of normalisation of its relations with the Western international community that had preceded the Darfur crisis. In 1999, for example, the European Union entered into a political dialogue with Sudan, noting improvements within the Sudanese situation.[1500] There had also been a similar regional shift in attitudes towards Sudan and the Sudanese conflict.[1501] In 2001, for example, Sudan held the presidency of both the regional Intergovernmental Authority on Development as well as the Community of Sahel-Saharan States, a body which brings together eleven North African states.[1502] The then newly-elected Bush administration and Sudan entered into a new relationship, with extensive Sudanese support in counter-terrorism both before and after the 11 September 2001 terrorist attacks within the United States.

What are the Obstacles?

There are, of course, a number of real or potential obstacles along any Darfur road-map to peace. One of the obstacles has already been touched upon. International perceptions of the crisis continue to be distorted by the sort of propaganda claims that go hand-in-hand with all war and particularly civil war – claims all too often echoed by a sensationalist media. Unrealistic international demands, often fuelled by superficial press coverage of the war, can result in the hardening of positions. The international community must take an objective, well-informed position on Darfur. Demands for 30-day "fixes" ill-serve the Darfur people and weaken the credibility of those countries and international institutions that stipulate such deadlines. "Megaphone diplomacy" by the US, especially when it is aimed at placating ill-informed domestic constituencies, is counterproductive. General Anyidoho was clear about the use of this sort of approach:

It is not the way to go. Americans give deadlines all the time. The threat of sanctions is also not enough. They have lived under these for so long that they have become normal. They are used to living in seclusion. Now, they have oil and a friend in the Security Council ... We can't solve these problems through weapons. We have to sit and talk, which is why it is important to look at how Côte d'Ivoire was solved after four years of fighting. Outsiders can never solve the problem for us. It's a distant misery for them. We have to do it for ourselves."[1503]

Bumper sticker-driven, US "advocacy" groups continue to pose not just an obstacle but a clear danger to a peaceful solution to the Darfur crisis. They have already indirectly served to prolong the conflict by fuelling rebel intransigence about peace-talks. Their demands for military intervention would greatly exacerbate Darfur's suffering. There are, of course, any number of political opportunists waiting to exploit any Western misjudgements on Darfur – not least of which are those Islamist extremists, internationally and within Sudan, who would welcome any foreign military intervention in the region as a pretext for another Iraq or Afghanistan-type conflict with the West. If Darfur is turned into the next Iraq or Afghanistan by these forces responding to Western mistakes then once again it will be the people of Darfur who will suffer the most.

Another possible obstacle, itself accentuated by undemanding reporting, is the superficial perception that the rebels are necessarily fighting against marginalisation and underdevelopment in Darfur. Alternative or concurrent objectives have been suggested by independent observers such as Ghazi Suleiman, and others. Suleiman has pointed to the continuing role played in Sudan and particularly Darfur by the Islamist leader Dr Turabi. Turabi had long been opposed to settling the civil war in the south and any engagement with the United States. The war in Darfur may well be an attempt by Islamists to derail reform in Sudan and Sudan's move towards the West. Should the objective of the Islamist rebels in Darfur be the overthrow of the present Khartoum government rather than power-sharing or devolution for Darfur, then the rebel movements are unlikely to negotiate in good faith. Mediators have already noted repeated rebel intransigence during peace talks.

The argument that some of the rebel factions may wish to see continuing war and chaos in Darfur is at least partly confirmed by their constant attacks on humanitarian convoys and their escalating obstruction, intimidation and murder of humanitarian aid workers. They have also continued to show ambivalence with regard to committing to or honouring humanitarian aid agreements. [1504] In these circumstances it will be difficult to persuade all the anti-rebel militias in Darfur to stand down. The noted absence of a coherent political agenda on the part of various factions of the Sudan Liberation Army is a growing concern as is the issue of growing political fragmentation and the question of rebel command and control over their forces, and the possibility of Somalia-esque warlordism.

How Do We Get to Where We Want to Go?

It is essential that all parties to the conflict attend internationally-mediated peace talks in good faith. If rebel motives for starting the conflict are to be taken at face value, then everything they have been fighting for is encapsulated in the Darfur Peace Agreement. The DPA can be reworked and renegotiated if necessary through mediation. All parties to the conflict must be held to account by the international community without prejudice, double-standards or hypocrisy. While Khartoum appears to be eager to resolve the Darfur issue, any rebel reluctance, by design, inability or by way of opportunism, to engage in the talks must be recognised and addressed by the international community. Any agreed ceasefire – and the separation of forces it envisages – must be enforced and monitored. The sorts of ceasefire monitoring and verification teams that so effectively policed the ceasefire in southern Sudan and the Nuba mountains in the lead-up to the 2005 CPA must also be introduced to Darfur.[1505] Khartoum must address the criminality and armed banditry that has undermined law and order in Darfur. A working definition of the "Janjaweed" phenomenon must be agreed – especially with regard to the regulation and disarmament of armed groups in the region. External involvement with, and support for, the Darfur rebels, from Eritrea and Chad for example, must stop. Only concerted international pressure can make this happen. The humanitarian needs of those who have been displaced must be met until those affected are able to return to their homes. A reconstruction fund of several hundred million dollars must be established.

Cutting through often sensationalist western media projections of Sudanese government positions regarding Darfur, it is important to record the stated position of the Government of Sudan. A Canadian university media study of the Sudanese government's position has done precisely that. The report stated that seven key themes characterise the response of the Government of Sudan to international pressure: Sudan is a sovereign nation and UN involvement constitutes meddling in Sudan's internal affairs, eroding Sudan's sovereignty; the Government of Sudan has the Darfur situation under control and does not need foreign help; it is dedicated to the peace process and progress is being made towards economic and social development in Darfur; foreign pressure on Sudan amounts to a hostile attack on the nation and a new form of recolonization; United Nations interest in the Darfur crisis serves a Western-Zionist agenda, is part of foreign conspiracies directed against Sudan, and is not motivated by genuine humanitarian concerns; the people of Sudan are opposed to UN intervention in their region and the solution to its problems lie in the hands of Darfur's people, who oppose foreign interference; Sudan will resist by force if necessary any efforts to station UN troops in Darfur; the African Union is fully capable of fulfilling its responsibilities in the Darfur region without UN reinforcements and those who belittle the African Union's abilities do so from anti-African motives; international attention to the Darfur crisis strengthens the bargaining position of the rebel groups and makes unlikely a lasting peace in the region.[1506] Any objective assessment of the government's stated positions would find that most of them are understandable and valid and to a greater or lesser extent borne out by various sections of this study. Without a full understanding of the Sudanese perspective on the Darfur issue there is the danger of Khartoum and parts of the international community continuing to talk at cross purposes.

Criticism of the Sudanese government for a number of its actions in Darfur is valid but it must be measured and properly focused. It seems to no longer be part of the problem. Knee-jerk responses by Western countries and other sections of the international community to sensationalist and often questionable claims about Darfur serve only to enflame an already tense situation. They also endanger the north-south peace process and have the potential of slowing Sudan's re-engagement with the West as well as adversely colouring the image of the West within the developing world. Darfur is not genocide. It is an African civil war and a humanitarian disaster and both can be addressed. The world's humanitarian community is holding the ring while a political solution is arrived at. All the ingredients for a peaceful settlement are in writing and on the table. Peace beckons in Darfur – if it is properly managed. If it is not, the fatal warlordism of Somalia could be replicated. Worse, international military intervention could spawn another Iraq.

Appendix One

Key Provisions of the Darfur Peace
Agreement (DPA)

5 May 2006

Permanent status of Darfur

The DPA provides that a referendum on whether to retain Darfur's three states or create a Darfur region is to be held within 12 months of the general elections (by July 2010). The Transitional Darfur Regional Authority (TDRA) is responsible for coordinating the implementation and follow-up of the DPA and facilitating better cooperation between the three state governments.

Participation in government

Pending elections, the SLM/A and JEM are to nominate people to the following posts, making a special effort to nominate women: one Special Assistant to the President, the fourth ranking national official (after the President and two Vice Presidents) who will also chair the TDRA, and 1 cabinet-level presidential advisor; 1 cabinet minister and 2 state ministers (in addition to 3 cabinet minister and 3 state minister posts which will continue to be filled by Darfurians); 12 seats in the National Assembly and chairmanship of one of the National Assembly's parliamentary committees; 1 ministerial position in the Khartoum State government; The governor of one of Darfur's states and deputy governor of each of the other two, plus 2 ministers and 1 advisor in each of the states and a senior member of each state ministry; 21 of the 73 seats in each state assembly, including the deputy speaker of each assembly: 6 local commissioners and 6 executive directors in Darfur. Membership of the Council of States is to be non-partisan and to follow consultation with Darfurians. 50 per cent of places in Darfurian universities and 15 per cent of places in Khartoum's universities are reserved for Darfurians.

Historical land rights (hawakeer) are recognised, subject to rulings by state-level Land Commissions.

Development priorities

The agreement provided for a Panel of Experts to establish a formula for allocation to Darfur of a fair portion of national revenues, including from the oil industry. It also establishes a new Darfur Reconstruction and Development Fund to manage rehabilitation, reconstruction, and development — to be funded by the national government at levels of $300 million in 2006 and $200 million each in 2007 and 2008, and also financed by international donors. A Compensation Commission with guidelines for determination and payment of compensation and other remedies for victims of the conflict was also established and it was agreed the national government will make an initial $30 million contribution to the Compensation Fund. A Joint Assessment Mission (JAM) is to determine priorities.

Protection and compensation

A Darfur Rehabilitation and Resettlement Commission (DRRC) is established to coordinate humanitarian provision and access and the safe and voluntary return of IDPs and refugees. A Property Claims Committees will resolve disputes. A Compensation Commission is established with an initial budget of US$30million.

A comprehensive ceasefire comes into force within 72 hours of signing; free movement of people, goods and services; the janjaweed is to disarm within 150 days; members of the rebel groups will be incorporated into the Sudanese military forces or assisted with their integration into civilian life, and the principal responsibility for law enforcement in Darfur will be returned to a reformed civilian police force. Armed forces are prohibited from displaced persons camps and other civilian areas, including humanitarian supply routes. The African Union-run Ceasefire Commission, are given expanded powers including to identify those responsible for ceasefire violations and to recommend measures against them by the AU Peace and Security Council. Provides that these security arrangements will be monitored by African Union peacekeeping forces. A Joint Humanitarian Facilitation and Monitoring Unit (including representatives of AMIS, the UN, the international community and the parties) is to monitor and report. 4000 former combatants from the movements are to be incorporated into the SAF; education and training are to be provided for a further 3000.

Dialogue and consultation

Darfur-Darfur Dialogue and Consultation (DDDC) is to serve as a mechanism for mobilizing support for, and implementing, the DPA. 60 per cent of delegates will be tribal and community representatives, the remaining 40 per cent from political parties, civil society, religious organizations and the diaspora. This process is to be organised by a Preparatory Committee appointed by the African Union and to include members of the rebel groups and the Government of Sudan, as well as tribal leaders and representatives of civil society and international organizations including the African Union, United Nations, and Arab League. The DDDC process is to be chaired by an "African of independence and integrity" and assisted by a team of elders from Darfur, and shall have between 800 and 1000 delegates, to include sheiks and tribal leaders, refugees, internally displaced persons, women, rebel groups, militias, civil society, and other local parties. The DDDC is empowered to make recommendations to the relevant local and national authorities, and to establish a permanent Peace and Reconciliation Council to continue its work.

Appendix Two

EXPLAINING THE MAY 2006 DARFUR PEACE AGREEMENT: AN OPEN LETTER FROM THE AFRICAN UNION MEDIATORS

We are writing this open letter to our dear friends and colleagues in the Sudan Liberation Movement/Army and Justice and Equality Movement, who are hesitating to support the Darfur Peace Agreement that was presented by the African Union Mediation to the Parties on 25 April, and which was enhanced with the support of the United States, United Kingdom, Canada and the European Union, and signed by Dr. Magzoub el Khalifa on behalf of the Government of Sudan and Mr. Minni Arkoy Minawi on behalf of the Sudan Liberation Movement/Army, on 5 May. Although we are members of the Mediation Team in Abuja, we are writing this as individuals who are deeply concerned with the situation in Darfur and committed to bringing about peace. We are concentrating on the actual paragraphs of the Darfur Peace Agreement, explaining its provisions, rather than exploring the wider political context and choices facing the leaders of the Movements.

We believe that the Darfur Peace Agreement represents a good deal for the Movements and for the people of Darfur. It is not perfect and it does not meet all the aspirations of the Movements. But it is a very strong deal in each of three main areas: power-sharing, wealth-sharing and security arrangements. And the Darfur Peace Agreement has stronger guarantees for implementation than any other peace agreement in this African continent.

In this open letter, let us explain some of the most important provisions of the Darfur Peace Agreement. We believe that many of the suspicions about this Agreement are based on misunderstanding and the fact that many of you have not had time to study the text in detail, and understand what it provides. The Darfur Peace Agreement does not demand that anyone gives up on their political demands. The SLM and JEM are still able to pursue their political objectives, by peaceful means, and they still have the opportunity to gain power in Darfur and establish governments at the level of State and Region, through democratic processes. At the moment you have nothing. Everything in the Agreement is a gain, and if you obtain the support of the people, you can gain still more.

Power-Sharing

A basic principle of the DPA is compromise. The Movements did not win the war and were not in a position to dictate their terms. The Government is in power and has no intention of handing over that power at the negotiating table. The Movements did not control a single state capital and controlled very few sizeable towns. The Mediation squeezed many concessions out of the Government. But we would never have been able to squeeze the Government so hard that it agreed to hand over a majority of control at any level of government.

If we could not find a means to provide the Movements with majority control of government structures in Darfur, what did we do for them? What the Darfur Peace Agreement does is create new structures especially for Darfur. Our solution to this problem was to set up a new position in the Presidency, a new Regional Authority with six subsidiary bodies, and enable the Movements to have at least equal representation in these. The purpose of all these bodies is to implement the Darfur Peace Agreement. Most of these bodies are directly supported by the international community. Most of them are transitional: they will be dismantled in a few years when their job is done. But in three years time, elections will be held. Whoever wins those elections, governs Darfur. A year after that, a referendum is held for the people of Darfur to decide whether Darfur should be a region or three states. The future will be decided democratically, depending on the decision of the people. Let us go into some more detail on the DPA proposals for power sharing.

The central proposal is the creation of the Transitional Darfur Regional Authority (TDRA). The TDRA is headed by a Chairperson, who is also the Senior Assistant to the President, and the fourth-ranking person in the Presidency. His competencies are equal to those of a Vice President. The TDRA has eleven members. The Senior Assistant to the President, who is chosen by the Movements, is the Chairperson. The three Governors are members—one from the Movements, two from the Congress Party. But the majority of members are the heads of the new bodies set up:

- The Darfur Rehabilitation and Resettlement Commission;
- The Darfur Reconstruction and Development Fund;
- The Darfur Land Commission;
- The Darfur Security Arrangements Implementation Commission;
- The Darfur Peace and Reconciliation Council; and
- The Darfur Compensation Commission.

In each case, the Senior Assistant to the President will nominate who is to be appointed. The heads of these Commissions should be individuals of integrity who enjoy the confidence of all Darfurians. This means that the TDRA has eight members nominated by the Movements and two by the National Congress Party. Examine for a moment the powers, competencies and resources available to the four Commissions, the Fund and the Council that fall under the TDRA. These are the bodies that will determine the real fate of the people of Darfur, which will decide how the key questions of rehabilitation and resettlement, reconstruction and development, land and compensation are decided.

The Security Arrangements Implementation Commission will oversee the integration of the Movements' combatants, the disarming of the Janjaweed and other militia, and the downsizing of the Popular Defence Forces. The DSAIC is also responsible for a thorough-going reform of the Police. Within it is a Security Advisory Team from a foreign country or an international organization. And it is to be chaired by a person of integrity who enjoys the confidence of all, who will be a nominee of the Movements, with the Movements and the Government equally represented under the Chairperson. These bodies will be well-funded. The DRDF in particular will have resources that completely dwarf what is available to states. The GoS has agreed to fund the DRDF to the tune of $300 million this year and $200 million for each of the following two years. How many times greater is this than the budget of a State Government? And that is just the GoS contribution: the international donors are likely to double the amount, at the minimum. Already, contributions are being offered. The head of the DRDF is nominated by the Movements. He reports to the TDRA which has eight out of ten members nominated by the Movements. And the President of Sudan is required to consult with the Senior Assistant to the President on every decision relating to Darfur.

The Movements demanded a Region for Darfur. The Darfur Peace Agreement does not give a Region today. But it sets up a process whereby the people of Darfur can vote to set up a Region. After four years there is a referendum that allows every Darfurian to vote for or against the creation of a region. Any Darfur Region will have the borders of Darfur as of 1 January 1956, one of the Movements' central demands. If we turn to the State Governments, here the Movements enjoy significant representation, but it is short of a majority. One of the three Governors is from the Movements, and the deputy Governors of the two other states. In each state, two of the eight ministers are from the Movements. The NCP has about 50% of the seats in the State Legislatures, with the Movements getting about 30% and the balance with the other parties including the SPLM. In six of the localities, the Movements nominate the Commissioner; in another six, they nominate the Executive Director. Clearly the Movements do not get a majority in the Darfur States, either in the executive or the legislature. But one Governor is a Movement nominee too. But, dear friends in the Movements, reflect on the comparative power and respective roles of the States and the TDRA. They are designed to do different things. The States continue to function with routine activities such as health and education. It is the TDRA that is responsible for the things that the displaced people, the victims of war, and the members of the

Movements themselves, care most about. What happens if the States try to block the programmes of the TDRA? At the specific request of the Movements, we built in a mechanism for breaking the deadlock and overcoming any such obstructionism. The matter is referred to the Presidency. And the President is required to consult the Senior Assistant to the President on all matters relating to Darfur.

This arrangement is in place for three years. Then there are elections and the winner governs. Many in the Movements are fearful that the Congress Party will use its influence to win those elections even though the people of Darfur's true loyalties may be elsewhere. But consider that the elections will be monitored and international donors have promised extensive funds for the SLM to transform itself into a political party and campaign in the elections.

Before leaving Power-Sharing, let us briefly examine four other issues. One is the post of Senior Assistant to the President. This is not the Vice Presidential post that the Movements demanded. In fact, it has more competencies. A Vice President functions at the request of the President. This position of Senior Assistant is specifically designed to have powers over Darfur. He will be the fourth-ranking member of the Presidency. A second point is representation in Khartoum. Paragraph 89 provides that one minister in Khartoum State should be a nominee of the Movements. An additional question is representation in the civil service. Here, a Panel of Experts under the National Civil Service Commission is to determine the correct representation of Darfurians, using the criteria of population size, affirmative action, and precedents (the Comprehensive Peace Agreement). This has to be done within a year. In the meantime, the Government is required to take action to put Darfurians in senior positions across the civil service. Related to this is the provision for education in paragraphs 86-88. There is a quota for Darfurians to be represented in universities, both in Darfur and in Khartoum. And education for Darfurians is to be free.

Lastly, we must mention the Darfur-Darfur Dialogue and Consultation. This will be an opportunity for every Darfurian voice to be heard, for all those who have not been at the table in the peace process to come and join in the peace process during its most important phase, which is implementation.

Wealth-Sharing

Turning to Wealth-Sharing, there is less to explain. The great majority of the text was agreed by the Movements. There are three key issues to elucidate. One of these issues is how much money is to be transferred from central government to the states, through the Fiscal and Financial Allocation Monitoring Commission (FFAMC). The FFAMC has been set up but has not yet completed its formula. Mindful of this delay, the DPA proposes that a panel of experts is appointed to work out a formula to enable the government to make an allocation from the National Revenue Fund to the States. The second issue has been the seed money for the Darfur Reconstruction and Development

Fund (DRDF). On this issue the DPA provides US$300 million for the year 2006 and US$200 million for 2007 and 2008 respectively. These amounts will be adjusted after the Joint Assessment Mission outcome and recommendations. Already donor governments have committed themselves to literally hundreds of millions of additional dollars for this fund and a big donor conference has been scheduled for September in Holland. Finally we have the most controversial issue of all: compensation for victims. Fourteen paragraphs in the DPA—from 199 to 213—provide the details for setting up a Compensation Commission. Agreement on this was reached only at the last moment, against strenuous opposition from the Government. The Government has agreed to $30 million as its first payment. Let us repeat: the DPA includes compensation. Let us repeat again: the Movements' demand for a Compensation Commission has been met. This is a victory for the Movements.

Security Arrangements

For the Movements, the security arrangements are the strongest part of the document. The first section of the Security Arrangements chapter is a comprehensive ceasefire and transitional security arrangements. The core of this is three phases over five months. In stage one, the Parties disengage their forces, to their respective areas of control. Demilitarized zones are created along humanitarian supply routes and around camps for internally displaced persons, and in buffer zones that separate the forces of the Parties. In the coming months, the GoS is required to neutralize the Janjaweed armed militia. Given that the GoS has been slow in proposing its plan for how to do this, the DPA has done most of the work of developing this plan. The first step is that all Janjaweed, militia and PDF must be confined to their camps, strictly designated areas or their own communities. Then all heavy weapons must be taken from them. Read Paragraphs 314-317. This is all to be verified by AMIS before the Movements are asked to withdraw their forces. There is also a special provision that they cannot be active in areas where civilians live or where the Movements are asked to redeploy their forces, in paragraphs 366-368. At long last, there is a clear plan for dealing with the problem of the Janjaweed. This is another victory for the Movements' negotiators in Abuja. The DPA also includes extensive measures for providing security to IDP camps including the creation of a community police force, which acts as a temporary guarantee of the safety of IDPs until such time as normality is restored.

The second section of the Security Arrangements is the long-term question of the final status of security in Darfur. This includes three main pillars, organized under a new institution which we are calling the Darfur Security Arrangements Implementation Commission, which is to be supported by a Security Advisory Team.

The first pillar is provisions for integrating former combatants from the Movements into the Sudan Armed Forces and other security services. This section is remarkably strong: 4,000 former combatants into the army, 1,000 into other security institutions, and 3,000 for special programmes of assistance and education. Read paragraphs 399-416 for the details. Equally important is a robust mechanism for disarming the Janjaweed and other armed militia. The obligation on the GoS to disarm the Janjaweed, contained in UN Security Council Resolution 1556, is given concrete form in Paragraph 457. Let us repeat: the Darfur Peace Agreement sticks to the principle that the Janjaweed must be disarmed, and creates a practical process whereby this can be accomplished. The third pillar is the reform of selected security institutions in Darfur, specifically those that have been expanded during the war as paramilitary branches of the army, such as the PDF and Border Intelligence. The aim is to return these to their normal size and function. (Paragraph 429.) Alongside this, the civilian police is to have its capacity built so that it can become the instrument of law enforcement in Darfur.

Guarantees

Most of the members of the Movements are deeply worried that the Government will not implement this agreement fairly and faithfully. You fear that implementation will lag behind or be blocked. You are looking for guarantees. The DPA in fact has some of the strongest guarantees of any peace agreement of recent times. There are four layers of guarantee. The first and the most important guarantee is the sequence of the implementation of the agreement itself. The Movements are not required to lay down their arms until the Sudan Armed Forces have withdrawn to its garrisons and the Janjaweed and other militia have been brought under strict control and disarmed. If the Government doesn't stick to its obligations, then the armed forces of the SLM do not have to do their part: they don't have to redeploy, or assemble, or disarm, until they are sure that the Government has done what it promises. Overall, the Agreement also has a Darfur Assessment and Evaluation Commission and the deadlock-breaking mechanisms of referring matters to the Presidency, where the Senior Assistant to the President has to be involved in every decision relating to Darfur. The second guarantee is the monitoring mechanisms of AMIS and the Ceasefire Commission. The Agreement strengthens all of these. Every stage needs to be verified. And we must not overlook one of the most important facts about this Agreement: now it is place, it is possible for the UN to send a force to Darfur. All of these mechanisms will be much stronger if the UN is involved. The DPA provides a Security Advisory Team from an international partner. The third layer of guarantee is international mechanisms at the African Union and the UN. This Agreement does not supercede any of the existing UN Security Council Resolutions relating to Darfur. There will be resolutions at the AU Peace and Security Council and the UN Security Council supporting it, and Resolution 1591, which provides for individuals who obstruct the peace process to be subjected to individual sanctions, can also be applied to individuals who obstruct the implementation of the DPA. Darfur will remain on the agenda of the Security Council until this agreement is fully implemented and normality has returned. Lastly, there are the bilateral guarantees of the international partners. There is no conflict in the world that has obtained more international attention than Darfur, and this will continue. There is no peace agreement that has obtained greater international recognition. The President of the United States, George W. Bush, wrote personal letters to both Abdel Wahid Nour and Minni Minawi, assuring them both that he would do his utmost to ensure the faithful implementation of the Agreement. What more guarantees could one have? One cannot go higher than the UN Security Council and the President of the United States. These are stronger guarantees than were provided to the CPA, stronger than any other peace process in Africa today.

In summary, we firmly believe that many of the reasons why members of the SLM and JEM have hesitated in accepting the Darfur Peace Agreement, are not based on an accurate reading of the actual text of the Agreement. It is understandable that many people have not had the time to read and analyze this long and complicated document fully. We hope that this open letter enables you to better understand how the DPA does indeed meet the core demands and concerns of the Movements, and can be the basis for a just and lasting peace in Darfur.

Yours very sincerely,

Sam Ibok
Boubou Niang
Noureddine Mezni
Alex de Waal
Abdul Mohammed
Dawit Toga

Appendix Three

Declaration of Principles for the Resolution of the Sudanese Conflict in Darfur

Preamble

1. We, the Government of the Sudan (hereinafter the GOS), the Sudan Liberation Movement/Army (SLM/A) and the Justice and Equality Movement (JEM), meeting in Abuja, Nigeria, under the auspices of the African Union (AU), as parts of the efforts to find a lasting solution to the conflict in Darfur,

2. Reiterating our commitment to our previous agreements, namely the Humanitarian Ceasefire Agreement signed in N'djamena, Chad, on April 2004, the agreement on modalities for the establishment of the Ceasefire Commission (CFC) and the Deployment of Observers signed in Addis Ababa, Ethiopia, on 28 May 2004, as well as the Protocols on the Improvement of the Humanitarian Situation in Darfur and the agreement on the Security situation signed in Abuja, Nigeria, on 9 November 2004

3. Reaffirming our commitment to the full implementation of relevant UN Security Council resolutions and African Union decisions stressing the need to reach a political solution in order to bring the conflict in Darfur to an end;

4. Convinced that the core of the current conflict in Darfur is political and socio-economic which can only be resolved through peaceful means and within the framework of a comprehensive settlement that addresses its various causes and aspects;

5. Stressing the commitment to respect international humanitarian law and promote and protect human rights, including the rights of women and children, as part of the efforts to address the prevailing situation in Darfur;

6. Recognizing that faith, traditional values and customs as well as family as the natural and basic nucleus of society, play a positive role;

7. Reaffirming our commitment to the unity, sovereignty, territorial integrity and independence of the Sudan;

8. Recognising that the signing of the Comprehensive Peace agreement (CPA) between the government of Sudan (GOS) and the Sudan Liberation Movement/Army,

on January 9, 2005, constitutes a significant step forward towards finding a just, peaceful and lasting solution to the conflict in the Sudan.

Agree that the following principles shall guide our future deliberations and constitute the basis for a just, comprehensive and durable settlement of the conflict in Darfur:

1. Respect for the diversity of the people of the Sudan is of paramount importance, as are the full recognition and accommodation of the multi-ethnic, multi-religious, multi-cultural situation, as well as the unity of the Sudan historically agreed by the free will of its people will be enhanced by the recognition and accommodation of such diversity

2. Democracy, political pluralism, freedom a vibrant and dynamic civil society, the rule of law, independence of judiciary, the freedom of the media, accountability and transparency, with justice and equality for all, regardless of ethnicity, religion and gender, are a basis for the effective participation of all Sudanese citizens in the management of their own affairs and decision making processes at all levels of governance.

3. Citizenship is the basis for civil and political rights and duties, including the freedom of expression and association for all Sudanese. No Sudanese shall be discriminated against on the basis of religion, belief, ethnicity, gender or for any other reason. This shall be incorporated into the National Constitution.

4. A federal system of government, with an effective devolution of powers and a clear distribution of responsibilities between the national and other levels of governance, is considered essential for ensuring effective local participation and fair administration of Sudan in general and Darfur in particular. In this context, issues relating to the Native Administration should be addressed.

5. Effective representation in all government institutions at the national level, including the legislative, judicial and executive branches, as well as economic and cultural institutions shall be ensured as effective participation by the citizens of Sudan, including those from Darfur.

6. National wealth shall be distributed equitably. This is essential to ensure the effectiveness of the devolution of power in Darfur, within the framework of a federal system of government, and to ensure that due consideration is given to the socio-economic needs of Darfur.

7. Power sharing and wealth sharing shall be addressed in accordance with a fair criteria to be agreed by the Parties.

8. Humanitarian assistance will be provided on the basis of humanitarian standards including those enshrined in International Humanitarian Law, UN norms and standards.

9. Refugees and internally displaced persons (IDPs) have an inalienable right to return to their places of origin in accordance with International Law and UN norms and standards. To this end, the Parties to the conflict and the international community shall take concrete measures to create a conducive environment to provide the necessary assistance to IDPs and Refugees.

10. Rehabilitation and reconstruction of Darfur is a priority; to that end, steps shall be taken to compensate the people of Darfur and address grievances for lives lost, assets destroyed or stolen, and suffering caused.

11. The promotion of reconciliation, the restoration of the traditional and time honoured peaceful coexistence among the communities of Darfur, based on the principle of mutual respect, and the commitment to prevent future divisions are essential to restore and sustain lasting peace and stability in Darfur.

12. Aiming at sustainable development, environmental degradation, water resources and land use shall be addressed. Tribal land ownership rights (hawakeer) and other historical rights shall be affirmed within their historical borders. Traditional mechanisms in Darfur will be considered consistent with the provisions of the national Constitution.

13. Broad security arrangements to consolidate the restoration of people of Darfur shall be addressed in the context of a Comprehensive Agreement.

14. Agreements reached by the Parties shall be presented to the people of Darfur to secure their support through Darfur-Darfur dialogue and consultation.

15. The guarantee of the AU and assistance of the international community shall be sought to ensure the implementation of Agreements reached for the resolution of the conflict in Darfur.

16. All Agreements reached by the Parties shall be incorporated into the national Constitution.

17. The Parties commit themselves to undertake negotiations to end the conflict in Darfur in good faith.

Abuja, July 5, 2005

Signed

For the Government of Sudan
Mohamed Yousif Abdallah, State Minister for Humanitarian Affairs

For the Sudan Liberation Movement/Army
Khamis Abdallah Abakar, Vice President

For the Justice and Equality Movement
Ahmed Mohamed Tugod Lissan, Head of Delegation
Witnessed by the AU Special Envoy Dr. Salim Ahmed Salim

Appendix Four

THE APRIL 2005 NDJAMENA HUMANITARIAN CEASEFIRE AGREEMENT ON THE CONFLICT IN DARFUR

19 April 2004

Under the auspices of His Excellency, Idriss Deby, President of the Republic of Chad, Head of State, assisted by the Chairperson of the Commission of the African Union, and in the presence of International Observers and Facilitators, The Government of the Republic of Sudan, the Sudan Liberation Movement/Army and the Sudan Justice and Equality Movement; hereinafter known as the Parties, have agreed on the following:

Political Preamble

Convinced of the necessity of the establishment in Darfur of a democratic political culture to guarantee to the populations of the region their political, economic and social rights; Convinced that only a global, just and durable solution negotiated peacefully can resolve the problems in Darfur; Convinced that a mechanism for a political solution should be envisaged as soon as possible;

1   The parties undertake to join their efforts in order to establish a global and definite peace in Darfur.
2   The parties agree to meet under the auspices of the Tchadian mediator in a period not exceeding two weeks, to negotiate a definitive settlement of the conflict and to discuss solutions to the problems of Darfur, with a view to finding a definite and global settlement in the framework of a conference between all the representatives of Darfur, especially in relation to its socio-economic development.
3   The parties undertake to create a conducive environment for negotiations and to cease all hostile media campaigns.

Humanitarian Questions

— Agreeing on the fact that any peaceful and durable settlement of the problem of Darfur can be achieved only through frank and sincere dialogue,
— Determined to give up the use of force as means of settling the problem of Darfur,

Article 1: The parties decide on the cessation of hostilities between them and specifically proclaim a cease-fire for a period of 45 days automatically renewable except if opposed by one of the parties. The ceasefire will be effective on land, and air, to allow on one hand, a fast and unrestricted humanitarian access to the needy populations of Darfur and on the other hand, to arrive at a just and durable solution to the problem in Darfur;

Article 2: The cessation of hostilities between all the forces of the parties will be effective 72 hours after the signing of this Agreement.

During the cease-fire, each party shall:
— Refrain from any recruitment operations;
— Refrain from any military action, and any reconnaissance operations
— Disengage and refrain from any deployment, movement or action which could extend the territory under its control or which could lead to a resumption of hostilities;
— Stop laying landmines; mark and sign post any danger areas and mine fields;
— Refrain from supplying or acquiring arms and ammunitions;
— Refrain from any act of violence or any other abuse on civilian populations;
— Stop any act of sabotage;
— Stop any restriction on the movement of goods and people;
— Stop any form of hostile act, including hostile propaganda;
— Ensure humanitarian access;
— Refrain from any military activity which, from the opinion of the Cease-fire Commission or the Joint Commission, could endanger the cease-fire;

Article 3: The parties shall establish a Cease-fire Commission composed of 2 high ranking officers from the Parties, the Tchadian mediation and the international community in accordance with the sovereignty of the Sudan.

Article 4: The mandate of the Cease-fire Commission shall consist of:
— planning, verifying and ensuring the implementation of the rules and provisions of the cease fire;
— defining the routes for the movement of forces in order to reduce the risks of incidents; the administrative movements shall be notified to the Cease-fire Commission. -assist with demining operations;

- receiving, verifying, analyzing, and judging complaints related to the possible violations of the cease-fire;
- developing adequate measures to guard against such incidents in the future violations
- the parties shall provide the head of the Cease-fire Commission, or his designated representative, immediately upon request information required for the implementation of this Agreement on the understanding that the information will be held confidentially.
- the parties shall give the Cease-fire Commission and its personnel unrestricted access throughout Darfur;
- determine clearly, the sites occupied by the combatants of the armed opposition and verify the neutralization of the armed militias.

The Cease-fire Commission shall report to a Joint Commission composed of the parties, the Tchadian mediation and the international community.

Article 5: The parties have decided to free all the prisoners of war and all other persons detained because of the armed conflict in Darfur;

Article 6: The parties shall ensure that all armed groups under their control comply with this Agreement. The forces of armed opposition should be assembled in clearly identified sites. The Sudanese Government shall commit itself to neutralize the armed militias.

Article 7: The parties have agreed to meet as soon as possible under the auspices of the Tchadian mediation and the international community to discuss pending points, notably about setting up the Joint Commission and the Cease-fire Commission mentioned in article 3 and 4 of the present agreement;

Article 8: The parties undertake to facilitate the delivery of humanitarian assistance and the creation of conditions favorable to supplying emergency relief to the displaced persons and other civilian victims of war and this, wherever they are in the Darfur region, in accordance with the appendix attached to the present Agreement;

Article 9: In case of non respect of the clauses of this Agreement by one of the parties, the other party will refer such a case to the Cease-fire Commission and if necessary the Joint Commission.

Article 10: This Agreement can be amended by agreement of the parties with the consent of the Cease-fire Commission. The parties may agree to renew this Agreement for an additional 45 days not later than 21 days before the expiry of the Agreement.

Any party may notify the Cease-fire Commission of its intention for renewal and if the parties agree, this Agreement shall be extended for an additional two months period;

Article 11: This Agreement shall take effect as from its date of signature. It is drafted in Arabic, in French and in English, all three texts being equally authentic.

Done at N'djamena, this 8th Day of April, 2004.

For the Sudan Liberation Movement/Army (SLM/A)
Mini Arkou Minawi, Secretary General

For the Government of Sudan (GOS)
Acherif Ahmad Oumar Badour, Minister for Investment

For the Sudanese Justice and Equality Movement (SJEM)
Nasradine Hussein Difallah, President
Mahamat Saleh Hamid, Deputy Secretary General

For the Tchadian Mediation
Nagoum Yamassoum, Minister of State, Ministry of Foreign Affairs and African Integration

For the African Union
Sam B. Ibok, Representative of the Chairperson of the Commission

Appendix Five

THE MAY 2004 AGREEMENT WITH THE SUDANESE PARTIES ON THE MODALITIES FOR THE ESTABLISHMENT OF THE CEASEFIRE COMMISSION AND THE DEPLOYMENT OF OBSERVERS IN THE DARFUR

I. TERMS OF REFERENCE

The Humanitarian Ceasefire Agreement on the conflict in the Darfur, signed in N'Djamena on 8 April 2004, provides, in its articles 3 and 4, for a Ceasefire Monitoring Committee, which shall report to a Joint Commission consisting of the Parties, the Chadian mediation and the international community. To implement the above provisions, the African Union is proposing that the Parties agrees on the followings:

1. Joint Commission

A. The Joint Commission shall operate on the basis of consensus and consist of two senior members each, from the Parties, the Chadian mediation, the African Union (AU), the US and the EU. The Chairman of the Joint Commission shall be selected by the AU from an African Union Member State. Other International Representatives from the UN and major contributors shall be invited to attend the meetings of the Joint commission as observers.

B. The Joint Commission shall comprise political leaders who should be mandated to take decisions and to deal with matters brought before it by CFC. The Joint Commission (JC) shall be located initially in N'Djamena, moving to Khartoum at a time to be agreed upon by the parties.

2. Ceasefire Commission

The CFC shall report to a Joint Commission consisting of the Parties, the Chadian Mediation and the international community in accordance with the sovereignty of Sudan.

II. COMPOSITION

1. The Ceasefire Commission (CFC) shall be composed as follows:
    a. Chairman, to be appointed by the AU, from an African Union Member State;
    b. Deputy Chairman (European Union);
    c. Chadian Mediation;
    d. Government of Sudan
    e. JEM
    f. SLM/A

2. The size of the CFC may be adjusted with the agreement of the Parties as necessary to carry out the objectives of the Agreement.

3. Other International Representatives from the UN, the EU and USA shall be invited to participate as observers.

4. The operational arm of the Ceasefire Commission shall be the African Union Monitoring Mission, composed of Observers from the Parties, the Chadian mediation, African Union Member States and other representatives of the International Community.

5. To ensure command and control, all Observers shall be answerable to the Chief Military Observer (CMO) to be designated by the AU, who, in turn, shall be answerable to the CFC. Additionally, and in order to ensure unity and discipline of command, all Observers participating in the monitoring, investigation and verification exercise, as well as members of the CFC, shall be funded through the budget of the CFC. No parallel reporting to other authority shall be allowed in the execution of responsibilities.

6. The Military Observers (MILOBS) may be lightly armed. The AU Monitoring Mission shall be deployed on the basis of the commitment of the Government of The Sudan, the JEM and the SLM/A to ensure the protection and the safety of the Observers. However, in the event that the Parties are unable to provide effective protection, the Chairmen of the Joint Commission (JC) and the Ceasefire Commission (CFC) shall request for the deployment of the protection element as envisaged in the decision of

the AU Peace and Security Council of 25th May 2004. The Protection element shall be drawn from AU Member States and shall number between 100 and 300.

III. MANDATE

i. The mandate of the CFC shall consist of:
- Planning, verifying and ensuring the implementation of the rules and provisions of the ceasefire;
- Defining the routes for the movement of forces in order to reduce the risks of incidents; the administrative movements shall be notified to the CFC;
- Requesting appropriate assistance with demining operations;
- Receiving, verifying, analyzing and judging complaints related to possible violations of the ceasefire;
- Developing adequate measures to guard against such incidents in the future;
- Determining clearly the sites occupied by the combatants of the armed opposition and verifying the neutralization of the armed militias.

ii. The CFC Headquarters shall be responsible for coordinating investigations, verifications, monitoring and reporting compliance in accordance with the Darfur Cease-fire Agreement and Implementation Modalities. The priority for the CFC is to investigate and report on violations of this Agreement

iii. The CFC Headquarters shall be located in El-Fisher (Darfur). Sectors sites shall be established at other locations, including, but not limited, to Nyala, El Geneina, Kabkabiyah, Tine, and Abeche. A liaison Office will be established in Khartoum.
Each Sector will be composed of two (2) Teams for verification and investigation comprising the Parties, the African Union, the Chadian Mediation and other members of the international community (see the deployment Plan). iv. The CFC support staff shall be part of the Headquarters and shall be organized as follows:
- Operations Team: Coordinates all activities of the CFC in Darfur. Maintains communications links with the Parties and the International community.
- Transportation/Logistics Team: Coordinates transportation, communications, supply and logistics requirements for the CFC.
- Information Team: Coordinates the dissemination of information to support and promote the Cease-fire Agreement among the people in Darfur, including information regarding activities of the CFC, freedom of movement, civic action, and others.
- Medical Support Team: Provides necessary health and medical care and advice to the CFC.

- Government of Sudan Team: Conducts liaison with the GoS.
- SLM Team: Conducts liaison with the SLM/A.
- JEM Team: Conducts liaison with the JEM.

IV. MODALITIES FOR MONITORING AND VERIFICATION

a. Under the orders of the Chairman, members of the CFC can be deployed anywhere in Darfur to monitor and report on compliance with the provisions of the Cease-fire Agreement and when necessary investigate any alleged violations of the Agreement. When deployed, the CFC shall organize itself as a team. The team leader will be designated by the Chairman/Deputy Chairman.

b. The CFC will investigate all credible reports of violations of the Ceasefire Agreement. The CFC may conduct its inspections and investigations by road or by air.

c. Each of the Parties and the international community shall provide two liaison officers per sector, to be available to participate in investigations at any time. The non-provision of liaison personnel by the Parties to investigate shall be considered as a violation of the Agreement.

d. Following an investigation, the CFC shall endeavor to reach its decisions by consensus. In the event that any of the parties disagrees with the final decision of the CFC, that Party will seek redress from the Joint Commission (JC).

e. The CFC shall seek to advance the process through confidence building visits in the region. The CFC will maintain regular liaison with the parties as well as UN Agencies, the ICRC and NGOs. The CFC will also visit IDP sites and other areas.

f. The parties shall provide the Chairman of the CFC, or his designated Representative, immediately upon request, information required for the implementation of the Darfur Ceasefire Agreement on the understanding that the information shall be held confidential by the Chairman.

g. The Parties shall give the CFC and its personnel unrestricted freedom of movement and access throughout Darfur. The Sector Commander shall inform all members of the Observer team of all their future movements. It will be the responsibility of Liaison Officers to inform their respective Commanders of such movements.

h. A Status of Mission Agreement (SOMA) will be signed with the Government of The Sudan.

Addis Ababa, 28 May 2004

For the Sudan Liberation Movement/Army:
Mini Arkou Minawi, Secretary General

For the Government of Sudan:
H.E. Osman Elsaïd, Ambassador of the Republic of the Sudan in Ethopia

For the Justice and Equality Movement:
Ahmed Mohamed Tugod Lissan

For the Chadian Mediation:
H.E. Maïtine Djoumbé, Ambassador of the Republic of Chad to Ethiopia

For the African Union:
H.E. Saïd Djinnit, Commissioner for Peace and Security

[A "PLAN FOR THE ESTABLISHMENT OF A CEASEFIRE COMMISSION AND
THE DEPLOYMENT OF OBSERVERS IN DARFUR" was also agreed]

Appendix Six

Protocol Between the Government of the Sudan (GoS), the Sudan Liberation Movement/Army (Slm/A) and the Justice and Equality Movement (Jem) on the Enhancement of the Security Situation in Darfur in Accordance with the N'djamena Agreement

Preamble

1   We, the Government of the Sudan (hereinafter the GoS), on one hand, the Sudan Liberation Movement/Army (SLM/A) and the Justice and Equality Movement (JEM) [hereinafter the SLM/A-JEM], on the other, henceforth referred to as the Parties, meeting in Abuja, Nigeria, under the auspices of the African Union (AU), as part of the efforts to find a lasting solution to the conflict in Darfur;

2   Expressing our utmost concern over the repeated violations of the relevant provisions of the Humanitarian Ceasefire Agreement, signed in N'djamena, Chad, on 8 April 2004 [hereinafter the N'djamena Agreement], and the prevailing insecurity in Darfur, notably the persistent attacks and other abuses against civilians and their property and livelihood;

3   Condemning all acts of violence against civilians and violations of human rights and international humanitarian law;

4   Cognizant of the need to restore confidence in Darfur, as part of the efforts to facilitate the voluntary return of the refugees and internally displaced persons (IDPs), alleviate the plight of the civilian population and create conditions for a lasting and comprehensive settlement of the conflict in Darfur;

5   Reiterating our commitment to the N'djamena Agreement, including the appended Protocol on the Establishment of Humanitarian Assistance in Darfur, the Agreement

on the Modalities for the Establishment of the Ceasefire Commission (CFC) and the Deployment of Observers in Darfur, signed in Addis Ababa, Ethiopia, on 28 May 2004 [hereinafter the Addis Ababa Agreement] and the Protocol on the improvement of the Humanitarian situation in Darfur, signed in Abuja on 9 November 2004;

6   Reaffirming our commitment to the sovereignty, unity, territorial integrity and independence of the Sudan;

7   Recalling the spirit and letter of resolutions 1556 (2004) and 1564 (2004) adopted by the UN Security Council on 30 July and 20 September 2004,

respectively, as well as relevant AU decisions, including the Communiqué adopted by the 18 th meeting of the Peace and Security Council (PSC) of the AU, held on 20 October 2004;

8   Recognizing that the magnitude of the crisis in Darfur is such that it requires sustained assistance and engagement by the international community and, in this regard, expressing our appreciation for its efforts to alleviate the humanitarian plight and promote lasting peace and security in Darfur;

9   Welcoming the leadership and the engagement of the African Union, including its decision to strengthen its Mission in the Sudan (CFC/AMIS), to provide more effective support to the efforts aimed at restoring peace and security in Darfur, and expressing our commitment to fully cooperate with the AU to that end;

10 Recording our agreement to address humanitarian issues, security issues, political questions, as well as economic and social affairs, in the course of the Inter-Sudanese Peace Talks on the crisis in Darfur;

Agree as Follows:

1. The Parties agree to strictly abide by the provisions of the N'djamena and Addis Ababa Agreements. In this respect, the Parties recommit themselves to ensure an effective ceasefire on land and air, in particular:

- refraining from all hostilities and military actions, any reconnaissance operations, deployment, movement, or any other action aimed at extending territories under their respective control, and any military activity which, in the view of CFC/AMIS, undermines the ceasefire;
- notifying all administrative movements to the CFC/AMIS.

2. The Parties agree to enhance and facilitate the implementation of the N'djamena Agreement, through, inter alia, the following:
- submitting to the Chairman of the CFC/AMIS, or his designated representative, all information needed to enable it to carry out its mandate

and tasks as agreed upon under the N'djamena and Addis Ababa Agreements. Such information shall be held confidentially;

— cooperating fully with the CFC/AMIS, to enable it develop, as soon as possible, a plan with a view to ensuring that no exchange of fire takes place and facilitating the effective monitoring of the ceasefire

— providing CFC/AMIS with the required information to enable it determine clearly the sites occupied by the forces on the ground;

— extending unreserved cooperation to AMIS to enable it discharge its mandate and operational tasks as spelt out in the communiqué adopted by the 18th meeting of the PSC held on 20 October 2004;

— refraining from conducting hostile military flights in and over the Darfur Region.

3   The Parties call upon the CFC/AMIS to accelerate the enforcement and full implementation of the N'djamena Agreement.

4. In compliance with Article 5 of the N'djamena Agreement, the Parties commit themselves to:

— release immediately and unconditionally all persons detained in relation to the hostilities in Darfur. This stipulation shall not apply to those convicted through the due process of law under para. 6 of resolution 1556 (2004);

— request the International Committee of the Red Cross (ICRC) to assist in this exercise in accordance with the Geneva Conventions; in this respect, further request CFC/AMIS to extend its full cooperation to the ICRC, in conformity with the latter's mandate as a neutral intermediary;

— abstain, in conformity with the N'djamena Agreement, from detaining or abducting persons.

5   In accordance with the N'djamena Agreement, relevant AU decisions and UN Security Council resolutions 1556 and 1564, the GoS undertakes to:

— expeditiously implement its stated commitment to neutralize and disarm the Janjaweed/armed militias, bearing in mind the relevant UN Security Council resolutions. Such a process shall be supervised and verified by the CFC/AMIS. For this purpose, the GoS shall provide all relevant information to the CFC/AMIS;

— identify and declare those militias over whom it has influence, and provide CFC/AMIS with all relevant details. The GoS shall ensure that these militias will refrain from all attacks, harassment, or intimidation.

6   The Parties agree to build confidence between themselves and restore trust among the local communities, including through:

- ensuring the security of commercial activities in Darfur, as well as to and from other parts of the country, and facilitating the provision of basic humanitarian services in Darfur;
- ensuring full control of the members of their respective forces at all levels to prevent all actions that would constitute violations of the ceasefire or undermine security.

7   Acknowledging the need for a sustained assistance and engagement by the international community, the Parties:

- commit themselves to fully cooperate with the AU to facilitate the process of strengthening AMIS as decided by 18th meeting of the PSC held on 20 October 2004;
- request the CFC to report on a regular basis, at least once every two weeks, to the Joint Commission on the progress made in the implementation of the present Protocol, in accordance with the N'djamena and Addis Ababa Agreements;
- agree on the urgent need to enhance the role of the Joint Commission, including by holding monthly meetings and ensuring adequate attendance at appropriate level;
- agree, in line with the Constitutive Act of the AU, to seek any additional assistance that may be needed from the AU to speed up the implementation of the above commitments.

8   The Parties shall refrain from recruiting children as soldiers or combatants, consistent with the African Charter on the Rights and Welfare of Children, the Convention on the Right of the Child (CRC) and the Optional Protocol to the CRC on the Involvement of Children in Armed Conflict.

9   The Parties request CFC and AMIS, in accordance with their mandates, to monitor and observe compliance with the present Protocol. In this respect, the CFC and AMIS shall, as necessary and in consultation with the Parties, determine modalities for discharging the responsibilities entrusted to them under the present Protocol.

10 The Parties agree to defer any disagreement on interpretation of the present Protocol to the AU Commission.

11 This Protocol shall take effect as from its date of signature.

12 The Chairperson of the AU Commission shall register the present Protocol with the Secretary-General of the United Nations, in accordance with Article 102 of the UN Charter.

Abuja, 9 November 2004.

For the Government of the Sudan
Dr. Magzoub El-Khalifa, Head of Delegation

For the Sudan Liberation Movement/Army
Minni Arkou Minawi, Secretary-General

For the Justice and Equality Movement
Ahmed Mohamed Tugod Lissan, General Coordinator,

The Federal Republic of Nigeria (Chair of the AU)
Amb. Oluyemi Adeniji, Minister of Foreign Affairs

The AU Commission
Amb. Sam B. Ibok

The Chadian Co-Mediation
Amb. Allam-Mi Ahmad

Appendix Seven

PROTOCOL BETWEEN THE GOVERNMENT OF THE SUDAN (GOS), THE SUDAN LIBERATION MOVEMENT/ARMY (SLM/A) AND THE JUSTICE AND EQUALITY MOVEMENT (JEM) ON THE IMPROVEMENT OF THE HUMANITARIAN SITUATION IN DARFUR

Preamble

We, the Government of the Sudan (hereinafter the GoS), on the one hand, the Sudan Liberation Movement/Army (SLM/A) and the Justice and Equality Movement (JEM) [hereinafter the SLA/M – JEM], on the other, and all the three parties referred to as the Parties, meeting in Abuja, Nigeria, under the auspices of the African Union (AU), as part of the efforts to find a lasting solution to the conflict in Darfur;

Expressing our utmost concern at the current humanitarian crisis in Darfur and its consequences for the civilian population, especially women and children, resulting in widespread human suffering;

Condemning all acts of violence and violations of human rights and international humanitarian law;

Reiterating our commitment to the Humanitarian Ceasefire Agreement, signed in N'djamena, Chad, on 8 April 2004 [hereinafter the N'Djamena Agreement], including the appended Protocol on the Establishment of Humanitarian Assistance in Darfur, and the Agreement on the Modalities for the Establishment of the Ceasefire Commission (CFC) and the Deployment of Observers in Darfur, signed in Addis Ababa, Ethiopia, on 28 May 2004 [hereinafter the Addis Ababa Agreement];

Recalling the spirit and letter of Resolution 1556 (2004) adopted by the UN Security Council, on 30 July 2004, as well as AU Decisions relevant to the humanitarian issues;

Upholding the noble traditions and values of the Sudanese people, including the principle of solidarity to assist and save the weak and vulnerable during times of difficulty;

Stressing the need to restore and uphold the rule of law, including investigating all cases of human rights violations and bringing to justice those responsible, in line with the AU's expressed commitment to fight impunity;

Recognizing that the magnitude of the crisis in Darfur is such that it requires sustained assistance and engagement by the international community;

Welcoming the leadership and the engagement of the AU, including through its Mission in Sudan (AMIS), to address the situation in Darfur and expressing our commitment to fully cooperate with the AU to achieve a lasting solution to the conflict;

Aware of the need to adhere to the humanitarian principles embodied in the UN Charter and other relevant international instruments, especially the principles of neutrality and impartiality of humanitarian assistance and aid workers;

Determined to do everything possible to halt the unfolding humanitarian crisis and to take the urgent steps required to create conditions conducive to a lasting and comprehensive solution to the conflict in Darfur;

Recording our agreement to address humanitarian issues, security issues, political questions, as well as economic and social affairs, in the course of the Inter-Sudanese Peace Talks on the crisis in Darfur.

Agree as follows:

1. *Free Movement and Access*
   - We commit ourselves to guarantee unimpeded and unrestricted access for humanitarian workers and assistance, to reach all needy people throughout Darfur, including:
   - The removal of all restrictions and procedures that may hinder free movement and access by land and air, without escort;
   - The authorization by the GoS, where deemed necessary by the UN, of cross-border humanitarian activities by international humanitarian agencies and organizations. In this respect, we commit ourselves to allow such assistance to proceed unimpeded;
   - Allowing the UN and other humanitarian assistance organizations, including Non-Governmental Organizations (NGOs), to travel along routes proposed by the UN, without restrictions or escorts, in order to deliver assistance to areas controlled by any Party, and facilitate all activities undertaken to that end;
   - Recognizing the right of the UN and other humanitarian assistance organizations, including NGOs, to administer and manage their operations, including the freedom to recruit and deploy their staff, without restrictions, interference or harassment by any Party;
   - Assigning a full time dedicated Contact Point, within the framework of the Joint Humanitarian Facilitation and Monitoring Unit, referred to in paragraph 4 of

the present Protocol, to work with the UN and other humanitarian assistance organizations to address issues related to free movement and access.

2. *Protection of Civilians*
We commit ourselves to:

— Take all steps required to prevent all attacks, threats, intimidation and any other form of violence against civilians by any Party or group, including the Janjaweed and other militias;
— Respect the property and livelihoods of individuals and communities;
— Ensure that the principle of voluntary return is fully respected and is not tampered with in any shape or form, consistent with general UN return principles;
— Maintain the civilian character of Internally Displaced Persons (IDPs) and refugee camps;
— Protect the rights of IDPs and refugees to return to their areas of origin;
— Protect the rights of IDPs and refugees in their areas of origin in order to enable them to return, should they choose to do so;
— Cooperate fully with the CFC and swiftly implement its recommendations;
— Ensure that all forces and individuals involved or reported to be involved in violations of the rights of IDPs, vulnerable groups and other civilians will be transparently investigated and held accountable to the appropriate authorities;
— Implement all commitments related to the protection of civilians in a manner consistent with the N'djamena and Addis Ababa Agreements. We request the AMIS to monitor the implementation of this commitment and to report thereon to the Joint Commission (JC), provided for in the N'djamena Agreement, on a regular basis.

3. *Role of the International Community*
Mindful of the crucial role of the international community in support of our efforts, we:

— Request the AU to urgently take the necessary steps to strengthen AMIS on the ground, with the requisite mandate, to ensure a more effective monitoring of the commitments we have made under the present Protocol and previous instruments, including the N'djamena and Addis Ababa Agreements, and those provisions of the Plan of Action for which AU's assistance has been requested. We undertake to extend full cooperation to the AU to that end;
— Appeal to the donors and the international community at large to extend full support to the UN and other humanitarian organizations in their endeavour to mitigate the humanitarian crisis in Darfur;

- Invite the international community to remain actively engaged in the efforts to alleviate the plight of the civilian population and promote a lasting solution to the current conflict;
- Welcome the deployment of UN human rights monitors and request the Office of the UN High Commission for Human Rights to expand the number of its human rights monitors in Darfur to assist the parties in their efforts to protect the human rights of the civilian population. We also commit ourselves to cooperate, as appropriate, with relevant and competent human rights organizations.

4. Implementation Mechanism

Within the framework of Article 8 of the N'djamena Agreement and in order to ensure full compliance with the provisions of this Protocol and implement them in good faith, we:

- Agree to form a Joint Humanitarian Facilitation and Monitoring Unit, based in El Fasher, under the leadership of the AMIS, comprising the UN, the members of the Joint Commission and other representatives of the international community invited by the AU. The Joint Humanitarian Facilitation and Monitoring Unit will report monthly to the Joint Commission on the progress made and the difficulties encountered;
- Endeavour, through the Joint Humanitarian Facilitation and Monitoring Unit, to identify ways and means of rebuilding confidence and trust in Darfur and defusing tensions among communities;
- Request the AU, working closely with the UN, to develop the detailed terms of reference and modalities for the functioning of the Joint Humanitarian Facilitation and Monitoring Unit.

Abuja, 9 November 2004

For the Government of the Sudan
Dr. Magzoub El-Khalifa, Head of Delegation

For the Sudan Liberation Movement/Army
Minni Arkou Minawi, Secretary-General

For the Justice and Equality Movement
Ahmed Mohamed Tugod Lissan, General Coordinator

Witnessed by:
The Federal Republic of Nigeria (Chair of the AU)
Amb. Oluyemi Adeniji, Minister of Foreign Affairs

The AU Commission
Amb. Sam B. Ibok

The Chadian Co-Mediation
Amb. Allam-Mi Ahmad

Appendix Eight

JOINT COMMUNIQUE BETWEEN THE GOVERNMENT OF SUDAN AND THE UNITED NATIONS ON THE OCCASION OF THE VISIT OF THE SECRETARY-GENERAL TO SUDAN

29 June – 3 July 2004

* Deeply concerned with the grave situation in the Darfur region of the Sudan;
* Alarmed by the number and severity of conditions of the internally displaced in Darfur and refugees in Chad which, if not addressed with urgency, may deteriorate to catastrophic levels;
* Aware of the urgent need to stop the continuing attacks on the targeted civilian population in Darfur, particularly by the Janjaweed and other outlaw armed groups, and to ensure security in the region consistent with the humanitarian ceasefire agreement signed by the government of Sudan and the rebel groups (SLM and JEM) in May;
* Convinced of the need to stop all human rights violations in the region;
* Convinced too of the urgency of resuming the talks between the Government of Sudan and the Darfur rebel groups (SLM and JEM) and speedily reach final settlement to address the root causes of the conflict;
* Aware of the positive impact the implementation of an eventual agreement on the South will have in the settlement of the conflict in Darfur and the establishment of durable peace in the Sudan as a whole;
* Recognizing the recent improvement in achieving humanitarian access to Darfur granted by the Government of Sudan to the United Nations, including humanitarian organizations and African Union monitors, as well as welcoming the increase in the provision of assistance to the internally displaced and other vulnerable groups by local and national authorities, international agencies and non-governmental organizations;

THE UNITED NATIONS:

1. Pledges to do its utmost to help alleviate the humanitarian need of the affected population in Darfur and Sudanese refugees in Chad consistent with its 90-day Humanitarian Action Plan.
2. Will assist in quick deployment of African Union ceasefire monitors
3. Stands ready to continue to help in the mediation on the South and on Darfur
4. Commits itself, subsequent to Security Council resolutions, to assist implement agreements reached on South Sudan and Darfur; to that end, the UN shall continue the preparations it has started for a possible peacekeeping role when agreements are reached.

THE GOVERNMENT OF SUDAN COMMITS ITSELF TO:

1. ON HUMANITARIAN ISSUES:
   Implement a 'moratorium on restrictions' for all humanitarian work in Darfur, and removes any other obstacles to humanitarian work, including:

   * Suspension of visa restrictions for all humanitarian workers and permitting freedom of movement for aid workers throughout Darfur.
   * Permitting immediate temporary NGO registration through a simple notification process that OCHA will offer to manage on behalf of NGOs; permanent registration shall be processed within 90 days.
   * Suspension of all restrictions for the importation and use of all humanitarian assistance materials, transport vehicles, aircraft and communication equipment.

2. ON HUMAN RIGHTS:

   * Undertake concrete measures to end impunity.
   * Undertake immediate investigation of all ceases of violations, including those brought to its attention by the UN, AU and other sources.
   * Ensure that the Independent Investigation Committee, established by presidential decree in May, receives the necessary resources to undertake its work and that its recommendations are fully implemented.
   * Ensure that all individuals and groups accused of human rights violations are brought to justice without delay.
   * Allow the deployment of human rights monitors.
   * Establish a fair system, respectful of local traditions, that will allow abused women to bring charges against alleged perpetrators.

3. ON SECURITY:

* Deploy a strong, credible and respected police force in all IDP areas as well as in areas susceptible to attacks.
* Train all police unit in human rights law and hold them responsible for upholding it;
* Ensure that no militias are present in all areas surrounding IDP camps.
* Immediately start to disarm the Janjaweed and other armed outlaw groups.
* Ensure that immediate action is taken to rebuild the confidence of the vulnerable population and that any return of the displaced to their homes is done in a truly voluntary manner in line with the current Humanitarian Ceasefire Agreement.

4. ON POLITICAL SETTLEMENT OF THE CONFLICT IN DARFUR:

* Resume the political talks on Darfur in the shortest possible time to reach a comprehensive solution acceptable to all
* As peace in Darfur is a requisite for peace in the South, welcome the international community's role in assisting the implementation of an eventual peace agreement in Darfur.

IMPLEMEMTATION MECHANISM:

1. The Government of Sudan and the United Nations agree to form a high level Joint Implementation Mechanism (JIM) for this agreement.
2. The Government of Sudan and the United Nations delegates to the JIM shall be lead by the Minister of Foreign Affairs for Sudan and the SRSG for the UN and its partners.
3. The JIM shall closely follow and appraise development and periodically report on the progress in the implementation of this agreement to the Government of Sudan and the United Nations.

KHARTOUM, 3 July 2004

Appendix Nine

GOVERNMENT LEGISLATIVE MEASURES ON DARFUR

KHARTOUM, July 06, 2004 (SUNA) — Following are the titles of the resolutions [issued by the representative of the Sudanese president in Darfur states and the minister of interior to restore law and order in western Sudan]: –

Resolution No. (1) for 2004 (To strengthen the security measures and protect the citizens in Darfur state.)

Resolution No. (2) for 2004 (Opening of police centers in the displaced camps and to strengthen the security measures in Darfur state.)

Resolution No. (3) for 2004 (To extend the necessary help to the committees and the African surveillance force.)

Resolution No. (4) for 2004 (Deployment of the armed force and the participating force and the security institutions in Darfur state to prevail security and protect the citizens and their properties in Darfur.)

Resolution No. (5) for 2004 (To facilitate the measures for granting entry visas to the workers of the voluntary organizations working in the sphere of humanitarian aid in Darfur state.)

Resolution No. (6) for 2004 (Exemption of all the humanitarian aid imports from any restrictions or customs tariff or any personal fee.

Resolution No. (7) for 2004 (Repeal of measures regarding the specifications on the humanitarian aid imports to Darfur state.)

Resolution No. (8) for 2004 (To facilitate the freedom of movement for those working in the humanitarian aid organizations in Darfur state.)

Resolution No. (9) for 2004 (To facilitate the flow of humanitarian aid to the displaced people in Darfur state.)

Resolution No. (10) for 2004 (Exemption of humanitarian aid from the health and medical measures in Darfur state.

Resolution No. (11) for 2004 (Exemption of agricultural inputs, fodders, and seeds in Darfur state from any restrictions or customs tariff or any personal fees)

Resolution No. (12) for 2004 (Exemption of humanitarian aid imports to Darfur state from any imports restrictions.)

Resolution No. (13) for 2004 (Exemption of humanitarian aid imports in Darfur state from the wounded stamp fee.)

Resolution No. (14) for 2004 (To activate the measures regarding the governments of Darfur states to guarantee the flow of the humanitarian aid and the humanitarian aid imports to the state and to ensure the return of the displaced to their villages)

Resolution No. (15) for 2004 (To facilitate the work of the facts finding committee in regard to the allegations of human rights violations committed by armed groups in Darfur state).

Appendix Ten

Joint Communique from the Ministry of Foreign Affairs and the Ministry of Humanitarian Affairs on the Facilitation of Humanitarian Access to Darfur

Khartoum, 20 May 2004

In fulfilment of its responsibilities and obligations toward its citizens and to ensure their well-being, and in adherence with the protocol on humanitarian access and the ceasefire agreement, both signed in N'Djamena, Chad in April 2004, the Government of Sudan recognizes the crucial need for immediate humanitarian assistance in the region and is determined to alleviate the suffering that has resulted as a byproduct of the war. This is one of the steps the Government is taking to enable the citizens of Darfur to return to their homes in time to prepare and plant their crops before the commencement of the rainy season. In efforts to facilitate the expected influx of assistance from various groups and partners, the Government of Sudan has decided the following:

1   To grant aid workers from various organizations, including the U.N., Red Cross, and NGOs, direct entry visas from Sudan missions abroad within forty-eight hours of application. The visas will be valid for three months.

2   To suspend the current system of travel permits required for travel to Darfur for three months. In its place the Government will require only that the aid workers have entry visas and provide the Ministry of Humanitarian Affairs with their names and itineraries.

3   To keep working on facilitating other procedures that will guarantee the delivery of the equipment and supplies needed for humanitarian work in Darfur.

4   These procedures will be effective Monday, May 24, 2004.
5   For more details references can be made to the Ministry of Humanitarian Affairs.

Based on the Government's open-ended vision to guarantee and facilitate humanitarian efforts, the Government calls on the African Union to prompt the deployment of the Cease-Fire Monitoring Team to Darfur. The presence of the Cease-Fire Monitoring Team will guarantee the flow of humanitarian aid and contribute to reinstating stability to the region. The Government also calls on the displaced persons and citizens of Darfur to return to their regions; the Government is committed to the Ministry of the Interior's security plan that guarantees their protection and security.

Appendix Eleven

[Published by the Government of Sudan, Khartoum, December 2004]

THE SUDAN GOVERNMENT VISION FOR A PEACEFUL SOLUTION IN DARFUR

Introduction:

1   The root causes of Darfur conflict are traced back to the competition between different groups of people over scarce natural and economic resources, such as water sources, pasture and arable and residential Land, in a society that, despite its religious harmony, is known for its tribal and linguistic diversity, in addition to the cross-border tribal ties with the neighbouring countries. As a result of the remoteness of the region which also lacks necessary infra-structure, coupled with the meagre resources and the lack of the international aid, the presence of law and security enforcement authorities in Darfur has been very weak. Therefore, in some parts of Darfur, traditional institutions, like the tribes, clans and armed groups enjoy people's loyalty and command greater influence than the state

2   In addition to the aforementioned reasons there have been other factors that have added to the complexity of the situation in Darfur, these are:

a-   The war in South of the Sudan that has lasted for more than twenty years. This war has wasted huge financial resources that could have been spent in developing the least developed regions of the Sudan, including Darfur. It has also contributed to the spread of culture of violence and incited some individuals and groups to believe that achieving their political objectives would be easier by raising arms against the state

b-   The armed conflicts in some of the neighbouring countries at different times led a number of armed groups to seek refuge in Darfur, some of them have their tribal extensions in the regions. This led to the spread of arms, given the long and not easy to monitor common borders c- An economic embargo that has been imposed on Sudan throughout the 1990s including the freezing of the country's legitimate rights in Lome and Cotonou Agreements As a result of this embargo which limited the state ability to execute social and economic developmental projects, the economic situation and living conditions in Sudan especially in the least developed regions, worsened. It should be noted, however, that most of the funds allocated to Sudan under, Lome Agreement, has been used in developmental projects in Darfur and other regions with similar conditions.

3   All these factors produced social and political congestions in some parts of Darfur. Different armed groups have emerged, some of them are organised robbery bandits, some are tribal militia for self-defence, and, of late, the anti-government armed groups came into being.

4   The Sudan Government acknowledges that there have been historical, objective domestic and external factors that made Darfur one of the least developed regions in Sudan. It also understands and shares the aspirations of Darfur people for economic and social development and equitable political participation. However, it must be made clear that raising arms against the state is not the appropriate method to achieve these legitimate ends. The Sudan Government reiterates that achieving sustainable and balanced development in all regions of the Sudan, and finding a political formula that secures equitable power sharing by its people have been on the top of its agenda. This has been manifested in the Naivasha Protocols that would lead to just and comprehensive peace agreement.

5   In recognition of this reality, the National Salvation Revolution has exerted considerable efforts in different fields of development and essential services in Darfur, including education, health, water supply, roads and airports, security and justice, The Government, however, admits that more efforts are still needed, given Darfur's vast area and the fact that the population is scattered throughout the region.

Principles of Peaceful Solution:

a   The Government of the Sudan calls for adoption of the following principles to resolve Darfur problem.

* Federal System of government which is the best for the Sudan.
* Acknowledging cultural and social diversity in the Sudan and considering it a support to the national unity.
* The equitable distributions of national wealth as a means to achieve the sustainable and balanced development of the whole country.

* Power devolution in appropriate way between different levels of government.
* Peaceful and democratic rotation of power and free political competition.

b The Government of Sudan views the agreed-upon agenda in Abuja talks under the AU auspices, namely: Humanitarian, Political, Security, Economic and Social affairs, respectively, as integral agenda that could lead to the resolution of Darfur Problem.

The positions of the Government of the Sudan on these agenda can be summed up as follows:

1 Humanitarian Affairs

To further enhance the internationally recognized progress and improvement in the humanitarian affairs, the Government believes that the agreed-upon protocol on the matter has covered all humanitarian aspects, and that it should be signed immediately to come into force. The Government of the Sudan reiterates its full commitment to implement this protocol to save the lives of its people who are affected by the conflict. It calls on the rebel movements in Darfur to sign and implement the protocol .

2 Security Affairs

The Government asserts that the responsibility of protecting civilians is an essential part of its duties that it spares no effort to fulfil. Addressing the question of security should take place in accordance with the Ndjamena Cease-Fire Agreement on 8th April 2004 and the AU Resolutions of 8th July 2004 in Addis Ababa. Had the rebels accepted a negotiated settlement to the problem and committed themselves to the signed agreements, the situation in Darfur would not have reached the current level. One of the major hindrances of improving the security situation is the failure of rebels to abide by the cease-fire agreement and their refusal to have their forces in specified areas as stipulated in Ndjamena Agreement and the AU resolutions. The Government has agreed to increase the African Union's monitors and their protection forces. This move is aimed at consolidating the cease-fire monitoring, helping confidence building and enhancing tranquillity in the camps of internally displaced persons and refugees to facilitate their voluntary return to their homes. At the same time, the rebel forces must be cantoned to protect them and to control their arms (see the appendix on security affairs)

3 Political Aspect

The Government's option is that the political aspect of Darfur problem is to be dealt with in the context of the federal system of government for all states in Northern Sudan and according to Naivasha Agreement, in particular the articles that cover the status of

Northern states. This agreement provides for holding multi-party elections at federal and state level including the direct election of state governors and legislative assemblies. It is the government's conviction that political solution to Darfur question should be based on a settlement accepted by all parties and supported by the people, provided that it should maintain the Sudan unity and ensure the widest popular participation on the basis of equality between all citizens.

The Government further believes that implementing and consolidating the federal system of government in the Northern states provides a real solution to the conflict in Darfur as it would ensure that:

* States shall have their own constitutions that do not contravene with the federal constitution.
* Elected State Governors.
* Elected Legislative Assemblies.

In the Government view, this solution would guarantee the Sudan unity and stability while enabling people of Darfur to run their own affairs in a direct and democratic manner beside enhancing their proactive participation in the government, administration, economy and all other public affairs.

Success of political solution in Darfur requires the full commitment and respect by the rebel to the cease-fire agreements, and they must also refrain from obstructing humanitarian activities for the sake of creating a conducive atmosphere for successfully peaceful settlement. Towards this end, political solution is to take place at two levels:

First level agreement between the Government and the two rebel movements on the above-mentioned fundamental principles

Second level A dialogue between the Government and people of Darfur as represented by their political, social, and tribal leaders beside armed groups, in the presence of representatives of Sudanese political powers, the AU, UN, Arab League, OIC, as monitors. The issues this conference will discuss include:

a- Issues of native, local, executive and political administration in Darfur within the federal framework
b- Issues of development and public service in Darfur.
c- Suitable formula of the region's participation in the central institutions.

Economic and Social Aspects:

Economic Aspects:

The Government of the Sudan recognizes that Sudanese citizen deserves an equitable share from the country's wealth and resources. The Government is keen on equitable distribution of wealth according to the following principles:

First   The aim of distribution of national wealth and resources is to attain decent living conditions for every and each citizen regardless of his/her gender, ethnicity, religion or political affiliation

Second   Each level of Government, federal state or local should be given enough resources that would enable it to fulfil its responsibilities

Third   All states and regions should get their equitable share of development to enable them reach a level that provides basic services and social development to have all states be on a par with the average standard.

Fourth   Special resources are to be allocated to regions affected by war and conflicts or those with meagre resources and economic backwardness with a view of providing them with developmental services and infra-structure to attain the desired growth. The Government views Naivasha Protocol on wealth sharing from this perspective. This protocol provides for the following:

1- The right of states to issue their own legislation, collect and utilize their resources including taxation.
2- Setting up of a fund for the national resources (non-state resources)
3- Setting up of a national council for the distribution of resources between the federal Government and the states. The states will be represented in this council by their Ministers of Finance. This council has the right to monitor payment of the state's dues from the national resources.
4- Setting up a fund for development and rehabilitation of the war-affected areas including Darfur. To overcome the aftermath of war in Darfur, he international community is required to contribute effectively in the development and rehabilitation efforts

Social Aspects

The following issues should be addressed:

1   Sewing up the social fabric through attaining reconciliation between different tribes and mending damages in keeping with heritage and traditions of the people of Darfur.

2   Holding a conference for Darfur tribal leaders to discuss the basis for peaceful co-existence and the requirements of social security and resolving conflicts over resources and land.

3   Holding inclusive conference on Darfur to endorse the resolutions of the tribal leaders conference, referred to above, to pave the way for reconciliation and mending the social fabric in Darfur.

4   In view of the root causes of the problem and its social and cultural dimensions, the Government believes that there is a need to create a commission for land to resolve disputes linked to tribal ancestral holdings, movement and routes of nomads and regulating land use and development.

Bibliography

A Note About the Bibliography

This book has relied heavily upon news wire services, especially Reuters, Agence France-Presse, Associated Press, Deutsche Presse-Agentur and the UN Integrated Regional Information Network. They have been used because they are generally perceived to be independent and credible sources of information. While much of the media coverage of Darfur has been undemanding, there have nevertheless been a number of outstanding journalists who have reported on the conflict, including Opheera McDoom of Reuters, the *Washington Post*'s Emily Wax and Jonathan Steele of *The Guardian*. Several universities and think-tanks have contributed greatly in making as much Darfur-related documentation as publicly accessible as possible. One such institution has been the South African-based Institute for Security Studies, one of Africa's leading human security research institutes. It has one of the most extensive databases of African and international documents relating to Darfur. These include all UN and African Union documents pertaining to Darfur, ranging from communiqués and reports of the AU Peace and Security Council and AU Ceasefire Commission reports, through to all relevant UN Security Council resolutions and reports as well as peace, ceasefire and humanitarian agreements and treaties signed in the course of the conflict. These documents are available at <http://www.issafrica.org/ index.php?link_id=14&tmpl_id=3&slink_id=2474&link_type=12&slink_type=12>. In addition to the growing literature on Darfur, a number of Darfur-oriented blogs have emerged. One of the most focused of these is the US Social Science Research Council's "Making Sense of Darfur", available at <http://www.ssrc.org/blog/ category/darfur/>. This blog addresses Darfur politics, the peace process, humanitarian issues, media and advocacy, climate and environment.

Books and Articles

Adam, Baballa Haroun Nor, "Ethnic Composition, Economic Pattern, and Armed Conflicts in Dar Fur", *Sudanese Human Rights Quarterly*, Number 8, July 1999.

Advertising Standards Authority, "Adjudication regarding Save Darfur Coalition t/a Globe for Darfur Aegis Trust advert", 8 August 2007, available at <http://www.asa.org.uk/asa/adjudications/Public/TF_ADJ_42993.htm>.

African Union, *Overview of AU's Efforts to Address the Conflict in the Darfur Region of the Sudan*, Conf/PLG/2 (I), 26 May 2005.

Ahmed A.M. and and S. Harir, *Sudanese Rural Society: Its Development and Dynamism*, (Arabic) University Khartoum Press, Khartoum, 1982.

Ahmed, Ismaeil Abakr, "Causes of Tribal Conflicts in Dar Fur", *Sudanese Human Rights Quarterly*, Number 8, July 1999.

Anderson, Scott, "How Did Darfur Happen?", *The New York Times* Magazine, 17 October 2004.

Burr, J. Millard and Robert O. Collins, *Africa's Thirty Years' War: Chad, Libya and the Sudan, 1963-1993*, Westview Press, Boulder, Co, 1999.

Burr, J. Millard and Robert O. Collins, *Darfur: The Long Road to Disaster*, Markus Wiener, Princeton N.J., 2006.

Cheadle, Don and John Prendergast, *"Not On Our Watch": The Mission To End Genocide in Darfur and Beyond*, Hyperion, New York, 2007.

Centre for Research on the Epidemiology of Disasters, *Darfur: Counting the Deaths. Mortality Estimates from Multiple Survey Data*, University of Louvain, Belgium, 26 May 2005, available at <www.cred.be>.

Centre for Research on the Epidemiology of Disasters *Darfur: Counting the Deaths (2). What are the Trends?* University of Louvain, Belgium, 15 December 2005, available at <www.cred.be>.

Coates, Ta-Nehisi, "Black, White, Read. Newspapers Are Serving Up the Sudan Conflict as a Race War. Sadly, It's Not That Simple", *The Village Voice* (New York), 28 September 2004.

Collins, Robert O., 'Disaster in Darfur', *African Geopolitics*, October 2004.

Daly, M.W., *Darfur's Sorrow: A History of Destruction and Genocide*, Cambridge University Press, Cambridge, 2007.

de Waal, Alex, *Famine that Kills: Darfur, Sudan, 1984-1985*, Oxford University Press, Oxford, 1989 (Revised 2005).

de Waal, Alex, "Counter-Insurgency on the Cheap", *London Review of Books*, Volume 26, Number 15, 5 August 2004.

de Waal, Alex, "Tragedy in Darfur: On Understanding and Ending the Horror", *Boston Review*, Volume 29, Number 5, October-November 2004.

de Waal, Alex, "Briefing: Darfur, Sudan: Prospects for Peace", *African Affairs*, Volume 104, Number 414, pp.127-35, London.

de Waal, Alex, *Who are the Darfurians? Arab and African Identities, Violence and External Engagement*, Justice Africa, London, 23 August 2005.

de Waal, Alex, "Are things getting worse in Darfur? There is no simple answer", 20 June 2007, Social Science Research Council Darfur weblog, available at <http://www.ssrc.org/blog/2007/06/20/are-things-getting-worse-in-darfur-there-is-no-simple-answer/>.

de Waal, Alex, "Deaths in Darfur: Keeping ourselves honest", 18 August 2007, Social Science Research Council Darfur weblog, available at <http://www.ssrc.org/blog/2007/08/16/deaths-in-darfur-keeping-ourselves-honest/>.

de Waal, Alex and Julie Flint, *Darfur: A Short History of a Long War*, Zed Books, London and New York, 2005.

de Waal, Alex (editor), *War in Darfur and the Search for Peace*, Harvard University Press, 2007.

de Waal, Alex, "Send in the Peacemakers", *Prospect*, London, October 2007.

de Waal, Alex and John Prendergast, "Duelling Over Darfur. A human rights activist and an Africa scholar disagree – vehemently – on the best way to help Sudan", *Newsweek* Online Forum, 8 November 2007, available at <http://www.newsweek.com/id/69004>.

de Waal, "Darfur and the failure of the responsibility to protect", *International Affairs*, Royal Institute of International Affairs, London, November 2007.

Dowden, Richard, "ICC in the Dock", *Prospect*, London, May 2007.

el-Baghir, Nima, "What's in a Name?", *Focus on Africa*, BBC, London, October-December 2004, London.

Fake, Steve and Kevin Funk, "Saving Darfur or Salvation Delusion?", *Foreign Policy in Focus*, 20 June 2007, available at <http://www.fpif.org/fpiftxt/4314>.

Fake, Steve and Kevin Funk, "Divestment: Solution or Diversion?", *Foreign Policy in Focus*, 6 October 2007, available at < http://www.fpif.org/fpiftxt/4581>.

Faris, Stephan, "The Real Roots of Darfur", *The Atlantic Monthly*, April 2007

Government of Sudan, *The Development of the Situation in Darfur and the State's Efforts to Deal With It*, Ministry of Foreign Affairs, Khartoum, 30 December 2003.

Government of Sudan, *Government's Efforts in the Areas of Development and Services in Darfur States*, Ministry of Cabinet Affairs, Khartoum, 2004, <http://www.sudan.gov.sd>.

Government of Sudan, *Commission of Inquiry to Investigate Alleged Human Rights Violations Committed by Armed Groups in the Darfur States*, Khartoum, January 2005. Also published as UN Document S/2005/80, 26 January 2005.

Government of the United States, *Sudan: Death Toll in Darfur*, Fact Sheet, Bureau of Intelligence and Research, Department of State, Washington-DC, 25 March 2005, available at <http://www.state.gov/s/inr/rls/fs/2005/45105.htm>.

Government of the United States, *Darfur Crisis: Death Estimates Demonstrate Severity of Crisis, but Their Accuracy and Credibility Could Be Enhanced*, United States

Government Accountability Office, Report Number GAO-07-24, Washington-DC, 11 December 2006.

Heinze, Eric A., "The Rhetoric of Genocide in U.S. Foreign Policy: Rwanda and Darfur Compared", *Political Science Quarterly*, Volume 122, Number 3, 2007

Hoile, David, *The Darfur Crisis: Looking Beyond the Propaganda*, European-Sudanese Public Affairs Council, London, March 2004, available at <http://www.espac.org/pdf/Beyond-Propaganda.pdf>.

Hoile, David, *Seven Myths Hindering Peace in Sudan*, European-Sudanese Public Affairs Council, London, 2004, available at <http://www.espac.org/usa_sudan_pages/seven_myths.asp>.

Humanitarian Policy Group, *Humanitarian Advocacy in Darfur: The Challenge of Neutrality*, Policy Brief 28, Overseas Development Institute, London, October 2007.

Ibrahim, F. N., *Ecological Imbalance in the Republic of the Sudan: With Special Reference to Desertification in Darfur*, Bayreuth, Germany, 1984.

Johnson, Douglas H., *The Root Causes of Sudan's Civil Wars*, James Currey, London, 2004, p.139.

Jooma, Mariam Bibi, "The International Criminal Court and Sudan – Opening a Pandora's Box", *ISS Today*, Institute for Security Studies, Tshwane (Pretoria), 6 March 2007.

Kuperman, Alan J., "Strategic Victimhood in Sudan", *The New York Times*, 31 May 2006.

Lobban, Richard, "Complexities of Darfur", *Sudan Tribune*, 3 August 2004, available at <http://www.sudantribune.com>.

Mamdani, Mahmood, "The Politics of Naming: Genocide, Civil War, Insurgency", *The London Review of Books*, Volume 29, Number 5, 8 March 2007, available at <http://www.lrb.co.uk/v29/n05/mamd01_.html>.

Mamdani, Mahmood, "Blue-Hatting Darfur", *The London Review of Books*, Volume 29, Number 17, 6 September 2007, available at <http://www.lrb.co.uk/v29/n17/mamd01_.html>

Marlowe, Jen, *Darfur Diaries. Stories of Survival*, Nation Books, New York, 2006.

Miniter, Richard, "The New Afghanistan and the Next Battlefield?", in *Shadow War: The Untold Story of How Bush is Winning the War on Terror*, Regnery Publishing, Washington-DC, 2004.

Moon, Ban-Ki, "A Climate Culprit in Darfur", *The Washington Post*, 16 June 2007

Nathan, Laurie, "No Dialogue, No Commitment. The Perils of Deadline Diplomacy for Darfur", The Sudan Human Security Baseline Assessment, Small Arms Survey, Geneva, December 2006.

O'Fahey, Sean, *State and Society in Darfur*, Hurst, London, 1980.

O'Fahey, Sean, "W. Sudan a Complex Ethnic Reality with a Long History", *Sudan Tribune*, 15 May 2004, available at <http://www.sudantribune.com>.

O'Neill, Brendan, "Darfur: Damned by Pity", *Spiked* online, London, 21 September 2006, available at <http://www.spiked-online.com/index.php?/site/printable/1687/>.

O'Neill, Brendan, "Darfur: pornography for the chattering classes", *Spiked* online, London, 14 August 2007, available at <http://www.spiked-online.com/index.php?/site/printable/3723/>.

Parrott, Louise, "The Role of the International Criminal Court in Uganda: Ensuring that the Pursuit of Justice does not come at the price of peace", *The Australian Journal of Peace Studies*, Volume 1, 2006.

Prunier, Gérard, *Darfur The Ambiguous Genocide*, Hurst, London, 2005.

Reeves, Eric, *A Long Day's Dying. Critical Moments in the Darfur Genocide*, The Key Publishing House, Toronto, 2007.

Rosenthal, John, "A Lawless Global Court. How the International Criminal Court Undermines the U.N. System", *Policy Review*, Hoover Institution, Stanford University, February-March 2004.

Ryle, John, "Disaster in Darfur", *The New York Review of Books*, Volume 51, Number 13, 12 August 2004.

Shekhdar, Kersap D., "Everything You Always Wanted to Know About Media Coverage of Darfur (But Where Afraid to Ask), *Online Journal*, 12 September 2004, available at <http://onlinejournal.com>.

Steele, Jonathan, "How the Media prolonged the war in Darfur", speech at the Royal United Services Institute, London, 6 July 2006.

Steidle, Brian and Steidle Wallace, Gretchen, *The Devil Came on Horseback: Bearing Witness to the Genocide in Darfur*, PublicAffairs, New York, 2007.

Tanner, Victor, "Rule of Lawlessness: Roots and Repercussions of the Darfur Crisis", Interagency Paper, Sudan Advocacy Coalition, 2005.

Tanner, Victor and Jérôme Tubiana, *Divided They Fall: The Fragmentation of Darfur's Rebel Groups*, Small Arms Survey, Graduate Institute of International Studies, Geneva, July 2007.

Totten, Samuel and Eric Markusen (editors), *Genocide in Darfur: Investigating the Atrocities in the Sudan*, Routledge, New York, 2006.

United Nations, *Report of the International Commission of Inquiry on Darfur to the United Nations Secretary-General*, United Nations, January 2005.

United Nations, *Darfur Mortality Rate Declines, But Remains "Extremely Fragile" – Survey*, United Nations Mission in Sudan Press Release, UNMIS, Khartoum, 28 June 2005.

Wax, Emily, "5 Truths About Darfur", *The Washington Post*, 23 April 2006.

Notes

Introduction

1 Alex de Waal, "Darfur and the failure of the responsibility to protect", *International Affairs*, Royal Institute of International Affairs, London, November 2007. Described by *The Observer* newspaper of London as a "world authority on the country", Dr de Waal is a human rights advocate who has published widely on Sudan. He was an adviser to the African Union during the Darfur peace talks in Abuja in 2006. He is a program director at the Social Science Research Council (SRRC), engaged in Emergencies and Humanitarian Action, HIV/AIDS and Social Transformation projects. He is also a fellow of the Global Equity Initiative at Harvard University, which is a partner in a consortium with the SSRC working on governance issues, and he is a director of Justice Africa, a human rights organisation based in London. De Waal was a founder and director of African Rights and chairman of Mines Advisory Group 1993-8 (co-laureate of the 1997 Nobel Peace Prize) In his twenty-year career, de Waal has studied the social, political and health dimensions of famine, war, genocide and the HIV/AIDS epidemic, especially in the Horn of Africa and the Great Lakes. He has been at the forefront of mobilising African and international responses to these problems. De Waal's books include: *Famine that Kills: Darfur, Sudan, 1984-5* (Oxford University Press, 1989), *Facing Genocide: The Nuba of Sudan* (African Rights 1995), *Who Fights? Who Cares? War and Humanitarian Action in Africa*, and *AIDS and Power: Why There is No Political Crisis Yet* (Zed, 2006). He is the editor of *War in Darfur and the Search for Peace*, Global Equity Initiative, Harvard University and Justice Africa, 2007, and *Islam and Its Enemies in the Horn of Africa*, Indiana, 2004. De Waal earned his doctorate in social anthropology from Oxford University.

2 "Darfur Violence is 'Demographic Catastrophe': Study", News Article by Agence France-Press, 1 October 2004.

3 *Darfur Humanitarian Profile*, United Nations, Khartoum, July 2007, p.3.

4 *Darfur Humanitarian Profile*, United Nations, Khartoum, September 2005, p.9.

5 "Darfur Humanitarian Crisis Seems to Have Eased – WHO", News Article by Reuters, 25 January 2005.

6 *Darfur 120-Day Plan Report September to December 2004*, Office of the United Nations Resident and Humanitarian Co-ordinator for the Sudan, Khartoum, January 2005.

7 *Darfur Humanitarian Profile*, United Nations, Khartoum, September 2005, p.9.

8 *Darfur 120-Day Plan Report September to December 2004, op. cit.*

9 *Darfur Humanitarian Profile*, United Nations, Khartoum, September 2005, p.5.

10 "SLA Rebels 'Destabilising' Darfur", News Article by BBC News, 5 September 2005.

11 *Darfur Humanitarian Profile,* United Nations, Khartoum, July 2007, p.5

12 See, for example, "AU condemns murder of Darfur peacekeepers", News Article by UN Integrated Regional Information Networks, UN Office for the Coordination of Humanitarian Affairs, Nairobi, 10 October 2005; "Secretary-General deplores murder of 5 African Union peacekeepers in Darfur", News Article by UN News Center, 2 April 2007, available at <http://www.un.org/apps/news/story.asp?NewsID=22097&Cr=sudan&Cr1=>; "Darfur rebels attack base, kill 10 peacekeepers", News Article by CNN, 30 September 2007, available at <http://www.cnn.com/2007/WORLD/africa/09/30/darfur.peacekeepers>.

13 "Death Rates Decline in Darfur", *The Los Angeles Times,* 26 August 2007.

14 Alex de Waal and Julie Flint, "In Darfur, From Genocide to Anarchy", *The Washington Post,* 28 August 2007. Flint is another long-standing anti-Khartoum activist. She was a London-based correspondent for *The Observer* from 1990-1992, focusing on the Middle East and the Horn of Africa. Since 1998, she has been a freelance journalist based in London and Beirut, concentrating since 2003 on Darfur.

15 "Darfur's Outdated Script", *The International Herald Tribune,* 9 July 2007.

16 Brendan O'Neill, "Darfur: Damned by Pity", *Spiked* online, London, 21 September 2006, available at <http://www.spiked-online.com/index.php?/site/printable/1687/>.

17 *Report of the International Commission of Inquiry on Darfur to the United Nations Secretary-General,* United Nations, January 2005. See, also, for example, "UN Clears Sudan of Genocide in Darfur", News Article by Associated Press, 31 January 2005.

18 *Commission of Inquiry to Investigate Alleged Human Rights Violations Committed by Armed Groups in the Darfur States,* Government of Sudan, Khartoum, January 2005. Also published as UN Document S/2005/80, 26 January 2005.

19 One of the direct dangers of any foreign military intervention has been pointed out by Professor Sean O'Fahey: "I am sceptical to large-scale outside intervention...to combine NGO activity with military intervention could lead to great difficulties. The recent decision of MSF to withdraw from Afghanistan illustrates the problem." ("Interview with Professor Sean O'Fahey", part of the "Asking the Right Questions about Darfur, Sudan" series, at Black Electorate.Com, 2004, <http://blackelectorate.com>). The dangers of foreign intervention have been outlined in a number of articles. See, for example, "Sudan Leaflets Vow Revenge on Foreign Troops", *The Daily Telegraph* (London), 27 July 2004; "Darfur Will be a Graveyard for Foreign Troops", *Sudan Vision* (Khartoum), 27 July 2004; "Sudan Warns Britain that Intervention Could Turn into Another Iraq", *The Daily Telegraph* (London), 23 July 2004; "Janjaweed Vow to Fight any Intervention by 'Infidels'", *The Sunday Telegraph,* 15 August 2004. See also, articles cautioning against intervention being urged by anti-government critics such as Peter Moszynski, "There Can be No Quick Fix in Sudan: After Iraq, Military Intervention is No Longer a Credible Option", *The Guardian* (London), 28 July 2004, and by *The Guardian*'s diplomatic editor, Ewen Macaskill,

"Power of Persuasion", *The Guardian* (London), 21 June 2004. Tim Hames of *The Times* has also challenged the notion, in any instance, of a moral obligation to intervene: "Our Forces Cannot be the Military Wing of Oxfam: The War in Iraq Places No Moral Obligation on Britain to Act in Sudan", *The Times* (London), 23 August 2004.

20 "Darfur, Saving Itself", *The Washington Post*, 3 June 2007.

21 Rebecca Hamilton and Chad Hazlett, "'Not on Our Watch': The Emergence of the American Movement for Darfur", in Alex de Waal (editor), *War in Darfur and the Search for Peace*, Global Equity Initiative, Harvard, and Justice Africa, 2007, p.362.

22 *Ibid*, p.344.

23 See, for example, "UK Advertising Regulator Says Ad Campaign's Darfur Deaths Claim Not Factual", News Article by Associated Press, 15 August 2007.

24 "Darfur's Outdated Script", *The International Herald Tribune*, 9 July 2007.

25 See, for example, "Did they plot to steal African's orphans of war?", *The Observer* (London), 4 November 2007; and Chris Bickerton, "Zoe's ark: the dangers of 'DIY humanitarianism'", *Spiked* online, London, 7 November 2007, available at <http://www.spiked-online.com/index.php?/site/printable/4052/>. Bickerton is Stipendiary lecturer in International Politics at Pembroke College, Oxford. He is co-editor of *Politics without Sovereignty: A Critique of Contemporary International Relations*, UCL Press, London, 2007.

26 "Do-Gooders Gone Bad. Activists have brought issues like Darfur into living rooms. But they may be doing more harm than good", *Newsweek*, 3 November 2007. See, also, "Packaging a Tragedy. What the Save Darfur movement did right, where it went wrong – and what its strategy can teach us about the future of political advocacy", *Newsweek* Web Exclusive, 26 October 2007.

27 Alex de Waal, "Darfur's Elusive Peace", in Alex de Waal (editor), *War in Darfur and the Search for Peace*, *op. cit.*, p.377.

28 *Ibid*.

29 *Ibid*.

30 "Repairing the Damage in Darfur", Comment is Free, *The Guardian* (London), 8 September 2006.

31 "All this moral posturing won't help Darfur", *The Independent* (London), 31 July 2007.

32 "General Martin Luther Agwai fears Darfur force will fail", *The Times* (London), 26 October 2007.

33 Paul Moorcraft, "How to Avoid Another Iraq in Sudan", *Business Day* (South Africa), 9 March 2006.

34 "Bin Laden Calls for Jihad against Darfur Peacekeepers", News Article by Associated Press, 23 October 2007.

35 "Death Rates Decline in Darfur", *The Los Angeles Times*, 26 August 2007.

36 *Ibid*.

37 "In Darfur, From Genocide to Anarchy", *The Washington Post*, 28 August 2007.

38 "Unseen by western hysteria, Darfur edges closer to peace", *The Guardian* (London), 10 August 2007.

39 *Monthly Report of the Secretary-General on Darfur*, S/2005/650, United Nations, New York, 14 October 2005, p.5.

40 Mahmood Mamdani, "Blue-Hatting Darfur", *The London Review of Books*, 6 September 2007, available at <http://www.lrb.co.uk/v29/n17/mamd01_.html>. Mamdani is the Herbert Lehman Professor of Government in the Departments of Anthropology and Political Science at Columbia University in the United States. He is also the Director of Columbia's Institute of African Studies. He is also the current President of the Council for Development of Social Research in Africa in Dakar, Senegal.

41 See, for example, "Political Negotiations the Only Way to Resolve Darfur Crisis, Sudan tells UN", News Article by UN News Service, 3 October 2007, available at <http://www.un.org/apps/news/printnews.asp?nid=24180>; Sudanese President Vows to End Darfur Conflict", *Sudan Tribune*, 3 September 2005, available at <http://www.sudantribune.com>; "Sudan to Seek Final Darfur Peace Deal at Abuja Talks: VP", News Article by Agence France-Presse, 30 August 2005.

42 "Vice President: To Work for Peace in Darfur, Unity in Sudan", News Article by Associated Press, 2 September 2005.

43 "Sudan's New FM Proposes Plan to End Darfur Conflict", News Article by Agence France-Presse, 25 September 2005.

44 Alex de Waal and Julie Flint, *Darfur: A Short History of a Long War*, Zed Books, London and New York, 2005, p.121.

45 See, for example, "UN Envoy Blames Darfur Rebels with Blocking Peace Talks", News Article by Associated Press, 22 November 2005, and "AU Threatens Sanctions against Darfur Rebels for Impeding Peace Talks", News Article by Agence France-Presse, 24 November 2005. The rebels had also largely ignored American attempts to encourage them to engage more constructively in the peace process – see "U.S. Convenes Peace Talks on Darfur, but Rebels are Mostly Absent", *The New York Times*, 9 November 2005.

46 "Sudan's Kiir Urges EU to Press Darfur Rebels on Peace", *Sudan Tribune*, 8 October 2005, available at <http://www.sudantribune.com>. See also, "Sudan Urges Int'l Community to Pressurize Darfur Rebels", News Article by Xinhua, 24 October 2005.

47 "Repairing the Damage in Darfur", Comment is Free, *The Guardian* (London), 8 September 2006.

48 See, for example, "Donor Fatigue Threatens Humanitarian Aid to Darfur", News Article by Reuters, 17 November 2005.

49 See, for example, "Darfur Peace Talks in Crisis after Boycott by Rebel Groups", *The Guardian* (London), 25 October 2007; and "Darfur Talks in Danger of Lacking Attendance", *The New York Times*, 25 October 2007.

50 "Sudanese President Demands Brown Apology", *The Guardian* (London), 31 October 2007.

51 "All this moral posturing won't help Darfur", *The Independent* (London), 31 July 2007.

52 "Exclusive Interview: In Defence of the United States", *The Independent* (London), 29 September 2006.

53 See, for example, "International Criminal Court Opens Investigation into Darfur", UN News Service, New York, 6 June 2005. The Sudanese government and judiciary have challenged the jurisdiction of the International Criminal Court – see "Sudan: Judiciary Challenges ICC over Darfur Cases", News Article by Integrated Regional Information Networks, UN Office for the Coordination of Humanitarian Affairs, Nairobi, 24 June 2005. The Sudanese president has publicly stated that Sudan will not allow any Sudanese citizens to stand trial before the ICC – see, for example, "President: No Sudanese to be Tried by ICC", News Article by UPI, 12 May 2005.

54 Christopher Caldwell, "It is best to stay out of Darfur", *The Financial Times* (London), 16 December 2006.

55 Jonathan Steele, "How the Media prolonged the war in Darfur", speech at the Royal United Services Institute, London, 6 July 2006.

56 Alex de Waal, "The book was closed too soon on peace in Darfur", *The Guardian* (London), 29 September 2006.

57 For an excellent historical background to Darfur, see Sean O'Fahey, *State and Society in Darfur*, Hurst, London, 1980.

58 See, for example, Baballa Haroun Nor Adam, "Ethnic Composition, Economic Pattern, and Armed Conflicts in Dar Fur", *Sudanese Human Rights Quarterly*, Number 8, July 1999, pp. 9-10.

59 See, for example, A.M. Ahmed, A. M. and S. Harir, *Sudanese Rural Society: Its Development and Dynamism*, (Arabic) University Khartoum Press, Khartoum, 1982.

60 See, for example, F. N. Ibrahim, *Ecological Imbalance in the Republic of the Sudan: With Special Reference to Desertification in Darfur*, Bayreuth, Germany, 1984.

61 See, for example, Roland Oliver and Anthony Atmore, *Medieval Africa 1250-1800*, Cambridge University Press, Cambridge, 2001, p.106.

62 Richard Lobban, "Complexities of Darfur", *Sudan Tribune*, 3 August 2004, available at <http://www.sudantribune.com>.

63 Sean O'Fahey, "W. Sudan a Complex Ethnic Reality with a Long History", *Sudan Tribune*, 15 May 2004, available at <http://www.sudantribune.com>.

64 Ismail Abakr Ahmed, "Causes of Tribal Conflicts in Dar Fur", *Sudanese Human Rights Quarterly*, Number 8, July 1999, p.24.

65 Sharif Harir and Terje Tvedt (editors), *Short-Cut to Decay: The Case of the Sudan*, Nordic Africa Institute, Uppsala, 1993.

66 *Commission of Inquiry to Investigate Alleged Human Rights Violations Committed by Armed Groups in the Darfur States*, Government of Sudan, Khartoum, *op. cit.*, pp.23-24.

67 John Ryle, "Disaster in Darfur", *The New York Review of Books*, Volume 51, Number 13, 12 August 2004. John Ryle, an anti-Government activist, is Chair of the Rift Valley Institute and a Research Associate of the Centre of African Studies at the University of London.

68 *Darfur: "Too Many People Killed For No Reason"*, Amnesty International, London, February 2004.

69 Gérard Prunier, *Darfur The Ambiguous Genocide*, Hurst, London, 2005, p. 152.

Chapter One

70 "Sudan Islamists use Darfur as Battleground", News Article by Reuters, 22 September 2004.

71 "How to Prevent the Next Darfur", *Time*, 26 April 2007, available at <http:// www.time.com/time/magazine/article/0,9171,1615171,00.html>.

72 Julian Borger, "Scorched", *The Guardian Weekend* (London), 28 April 2007.

73 The Sudan Liberation Army, which originally called itself the Darfur Liberation Front, is also known as the Sudan Liberation Movement (SLM). To avoid confusion this study will refer to the Sudan Liberation Army, or SLA.

74 Prunier, *op. cit.*, p.96.

75 "Sudan: Rage Finds Outlet in Rebel Camps", *Mail and Guardian* (Johannesburg), 28 August 2004.

76 "New Rebel Group Seizes West Sudan Town", News Article by Agence France-Presse, 26 February 2003.

77 "The Escalating Crisis in Darfur", News Article by Integrated Regional Information Networks, UN Office for the Coordination of Humanitarian Affairs, Nairobi, 31 December 2003.

78 See, for example, "Sudan Accuses Southern Separatists of Supplying Arms to Darfur Rebels", News Article by Agence France-Presse, 28 April 2003, and "Sudanese Armed Forces Attack an Unidentified Plane for Helping Western Rebels", News Article by Associated Press, 28 August 2003.

79 See, for example, *Report of the International Commission of Inquiry on Darfur to the United Nations Secretary-General*, United Nations, January 2005.

80 Julie Flint, "Darfur's Armed Movements", in Alex de Waal (editor), *War in Darfur and the Search for Peace*, Global Equity Initiative, Harvard, and Justice Africa, 2007, pp. 153-4.

81 "Widespread Insecurity in Darfur Despite Ceasefire", News Article by Integrated Regional Information Networks, UN Office for the Coordination of Humanitarian Affairs, Nairobi, 3 October 2003.

82 Victor Tanner, "Rule of Lawlessness: Roots and Repercussions of the Darfur Crisis", Interagency Paper, Sudan Advocacy Coalition, 2005.

83 Victor Tanner and Jérôme Tubiana, *Divided They Fall: The Fragmentation of Darfur's*

Rebel Groups, Small Arms Survey, Graduate Institute of International Studies, Geneva, July 2007, p.38.

84 See, for example, "Khartoum Forces Free Tribal Leaders Held Hostage in Darfur: Press", News Article by Agence France-Presse, 30 March 2003 and "Arab Leaders Killed by Sudan Insurgents", News Article by Agence France-Presse, 24 March 2004.

85 See "Sudan, Darfur Rebels Sign Pacts to End Hostilities, Aid Refugees", *USA Today*, 9 November 2004; "Sudan Signs Pacts with Rebels in Darfur Region", *The New York Times*, 9 November 2004.

86 All this should be compared with the fact that there were only three primary schools in Darfur in 1935.

87 This compares with Darfur opposition leader Ahmed Ibrahim Diraige's comment that up until 1965 there had not been a single minister from either Darfur or Kordofan, in *Management of the Crisis in the Sudan, Proceedings of the Bergen Forum*, 23-24 February 1989, University of Bergen.

88 Various government publications, including *The Development of the Situation in Darfur and the State's Efforts to Deal With It*, Ministry of Foreign Affairs, Khartoum, 30 December 2003. See, also, *Understanding the Darfur Conflict*, Khartoum, December 2004, <http//www.reliefweb.org> and *Government's Efforts in the Areas of Development and Services in Darfur States*, Ministry of Cabinet Affairs, Khartoum, 2004, <http://www.sudan.gov.sd>.

89 *Ibid.*

90 "Darfur Rebel Attack Stops Water Supply Project", *Sudan Vision* (Khartoum), 7 June 2004.

91 "Darfur Leaders Condemn Rebel Attacks on Development Projects", *Sudan Vision* (Khartoum), 28 October 2004.

92 *Highlights on the Problems of Darfur*, Government of North Darfur State, al-Fasher, May 2005.

93 "Darfur Governor Links Khartoum Plot with Rebels", News Article by Reuters, 26 September 2004. Ghazi Suleiman is the chairman of the Sudanese Human Rights Group. He was been arrested and detained by the Sudanese government on more than a dozen occasions. He became a SPLA member of parliament in 2005.

94 Sudarsan Raghavan, "Sudan Violence is Part of Power War", News Article by Knight-Ridder News Service, 20 August 2004.

95 "Sudan Islamists use Darfur as Battleground", News Article by Reuters, 22 September 2004.

96 Alex de Waal, "Tragedy in Darfur: On Understanding and Ending the Horror", *Boston Review*, Volume 29, Number 5, October-November 2004.

97 Idriss Déby is a Zaghawa of the Bedeyat clan from north-east Chad.

98 *Situation of Human Rights in the Darfur Region of the Sudan*, E/CN.4/2005/3, UN Commission on Human Rights, Geneva, 7 May 2004, paragraph 53.

99 Prunier, *op. cit.*, p.48.

100 Douglas H Johnson, *The Root Causes of Sudan's Civil Wars*, James Currey, London,

2004, p.139. A critic of the Sudanese government, Johnson is the author of *Nuer Prophets* (1994), co-author of *Operation Lifeline Sudan (OLS): A Review* (1996) and editor of the British Documents on the End of Empire *Sudan* volume (1998).

101 Sharif Harir and Terje Tvedt *op. cit.*

102 Alex de Waal, "Tragedy in Darfur: On Understanding and Ending the Horror", *Boston Review*, October-November 2004.

103 See, for example, "Islamist Turabi Fears U.S. Dominates Sudan", News Article by Reuters, 26 March 2002, and "Toppling Government is First Item in Programme of Hasan al-Turabi's Party: Interview", *Sudan Tribune*, 18 February 2004, available at <http://www.sudantribune.com>.

104 Sudarsan Raghavan, "Sudan Violence is Part of Power War", News Article by Knight-Ridder News Service, 20 August 2004.

105 *Ibid.*

106 "Darfur Governor Links Khartoum Plot with Rebels", News Article by Reuters, 26 September 2004.

107 "What Kind of Intervention Will Work in Darfur?", News from Africa, Nairobi, August 2004.

108 "Power Struggle: Darfur's Janjaweed Militia Aren't the Only Ones Sowing Chaos and Death. Meet the Two Rebel Factions Threatening Yet Another Civil War", *Time*, 31 October 2004.

109 *Darfur Rising: Sudan's New Crisis*, International Crisis Group, Africa Report Number 76, Brussels, 25 March 2004.

110 *Emir* is a title of leadership. In Sudan it was particularly used for Mahdist military commanders.

111 Victor Tanner and Jérôme Tubiana, *Divided They Fall: The Fragmentation of Darfur's Rebel Groups, op. cit.*, p.33.

112 "Sudanese Government Warns Opposition Party to Stop 'Sedition' in West", News Article by Associated Press, 23 November 2003.

113 "Peace Still Some Way Off in Sudan", *Middle East International* (London), 8 January 2004.

114 "Al-Turabi Denounces US Role in Peace Process", News Article by *Al-Hayat* (London), 26 January 2004.

115 "Sudanese Peace Talks flounder over the Legal status of the Capital Khartoum", *al-Ahram* (Cairo), Issue Number 686, 15-21 April 2004. Turabi's Popular National Congress soon changed its name to the Popular Congress.

116 "Plot Thickens Around Darfur", *Al-Ahram* (Cairo), Issue No 684, 1-7 April 2004.

117 *Darfur Rising: Sudan's New Crisis*, International Crisis Group, Africa Report Number 76, Brussels, 25 March 2004.

118 See, for example, "The Darfur Conflict: Crimes Against Humanity in Sudan", Crimes of War Project, <http://crimesofwar.org>.

119 Alex de Waal, "Counter-Insurgency on the Cheap", *London Review of Books*, Volume 26, Number 15, 5 August 2004.

120 *Darfur Rising: Sudan's New Crisis, op. cit.*

121 *Ibid.*

122 "Darfur Crisis Has Complex Roots with No Immediate Solution", News Item by Voice of America, 17 December 2004.

123 "Rebel Groups in Sudan's Darfur", News Article by Agence France-Presse, 18 December 2004.

124 Victor Tanner and Jérôme Tubiana, *Divided They Fall: The Fragmentation of Darfur's Rebel Groups, op. cit.*

125 "Sudan Says Troubled Darfur Region is Now Stable", News Article by Reuters, 17 May 2004.

126 "Darfur Governor Links Khartoum Plot with Rebels", News Article by Reuters, 26 September 2004.

127 See, for example, "Sudan Links Rebels to Plot to Attack in Capital", News Article by Reuters, 3 April 2004; "Sudanese Islamist Leader Arrested", News Article by BBC Online, 31 March 2004.

128 "Sudanese Claim Terrorism Plot Exposed", News Article by Reuters, 4 April 2004.

129 See, for example, "Sudan Accuses Opposition of Coup Attempt, News Article by *The Guardian* (London), 25 September 2004; "Sudan Finds Arms Cache for Coup Plot", News Article by Reuters, 25 September 2004; "Darfur Governor Links Khartoum Plot with Rebels", News Article by Reuters, 26 September 2004; and "Sudan Arrests 14 Islamists for Sabotage Plot", News Article by Reuters, 8 September 2004.

130 *Unifying Darfur's Rebels: A Prerequisite for Peace*, Africa Briefing Number 32, International Crisis Group, 6 October 2005, p.7. See also, claims of JEM involvement in "Sudanese Rebel Group Claims Involvement in Alleged Coup Plot", *Al-Quds*, 29 November 2004.

131 "Sudan Court Charges 21 Soldiers over Alleged 2004 Coup Attempt", News Article by Agence France-Presse, 5 January 2005.

132 "Darfur Governor Links Khartoum Plot with Rebels", News Article by Reuters, 26 September 2004. See, also, "Sudan Arrests 14 Islamists for Sabotage Plot", News Article by Reuters, 8 September 2004.

133 "Sudan Starts Trial of 78 Suspected Coup Plotters", News Article by Reuters, 16 December 2004.

134 "Sudan Court Charges 21 Soldiers over Alleged 2004 Coup Attempt", News Article by Agence France-Presse, 5 January 2005

135 "Sudan Steps Up Campaign against Islamists, Under Fire from Rights Groups", News Article by Agence France-Presse, 2 April 2004.

136 "The Black Book History or Darfur's Darkest Chapter," *The Financial Times* (London) 21 August 2004.

137 Prunier, *op. cit.*, p.93.

138 Alex de Waal, "Tragedy in Darfur: On Understanding and Ending the Horror", *Boston Review*, October-November 2004

139 "Ethnic Cleansing in Darfur: A New Front Opens in Sudan's Bloody War", Testimony Before the House of Representatives International Relations Committee by Charles Snyder, Acting Assistant Secretary of State for African Affairs, Washington, DC, May 6, 2004.

140 *Darfur Rising: Sudan's New Crisis, op. cit.*

141 "Sudanese Rebels Want Jailed Islamist Leader at Peace Ceremony", News Article by Agence France-Presse, 6 January 2005.

142 Prunier, *op. cit.*, p.93.

143 "Fighting Erupts in Eastern Sudan", News Article by BBC News, 21 June 2005.

144 "Khartoum Says New Islamist Rebellion Emerges in Central Sudan", News Article by Agence France-Presse, 21 October 2004.

145 "A Hostile Climate. Did Global Warming Cause a Resource War in Darfur?", *Seed* Magazine, 2 August 2006, available at <http://seedmagazine.com/news/2006/08/a_hostile_climate.php>.

146 "A Climate Culprit in Darfur", *The Washington Post*, 16 June 2007. See, also, "UN Chief says Drought is the Cause of Darfur Crisis", *Sudan Tribune*, 4 September 2007.

147 "Darfur Conflict Heralds Era of Wars Triggered by Climate Change, UN Report Warns", *The Guardian* (London), 23 June 2007.

148 Stephan Faris, "The Real Roots of Darfur", *The Atlantic Monthly*, April 2007.

149 *Ibid*.

150 Julian Borger, "Scorched", *The Guardian Weekend* (London), 28 April 2007.

151 "How to Prevent the Next Darfur", *Time*, 26 April 2007, available at <http://www.time.com/time/magazine/article/0,9171,1615171,00.html>.

152 Cited in "A Hostile Climate. Did Global Warming Cause a Resource War in Darfur?", *Seed* Magazine, 2 August 2006, available at <http://seedmagazine.com/news/2006/08/a_hostile_climate.php>.

153 "How to Prevent the Next Darfur", *Time, op. cit.*

154 "U.K.'s Reid Warns of Looming Water Wars", News Article by UPI, 28 February 2007.

155 Cited in "Could Global Warming Cause War?", *Christian Science Monitor*, 19 April 2007

156 "Now the Pentagon tells Bush: climate change will destroy us", *The Observer* (London), 22 February 2004.

157 "National Security and the Threat of Climate Change", The CNA Corporation, Alexandra, Virginia, April 2007, available at <http://www.npr.org/documents/2007/apr/security_climate.pdf>.

158 "How to Prevent the Next Darfur", *Time, op. cit.*

159 Dr Emeka E. Obioha, "Climate Change, Population Drift and Violent Conflict Over Land Resources in North Eastern Nigeria", Paper presented at "Human Security

and Climate Change An International Workshop", Norway, 21-23 June 2005, organised by Centre for the Study of Civil War and the International Peace Research Institute, Oslo; Centre for International Environmental and Climate Research at the University of Oslo for the Global Environmental Change and Human Security Program. Dr Obioha's study addressed the nature of violent conflicts in the northeast area of Nigeria, the extent to which continuous climatic change has contributed to the scenario, the patterns of the climatically induced violent conflicts, the major actors and the security implications of the conflict in the sub region. Available at <www.cicero.uio.no/humsec/papers/Obioha.pdf>.

160 "Kenya: Conflict over resources in border areas", News Article by Integrated Regional Information Networks, UN Office for the Coordination of Humanitarian Affairs, Nairobi, 1 August 2005.

161 "Northern Kenyan and Ugandan Ethnic Groups Fight Over Pasture Land", News Item by Voice of America, 8 May 2006.

162 "More People at Risk as Land Clashes Persist", News Article by Integrated Regional Information Networks, UN Office for the Coordination of Humanitarian Affairs, Nairobi, 29 March 2007.

163 "New Rebel Group Seizes West Sudan Town", News Article by Agence France-Presse, 26 February 2003.

164 See, for example, "Sudan Accuses Southern Separatists of Supplying Arms to Darfur Rebels", News Article by Agence France-Presse, 28 April 2003, and "Sudanese Armed Forces Attack an Unidentified Plane for Helping Western Rebels", News Article by Associated Press, 28 August 2003.

165 "Dozens Reported Killed or Wounded in Attack in Western Sudan", News Article by Agence France-Presse, 6 October 2003.

166 See, for example, "Sudan Accuses Eritrea of Involvement in Darfur Crisis", News Article by Agence France-Presse, 31 July 2004; "Eritrea Shipping Arms to Darfur Rebels: Report", News Article by Agence France-Presse, 5 December 2004. The International Crisis Group has also confirmed Eritrean military assistance to the rebels – see *Unifying Darfur's Rebels: A Prerequisite for Peace*, op. cit., p. 17. Eritrea's clear involvement in Darfur was also mentioned in a keynote article by Senator Jon Corzine and Richard Holbrooke, the Clinton Administration's former ambassador to the United Nations. They stated that the rebels "receive outside assistance, primarily from Sudan's eastern neighbour, Eritrea, which…has shown…a surprising aggressiveness towards its much larger neighbors." ("Support the African Union in Darfur", *The Washington Post*, 10 September 2004.)

167 See, for example, "Sudan Calls on U.N. to Take Action against Eritrea", News Article by Deutsche Presse-Agentur, 5 January 2004; and "AU to Consider Sudan Complaint Against Eritrea", News Article by Agence France-Presse, 10 January 2004.

168 See, for example, "Sudan Rebels Form Alliance against Khartoum Government", News Article by Africa Online, 28 January 2004.

169 *Unifying Darfur's Rebels: A Prerequisite for Peace, op. cit.*, pp. 9, 14-15.

170 *Report of the Panel of Experts established pursuant to paragraph 3 of resolution 1591 (2005) concerning the Sudan*, United Nations, S/2006/65, 30 January 2006.

171 *Report of the Panel of Experts established pursuant to paragraph 3 of resolution 1591 (2005) concerning the Sudan*, United Nations, S/2007/584, 3 October 2007.

172 See, for example, "The New Afghanistan and the Next Battlefield?", in Richard Miniter, *Shadow War: The Untold Story of How Bush is Winning the War on Terror*, Regnery Publishing, Washington-DC, 2004.

173 Roland Marchal, "The Unseen Regional Implications of the Crisis in Darfur", in Alex de Waal (editor), *War in Darfur and the Search for Peace*, Global Equity Initiative, Harvard, and Justice Africa, 2007, p.195.

174 *Unifying Darfur's Rebels: A Prerequisite for Peace, op. cit.*, p.7, footnote 40. See also, "Sudan Says Darfur Rebel Groups Full of Foreigners", *Sudan Tribune*, 11 October 2005, available at <http://www.sudantribune.com>.

175 *Report of the Panel of Experts established pursuant to paragraph 3 of resolution 1591 (2005) concerning the Sudan*, United Nations, S/2007/584, 3 October 2007.

176 See, for example, J. Millard Burr and Robert O. Collins, *Africa's Thirty Years' War: Chad, Libya and the Sudan, 1963-1993*, Westview Press, Boulder Co, 1999.

177 *Ibid*.

178 *Report of the Panel of Experts established pursuant to paragraph 3 of resolution 1591 (2005) concerning the Sudan*, United Nations, S/2006/65, 30 January 2006.

179 *Sudan Now or Never*, International Crisis Group, Africa Report No 80, Brussels, 21 May 2004.

180 Victor Tanner and Jérôme Tubiana, *Divided They Fall: The Fragmentation of Darfur's Rebel Groups, op. cit.*, p.13.

181 *Darfur: A Short History of a Long War, op. cit.*, p.81.

182 *Ibid*, p.82.

183 *Report of the Panel of Experts established pursuant to paragraph 3 of resolution 1591 (2005) concerning the Sudan*, United Nations, S/2006/65, 30 January 2006.

184 Julie Flint, "Darfur's Armed Movements", in Alex de Waal (editor), *War in Darfur and the Search for Peace*, Global Equity Initiative, Harvard, and Justice Africa, 2007, p.152.

185 "Sudan's Southern Rebels deny Involvement in Crisis in Darfur Region", News Article by Agence France-Presse, 16 September 2004.

186 Eric S. Margolis, "No Time for a Crusade in Sudan", 12 August 2004, available at <http://www.bigeye.com>.

187 See, "Sudan's President Blames U.S. for Darfur Conflict", News Article by Deutsche Presse-Agentur, 30 September 2004, and "Sudanese President Accuses US of Arming Darfur Rebels", News Article by Xinhua, 30 September 2004.

188 "Sudan President says Darfur Rebels Western-backed", News Article by Reuters, 16 February 2007.

189 See, for example, reporting of American financial assistance to the SLA in "Sudan

Government's Attacks Stoke Rebels' Fury", *The New York Times*, 11 September 2004.
190 "US 'Hyping' Darfur Genocide Fears", *The Observer* (London), 3 October 2004.
191 *Report of the Panel of Experts established pursuant to paragraph 3 of resolution 1591 (2005) concerning the Sudan*, United Nations, S/2007/584, 3 October 2007, p.28.
192 Denis M. Tull and Andreas Mehler, "The Hidden Costs of Power-Sharing: Reproducing Insurgent Violence in Africa", *African Affairs* (London), July 2005, Volume 104, Number 416, pp.375-98. See, also, Mary B. Anderson, *Do No Harm: How Aid Can Support Peace or War*, Lynne Rienner, Boulder, Co, 1999.

Chapter Two

193 "Sudan Govt, SLA Rebels Peace Talks Break Down in Chad", News Article by Associated Press, 16 December 2003.
194 Quoted in Scott Anderson, "How Did Darfur Happen?", *The New York Times Magazine*, 17 October 2004.
195 "U.N. Says Darfur Rebel Threat Spells Disaster", News Article by Reuters, 5 January 2005.
196 See, as but two examples, "Government Prefers Political Solution to Darfur Problem, Sudan's FM Says", News Article by Agence France-Presse, 20 January 2004 and "Gov't Stresses Commitment to Just and Peaceful Solution to Darfur Conflict", News Article by Integrated Regional Information Networks, UN Office for the Coordination of Humanitarian Affairs, Nairobi, 24 March 2004.
197 See, for example, "Sudan Declares Cease-Fire at Darfur Peace Talks", *The New York Times*, 28 October 2007.
198 See, for example, "Sudan Hopes Peace Deal Ends Darfur Crisis", News Article by Associated Press, 8 January 2005 and "Sudan Committed to Peace in South and Pursuing Solution to Darfur Crisis", News Article by Agence France-Presse, 2 January 2005.
199 "Nigerian Leader Vows AU Will Secure Darfur Peace", News Article by Reuters, 8 January 2005.
200 See, for example, "Sudanese President Vows to End Darfur Conflict", *Sudan Tribune*, 3 September 2005, available at <http://www.sudantribune.com>; "Sudan to Seek Final Darfur Peace Deal at Abuja Talks: VP", News Article by Agence France-Presse, 30 August 2005.
201 "Sudanese VP Pledges To Hold Soon Talks With Darfur Rebels", News Article by Sudan News Agency, 14 January 2004. Vice-President Taha's involvement has been welcomed by the United States: "US Hail Choice of Sudan's VP to Conduct Peace Talks with Darfur Rebels", News Article by Sudan Media Center (Khartoum), 15 January 2005.
202 "Sudan's VP: Darfur Easier to Resolve than South War", News Article by Associated Press, 17 January 2005.
203 See, for example, "Sudanese Govt, Opposition Alliance to Work Together to End

Darfur Conflict", News Article by Associated Press, 18 January 2005. The government has already agreed a joint approach with the opposition Umma Party, see "Shared Vision Between the National Congress and Umma Party on the Problem of Darfur", in the Umma File on Darfur, <http://www.umma.org>.

204 See, for example, "African Union to Deploy Darfur Ceasefire Monitors", News Article by Reuters, 14 April 2004; "Sudan Agrees to 3,500 Extra AU Troops – AU Source", News Article by Reuters, 1 October 2004, and "Sudan Urges AU to Fulfil Commitment on Darfur", News Article by Xinhua News Agency, 30 November 2004.

205 "Nigerian Leader Vows AU Will Secure Darfur Peace", News Article by Reuters, 8 January 2005.

206 See, for example, "Sudan to Hold Conference in Bid to Quell Tribal Violence in Darfur", News Article by Associated Press, 22 February 2003.

207 "West Sudan Rebels Agree to Face-to-Face Aid Talks", News Article by Reuters, 3 February 2004.

208 "Sudan Vice-President Holds Talks With Rebel Leader", News Article by Xinhua News Agency, 24 January 2004.

209 "Sudan Says Ready to Talk Peace to Darfur Rebels", News Article by Reuters, 13 January 2004.

210 See, for example, "Sudan Seeks Talks with New Rebel Groups in Darfur: SUNA", News Article by Agence France-Presse, 8 December 2004: "Sudan Starts Talks with 3rd Darfur Rebel Group", News Article by Reuters, 14 December 2004; "Third Darfur Rebel Group Signs Peace Pact with Sudan Government", News Article by Agence France-Presse, 17 December 2004 and "Sudanese Government Agrees Dialogue with New Darfur Rebel Group", News Article by Xinhua News Agency, 6 December 2004.

211 "Sudan Hails New Chad Mediation in Rebellion-hit Western Darfur: Report", News Article by Agence France-Press, 3 February 2004.

212 "Sudan Govt, SLA Rebels Peace Talks Break Down in Chad", News Article by Associated Press, 16 December 2003.

213 *Darfur Rising: Sudan's New Crisis, op. cit.*

214 "Peace Talks Break Off Between Sudan Government and Darfur Rebels", News Article by Agence France-Presse, 16 December 2003.

215 "Sudan Charges That Meddling Sabotaged Chad-Hosted Peace Talks", News Article by Agence France-Presse, 17 December 2003.

216 "Sudan Accuses Eritrea, Popular Congress Party of Supporting Darfur Rebels", News Article by Agence France-Press, 19 December 2003.

217 "W. Sudan Rebels Say Killed 1,000 Govt Troops, Militia", News Article by Reuters, 19 January 2004.

218 "Sudan: Government Stresses Commitment to Just and Peaceful Solution to Darfur Conflict", News Article by Integrated Regional Information Networks, UN Office for the Coordination of Humanitarian Affairs, Nairobi, 24 March 2004.

219 "Khartoum Blames Darfur Rebels for Blocking Aid", News Article by Agence France-Presse, 24 March 2004

220 "Government and Rebels Agree 45-day Ceasefire", News Article by Integrated Regional Information Networks, UN Office for the Coordination of Humanitarian Affairs, Nairobi, 9 April 2004.

221 *Ibid.*

222 "Sudan Welcomes African Ceasefire Monitoring Teams for Darfur", News Article by Sudan News Agency, 16 April 2004.

223 "African Union to Deploy Darfur Ceasefire Monitors", News Article by Reuters, 14 April 2004.

224 "Uncertainty Over Peace Talks with W. Sudan Rebels", News Article by Reuters, 17 April 2004.

225 *Sudan Now or Never, op. cit.* See also "Talks on Sudan's Darfur Conflict Postponed a Day as Rebel Split Appears", News Article by Agence France-Presse, 20 April 2004.

226 *Sudan Now or Never, op. cit.*

227 "W. Sudan Rebels Say Unlikely to go to Peace Talks, Want Eritrean Mediation", News Article by Reuters, 15 April 2004.

228 "US Warns Sudan Rebels Against Boycott of Darfur Peace Talks", News Article by Agence France-Presse, 17 April 2004.

229 "Darfur Rebels Reject Invitation to Hold Talks with Sudan's Government in Ethiopia", *Sudan Tribune*, 22 May 2004, available at <http://www.sudantribune.com>.

230 *Overview of AU's Efforts to Address the Conflict in the Darfur Region of the Sudan*, Conf/PLG/2 (I), African Union, 26 May 2005, p.3.

231 "Khartoum, Observers Sign Deal on Monitoring Darfur Ceasefire", News Article by Agence France-Presse, 4 June 2004.

232 "African Observers Open HQ in Darfur", News Article by Agence France-Presse, 9 June 2004.

233 "Darfur Rebels Say Won't Attend Peace Talks", News Article by Reuters, 2 July 2004.

234 "Darfur Rebel Group Rejects Call for Negotiations", News Article by Agence France-Presse, 3 July 2004.

235 "Violence Anew in Sudan's South and West", News Article by UPI, 9 July 2004.

236 "Darfur Peace Moves Collapse as Rebels Quit", News Article by al-Jazeera, 18 July 2004.

237 "Sudanese Rebels Urged to Return Vehicles Seized from British Charity", News Article by Deutsche Presse-Agentur, 13 July 2004.

238 "Text of Statement Issued by Minister of Information and Official Government Spokesman", News Article by Sudan News Agency, 27 July 2004.

239 "African Union to Deploy Peacekeeping Force in Sudan's Darfur Region: AU", News Article by Agence France-Presse, 4 August 2004.

240 "Sudan Vows Open Mind in Darfur Talks – But No Magic Wand in Sight", News Article by Agence France-Presse, 20 August 2004.

241 "Sudan Peace Talks Deadlocked as Rebels Backtrack on Agenda", News Article by Agence France-Presse, 24 August 2004.

242 "Sudan Agrees That AU Troops Can Disarm Rebels, Talks Reopen", News Article by Agence France-Presse, 25 August 2004.

243 "Sudan Peace Talks Delayed as Rebels Refuse Demobilisation", News Article by Agence France-Presse, 25 August 2004.

244 Scott Anderson, "How Did Darfur Happen?", *The New York Times* Magazine, 17 October 2004.

245 "Misreading the Truth in Sudan", *The New York Times*, 9 August 2004.

246 "Sudan's Foreign Minister Says UN SC Measure on Darfur Will Encourage Rebels", News Article by United Nations News Service, 23 September 2004.

247 "Sudan Agrees to 3,500 Extra AU Troops – AU Source", News Article by Reuters, 1 October 2004.

248 "Blaming Rebels, UN Envoy to Sudan Warns That Security Remains Elusive in Darfur", New Article by UN News Service (New York), 28 October 2004.

249 "Darfur Peace Talks restart, but Rebels Not Prepared to Sign Humanitarian Protocol", News Article by Xinhua News Agency, 26 October 2004.

250 "Darfur Rebels Storm Out of Sudan Security Meeting", News Article by Agence France-Presse, 25 October 2004.

251 "Peace Talks on Darfur Overcome Walkout by Rebels", News Article by Deutsche Presse-Agentur, 25 October 2004.

252 "Sudanese Darfur Rebels Block Aid Pact for Refugees", News Article by Reuters, 26 October 2004.

253 "Darfur Peace Talks Restart, but Rebels Not Prepared to Sign Humanitarian Protocol", News Article by Xinhua News Agency, 26 October 2004.

254 See, for example, "Sudan, Rebels Reach Darfur Accords", News Article by Associated Press, 9 November 2004 and "Sudan: Darfur Deal Doesn't Exclude Right of Self-Defense", News Article by al-Jazeera, 11 November 2004.

255 *Third Round of the Inter-Sudanese Peace Talks on Darfur: Abuja Nigeria 21 October – 9 November 2004: Chairman's Conclusions*, African Union, Addis Ababa, 9 November 2004.

256 "Tensions Rise in Sudan as Rebels and Government Begin to Lose Control, UN Says", News Article by the UN News Centre, New York, 4 November 2004.

257 "Sudan Accuses United Nations of Criticizing Government While Ignoring Rebel Violence", News Article by Associated Press, 6 November 2004.

258 "Press Release No. 112/2004", African Union, Addis Ababa, 10 December 2004.

259 "Renewed Fighting Shuts Down WFP Operations in North Darfur", Statement by World Food Programme, Nairobi, 25 November 2004.

260 "UN Condemns Darfur Rebel Attacks", News Article by United Nations News Centre, 24 November 2004.

261 "Sudan Says 22 Policemen, a Doctor and two Civilians were Killed in Rebel Attacks", News Article by Associated Press, 24 November 2004.

262 "Darfur Rebels Defy Ceasefire", News Article by Associated Press, 23 November 2004.

263 *Report of the Ceasefire Commission on the Situation in Darfur*, African Union, Addis Ababa, 4 October 2004.

264 "Achievements on Humanitarian Access in Darfur 'Fast Falling Apart'", Press Release by Oxfam UK, 18 November 2004.

265 News at 7pm, Channel Four TV (London), 16 December 2004.

266 "Renewed Fighting Shuts Down WFP Operations in North Darfur", Statement by World Food Programme, Nairobi, 25 November 2004.

267 "Fresh Violence Engulfs Darfur", *The New York Times*, 27 November 2004.

268 "UN Envoy Blames Rebels for Renewed Fighting in North Darfur", News Article by Associated Press, 26 November 2004.

269 "World Should Hold Darfur Rebels Accountable – UN's Pronk", News Article by Reuters, 25 November 2004.

270 "US Blames Darfur Rebels for New Fighting", News Article by UPI, 24 November 2004. See also, for example, "U.S. Warns Rebels to Curb Attacks in Darfur", News Article by Reuters, 29 October 2004; "U.S., U.N. Condemn Sudan Attacks", News Article by CNN, 24 November 2005 and "France Condemns SLA Rebel Attack in Sudan's Darfur", News Article by KUNA, 26 November 2004.

271 News at 7pm, Channel Four TV (London), 16 December 2004.

272 "Helicopter Attack Hits African Union's Bid for Sudan Peace", *The Independent* (London), 21 December 2004.

273 "Leader of Darfur Rebels Resorts to Damage Control", *The New York Times*, 5 December 2004.

274 "Sudan Says Rebels Kill 89", News Article by Reuters, 5 December 2004.

275 "Government Accuses Rebels of Increasing Attacks on Major Roads in Darfur", News Article by Associated Press, 5 December 2004.

276 "Darfur: Sudan Gives Fresh Conditions for Peace Talks", *Daily Trust* (Abuja), 30 December 2004.

277 *Report of the United Nations Secretary-General on the Sudan Pursuant to Paragraphs 6, 13 and 16 of Security Council Resolution 1556 (2004), Paragraph 15 of Resolution 1564 (2004) and Paragraph 1574 (2004)*, S/2005/10, United Nations, New York, 7 January 2005.

278 The Secretary-General also noted in his report that the "AU clarified later that although it had some reservations initially, it had not totally rejected the offer and consideration was being given to the possibility of working with Sudanese police in protecting roads in Darfur."

279 *Report of the United Nations Secretary-General on the Sudan Pursuant to Paragraphs 6, 13 and 16 of Security Council Resolution 1556 (2004), Paragraph 15 of Resolution 1564 (2004) and Paragraph 1574 (2004)*, S/2005/10, United Nations, New York, 7 January 2005.

280 Dr Mustapha Osman Ismail quoted in "Sudan's Foreign Minister Urges Complete Deployment of African Union Troops to Darfur", News Article by Associated Press, 13 January 2005.

281 *Report of the United Nations Secretary-General on the Sudan Pursuant to Paragraphs 6, 13 and 16 of Security Council Resolution 1556 (2004), Paragraph 15 of Resolution 1564 (2004) and Paragraph 1574 (2004)*, S/2005/10, United Nations, New York, 7 January 2005, p.2.

282 "Sudan Expects Darfur Peace Settlement in Two Months: Minister", News Article by Agence France-Presse, 7 December 2004.

283 "Sudan Accuses Rebels of Attacks in Darfur", News Article by Associated Press, 3 December 2004.

284 "Leader of Darfur Rebels Resorts to Damage Control", *The New York Times*, 5 December 2004.

285 "Sudan Split on Peace Chances", News Article by Reuters, 9 December 2004.

286 "AU in desperate move to save peace talks on Darfur crisis after rebels' boycott", News Article by Agence France-Presse, 14 December 2004.

287 "Violence Pushes Peace Talks off Track", News Article by UN Integrated Regional Information Networks, UN Office for the Coordination of Humanitarian Affairs, Nairobi, 13 December 2004.

288 "Darfur Rebels Suspend Participation in Sudan Peace Talks", News Article by Agence France-Presse, 13 December 2004.

289 See, for example, "AU Says Sudan has Started Darfur Troop Withdrawal", News Article by Reuters, 18 December 2004 and "Sudan Withdrawing Forces from Darfur", News Article by Agence France-Presse, 18 December 2004.

290 "Sudan Rebels Reject Libyan Proposal on Darfur, Talks to End Tuesday", News Article by Agence France-Presse, 20 December 2004.

291 "Sudan Rebels Vow No New Attacks", News Article by Associated Press, 21 December 2004.

292 "Stalled Darfur Peace Talks Suspended Until January", News Article by Agence France-Presse, 22 December 2004.

293 "Fighting in Ghubaysh Hinders Humanitarian Assistance", Press Release by Office of the Special Representative of the UN Secretary-General for Sudan, Khartoum, 28 December 2004.

294 "Darfur Rebel Group Rejects Return to Talks", News Article by Reuters, 24 December 2004.

295 See, for example, "Rebels Withdraw from the Negotiations: Khartoum Proposes Federation for Darfur", News Article by Arabic.News, 27 December 2004.

296 "Sudanese Govt Urges Rebels' Commitment to Darfur Peace Talks", News Article by Xinhua News Agency, 29 December 2004.

297 "U.N. Says Darfur Rebel Threat Spells Disaster", News Article by Reuters, 5 January 2005.

298 *Ibid.*

299 "At Least Seven Killed in Darfur Clashes: Sudan Police", News Article by Agence France-Presse, 13 January 2005.

300 See, "New Rebel Group Claims Sudan Oil Attack", News Article by Reuters, 20 December 2004 and "Sudan Rebels Say Attack Government Near Darfur", News Article by Reuters, 27 December 2004.

301 "Nigerian Leader Vows AU Will Secure Darfur Peace", News Article by Reuters, 8 January 2005.

302 "Sudan Says Darfur Rebel Groups Involved in Attack", News Article by Reuters, 30 December 2004.

303 "Sudan's Foreign Minister Urges Complete Deployment of African Union Troops to Darfur", News Article by Associated Press, 13 January 2005.

304 "Sudan Urges AU to Fulfil Commitment on Darfur", News Article by Xinhua News Agency, 1 December 2004.

305 Statement to the Security Council by Mr Jan Pronk, Special Representative of the Secretary-General of the United Nations to Sudan, New York, 8 February 2005.

306 *Report of the Secretary-General on the Sudan pursuant to paragraphs 6, 13 and 16 of Security Council resolution 1556 of 30 July 2004, paragraph 15 of Security Council resolution 1564 of 19 September 2004, and paragraph 17 of Security Council resolution 1574 of 18 November 2004,* United Nations, S/2005/68, New York, 5 February 2005.

307 See, for example, "East of the Border", *Africa Confidential* (London), Volume 46, Number 4, 18 February 2005.

308 *Monthly Report of the Secretary-General on Darfur,* S/2005/240, United Nations, New York, 12 April 2005, p.3.

309 *Ibid.*

310 *Monthly Report of the Secretary-General on Darfur,* S/2005/378, United Nations, New York, 9 June 2005, p.1-2.

311 *Monthly Report of the Secretary-General on Darfur,* S/2005/240, United Nations, New York, 10 May 2005, p.2.

312 "Darfur Rebels Attack Bedouin Village", News Article by Xinhua, 25 May 2005.

313 *Monthly Report of the Secretary-General on Darfur,* S/2005/378, United Nations, New York, 9 June 2005.

314 See, for example, "Libya to Host Six-Way Summit on Sudan's Darfur Issue", News Article by Xinhua, 16 May 2005; "Darfur Summit to Open in Libya Without Rebels", News Article by Agence France-Press, 16 May 2005.

315 "Darfur Talks to Resume in Nigeria, Long Road Ahead", News Article by Reuters, 8 June 2005.

316 "Interview – Darfur Rebel Rifts are Big Obstacle for Talks – Chad", News Article by Reuters, 3 July 2005. See also, "Darfur Rebels Urged to Accept Chadian Mediation", News Article by Agence France-Presse, 20 June 2005. Chad resumed its role as joint mediator in the Darfur talks during the September 2005 round of peace negotiations

(See, "Chad Resumes Mediation Role in Darfur Talks", News Article by Agence France-Presse, 25 September 2005).

317 *Monthly Report of the Secretary-General on Darfur*, S/2005/467, United Nations, New York, 18 July 2005, pp. 9-10.

318 The rebels had previously signed Libyan mediated agreements – see, for example, "Darfur Rebels Pledge Cooperation to Solve the Crisis", News Article by Associated Press, 12 May 2005.

319 See, for example, "Darfur Rebels Call for Delay to Peace Talks", News Article by Agence France-Presse, 9 August 2005; "Khartoum Deplores Darfur Rebels' Call to Delay Talks", News Article by Agence France-Presse, 11 August 2005.

320 "Sudan: Interview with Amb Baba Gana Kingibe, Head of AMIS", News Article by Integrated Regional Information Networks, UN Office for the Coordination of Humanitarian Affairs, Nairobi, 19 July 2005.

321 *Ibid*.

322 See, for example, "Sudanese Army Accuses Darfur Rebels of Launching New Attack", News Article by Xinhua, 25 July 2005; "Government Forces, Rebels Clash in Darfur", News Article by Reuters, 26 July 2005.

323 "AU Says Darfur Rebels Attacked Government Convoy", News Article by Reuters, 27 July 2005.

324 "Sudan: Interview with UN Special Representative Jan Pronk", Integrated Regional Information Networks, UN Office for the Coordination of Humanitarian Affairs, Nairobi, 4 August 2005.

325 *Monthly Report of the Secretary-General on Darfur*, S/2005/467, United Nations, New York, 18 July 2005, p.11.

326 *Monthly Report of the Secretary-General on Darfur*, S/2005/523, United Nations, New York, 11 August 2005, p.1.

327 *Ibid*., p.6.

328 "UNICEF: Bandits Hit Vital Aid Convoys in Darfur", *Sudan Tribune*, 31 August 2005, available at <http://www.sudantribune.com>.

329 See, for example, "Bandits in Darfur Attack AU, Obstruct Aid", News Article by Reuters, 29 August 2005.

330 See, for example, "Attack on IAS Team in Darfur", Press Release, International Aid Services, 1 September 2005; and "AU Condemns Renewed Raids Against Relief Convoy in Darfur", *Sudan Tribune*, 5 September 2005, available at <http://www.sudantribune.com>.

331 The Special Representative of the Chairperson of the Commission of the African Union Condemns the SLA/M Attack on Al Malam, Press Statement, African Union, Khartoum, 2 September 2005.

332 "AU Official: Darfur Rebels are Thieves", *Sudan Tribune*, 6 September 2005, available at <http://www.sudantribune.com>. See also, "Darfur Rebel Attacks are Banditry, AU Official Says", News Article by Reuters, 3 September 2005.

333 "Sudanese Troops Drive Rebels from Southern Darfur, Inflict Heavy Losses", News Article by Associated Press, 21 September 2005.

334 *Monthly Report of the Secretary-General on Darfur*, S/2005/592, United Nations, New York, 19 September 2005, p.1.

335 *Ibid*.

336 "Darfur Commission Condemns Rebel Attacks in Sudan", News Article by Associated Press, 9 September 2004.

337 "Sudan: Darfur Risks Descending into Anarchy – Observers", Integrated Regional Information Networks, UN Office for the Coordination of Humanitarian Affairs, Nairobi, 14 September 2005.

338 "Thousands Flee as Darfur Rebels Renew Attacks", *The Guardian* (London), 26 September 2005.

339 "SLA Rebels 'Destabilising' Darfur", News Article by BBC News, 5 September 2005.

340 *Monthly Report of the Secretary-General on Darfur*, S/2005/650, United Nations, New York, 14 October 2005, pp.5-6. See, also, "SLA Minnawi Faction Withdraws from Darfur Talks", News Article by Reuters, 2 September 2005; "African Union Says Uncooperative Darfur Rebels Threaten Talks", News Article by Agence France Press, 5 September 2005; "Darfur Rebels Want Peace Talks Put Off – Again", News Article by Agence France-Presse, 6 September 2005; "Darfur Rebels Split on Participation in Peace Talks", News Article by Agence France-Presse, 17 September 2005; "Darfur Rebels Say Won't Attend Peace Talks", News Article by Agence France-Presse, 14 September 2005.

341 *Monthly Report of the Secretary-General on Darfur*, S/2005/650, United Nations, New York, 14 October 2005, pp.5-6.

342 "Sudanese Rebels Capture Southern Darfur Town", News Article by Associated Press, 20 September 2005.

343 "Sudanese Government Accuses Rebels of Sabotaging Talks", News Article by Agence France-Presse, 21 September 2005.

344 "Rebel Division a Stumbling Block to Darfur Peace Talks: AU", News Article by Xinhua, 17 October 2005.

345 *Communiqué Issued by the Parties Attending the Sixth Round of the Inter-Sudanese Peace Talks on the Conflict in Darfur – Sudan*, African Union, Addis Ababa, 20 October 2005.

346 "Security Problems Hinder Darfur Relief Efforts", Voice of America Radio, 19 October 2005, available at <http://www.voanews.com/english/Africa/2005-10-19-voa46.cfm>.

347 *Unifying Darfur's Rebels: A Prerequisite for Peace*, Africa Briefing Number 32, International Crisis Group, 6 October 2005, p.1.

348 "Darfuris Urge Rebel Leaders to United and Make Peace", News Article by Reuters, 27 October 2005.

349 Alex de Waal, 'I will not sign', *London Review of Books*, Volume 28, Number 23, London, 30 November 2006.

350 Alex de Waal, "Darfur Peace Agreement: So Near, So Far", Open Democracy, 29 September 2006.

351 "Government and main rebel group set to sign Darfur deal", *The International Herald Tribune*, 5 May 2006.

352 Robert B. Zoellick, Deputy Secretary of State, "Briefing on Abuja Peace Agreement for Darfur", Abuja, Nigeria, May 5, 2006, U.S. State Department document available at <http://www.state.gov/s/d/former/zoellick/rem/2006/65933.htm>.

353 "Largest Faction of Darfur Rebels Signs Peace Pact", *The New York Times*, 6 May 2006.

354 "Darfur rebels told to sign peace or face sanctions", New Article by Afrol News, 4 May 2006, <http://www.afrol.com/articles/19090>.

355 Alex de Waal, "Darfur's Deadline: The Final Days of the Abuja Peace Process", in Alex de Waal (editor), *War in Darfur and the Search for Peace*, Global Equity Initiative, Harvard, and Justice Africa, 2007.

356 "Darfur rebels told to sign peace or face sanctions", New Article by Afrol News, 4 May 2006, <http://www.afrol.com/articles/19090>.

357 Alex de Waal, 'I will not sign', *London Review of Books, op. cit.*

358 Alex de Waal, "The book was closed too soon on peace in Darfur", *The Guardian* (London), 29 September 2006.

359 Laurie Nathan, "No Dialogue, No Commitment. The Perils of Deadline Diplomacy for Darfur", The Sudan Human Security Baseline Assessment, Small Arms Survey, Geneva, December 2006. Nathan is a Research Fellow with the Crisis States Research Centre at the London School of Economics and the Department of Environmental and Geographical Sciences at the University of Cape Town. He was a member of the AU Mediation Team for Darfur during the Abuja peace talks.

360 Julie Flint, "Darfur's Armed Movements", in Alex de Waal (editor), *War in Darfur and the Search for Peace*, Global Equity Initiative, Harvard, and Justice Africa, 2007, p.142.

361 Comments by Abd al-Wahid al-Nur, press conference, Paris, 16 January 2007.

362 "Largest Faction of Darfur Rebels Signs Peace Pact", *The New York Times*, 6 May 2006.

363 Comments made by Andrew Natsios before the Senate Foreign Relations Committee, Washington-DC, 11 April 2007.

364 *Ibid.*

365 "AU Welcomes Inauguration of Darfur Transitional Authority", News Article by Xinhua News Agency, 24 April 2007.

366 "Libya slams rebels over internationalization of Darfur crisis", News Article by Reuters, 29 April 2007.

367 "Sudan admits the signing of Darfur agreement was a mistake", *Sudan Tribune*, 14 May 2007.

368 "Sudan says Darfur Rebels Killed 41 Police in Kordofan Raid", News Article by Associated Press, 1 September 2007.

369 Alex de Waal, "New (and Different) Hostilities in Darfur", SSRC Making Sense of Darfur weblog, 19 September 2007, available at <http://www.ssrc.org/blog/2007/09/19/new-and-different-hostilities-in-darfur/>.

370 "Sudan's Beshir Offers Darfur Ceasefire", News Article by Agence France-Presse, 14 September 2007.

371 "10 African peacekeepers killed in Darfur attack", News article by Agence France-Presse, 30 September 2007.

372 "Ban Ki-Moon Voices Outrage at Deadly Attacks on AU Peacekeepers in Darfur", Article by UN News Service, New York, 1 October 2007.

373 Alex de Waal, "In Defense of the African Union", SSRC Making Sense of Darfur weblog, 3 October 2007, available at <http://www.ssrc.org/blog/2007/10/03/in-defense-of-the-african-union/>.

374 *Ibid.*

375 "Six Darfur rebel factions to boycott Libya peace talks", News Article by Agence France-Presse, 23 October 2007.

376 *Ibid.*

377 "In Sudan, Darfur rebels risk obstructing peace", *The Christian Science Monitor*, 16 October 2007.

378 See, for example, "Sudanese President Sets Up Fact-Finding Committee for Darfur", News Article by Sudan News Agency, 9 May 2004; "Bashir Sets Up Panel to Probe Human Rights Abuses in Darfur", News Article by PANA, 9 May 2004.

379 *Monthly Report of the Secretary-General on Darfur*, S/2005/305, United Nations, New York, 10 May 2005, p.4.

380 "Ministry of Information Issues Statement on Darfur", News Article by Sudan News Agency, 24 July 2004.

381 *Monthly Report of the Secretary-General on Darfur*, S/2005/240, United Nations, New York, 12 April 2005.

382 *Monthly Report of the Secretary-General on Darfur*, S/2005/467, United Nations, New York, 18 July 2005, p.15.

383 "Sudan Adopts New Measures to Facilitate Delivery of Humanitarian Aid in Darfur", News Article by Sudan News Agency, 20 May 2004.

384 "Sudan's Ruling Party Approves Nomination of a Presidential Representative in Darfur", News Article by Sudan News Agency, 25 June 2004.

385 "Government Measures to Alleviate the Darfur Crisis", News Article by Sudan News Agency, 6 July 2004.

386 *Report of the Secretary-General Pursuant to Paragraphs 6 and 13 of Security Council Resolution 1556 (2004)*, S/2004, United Nations, New York, 30 August 2004.

387 *Ibid.*

388 "Combined Police Force Heads for Troubled Darfur", News Article by Pan African News Agency, 12 July 2004.

389 "Sudan Deploys Additional 2,000 Policemen in Darfur", News Article by Xinhua News Agency, 17 August 2004.

390 *Report of the Secretary-General Pursuant to Paragraphs 6 and 13 of Security Council Resolution 1556 (2004)*, S/2004, United Nations, New York, 30 August 2004.

391 *Ibid.*

392 "Leaders of Six Darfur Tribes Sign Pact to Cease Fire, Waive Claims Against Each Other and Not to Hide Fighters", News Article by Associated Press, 16 February 2005.

393 Letter dated 19 April 2006 from the Chairman of the Security Council Committee established pursuant to resolution 1591 (2005) concerning the Sudan addressed to the President of the Security Council, United Nations, S/2006/250, 19 April 2006.

394 Alex de Waal and Julie Flint, *op. cit.*, p.123.

395 *Ibid.*

396 *Monthly Report of the Secretary-General on Darfur*, S/2005/240, United Nations, New York, 10 May 2005, pp.1-2.

397 *Monthly Report of the Secretary-General on Darfur*, S/2005/592, United Nations, New York, 19 September 2005, p.1.

398 *The Special Representative of the Chairperson of the Commission of the African Union Condemns the SLA/M Attack on Al Malam*, Press Statement, African Union, Khartoum, 2 September 2005.

399 "Sudan: Major Clash in Darfur Reportedly Kills More than 40", News Article by Integrated Regional Information Networks, UN Office for the Coordination of Humanitarian Affairs, Nairobi, 20 September 2005.

400 "Thousands Flee as Darfur Rebels Renew Attacks", *The Guardian* (London), 26 September 2005.

401 *Unifying Darfur's Rebels: A Prerequisite for Peace, op. cit.*

402 *Ibid.*, footnote 24, p.5.

403 Alex de Waal and Julie Flint, *op. cit.*, p.85.

404 *Ibid.*, p.86.

405 *Unifying Darfur's Rebels: A Prerequisite for Peace, op. cit.*, p.4.

406 *United Nations Sudan Situation Report*, United Nations Mission in Sudan, 15 November 2005, Khartoum.

407 Alex de Waal and Julie Flint, *op. cit.*, pp.83-84.

408 *Ibid.* p.87.

409 *Ibid.*

410 *Ibid.*

411 *Unifying Darfur's Rebels: A Prerequisite for Peace, op. cit.*, p.3.

412 Julie Flint, "Darfur's Armed Movements", in Alex de Waal (editor), *War in Darfur and the Search for Peace*, Global Equity Initiative, Harvard, and Justice Africa, 2007, p.155.

413 "Darfur Rebel SLA Holds Unity Congress to Repair Splits", *Sudan Tribune*, 28 October 2005.

414 See, for example, "Darfur Rebel Faction Snubs Reconciliation Meeting", News Article by Agence France-Presse, 28 October 2005.

415 See, for example, "Darfur Unity Meeting May Further Divide Rebels", *Sudan Tribune*, 1 November 2005; and "Sudan: Darfur's Main Rebel Group Set to Split", News Article by Agence France-Presse, 2 November 2005.

416 "Sudan: Darfur Unity Meeting May Further Fracture Rebels", News Article by Reuters, 1 November 2005.

417 *Sudan Now or Never*, *op. cit.*

418 See, for example, "Sudan's Foreign Minister Backs Darfur Autonomy", News Article by Reuters, 27 September 2004 and "Sudan Supports Darfur Federal Rule, Local Laws", News Article by Reuters, 3 October 2004.

419 *Sudan Now or Never*, *op. cit.*

420 "Power Struggle: Darfur's Janjaweed Militia Aren't the Only Ones Sowing Chaos and Death. Meet the Two Rebel Factions Threatening Yet Another Civil War", *Time*, 31 October 2004.

421 "New Guerilla Factions Snarl Sudan Peace Talks", *The New York Times*, 26 October 2004.

422 "Leader of Darfur Rebels Resorts to Damage Control", *The New York Times*, 5 December 2004.

423 "UN Warns That Darfur Could Descend into Anarchy with Warlords", News Article by Associated Press, 4 November 2004.

424 "Tensions Rise in Sudan as Rebels and Government Begin to Lose Control, UN Says", News Article by the UN News Centre", 4 November 2004.

425 "U.S., U.N. Condemn Sudan Attacks", News Article by CNN, 24 November 2005.

426 "Independence of Darfur Rebel Commanders Threatens Peace Efforts", News Article by Knight-Ridder News Service, 4 December 2004.

427 "U.S., U.N. Condemn Sudan Attacks", News Article by CNN, 24 November 2005.

428 "Independence of Darfur Rebel Commanders Threatens Peace Efforts", News Article by Knight-Ridder News Service, 4 December 2004.

429 "Fresh Violence Engulfs Darfur", *The New York Times*, 27 November 2004.

430 *Ibid.*

431 *Unifying Darfur's Rebels: A Prerequisite for Peace*, *op. cit.*

432 "Darfur Rebels Beset by Problems", News Article by BBC News, 28 October 2005.

433 Alex de Waal and Julie Flint, *op. cit.*, p.122.

434 *Ibid.*

435 "Sudanese Government Not the Only Obstacle to Darfur Agreement", News Article by Reuters, 16 August 2004.

436 *Ibid.*

437 Victor Tanner and Jérôme Tubiana, *Divided They Fall: The Fragmentation of Darfur's Rebel Groups*, *op. cit.*

438 *Ibid.*

439 See, for example, "How Credible is Darfur's Third Rebel Movement?", News Article by Integrated Regional Information Networks, UN Office for the Coordination of Humanitarian Affairs, Nairobi, 13 January 2005. NMRD was said to have some 1,000 fighters under arms.

440 "Clashes between Darfur Rebels Leaves 20 Dead: SMC", News Article by Agence France-Presse, 4 November 2004.

441 "Sudanese Government Not the Only Obstacle to Darfur Agreement", News Article by Reuters, 16 August 2004.

442 See, also, for example, "Two New Rebel Factions Threaten Peace Efforts in Darfur", News Article by Reuters, 24 October 2004; "New Guerilla Factions Snarl Sudan Peace Talks", *The New York Times*, 26 October 2004; "New Armed Militias Emerge in Sudan's Darfur Region", News Article by *al-Hayat* (Khartoum), 27 October 2004.

443 "Nigerian Leader Vows AU Will Secure Darfur Peace", News Article by Reuters, 8 January 2005.

444 Julie Flint, "Darfur's Armed Movements", *op. cit.*

445 *Ibid*, p.163.

446 *Sudan Now or Never, op. cit.*

447 "Darfur Rebels Split Over Secular State Demands", News Article by Reuters, 31 October 2004.

448 "Leader of Darfur Rebels Resorts to Damage Control", *The New York Times*, 5 December 2004.

449 "Darfur Rebels Split Over Secular State Demands", News Article by Reuters, 31 October 2004.

450 *Report of the Chairperson of the Commission on the Situation in the Darfur Region of the Sudan*, PSC/PR/2 (XXVIII), African Union, 28 April 2005, p.5.

451 *Press Release on the Deteriorating Security Situation in South Darfur*, Press Release by African Mission in Sudan, Khartoum, 6 June 2005.

452 *Monthly Report of the Secretary-General on Darfur*, S/2005/240, United Nations, New York, 12 April 2005.

453 *Report of the Chairperson of the Commission on the Situation in the Darfur Region of the Sudan, op. cit.*, p.6.

454 *Report of the United Nations Secretary-General on the Sudan Pursuant to Paragraphs 6, 13 and 16 of Security Council Resolution 1556 (2004), Paragraph 15 of Resolution 1564 (2004) and Paragraph 1574 (2004)*, S/2005/10, United Nations, New York, 7 January 2005, p.2.

455 *Ibid.*, pp. 11-12.

456 *Ibid.*, p.2.

457 *Report of the Chairperson of the Commission on the Situation in the Darfur Region of the Sudan*, PSC/PR/2 (XXVIII), African Union, 28 April 2005, p.14.

458 *Ibid.*, p.30.

459 *Report of the United Nations Secretary-General on the Sudan Pursuant to Paragraphs 6, 13 and 16 of Security Council Resolution 1556 (2004), Paragraph 15 of Resolution 1564*

(2004) and Paragraph 1574 (2004), S/2005/140, United Nations, New York, 4 March 2005, p.10.

460 *Monthly Report of the Secretary-General on Darfur*, S/2005/378, United Nations, New York, 9 June 2005, p.2.

461 "UN Envoy Says Darfur Rebels not Cooperating with AU Truce Mission", News Article by Agence France-Presse, 25 May 2005.

462 *Communiqué*, PSC/PR/Comm (XLI), African Union, 10 October 2005.

463 *Report of the United Nations Secretary-General on the Sudan Pursuant to Paragraphs 6, 13 and 16 of Security Council Resolution 1556 (2004), Paragraph 15 of Resolution 1564 (2004) and Paragraph 1574 (2004)*, S/2005/140, United Nations, New York, 4 March, pp.2-3.

464 *Report of the Chairperson of the Commission on the Situation in the Darfur Region of the Sudan*, PSC/PR/2 (XXVIII), African Union, 28 April 2005, p.9.

465 *Monthly Report of the Secretary-General on Darfur*, S/2005/378, United Nations, New York, 9 June 2005, p.2.

466 *Monthly Report of the Secretary-General on Darfur*, S/2005/467, United Nations, New York, 18 July 2005, p.5.

467 "AU Condemns Killing of its Soldiers in Sudan's Darfur", News Article by Agence France-Presse, 9 October 2005.

468 "Darfur Rebels Release 36 African Union Personnel, Including American", News Article by Associated Press, 10 October 2005.

469 *Ibid*.

470 Letter dated 19 April 2006 from the Chairman of the Security Council Committee established pursuant to resolution 1591 (2005) concerning the Sudan addressed to the President of the Security Council, United Nations, S/2006/250, 19 April 2006.

471 "Press Release on the incidents affecting the African Union Mission in Sudan (AMIS), Press Release by AMIS, Khartoum, 2 April 2007.

472 *Sudan Now or Never, op. cit.*

473 Personal conversation with journalists.

474 "Sudan: Interview with UN Special Representative Jan Pronk", Integrated Regional Information Networks, UN Office for the Coordination of Humanitarian Affairs, Nairobi, 4 August 2005.

475 See, for example, "Darfur Rebel Leader Urges Immediate US-British Military Intervention", News Article by Agence France-Presse, 11 August 2004.

Chapter Three

476 "Interview with UN's Jan Egeland on the Situation in Darfur", News Article by UN Integrated Regional Information Networks, UN Office for the Coordination of Humanitarian Affairs, Nairobi, 5 July 2004.

477 "Press Briefing", Office of the Spokesman, United Nations Advance Mission in the Sudan, 15 December 2004.

478 Anti-Sudan voices claimed that delays or obstacles in aid arriving at Port Sudan were deliberate. The reality is that the same sort of initial bureaucratic difficulties encountered in relief aid deliveries in the early days of the Darfur crisis were subsequently seen in American bureaucratic inertia following the Hurricane Katrina disaster in Louisiana in 2005. *The Washington Post*, for example, reported that millions of dollars worth of perishable food aid donated by Britain, including 400,000 packaged meals, was not delivered because of "cumbersome bureaucracy" involving six government agencies – see, "Katrina Food Aid Blocked by U.S. Rules", 14 October 2005.

479 "Agreement Reached Allowing Humanitarian Access to Darfur Region of Sudan", Press Release by United Nations Office for the Coordination of Humanitarian Affairs, New York, 17 September 2003.

480 Figures provided by the UN press office, Khartoum.

481 *Darfur Humanitarian Profile*, United Nations, Khartoum, 1 January 2005.

482 *Darfur Humanitarian Profile*, United Nations, Khartoum, September 2005, p.5.

483 *Darfur 120-Day Plan Report September to December 2004*, Office of the United Nations Resident and Humanitarian Co-ordinator for the Sudan, Khartoum, January 2005, pp.2-3.

484 "Darfur: Humanitarian Emergency Fact Sheet Number 24", US Agency for International Development, 1 October 2004.

485 "Interview with Kevin Kennedy, Outgoing Acting UN Humanitarian Coordinator for Sudan", News Article by UN Integrated Regional Information Networks, UN Office for the Coordination of Humanitarian Affairs, Nairobi, 23 June 2004.

486 "Interview with UN's Jan Egeland on the Situation in Darfur", News Article by UN Integrated Regional Information Networks, UN Office for the Coordination of Humanitarian Affairs, Nairobi, 5 July 2004.

487 "Darfur: Humanitarian Emergency Fact Sheet Number 24", US Agency for International Development, 1 October 2004.

488 See, for example, "Sudanese Darfur Rebels Block Aid Pact", News Article by Reuters, 26 October 2004 and "Darfur Rebels Threaten Humanitarian Aid Workers", News Article by UPI, 23 October 2004.

489 "Widespread Insecurity Reported in Darfur", News Article by Integrated Regional Information Networks, UN Office for the Coordination of Humanitarian Affairs, 30 July 2003.

490 "Aid for Sudan Ending Up With SPLA: Relief Workers", News Article by Agence France-Presse, 21 July 1998.

491 "Darfur – War or Humanitarian Crisis?", News Report by Voice of America, 5 January 2005.

492 "U.N. Agency Suspends Food Convoys to Sudan", News Article by Associated Press, 29 December 2004.

493 *Ibid.*

494 "Workers in Sudan Aid Convoy Killed", News Article by BBC News, 28 October 2003.

495 Robert D. Kaplan, *Surrender or Starve: Travels in Ethiopia, Sudan, Somalia, and Eritrea*, Vintage Books, New York, 2003, p.190.

496 "Sudanese Government Accuses Rebels of Murdering its Relief Workers", News Article by Agence France-Presse, 17 November 2003.

497 "Aid Workers Unable to Reach Most War Zones in Darfur, Western Sudan", News Article by Deutsche Presse-Agentur, 13 January 2004.

498 "Authorities Forcibly Close IDP Camps in Southern Darfur", News Article by Integrated Regional Information Networks, UN Office for the Coordination of Humanitarian Affairs, 16 January 2004.

499 "Feature – Death and Destruction in Darfur", News Article by Integrated Regional Information Networks, UN Office for the Coordination of Humanitarian Affairs, 11 December 2003.

500 "USAID Seeks Security for Aid Convoys to War-Torn Area of Sudan", News Article by Agence France-Presse, 26 October 2003.

501 "Sudanese Government Accuses Rebels of Murdering its Relief Workers", News Article by Agence France-Presse, 17 November 2003.

502 "Rebel Faction Admits Abducting Relief Workers in Sudan", News Article by Agence France-Presse, 20 November 2003.

503 "Relief Organisations Warn of Humanitarian Catastrophe in west Sudan", News Article by Deutsche Presse-Agentur, 17 February 2004.

504 "Government Opens Corridors to Deliver Aid to Rebellion-hit Darfur", News Article by Associated Press, 12 February 2004.

505 "Sudan Says Trying to Secure Access for Relief to Darfur Region", News Article by Agence France-Presse, 7 January 2004.

506 "UN Said Access to Sudan's War-torn West Improves", News Article by Reuters, 10 February 2004.

507 "UN Hails Sudan's Agreement to let Aid Workers in Troubled Darfur Region", News Article by Integrated Regional Information Networks, UN Office for the Coordination of Humanitarian Affairs, Nairobi, 10 February 2004.

508 "UN Says Aid Team in Sudan's Troubled Darfur Region", News Article by Agence France-Presse, 18 February 2004.

509 "Western Sudan Too Dangerous for Road Convoys", News Article by UPI, 17 February 2004.

510 "Khartoum Blames Darfur Rebels for Blocking Aid", News Article by Agence France-Presse, 24 March 2004

511 "Sudan Says Darfur Rebels Attack Relief Convoys, Denounce Ceasefire Violation", News Article by Sudan News Agency, 29 April 2004.

512 *Sudan Now or Never, op. cit.*

513 "Rebel Group Abducts 16 Relief Workers in Sudan's Darfur Region", News Article by Associated Press, 5 June 2004.

514 "Top UN Relief Official Welcomes Release of Aid Workers, Calls Their Detention 'Totally Unacceptable'", Press Statement by UN Office for the Coordination of Humanitarian Affairs, Geneva, 6 June 2004.

515 "Rebels Commandeer Relief Trucks in Sudan's Darfur Region", News Article by Agence France-Presse, 8 June 2004.

516 "Sudan's Govt Accuses Darfur Rebels of Attacking FAO Food Convoy", News Article by Associated Press, 30 June 2004.

517 "Sudanese Rebels Urged to Return Vehicles Seized from British Charity", News Article by Deutsche Presse-Agentur, 13 July 2004.

518 "Rebels Attack Towns in North Darfur", News Article by *Sudan Vision* (Khartoum), 12 July 2004.

519 "Sudanese Militia Kidnap 32 Children in Darfur", News Article by Middle East News Agency, 11 July 2004.

520 *Report of the Ceasefire Commission on the Situation in Darfur*, African Union, Addis Ababa, 4 October 2004.

521 "Abducted WFP Staff Released By Rebels in Darfur", Press Release by World Food Programme, Rome, 1 September 2004.

522 *Ibid.*

523 "Darfur Disarmament Plan Laid Out", News Article by Reuters, 22 August 2004.

524 "New Guerilla Factions Snarl Sudan Peace Talks", *The New York Times*, 26 October 2004.

525 "Darfur Rebels Threaten Humanitarian Aid Workers", News Article by UPI, 23 October 2004.

526 "UN Envoy Blames Darfur Rebels for Deaths of Aid Officials", News Article by Agence France-Presse, 28 October 2004.

527 *Ibid.*

528 "Humanitarian Aid in Sudan Limited By Insecurity, Road Closures, Says UN Mission", News Article by UN News Service (New York), 27 October 2004.

529 "UN Envoy Blames Rebels for Continuing Insecurity in Darfur", News Article by Integrated Regional Information Networks, UN Office for the Coordination of Humanitarian Affairs, Nairobi, 29 October 2004.

530 "U.N. says 200,000 Denied Aid as a Result of Darfur Violence", News Article by Deutsche Presse-Agentur, 14 November 2004.

531 "Despite Pact, New Violence Stymies Aid in Sudan", *The New York Times*, 28 November 2004.

532 "Doctor Killed, Four Injured in Sudan's Darfur", News Article by *Al-Rai Al-Amm* (Khartoum), 8 November 2004.

533 See, for example, "Foreign Aid Groups Flee Rebel Attacks in Sudan's Darfur: Report", News Article by Agence France-Presse, 7 November 2004.

534 "MSF Spain Flees Rebel Attacks in Sudan's Darfur", News Article by Agence France-Presse, 7 November 2004.

535 "Fresh Violence Engulfs Darfur", *The New York Times*, 27 November 2004.

536 "Armed Groups Must Stop Targeting Civilians and Humanitarian Convoys", Press Release by Amnesty International, New York, 3 November 2004.

537 "Moral Clarity Blurs in Darfur Crisis", *The Christian Science Monitor* (Boston), 10 December 2004. See also, "Crisis in Sudan's Darfur Deepens as New Violence Prevents Food Deliveries", News Article by Knight-Ridder News Service, 23 November 2004 and "16 Killed in Darfur, Humanitarian Aid Road Closed: UN Spokesman", News Article by Agence France-Presse, 17 November 2004.

538 "Staff Murders Stop Aid Work in South Darfur", *The Guardian* (London), 14 December 2004.

539 "Arms Pouring into Darfur, Officials Say: African Union Calls Region a 'Time Bomb'", News Article by Reuters, 17 December 2004.

540 "UN Points at Rebels for Darfur Aid Workers' Death", News Article by Reuters, 15 December 2004.

541 "UN Suspends Aid Operations in South Darfur after Killings: Two Workers Fatally Shot in Convoy Attack", News Article by Associated Press, 14 December 2004.

542 "Rebel Attacks Raise Insecurity Cuts Darfur Refugees Off From Aid", *The Washington Post*, 21 November 2004.

543 "Sudan Expects Darfur Peace Settlement in Two Months: Minister", News Article by Agence France-Presse, 7 December 2004.

544 "Press Briefing", Office of the Spokesman, United Nations Advance Mission in the Sudan, Khartoum, 15 December 2004.

545 "United Nations Darfur Situation Report", United Nations Advance Mission in the Sudan Khartoum, 21 December 2004

546 "Sudan and Rebels Suspend Peace Talks, as Aid Group Withdraws", *The New York Times*, 22 December 2004.

547 "Fighting in Ghubaysh Hinders Humanitarian Assistance", Press Release by Office of the Special Representative of the UN Secretary-General for Sudan, Khartoum, 28 December 2004.

548 "Clashes Force WFP to Suspend Food Convoys to Darfur", News Article by Integrated Regional Information Networks, UN Office for the Coordination of Humanitarian Affairs, Nairobi, 29 December 2004.

549 *Ibid*.

550 "UN condemns Sudan Rebel Attacks in Darfur, Calls for halt to all Fighting", News Article by Associated Press, 24 November 2004.

551 See, for example, "U.N. Envoy, Britain Blame Rebels for Renewed Fighting in Darfur; World Food Program Pulls Out", 25 November 2004; "World Should Hold Darfur Rebels Accountable – UN's Pronk", News Article by Reuters, 25 November 2004.

552 "British Aid Agency Quits Sudan's Darfur", News Article by Reuters, 21 December 2004.

553 "Armed Groups Must Stop Targeting Civilians and Humanitarian Convoys", Press Release by Amnesty International, 3 November 2004.

554 "Rebel Raids Block UN Aid to Darfur", *The Daily Telegraph* (London), 31 December 2004.

555 *Report of the United Nations Secretary-General on the Sudan Pursuant to Paragraphs 6, 13 and 16 of Security Council Resolution 1556 (2004), Paragraph 15 of Resolution 1564 (2004) and Paragraph 1574 (2004)*, S/2005/10, United Nations, New York, January 2005.

556 *Report of the Secretary-General on the Sudan pursuant to paragraphs 6, 13 and 16 of Security Council resolution 1556 of 30 July 2004, paragraph 15 of Security Council resolution 1564 of 19 September 2004, and paragraph 17 of Security Council resolution 1574 of 18 November 2004*, S/2005/68, United Nations, New York, 5 February 2005.

557 *Report of the United Nations Secretary-General on the Sudan Pursuant to Paragraphs 6, 13 and 16 of Security Council Resolution 1556 (2004), Paragraph 15 of Resolution 1564 (2004) and Paragraph 1574 (2004)*, S/2005/10, United Nations, New York, 7 January 2005, p.9.

558 *Ibid.*, p.10.

559 *Ibid.*

560 *Report of the United Nations Secretary-General on the Sudan Pursuant to Paragraphs 6, 13 and 16 of Security Council Resolution 1556 (2004), Paragraph 15 of Resolution 1564 (2004) and Paragraph 1574 (2004)*, S/2005/68, United Nations, New York, 4 February 2005, p.6.

561 *Report of the United Nations Secretary-General on the Sudan Pursuant to Paragraphs 6, 13 and 16 of Security Council Resolution 1556 (2004), Paragraph 15 of Resolution 1564 (2004) and Paragraph 1574 (2004)*, S/2005/140, United Nations, New York, 4 March, pp.2-3.

562 *Ibid.*, p.10.

563 *Monthly Report of the Secretary-General on Darfur*, S/2005/240, United Nations, New York, 12 April 2005, p.6.

564 *Report of the Chairperson of the Commission on the Situation in the Darfur Region of the Sudan*, PSC/PR/2 (XXVIII), African Union, 28 April 2005, p.30.

565 *Monthly Report of the Secretary-General on Darfur*, S/2005/378, United Nations, New York, 9 June 2005.

566 *Ibid.*, p.3.

567 *Monthly Report of the Secretary-General on Darfur*, S/2005/467, United Nations, New York, 18 July 2005, p.5.

568 *Ibid.*

569 *Monthly Report of the Secretary-General on Darfur*, S/2005/523, United Nations, New York, 11 August 2005, p.1.

570 *Press Briefing*, Office of the Spokesman, UNIMIS, Khartoum, 12 October 2005.

571 *Darfur: Humanitarian Aid Under Siege*, Human Rights Watch, New York, May 2006, available at <http://hrw.org/backgrounder/africa/sudan0506/6.htm>.

572 "The Special Representative of the Secretary General in Sudan Jan Pronk appeals to SLM/A to stop attacks on humanitarian workers in north Darfur," UNMIS Press Release, 28 April 2006, available at <http://www.reliefweb.int/rw/RWB.NSF/db900SID/LSGZ-6PDBAD?OpenDocument&rc=1&emid=ACOS-635PJQ>.

573 "Monthly Report of the Secretary-General on Darfur," United Nations Security Council, 10 May 2005, available at <http://daccessdds.un.org/doc/UNDOC/GEN/N05/337/43/PDF/N0533743.pdf?OpenElementt>.

574 "Monthly Report of the Secretary-General on Darfur," United Nations Security Council, 23 December 2005, available at <http://daccessdds.un.org/doc/UNDOC/GEN/N05/648/57/PDF/N0564857.pdf?OpenElement>.

575 *Darfur Humanitarian Profile*, United Nations, Khartoum, 1 October 2006.

576 *Ibid.*

577 *Darfur Humanitarian Profile*, United Nations, Khartoum, 1 April 2007.

578 *Ibid.*

579 "Darfur Rebels Pledge to Allow Aid Delivery", News Article by Integrated Regional Information Networks, UN Office for the Coordination of Humanitarian Affairs, Nairobi, 6 August 2007.

580 "Sudan Advises Aid Agencies to Accept Military Escort Offer", News Item by Voice of America, 25 September 2007.

581 *Darfur Humanitarian Profile*, United Nations, Khartoum, 1 April 2007.

582 *Report of the Chairperson of the Commission on the Situation in the Darfur Region of the Sudan*, PSC/AHG/4 (XXIII), African Union, 10 January 2005, p.10.

583 *Monthly Report of the Secretary-General on Darfur*, S/2005/523, United Nations, New York, 11 August 2005, p.4.

584 "Armed men attack police in Darfur refugee camp", News Article by Reuters, 20 August 2007.

585 *Monthly Report of the Secretary-General on Darfur*, S/2005/650, United Nations, New York, 14 October 2005, p.8.

586 *Monthly Report of the Secretary-General on Darfur*, S/2006/764, United Nations, 26 September 2006.

587 *Darfur Humanitarian Profile*, United Nations, Khartoum, 1 January 2007.

588 "Violence flares in Darfur's Kalma refugee camp as a new cycle of violence begins", *The Guardian* (London), 27 October 2007.

Chapter Four

589 "Prospects for Peace", Justice Africa Briefing, London, July 2004, <http://justiceafrica.org>.

590 Nima el-Baghir, "What's in a Name?", *Focus on Africa*, BBC, London, October-December 2004, London.

591 Ali Haggar, "The Origins and Organization of the Janjawiid in Darfur", in Alex de Waal (editor), *War in Darfur and the Search for Peace*, Global Equity Initiative, Harvard, and Justice Africa, 2007, p.127. Haggar is a senior researcher at the University of Omdurman who is active in the search for peace in Darfur.

592 *Report of the International Commission of Inquiry on Darfur to the United Nations Secretary-General*, United Nations, January 2005, Paragraphs 103-104, pp. 32-33.

593 "The Escalating Crisis in Darfur", News Article by Integrated Regional Information Networks, UN Office for the Coordination of Humanitarian Affairs, Nairobi, 31 December 2003.

594 Meeting with journalists, al-Fasher, 30 November 2004.

595 Interview with media, 13 September 2005.

596 Interview with media, 4 December 2004.

597 See, for example, *The Darfur Crisis: Looking Beyond the Propaganda*, European-Sudanese Public Affairs Council, London, March 2004, available at <http://www.espac.org>.

598 *Empty Promises? Continuing Abuses in Darfur, Sudan*, Briefing Paper, Human Rights Watch, New York, 11 August 2004.

599 "Sudan: Interview with UN Special Representative Jan Pronk", Integrated Regional Information Networks, UN Office for the Coordination of Humanitarian Affairs, Nairobi, 4 August 2005.

600 *Ibid*.

601 "Widespread Insecurity in Darfur Despite Ceasefire", News Article by Integrated Regional Information Networks, UN Office for the Coordination of Humanitarian Affairs, Nairobi, 3 October 2003.

602 *Darfur Deadline: A New International Action Plan*, Africa Briefing Number 83, International Crisis Group, 23 August 2004, p.7.

603 *Ibid*., p.12.

604 See, for example, "Sudan: State of Emergency after Southern Darfur Tribal Clashes", News Article by Integrated Regional Information Network, UN Office for the Coordination of Humanitarian Affairs, Nairobi, 22 May 2002.

605 "Janjawid Militia in Western Sudan Appears to be Out of Control", News Article by United Nations Integrated Regional Information Networks, UN Office for the Coordination of Humanitarian Affairs, Nairobi, 14 May 2004.

606 Ali Haggar, "The Origins and Organization of the Janjawiid in Darfur", *op. cit.*, p.128.

607 Julie Flint, "Darfur's Armed Movements", *op. cit.*

608 "Sudan and Chad Agree to Disarm Militias", News Article by Reuters, 23 June 2004.

609 "The Last Straw", *Al-Haram* (Cairo), Issue Number 686, 15 – 21 April 2004.

610 See, for example, "Janjawid Militia in Darfur Appears to be out of Control", News Article by Integrated Regional Information Network, UN Office for the Coordination of Humanitarian Affairs, Nairobi, 14 May 2004.

611 *Commission of Inquiry to Investigate Alleged Human Rights Violations Committed by Armed Groups in the Darfur States*, Government of Sudan, Khartoum, January 2005. Also published as UN Document S/2005/80, 26 January 2005, p.30.

612 "Sudan: Darfur Nomads Face Adversity in Isolation", News Article by Integrated Regional Information Network, UN Office for the Coordination of Humanitarian Affairs, Nairobi, 19 October 2005. See also, "The Forgotten Nomads of Darfur", News Article by Integrated Regional Information Network, UN Office for the Coordination of Humanitarian Affairs, Nairobi, 28 July 2005; and "Darfur's Nomads Under Threat", News Article by BBC, 2 September 2005.

613 See "Sudan's New Killing Fields", Middle East International (London), 27 May 2004, and also Darfur: What Hope for the Future? Civilians in Urgent Need of Protection, Amnesty International, London, 15 December 2004.

614 See, for example, *Darfur: What Hope for the Future? Civilians in Urgent Need of Protection*, Amnesty International, London, 15 December 2004.

615 *Report of the International Commission of Inquiry on Darfur to the United Nations Secretary-General*, United Nations, January 2005, p. 108.

616 *Ibid.*, p.75.

617 See, for example, *Commission of Inquiry to Investigate Alleged Human Rights Violations Committed by Armed Groups in the Darfur States*, Government of Sudan, Khartoum, January 2005. Also published as UN Document S/2005/80, 26 January 2005, p.46.

618 *Darfur – Humanitarian Emergency*, Fact Sheet Number 52, USAID, Washington-DC, 23 September 2005; see, also, "Chaos Spreads in Embattled Darfur", *The New York Times*, 19 October 2005.

619 Cited in *Response to the Report of the International Community of Inquiry on Darfur to the United Nations Secretary-General*, Government of Sudan, Khartoum, February 2005.

620 See, for example, "Tora Bora Army Strikes Back at the Janjaweed", *The Independent* (London), 16 August 2004. This article mentions Janjaweed attacks on the Arab Ma'aliyah tribe.

621 *Report of the International Commission of Inquiry on Darfur to the United Nations Secretary-General*, United Nations, January 2005, p.109.

622 "Janjawid Militia in Western Sudan Appears to be Out of Control", News Article by Integrated Regional Information Network, UN Office for the Coordination of Humanitarian Affairs, Nairobi, 14 May 2004.

623 "Chadian Soldiers Kill 69 Sudanese Arab Militiamen", News Article by Associated Press, 18 June 2004.

624 "Special Report II: Chad and the Darfur Conflict", News Article by Integrated Regional Information Networks, UN Office for the Coordination of Humanitarian Affairs Nairobi, 16 February 2004.

625 "Janjawid Militia in Western Sudan Appears to be Out of Control", News Article

by United Nations Integrated Regional Information Network, UN Office for the Coordination of Humanitarian Affairs, Nairobi, 14 May 2004.

626 *Ibid*.

627 "Sudan's President Orders Darfur Crackdown on Armed Groups, Including Militia", News Article by Agence France-Presse, 19 June 2004.

628 "Sudan and Chad Agree to Disarm Militias", News Article by Reuters, 23 June 2004.

629 See, for example "Sudan, US Agree to Crush Militia", News Article by *Sudan Vision* (Khartoum), 1 July 2004.

630 Nima el-Baghir, "What's in a Name?", *Focus on Africa*, BBC, October-December 2004, London.

631 Ali Haggar, "The Origins and Organization of the Janjawiid in Darfur", *op. cit.*, p.127.

632 "Squabble Over Words Obscures Sudan Violence", *The Los Angeles Times*, 6 November 2004.

633 "Militia Chief Scorns Slaughter Charge", *The Guardian* (London), 16 July 2004.

634 *Ibid*.

635 "We Fight On, Says the Demon of Darfur", *The Sunday Times* (London), 25 July 2004. These warnings were also echoed in another article, "Janjaweed Vow to Fight Any Intervention by 'Infidels'", *The Sunday Telegraph* (London), 15 August 2004.

636 "We Fight On, Says the Demon of Darfur", *The Sunday Times* (London) 25 July 2004.

637 "Squabble Over Words Obscures Sudan Violence", *The Los Angeles Times*, 6 November 2004.

638 "Sudan: Interview with UN's Jan Egeland on the Situation in Darfur", News Article by UN Integrated Regional Information Networks, UN Office for the Coordination of Humanitarian Affairs, Nairobi, 5 July 2004.

639 "Tensions Rise in Sudan as Rebels and Government Begin to Lose Control, UN Says", News Article by the UN News Centre, New York, 4 November 2004.

640 Statement to the Security Council by Jan Pronk, Special Representative of the Secretary-General of the United Nations to Sudan, New York, 8 February 2005.

641 *Sudan Briefing*, Justice Africa, London, July 2004, <http://www.justiceafrica.org/July04.htm>.

642 Ali Haggar, "The Origins and Organization of the Janjawiid in Darfur", *op. cit.*, p.127.

643 See, for example, "Sudan Must Act on Darfur in 30 Days or Face Measures, Security Council Warns", News Article by the United Nations News Center, New York, 30 July 2004.

644 "U.S. Diplomat Says it May Take 2 Years to Disarm Militias in Sudan", News Article by Associated Press, 24 September 2004.

645 Alex de Waal, "Tragedy in Darfur: On Understanding and Ending the Horror", *Boston Review*, Volume 29, Number 5, October-November 2004.

646 *Report of the Secretary-General Pursuant to Paragraphs 6 and 13 of Security Council Resolution 1556 (2004)*, S/2004, United Nations, New York, 30 August 2004.

647 *Ibid.* See also, for example, "Sudan Says Disarmament of Militias Taking Place in Darfur", News Article by Deutsche Presse-Agentur, 19 August 2004; "UN Witnesses Arms Handover by Government-backed Group in Darfur", News Article by United Nations News Service, 27 August 2004.

648 See, for example, "Sudan Jails Darfur Militiamen", News Article by Reuters, 19 July 2004.

649 "We Fight On, Says the Demon of Darfur", *The Sunday Times* (London) 25 July 2004.

650 "Prospects for Peace", Justice Africa Briefing, London, July 2004, <http://justiceafrica.org>.

651 See, for example, "US Tells Sudan: Disarm Darfur Militias", News Article by Agence France-Presse, 3 June 2005.

652 The presence of militias in Iraq has been well documented. See, for example, "Iraqi Militias Will 'Undermine Government'", News Article by Reuters, 26 May 2004; "Delicate Challenge of Taming Iraq's Militias", *Christian Science Monitor*, 13 April 2004; "New Factor in Iraq: Irregular Brigades Fill Security Void", *Wall Street Journal* (New York), 16 February 2005; "Invisible Militias in Iraq", Article by UPI, 9 March 2005; "Unravelling Iraq's Secret Militias", *Z Magazine* Online, May 2005, available at <http://zmagsite.zmag.org/Images/guptapr0505.html; "Iraq: Militias' Law Rules", News Article by Aljazeera.net, 11 March 2004.

653 "Q&A: Iraq's Militias", *The New York Times*, 9 June 2005.

654 "Iraq's Militias: Many Little Armies, One Huge Problem", *The New York Times*, 9 March 2006.

655 "Sadr Strikes", *Newsweek*, 10 April 2006.

656 "Can Iraq's Militia's be Tamed?", *Time*, 10 April 2006.

Chapter Five

657 "Violence in the Sudan Displaces Nearly 1 Million. An Aid Worker Describes the Gravity of the Humanitarian Crisis", News Article by MSNBC, 16 April 2004.

658 "Thousands Die as World Defines Genocide", *The Financial Times* (London), 6 July 2004. See also Bradol's views in "France Calls on Sudan to Forcibly Disarm Darfur Militias", News Article by Agence France-Presse, 7 July 2004.

659 For a full transcript of Powell's comments see "Powell Says Talks with Sudan Government Yielded Agreement", 1 July 2004 at <http://allafrica.com/stories/200407010005.html>.

660 Alex de Waal, "What does adding the 'Genocide' Label to the Darfur Crisis Really Mean?", *Index on Censorship*, February 2005.

661 Mahmood Mamdani, "The Politics of Naming: Genocide, Civil War, Insurgency", *The London Review of Books*, 8 March 2007.

662 "Sudanese Plant 'Not Built for Weapons'", *The Observer* (London), 30 August 1998.

663 See, for example, Richard Miniter, "The False Promise of Slave Redemption", The Atlantic Monthly, July 1999.

664 "The Great Slave Scam", *The Irish Times*, 23 February 2002; "Scam in Sudan – An Elaborate Hoax Involving Fake African Slaves and Less-than-Honest Interpreters is Duping Concerned Westerners", *The Independent on Sunday* (London), 24 February 2002; "Ripping Off Slave 'Redeemers': Rebels Exploit Westerners' Efforts to Buy Emancipation for Sudanese", *The Washington Post*, 26 February 2002; "Sudan Rip-Offs Over Phony Slaves", *International Herald Tribune*, 27 February 2002. See, also, *The Reality of Slave Redemption*, European-Sudanese Public Affairs Council, London, March 2001.

665 "The Great Slave Scam", *The Irish Times*, 23 February 2002.

666 See, for example, Peter Hallward's observation in *The Guardian*: "Bush's opportunity to adopt an election-season cause that can appeal, simultaneously, to fundamentalist Christians, the National Association for the Advancement of Coloured People, multilateralist liberals and the altruistic 'left' may now be too tempting to pass up." ("Enough Imperial Crusades", *The Guardian*, 18 August 2004.)

667 "Too Close to Call? Maybe", *Newsweek*, 6-13 September 2004. This was not lost on outside observers. The Germany newspaper, *Berliner Zeitung*, for example, editorialised to this effect on 11 September 2004: "The U.S. election is the real reason for the verbal escalation of the Darfur diplomacy."

668 "Fierce Fighting Returns to Sadr City as Mahdi Army Battles US Troops", *The Guardian* (London), 8 September 2004; "Worsening Security Hampers Reconstruction Efforts in Iraq", *The Financial Times* (London), 9 September 2004; "Aid Agencies Say That They Might Pull Out of Iraq", *The Guardian* (London), 9 September 2004.

669 "US Military Death Toll in Iraq Hits 1,000", *The Guardian* (London), 8 September 2004.

670 Rebecca Hamilton and Chad Hazlett, "'Not on Our Watch": The Emergence of the American Movement for Darfur", in Alex de Waal (editor), *War in Darfur and the Search for Peace*, Global Equity Initiative, Harvard, and Justice Africa, 2007, p.341.

671 "Stop the Killing in Sudan", remarks of Frank R. Wolf in the U.S. House of Representatives, 108th Cong., 2nd sess., *Congressional Record* 150, 2 April 2004, E 518.

672 U.S. House, "Declaring Genocide in Darfur, Sudan", 108th Cong., 2nd session, 2004, H. Doc. 467; U.S. Senate, "Declaring Genocide in Darfur, Sudan", 108th Cong., 2nd session, 2004, S. Doc. 133. One of the few voices of dissent within the United States Congress with regard to Sudan and Darfur has been Texas Congressman Ron Paul. Speaking in the US House of Representatives on 23 July, he warned that in calling for military intervention in Sudan the resolution was "incredibly dangerous legislation" and that his colleagues should "not fooled by the title of this bill, 'Declaring genocide in Darfur, Sudan.' Representative Paul stated that "this resolution is no statement of

humanitarian concern for what may be happening in a country thousands of miles from the United States. Rather, it could well lead to war against the African country of Sudan." Paul also pointed to the underhand way in which the resolution was passed: "This resolution was never marked-up in the House International Relations Committee, on which I serve. Therefore, Members of that committee had no opportunity to amend it or express their views before it was sent to the Floor for a vote. Like too many highly controversial bills, it was rushed onto the suspension calendar (by House rules reserved for 'non-controversial' legislation) at the last minute. Perhaps there was a concern that if Members had more time to consider the bill they would cringe at the resolution's call for US military action in Sudan – particularly at a time when our military is stretched to the breaking point." (Ron Paul's comments are available at <http://www.lewrockwell.com/paul/paul195.html>). He has subsequently cautioned that "we do not know and cannot understand the complexities of the civil war in Sudan" and noted the "very simplistic characterization of the conflict" in Darfur. He observed that "It seems as if this has been all reduced to a few slogans, tossed around without much thought or care about real meaning or implication. We unfortunately see this often with calls for intervention." He warned that unbalanced American involvement "will do little to solve the crisis". See, *Congressional Record*, United States House of Representatives, Washington-DC, 19 November 2004.

673 Deborah Murphy, "Narrating Darfur: Darfur in the U.S. Press, March-September 2004", in Alex de Waal (editor), *War in Darfur and the Search for Peace*, Global Equity Initiative, Harvard, and Justice Africa, 2007, pp. 314-17.

674 "Hearing of the Senate Foreign Relations Committee on the Current Situation in Sudan and Prospects for Peace, Testimony of Secretary of State Colin Powell", Federal News Service, 9 September 2004.

675 "President's Statement on Violence in Darfur, Sudan", News Release News Release by White House, Office of the Press Secretary, Washington-DC, 9 September 2004.

676 Transcript of the Presidential Debate between President George W. Bush and Senator John Kerry, Commission on Presidential Debates, 30 September 2004.

677 "Is Genocide Just a Word in Darfur Dilemma?", Special to CNN.com, 13 September 2004.

678 Transcript of the Presidential Debate between President George W. Bush and Senator John Kerry, Commission on Presidential Debates, 30 September 2004.

679 Rebecca Hamilton and Chad Hazlett, "'Not on Our Watch': The Emergence of the American Movement for Darfur", *op. cit.*, p.361.

680 *Ibid.*

681 *Ibid.*, p.365.

682 Alex de Waal, "What does adding the 'genocide' Label to the Darfur Crisis Really Mean?", *Index on Censorship*, February 2005.

683 *Ibid.*

684 "Bush Once Again Cites 'Genocide' in Darfur, News Article by IPS, 1 June 2005.

685 Alex de Waal, *Who are the Darfurians? Arab and African Identities, Violence and External Engagement*, Justice Africa, 23 August 2005, p.15 available at <http://justiceafrica.org/the_darfurians.htm>.

686 "Never Again" BBC Panorama Programme, 3 July 2005. See also, "Danforth Described Darfur as 'Genocide' to Please Christian Right", *The Independent* (London), 5 July 2005.

687 "Zoellick reluctant to describe Darfur violence as genocide", *The Financial Times*, 15 April 2005, available at <http://www.ft.com/cms/s/0/4bed5bba-ad4b-11d9-ad92-00000e2511c8.html>.

688 Samuel Totten and Eric Markusen (editors), *Genocide in Darfur: Investigating the Atrocities in the Sudan*, Routledge, New York, 2006, p.184.

689 Rebecca Hamilton and Chad Hazlett, "'Not on Our Watch": The Emergence of the American Movement for Darfur", *op. cit.*, p.343.

690 Although, it must be said in defence of the US intelligence community, they may well have been kept out of any of the discussions within the White House that chose to make the declaration essentially for political reasons – just as the decision to attack the al-Shifa pharmaceutical factory in Sudan was made by political appointees in the Clinton White House, virtually excluding any significant intelligence input, see Seymour Hersh, "Annals of National Security: The Missiles of August", *The New Yorker*, 12 October 1998, pp.34-41.

691 "'Foot in mouth' prize for Rumsfeld", News Item by CNN, 1 December 2003.

692 This was a point made by the Sudanese Foreign Minister, Dr Mustapha Osman Ismail, shortly after Powell's "declaration": "Look at what is going on in Iraq. The United States kept saying there were weapons of mass destruction. The same thing as genocide. After six months, it will say there is no genocide (in Sudan)" ("Sudanese FM Refutes US Stance on Darfur Issue", News Article by Xinhua News Agency, 13 September 2004.)

693 For a record of Powell's allegations, see "Transcript of Powell's U.N. presentation", News Article by CNN, 6 February 2003, available at <http://www.cnn.com/2003/US/02/05/sprj.irq.powell.transcript/index.html>. A video recording of his presentation is available at <http://www.whitehouse.gov/news/releases/2003/02/20030205-1.v.html>.

694 "CIA's final report: No WMD found in Iraq", News Article by MSNBC, 25 April 2005, available at <http://www.msnbc.msn.com/id/7634313/>.

695 See, for example, "Powell regrets UN speech on Iraq WMD", News Article by ABC, 9 September 2005, available at <http://www.abc.net.au/news/newsitems/200509/s1456650.htm>; "Powell Admits his Iraq WMD Claim is "Painful Blot", *The Daily Telegraph* (London), 10 September 2005.

696 See, "Following Orders is No Excuse. Colin Powell's Career as a 'Yes Man'", *Counterpunch*, 7 February 2006.

697 Brendan O'Neill, "Genocide? What genocide?", Comment is Free, *The Guardian*

(London), 4 May 2006, available at <http://commentisfree.guardian.co.uk/brendan_oneill/2006/05/stop_using_the_holocaust.html>.

698 Prunier, *op. cit.*, p. 140.

699 Gerald Caplan, "From Rwanda to Darfur: Lessons Learned", in Samuel Totten and Eric Markusen (editors), *Genocide in Darfur: Investigating the Atrocities in the Sudan*, Routledge, New York, 2006, p.171.

700 Arianna Huffington, "White House chutzpah: The administration that came to power talking about humility has become gallingly arrogant and drunk with power", *Salon.com*, 12 December 2002, available at <http://dir.salon.com/story/news/col/huff/2002/12/12/bush/>.

701 David Corn, *The Lies of George W. Bush. Mastering the Politics of Deception*, Three Rivers Press, New York, 2003, p.1.

702 "U.S. Calls Killings In Sudan Genocide", *The Washington Post*, 10 September 2004.

703 Andrew Natsios, "Moving Beyond the Sense of Alarm", in Samuel Totten and Eric Markusen (editors), *Genocide in Darfur: Investigating the Atrocities in the Sudan, op. cit.*, p.39.

704 *Darfur: Counting the Deaths. Mortality Estimates from Multiple Survey Data*, Centre for Research on the Epidemiology of Disasters, University of Louvain, Belgium, 26 May 2005, p.7, available at <http://www.cred.be/docs/cedat/DarfurCountingTheDeaths-withClarifications.pdf>.

705 *Darfur Crisis: Death Estimates Demonstrate Severity of Crisis, but Their Accuracy and Credibility Could Be Enhanced*, GAO-07-24 U.S. Government Accountability Office, Washington-DC, 11 December 2006., available at <http://www.gao.gov/new.items/d0724.pdf>.

706 "Holding Khartoum Accountable in Darfur", *The Boston Globe*, 8 September 2007.

707 "Zoellick reluctant to describe Darfur violence as genocide", *The Financial Times*, 15 April 2005, available at <http://www.ft.com/cms/s/0/4bed5bba-ad4b-11d9-ad92-00000e2511c8.html>.

708 "U.S. Blocks U.N. Briefing on Atrocities in Sudan", News Article by Reuters, 10 October 2005.

709 "US Backs Away from Genocide Charge in Darfur", News Article by Agence France-Presse, 3 February 2006.

710 "'Genocide' Continues in Darfur – Rice", News Article by Agence France-Presse, 17 February 2006.

711 "Natsios describes on-going Sudanese crisis", *The Georgetown Voice*, 8 February 2007. Natsios is a professor at Georgetown University.

712 See, for example, "U.S. Says Darfur Genocide Continues, Rights Abuses Rife", News article by Reuters, 7 March 2007.

713 "U.S. Special Envoy to Sudan Dodges Senator's Questions on Darfur. Natsios refuses to give Menendez straightforward answers on start to Plan-B, genocide", Press Release by Senator Menendez, 11 April 2007.

714 See, "President Bush Participates in United Nations Security Council Meeting on Africa", News Release by White House, Office of the Press Secretary, Washington-DC, 25 September 2007.

715 "Powell 'Disappointed' US Stands Alone on Darfur Genocide Determination", News Article by Agence France-Presse, 29 September 2004.

716 "No Genocide in Sudan, Annan Says", News Article by Deutsche Presse-Agentur, 17 June 2004.

717 Communiqué of the 12th Meeting of the Peace and Security Council, The Peace and Security Council of the African Union, Meeting in its 12th Meeting, at ministerial level, PSC//MIN/Comm. (XII), para. 2, 4 July 2004.

718 "Nigeria's Obasanjo Unconvinced on US Call of 'Genocide' in Darfur", News Article by Agence France-Presse, 3 December 2004.

719 See, for example, "EU Mission Sees Abuses, But Not Genocide, in Darfur", News Article by Reuters, 9 August 2004; "EU Mission Finds No Evidence of Darfur Genocide", News Article by al-Jazeera, 10 August 2004.

720 See, for example, "Israel to turn away Darfur Refugees", News Article by Associated Press, 19 August 2007.

721 *Report of the International Commission of Inquiry on Darfur to the United Nations Secretary-General*, United Nations, January 2005.

722 See, for example, "Doctors Without Borders/Médecins Sans Frontières Challenges US Darfur Genocide Claims", Mediamonitors, 5 October 2004, available at <http://www.mediamonitors.net>.

723 *Messages*, Number 132, Médecins Sans Frontières, Paris, October-November 2004.

724 *Messages*, Number 132, Médecins Sans Frontières, Paris, October-November 2004.

725 "Thousands Die as World Defines Genocide", *The Financial Times* (London), 6 July 2004. See also, Bradol's views in "France Calls on Sudan to Forcibly Disarm Darfur Militias", News Article by Agence France-Presse, 7 July 2004.

726 "Violence in the Sudan Displaces Nearly 1 Million. An Aid Worker Describes the Gravity of the Humanitarian Crisis", News Article by MSNBC, 16 April 2004.

727 See, for example, MSF's own briefing: "Médecins Sans Frontières has been working in Darfur since December 2003. Today, 90 international volunteers and nearly 2,000 Sudanese staff provide medical and nutritional care in areas with more than 400,000 displaced people. Medical teams conduct medical consultations and hospitalisation, treat victims of violence, care for severely and moderately malnourished children, and provide water, blankets, feeding and other essential items in Mornay, Zalingei, Nyertiti, Kerenik, El Genina, Garsila, Deleig, Mukjar, Bindisi, and Um Kher in West Darfur State; Kalma Camp near Nyala and Kass in South Darfur State; and Kebkabiya in North Darfur State. MSF also continues to assess areas throughout Darfur. Additional teams provide assistance to Sudanese who have sought refuge in Chad in Adre, Birak and

Tine, Iriba and Guereda." – "We are looking at a second catastrophe", Darfur feature article on MSF Australia Website, <http://www.msf.org.au/tw-feature/045twf.html>.

728 Medécins Sans Frontières has received, amongst others, the following international awards for their activities: 1999, the Nobel Peace Prize; 1998, the Conrad Hilton Prize; 1997, *Prix International – Primo Levi*; 1997, *Prix International Sebetiater*; 1996, *Prix International pour la Paix et l'Action Humanitaire*; 1997, Indira Gandhi Prize; 1996, *Prix Seoul pour la Paix*; 1993, the European Parliament's *Prix pour la liberte de l'Esprit Prix Sakharov*, 1993, the United Nations High Commission for Refugees' Nansen Medal; 1992, the Council of Europe's *Prix Europeen des Droits de l'Homme*.

729 *Messages*, Number 132, Médecins Sans Frontières, Paris, October-November 2004.

730 "War Surgeon Gino Strada: 'Media Not Interested in Human Tragedies' of War", Interview on DemocracyNow.org, 8 April 2005, available at <http://www.democracynow.org/article.pl?sid=05/04/08/1346222>.

731 "'Elders' criticize West's response to situation in Darfur. Brahimi says West 'pampered' rebels, while Carter calls US's use of term 'genocide' to describe violence 'unhelpful'", *The Christian Science Monitor* (Boston), 6 October 2007, available at <http://www.csmonitor.com/2007/1005/p99s01-duts.html>.

732 "Jimmy Carter confronts Sudan officials", News Article by Associated Press, 3 October 2007.

733 Dr Eric A. Heinze, "The Rhetoric of Genocide in U.S. Foreign Policy: Rwanda and Darfur Compared", *Political Science Quarterly*, Volume 122, Number 3, 2007, p.361.

734 *Ibid*.

735 *Ibid*.

736 "Darfur and African State-Building", *The American Interest* online, 26 October 2006.

737 Mahmood Mamdani, "The Politics of Naming: Genocide, Civil War, Insurgency", *The London Review of Books*, 8 March 2007.

738 "Mahmood Mamdani on Darfur: 'The Politics of Naming: Genocide, Civil War, Insurgency'", Interview on DemocracyNow.org, 4 June 2007, available at <http://www.democracynow.org/article.pl?sid=07/06/04/1334230 >.

739 Mahmood Mamdani, "The Politics of Naming: Genocide, Civil War, Insurgency", *The London Review of Books*, 8 March 2007. Four million people have died in the Congo since 1998, half of them children under 5, according to the International Rescue Committee. It was estimated that twice as many people will die in 2007 in the Congo as may have died in the entire Darfur conflict since it began in 2003. See, also, "The Lancet Publishes IRC Mortality Study from DR Congo; 3.9 Million Have Died: 38,000 Die per Month", International Rescue Committee, 6 January 2006.

740 See, "Mamdani's Darfur Lobby", *The Current*, Columbia University, New York, Spring 2007.

741 "Slavery, Genocide and the Politics of Outrage", *Middle East Report*, Spring 2005.

742 Wiesel has been very active on behalf of the Save Darfur movement, and has spoken at a number of meetings. See, for example, "Groups Plan Rally on Mall To Protest Darfur Violence. Bush Administration Is Urged to Intervene in Sudan", *The Washington Post*, 27 April 2006.

743 Norman Finkelstein, *The Holocaust Industry: Reflections on the Exploitation of Jewish Suffering*, Verso, New York, 2000.

744 See, "The Israeli government put pressure upon [Wiesel] to drop the Armenian genocide. They allowed the others, but not the Armenian one. He was pressured by the government to withdraw, and being a loyal commissar as he is, he withdrew...That gives an indication of the extent to which people like Elie Wiesel were carrying out their usual function of serving Israeli state interests" in Noam Chomsky, *Chronicles of Dissent*, Common Courage Press, Monroe, ME, 1992. Wiesel has been criticised on several occasions for his support for Israel. See, for example, Christopher Hitchens, "Wiesel Words", *The Nation*, Washington-DC, 19 February 2001, available at <http://www.thenation.com/doc/20010219/hitchens>.

745 See, for example, "Nobel Laureates Call For Turkish-Armenian Reconciliation", The Elie Wiesel Foundation for Humanity, 9 April 2007.

746 Glen Ford, "A Tale of Two Genocides, Congo and Darfur: The Blatantly Inconsistent US Position", 19 July 2007, available at dissidentvoice.org <http://www.dissidentvoice.org/2007/07/a-tale-of-two-genocides-congo-and-darfur-the-blatantly-inconsistent-us-position/>. See, also, Kim Petersen, "Bleaching the Atrocities of Genocide. Linguistic Honesty is Better with a Clear Conscience", 7 June 2007, available at <http://www.dissidentvoice.org/2007/06/bleaching-the-atrocities-of-genocide/>.

747 See, for example, Conor Foley, "Disturbing reading", 9 November 2006, available at <http://commentisfree.guardian.co.uk/conor_foley/2006/11/the_flat_earth_society.html>; See, also, "Stop using the G-word", 21 September 2006, available at <http://commentisfree.guardian.co.uk/conor_foley/2006/09/stop_using_the_g_word_about_da.html>; "Who defines genocide?", 22 May 2006, available at <http://commentisfree.guardian.co.uk/conor_foley/2006/05/who_defines_genocide_1.html>, and "Muddled thinking on Darfur", 16 April 2007, available at <http://commentisfree.guardian.co.uk/conor_foley/2007/04/no_tony_blair_this_is_not_abou.html>.

748 "The War on Genocide", 11 September 2004, available at <http://blogs.zmag.org/ee_links/neocolonial_studies1>.

749 "US 'Hyping' Darfur Genocide Fears", *The Observer* (London), 3 October 2004.

750 See, for example, "Hidden War that Claims 1,000 Lives a Day: Fighting Threatens to Escalate in the Democratic Republic of Congo, Where Six Years of Turmoil have Resulted in 'the World's Worst Conflict Since 1945'", *The Daily Telegraph* (London), 10 December 2004. In October 2004, the UN Under-Secretary-General for Humanitarian Affairs, Jan Egeland, has declared the situation in northern Uganda the "world's greatest neglected humanitarian crisis" and a "moral outrage".

751 "US 'Hyping' Darfur Genocide Fears", *The Observer* (London), 3 October 2004. For a critique of USAID and Natsios' previous involvement in Sudan, see *USAID Chief Natsios on Sudan: Inept and Partisan*, European-Sudanese Public Affairs Council, London, November 2001, available at <http://www.espac.org>.

752 Millard Burr, *Quantifying Genocide in the southern Sudan 1983-1993*, US Committee for Refugees, Washington-DC, October 1993.

753 Douglas H. Johnson, *The Root Causes of Sudan's Civil Wars*, James Currey, London, 2004, p.143, note 1. In his report Burr stated that 1.3 million had died by 1993. Johnson's concern about the accuracy of Burr's claims also hold for any of the so-called statistical claims made by similarly funded and propagandistic reports on Darfur: "The first difficulty in accepting Burr's figure is the unreliability of demographic data coming out of Sudan...The multipliers then applied to extrapolate a total figure from these data present yet another problem...Since the publication of Burr's report, the figure of war-related deaths has grown with each citation, and now figures of 2.5 and even 3 million are commonly cited and accepted. Adding this to other frequently noted numbers for displaced and enslaved persons gives a total which equals or even exceeds the recorded population of the Southern Region in 1983."

754 David Henige, *Numbers from Nowhere*, Norman, Oklahoma, 1998, p.20

755 Colin Powell's declaration of "genocide" in Darfur, for example, was based in large part – he claimed – on a study, commissioned and funded by sections of the American government and carried out by the New York-based Physicians for Human Rights.

756 *Darfur 120-Day Plan Report September to December 2004*, Office of the United Nations Resident and Humanitarian Co-ordinator for the Sudan, Khartoum, January 2005.

757 See, for example, "100,000 Excess Civilian Deaths after Iraq Invasion", *The Lancet* (London), 29 October 2004.

758 "Press Conference by UN Special Adviser on Prevention of Genocide", News Article by UN News Centre, available at <http://www.un.org/News/briefings/docs/2006/060407_Mendez_PC.doc.htm >.

759 "Resort to the G World takes place of action in Darfur", *The Financial Times* (London), 5 January 2005.

760 Jonathan Steele, "Darfur Wasn't Genocide and Sudan is not a Terrorist State", *The Guardian* (London), 6 October 2005.

761 "Why Genocide is Difficult to Prosecute", *The Christian Science Monitor*, 20 April 2007.

762 Susan Moeller, *Compassion Fatigue: How the Media Sell, Disease, Famine, War and Death*, Routledge, New York and London, 1999, p.229.

763 Charles Lane, "When Is It Genocide?", *Newsweek*, 17 August 1992, p.27.

764 David White, "Darfur is Part of a Wider Problem", *The Financial Times* (London), 13 June 2004.

765 Peter Quayle, "Grave Crimes", *The World Today*, Volume 61, Number 1, The Royal Institute of International Affairs, London, January 2005.

766 Michael Clough, "It's hell in Darfur, but is it genocide? The Sudanese government has targeted villagers, but not a whole race", *The Los Angeles Times*, 14 May 2006.

767 *Ibid.*

768 *Ibid.*

769 *Ibid.*

770 "Darfur rebel group leader offers olive branch to foes", News Article by *People's Daily Online*, 9 November 2005, available at <http://english.people.com.cn/>.

771 "Interview: SLM Leader Rejects Darfur Peace Talks with Sudan", Sudan Tribune, 2 January 2007.

772 Alex de Waal, 'I will not sign', *London Review of Books*, Volume, 28, Number 23, London, 30 November 2006.

773 Emily Wax, "5 Truths About Darfur", *The Washington Post*, 23 April 2006.

774 See, "Virtual Genocide", *Focus on Africa*, BBC, London, January-March 2007.

775 "In Darfur, From Genocide to Anarchy", *The Washington Post*, 28 August 2007.

776 See, for example, "Arab Militias Destroying Schools in Sudan to Wipe out Black Culture", News Article by Knight-Ridder News Service, 20 August 2004.

777 "In Sudan, No Clear Difference between Arab and African", *The New York Times*, 3 October 2004.

778 Prunier, *op. cit.*, p.4.

779 "Empty Villages Mark Trail of Sudan's Hidden War", *The Observer* (London), 30 May 2004.

780 "The Escalating Crisis in Darfur", News Article by Integrated Regional Information Networks, UN Office for the Coordination of Humanitarian Affairs, Nairobi, 31 December 2003.

781 John Ryle, "Disaster in Darfur", *The New York Review of Books*, Volume 51, Number 13, 12 August 2004.

782 Nicholas Kristof, "Cruel Choices", *The New York Times*, 14 April 2004.

783 "In Sudan, No Clear Difference between Arab and African", *The New York Times*, 3 October 2004.

784 See, Nicholas Kristof, "Driving Up the Price of Blood", *The New York Times*, 17 April 2007.

785 Comments made by Dr Eltigani Ateem Seisi at the seminar "Confronting the Crisis in Darfur: A Transatlantic Assessment", Transatlantic Institute, Brussels, 12 May 2004. Dr Seisi is the head of Darfur UK, an anti-government group based in Britain.

786 "Darfur's Deep Grievances Defy all Hopes for an Easy Solution", *The Observer* (London), 25 July 2004.

787 Alex de Waal, "Tragedy in Darfur: On Understanding and Ending the Horror", *Boston Review*, Volume 29, Number 5, October-November 2004.

788 See, as but two examples, "Sudan: Government Commits 'Ethnic Cleansing' in

Darfur", Human Rights Watch, 7 May 2004 and "Ethnic Cleansing Blights Sudan", News Article by BBC News Online, 27 May 2004.

789 "Bashir Sets Up Panel to Probe Human Rights Abuses in Darfur", News Article by PANA, 9 May 2004.

790 "Interview with UN's Jan Egeland on the Situation in Darfur", News Article by UN Integrated Regional Information Networks, UN Office for the Coordination of Humanitarian Affairs, Nairobi, 5 July 2004.

791 "Sudan 'Neglecting' Darfur Crisis", News Article by BBC News Online, 8 June 2004, available at <http://news.bbc.co.uk/go/pr/fr/-/1/hi/world/africa>.

792 Charles King, "How 'Ethnic' is Ethnic Conflict?", *Harvard International Review*, Volume 28, Number 4, Winter 2007, pp.68-69.

793 Prunier, *op. cit.*, p. 157.

794 *Report of the Secretary-General on the Sudan pursuant to paragraphs 6, 13 and 16 of Security Council resolution 1556 of 30 July 2004, paragraph 15 of Security Council resolution 1564 of 19 September 2004, and paragraph 17 of Security Council resolution 1574 of 18 November 2004*, United Nations, S/2005/68, New York, 5 February 2005.

795 "Sudan Claims 270,000 Displaced from Darfur Return Voluntarily", News Article by Agence France-Presse, 10 November 2004.

796 *Darfur 120-Day Plan Report September to December 2004*, Office of the United Nations Resident and Humanitarian Co-ordinator for the Sudan, Khartoum, January 2005.

797 "Sudan: Gov't Trying to Force Darfur's Displaced to Return Home – UN Agencies", News Article by Integrated Regional Information Networks, UN Office for the Coordination of Humanitarian Affairs, Nairobi, 20 July 2004.

798 Alex de Waal, "Briefing: Darfur, Sudan: Prospects for Peace", *African Affairs*, Volume 104, Number 414, pp. 127-35.

799 Alex de Waal, *Who are the Darfurians? Arab and African Identities, Violence and External Engagement*, Justice Africa, 23 August 2005, p.15 available at <http://justiceafrica.org/the_darfurians.htm>.

800 Emily Wax, "5 Truths About Darfur", *The Washington Post*, 23 April 2006.

801 "Press Conference by UN Special Adviser on Prevention of Genocide", UN News Service, New York, 7 April 2006.

802 See, for example, "Chad Says Darfur Rebel JEM is Scheming", News Article by Agence France-Presse, 22 June 2005.

803 Prunier, *op. cit.*, p. 152.

804 *Ibid*, p. 154.

805 *Ibid*, pp.103-04

806 Brendan O'Neill, "Genocide? What genocide?", Comment is Free, *The Guardian* (London), 4 May 2006, available at <http://commentisfree.guardian.co.uk/brendan_oneill/2006/05/stop_using_the_holocaust.html>.

Chapter Six

807 Michael Clough, "It's hell in Darfur, but is it genocide? The Sudanese government has targeted villagers, but not a whole race", *The Los Angeles Times*, 14 May 2006.

808 Professor Debarati Guha-Sapir, "Sensational Numbers Do Not Help the Darfur Cause", Letter to the Editor, *The Financial Times* (London), 7 May 2005.

809 "UN: Mortality Rates Drop in Darfur, But Food Insecurity a Major Issue", News Item by Voice of America, 21 October 2006.

810 Alex de Waal, "Deaths in Darfur: Keeping ourselves honest", 18 August 2007, Social Science Research Council Darfur weblog, available at <http://www.ssrc.org/blog/2007/08/16/deaths-in-darfur-keeping-ourselves-honest/>.

811 Sudan's President, Omer al-Bashir, has stated that some 9,000 people may have died in Darfur ("Sudan's Bashir Defends Record in Darfur", News Article by Reuters, 24 February 2007: anti-Sudan activist Eric Reeves has claimed 500,000 deaths (Quantifying Genocide in Darfur: April 28, 2006 (Part 1), 29 April 2006, available at <www.sudanreeves.org>.

812 See, for example, the Save Darfur Coalition's campaign in newspapers such as *The Washington Post* and *The New York Times* in the United States and *The Times*, *The Guardian*, *The Financial Times* and *The Independent* in Great Britain.

813 "300,000 Deaths Foretold", *The Washington Post*, 7 June 2004.

814 "Mortality Projections for Darfur", Media Briefing by David Nabarro, WHO Representative in Sudan, Geneva, 15 October 2004.

815 *Darfur 120-Day Plan Report September to December 2004*, Office of the United Nations Resident and Humanitarian Co-ordinator for the Sudan, Khartoum, January 2005.

816 See, for example, The Knight-Ridder news service reported on 9 January 2005 that "the war in Darfur has taken an estimated 70,000 lives." On 11 January 2005, Associated Press stated that "about 70,000 people have died through disease, hunger and attacks in Darfur." On 12 January 2005, Reuters stated that "70,000 are estimated to have died in Darfur." On the same day the BBC reported that "about 70,000 people" had died. The Voice of America reported on 14 January 2005 that "two years of fighting between rebels and government-backed militias have claimed an estimated 70,000 lives. On 16 January 2005, Agence France-Presse wrote that the conflict "has claimed the lives of 70,000 people".

817 "Over 180,000 Darfur Deaths in 18 Months – U.N. Envoy", News Article by Reuters, 15 March 2005.

818 CRED is a non-profit research institution and a World Health Organization Collaborating Centre based in the School of Public Health of the Université Catholique de Louvain in Brussels. CRED conducted two death estimates: one for the period of September 2003-January 2005 and another for the period of February-June 2005.

819 "Viewpoint: Counting Darfur's Dead isn't Easy", News Article by Reuters, 18 March 2005.

820 *Sudan: Death Toll in Darfur*, Fact Sheet, US Department of State, Bureau of Intelligence and Research, Washington, DC, 25 March 2005, available at <http://www.state.gov/s/inr/rls/fs/2005/45105.htm>.

821 *Ibid.*

822 Professor Debarati Guha-Sapir, "Sensational Numbers Do Not Help the Darfur Cause", Letter to the Editor, *The Financial Times* (London), 7 May 2005.

823 *Darfur: Counting the Deaths. Mortality Estimates from Multiple Survey Data*, Centre for Research on the Epidemiology of Disasters, University of Louvain, Belgium, 26 May 2005, p.36, available at <www.cred.be>.

824 *Ibid.*, p.7.

825 *Ibid.*, p.9.

826 Alex de Waal, "Deaths in Darfur: Keeping ourselves honest", *op. cit.*

827 *Darfur Mortality Rate Declines, But Remains "Extremely Fragile" – Survey*, United Nations Mission in Sudan Press Release, UNMIS, Khartoum, 28 June 2005.

828 *Mortality in Darfur: Second Mortality Survey Greater Darfur Region, Sudan*, Khartoum, World Health Organization, *July 2005; Preliminary Findings of Survey Conclude Deaths in Darfur are Below Emergency Threshold and Health situation in Darfur Dramatically Improved since Last Year*, World Health Organization Press Release, Khartoum, July 2005.

829 "Sudan: Interview with UN Special Representative Jan Pronk", News Article by Integrated Regional Information Networks, UN Office for the Coordination of Humanitarian Affairs, Nairobi, 4 August 2005

830 See, for example, "UN Envoy Criticises Security Council and Khartoum", News Item by Radio Netherlands, 6 April 2006; "Je Kunt er Niet op Los Slaan, Je Hebt die Schurken Nodig", *NRC Handelsblad* (Amsterdam), 9 March 2006

831 *Darfur: Counting the Deaths (2). What are the Trends?* Centre for Research on the Epidemiology of Disasters, University of Louvain, Belgium, 15 December 2005, p.8.

832 *Darfur Morbidity and Mortality Bi-Annual Report 22 May 2004 – 30 December 2005*, World Health Organization, Sudan Country Office, Khartoum available at <http://www.emro.who.int/sudan/media/pdf/WMMB%20bi-annual%20report.pdf>.

833 *Weekly Morbidity and Mortality Bulletin*, Epidemiological Week Number 49, 3-9 December 2006, World Health Organization, available at <http://www.emro.who.int/sudan/InformationCentre.htm#wmmb>.

834 "Darfur, Saving Itself", *The Washington Post*, 3 June 2007.

835 *Massive Aid Effort Contains Growth of Malnutrition in Darfur*, Statement by UNICEF, 19 October 2006, available at <http://www.unicef.org.uk/press/news_detail.asp?news_id=817>.

836 Alex de Waal, "Deaths in Darfur: Keeping ourselves honest", *op. cit.*

837 *Ibid.*

838 Alex de Waal, "Are things getting worse in Darfur? There is no simple answer", 20 June 2007, Social Science Research Council Darfur weblog, available at <http://

www.ssrc.org/blog/2007/06/20/are-things-getting-worse-in-darfur-there-is-no-simple-answer/>.

839 *Ibid.*

840 *Ibid.*

841 *Ibid.*

842 Dr Jean-Hervé Bradol and Fabrice Weissman, "An Appeal for Darfur: Killings and Demagogy", *Liberation* (Paris), 23 March 2007.

843 Eric Reeves, an English teacher at Smith College in Massachusetts, in the United States, has been active for some time in a campaign against Sudan during which he has written dozens of articles making serious allegations about events within Sudan. His claims have been exposed as either consciously dishonest or at the very least unforgivably naïve. Several measured criticisms of Reeves' approach, methodology – and especially the sources he has relied upon for his claims – have been published and republished. Reeves continues to make, or repeat, serious claims about the situation in Sudan – most recently focusing on Darfur – without any means of verifying them. For a detailed critique of Reeves' repeated abuse of statistics, see *"Lies, Damned Lies, and Statistics": Eric Reeves on Darfur,* European-Sudanese Public Affairs Council, London, 2005, available at <http://darfurinformation.com/publications-of-interest/book12.asp>. For critiques of Reeves' earlier claims about Sudan see, for example, *The Return of the 'Ugly American': Eric Reeves and Sudan,* European-Sudanese Public Affairs Council, London, December 2000, available at <http://www.espac.org/oil_pages/the_ugly_american.html> and *Smith College, Eric Reeves and Sudan: What Price a Reputation?"*, European-Sudanese Public Affairs Council, London, August 2001, available at <http://www.espac.org/oil_pages/smith_college.htm> as well as *Eric Reeves' 'Reporting Credibility' on Sudan Devastated by Reuters Report,* European-Sudanese Public Affairs Council, London, 16 February 2001, available at <http://www.espac.org>; *Eric Reeves, The World Food Programme and Displacement,* European-Sudanese Public Affairs Council, London, 23 February 2001, available at <http://www.espac.org>; *Allegations of Oil Development Displacement Assessed Against Independent Sources,* European-Sudanese Public Affairs Council, London, March 2001, available at <http://www.espac.org>; *Eric Reeves' Credibility on Sudan Further Damaged by British Satellite Picture Analysis of Sudanese Oil Fields,* Media Monitors Network, May 2001; *Eric Reeves Against Africa,* Media Monitors Network, May 2001; *Eric Reeves, Sudan, Displacement and Double Standards,* European-Sudanese Public Affairs Council, London, 15 June 2001, available at <http://www.espac.org>.

844 See, Eric Reeves, "Darfur Mortality Update", 18 January 2005, available at <http://sudanreeves.org>.

845 Eric Reeves, "Quantifying Genocide in Darfur: A Summary and Update", 28 June 2004 available at <http://sudanreeves.org>.

846 *Darfur Crisis: Death Estimates Demonstrate Severity of Crisis, but Their Accuracy and*

Credibility Could Be Enhanced, United States Government Accountability Office, Report Number GAO-07-24, Washington-DC, 11 December 2006.

847 The GAO is the investigative arm of the U.S. Congress. As the congressional watchdog it is independent and non-partisan. It studies how the federal government spends taxpayer dollars. GAO advises Congress and the heads of executive agencies about ways to make government more effective and responsive. GAO evaluates federal programs, audits federal expenditures, and issues legal opinions. When GAO reports its findings to Congress, it recommends actions.

848 Alex de Waal, "Deaths in Darfur: Keeping ourselves honest", *op. cit.*

849 The following international experts participated in the assessment: Jana Asher, American Association for the Advancement of Science; Richard Brennan, Health Unit, International Rescue Committee; Francesco Checchi, London School of Hygiene and Tropical Medicine; Allan Hill, Harvard School of Public Health, Harvard University; Arif Husain, Vulnerability Analysis and Mapping Unit, United Nations World Food Program; Mark Myatt, University College of London; W. Courtland Robinson, Bloomberg School of Public Health, Johns Hopkins University; William Seltzer, Department of Sociology and Anthropology, Fordham University; Romesh Silva, Human Rights Data Analysis Group, The Benetech Initiative; Michael Van Rooyen, Program on Humanitarian Crises and Human Rights, Harvard University; Ronald Waldman, Mailman School of Public Health, Columbia University; Bradley Woodruff, Maternal and Child Nutrition Branch, U.S. Centers for Disease Control and Prevention. The following experts participated in the meeting by phone for parts of the day: Bushra Gamar Hussein, Darfur Region, Sudan Social Development Organization and Jennifer Leaning, Harvard School of Public Health, Harvard University.

850 CRED is a non-profit research institution and a World Health Organization Collaborating Centre based in the School of Public Health of the Université Catholique de Louvain in Brussels. CRED conducted two death estimates: one for the period of September 2003-January 2005 and another for the period of February-June 2005.

851 The Coalition for International Justice was an organisation that advocated international war crimes tribunals. It closed its operations in March 2006. John Hagan, a professor of law and sociology at Northwestern University in the United States, produced his estimate with his colleagues, Wynnona Rymond-Richmond and Patricia Parker.

Chapter Seven

852 The report notes that: "to estimate an "excess" number of deaths directly attributable to the conflict, some researchers subtract a baseline mortality rate – that is, an expected number of deaths that would have occurred absent the conflict—from the total number of deaths estimated for the time period and population." The report further noted that "In acute emergencies, when mortality may change significantly during a short time

interval, mortality rates are often expressed as the number of deaths per 10,000 people per day. Typically, a crude mortality rate – that is, the rate of death for the entire population, including both sexes and all ages – is reported, as well as mortality rates for specific groups (such as those younger than 5 years or of a specific sex)." The U.S. National Center for Health Statistics, for example, assumed a baseline crude mortality rate for 2003 in the United States to be about 0.23 deaths per 10,000 per day. CRED assumed a baseline crude mortality rate of 0.3 based on the national average provided by the United Nations Children's Fund (UNICEF), as did Reeves; the Department of State, WHO and Dr Coeberg all assumed a baseline crude mortality rate of 0.5 (the State Department accepted a WHO estimate for sub-Saharan African populations); the Coalition estimate did not apply a baseline mortality rate. The Red Cross supported Sphere Project states that the daily crude mortality rate is the most specific and useful health indicator to monitor in a disaster situation. The Sphere handbook, *Humanitarian Charter and Minimum Standards in Disaster Response* (The Sphere Project, Geneva, 2004), states that a doubling of the baseline crude mortality rate indicates a significant public health emergency, requiring an immediate response. It states that if the baseline rate is unknown, health agencies should aim to maintain the crude mortality rate at below 1.0 per 10,000 per day. The Sphere Project was launched in 1997 by the Red Cross and several humanitarian NGOs. It developed minimum standards to be attained in disaster assistance in five sectors: water supply and sanitation, nutrition, food aid, shelter, and health services.

853 Alex de Waal, "Tragedy in Darfur: On Understanding and Ending the Horror", *Boston Review*, Volume 29, Number 5, October-November 2004.

854 See, for example, "Sudan Admits Rights Abuses, Including Rape, by Allies in Darfur", News Article by Agence France-Presse, 22 August 2004 and "Sudan Committee Acknowledges Rights Abuse in Darfur but Rejects Genocide", News Article by Agence France-Presse, 20 January 2005.

855 "The Escalating Crisis in Darfur", News Article by Integrated Regional Information Networks, UN Office for the Coordination of Humanitarian Affairs, Nairobi, 31 December 2003.

856 "Statement to the Security Council on the Situation of Human Rights in Darfur by Ms Louise Arbour, High Commissioner for Human Rights", United Nations, October 2004.

857 *Report of the International Commission of Inquiry on Darfur to the United Nations Secretary-General*, United Nations, January 2005, p.11.

858 *Ibid.*, p.106.

859 "The Escalating Crisis in Darfur", News Article by Integrated Regional Information Networks, UN Office for the Coordination of Humanitarian Affairs, Nairobi, 31 December 2003.

860 "Pressure Seen as Key to Ending Sudan's Western War", News Article by Reuters, 28 January 2004.

861 "War in Western Sudan Overshadows Peace in the South", *The New York Times*, 17 January 2004.

862 See, for example, "Janjawid Militia in Darfur Appears to be out of Control", News Article by Integrated Regional Information Networks, UN Office for the Coordination of Humanitarian Affairs, Nairobi, 14 May 2004.

863 "Statement to the Security Council on the Situation of Human Rights in Darfur by Ms Louise Arbour, High Commissioner for Human Rights", United Nations, October 2004.

864 See, for example, *Darfur Destroyed: Ethnic Cleansing by Government and Militia Forces in Western Sudan*, Human Rights Watch, New York, 7 May 2004.

865 "Sudanese Gov't 'Largely Responsible' for Abuses in Darfur, Says Watchdog", News Article by Integrated Regional Information Networks, UN Office for the Coordination of Humanitarian Affairs, Nairobi, 27 November 2003.

866 See, for example, "Violence in the Sudan Displaces Nearly 1 Million. An Aid Worker Describes the Gravity of the Humanitarian Crisis", News Article by MSNBC, 16 April 2004.

867 See, for example, "We Must Halt the Genocide in Darfur, Sudan Now", Human Rights Discussion Paper, The Jacob Blaustein Institute for the Advancement of Human Rights, June 2005.

868 See, for example, *Eulogy for a Sudanese War Criminal: Jemera Rone, Human Rights and Double Standards*, European-Sudanese Public Affairs Council, London, 2001, available at <http://www.espac.org>.

869 *Darfur in Flames: Atrocities in Western Sudan*, Human Rights Watch, New York, 2 April 2004.

870 "Widespread Insecurity Reported in Darfur", News Article by Integrated Regional Information Networks, UN Office for the Coordination of Humanitarian Affairs, Nairobi, 30 July 2003.

871 "Workers in Sudan Aid Convoy Killed", News Article by BBC News, 28 October 2003.

872 "USAID Seeks Security for Aid Convoys to War-Torn Area of Sudan", News Article by Agence France-Presse, 26 October 2003.

873 "Sudanese Government Accuses Rebels of Murdering its Relief Workers", News Article by Agence France-Presse, 17 November 2003.

874 *Ibid*.

875 "Rebel Faction Admits Abducting Relief Workers in Sudan", News Article by Agence France-Presse, 20 November 2003.

876 "Western Sudan Too Dangerous for Road Convoys", News Article by UPI, 17 February 2004.

877 See, for example, "Khartoum Blames Darfur Rebels for Blocking Aid", News Article by Agence France-Presse, 24 March 2004

878 See, for example, "Sudan: Peace, But at What Price? Testimony by Julie Flint Before U.S. Senate Foreign Relations Committee", Human Rights Watch, New York,

2004, available at <http://www.hrw.org>. Flint has never hidden her opposition to the Government of Sudan.

879 "A Year Gone By in Darfur, and the Despair Has Deepened", *The Daily Star* (Beirut), 30 December 2004.

880 See, for example, interview with Associate Director of Human Rights Watch, Carroll Bogert, in *Der Spiegel*, 14 January 2005.

881 "A Year Gone By in Darfur, and the Despair Has Deepened", *op. cit.*

882 "Sudan" section in *World Report 2004*, Human Rights Watch, London, January 2004.

883 "Sudan Govt, SLA Rebels Peace Talks Break Down in Chad", News Article by Associated Press, 16 December 2003.

884 *Darfur: "Too Many People Killed For No Reason"*, Amnesty International, London, February 2004.

885 "Sudan Crisis – Background", Amnesty International, <http://www. amnesty.org>.

886 *Deliberate and Indiscriminate Attacks against Civilians in Darfur*, AI Index AFR 54/034/2004, Amnesty International, 7 April 2004, <http://www.amnesty.org>.

887 *Arming the Perpetrators of Grave Abuses in Darfur*, Amnesty International, 2004, <http://www.amnesty.org>.

888 *Open Letter to All Members of the Security Council*, AI Index AFR 54/162/2004, Amnesty International, 2004, <http://www.amnesty.org>.

889 See, for example, Eric Reeves, "Sudan's Reign of Terror", *Amnesty Now*, New York, Summer 2004.

890 See, for example, *The Displacement of Truth: Amnesty International, Oil and Sudan*, European-Sudanese Public Affairs Council, London, 2000, and *Amnesty International, Child Soldiers and War Criminals: Troubling Questions*, European-Sudanese Public Affairs Council, London, 2001, both available at <http://www.espac.org>.

891 Paul de Rooij, "Double Standards and Curious Silences. Amnesty International: A False Beacon?", *Counterpunch*, 13 October 2004, available at <http://www.counterpunch.org/rooij10132004.html>.

892 "Court Sentences 24 to Death for Killing 35 People in Tribal Raid", News Article by Associated Press, 27 April 2003.

893 "Forty-four Sudanese Killed, 22 Hurt in Tribal Clashes in Darfur", News Article by Agence France-Presse, 24 April 2003.

894 "Sudan Sentences 14 to Death for Arson in Turbulent Western Province", News Article by Agence France-Presse, 16 October 2003.

895 "State of Emergency after Southern Darfur Tribal Clashes", News Article by Integrated Regional Information Networks, UN Office for the Coordination of Humanitarian Affairs, Nairobi, 22 May 2002.

896 "Sudan: Urgent Call for Commission of Inquiry in Darfur as Situation Deteriorates", Press Release by Amnesty International, London, 21 February 2003.

897 "Khartoum Stepping Up Arrests in Strife-Torn Darfur: Amnesty", News Article by Agence France-Presse, 6 August 2003.

898 See, for example, "Sudan: Alarming Increase in Executions in Darfur Region", Press Release by Amnesty International, London, 28 June 2002.

899 See, for example, *Darfur: What Hope for the Future? Civilians in Urgent Need of Protection*, Amnesty International, London, 15 December 2004.

900 *Q & A: Crisis in Darfur*, Human Rights Watch, New York, June 2004.

901 "Leader of Darfur Rebels Resorts to Damage Control", *The New York Times*, 5 December 2004.

902 See, for example, "Sudan: Peace, But at What Price? Testimony by Julie Flint Before U.S. Senate Foreign Relations Committee", Human Rights Watch, New York, 2004, available at <http://hrw.org/english/docs>.

903 Prunier, *Darfur The Ambiguous Genocide, op. cit.*, p.96.

904 "Sudan Governor Accuses Darfur Rebels of Rape and Pillage", News Article by Agence France Press, 5 December 2004.

905 "Sudan Army: Rebels Burned Eight Villages, Killed Civilians in South Darfur", News Article by Associated Press.

906 See, for example, Amnesty International *Sudan* report, 2004.

907 Rob Crilly, South of West A Journalist in Africa weblog, 30 September 2007, available at <http://robcrilly.wordpress.com/2007/09/30/shades-of-grey/>.

908 *Report of the High-Level Mission on the situation of human rights in Darfur pursuant to Human Rights Council decision S-4/101*, A/HRC/4/80, 7 March 2007.

909 *"If We Return, We Will Be Killed" Consolidation of Ethnic Cleansing in Darfur, Sudan*, Human Rights Watch, New York, 2004, n.74.

910 "Sudan: Many Reported Killed During New Hostilities in Darfur", News Article by Integrated Regional Information Networks, UN Office for the Coordination of Humanitarian Affairs, Nairobi, 27 January 2005.

911 "Decision Time in Sudan", *The Economist*, 28 August 2004.

912 "The Other Rebels Causing Carnage in Sudan", *The Daily Telegraph* (London), 13 August 2004.

913 "Tora Bora Army Strikes Back at the Janjaweed", *The Independent* (London), 16 August 2004.

914 "We Are Victims Too, Say Darfur's Arab Refugees", *The Independent* (London), 13 August 2004.

915 "Sudan Says Rebels Kill 89", News Article by Reuters, 5 December 2004.

916 "Darfur: Sudan Gives Fresh Conditions for Peace Talks", *Daily Trust* (Abuja), 30 December 2004.

917 *"If We Return, We Will Be Killed" Consolidation of Ethnic Cleansing in Darfur, Sudan, op. cit.*

918 See, for example, "AU Says Rebels Attacked Convoy of Nigerian Pilgrims, Killing Seven People", News Article by Associated Press, 4 November 2004; and "Sudanese Rebels Attack Convoy of Nigerian Pilgrims", News Article by PANA, 6 November 2004.

919 "Armed groups must stop targeting civilians and humanitarian convoys", Press Release by Amnesty International, 3 November 2004.

920 *"If We Return, We Will Be Killed" Consolidation of Ethnic Cleansing in Darfur, Sudan, op. cit.*

921 *Ibid.*

922 "Workers in Sudan Aid Convoy Killed", News Article by BBC News, 28 October 2003.

923 "Sudanese Government Accuses Rebels of Murdering its Relief Workers", News Article by Agence France-Presse, 17 November 2003.

924 "Rebel Faction Admits Abducting Relief Workers in Sudan", News Article by Agence France-Presse, 20 November 2003.

925 "Rebels Commandeer Relief Trucks in Sudan's Darfur Region", News Article by Agence France-Presse, 8 June 2004.

926 "Sudan's Govt Accuses Darfur Rebels of Attacking FAO Food Convoy", News Article by Associated Press, 30 June 2004.

927 *Report of the Ceasefire Commission on the Situation in Darfur*, African Union, Addis Ababa, 4 October 2004.

928 "Abducted WFP Staff Released By Rebels in Darfur", Press Release by World Food Programme, Rome, 1 September 2004.

929 "UN Envoy Blames Darfur Rebels for Deaths of Aid Officials", News Article by Agence France-Presse, 28 October 2004.

930 *Ibid.*

931 "Humanitarian Aid in Sudan Limited By Insecurity, Road Closures, Says UN Mission", News Article by UN News Service (New York), 27 October 2004.

932 "U.N. says 200,000 Denied Aid as a Result of Darfur Violence", News Article by Deutsche Presse-Agentur, 14 November 2004.

933 "Despite Pact, New Violence Stymies Aid in Sudan", *The New York Times*, 28 November 2004.

934 "Doctor Killed, Four Injured in Sudan's Darfur", News Article by *Al-Rai Al-Amm* (Khartoum), 8 November 2004.

935 See, for example, "Foreign Aid Groups Flee Rebel Attacks in Sudan's Darfur: Report", News Article by Agence France-Presse, 7 November 2004; "MSF Spain Flees Rebel Attacks in Sudan's Darfur", News Article by Agence France-Presse, 7 November 2004.

936 "Armed Groups Must Stop Targeting Civilians and Humanitarian Convoys", Press Release by Amnesty International, 3 November 2004.

937 "Staff Murders Stop Aid Work in South Darfur", *The Guardian* (London), 14 December 2004.

938 See, for example, "UN Points at Rebels for Darfur Aid Workers' Death", News Article by Reuters, 15 December 2004.

939 "UN Points at Rebels for Darfur Aid Workers' Death", News Article by Reuters, 15 December 2004.

940 "U.N. Agency Suspends Food Convoys to Sudan", News Article by Associated Press, 29 December 2004.

941 *"If We Return, We Will Be Killed" Consolidation of Ethnic Cleansing in Darfur, Sudan, op. cit.*

942 "Sudanese Rebels Claim New Talks are Last Hope for Peace", *The Independent* (London), 15 September 2004. See also, "Sudan Government's Attacks Stoke Rebels' Fury", *The New York Times*, 11 September 2004, which also confirmed that rebel ranks are "filled" with child soldiers, some no more than 13.

943 *"If We Return, We Will Be Killed" Consolidation of Ethnic Cleansing in Darfur, Sudan, op. cit.*

944 "Violence in Sudan is Bringing Quick End to Many Childhoods", *The International Herald Tribune*, 16 August 2004.

945 *Report of the Ceasefire Commission on the Situation in Darfur*, African Union, Addis Ababa, 4 October 2004. See also "Sudan's Ragtag Rebels", *The Washington Post*, 7 September 2004.

946 "Sudanese Rebel Fighters Braced for Attack", *The Independent* (London), 14 August 2004.

947 "Darfur Rebels Roam Empty African Plains", News Article by Reuters, 9 February 2005.

948 "Sudan: Darfur Rebels Use Human Shields", News Article by Reuters, 19 October 2004.

949 See, "Sudan Rebels Say Air Strike Kills 25 Fighters", News Article by Reuters, 24 November 2004; "Sudan Rebels Retreat under Government Air Attack", News Article by Reuters, 24 November 2004.

950 News at 7pm, Channel Four TV (London), 16 December 2004.

951 "Power Struggle: Darfur's Janjaweed Militia Aren't the Only Ones Sowing Chaos and Death. Meet the Two Rebel Factions Threatening Yet Another Civil War", *Time*, 31 October 2004.

952 *Situation of Human Rights in the Darfur Region of the Sudan*, E/CN.4/2005/3, UN Commission on Human Rights, Geneva, 7 May 2004.

953 "Rebels from Displaced Camp Attack Relief Convoy", *Sudan Vision* (Khartoum), 2 October 2004.

954 "Renewed Fighting Shuts Down WFP Operations in North Darfur", Statement by World Food Programme, Nairobi, 25 November 2004.

955 See, for example, "Darfur Rebels Attack Convoy, Police – Sudan Official", News Article by Reuters, 16 December 2004.

Chapter Eight

956 "A Losing Strategy on War Crimes", *The International Herald Tribune*, 12-13 February 2005.

957 André-Michel Essoungou, "Uganda. Justice or Peace?", *The International Herald Tribune*, 21-22 April 2007.

958 Established on 1 July 2002, the ICC is based on the *Rome Statute of the International Criminal Court*, which was adopted after the UN Diplomatic Conference of Plenipotentiaries on the Establishment of a Permanent International Criminal Court in Rome on 17 July 1998. The statute states that the ICC is able to prosecute crimes of genocide, crimes against humanity, and war crimes.

959 See, for example, "No Darfur Solution without Arrest of Minister: ICC", News Article by Agence France-Presse, 24 September 2007.

960 "Sudan Stages 'Million-man' March against UN War Crimes Trial", News Article by Agence France-Presse, 5 April 2005, available at <http://www.sudantribune.com/article.php3?id_article=8891>.

961 "Sudan refuses questioning of top official over Darfur", News Article by Agence France-Presse, 26 March 2007.

962 "Warrants of arrest for the Minister of State for Humanitarian Affairs of Sudan, and a leader of the Militia/Janjaweed", International Criminal Court, The Hague, ICC-20070502-214-En, 2 May 2007.

963 "ICC judges issue arrest warrants for Darfur suspects", News Article by Reuters, 2 May 2007.

964 John Rosenthal, "A Lawless Global Court. How the International Criminal Court Undermines the U.N. System", *Policy Review*, Hoover Institution, Stanford University, February-March 2004.

965 David Scheffer, "International Criminal Court: The challenge of jurisdiction", speech to the American Society of International Law, 26 March 1999, cited in P. Scharf, "The United States and the International Criminal Court: The ICC's Jurisdiction over Nationals of Non-party States: A Critique of the US Position", *Law and Contemporary Problems*, No. 64, 2001, p 68.

966 David Scheffer, speaking to the Subcommittee on International Operations of the Senate Committee on Foreign Relations of the United States Senate, 23 July 1998, 105th Cong, 2d Sess, S Rep No 105 724, cited in Scharf, *op. cit.*, p. 68.

967 "Frequently Asked Questions About the U.S. Government's Policy Regarding the International Criminal Court (ICC)", Fact Sheet, Bureau of Political-Military Affairs, US Department of State, Washington, DC, 30 July 2003, available at <http://www.state.gov/t/pm/rls/fs/23428.htm>.

968 *Ibid.*

969 "Africa and the International Criminal Court", Council on Foreign Relations, New York, 17 November 2006.

970 See, for example, "ICC, Darfur and a Flawed U.S. Foreign Policy", Partnership for a Secure America, available at <http://blog.psaonline.org/2007/08/02/icc-darfur-and-a-flawed-us-foreign-policy/>, 2 August 2007. Mark Goldberg, writer in residence of the United Nations Foundation put in a Freedom of Information Act

request for cable traffic and other items relating to the State Department's Darfur policy.

971 Max du Plessis and Christopher Gevers, "Darfur Goes to the International Criminal Court (Perhaps)", *African Security Review*, Volume 14, Number 2, South Africa, 2005.

972 "A Losing Strategy on War Crimes", *The International Herald Tribune*, 12-13 February 2005.

973 John Rosenthal, "A Lawless Global Court. How the International Criminal Court Undermines the U.N. System", *Policy Review*, Hoover Institution, Stanford University, February-March 2004.

974 Max du Plessis and Christopher Gevers, "Darfur Goes to the International Criminal Court (Perhaps)", *op. cit.*

975 Paragraph 648, *Report of the International Commission of Inquiry on Darfur to the United Nations Secretary-General*, United Nations, January 2005.

976 Louise Parrott, "The Role of the International Criminal Court in Uganda: Ensuring that the Pursuit of Justice does not come at the price of peace", *The Australian Journal of Peace Studies*, Volume 1, 2006.

977 "Africa and the International Criminal Court", Council on Foreign Relations, New York, 17 November 2006.

978 See "Joint Statement by ICC Chief Prosecutor and the visiting Delegation of Lango, Acholi, Iteso and Madi Community Leaders from Northern Uganda," The Hague, April 16, 2005, <http://www.icc-cpi.int/press/pressreleases/102.html>.

979 "Will ICC prosecutions threaten Ugandan peace process?", Institute for War and Peace Reporting, Africa Report Number 46, 16 November 2005.

980 "Uganda: Give peace a chance, northern leaders tell ICC", News Article by Integrated Regional Information Networks, UN Office for the Coordination of Humanitarian Affairs, Nairobi, 2 June 2006.

981 "Uganda: ICC indictments to affect northern peace efforts, says mediator", News Article by Integrated Regional Information Networks, UN Office for the Coordination of Humanitarian Affairs, Nairobi, 10 October 2005.

982 "African Search for Peace Throws Court into Chaos", *The Guardian* (London), 9 January 2007.

983 "Africa and the International Criminal Court", Council on Foreign Relations, New York, 17 November 2006.

984 "Uganda's war victims prefer peace over punishment", News Article by Reuters, 30 April 2007.

985 André-Michel Essoungou, "Uganda. Justice or Peace?", *The International Herald Tribune*, 21-22 April 2007.

986 "Uganda's Government Wants Rebels Tried Locally", News Item by Voice of America, 12 September 2007.

987 Mahnoush Arsanjani and Michael Reisman, "The Law-In-Action of the International Criminal Court", *American Journal of International Law*, Number 99, 2005, p.393.

988 *Ibid.*

989 Richard Dowden, "ICC in the Dock", *Prospect*, London, May 2007.

990 *Ibid.*

991 *Ibid.*

992 "African Search for Peace Throws Court into Chaos", *The Guardian* (London), 9 January 2007.

993 Christopher Caldwell, "It is best to stay out of Darfur", *The Financial Times* (London), 16 December 2006.

994 Mariam Bibi Jooma, "The International Criminal Court and Sudan – Opening a Pandora's Box", *ISS Today*, Institute for Security Studies, Tshwane (Pretoria), 6 March 2007.

995 "Africa and the International Criminal Court", Council on Foreign Relations, New York, 17 November 2006.

996 Jooma, *op. cit.*

997 "UN concerned about staff security after ICC accuses Sudanese of war crimes", News Item by United Nations Radio, 28 February 2007.

998 Cited in "Sudan Morning News", 28 February 2007, Public Affairs Section, US Embassy, Khartoum.

999 Jooma, *op. cit.*

1000 Rosenthal, *op. cit.*

1001 *Ibid.*

1002 "Africa and the International Criminal Court", Council on Foreign Relations, New York, 17 November 2006.

1003 Dilip Lahiri, "Explanation of vote on the adoption of the Statute of the International Criminal Court", Embassy of India, 17 July 1998, Washington, D.C.

1004 Parrott, *op. cit.*

1005 *Ibid.*

1006 Allison Danner, "Enhancing the Legitimacy and Accountability of Prosecutorial Discretion at the International Criminal Court", *American Journal of International Law*, Number 97, 2003.

1007 Parrott, *op. cit.*

1008 *Ibid.*

1009 See, for example, President Museveni's interview with Integrated Regional Information Networks, on 9 June 2005: "The involvement of the ICC in hunting Kony is very important, mainly because it enables us to deal with Khartoum. Khartoum is fully aware of the consequences of dealing with somebody under the ICC's indictment. If Kony is in Uganda or in the areas of Sudan where Khartoum has allowed us to operate, then we do not need assistance – we shall catch him ourselves. But if Kony goes deeper into Sudan, beyond where Sudan has allowed us to pursue him, we need the ICC's assistance to get the Sudanese government to cooperate with us and help us to get him. That is why we need the ICC.", "Uganda: Interview with President Yoweri

Museveni," News Article by Integrated Regional Information Networks, UN Office for the Coordination of Humanitarian Affairs, Kampala, 9 June 2005, available at <http://www.irinnews.org/S_report.asp?ReportID=47569>.

1010 "African Search for Peace Throws Court into Chaos", *The Guardian* (London), 9 January 2007.

1011 *Ibid.*

1012 "Africa and the International Criminal Court", Council on Foreign Relations, New York, 17 November 2006.

1013 *Ibid.*

1014 Parrott, *op. cit.*

Chapter Nine

1015 Martin Bell, *Through Gates of Fire: A Journey into World Disorder*, Weidenfeld and Nicholson, London, 2003, p.26.

1016 Andrew Natsios, "Illusions of Influence: The CNN Effect in Complex Emergencies", in Robert I. Rotberg and Thomas G. Weiss (Editors), *From Massacres to Genocide. The Media, Public Policy, and Humanitarian Crises*, The Brookings Institution, Washington-DC and The World Peace Foundation, Cambridge, Massachusetts, 1996, p.164.

1017 News at 7pm, Channel Four TV (London), 16 December 2004.

1018 "Sudan Rebels Accuse Government of Using Chemical Weapons", News Article by Reuters, 30 July 1999.

1019 See, "Sudan 'Chemical' Attack on Rebels", News Article by BBC Online News, 31 July 1999; "Sudan Denies 'Chemical' Attack", News Article by BBC Online News, 1 August 1999; "UN Teams Investigate Sudan Gas Attack", News Article by BBC Online News, 5 August 1999; "UN Investigates 'Chemical' Attack", News Article by BBC Online News, 5 August 1999; and "Warning On Sudanese 'Chemical Attack'", News Article by BBC Online News, 23 August 1999. For a critique of the British media's lacklustre reporting of this issue, see *Irresponsible Journalism: British Media Reporting of Allegations of Chemical Weapons in Sudan*, European-Sudanese Public Affairs Council, London, February 2000, available at <http://www.espac.org>. For a study of similarly unfounded claims of the use of chemical weapons, see *"Chemical Weapons in Sudan": The Baroness Cox Fiasco*, European-Sudanese Public Affairs Council, London, June 2000, available at <http://www.espac.org>.

1020 "Note for the Spokesman of the Secretary-General on Sudan", Note delivered by the United Nations Resident Coordinator, Mr Philippe Borel, to the Sudanese Foreign Ministry, 17 October, 1999. The on-site inspection by United Nations medical teams had also found no evidence to support the claims made by Norwegian Peoples Aid: see, "UN: No Evidence of Serious Symptoms in Alleged Chemical Attack", News Article by CNS, 13 August 1999.

1021 Richard Miniter, "The False Promise of Slave Redemption", *The Atlantic Monthly*, July 1999.

1022 See, for example, "The Great Slave Scam", *The Irish Times*, 23 February 2002; "Scam in Sudan – An Elaborate Hoax Involving Fake African Slaves and Less-than-Honest Interpreters is Duping Concerned Westerners", *The Independent on Sunday* (London), 24 February 2002; "Ripping Off Slave 'Redeemers': Rebels Exploit Westerners' Efforts to Buy Emancipation for Sudanese", *The Washington Post*, 26 February 2002; "Sudan Rip-Offs Over Phony Slaves", *International Herald Tribune*, 27 February 2002.

1023 "Syrien Testet Chemische Waffen an Sudanern", *Die Welt* (Berlin), 14 September 2004.

1024 See, for example, restating of claims, "Syria Tested Chemical Arms on Civilians in Darfur Region: Press", Agence France-Presse, 14 September 2004, and the discounting of the allegations: "Germany Questions Report Syria Tested Chemical Weapons", News Article by Deutsche Presse-Agentur, 16 September 2004, and "US Doubts Report on Syrian Chemical Weapons Testing in Darfur", News Article by Agence France-Presse, 15 September 2004.

1025 See, for example, "Sudan Chemical Weapons Allegations from Norway, Germany", News Article by afrol News, 15 September 2004, available at <http://www.afrol.com/articles/13956>.

1026 House of Lords *Hansard*, Written Parliamentary Answer, 16 November 2004, column WA 130.

1027 For a detailed study of Norwegian Peoples Aid see *Perpetuating Conflict and Sustaining Repression: Norwegian Peoples Aid and the Militarisation of Aid in Sudan*, European-Sudanese Public Affairs Council, London, March 2000, available at <http://www.espac.org>.

1028 Susan Moeller, *Compassion Fatigue: How the Media Sell, Disease, Famine, War and Death*, Routledge, New York and London, 1999, p.106-7.

1029 Deborah Murphy, "Narrating Darfur: Darfur in the U.S. Press, March-September 2004", in Alex de Waal (editor), *War in Darfur and the Search for Peace*, Global Equity Initiative, Harvard, and Justice Africa, 2007, pp. 314-17.

1030 Deborah Murphy, "Narrating Darfur: Darfur in the U.S. Press, March-September 2004", *op. cit.*, p.316.

1031 Herbert Gans, *Deciding What's News*, Random House, New York, 1980, p.133.

1032 Judith Miller, quoted in Michael Massing, "Now They Tell Us", *The New York Review of Books*, 26 February 2004.

1033 Jonathan Steele, "How the Media prolonged the war in Darfur", speech at the Royal United Services Institute for Defence and Security Studies, London, 6 July 2006.

1034 Moeller, *op. cit.*, p.106.

1035 *Darfur 120-Day Plan Report September to December 2004*, Office of the United Nations Resident and Humanitarian Co-ordinator for the Sudan, Khartoum, January 2005.

1036 "As Darfur War Rages On, Disease and Hunger Kill", *The New York Times*, 31 May 2006.

1037 See, for example, "U.S. Weighs Moves Against Sudan Over U.N. Force", *The Washington Post*, 28 September 2006".

1038 "Darfur Death Toll is Hundreds of Thousands Higher than Reported, Study Says", *National Geographic News*, New York, 14 September 2006.

1039 "The next Rwanda?", *The Times* (London), 5 September 2006.

1040 See, for example, "Sudan. A Triumph Marred by Terror", *The Economist*, 29 May 2004; *The Sunday Telegraph* (London), 16 May 2004; "Inside Sudan's Rebel Army", Philip Cox, BBC *Focus On Africa*, 5 April 2004. Cox also appeared on "Inside Africa: Battle for Sudan's Western Darfur Region", Report by CNN, 17 April 2004.

1041 "Pressure Seen as Key to Ending Sudan's Western War", News Article by Reuters, 28 January 2004.

1042 See, for example, *Questionable Sources, Questionable Journalism: The Observer and Sudan*, The British-Sudanese Public Affairs Council, London, May 2000, available at <http://www.espac.org>.

1043 "And With Darfur's Rebels", *The Sunday Herald*, 8 August 2004. This piece was written by the newspaper's foreign editor, David Pratt.

1044 Mahmood Mamdani, "The Politics of Naming: Genocide, Civil War, Insurgency", *The London Review of Books*, 8 March 2007.

1045 *Ibid*.

1046 Jonathan Steele, "How the Media prolonged the war in Darfur", *op. cit.*

1047 Alex de Waal, "The book was closed too soon on peace in Darfur", *The Guardian* (London), 29 September 2006.

1048 Jonathan Steele, "How the Media prolonged the war in Darfur", *op. cit.*

1049 Andrew Buckoke, *Fishing in Africa: A Guide to War and Corruption*, Picador, London, 1992, p.42.

1050 *Ibid.*, p.44.

1051 *Ibid.*, p.43.

1052 *Ibid.*, p.44.

1053 *Ibid.*, p.44.

1054 Prunier, *op. cit.*, p. 127.

1055 *Ibid.*, pp. 127-8.

1056 *Ibid.*, p. 156.

1057 See, for example, Nicholas Kristof's, "Will We Say 'Never Again' Yet Again?", *The New York Times*, 27 March 2004, "Don't Let Sudan's Ethnic Cleansing Go On", *The New York Times*, 25 March 2004.

1058 Marc Lacey, "In Sudan, Militiamen on Horses Uproot a Million", *The New York Times*, 4 May 2004.

1059 Nicholas Kristof, "Will We Say 'Never Again' Yet Again?", *op. cit.* See also, for example, repeated claims of genocide in "He Ain't Heavy...", *The New York Times*, 20

October 2004; "Saying No to Killers", *The New York Times*, 21 July 2004, "Sudan's Final Solution", *The New York Times*, 19 June 2004, "Dare We Call it Genocide?", *The New York Times*, 16 June 2004.

1060 Nicholas Kristof, "Cruel Choices", *The New York Times*, 14 April 2004.

1061 "In Sudan, No Clear Difference between Arab and African", *The New York Times*, 3 October 2004.

1062 "'New York Times' on Africa: A tradition of Pessimism Continues", News Opinion Piece by Afrol News, 4 June 2003, <http://www.afrol.com/articles/12907>

1063 See, for example, "Times Columnist Humiliated", *Media Monitor*, Accuracy in Media, Washington-DC, 18 August 2004, and "Another Embarrassment for Kristof", *Media Monitor*, Accuracy in Media, Washington-DC, 17 October 2002. See also, "Another Black Eye for a Times Columnist", *Media Monitor*, Accuracy in Media, Washington-DC, 11 March 2003.

1064 "War in Western Sudan Overshadows Peace in the South", *The New York Times*, 17 January 2004. Even long-standing anti-Sudan activists such as Eric Reeves has admitted to making serious allegations about Darfur while at the same time acknowledging that such claims are based on "second-hand accounts" and "fragmentary" accounts: "There have been virtually no first-hand accounts by journalists, and the observations by humanitarian organizations are necessarily scattered" (see, 'The Accelerating Catastrophe in Darfur (Sudan): Khartoum Fixes Upon a Policy of War and Civilian Destruction', 24 November 2003).

1065 Moeller, *op. cit.*, p.108.

1066 *Ibid*.

1067 Michael Maren, "Feeding a Famine", *ForbesMediaCritic*, Volume 2, Number 1, 1994, p.32.

1068 Mahmood Mamdani, "The Politics of Naming: Genocide, Civil War, Insurgency", *op. cit.*

1069 *Ibid*.

1070 *Ibid*.

1071 "Cut and Walk", *The International Herald Tribune* (New York), 6 December 2006.

1072 "Darfur and the Genocide Debate", *Foreign Affairs*, January-February 2005, Council on Foreign Relations, New York.

1073 Moeller, *op. cit.*; Senator Paul Simon. "Letters to the Editor", *ForbesMediaCritic*, Volume 2, Number 2, 1994-95.

1074 The full citation is available at <http://www.pulitzer.org/year/2006/commentary/>.

1075 See, Mark von Hagen, "The Pulitzer Prize the NYT Should Not Have Won", History News Network, 23 October 2003, available at <http://hnn.us/articles/1754.html>, and "Times Should Lose Pulitzer From 30's, Consultant Says", *The New York Times*, 23 October 2003.

1076 See, for example, "As Genocide Unfolds", *The Washington Post*, 20 June 2004;

"'Realism' and Darfur", *The Washington Post*, 1 August 2004; "The Killing Continues", *The Washington Post*, 17 October 2004; "Diplomacy and Darfur", *The Washington Post*, 17 November 2004; "Inaction's Consequence", 9 December 2004; "US Shift on Darfur Policy", *The Washington Post*, 27 December 2004.

1077 Severine Autesserre, "United States 'Humanitarian Diplomacy' in South Sudan", *Journal of Humanitarian Assistance*, 18 March 2002.

1078 "Millions Still in Need in Sudan", *The Guardian* (London), 25 April 1998.

1079 "Chapter 4: Overview of the Humanitarian Response", *Evaluation of Danish Humanitarian Assistance to Sudan 1992-98*, Royal Danish Ministry of Foreign Affairs, Copenhagen, 1999.

1080 *Ibid*.

1081 See, for example, "Aid for Sudan Ending up with SPLA: Relief Workers", News Article by Agence France-Presse, 21 July 1998.

1082 "Emergency Assistance to the Sudan", UN General Assembly Resolution A/RES/53/1 O, 17 December 1998.

1083 *Darfur: "Too Many People Killed For No Reason"*, Amnesty International, London, February 2004.

1084 "'Realism' and Darfur", *The Washington Post*, 1 August 2004

1085 "The Killing Continues", *The Washington Post*, 17 October 2004

1086 "Diplomacy and Darfur", *The Washington Post*, 17 November 2004

1087 See, for example, "US Shift on Darfur Policy", *The Washington Post*, 27 December 2004.

1088 "100,000 Civilian Deaths Estimated in Iraq", *The Washington Post*, 29 October 2004.

1089 "Study Claims Iraq's 'Excess' Death Toll Has Reached 655,000", *The Washington Post*, 11 October 2006.

1090 "Poll: Civilian toll in Iraq may top 1M. A British survey offers the highest estimate to date", *The Los Angeles Times*, 14 September 2007.

1091 See, for example, "U.S. Weighs Moves Against Sudan Over U.N. Force", *The Washington Post*, 28 September 2006".

1092 Alex de Waal, Social Science Research Council weblog, 28 August 2007, available at <www.ssrc.org/blog/category/darfur/>.

1093 "Sudan: Interview with UN's Jan Egeland on the Situation in Darfur", News Article by Integrated Regional Information Networks, UN Office for the Coordination of Humanitarian Affairs, Nairobi, 5 July 2004.

1094 "Sudan: Interview with Kevin Kennedy, Outgoing Acting UN Humanitarian Coordinator for Sudan", News Article by UN Integrated Regional Information Networks, UN Office for the Coordination of Humanitarian Affairs, Nairobi, 23 June 2004.

1095 "Two Million Darfur Children Get Measles Shot", Press Release by UNICEF, Geneva, 6 July 2004.

1096 See, for example, "The Missiles, the Bungling Pentagon and the Nerve Gas Factory That Never Was", *The Observer* (London), 30 August 1998; "Sudan Attack Blamed on US Blunders", *The Times* (London) 22 September 1998; "Dubious Decisions on the Sudan", Editorial, *The New York Times*, 23 September 1998; "Experts Find No Arms Chemicals at Bombed Sudan Plant", *The New York Times*, 9 February 1999.

1097 "Genocide", *The Independent* (London), 10 September 2004; It also published another front-page banner headline reading, "Darfur: Never Again?", *The Independent* (London), 26 January 2005.

1098 See, for example, "An Impressive Show; But Mr Powell Failed to Make the Case for a War on Iraq", Editorial, *The Independent* (London), 6 February 2003; "Colin Powell and the Failure of US Diplomacy", *The Independent* (London), 5 August 2003. *The Independent* has also reported on proven inaccuracies in Powell's claims: "Powell Withdraws al-Qa'ida Claim as Hunt for Saddam's WMD Flags", *The Independent* (London), 11 January 2004.

1099 "Danforth Described Darfur as 'Genocide' to Please Christian Right", *The Independent* (London), 5 July 2005.

1100 See, for example, "A World against the War", *The Independent* (London), 19 January 2003; "Stop. Think Listen", *The Independent* (London), 26 January 2003 "We Can Still Stop This Blind March to Disaster", *The Independent* (London), 2 February 2003; "Revealed: How the Road to War was Paved with Lies", *The Independent* (London), 27 April 2003.

1101 "Focus: Part One The Human Cost – 'Does Tony Have Any Idea What the Flies are Like That Feed Off the Dead?'", *The Independent* (London), 26 January 2003.

1102 "No Weapons, No Programmes: Nothing to Justify the Invasion", *The Independent* (London), 7 October 2004; "Lies, Mischief and the Myth of Western Intelligence Services", *The Independent* (London), 28 September 2003; "WMD Just a Convenient Excuse for War, Admits Wolfowitz", *The Independent* (London), 30 May 2003; "20 Lies About the War", *The Independent* (London), 13 July 2003; "Bit by Bit, How Case for War has Unravelled, Leaving Blair Dangerously Exposed", *The Independent* (London), 31 January 2004.

1103 "Iraq is Now al-Qa'ida's Battleground, Say MPs", *The Independent* (London), 29 July 2004; "Iraq cannot be Forgotten or Forgiven", *The Independent* (London), 16 September 2004; "Is the World Safer Now?", *The Independent* (London), 28 January 2005; "The Final Judgement", *The Independent* (London), 7 October 2004.

1104 See, for example, "The Prime Minister Led Us into an Illegal War", *The Independent* (London), 14 October 2004.

1105 "Britain Must Not be Suckered a Second Time by the White House", *The Independent* (London), 30 May 2003.

1106 "The Belated Recognition of Reality in Sudan", *The Independent* (London), 10 September 2004.

1107 "Sudan is Another Rwanda in the Making", *The Independent* (London), 23 April 2004.

1108 "Would We Have Acted Long Ago if the Victims of this Mass Murder were White?", *The Independent* (London), 25 August 2004.

1109 "How some of the World's Biggest Corporations are Fuelling the Genocide in Darfur", *The Independent* (London), 19 November 2004.

1110 "Would We Have Acted Long Ago if the Victims of this Mass Murder were White?", *The Independent* (London), 25 August 2004.

1111 "How Some of the World's Biggest Corporations are Fuelling the Genocide in Darfur", *The Independent* (London), 19 November 2004.

1112 "The Great Betrayal: How the World is Ignoring the Victims of Racist Slaughter", *The Independent* (London), 24 December 2004. The UN had said that "by 31 December 2004 the humanitarian situation for most of the 2.2 million people affected is stabilized": *Darfur 120-Day Plan Report September to December 2004*, Office of the United Nations Resident and Humanitarian Co-ordinator for the Sudan, Khartoum, January 2005.

1113 "The First Genocide of the Twenty-First Century is Drawing to an End", *The Independent* (London), 4 October 2005.

1114 "First In and Last Out of the World's Danger Zones", *The Independent* (London), 29 July 2004.

1115 "Sudan's Bombing of Darfur 'Breaks Ceasefire'", *The Independent* (London), 28 January 2005.

1116 "Charity Pulls Out of Darfur after Murders", *The Independent* (London), 21 December 2005; "Aid Workers Killed in Darfur Convoy Attack", *The Independent* (London), 14 December 2004.

1117 "The Withdrawal of Aid Workers Adds to Darfur's Despair", *The Independent* (London), 23 December 2004.

1118 House of Commons *Hansard*, London, 14 December 2004.

1119 "Never Again", Panorama, BBC 1 (TV), 3 July 2005.

1120 Prunier, *op. cit.*, p. 157.

1121 *Ibid.*, p.156.

1122 Ta-Nehisi Coates, "Black, White, Read. Newspapers Are Serving Up the Sudan Conflict as a Race War. Sadly, It's Not That Simple", *The Village Voice* (New York), 28 September 2004.

1123 Kersap D. Shekhdar, "Everything You Always Wanted to Know About Media Coverage of Darfur (But Where Afraid to Ask), *Online Journal*, 12 September 2004 <http://onlinejournal.com>.

1124 Eric Reeves, Darfur Mortality Update", 18 January 2005, <http://sudanreeves.org>.

1125 Kersap D. Shekhdar, "Everything You Always Wanted to Know About Media Coverage of Darfur (But Where Afraid to Ask), *op. cit.*

1126 Moeller, *op. cit.*, p.314.

1127 Interview cited in Moeller, *op. cit.*, p.315.

1128 Natsios, *op. cit.*, pp, 164-65.

1129 *Ibid.*, p.164.

1130 See, for example, Pieter Tesch, "Unravelling Sudan: The Media Should Not Get Embedded with NGOs", *Press Gazette* (London), 3 September 2004, p.17.

1131 Pieter Tesch, "Darfur Deserves Analysis, Not Clichés", Letters Page, *Press Gazette*, 7 January 2005.

1132 Moeller, *op. cit.*, p.48.

1133 "Darfur Overshadows the Peace Process in South Sudan", News Article by IPS, 2 September 2004.

1134 Moeller, *op. cit.*, p.321.

1135 See <www.beawitness.org>.

1136 Brendan O'Neill, "Darfur: pornography for the chattering classes. Why have the British media been silent about the Advertising Standards Authority's damning judgement against the Save Darfur Coalition?", *Spiked* online, London, 14 August 2007, available at <http://www.spiked-online.com/index.php?/site/printable/3723/>.

Chapter Ten

1137 Dimitri K. Simes, "Unrealists", *The National Interest*, Washington-DC, Summer 2006. Simes is the publisher of *The National Interest*.

1138 George Washington, *Observations on July 28, 1791*, from the collection by Edward S. Morgan, reprinted in *The New York Times*, 22 February 1981.

1139 "Asking the Right Questions about Darfur, Sudan", Part IV, Exclusive Q&A with Salih Booker, Executive Director, Africa Action, available at <www.blackelectorate.com>.

1140 Cited in Christopher Caldwell, "It is best to stay out of Darfur", *The Financial Times* (London), 16 December 2006.

1141 Alex de Waal, "Darfur Peace Agreement: So Near, So Far", Open Democracy, 29 September 2006.

1142 Alan J. Kuperman, "Strategic Victimhood in Sudan", *The New York Times*, 31 May 2006.

1143 *Ibid.*

1144 Michael Clough, "It's hell in Darfur, but is it genocide? The Sudanese government has targeted villagers, but not a whole race", *The Los Angeles Times*, 14 May 2006.

1145 *Ibid.*

1146 The extent to which skewed perspectives of the Darfur crisis have worked their way into American popular culture is also clear. Several episodes of the television show "ER", and featuring several major characters, have been set in the Darfur region. "Internal Displacement", an episode in the seventh season of the television show "The West Wing", features a garbled version of the conflict in Darfur. West Wing actor Bradley Whitford subsequently called for international intervention in Darfur.

1147 Similar questionable claims about Darfur featured in advertisements run on the MTV music channel. The US CW show "7th Heaven", has dedicated two episodes to the crisis. Darfur has also been reduced to comic-book simplicity. A distorted picture of the conflict is featured in the comic book "Squadron Supreme: Hyperion vs. Nighthawk", published by Marvel Comics, which is set in the region.

1148 Gal Beckerman, "US Jews leading Darfur rally planning", *The Jerusalem Post*, 27 April 2006.

1149 See, for example, the Save Darfur Coalition website <http://www.savedarfur.org>.

1150 See, Save Darfur Coalition website <http://www.savedarfur.org/section/about/>.

1151 Rebecca Hamilton and Chad Hazlett, "'Not on Our Watch": The Emergence of the American Movement for Darfur", in Alex de Waal (editor), *War in Darfur and the Search for Peace*, Global Equity Initiative, Harvard, and Justice Africa, 2007, p.362.

1152 Cited in Rebecca Hamilton and Chad Hazlett, *op. cit.*, p.344.

1153 Anne Bartlett, "Why a Reality Check is Needed on Darfur", *Sudan Tribune*, 21 September 2007 available at <http://www.sudantribune.com/spip.php?article23863>.

1154 David Rieff, "The Darfur Deception", *The Los Angeles Times*, 7 October 2007. Rieff is a Fellow at the World Policy Institute, a Contributing Editor, *The New Republic* Magazine; Board Member, the Arms Project of Human Rights Watch; and a Fellow of the New York Institute for the Humanities at New York University. His books have included *At the Point of a Gun: Democratic Dreams and Armed Intervention*, *A Bed for the Night: Humanitarianism in Crisis*, and *Slaughterhouse: Bosnia and the Failure of the West*. He is a frequent contributor to *The New Republic*, *The New York Times*, *The Los Angeles Times*, and the *Times Literary Supplement*.

1155 Brendan O'Neill, "Darfur: pornography for the chattering classes. Why have the British media been silent about the Advertising Standards Authority's damning judgement against the Save Darfur Coalition?", *Spiked* online, London, 14 August 2007, available at <http://www.spiked-online.com/index.php?/site/printable/3723/>.

1156 Mahmood Mamdani, "The Politics of Naming: Genocide, Civil War, Insurgency", *The London Review of Books*, 8 March 2007.

1157 See, Save Darfur Coalition website <http://www.savedarfur.org/pages/faq>.

1158 David Rieff, "Good vs good in Darfur", *The Los Angeles Times*, 24 June 2007.

1159 Mahmood Mamdani, "The Politics of Naming: Genocide, Civil War, Insurgency", *op. cit.*

1160 Steve Fake and Kevin Funk, "Saving Darfur or Salvation Delusion?", Foreign Policy in Focus, 20 June 2007, available at <http://www.fpif.org/fpiftxt/4314>.

1161 See, for example, "UK Advertising Regulator Says Ad Campaign's Darfur Deaths Claim Not Factual", News Article by Associated Press, 15 August 2007.

1162 Sam Dealey, "An Atrocity That Needs No Exaggeration", *The New York Times*, 12 August 2007, available at <http://www.nytimes.com/2007/08/12/opinion/12dealey.html?_r=1&oref=slogin>. Dealey has reported on Africa for *Time* magazine.

1163 *Ibid.*

1164 Brendan O'Neill, "Darfur: pornography for the chattering classes. Why have the British media been silent about the Advertising Standards Authority's damning judgement against the Save Darfur Coalition?"

1165 Reuters, "Thousands March to Stop Darfur Killing", News Article by Reuters, 30 April 2006.

1166 "Groups Plan Rally on Mall To Protest Darfur Violence. Bush Administration Is Urged to Intervene in Sudan", *The Washington Post*, 27 April 2006.

1167 Gal Beckerman, "US Jews leading Darfur rally planning", *The Jerusalem Post*, 27 April 2006.

1168 *Ibid.*

1169 Anne Bartlett, "Why a Reality Check is Needed on Darfur", *Sudan Tribune*, 21 September 2007 available at <http://www.sudantribune.com/spip.php?article23863>. Anne Bartlett is a sociologist who has also been involved in rights based issues for over 20 years. She has worked with the Fur Diaspora in London as part of a research project since January 2003 and has been actively involved in the campaign to protect Darfur. She travelled with the Darfur delegation to the UN Human Rights Commission in Geneva where she chaired a session and spoke on the crisis in 2004 and 2005. She has also been instrumental in organising grassroots protests and other activities to highlight the situation in Darfur.

1170 "Can the Glitterati Save Darfur?", *The Boston Globe*, 10 September 2007.

1171 Brendan O'Neill, "Darfur: pornography for the chattering classes. Why have the British media been silent about the Advertising Standards Authority's damning judgement against the Save Darfur Coalition?", *op.cit.*

1172 See "Unity Statement", on Save Darfur website available at <http://www.savedarfur.org/pages/unity_statement>.

1173 *Ibid.*

1174 See, for example, *Darfur Crisis: Death Estimates Demonstrate Severity of Crisis, but Their Accuracy and Credibility Could Be Enhanced*, United States Government Accountability Office, Report Number GAO-07-24, Washington-DC, 11 December 2006. The experts were asked further questions. Eleven out of twelve experts stated that Hagan had used inappropriate extrapolations, 6 stating he had used "very inappropriate" extrapolations. Ten out of twelve experts stated that he had made unreasonable assumptions, with 6 experts further stating he had used very unreasonable assumptions; When asked whether Hagan had sufficiently or insufficiently described appropriate limitations, including sources of possible over or under estimation, 9 out of 12 experts stated that his descriptions were insufficient, of which 8 experts stated he had very insufficiently described these limitations. Hagan's peers had previously found that his estimates, in the words of the GAO report, "used unrealistic extrapolations and assumptions to fill information gaps and estimate total deaths." Hagan's work had "relied on two few data points extrapolated to an excessive degree. As a result of this type of extrapolation, the experts observed, a sensitivity analysis changing one or two assumptions could swing the total number of deaths from 100,000 to half a million, making the estimates unreliable." Several experts had also believed that Hagan had "inappropriately assumed constant rates of mortality for different population groups in Darfur at different periods in the conflict".

1175 Alan J. Kuperman, "Strategic Victimhood in Sudan", *The New York Times*, 31 May 2006.

1176 Brendan O'Neill, "Darfur: pornography for the chattering classes. Why have the British media been silent about the Advertising Standards Authority's damning judgement against the Save Darfur Coalition?" *op. cit.*

1177 Yoshie Furuhashi, "Who Wants Peace in Darfur?", *Monthly Review*, 30 April 2006, available at <http://mrzine.monthlyreview.org/furuhashi300406.html>.

1178 Cited in Rebecca Hamilton and Chad Hazlett, *op. cit.*, p.344.

1179 Anne Bartlett, "Why a Reality Check is Needed on Darfur", *op. cit.*

1180 "Mahmood Mamdani on Darfur: 'The Politics of Naming: Genocide, Civil War, Insurgency'", *op, cit.*

1181 *Ibid.*

1182 "Saving Darfur, Multiple Steps at a Time", *The Washington Post*, 1 June 2007.

1183 "Bush's Special Sudan Envoy says that Save Darfur Coalition's Efforts may be Outdated", *The Boston Herald*, 10 September 2007.

1184 "Duelling Over Darfur. A human rights activist and an Africa scholar disagree – vehemently – on the best way to help Sudan", Newsweek Online Forum, 8 November 2007, available at <http://www.newsweek.com/id/69004>.

1185 *Ibid.*

1186 "Do-Gooders Gone Bad. Activists have brought issues like Darfur into living rooms. But they may be doing more harm than good", *Newsweek*, 3 November 2007. See, also, "Packaging a Tragedy. What the Save Darfur movement did right, where it went wrong – and what its strategy can teach us about the future of political advocacy", *Newsweek* Web Exclusive, 26 October 2007.

1187 David Kelsey, "Jewish Leadership on Darfur", 17 April 2006, available at <http://jewschool.com/?p=10451>.

1188 A standard Google search for Darfur Zionist plot, for example, will bring up thousands of pages. See, for example, from one website, Ned Goldstein, "Save Darfur: Zionist Conspiracy? Exploiting African Genocide for Propaganda", WW4 Report, available at <http://ww4report.com/node/2582>; "Save Sudan: The Zionist Lobby and Coordinated Media", 27 April 2007 on the <pittsburghindymedia,org> site; and David Hoffman, "Zionist and anti-Zionist Spinning of Darfur Crisis", WW4 site, 4 October 2006, available at <http://ww4report.com/node/2585#comment-289444>.

1189 Paul de Rooij, "The Useful Fools of Empire. Humanitarian Wars and Associated Delusions", *Counterpunch*, 14 August 2007, available at <http://www.counterpunch.org/rooij08142007.html>.

1190 "Sudan: Jews behind Darfur conflict. Sudanese defense minister says '24 Jewish organizations fuelling conflict in Darfur'", News Article by Ynetnews, 29 July 2007, available at <http://www.ynetnews.com/articles/0,7340,L-3431281,00.html>. See, also, for example, "Sudan FM: Israel escalates Darfur Crisis", News Article by Arabicneww.com, 9 August 2004, available at <http://www.arabicnews.com/ansub/Daily/Day/040809/2004080903.html>; Sudan has also accused Israel of having supported southern Sudanese rebels: "Sudan: Israel backs the rebels", News Article by Arabicneww.com, 16 September 2002, available at <http://www.arabicnews.com/ansub/Daily/Day/020916/2002091607.html>.

1191 See comments made at "Darfur Rally To Be Held in D.C.", *The Washington Post* website, available at <http://www.washingtonpost.com/wp-dyn/content/discussion/2006/04/24/DI2006042401049_pf.html>.

1192 See, for example, "Israeli government criticized for deporting Darfur refugees", *The International Herald Tribune*, 20 August 2007.

1193 See, for example, <http://www.standnow.org/learn/situation>.

1194 See, for example, the STAND website at <http://www.standnow.org>.

1195 See Aegis Trust website <http://www.aegistrust.org/index.php?option=com_content&task=view&id=437&Itemid=88>.

1196 See, for example, statements made on Aegis Trust website <http://www.protectdarfur.org/Statement/Read_The_Protect_Darfur_Campaign_Statement.htm>.

1197 See Aegis Trust website <http://www.protectdarfur.org/Background/Background_And_Timeline.htm>.

1198 See Aegis Trust website <http://www.protectdarfur.org/>.

1199 See Sudan Divestment UK website <http://www.sudandivestment.co.uk/>.

1200 See, for example, "In the west of Sudan, fears of economic and political isolation catalysed the formation last year of the Sudanese Liberation Army (SLA) and the Justice and Equality Movement (JEM)", James Smith, "'Cleansing' in Sudan may soon become Genocide", *The Times* (London), 18 May 2004.

1201 See, for example, the *Urgence Darfour* European petition, available at <http://www.urgencedarfour.info/index.php?name=Petitions>.

1202 Dr Jean-Hervé Bradol and Fabrice Weissman, "An Appeal for Darfur: Killings and Demagogy", *Liberation* (Paris), 23 March 2007.

1203 *Ibid.*

1204 Robert Ménard and Stephen Smith, "Darfour: faisons la paix, pas le guerre!", *Le Monde* (Paris), 29 March 2007, available at <www.aidh.org/darfur/pdv13.htm>. For a useful study of the debate on Darfur within French intellectual circles, see K.A. Dilday, "The Darfur Conundrum", Open Democracy, 3 April 2007, available at <www.opendemocracy.net>.

1205 "Did they plot to steal African's orphans of war?", *The Observer* (London), 4 November 2007.

1206 *Ibid.*

1207 "Anger in Chad after 'kidnapping'", News Article by BBC News, 31 October 2007.

1208 "Did they plot to steal African's orphans of war?", *op. cit.*

1209 *Ibid.*

1210 Chris Bickerton, "Zoe's ark: the dangers of 'DIY humanitarianism'", *Spiked* online, London, 7 November 2007, available at <http://www.spiked-online.com/index.php?/site/printable/4052/>. See, also, Jean-Phillipe Rémy, "Arche de Zoé: du messing à la faute", *Le Monde* (Paris), 3 November 2007.

1211 *Ibid.*

1212 *Ibid.*

1213 See, for example, the Save Darfur/Globe for Darfur advertisements in *The Guardian* (London) on 30 November 2006.

1214 "Groups Plan Rally on Mall To Protest Darfur Violence. Bush Administration Is Urged to Intervene in Sudan", *The Washington Post*, 27 April 2006.

1215 Nicholas Kristof has cited Steidle on several occasions. See, for example, Nicholas Kristof, "The Secret Genocide Archive", *The New York Times*, 23 February 2005.

1216 Brian Steidle with Gretchen Steidle Wallace, *The Devil Came on Horseback. Bearing Witness to the Genocide in Darfur*, Public Affairs, New York, 2007.

1217 *Ibid.*, p.209.

1218 *Ibid.*, p.93.

1219 Rob Crilly, South of West A Journalist in Africa weblog, 30 September 2007, available at <http://robcrilly.wordpress.com/2007/09/30/shades-of-grey/>.

1220 *Ibid.*, p.46.

1221 "Sudan: Many Reported Killed During New Hostilities in Darfur", News Article by Integrated Regional Information Networks, UN Office for the Coordination of Humanitarian Affairs, Nairobi, 27 January 2005.

1222 It is a matter of record that systematic rebel attacks on civilians in the vicinity of Malam continued into 2005. Both the UN and AMIS reported, for example, in September 2005 that the SLA had once again attacked nomadic herders near the Malam in South Darfur, abducting seven people and stealing over three thousand camels. The UN noted that the SLA refused to assist AMIS with its enquiries. Regrettably, having waited in vain for AMIS intervention, the nomad communities in question chose to take the law into their own hands and attempted to recover the abducted members of their tribe as well as the stolen livestock. Forty people died in the clash. A source within the nomadic community stated: "Following a week-long truce, the AU was unable to convince the SLA to return the camels. A few evenings after the truce ended, a large group of nomads attacked an SLA stronghold in the Jebel Marra mountain area." *The Guardian* newspaper had also noted that the Malam incident had "sparked a chain of clashes" and confirmed that tribal leaders had appealed to the AU for assistance. When that was not forthcoming the nomads tried to forcibly recover their livestock. The International Crisis Group also noted deliberate provocation regarding Malam on the part of the rebels, stating that "An outbreak of fighting in early and mid-September...The looting at the beginning of that month of several thousand cattle from Arab nomads near Malam was committed by SLA soldiers...The camels were taken to Jebel Marra, leading to retaliatory attacks by Arab tribes." This would doubtless once again qualify as genocidal behaviour according to Steidle.

1223 Brian Steidle with Gretchen Steidle Wallace, *op. cit.*, p.216.

1224 *"If We Return, We Will Be Killed" Consolidation of Ethnic Cleansing in Darfur, Sudan*, Human Rights Watch, New York, 2004, n.74.

1225 Brian Steidle with Gretchen Steidle Wallace, *op. cit.*, p.116.

1226 *Ibid.*, p.218.

1227 Brian Steidle, "In Darfur, My Camera Was Not Nearly Enough", *The Washington Post*, 20 March 2005.

1228 Brian Steidle with Gretchen Steidle Wallace, *op. cit.*, p.164.

1229 *Ibid.*, pp. 130-31.

1230 *Ibid.*, p.133.

1231 *Ibid.*, p.210.

1232 *Ibid.*, pp. 148-49.

1233 *Ibid.*, pp. 195-202

1234 *Ibid.*, p.186.

1235 *Ibid.*, p.82.

1236 It is interesting to note that when veteran American investigative journalist Seymour Hersh was asked about the similarly crude forgeries that were at the centre of the Bush administration's false allegations of Iraqi purchases of uranium from Niger, he said that CIA stations around the world had "falsified documents all the time. That's what they did for a living. That's part of the tradecraft." (See, "Behind the 'Mushroom Cloud'", *The New Yorker*, 21 October 2003.)

1237 Brian Steidle with Gretchen Steidle Wallace, *op. cit.*, pp.186-90.

1238 *Ibid.*, pp. 103-4.

1239 *Ibid.*, p.114.

1240 *Ibid.*, pp. 176-77.

1241 *Ibid.*, p.178.

1242 Reviewed By Laura Kyle, and available at eFilmcritic.com <http://efilmcritic.com/review.php?movie=15875&reviewer=369>.

1243 Keith Harmon Snow, "Oil in Darfur? Special Ops in Somali? New Old 'Humanitarian' Warfare in Africa", Centre for Research on Globalization, Canada, 9 February 2007, available at <www.globalresearch.ca>. Keith Harmon Snow is an independent researcher and investigative journalist. He has worked on Horn of Africa issues as a consultant on genocide and humanitarian aid for the United Nations (2005), and he worked in Ethiopia, Sudan and the Congo as a human rights researcher and genocide investigator for Genocide Watch (2004, 2005) and Survivors Rights

International (2004, 2005). He has also worked extensively (2004-2006) with the multinational peacekeeping forces of the United Nations Observers Mission for Congo (MONUC). Snow is a four-time 'Project Censored' award-winner, In 2001 he reported from the International Criminal Tribunal on Rwanda, and he has worked or reported from 17 countries in Africa.

1244 Brian Steidle with Gretchen Steidle Wallace, *op. cit.*, p.226.

1245 See Steidle's own homepage at <http://www.briansteidle.com/>.

1246 See, for example, "Steidle...wholeheartedly endorses the divestment campaign." Katharine Mieszkowski, "No Oil for Blood", 29 April 2006, Salon.com news available at <http://www.salon.com/news/feature/2006/04/29/darfur/>.

1247 Don Cheadle and John Prendergast, *Not on Our Watch. The Mission to End Genocide in Darfur and Beyond*, Hyperion, New York, 2007.

1248 *Ibid.*, p.39.

1249 *Ibid.*, pp. 2-3.

1250 *Ibid.*, p. 2.

1251 For an examination of Prendergast's shortcomings as a Sudan analyst, see, for example, *"No Lesson Learned": A Review of John Prendergast's 'God, Oil and Country: Changing the Logic of War in Sudan*, The European-Sudanese Public Affairs Council, London, 20 February 2002 available at <http://www.espac.org/oil_pages/no_lesson_learned.html>. Prendergast and Cheadle have also shared their views on U.S.-Sudanese counter-terrorism, see, for example, *John Prendergast on Sudan and Counter-Terrorism: Self-Serving Dishonesty and Rank Hypocrisy*, The European-Sudanese Public Affairs Council, London, 17 March 2006, available at <http://www.sudan.net/news/press/postedr/343.shtml>.

1252 Letter from Cynthia McKinney to U.S. President William Jefferson Clinton, 31 August 1999, available at <http:www.africa2000.com/UGANDA/mckinney.html>.

1253 "Sierra Leone, the last Clinton betrayal: Where Angels Fear to Tread", *The New Republic*, 24 July 2000.

1254 In assessing Prendergast's abysmal record, one cannot help recalling the comments made by Lawrence Kaplan: "Were foreign policy intellectuals held to the same standards of accountability as doctors and lawyers, a substantial slice of the commentariat would have been sued for malpractice or disbarred". Cited in Dimitri K. Simes, "Unrealists", *The National Interest*, Washington-DC, Summer 2006.

1255 See David Hoile, *Farce Majeure: The Clinton Administration's Sudan Policy 1993-2000*, The European-Sudanese Public Affairs Council, London, 2000, available at <http://www.espac.org/usa_sudan_pages/farce_majeure.html>. See also articles such as Michael Kelly, "U.S. Handiwork in Sierra Leone", *The Washington Post*, 19 July 2000; and, regarding the bin Laden offer, "Sudan Offered Up bin Laden in '96", *The Washington Post*, 3 October 2001.

1256 "Duelling Over Darfur. A human rights activist and an Africa scholar disagree –

vehemently – on the best way to help Sudan", Newsweek Online Forum, 8 November 2007, available at <http://www.newsweek.com/id/69004>.

1257 *Ibid.*

1258 Cheadle and Prendergast, *op. cit.*, p.204

1259 "'Hotel Rwanda' is "Inaccurate" Says President", News Article by WENN, 5 June 2006.

1260 See, for example, "Clooney urges U.N. action on Darfur", News Article by Association Press, 15 September 2006.

1261 "Clooney calls on Bush to act over Darfur crisis", *The Times* (London), 28 April 2006.

1262 De Waal was commenting on "Vanity Fair or Fair Vanity? Bono's Africa Issue" in his weblog, "Making Sense of Darfur", available at <http://www.ssrc.org/blog/2007/06/13/vanity-fair-or-fair-vanity-bonos-africa-issue/>.

1263 "'Actorvists' Make People Care", *The Politico*, 12 June 2007, available at <www.dyn.politico.com>.

1264 "Clooney calls on Bush to act over Darfur crisis", *The Times* (London), 28 April 2006.

1265 Laurie Nathan, "The Making and Unmaking of the Darfur Peace Agreement", in Alex de Waal (editor), *War in Darfur and the Search for Peace*, Global Equity Initiative, Harvard, and Justice Africa, 2007.

1266 De Waal was commenting on "Vanity Fair or Fair Vanity? Bono's Africa Issue" in his weblog, "Making Sense of Darfur", available at <http://www.ssrc.org/blog/2007/06/13/vanity-fair-or-fair-vanity-bonos-africa-issue/>. Clooney's position has come in for considerable criticism. See, for example, Jonathan Steele, "Sorry George Clooney, but the last thing Darfur needs is western troops", *The Guardian* (London), 19 September 2006; and Brendan O'Neill, "The Hollywood Actor's Burden", *Spiked* online, 4 May 2006, available at <http://www.spiked-online.com/Articles/0000000CB04A.htm>.

1267 Nina Shea, "Clooney Does Darfur", *National Review*, 2 May 2006.

1268 "Interview: Tony Allen-Mills talks to George Clooney", *The Sunday Times* (London), 11 December 2005.

1269 Brendan O'Neill, "The Hollywood Actor's Burden", *op. cit.*

1270 "Interview: Tony Allen-Mills talks to George Clooney", *The Sunday Times* (London), 11 December 2005.

1271 De Waal, "Vanity Fair or Fair Vanity? Bono's Africa Issue", *op. cit.*

1272 See previous notes.

1273 See, for example, Eric Reeves, "African Auschwitz: The Concentration Camps of Darfur; The UN and the International Community Are Acquiescing in Genocide", 12 May 2004, <http://sudanreeves.org>; "Stopping Genocide in Darfur: What Must Be Done", 17 May 2004, <http://sudanreeves.org>; "The Data of Destruction: Accelerating Genocide in Darfur", 27 May 2004, <http://sudanreeves.org>.

1274 See, for example, Eric Reeves, "Rwanda Redux? As the Catastrophe in Darfur

Continues to Accelerate, There Are Still No Signs of International Humanitarian Intervention", 22 March 2004, <http://sudanreeves.org>.

1275 See, Eric Reeves, "Darfur Mortality Update", 18 January 2005, <http://sudanreeves.org>.

1276 See, "Darfur Crisis has Activist 'Angry' all the Time", *USA Today*, 19 March 2007.

1277 Eric Reeves, "Quantifying Genocide in Darfur: A Summary and Update", 28 June 2004, <http://sudanreeves.org>.

1278 Eric Reeves, "The Accelerating Catastrophe in Darfur (Sudan): Khartoum Fixes Upon a Policy of War and Civilian Destruction", 24 November 2003, <http://sudanreeves.org>.

1279 See, as just a few examples, Eric Reeves, "Unnoticed Genocide", *The Washington Post*, 25 February 25 2004 ; Eric Reeves, "Sudan's Reign of Terror", *Amnesty Now*, Summer 2004; Eric Reeves, "Darfur Mortality Update", 27 August 2004, (four references); Eric Reeves, "Darfur Mortality Update", 15 July 2004, <http://sudanreeves.org> (five references); Eric Reeves, "The Data of Destruction: Accelerating Genocide in Darfur", 27 May 2004", http://sudanreeves.org>; Eric Reeves, "As the Darfur Catastrophe Deepens, Genocidal Destruction Intensifies: Diplomatic Confusion Increases, With No Humanitarian Intervention in Sight", 20 February 2004, <http://sudanreeves.org>.

1280 See, for example, Reeves' profile at <http://www.giraffe.org/giraffe_heroes/Eric_reeves.html>.

1281 Eric Reeves, "The Overdue Journey", *NewsSmith*, Smith College, Spring 2003.

1282 Eric Reeves, "Genocide in Darfur: A Growing International Strategy of Equivocation; In Place of Humanitarian Intervention, Studied Avoidance of Moral Responsibility", 6 December 2004, <http://sudanreeves.org>.

1283 See, for example, Eric Reeves, "Human Rights Watch Appeal on Factional Fighting in Southern Sudan", 4 February 2001, <http://sudanreeves.org>.

1284 E-mail publication by Jemera Rone via <Darfur_task_force @yahoogroups.com>, 1 July 2004.

1285 See, for example, Eric Reeves, "Humanitarian Aid in Darfur Threatened with Utter Collapse", 17 December 2004, <http://sudanreeves.org>. The murders were condemned by the international community: "UN envoy for Sudan condemns 'brutal' murder of humanitarian workers in Darfur", Press Release by UN News Center, New York, 13 December 2004.

1286 "UN Envoy Blames Darfur Rebels for Deaths of Aid Officials", New Article by Agence France-Presse, 27 October 2004.

1287 "Darfur Rebels Threaten Humanitarian Aid Workers", News Article by UPI, 23 October 2004.

1288 *Report of the United Nations Secretary-General on the Sudan Pursuant to Paragraphs 6, 13 and 16 of Security Council Resolution 1556 (2004), Paragraph 15 of Resolution 1564 (2004) and Paragraph 1574 (2004)*, S/2005/10, United Nations, New York, January 2005.

1289 "China Puts '700,000 Troops' on Sudan Alert", *The Sunday Telegraph* (London), 26 August 2000.

1290 Eric Reeves, "China 'Flexing Its Muscle' in Sudan: Its time for SEMA!", 30 August 2000, <http://sudanreeves.org>.

1291 House of Lords *Hansard*, Written Parliamentary Answer, 5 March 2001, column WA 10.

1292 "U.S.: Reports of China's Role in Sudanese War Are Overstated", News Article by UPI on 29 August 2000.

1293 Eric Reeves, "An Up-Dated Report on the Government of Sudan Attack on the Elementary School in Upper Kaoda", 25 February 2000, <http://sudanreeves.org>.

1294 "African Christian Faith in Action", <http://www.liaafrica.org>. Hammond's exaggerations are obvious: he also claimed that "Christians make up...over 80% of Southern Sudan." (This figure should be compared with the figures of 10-15 percent carried in official American government studies, Economist Intelligence Unit briefings or Human Rights Watch material).

1295 See, for example, "Sudan's Reign of Terror", *Amnesty Now*, New York, Summer 2004.

1296 Kersap D. Shekhdar, "Everything You Always Wanted to Know about Media Coverage of Darfur (But Were Afraid to Ask), *Online Journal*, 12 September 2004 <http://onlinejournal.com>.

1297 For an overview of propaganda within the Sudanese conflict see, David Hoile, *Images of Sudan: Case Studies in Misinformation and Propaganda*, European-Sudanese Public Affairs Council, London, 2003, available at <http://www.espac.org/pdf/images_of_sudan.pdf>.

1298 "The Escalating Crisis in Darfur", News Article by Integrated Regional Information Networks, UN Office for the Coordination of Humanitarian Affairs, Nairobi, 31 December 2003.

1299 See, for example, "Syria Tested Chemical Arms on Civilians in Darfur Region: Press", Agence France-Presse, 14 September 2004.

1300 "US Doubts Report on Syrian Chemical Weapons Testing in Darfur", News Article by Agence France-Presse, 15 September 2004.

1301 "Darfur Rebels Deny Police Killings that Led to State of Emergency", News Article by Agence France-Presse, 24 November 2004.

1302 See, for example, "U.S. and U.N. Blame Rebels in Upsurge of Violence in Sudan's Darfur Region", News Article by Associated Press, 23 November 2004; "UN Condemns Sudan Rebel Attacks in Darfur, Calls for Halt to all Fighting", News Article by Associated Press, 24 November 2004; "Africa Union Urges Sudan Rebels to End Truce Violations in Darfur", News Article by Agence France-Presse, 26 November 2004.

1303 "W. Sudan Rebels Say Killed 1,000 Govt Troops, Militia", News Article by Reuters, 19 January 2004.

1304 See, for example, "Sudan Chemical Weapons Allegations from Norway,

Germany", News Article by Afrol News, 15 September 2004, available at <http://www.afrol.com/articles/13956>.

1305 "Credibility where it's due", Comment is Free, *The Guardian* (London), 25 June 2007, available at <http://commentisfree.guardian.co.uk/julie_flint/2007/06/credibility_where_its_due.html>.

1306 See, Dimitri Oram, "Whitewashing Western Intervention. Samantha Power's *A Problem from Hell*", Swans Commentary, Swans.com, 26 February 2007.

1307 David Morse interviews Samantha Power, Talk Nation Radio, 1 December 2006, available at <www.talknationradio.com/?p=59>.

1308 "Rwanda's Genocide: Looking Back", Statement of Samantha Power, House Committee on International Relations Subcommittee on Africa, Washington-DC, 22 April 2004.

1309 See, "Peacekeepers alone can't help Darfur – UNHCR chief ", *Sudan Tribune*, 25 April 2007.

1310 Paul de Rooij, "The Useful Fools of Empire. Humanitarian Wars and Associated Delusions", *op. cit.*

1311 Brendan O'Neill, "Darfur: pornography for the chattering classes. Why have the British media been silent about the Advertising Standards Authority's damning judgement against the Save Darfur Coalition?", *op. cit.*

Chapter Eleven

1312 Ambassador Joseph Wilson, *The Politics of Truth*, Carroll and Graf, New York, 2004.

1313 Cited in "Iraq Casts Shadow on Darfur Options", *The Financial Times* (London), 13 December 2006.

1314 Alex de Waal, "The book was closed too soon on peace in Darfur", *The Guardian* (London), 29 September 2006.

1315 See, for example, "US Begins Quest for Approval for UN Force for Sudan's Darfur", News Article by Reuters, 2 February 2006; "US Hopes UN Force for Darfur This Month", News Article by Agence France-Presse, 1 February 2006.

1316 "Bush Signals Expanded NATO Role in Sudan – NYT", *The New York Times*, 19 February 2006. See, also, "Bush: Double Peacekeeping Troops Needed in Darfur", News Article by Reuters, 17 February 2006.

1317 "NATO Mulls More Help for African Peacekeepers in Sudan's Darfur", News Article by Associated Press, 21 February 2006.

1318 "Bush Presses Chirac on NATO Involvement in Darfur", News Article by Reuters, 23 February 2006.

1319 "US Alone in Pushing for UN Peacekeeping Mission in Darfur", News Article by Associated Press, 25 February 2006.

1320 "NATO Role in Darfur on Table", *The Washington Post*, 10 April 2006.

1321 "Annan Wants US Troops for UN Darfur Force", News Article by Reuters, 9 February 2006.

1322 See, for example, "U.S. and NATO Balk on Troops for Lebanon Force", *The New York Times*, 25 July 2006; "Bolton Questions UN Troops in Timor", *The Daily Telegraph* (London), 20 June 2006.

1323 "Annan Recommends against Deployment of U.N. Peacekeeping Forces in Chad and Central African Republic", News Article by Associated Press, 3 January 2007.

1324 Glen Ford, "A Tale of Two Genocides, Congo and Darfur: The Blatantly Inconsistent US Position", 19 July 2007, available at dissidentvoice.org <http://www.dissidentvoice.org/2007/07/a-tale-of-two-genocides-congo-and-darfur-the-blatantly-inconsistent-us-position/>. See, also, Kim Petersen, "Bleaching the Atrocities of Genocide. Linguistic Honesty is Better with a Clear Conscience", 7 June 2007, available at <http://www.dissidentvoice.org/2007/06/bleaching-the-atrocities-of-genocide/>.

1325 "The Lancet Publishes IRC Mortality Study from DR Congo: 3.9 Million Have Died: 38,000 Die per Month", International Rescue Committee, 6 January 2006.

1326 See, for example, Kim Petersen, "Bleaching the Atrocities of Genocide. Linguistic Honesty is Better with a Clear Conscience", *op. cit.*

1327 "UN says thousands dying every day in DR Congo, urges world to act", News Article by Agence France-Presse, 3 September 2005.

1328 "Congo war tops AlertNet poll of 'forgotten' crises", News Article by AlertNet, 10 March 2005.

1329 "War in northern Uganda world's worst forgotten crisis: UN", News Article by Agence France-Presse, 11 November 2003.

1330 "UN says thousands dying every day in DR Congo, urges world to act", News Article by Agence France-Presse, 3 September 2005.

1331 "Factsheet: AlertNet top 10 'forgotten' emergencies", News Article by AlertNet, 9 March 2005.

1332 Gilbert Burnham, Riyadh Lafta, Shannon Doocy, and Les Roberts, "Mortality after the 2003 invasion of Iraq: a cross-sectional cluster sample survey", *The Lancet*, Number 368, 21 October 2006, pp. 1421-1428.

1333 See, for example, Gideon Polya, "US Iraqi Holocaust and One Million Deaths", *Countercurrents*, 7 February 2007.

1334 "As Somali Crisis Swells, Experts See a Void in Aid", *The New York Times*, 20 November 2007.

1335 Wikipedia has this to say about the Project for the New American Century's role in promoting the invasion of Iraq: "Commentators from divergent parts of the political spectrum—such as Democracy Now! and American Free Press, including Nobel Peace Prize Laureate Jody Williams and former Republican Congressmen Pete McCloskey and Paul Findley—have voiced their concerns about the influence of the PNAC on the decision by President George W. Bush to invade Iraq. Some have regarded the

PNAC's January 16, 1998 letter to President Clinton, which urged him to embrace a plan for 'the removal of Saddam Hussein's regime from power,' and the large number of members of PNAC appointed to the Bush administration as evidence that the 2003 invasion of Iraq was a foregone conclusion. The television program Frontline, broadcast on PBS, presents the PNAC's letter to President Clinton as a notable event in the leadup to the Iraq war. Media commentators have found it significant that signatories to the PNAC's January 16, 1998 letter to President Clinton (and some of its other position papers, letters, and reports) include such Bush administration officials as Donald Rumsfeld, Paul Wolfowitz, Richard Perle, John Bolton, Richard Armitage, and Elliott Abrams."

1336 William Kristol and Vance Serchuk, "End the Genocide Now", *The Washington Post*, 22 September 2004.

1337 See, "Darfur's Fleeting Moment", *The New York Times*, 21 May 2006.

1338 "Gen. Wesley Clark Weighs Presidential Bid: 'I Think About it Everyday'", Interview on DemocracyNow.org, 2 March 2007, available at <http://www.democracynow.org/article.pl?sid=07/03/02/1440234>.

1339 Cited in John Walsh, "Neocon Advocates Civil War in Iraq as 'Strategic' Policy. Daniel Pipes Finds Comfort in Muslims Killing Muslims", *Counterpunch*, n.d.

1340 "Security Holds the Key to the Tehran Tangle", *The Financial Times* (London), 2 February 2006.

1341 See, for example, "Sudan Reiterates Opposition to UN Peacekeepers for Darfur", News Article by Associated Press, 7 February 2006.

1342 "Gadhafi: U.N. Darfur Force is Ruse to Grab Sudan's Oil", News Article by Reuters, 21 November 2006.

1343 "Now the Pentagon tells Bush: climate change will destroy us", *The Observer* (London), 22 February 2004.

1344 Gum Arabic is an essential material to many industries including beverages, pharmaceuticals, confections and baked goods, encapsulated flavours, cosmetics, printing, textiles and has many other applications. In short, Coke and Pepsi could not be made without it, nor would any number of medications. Gum Arabic is excluded from the otherwise comprehensive US economic sanctions on Sudan.

1345 "What's Behind the Darfur campaign", *Workers World*, 17 July 2006 available at <www.workers.org>.

1346 "British lawmaker: Iraq war was for oil", News Article by Al-Jazeera, 22 May 2005.

1347 Christopher Caldwell, "It is best to stay out of Darfur", *The Financial Times* (London), 16 December 2006.

1348 "In Iraqi War Scenario, Oil Is Key Issue. U.S. Drillers Eye Huge Petroleum Pool", *The Washington Post*, 15 September 2002.

1349 Yoshie Furuhashi, "Who Wants Peace in Darfur?", *Monthly Review*, 30 April 2006, available at <http://mrzine.monthlyreview.org/furuhashi300406.html>. China has a $4 billion investment in Sudan – which is widely believed to have the largest untapped oil reserves in Africa. The China National Petroleum Corporation has a 40% stake in Greater Nile Petroleum, which owns oil fields, a pipeline, a large refinery and a port. Last year, China purchased more than half of Sudan's oil exports. Conversely, Sudan accounted for 6% of China's oil imports, about 200,000-plus barrels a day. (Jon D. Markman, "How China Is Winning the Oil Race", MSN Money, 25 April 2006.)

1350 "Oil Discovery Adds New Twist to Darfur Tragedy", New Article by Alert Net, 15 June 2005. Alert Net is a syndicated on-line journal which positions itself as a leader in "alerting humanitarians to emergencies." Published in London by the highly respected Reuters Foundation, the award-winning AlertNet was launched in 1997 "to provide support services for aid agencies" and it reports current membership of over 300 leading agencies in some 80 countries.

1351 Dr Jean-Hervé Bradol, *Messages*, Number 132, Médecins Sans Frontières, Paris, October-November 2004.

1352 "UN Envoy Criticises Security Council and Khartoum", News Item by Radio Netherlands, 6 April 2006.

1353 Alex de Waal, 'I will not sign', *London Review of Books*, Volume 28, Number 23, London, 30 November 2006.

1354 Alex de Waal, "The book was closed too soon on peace in Darfur", *The Guardian* (London), 29 September 2006.

1355 Christopher Caldwell, "It is best to stay out of Darfur", *The Financial Times* (London), 16 December 2006. Caldwell is a senior editor at the American neo-conservative magazine, *The Weekly Standard*. He is a regular contributor to *The Financial Times* and *Slate*. His essays and reviews appear in *The New York Times*, *The Wall Street Journal*, and *The Washington Post*.

1356 "Peacekeepers alone can't help Darfur – UNHCR chief ", News Article by Reuters, 24 April 2007.

1357 Julie Flint, "Sending the UN into Darfur is No Solution at All", *Daily Star* (Lebanon), 4 March 2006.

1358 See, for example, "Sudan Reiterates Opposition to UN Peacekeepers for Darfur", News Article by Associated Press, 7 February 2006.

1359 See, for example, "Sudan Renews Opposition to UN Forces for Darfur", News Article by Agence France-Presse, 23 February 2006.

1360 "Non-African Troops in Darfur Risk 'Iraq': Sudan", News Article by Reuters, 20 March 2006.

1361 See, for example, "Ex-Sudan Opposition MPs Reject UN Darfur Force, Blame Government", *Sudan Tribune*, 23 February 2006; and "Sudan's Parliament Rejects Deployment of UN Forces in Darfur", News Article by Xinhua, 23 February 2006.

1362 "Big Country, Big Problem", News Item by BBC, 10 June 2004.

1363 Dr Jean-Hervé Bradol and Fabrice Weissman, "An Appeal for Darfur: Killings and Demagogy", *Liberation* (Paris), 23 March 2007.

1364 *Ibid*.

1365 See, for example, "UK Supports Darfur No-Fly Zone", News Article by BBC News, 14 December 2006.

1366 "Darfur no-fly zone unworkable – top EU soldier", News Article by Reuters, 22 May 2007.

1367 Alex de Waal, "Making Sense of Darfur, Peacekeeping: Is it Worth Trying a No-Fly Zone?", 11 July 2007, Social Science Research Council Darfur weblog, available at <http://www.ssrc.org/blog/2007/07/11/is-it-worth-trying-a-no-fly-zone/>.

1368 "Darfur's Outdated Script", *The International Herald Tribune*, 9 July 2007.

1369 Francis Fukuyama, "After Neoconservatism", *The New York Times*, 19 February 2006.

1370 "UN vote backs Lebanon ceasefire", News Article by BBC, 12 August 2006.

1371 "Heavy Burden. UN and the Middle East", *The World Today*, Volume 63, Number 7, July 2007, Royal Institute of International Affairs, London,

1372 "UN no longer seen as neutral, says former chief ", *The Independent* (London), 25 June 2007.

1373 "Je Kunt er Niet op Los Slaan, Je Hebt die Schurken Nodig", *NRC Handelsblad* (Amsterdam), 9 March 2006.

1374 "Peacekeeping boom strains United Nations", News Article by Reuters, 25 August 2006.

1375 "The Strains Tell on UN Peacekeeping. Too Few Forces, Too Little Oversight", *The Economist*, 4 March 2006. See also, "The Limits of Peacekeeping. The U.N. Finds itself Stretched Thin by Conflicts in Africa and Elsewhere", *The Los Angeles Times*, 1 March 2006.

1376 "Peacekeeping Blues", *The Financial Times* (London), 9-10 December 2006.

1377 "UN's Sudan Peacekeeping Could Cost $1.7 Bln a Year", News Article by Reuters, 2 September 2006.

1378 Bruce Jones, "The Limits of Peacekeeping. The U.N. finds itself stretched thin by conflicts in Africa and elsewhere", *The Los Angeles Times*, 1 March 2006.

1379 See, for example, "UN Shame over Sex Scandal", *The Independent on Sunday* (London), 7 January 2007, and "At least 300 UN Peacekeeping Staff Faced Sexual Exploitation Allegations", News Article by Newsblaze.com.

1380 "UN Troops in south Sudan Raping Children – Report", News Article by Reuters, 2 January 2007.

1381 See, for example, "UN Probes Report of Force's Role in Congo Massacre", News Article by Reuters, 21 June 2006, and "Haiti Deaths Blamed on UN Troops", *The Observer* (London), 1 April 2007.

1382 Damien Lewis, *Operation Certain Death*, Arrow Books, London, 2005, p.18.

1383 *Ibid.*, pp.331-32.

1384 *Ibid.*, pp.618-20.

1385 *Ibid.*, p.619.

1386 *Ibid.*, pp.610-11.

1387 "Sudan President Stands Firmly Against UN Force", News Article by Associated Press, 29 March 2007.

1388 "Sudan Army's Anger Over UN 'War'", News Article by BBC, 2 August 2004.

1389 See, for example, "Thousands of Sudanese Protest against UN Force", News Article by Reuters, 8 March 2006; "Sudanese Protest UN Takeover in Darfur", News Article by Agence France-Presse, 8 March 2006.

1390 Simon Jenkins, "We Cannot Save Darfur at the Point of a Gun", *The Times* (London), 28 July 2004.

1391 "'Jihad' Threatened if UN Force Comes to Darfur. Security Council envoys face opposition in war-torn Sudan region", News Article by CNN, 9 July 2006.

1392 Article in *Al-Rai Al-Amm* (Khartoum), posted on Rumbek Online Hall at <http://members3.boardhost.com/Administrator/msg/1264.html>.

1393 "NATO-led Force in Darfur Would be 'Recipe for Disaster'", News Article by Agence France-Presse, 28 February 2006.

1394 *Ibid.*

1395 Jan Pronk's weblog, Weblog Number 16, 13 March 2006.

1396 *Ibid.*

1397 "Pronk – Growing Climate of Distrust of UN Looms in Sudan", News Article by United Press International, 28 February 2006.

1398 "A Deadly Confusion", *Messages*, Number 132, Médecins Sans Frontières, Paris, October-November 2004.

1399 Dr Jean-Hervé Bradol and Fabrice Weissman, *op. cit.*

1400 "UN Force in South Sudan Still Running Late", *Sudan Tribune*, 15 March 2006.

1401 See, for example, "International Engagement Needed to Save Peace Pact – ICG", News Article by Integrated Regional Information Networks, UN Office for the Coordination of Humanitarian Affairs, Nairobi, 6 April 2006.

1402 Patrick Buchanan, "Time for an 'Agonizing Reappraisal'", *The American Conservative*, 3 July 2006.

1403 "Bush Team 'Causing Chaos in Arab World'", *The Daily Telegraph* (London), 6 April 2005.

1404 "Bush Denies Iraq is in Civil War", News Article by BBC News, 21 March 2006.

1405 John Harper, "Anatomy of a Habit: America's Unnecessary Wars", *Survival*, International Institute for Strategic Studies, Volume 47, Number 2, Summer 2005, p.76.

1406 "We Did Go to War on Faulty Intelligence, Bush Admits", *The Times* (London), 15 December 2005.

1407 "Security Holds the Key to the Tehran Tangle", *The Financial Times* (London), 2 February 2006.

1408 "Rice Admits U.S. Underestimated Hamas Strength", *The New York Times*, 30 January 2006.

1409 Fareed Zakaria, "Caught by Surprise. Again", *Newsweek*, 6 February 2006.

1410 "Iraq in Civil War, Says Former PM", News article by BBC News, 19 March 2006.

1411 "Bush Denies Iraq is in Civil War", News Article by BBC News, 21 March 2006.

1412 "US Envoy to Iraq: 'We Have Opened the Pandora's Box", *The Guardian* (London), 8 March 2006.

1413 "Chaos and the Coalition", *The Daily Telegraph* (London), 3 April 2006.

1414 "Murder is Certain. Three Years After America Invaded, Iraq is as Violent as Ever", *The Economist*, 25 March 2006.

1415 See, for example, "US Made Thousands of Mistakes Over Iraq, Admits Rice", *The Times* (London), 1 April 2006; "'Tactical Errors' Made in Iraq, Rice Concedes", *The Washington Post*, 1 April 2006.

1416 Sidney Blumenthal, "The Tethered Goat Strategy", *The Guardian* (London), 6 April 2006.

1417 "The March of Folly, That Has Led to a Bloodbath", *The Independent* (London), 20 March 2006.

1418 "Iraq Reconstruction Projects 'Fall Apart'", *CityAM* (London), 1 May 2007.

1419 "Afghanistan More Dangerous than Iraq", News Article by Pakistan Times Online, 25 February 2006.

1420 "A Risky Feud", *Newsweek*, 20 March 2006.

1421 "The Taliban will be Back in Power if the West Doesn't Narrow its Ambitions", *The Guardian* (London), 11 September 2006.

1422 "Afghanistan Close to Anarchy, Warns General", *The Guardian* (London), 22 July 2006.

1423 "Old Alliance, New World. NATO's Increasing Role in Afghanistan is Testing the Will of its Member Nations – and redefining its Role", *Time*, 6 February 2006.

1424 Charles D. Ferguson, "Been There, Botched That", *The Boston Globe*, 14 February 2006.

1425 Andrew Sullivan, "General Bush's Lose-Lose Iranian War Options", *The Sunday Times* (London), 16 April 2006.

1426 "Plot Thickens Around Darfur", *Al-Ahram* (Cairo), Issue Number 684, 1-7 April 2004.

1427 Eric S. Margolis, "No Time for a Crusade in Sudan", 12 August 2004, available at <http://www.bigeye.com>.

1428 Paul Moorcraft, "How to Avoid Another Iraq in Sudan", *Business Day* (South Africa), 9 March 2006.

1429 See, "The New Killing Fields", BBC Panorama programme, 11 November 2004, available at <http://news.bbc.co.uk/1/hi/programmes/panorama/4647011.stm>.

1430 "NATO Mulls More Help for African Peacekeepers in Sudan's Darfur", News Article by Associated Press, 21 February 2006.

1431 "Bin Laden Call for Darfur Jihad Clouds UN Mission", News Article by Reuters, 24 April 2006.

1432 "UN Peacekeepers Could be at Risk if Deployed to Darfur – Minister", News Article by Associated Press, 27 February 2006.

1433 Gen. Tony Zinni and Tony Koltz, *The Battle for Peace: A Frontline Vision of America's Power and Purpose*, Palgrave Macmillan, New York, 10 April 2006.

1434 See, also, for example, "Northeast Africa: Al-Qaeda's New Battleground, *Jane's Islamic Affairs Analyst*, 23 March 2004; "U.S. Guerrillas in Sahara Desert Hunting Militants Tied to Al-Qaeda", *The Boston Globe*, 12 March 2004; "U.S. Military Fears Al-Qaeda May be Eyeing Africa", News Article by Associated Press, 6 March 2004; "Niger: Army Claims Deaths of Algerian Militants", *The New York Times*, 1 May 2004; "U.S. Training African Forces to Uproot Terrorists", *The New York Times*, 11 May 2004; "US Says Militants Lurk in Horn of Africa", News Article by Reuters, 28 December 2004.

1435 See, for example, "Chad 'Defeats' Algerian Muslim Extremists", News Article by Associated Press, 26 March 2004, and "US Applauds Chad Offensive on Islamic Militants", News Article by Reuters, 13 March 2004.

1436 Richard Miniter, *Shadow War: The Untold Story of How Bush is Winning the War on Terror*, Regnery Publishing, Washington-DC, 2004, pp. 98-99.

1437 "Pentagon Says Al-Qaida Growing after 'Merger' in North Africa", News Article by AHN, 14 July 2007. See, also, "Policing the undergoverned spaces: The Americans are intensifying their hunt for al-Qaeda in the Sahara and beyond", *The Economist*, 14 June 2007, and "Al Qaeda Strikes Back", *Foreign Affairs*, May-June 2007.

1438 There is no doubt that there are a number of stark social, political and geographical similarities with Afghanistan. Compare Darfur, for example, with this background to Afghanistan: "The geographical features of Afghanistan have had a great impact on the cultural development of its people. An insufficient transportation system has impeded internal communications and, because of this, economic, social, and political integration has been slow…The mountainous features of Afghanistan make it necessary for many villages to be self-sufficient. They build their houses, grow their crops, and protect their community. Trade is primarily on the regional level, rather than national; for centuries the regional market economy was the primary source of commerce. Therefore, Afghanistan has never been able to integrate regional economies on a national scale…On the ethnic level the members of an ethnic group, in particular within a tribe, share 'a common ancestor, a common leader and a common territory in a positive way and harbour negative attitudes towards members of other tribes.'…Because of highly ethnic and communal diversities and because of inefficient transportation and communications systems, the linkage between governmental centers (mostly located in the towns) and rural areas was very weak. Through the course of time, this geographical and ethnic situation created a social environment that was closed to outsiders…Often the role of the central government in the daily affairs of the rural communities was marginal. Many villages not only produced their food without outside help but also managed their administrative affairs such as marriage, divorce, conflict over land, and business… Usually, the government representatives, without the help from local leaders, were seen as outsiders." (Neamatollah Nojumi, *The Rise of the*

Taliban in Afghanistan: Mass Mobilization, Civil War, and the Future of the Region, Palgrave, New York, 2002, pp 5-6.) See, also, Diego Cordovez and Selig S. Harrison, *Out of Afghanistan*, Oxford University Press, London, 1995, and Beattie Hugh, *Afghanistan Studies*, Volumes 3 and 4, Society for Afghanistan Studies – British Academy, 1982.

1439 "UN Force in Sudan 'Will Raise al-Qa'eda Threat'", *The Daily Telegraph* (London), 20 March 2006.

1440 "Bin Laden calls for war against UN peacekeepers", *The Times* (London), 24 April 2006; "Bin Laden calls for jihad in Darfur", News Article by Reuters, 23 April 2006; and "In Tape, Bin Laden Urges Fighters to Sudan", News Article by Associated Press, 23 April 2006.

1441 "Qaeda urges attacks on Darfur force, talks questioned", News Article by Reuters, 20 September 2007.

1442 "Bin Laden Calls for Jihad against Darfur Peacekeepers", News Article by Associated Press, 23 October 2007.

1443 "Al Qaeda is Entrenched in Sudan, U.N. Envoy Warns", *New York Sun*, 1 March 2006. See also "Sudan Rejects UN Forces in Darfur; Envoy Cites Al-Qaeda Threat", News Article by Bloomberg, 28 February 2006.

1444 "Al-Qaeda Said Angry at Sudan for Passing Data to US", *Al-Sharq al-Awsat* (London), 18 June 2006.

1445 "Al-Qaeda Will Retreat to Africa, Says US General", *Mail and Guardian* (Johannesburg), 30 August 2005.

1446 "Situation in Sudan's Dafour Region 'Very Serious', Says UN Envoy", News Article by Africa Online, 16 January 2004.

1447 Ali Ali-Dinar, "Why Khartoum Wants a War in Darfur", *Sudan Tribune*, 30 July 2004, available at <http://www.sudantribune.com>.

1448 Sudarsan Raghavan, "Sudan Violence is Part of Power War", News Article by Knight-Ridder News Service, 20 August 2004.

1449 Richard A. Clarke, *Against All Enemies: Inside America's War on Terror*, Free Press, New York, 2004, p.136.

1450 "US Targets Three More Countries", *The Sunday Times* (London), 25 November 2001.

1451 Gamal Nkrumah, "Plot Thickens Around Darfur", *Al-Ahram* (Cairo), Issue Number 684, 1-7 April 2004.

1452 See, for example, "Tora Bora Army Strikes Back at the Janjaweed", *The Independent* (London), 16 August 2004.

1453 "Sudanese Authorities Fear al-Qaeda Attacks on Western Aid Agencies", *Sunday Tribune* (Dublin).

1454 "Two Darfur Refugees Killed in Chad Amid Tensions With Aid Groups: UN", News Article by Agence France-Presse, 25 July 2004.

1455 See, for example, "Khartoum Accuses Darfur Rebels of Killing Two Police in

Truce Breach", News Article by Agence France-Presse, 26 September 2004; "Sudan Says More Than 30 Police Killed in Darfur", News Article by Reuters, 23 November 2004; "Seven Police Officers Injured in Rebel Attack in Darfur: Sudanese Govt", News Article by Associated Press, 12 December 2004; "Darfur Rebels Attack Convoy, Police – Sudan Official", News Article by Reuters, 16 December 2004.

1456 *Report of the United Nations Secretary-General on the Sudan Pursuant to Paragraph 15 of Resolution 1564 (2004) and Paragraphs 6, 13 and 16 of Security Council Resolution 1556 (2004)*, S/2004/787, United Nations, New York, 4 October 2004.

1457 *Report of the United Nations Secretary-General on the Sudan Pursuant to Paragraph 15 of Resolution 1564 (2004) and Paragraphs 6, 13 and 16 of Security Council Resolution 1556 (2004)*, S/2004/881, United Nations, New York, November 2004.

1458 "War Weary Darfur on the Brink of Deadly Famine", *Sunday Tribune* (Dublin), 5 December 2004.

1459 *Report of the Ceasefire Commission on the Situation in Darfur*, African Union, Addis Ababa, 4 October 2004.

1460 "Independence of Darfur Rebel Commanders Threatens Peace Efforts", News Article by Knight-Ridder News Service, 4 December 2004.

1461 *"If We Return, We Will be Killed"*, Human Rights Watch, New York, November 2004.

1462 See, for example, "Liberia: Islamic Militants Launch Fresh Attacks on Police Stations", News Article by Integrated Regional Information Networks, UN Office for the Coordination of Humanitarian Affairs, Nairobi, 22 September 2004; "Nigerian Islamist Rebels Attack Police, Taken Officers Hostage", News Article by Agence France-Presse, 9 October 2004; "Radical Sect Attacks Police Convoy in Nigeria; 3 Officers Killed", News Article by Associated Press, 10 October 2004.

1463 See, for example, reporting of American financial assistance to the SLA in "Sudan Government's Attacks Stoke Rebels' Fury", *The New York Times*, 11 September 2004.

1464 "Battle for Hearts in Bandit Country", *The Guardian* (London), 3 March 2006.

1465 "Somali Warlords Battling Islamists. Fighting Seen as Proxy War", *The Washington Times*, 10 April 2006.

1466 "Islamist insurgency grows in Somalia", *The Guardian* (London), 19 November 2007.

1467 "11m Face Death as Drought Worsens", *Metro* (London), 6 March 2006.

1468 See, for example, "Nigerian Fundamentalist Group Kills 12 Police Officers in North", *The Washington Post*, 18 April 2007, and "Nigerian Troops Kill 25 Suspected Militants", *International Herald Tribune* (New York), 19 April 2007.

1469 See, for example, "Suicide Bombers Strike N. Africa Again", *The Washington Post*, 15 April 2007.

1470 "Africans Risk Death at Sea for New Life Abroad. Mauritania Becomes a Gateway to Europe", *The Washington Post*, 1 April 2006.

1471 "Spy Agencies Say Iraq War Worsens Terrorism Threat", *The New York Times*, 24 September 2006.

1472 "A New Afghanistan? Exploring the Iraqi Jihadist Training Ground", *Jane's Intelligence Review*, London, July 2006, at <www.jir.janes.com>.

1473 Scheuer used this description in several publications. See, for example, his interview with NBC's Andrea Mitchell "CIA Insider says US fighting war", NBC, available at <http://www.msnbc.msn.com/id/5279743/>.

1474 "Bush: I Made Terror Attacks More Likely", *The Daily Mail* (London), 15 January 2007.

1475 "Iraq Terror Backlash in UK 'for Years'", *The Sunday Times* (London), 2 April 2006.

1476 "Muslim Leaders say Foreign Policy Makes UK Target", *The Guardian* (London), 12 August 2006.

1477 "Iran Suicide Bombers 'Ready to Hit Britain'", *The Sunday Times* (London), 16 April 2006.

1478 Christopher Caldwell, "It is best to stay out of Darfur", *The Financial Times* (London), 16 December 2006.

1479 Simon Jenkins, "The inhumane folly of our interventionist machismo", *The Guardian* (London), 20 September 2006.

1480 "Enough Imperial Crusades. The Alternative to Armed Intervention in Darfur is not Passive Resignation, but Support for an African Union-led Solution", *The Guardian* (London), 18 August 2004.

Chapter Twelve

1481 Julie Flint, "Sending the UN into Darfur is No Solution at All", *Daily Star* (Lebanon), 4 March 2006.

1482 "Darfur Peace Lies in Separate Southern Deal – U.S.", News Article by Reuters, 23 September 2004.

1483 "Sudanese Govt Urges Rebels' Commitment to Darfur Peace Talks", News Article by Xinhua News Agency, 29 December 2004.

1484 Douglas H. Johnson, *The Root Causes of Sudan's Civil Wars*, James Currey, London, 2004, xviii.

1485 Michael Fellman, *Inside War: The Guerilla Conflict in Missouri During the American Civil War*, New York, 1989, pp. 251, 266.

1486 Richard Dowden, "Darfur Can Best be Resolved by Africans", *The Independent* (London), 26 July 2004.

1487 Mahmood Mamdani, "Blue-Hatting Darfur", *The London Review of Books*, 6 September 2007, available at <http://www.lrb.co.uk/v29/n17/mamd01_.html>. General Anyidoho was a member of the initial AMIS joint assessment mission to Darfur in 2005. He had also served as the UN deputy force commander in Rwanda at the time of the genocide.

1488 See "Sudan Government, Darfur Rebels Sign Ceasefire Deal", News Article by Agence France-Presse, 9 April 2004.

1489 See "Sudan, Darfur Rebels Sign Pacts to End Hostilities, Aid Refugees", *USA Today*, 9 November 2004.

1490 "Sudan's Government Expresses Optimism Reaching Solution with Rebels on Darfur", Associated Press, 31 October 2004.

1491 "Sudan Government, Rebels Meet with AU to Set Agenda for Peace Talks", News Article by Agence France-Presse, 24 August 2004.

1492 "Ceasefire Reportedly Breaks Down in Darfur", News Article by Integrated Regional Information Networks, UN Office for the Coordination of Humanitarian Affairs, Nairobi, 20 March 2003.

1493 *The Sudan Government's Vision for Peaceful Solution in Darfur*, Government of Sudan, November 2004.

1494 "Interview: Sudan's Foreign Minister Backs Darfur Autonomy", News Article by Reuters, 27 September 2004.

1495 "Sudan Supports Darfur Federal Rule, Local Laws", News Article by Reuters, 3 October 2004.

1496 See, for example, "Highlights of the Sudanese Peace Process", News Article by Agence France-Presse, 9 January 2005.

1497 "Sudan 'Welcomes' Darfur Autonomy", News Article by BBC News Online, 24 September 2004.

1498 "Darfur Peace Lies in Separate Southern Deal – U.S.", News Article by Reuters, 23 September 2004.

1499 Alex de Waal, "The book was closed too soon on peace in Darfur", *The Guardian* (London), 29 September 2006.

1500 See, for example, "Sudan's Government in Favour of Ceasefire in 18-year Civil War", News Article by Agence France-Presse, 22 April 2001 and "Government Ready for a Ceasefire", News Article by United Nations Integrated Regional Information Network, UN Office for the Coordination of Humanitarian Affairs, Nairobi 15 May 2001.

1501 "EU and Sudan Agree to Mend Rifts Through Dialogue", *Middle East Times*, 19 November 1999. See, also, "EU Seeks to Renew Dialogue with Sudan Broken Off in 1996", News Article by Agence France-Presse, 10 November 1999. In July 2000, the countries of Africa also selected Sudan to represent the continent as a non-permanent member of the United Nations Security Council. The fifty-three African nations chose Sudan over Mauritius and Uganda to succeed Namibia as the African representative on the Security Council. The United States blocked Sudan's election.

1502 Sudan has over the past several years emerged as a leader of the region, developments which culminated in Sudan's hosting of the Eighth Heads of State summit of the regional Intergovernmental Authority on Development (IGAD) body, as well as the February 2001 Heads of State summit of the Community of Sahel-Saharan States.

1503 Sudan was amongst the first nine of 20 Common Market of East and Southern Africa member states to implement the first stage of the envisaged Free Trade Area. This is Africa's first step towards full regional integration and a common currency by 2025. See "Sudan to Join African Free Trade Area", News Article by Reuters, 30 October 2000.

1504 Mahmood Mamdani, "Blue-Hatting Darfur", *op. cit.*

1505 See, for example, "Sudanese Darfur Rebels Block Aid Pact", News Article by Reuters, 26 October 2004.

1506 Numerous observers have confirmed that this monitoring process was a success. See, for example, "Sudan Successful Ceasefire Monitoring in Southern Sudan", Press Release by Refugees International – USA, 3 January 2005.

1507 *Sudan Media Study Summary: Mass Atrocity Crimes in Darfur and the Response of Government Sudan Broadcasters to International Pressure*, Concordia University, Montreal, 8 September 2006, available at <http://mediarelations.concordia.ca/pressreleases/archives/2006/09/sudan_media_study_summary.php>.

Index